J. D. Bern:
The Sage of S

Andrew Brown is an English radiation oncologist practising in New Hampshire. His previous publications include *The Neutron and the Bomb* (a biography of Sir James Chadwick, discoverer of the neutron) He is also a research fellow at the Belfer Center for Science and International Affairs at Harvard University

'Bernal was himself a Colossus, and Andrew Brown has written a biography to match. It should stand as a classic.'
Walter Gratzer, *Current Biology*

'Apart from taking its place as the best account of Bernal's life and work, Brown's book provides an inspiring introduction to the academic culture of the 1920s and 1930s, a period which to those living through it seemed to overflow with hope, challenge, and passion.'
Richard Barnett, *Lancet*

'Andrew Brown does an outstanding job of weaving together the many strands of Bernal's complicated life to create a hugely entertaining and enjoyable biography'
BBC Focus Magazine

'J.D.Bernal: The Sage of Science is a clever and engaging book and a worthy tribute to the life of one of the most influential and bright personalities the 20th century has offered humanity'
Richard A. Stein, *Journal of the American Medical Association*

'There are two reasons for reading the biography of this brilliant and tragic figure: sheer human curiosity about an individual recognisable even at first sight as singular and fascinating, and ... the need to understand the scientific, socio-political and cultural revolutions of the 20th century.'
Eric Hobsbawm, *London Review of Books*

'Brown recounts [Bernal's legendary life] with fresh detail and in a succinct and vivid style.'
Soraya de Charadevian, *Science*

'This is a very fine (and large) book. Much more than a biography, because of Bernal's involvement in so many sociological issues of his day, it takes the form of a social history of the first half of the twentieth century.'
Kenneth C. Holmes, *Nature*

'...[an] admirable book...'
Graham Farmelo, *Sunday Telegraph*

'...marvellous book...'
Brian Cathcart, *New Statesman*

'... a fine achievement...'
Times Higher Education Supplement

'Andrew Brown is a fine storyteller with an easy flowing style.'
Richard Collins, *Sunday Business Post, Dublin*

'Bernal was an impressive and fascinating figure, often for conflicting reasons. Brown's biography is a vivid and balanced account of this full and colourful life and its times. The book makes compelling reading, whether one is interested in molecular biology or not. The chapter entitled "The physical basis of life" alone provides a good overview of the development of molecular biology, in which Bernal played a vital pioneering role.'
Gordon Fraser, *PhysicsWeb*

'Brown's fine biography of Bernal is a scholarly account of the whole man'
Derry Jones, *Chemistry World*

J. D. Bernal

The Sage of Science

ANDREW BROWN

OXFORD

UNIVERSITY PRESS

OXFORD
UNIVERSITY PRESS

Great Clarendon Street, Oxford OX2 6DP

Oxford University Press is a department of the University of Oxford.
It furthers the University's objective of excellence in research, scholarship,
and education by publishing worldwide in

Oxford New York

Auckland Cape Town Dar es Salaam Hong Kong Karachi
Kuala Lumpur Madrid Melbourne Mexico City Nairobi
New Delhi Shanghai Taipei Toronto

With offices in

Argentina Austria Brazil Chile Czech Republic France Greece
Guatemala Hungary Italy Japan Poland Portugal Singapore
South Korea Switzerland Thailand Turkey Ukraine Vietnam

Oxford is a registered trade mark of Oxford University Press
in the UK and in certain other countries

Published in the United States
by Oxford University Press Inc., New York

British Library Cataloguing in Publication Data

Data available

Library of Congress Cataloging in Publication Data

Data available

Typeset by SPI Publisher Services, Pondicherry, India
Printed in Great Britain
on acid-free paper by
Clays Ltd., St. Ives plc

ISBN 978-0-19-920565-3

1

Contents

Contents

For Tom Shields
and
In memory of my parents

Acknowledgements

For the past five years I have led the double life of a biographer, and Desmond Bernal (Sage) has proved to be the most engrossing and stimulating of companions. I was fortunate to be able to interview many of his friends and distinguished colleagues. Readers will discover that his domestic arrangements were unconventional, and my first thanks are to Jane and Martin Bernal for supplying family information. Martin's mother, Margaret Gardiner, who was then in her late nineties and still occupying the house that was such a lively venue for intellectuals in the 1930s, was mystified that Des was going to join her other close friends, W.H. Auden, Barbara Hepworth, and Solly Zuckerman as a biographical subject. She gave me good-humoured advice on traps to avoid, before describing with chilling detail the visit to the USSR in 1934 and the threatening atmosphere, to which Bernal seemed impervious.

Bernal's greatest legacy was the next generation of scientists that he inspired to extend the many trails he started. Max Perutz, who said that Bernal was the most fascinating talker he ever encountered, described Bernal's lab at Cambridge as though he had first set foot in it a few weeks (rather than 65 years) earlier. He explained some of the technical aspects of X-ray crystallography with such lucidity that the hair stood up on the back of my neck, and I glimpsed the amazing world of three-dimensional symmetry and reciprocal space. Perutz referred to Dorothy Hodgkin (another Bernal protégée) as having saintly qualities: after he described the twenty-five years of utter frustration he endured before beginning to unravel the structure of haemoglobin, I formed the impression that saintliness was a prerequisite in crystallography – at least until the advent of automation. Sir Aaron Klug left me in no doubt about the brilliance of Bernal as an experimenter and his stature as one of the founding fathers of molecular biology. His account of the groundbreaking research into the structure of viruses, begun at Birkbeck with Rosalind Franklin, was revelatory. Klug and Alan Mackay both recalled the hazards and squalor of the labs at Birkbeck during the 1950s, and Bernal's strengths and weaknesses as a director. Alan, who is a true disciple of Bernal's in his approach to the history of science and its social implications, has been a bountiful source of obscure articles and of contacts around the world. John Finney helped me to understand Bernal's contributions to the structure of liquids.

Bernal was one of the crucial British 'boffins', who contributed so much in World War Two. During the war, with Solly Zuckerman and others, he extended the nascent field of operational research to study the effects of bombing on cities. Brenda Swann (Ryerson) and Renée Brittan were firsthand witnesses to those efforts. Sage's *pièce de résistance* was the planning of D-Day – a contribution that has given rise to some controversy. I was extremely fortunate to track down Major-General Logan Scott-Bowden, who heroically tested Bernal's hypotheses about the nature of the Normandy beaches in the months prior to the invasion. His early morning phone call was the most vivid account of the landings I have ever heard or read.

In addition to those already mentioned, I would like to thank the following, who knew Bernal and generously provided information: Paul Barnes, Gofty Bernal, Mike Bernal, Andrew Booth, Hugh Bunting, Ian Cherry, Francis Crick, John Finch, Ully Harris, Ken Holmes, Olga Kennard, John Kerridge, Stan Lenton, Andrew Malleson, John Mason, Vivien Pixner, Romila Thapar, Peter Trent, Norman Waddleton, James D. Watson and Maurice Wilkins. With the passing of the years, some of these remarkable people are, alas, no longer alive.

The raw material for this book mostly came from the Bernal archive in Cambridge University Library, where I was well served by Godfrey Waller and his staff. Here are the unpublished letters, diaries and travelogues that show Bernal consumed with the stuff of life from the atomic level to global politics. One unpublished note contains Bernal's beautiful inductive argument for the replication of genetic material being essentially a linear process at the critical instant – an insight that would occur to Crick more than two decades later, when, as he wrote to me, he knew a lot more about proteins than Sage did in 1931. Although there are still six boxes of Sage's love letters sealed until 2021, there were enough indiscretions in his early diaries to reflect his libidinous ways. As president of the World Peace Council, Bernal's papers reveal a genuine personal relationship with Khrushchev. I will deposit transcripts of my interviews in the Bernal archive for the use of future historians.

In addition to the Cambridge University collection, I obtained valuable material from the American Institute of Physics, Birkbeck College London, Emmanuel College Cambridge, the Harvard University libraries, the archives of Dorothy Hodgkin and John Kendrew at the Bodleian Library Oxford, the Mountbatten papers in the Hartley Library at the University of Southampton, the Ava Helen and Linus Pauling Archive at Oregon State University, the National Portrait Gallery, the Public Record Office at Kew, the Royal Society, and the Zuckerman Archives at the University of East Anglia. I am extremely grateful to the archivists and librarians in all these places, who were uniformly generous in their cooperation and spent considerable time hunting down small items for me, sometimes in response to whimsical email requests. I am indebted to all the above institutions for their permission to publish various letters and photographs.

Lorna Arnold proved to be the most alert, encouraging and informed listener. John Ballantyne and Michael St. Clair read and provided improving comments on every chapter (many of which were patiently scrutinized by the scientists involved). Others who helped in myriad ways include Will Bernal, Giovanna Bloor, Frank Bunn, Tim and Celia Charlton, Jeremy Karl Cock-croft, Neal Desjardins, Jeremy Elston, Sebastian Faulks, Istvan Hargittai, Graham and Betty Hines, Luke and Stephanie Hughes-Davies, Bruce Kupelnick, Julian Lewis, Victor Mcelheny, Robert Olby, John Streather, and numerous medical colleagues in New Hampshire. I have an uneasy feeling that I have forgotten someone important, in which case I apologize now.

At Oxford University Press, the book was commissioned by Susan Harri-son. Susan was succeeded by Michael Rodgers, before I eventually arrived at the overflowing desk of Latha Menon. She imposed a needed deadline and then applied her justly celebrated editorial touch to the manuscript. My thanks to her, James Thompson, Deborah Protheroe, Mike Nugent, Rachel Woodforde and all the other OUP staff who have brought the book to fruition. My thanks are also due to David Carles, and to Anne Holmes and Rob Rudnick for the index. Any remaining errors remain the sole property of the author.

Lastly, this biography would not have been started or finished without the love, patience and cooking of Jane Ballantyne MD.

List of Illustrations

Abbreviations

Abbreviations abound in military planning, science and ad hoc socialist politics, and were therefore unavoidable in writing about Bernal.

ARC	Agricultural Research Council
ARP	Air-Raid Precautions
AScW	Association of Scientific Workers
BAAS	British Association for the Advancement of Science
BRS	Building Research Station
CAS	Chief of the Air Staff
CCO	Chief of Combined Operations
CIGS	Chief of Imperial General Staff
CND	Campaign for Nuclear Disarmament
CO	Combined Operations
COHQ	Combined Operations Headquarters
COS	Chiefs of Staff
COSSAC	Chiefs of Staff Supreme Allied Command
CPGB	Communist Party of Great Britain
CSAWG	Cambridge Scientists Anti-War Group
CUSS	Cambridge University Socialist Society
DNA	Deoxyribonucleic acid
DSIR	Department of Scientific and Industrial Research
FAS	Federation of American Scientists
FIL	For Intellectual Liberty
FRS	Fellow of the Royal Society
HE	High Explosive
ICBM	Inter-Continental Ballistic Missile
ICDP	International Confederation for Disarmament and Peace
IRA	Irish Republican Army
IRD	Information Research Department
IUCr	International Union of Crystallography
JTWC	Joint Technical Warfare Committee
MP	Member of Parliament
MRC	Medical Research Council

MTB	Motor Torpedo Boat
OR	Operational Research
RAF	Royal Air Force
RF	Rockefeller Foundation
RI	Royal Institution
RNA	Ribonucleic acid
SAC	Supreme Allied Commander
SACSEA	Supreme Allied Commander South-East Asia
SANE	National Committee for a Sane Nuclear Policy
SEAC	South-East Asia Command
SHAEF	Supreme Headquarters Allied Expeditionary Force
TBSV	Tomato Bushy Stunt Virus
TIS	Theatre Intelligence Section
TMV	Tobacco Mosaic Virus
TUC	Trades Union Congress
UNESCO	United Nations Educational, Scientific and Cultural Organization
UXB	Unexploded Bomb
WPC	World Peace Council
WFSW	World Federation of Scientific Workers

1

A Long Way to Go

The newest and grandest liner in the White Star fleet, *Celtic*, sailed from Queenstown harbour without fanfare. She cut through the grey waves, rounding the Head of Kinsale as the late November sun slipped beneath the Atlantic Ocean. The coastline of southern Ireland became a faint black line, and the little boy who had been watching it intently turned to his mother and inquired, 'Mammy, we will go back now?' She replied, in French, 'No, Desmond, they must go on to America, they won't turn back now.' 'Not even for you, Mammy?'[1]

Unlike most of the passengers, Elizabeth Bernal was not sailing away to seek a life in the New World. Her own mother, who was born into a land-owning Protestant family in County Antrim, had been taken to the United States as a child. She subsequently met and married a man in the small town of Knoxville, Illinois, but was soon widowed. The local Presbyterian minister, the Reverend William Young Miller, whose family came from New England, befriended her, and they married. Elizabeth (Bessie), one of their six children, was born in 1869. When her father retired from the ministry in 1883, he moved the family west to the new city of San Jose in California.[2] Bessie and her sister, Laetitia, were sent to Mme Bovet's Academy for young ladies in New Orleans for the type of refined education that was not available in the rugged West. Both were good students and Bessie excelled at languages. By extraordinary good fortune, the Californian railway magnate and US Senator, Leland Stanford, founded his university just a short buggy ride from San Jose. When its doors first opened in 1891, women were admitted, and Bessie enrolled there for lectures the following year.[3] She did not complete a degree course, but instead made the Grand Tour of Europe with Laetitia, concentrating on the great centres of Renaissance art in Italy as well as visiting Germany and France. Bessie strengthened her French by studying at the Sorbonne, but she continued to speak it with a twanging New Orleans accent.

A few years later, she returned to France with her older brother, John Johnston Miller MD. He was a physician in San Jose and also served as the County Health Officer,[4] a role that brought him a particular responsibility for the control of infectious diseases. He came to Europe to make a study of hospitals and public health services, and the presence of his bright sister, fluent in French, Italian and German, was a great asset. They travelled by train and bicycle for six months, before he returned to California. The following summer of 1898, Bessie was still in Belgium, where she met and fell in love with Samuel Bernal, an Irish farmer.

The long sea voyage gave Bessie ample opportunity to reflect on her changed circumstances. In the six years since she left California, she had converted to Rome, married Samuel and borne him two sons.[5] The eldest, Desmond, was now two-and-one-half years, and she had left his eleven-month-old brother, Kevin, at home with their father. Her own father had died soon after her marriage, and she received the sad news on the day that she and Samuel moved into their farmhouse, Brookwatson. Even without such a loss, it seems improbable that Bessie would have been ecstatic about her new home. Having grown up in the warmth of California and New Orleans and spent languid, sun-filled months in France and Italy, the raw, damp climate of County Tipperary was bound to depress her. Her new husband was cheerful and full of dreams for their life together, but had no time for books and no knowledge of art or architecture. He was loquacious, but as happy to talk to his cattle as to converse with his wife. There was no one to share her intellectual passions, and the realities of farm life at times offended her sensibilities.

Samuel Bernal was a broad-shouldered man, with a flowing dark moustache. Five years older than Bessie, he came from Limerick, where his father had been a successful auctioneer. During Samuel's boyhood in the 1870s, there had been a series of failed potato harvests which, while not causing a repeat of the famine of thirty years earlier, led to widespread evictions of tenant farmers and the subsequent Land Wars.[6] In 1881, as a teenager, he might have seen mounted Dragoons, with sabres drawn, charge through the streets of Limerick to quell rioting. Despite the parlous state of farming, Samuel studied at the Royal Albert Agricultural College in Dublin. After graduating in 1884, he fell out with his father and showing frontier spirit of his own, Samuel sailed to Australia. He remained there for the next fourteen years, working on a sheep farm, and returned to Ireland only after his father's death.[7] Then he went to live with his older sister, Mrs Riggs Miller, who owned land near Nenagh, Co. Tipperary, a town about twenty-five miles north-east of Limerick. After his experience in Australia, Samuel was well qualified to manage his sister's estates.

Mrs Riggs Miller was an enthusiastic traveller in her own right, and persuaded Samuel to accompany her to the fashionable Belgian summer resort of Blankenberg. While walking along the beach he was attracted by a tall, slender young woman wearing the latest fashion in long bathing dresses. To his astonishment she suddenly disappeared beneath the waves and without a second thought he rushed in to rescue her. Bessie Miller had just submerged to sit on the sandy bottom for a moment, when she found herself in the powerful arms of Samuel Bernal.[8] Following such an abrupt and intimate introduction, their relationship flourished: they were engaged to be married after one month and the wedding took place in January 1900, after Bessie had been received into the Catholic Church.

In the time Sam had been away in Australia, there had been huge changes in the Irish agricultural community.[9] These largely flowed from Gladstone's second Land Act of 1881, which sought to remove some of the inherent injustices in the landlord–tenant system that had led to the state of near insurrection in rural Ireland. The Act had established rent tribunals and statutory tenure for tenants who paid the agreed fair rents. The returns on farming continued to decline through the 1880s, but the new rents fell in lockstep. As a result the landlords were the ultimate losers and by the 1890s many were keen to sell the lands they had once so ruthlessly administered. The transfer of ownership was facilitated by a government scheme to grant low interest mortgages to tenants. Sam took advantage of this system to purchase 'Brookwatson', a dilapidated farmhouse near Nenagh, where he planned to run his own dairy farm. He was able to buy and restore the property because Bessie had brought a considerable dowry of £1,600.

The Catholic Bernal family was unusual among the Anglo-Irish Protestant landowners of Tipperary. Sam soon established a thriving farm at Brookwatson and took particular pride in the appearance of the gardens. Bessie was sociable, she loved parties and dances, and joined the local tennis club. Friendships were forged on the basis of social class rather than religion. She and Samuel were both over thirty years old at the time of their marriage, and he was intent on a large family. Their first child, John Desmond, was born at Brookwatson on 10 May 1901. Sensing that he could become her soul-mate as well as her son, Bessie doted on the child, reading him French fairy stories, talking to him constantly, and answering his endless questions.

Desmond's precocity astounded the passengers during the trans-Atlantic voyage. After *Celtic* docked in New York, he and his mother continued their stately progress westwards by train. The journey was so long and confining that it left an indelible mark on the young boy's memory.[10] He took particular delight in the friendly black stewards, who would come every night to transform the seats into bunks. Apart from a short break in Chicago, they were on the train for over a week. When Desmond finally arrived at his grandmother's house, the Miller family was captivated by the silver-haired little boy, who talked to them, with equal ease, in English or French. For his part, the most lasting impression was to be surrounded by ladies in dresses of white, pink and blue that swept along the ground as they glided past.

The long return journey to Ireland, some weeks later, seemed less momentous. Desmond was preoccupied with the idea that he was going to receive a green pony, as a reward for his endurance, when he arrived home. He was disappointed when the mythical creature never materialized. Over the next year or so, there were fixed events and repeated rhythms that brought a pattern to his life. He would be woken each morning by the sound of milking and on running to his mother's bedroom could watch the sun rise over the purple mountain called the Devil's Bit. In the evening, the men would lead the horses back into the farmyard, as the sun set over the Arra Mountains. During the day, he and his constant companion, Kevin, were free to play with almost no restrictions. Their delights were 'to play in lofts, or hay sheds, to walk down to the Holy Well to see the rushing water of the weir'. The lack of adult supervision seems staggering today, and there was at least one nearly fatal accident. The field in front of the house contained a grass-covered mound and the two boys decided to tunnel through it. After they had burrowed some distance in, the unsupported tunnel collapsed, and they were lucky to be able to claw their way out.

Desmond soon understood that his mother controlled the children and domestic staff, while his jolly father was in charge of the farm. It was through his intense relationship with his mother that Des began to realize 'the outside world of beauty in form and language'. He constantly implored her to 'Tell me t'ings'.[11] On those occasions when he misbehaved, he asked always to be scolded in French, 'a language of gentleness'. His father was down-to-earth and a fine man in Desmond's estimation: 'a good Catholic and a good husband, ruling the house and beating his children because he knew it was his duty, though it did not fit his easy and kindly nature.'[12] The servants included a nurse called Daisy, who was responsible for the boys' everyday welfare. Desmond and Kevin took their meals with her in the kitchen; the staple diet was buttered potatoes washed down with fresh milk. In a free and happy childhood, the only trauma seems to have been a trip to Dublin to have his tonsils removed. He remembered ruining his mother's blue dress by spitting blood, after she took him from the hospital; his hurt was forgotten when they were met at Nenagh station by his father in the high trap, 'it was dark and frosty and the horse's heels clattered on the stones'.

As a natural complement to his physical and social world, Desmond soon constructed a clear image of a spiritual universe.[13] The family went to Mass every Sunday, and Desmond was a good boy who knew his catechism well. There was God, the Father, Son and Holy Ghost. There was the world of this life with air, earth and water, and its inhabitants (birds, beasts and fishes), and the other worlds, Heaven, Purgatory and Hell, with angels, souls of men and devils. To Desmond 'it was very beautiful and simple', but he did not know what to do about worms and the souls of animals. Kevin, who 'had a raging temper and told lies', was much less devout and enjoyed asking 'Who made the world?' – invariable response, 'God made the World' – so that he could put the defiant, supplementary question 'Who made God?' To this, of course, there was no satisfactory answer, and Desmond shared the family's horror at his little brother's wickedness.

Desmond was taught his letters and rudimentary arithmetic by a tiny nun, Sister Mary Rose, on Sundays after Mass. His formal schooling began at the age of five; the three-year-old Kevin was also judged to be ready for the experience and so would be Desmond's constant schoolmate over the next dozen years. Their mother decided that the local Christian Brothers Academy was too crowded, and fearing lice and infectious diseases, she sent her sons to the Protestant diocesan school in Nenagh. The brothers were taught by Miss Dagg in the upstairs room, and Desmond instantly found learning exciting and particularly liked arithmetic. He was fascinated by numbers, which became like friends, each with its own character. He liked 3 the best, then 9. He thought even numbers were like girls and rather despised them. 12 was 'awfully important', and while 5 and 10 were too easy, 7 was a terrible puzzle – it was nobody's relation. 11 was 'an awfully jolly number'. He soon progressed from the kindergarten to the big school, where there were still only about twenty boys and girls, each proceeding at their own pace. Desmond soon progressed to geometry and found 'the first lesson in Euclid wonderful even though I thought "obvious" meant "impossible"'.[14]

Although discipline was strict, 'we were caned every day or oftener if we were bold', it did nothing to quell boisterous behaviour. At lunchtimes, the masters went home to eat, and the boys would stage 'grand fights' in the schoolyard. These involved laying siege to buildings, using makeshift battering rams; covering fire was provided with stones and water pistols. While a lookout was always posted for a returning master, there was no disguising the collateral damage of broken windows, and afternoon canings followed with regularity.

There were two new additions to the family at Brookwatson during the year the boys started school. One was a baby sister, Geraldine (always known as Gigi) and the other was Bessie's younger sister Laetitia (called Cuddie by the Bernal children), who came to live with them after the death of her mother. She took on the role of devoted maiden aunt, although some years before she had been engaged to a Scottish MP, Mr McLaren, who died suddenly shortly before the planned wedding. According to her brother,[15] it was a blow from which she never recovered, and may explain Desmond's observation that she took 'God on hard terms'. She remained a Protestant and made no concession to her sister's new religion nor to the Irish, whom she loathed for 'their laziness, their dirt and their dishonesty': but she was equally unable 'to escape the charm of their language and the ingenuity of their evasions'.[16]

Signs of curiosity about the physical world were evident in Desmond from an early age. When Gigi was at the crawling stage, and he was therefore about seven years old, she impaled her knee on a needle, dropped on the floor. Part of the needle broke off beneath the skin, and she was taken to Limerick hospital to have it removed. Desmond was told that the surgeon had taken an X-ray photograph of Gigi's knee in order to see exactly where the needle was. This set his imagination racing and although he did not know what an X-ray was, he reasoned that it must be an intense form of light that would illuminate structures beneath the skin. The brightest light available to him was the paraffin lamp that he was allowed to use for reading in bed. He opened a number of his books and stood them up around the lamp so that its light might be concentrated by reflection from their white pages. He then attempted to see the bones in his hand by holding his hand across a small gap between two of the books. Unfortunately he knocked one of the books over and 'the whole affair came down with a terrific crash [and] knocked the lamp off the table'. While the glass lamp broke and its oil ran over the floor, it luckily did not catch fire; Sam Bernal, who came racing upstairs, was caught between relief and fury when he saw what had happened and administered his son 'a very bad beating'.[17]

His first experiment in chemistry, undertaken at about the same age, again might have easily caused serious injury, but fortunately left only a mental impression. Desmond had read a lecture for children on 'The chemistry of the candle', delivered by Michael Faraday in London in the early nineteenth century. In his talk, Faraday had demonstrated how to make hydrogen gas by mixing granulated zinc with dilute sulphuric acid in a Florence flask. Desmond had no idea what all these terms meant, but persuaded his mother to write a letter to the local chemist so that he could acquire the raw materials. For the flask, he used a straw-covered Chianti bottle, which he found in a cupboard. Bessie had only one rule – no experiments in the house – so the mixing took place outside, with a tree stump serving as the benchtop. It was cold and getting dark, and he was very disappointed when absolutely nothing appeared to happen. Before going to bed, he slipped out of the back door for one more look, but it was now impossible to see: 'Well, I thought, I must have a look at it, so I took a box of matches out of my pocket and lit a match. And as I brought the match near it there was a most magnificent explosion and everything went to blazes!'[18]

Desmond's precocious talents continued to flourish: on New Year's Day 1909 he began the first of a series of daily diaries, a form of record he would maintain with remarkable consistency as a teenager and young adult. The first volume is entitled 'An autobiography for 1909–10 by Desmond Bernal aged eight next May';[19] its opening sentence continued the serious tone: 'When we were going to Mass on New Year's morning my hat fell off twice.' The next day, we learn, he was sick after breakfast and read *Black Beauty* for a while, until going outside with Kevin to play hockey and Mohawk Indians with bow and arrows. Once the school term started, it is remarkable to see how many subjects he was studying and how closely his performance was monitored. There were daily scores faithfully recorded: a typical list gave him eight marks out of ten for writing, reading, spelling, arithmetic, poetry and geography, while for conduct he received a seven. There were short entries in French, but the autobiography came to an abrupt halt in March. He did include a charming poem, the first verse of which was:

> I'm a mariner on the ocean
> I'm a mariner on the ocean
> And I make the most commotion
> That ever the world did see

The Bernals had another baby daughter, Fiona, in 1908, but in a cruel realization of Bessie's worst fears, the boys contracted whooping cough at school and Fiona succumbed to the infection. A last son, Godfrey, was born in 1910. The following summer Desmond and Kevin went to stay with friends at Royan, on the Gironde estuary, in a house surrounded by resinous pine-woods. This was an opportunity for them to improve their French, and both Sam and Bessie wanted to expand the limited perspective offered to their sons by a purely Irish upbringing. One scene from the Gironde stayed in Desmond's memory as fresh as an oil painting:

The midnight of the full moon was the great pêche. All the peasants went out with wine in their bullock carts. The men waded in up to their necks at the head of the long net, the women to the top of their black skirts. They swept back and forwards, and gleaming writhing fish piled on to the moonlit sand. Great stingrays, turbot and the small fry that were slung into the waves again, the men and women sang songs and we went to sleep lying on the straw.[20]

In Desmond's mind, that summer marked the end of childhood because in the early autumn he and Kevin were sent across the Irish Sea to go to school in England. While this decision was taken by Sam in order to expand his sons' horizons, it was opposed by Bessie and Cuddie. It is easy to imagine their reasons for resisting because Desmond and Kevin were blissfully happy with life on the farm, and the boys were the centre of the women's lives. In the sisters' homeland there was no tradition of sending children away to school at such tender ages (Kevin was only eight years old). The school chosen was

Hodder, in Lancashire, which was a preparatory school for the Jesuit college of Stonyhurst. The logic of Sam's choice was that Hodder and Stonyhurst would provide a superior education for his sons in the Catholic tradition, at a place in England accessible from the port of Liverpool. Despite his choice of a Jesuit school, Sam's roots were not deeply embedded in the Catholic religion. The Bernals were originally Sephardic Jews,[21] who fled from Spain after two of the family were burned at the stake at Cordoba in the Inquisition of the 1650s. The earliest record of the name was an apothecary named Bernal who sailed with Columbus on his third voyage to the Americas in 1502. After fleeing Spain, the family settled in Amsterdam and some members then migrated to England. Various Bernals were successful as landowners in the West Indies and as English politicians. The Irish branch of the family was established as recently as the early nineteenth century, which is when the conversion to Catholicism took place. Desmond made his own first Communion in April 1910 and his mother wrote in her diary: 'God bless the poor little boy. He was over-excited, very fervent, very serious. May he always remain an honest and sincere man.'

After his initial homesickness, Desmond settled in well at Hodder and wrote to Aunt Mod (one of Sam's sisters) on 11 November 1911: 'I'm rather happy here. I go to Holy Communion every day and to confession every week.'[22] He reported that he had come second in an oral exam in French, and sent love to all members of the family plus 'kind regards to all the servants'. The religiosity of school life, under the gentle direction of Father Cassidy, found an eager receptacle in Desmond's soul: 'We played and learned and were good boys. Too good. I bought a missal, flagellated myself with nails, and had a knotted rope tied round my middle until I found, by the anger that was roused in me when I was bumped into, that it was rather an occasion of sin than a penance. I started the practice of cutting grottoes to Our Lady in the hillside, and a fraternity of Perpetual Adoration of the Sacred Heart.'[23]

The following September, Desmond transferred to Stonyhurst College, which he found to be as cold and imposing a place as it sounds. Despite coming top in every subject, Desmond hated it and left after just one term. He later wrote that at Stonyhurst, 'I learned nothing but the joys of prison life. A regularity that even extended to defaecation. Dark corridors, wandering priests, terrible sermons on sins that must not be named lest they be practised. But against that there were forests of flaming candles, golden vestments, and the resonant chanting that tore out the soul for God.'[24] Bessie was concerned that her eldest son's piety was becoming so extreme that he would finish up in the priesthood, and whatever Sam's opinion on the matter, the boys did not return to Stonyhurst following the Christmas holiday. As a temporary measure the boys returned to their previous school in Nenagh, which was not a satisfactory solution either. Desmond was already showing an increasing preoccupation with science; after Christmas, he bought himself a microscope with money he had saved. At the school in Nenagh, there was one textbook that had some extracts from Faraday's lectures, but there was no formal science teaching. Bessie undertook a search for a public school that was strong in science and came up with Bedford School in the English Midlands. The Bernal brothers were accepted and began their careers there in January 1914.

From the first, Desmond seemed to adjust easily to life at Bedford and was soon showing a precocious, if uneven, talent for science. He wrote to his mother in October 1914 that he had started 'la trigonometrie, c'est asssez facile' but kept the letter short because 'J'ai une violine [deep purple] migraine.'[25] In early 1915, he was studying lines of force, the law of inverse squares, finding the moment of a magnet and using electroscopes. In the end-of-year examinations, he won a scholarship in physics for designing and executing an experiment to find the electrical resistance of a piece of wire. Surprisingly he found the mathematics exam very hard and managed only one problem out of eight. Apart from his studies, Desmond was an enthusiastic boxer, a disappointed cricketer and a good shot with a rifle.[26]

The brothers' first year at Bedford was of course overshadowed by the outbreak of war in Europe. The first reference to the hostilities appeared in Desmond's diary entry on 7 May 1915: '*Lusitania* torpedoed off Kinsale, 703 lives saved.' Many of the senior boys were joining the army as soon as school was over for the year, and the next mention of them at school assemblies would be news of their deaths in France. The sinking of the *Lusitania* was a particularly shocking event and was taken to heart by Desmond, who remembered sailing off Kinsale in a transatlantic liner. More immediately, he had to sail on a ferry across the Irish Sea to go home for the school holidays. In the event, the most memorable part of his journey home was being met by his father at Nenagh station in a new motor car, then a rare mode of transport in County Tipperary. After a carefree summer, he returned to Bedford at the end of September, and was soon immersed in organized activities. He took up rowing in addition to other sports, and there was also daily military drill, which with each passing season must have taken on heavier significance. The school days were long, with lessons from nine in the morning until five-thirty in the afternoons, and there was also school on Saturday mornings. In the evenings Desmond often took the chair at meetings of the science society. Nocturnal guerilla warfare between the dormitories was incessant, with raids and counter raids; Desmond was a spirited participant in such 'ragging', as well as its leading chronicler.

Back at Brookwatson, the new year of 1916 opened uneventfully, as Desmond helped with the milking and planted rows of fruit trees with his father.

He took long walks through the countryside, and there were novel outings in the car. Each day he would find several hours to read and to study local flora and fauna with his microscope or to carry out a chemistry experiment in his makeshift laboratory. Nor was the routine very different during the Easter break, but on 26th April Desmond noted in his diary: 'There is very little news of the Sinn Fein.'[27] The inhabitants of Brookwatson, like the rest of Ireland, had been astonished by the news that a small ragged army of revolutionary Irish Volunteers and Sinn Feiners had staged an armed rebellion in Dublin on Easter Monday, and that they now controlled the city centre. From the time of Gladstone's second premiership thirty years earlier, the Irish Nationalists had been engaged in a series of ungainly independence minuets on the dance floor at Westminster, with successive Liberal governments.[28] The dance never seemed to reach a conclusion, either because the Conservatives in the House of Lords stopped the music with a veto, or the Protestants of Ulster threatened a fight outside the ballroom at the prospect of being forced to partner their Catholic countrymen. After two elections in 1910 when Asquith could sustain power only with the acquiescence of the Irish Nationalist MPs, the Liberals removed the veto power of the House of Lords in the Parliament Act of 1911. The minuet could at last be concluded and so the Home Rule Bill passed into law in 1914.

In Ulster, crowds of increasing size and bellicosity protested against the new law, and a disciplined, well-armed Ulster Volunteer Force took shape, unnerving Prime Minister Asquith. He realized that he could not quell their anger nor make them accept 'Rome Rule', as they called it. After bowing politely to his former Irish Nationalist partners, Asquith was forced to explore amendments that might appease the Ulstermen and their determined leader, Sir Edward Carson. The most likely solution seemed to be to exclude the six counties of Ulster from the Home Rule agreement and let them form a self-governing, northern province.[29] No such compromise was agreed by the two Irish sides, who were becoming increasingly antagonistic. Only the outbreak of the much larger conflict in Europe had the effect of 'pouring oil on the stormy Irish waters', in Asquith's words, and instead of fighting each other, Irishmen from both camps volunteered to fight the Germans.[30]

The Home Rule Bill was suspended for at least a year or until the end of the war (whichever was longer), causing one Nationalist leader to describe it 'as a cheque continually post-dated'.[31] Other Nationalists were already disaffected by the attempts at constitutional change that had ground on for so many years without tangible result. To them the notion of proving the Irish worthiness of nationhood by fighting side by side with the British troops in France was anathema, and indeed they inclined towards the basic viewpoint that my enemy's enemy is my friend. Thus it was, with the promise of arms from

Germany, that the revolutionary Irish Volunteers and Sinn Fein planned the Easter rebellion in 1916. A proclamation of national independence was read from the steps of the General Post Office, their headquarters. While the British authorities had found themselves taken completely unawares by the uprising, within days they were able to bring in heavy reinforcements to throw a cordon around the city and bombard the city centre, reducing major buildings to smoking rubble.[32] By 30th April, news reached Brookwatson farm that most of the Sinn Feiners had surrendered. There seemed to be little further discussion there about the rebellion or about the executions of fifteen rebel leaders that followed over the next ten days. During that period of inflamed passions and continued violence, Sam took his two sons to Dublin on the way back to Bedford. Desmond recorded that 'we had lunch and looked at the ruin of Sackville Street'*.[33] They needed to get passes from the Town Hall in order to board the ferry at Kingstown; at the port they encountered a fierce military officer with a revolver and had their luggage searched.

Once back at Bedford, Desmond's thoughts were dominated by the demands and pressures of school. His physics course that summer term included optics, a subject whose mathematical intricacy and simple beauty instantly appealed to him. He was already a keen historian of science and would have been familiar with Newton's famous demonstration of the spectrum of light in 1665. Desmond understood that the dispersion of sunlight as it passes through a glass prism is due to the fact that the constituent colours are refracted (bent) to different degrees depending on their wavelengths. The index of refraction is higher for shorter wavelengths so that blue light is bent more than red. Nearly two hundred years after Newton, Kirchhoff and Bunsen had discovered that if certain elements were heated in a flame they produced spectra that were not continuous, but consisted of bright lines interspersed by lengths of darkness.[34] These line spectra are unique for each element so that the wavelengths of the lines act as a fingerprint for that substance, enabling its presence to be detected as a trace component of any compound. In May 1916, Bernal used the spectroscope in the dark room at school and saw the spectra for potassium, sodium, calcium, sulphur and barium. At the end of the week, he managed to come second in the chemistry exam but only fifth in physics. In addition to formal laboratory experiments, Bernal and his friends from the science society were active astronomers and were allowed to borrow telescopes from Mr Tearle, his housemaster, who christened Bernal his 'Astronomer Royal'. The housemaster would argue with his favourite student 'for hours on scientific and political subjects' and lend him interesting books. However much he enjoyed the burgeoning intellects of his charges, Mr Tearle

---

* Then the official name of O'Connell Street, site of the burnt-out General Post Office.

also bore the unenviable responsibility of needing to keep order in the dormitory. Bernal, despite his special relationship with Mr Tearle, was not above the juvenile fray and towards the end of the summer term received 'four with a gym shoe' from two prefects for ragging. This punishment was not resented by Bernal in any way, and he took the view that Mr Tearle was 'on the whole a kind and obliging man, though the house thinks he is the opposite'.[35]

The Great War consumed lives at an unprecedented and rising rate throughout 1916. More Irishmen were killed on 1st July, the first day of the Battle of the Somme, than on any other day in history. The New Year of 1917 brought only bleak prospects and very cold weather. In early February war rations were introduced at Bedford School: 'one slice of bread at breakfast, half at dinner, two at tea and one for supper.'[36] The only compensation for the cold was skating on the river – Desmond fell through the ice on 1st February, just after announcing to his friends, 'It's perfectly safe'! His diary, a week later, nonchalantly informs us that a total of seven were drowned; the following day a biplane, flying low, crashed into some trees behind the school. The machine caught fire and 'burned brightly': the boys, much to their disappointment, were not let out of school to watch. While in Ireland for Christmas, he and Kevin had bought some 'dog' bombs, small explosive devices, which they threw around with irresponsible abandon. They brought some back to school and the chemistry master even analysed one in a lab class, showing that it contained potassium chlorate and antimony sulphide. When one exploded during prep, they were made to hand over their remaining stock, and Mr Tearle gave 'the whole house a frightful jaw' without singling out the Bernal brothers for special punishment.

Desmond's passion for science intensified as his knowledge increased. He later said his reading was indiscriminate – by going to the school library every Sunday after Mass, he managed to devour the whole collection of books, without ever bothering to note any author's name. He continued to study the heavens at every available opportunity, and while at home on 8th January 1917, he got up early to see his first eclipse of the moon, (noting the moon was 'a light reddish brown'). The following week at Bedford, he observed 'two large sunspots on the lower left limb of the sun'. One night in March, Mrs Tearle made him come into the dormitory to sleep, causing him to miss the opportunity to see Saturn. He continued to be fascinated by spectroscopy and on the last day of the Easter term 'saw the Fraunhofer lines for the first time though I had to lie on the floor to do so'. Fraunhofer lines are thin dark lines that interrupt the continuous solar spectrum. These lines had been invisible to Newton, not only because of his poor eyesight, but because the quality of glass in his prism was not uniform enough to produce sharply defined spectra. A young Bavarian optician, Joseph von Fraunhofer, first observed the numerous lines in 1814 and accurately measured their constant wavelengths. The Fraunhofer lines are again examples of atomic line spectra, but unlike the bright lines Bernal saw a year before, the dark Fraunhofer lines result from discrete energy absorption, for example by sodium atoms, as light passes through the cool vapours surrounding the sun.

It took the genius of Danish physicist, Niels Bohr, to realize that these line spectra were the key to understanding the way electrons surrounding the atomic nucleus were constrained to travel in stationary or fixed orbits. This key insight formed the basis of his quantum model of the atom in 1913.[37] Bohr's audacious idea was that when an electron moves from one stationary state to another in an atom, a quantum of energy will be absorbed or emitted corresponding to a light photon of fixed frequency. He presented his theory at the British Association meeting in 1913 and there was a full report in *The Times* so that although Bernal does not refer to Bohr directly, it is quite possible that he knew of it; spectroscopy carried the extra excitement of being at the leading edge of physics. Two days after arriving home for the Easter holiday, Bernal had 'rigged up a spectroscope which worked moderately well'.[38]

Aside from spectroscopy, Desmond sampled a cornucopia of scientific and pastoral activities that Easter. He took more pleasure in the great paper-chases over the countryside, when a pair of human hares set off in advance, leaving a meagre trail of paper for the pursuers to follow. On a splendid outing that April, Desmond waded through a fast flowing river with water up to his waist and then stumbled into a field where he was confronted by a disgruntled bull. Two days after assembling the spectroscope, Desmond turned his hand to chemistry experiments and 'went down to the weir and got some plastic clay and bog iron ore. I made little crucibles with the clay and heated chalk and sulphur in them and made a sulphide that gave off hydrogen sulphide with water. I got ferric oxide out of the ore.'[39] In the evenings, he would work with his microscope and now started to be fascinated by the study of *diatoms*. These are single-celled algae that are extremely abundant in freshwater and marine ecosystems. Besides forming the basis of many food chains, *diatoms* contain chlorophyll so that they undertake photosynthesis, producing much atmospheric oxygen. Their appeal to the microscopist lies in their silica exoskeleton: a two-part shell that fits together like a shoe-box to enclose each organism. The silica gives the diatom a glassy appearance, and the skeletons come in a wonderful variety of geometrical shapes, both symmetrical and slightly asymmetrical, with intricately grooved and perforated surfaces. Desmond collected his first samples from a drain on the farm and started a catalogue of drawings. He was delighted to find that a farmer in the neighbourhood, Mr Launcelot Bayly, was a fellow enthusiast. Desmond rode

his bicycle over to visit Bayly's laboratory: 'he showed me several beautiful
diatoms and then some minerals under the polariscope. The colours were
simply gorgeous.'[40]

The Easter holiday lasted two days longer than scheduled for the Bernal
boys because all the Irish ports were closed temporarily owing to U-boat
activity. When they did sail from Kingstown on 4th May, there was a flat sea
and a beautiful full moon so they spent the entire night on deck. The crossing
was put to good use by Desmond: 'I had an excellent opportunity of studying
wave formation in the wake of the ship.'[41] No doubt he was thinking about
diffraction (the process by which waves bend around an object) and interference (where secondary wavelets bouncing off the ship either overlap in phase
with their respective troughs and crests superimposed to give a heightened
pattern due to *constructive interference,* or where the overlapping wavelets
cancel each other out as the crest of one is superimposed on the trough of
another in *destructive interference*). Fortunately, there was no destructive
interference from German U-boats.

Desmond celebrated his sixteenth birthday at Bedford and was given the
news that the school thought he should take a Cambridge scholarship examination in mathematics with a view to a degree in Natural Sciences. He
remained in the thick of school activities for the remainder of the year. A
typical day involved science experiments, boxing followed by an outing on the
river, military drill, and then perhaps some star gazing after prep. The
astronomical highlight was seeing 'the moon, some double stars and Jupiter
and four of his moons. I could make out the bands on Jupiter quite well.'[42] At
the beginning of 1916, conscription had been introduced in England, Wales
and Scotland, but not in Ireland. This meant that older boys at Bedford did
not stay to complete their senior year, passing from the Officer Training Corps
to leadership of men in the trenches, with little or no intervening preparation.
On 12th December, Desmond wrote that his 'oldest pal' Mayne had been
killed. While almost every British family was mourning the loss of a friend or
relative by this stage in the war, the civilian population as a whole remained
virtually immune to direct attacks. The notion of the homeland as safe
territory was starting to erode just a little since the Germans had started
to mount sporadic, daylight air raids on London with Gotha bombers.[43]
Desmond was caught in one of these during his homeward journey for
Christmas. On 18th December, he spent three hours in the Euston underground station listening to the noise of anti-aircraft fire and exploding bombs.

Yuletide 1917 was a lethal festival for British seamen.[44] Five days after
Desmond and Kevin sailed across to Kingstown, an armed British steamer,
Stephen Furness, was torpedoed in the Irish Sea by a German submarine and
sank with the loss of a hundred men. The same day three British destroyers

ran into a German minefield in the North Sea and two hundred and fifty more
sailors died. The worst tragedy came a week later, when another destroyer,
Attack, picking up survivors from a troopship that had been torpedoed,
herself struck a mine and sank. The Bernals decided it was unjustifiable to
expose their sons to such risks and they did not return to Bedford in January
1918. Initially Desmond was to go back to the old Diocesan school in Nenagh
with Kevin, and was delighted with the prospect of living at home for the
spring. After one day it became apparent to the schoolmistress that she had
nothing to teach Desmond, and so his mother took him to Mountjoy School
in Dublin.[45] They had an interview with the headmaster there, who, sensing
that his school could not meet Desmond's requirements either, suggested that
they should engage the services of a special tutor or 'grinder' to teach him
mathematics and science in preparation for the Cambridge scholarship. So
they found themselves at Trinity College, interviewing a rather desiccated
character named Mr Moore, who was engaged to grind Desmond 'from now
till Easter, five hours a week, for a fee of twelve guineas'.[46] Desmond would live
on his own in a hotel and attend Mr Moore in his room at Trinity for an hour
each afternoon. Even for a young man as studious and self-motivated as
Desmond, the expanse of free time was impossible to occupy. He would
walk for hours, through the parks, through the city, watching the reconstruction take shape where buildings had disappeared in the Easter uprising. Some
hours could be whiled away in the cinema and there were daily trips to
museums, but there were still hours of solitude. One Saturday morning in
January, he bought some books, but had read them all by 3.30 pm 'so there is
seven-and-sixpence wasted'. By that evening he was 'bored to death with this
hotel, I have hardly spoken twenty words all day'.

After the Battle of the Somme the previous summer, there had been an
understandable reluctance, unmistakable in the South of Ireland, to enlist
voluntarily in the British Army. While conscription had not been applied to
the Irish, there was talk of it in 1917, and just the threat of such coercion was
deeply resented by the constitutional Nationalists and used as an effective
rhetorical lever by Sinn Fein.[47] The Dublin in which Desmond found himself
in the winter of 1918 was bristling with anti-English sentiment that had not
been in the air even at the time of the Easter rebellion, two years before. He
was experiencing this change in public mood for the first time, and the new
political ardour left him cold. After attending Mass on 27th January, 'there
seemed to be a sort of flag-day on so I bought a flag. It was green and had
something Irish written on it so I suppose it was Sinn Fein. The worst of these
flag days is that they never tell you what they are for.'[48] Hardly the words of a
young revolutionary committed to throwing off the British yoke. Sinn Fein
had a new leader, Eamonn de Valera, who was the most senior commandant

of the 1916 uprising to escape execution (probably because he was an American citizen). Garnering support from many quarters, including the Catholic church by stressing that 'religion and patriotism were combined',[49] de Valera had won a landslide victory in a bye-election in East Clare in 1917. Further success at the polls followed; on Saturday, 2nd February 1918, Desmond was disturbed by cheering in the streets while he was working on a planet chart. He 'immediately suspected that the Sinn Feiners had won the Armagh Election'. Walking outside, he 'saw a huge crowd outside the Sinn Fein bank cheering like anything'. Not everyone in Dublin believed that Sinn Fein would renounce violence: Mr Moore 'punctuated his trigonometrical arguments with references to the Sinn Feiners and their atrocities'.[50]

The Bernal brothers were not the only Irish boys who did not return to Bedford at the beginning of 1918. Desmond ran across a fellow student in Dublin named 'Tulip' French. Tulip was attending another grinder in preparation for the army examinations to allow him to attend Military College at Woolwich and be commissioned. Desmond offered to help him with science and concluded after a few days that he was 'an Absolute Idiot'. He was good company though and together they would occasionally go to the Abbey Theatre or to the opera (which Desmond found wonderful). Tulip's home was in Bray, on the coast south of Dublin, and he would take Desmond there for weekends, when they would go off hiking and rock climbing in the Wicklow Mountains. Tulip was not such an idiot that he was not useful to the army, and he would be killed before the end of the year.

Desmond left Dublin at the end of March having enjoyed 'a very free and pleasant life there'. After a month at Brookwatson, he and Kevin returned to England on board a ferry camouflaged in black and white stripes. The Irish Sea was rough and they shared the boat with a large number of cattle, which resulted in smells familiar to them but not welcome to most other passengers. Arriving at Bedford, Desmond was mobbed by friends and resumed the office of house prefect, enforcing the rules with some vigour. On 4th June, 'I went up to the dorm tonight and slippered Whistler for being out of bed, it was 10 pm.'[51] The rule of law and Desmond's attempts to project authority did not always run smoothly. A new boy, who was ordered by Bernal to bend over to receive the customary punishment for not being in bed, 'refused . . . started arguing . . . argued and demanded justice all the time'. A few weeks later, the unhappy boy carried out a complicated escape plan, which involved stealing a motorbike, money and clothes.

In June 1918, King George V and Queen Mary visited the school.[52] The King inspected the ranks of the Officer Training Corps after taking the salute. In Desmond's mind he was not much of a king in appearance: 'he looks shifty and weak and his voice is curiously husky.' The shortage of able-bodied young men was now an acute problem for farmers, who needed casual labour at harvest times. In the first week of July, the weather was sunny and boys were sent to local farms to help with haymaking. Although Desmond had been rowing every afternoon and was used to farm work at Brookwatson, he felt utterly worn out after the first day and did not see how they were going to survive the week. That week too, another ominous shadow was cast over the school by the arrival of the 'Spanish fever', which 'laid out a number of victims'.

The influenza epidemic continued for months, and on 1st November 1918, Bernal fell ill. He was put to bed in the sick bay 'with three other victims',[53] and given a diet of fluids. The only consolation was the presence of 'a funny little night nurse...she has bobbed hair and is quite pretty'.[54] He was still unwell with a fever on 11th November when the end of the war was finally announced, but his thoughts on hearing the news were lucid:

Peace at last. Mrs Tearle rushed into the sick room before eleven this morning saying that the armistice had been signed and the fighting had stopped and we all cheered. I cannot explain my feelings at the news. There seemed to be a kind of relief but no joy, in fact I think I did not realize peace any more than I did the war, it was all a dream and now it was over. Individually it affects me quite a lot. I will now not have to try for a temporary commission and will be able to go up to Cambridge in due course in October 1919 if I get a scholarship, what next I do not know. I had quite counted on being killed in the war so I had made no plans for the immediate future except of course my dreams which seem to recede as I approach the time of their fulfillment. Am I to fail or have I failed already? I have certainly done so in my efforts at authority here, but is that a guarantee that I will do the same in the outside world. Do the same forces act and will I react on them in the same way? I do not know so I have recourse to the weak policy of 'Wait and See'.[55]

He was not allowed outside to join in the general rejoicing, but could hear bells ringing, cheering and, later, fireworks popping. He recovered steadily and two weeks later made a return to the boxing ring, where not surprisingly he was 'hardly ten seconds in the ring' before being tired out.

While Bernal was aware of his lack of authority as a prefect and worried to some extent about his relationships with other students at Bedford, perhaps the only unusual aspect of his behaviour as a seventeen-year old was to commit these anxieties to paper in his voluminous diaries. As one might expect at that age, another more perplexing force was beginning to disturb him. The time for his Cambridge scholarship examinations was rapidly approaching, and one of his friends introduced him to his sister, who lived in Cambridge: 'She is a very pleasant girl but as usual I was so perturbed that I made an absolute idiot of myself.'[56] Desmond in fact had been exposed to female company as much as any other young gentleman of the day. There were often parties at home, and his mother was friendly with Miss Gaskell, 'a pretty young dancing mistress' from Dublin, who was a frequent visitor to Brookwatson. She would give lessons to the children and organize dances, which Desmond had enjoyed hugely as a young boy, once describing Irish jigs to his mother as 'the mathematics of the feet'.[57] Now with the insecurities of adolescence weighing on him, he was more aware of the 'humiliating proficiency' of his dance partners and an accompanying 'vague, indefinable distraction that did not even become sexual'.[58]

The extent of his embarrassment became plain when he spent the first week of December in Cambridge, trying for admission to Emmanuel College. Another Bedford student, Broughton 'Twam' Twamley, was his companion and together they explored the streets around the University. They looked at all the colleges they came across, but where Twam would walk boldly into the quadrangles, Desmond stayed back, in case it was a women's college. When they discovered Newnham College later in the week, the audacious Twam watched some young ladies playing fives, while Desmond waited nervously down the street.[59]

They stayed in rooms in the town and had their first experience of Emmanuel, with the other scholarship candidates, the night before the examinations began. Dinner was taken at long tables with half a dozen students sitting each side on heavy polished oak benches. Before the meal a procession of dons filed into the panelled hall and took their places at the high table: 'Then one of them said a long Latin grace at breakneck pace and we all fell to.'[60] The dinner was not elaborate and contained no meat because of continuing wartime shortages, but Desmond was pleased to find the food 'infinitely superior' to that served at Bedford. He talked to some of his competitors and formed the opinion that about half were from the larger public schools and 'the rest from obscure grammar schools or board schools'. He also met a mathematics tutor, P.W. Wood, who assured him that the papers were not half as bad as they looked. He left feeling quite cheery about his prospects for the morrow.

By the next morning, he was too nervous to eat breakfast. He found the first paper very easy, but attempted only seven questions out of ten. Things got worse on the second day – 'algebra, trigonometry and differential calculus... made an awful mess of it, forgetting even how to do continued fractions.' The next morning brought a note of triumph as he wrote 'a startling essay' on the newly formed League of Nations. That afternoon the candidates were entertained to tea and given a tour of Emmanuel by the Master's wife. No doubt she told them that the College was founded by the Charter of Queen Elizabeth in 1584, and from the first earned a reputation as a stronghold of Puritanism. The College chapel, designed by Sir Christopher Wren, rises above a long gallery flanking either side, the whole supported on cloisters. The architecture did not immediately appeal to Bernal, perhaps still trying to come to terms with the anti-Catholic tradition of the College that he was seeking to join, and he found the chapel 'not a very imposing one'.

Back at Bedford, Desmond was excused from the end of term school exams and amused himself by studying crystallography. As a microscopist, he would of course appreciate the beautiful colours and forms of crystals, but what really engrossed him was the regularity of their shapes, their external symmetries. Mineralogists had long known that each crystal type shows a characteristic and constant angle between adjacent faces, and for a crystal of a given chemical composition that angle will not change regardless of the size of the crystal. There was also a firm belief that these invariant external features of a crystal were determined by its internal structure. A French crystallographer, Delafosse, wrote in 1843 that 'This [atomic] structure, as we are considering it here, appears without question to be the primary characteristic in crystals, that which dominates all others. External form, which until today has been privileged to absorb all the attention of crystallographers, is in our eyes now but a secondary characteristic, of importance only because modifications to it are always found to be subordinated to the particular laws of the internal structure and of the molecular constitution of the crystallized body.'[61]

Although nineteenth-century science had not been able to supply much knowledge about the molecular construction of crystals, studies of their physical qualities, such as the optical properties, had led to the realization that crystals were solids with homogeneous structures, and that this homogeneity resulted from the repetition of identical components in a three-dimensional array.[62] This property of homogeneity in space allowed geometers to analyse the varieties of crystal shapes, regardless of the nature of the material comprising them. From a general consideration of the possible symmetry of solid plane-faced structures, a German mathematician named Hessel had deduced that there were only thirty-two possible crystal shapes. His work though published in 1830, at a time when many of the crystal shapes he described had not yet been discovered in nature, did not gain any attention until it was unearthed sixty years later. By the beginning of the twentieth century, Hessel's observations were recognized by mineralogists and chemists as providing a way of classifying crystals. Bernal spent his time drawing crystal structures, exploring the thirty-two symmetry classes and also making two-dimensional projections, whereby the faces of any crystal can be represented by points within a circle. Crystallography appealed to him as a naturalist, a mathematician, a physicist and a chemist.

A week after sitting the examinations in Cambridge, Bernal received a telegram informing him that he had been awarded a scholarship for £60 to

Emmanuel, but 'strange to say I was not as elated as I ought to have been, in fact I was more depressed than anything else'.[63] End of term fighting started on a large scale, and Bernal was at first the irritated victim of high spirits running through the house: 'I was mobbed a few times by the kids and then someone hit on the brainy idea of putting me in a clothes basket. It was a tight fit but John Gates' weight on the lid eventually squashed me in.' Later that night, Bernal had given up any attempt at imposing order and was the leader of a raid on an adjoining dorm. He was captured after a fight, stripped, and doused with cold water – an experience he found 'refreshing rather than otherwise'. On the final morning of term, Mr Tearle received a letter from Emmanuel describing Bernal's performance as very uneven. 'He wrote a miserably poor essay on the League of Nations (a poor subject to choose). Had you not vouched for his general intelligence, I would have thought him a mathematical grub.' Desmond seems to have been unmoved by these unflattering remarks and on New Year's Eve wrote that 1918 had been an *annus mirabilis* for the whole world but especially for him. It had been the 'most glorious year of my life thus far', and he felt the Cambridge scholarship 'will make my future career'.

Bernal's strengths in science and mathematics had been achieved at the expense of more conventional study of classics. He had tried to teach himself Greek, but at the scholarship examinations in December had managed to translate just one sentence. He was therefore required to go back to Cambridge in the spring of 1919 to take the 'Little Go' exam in Latin, which he duly passed. When he returned to Bedford, he was devastated to find that his closest friend, Lovell Hodgkinson, had died from influenza. The two had planned to start a school magazine, and in a letter home Hodgkinson once described Bernal as 'the cleverest chap in the school...He is not a bit conceited – he has got a very keen sense of humour and is simply a topping chap.'[64]

During the Easter break, Desmond concentrated on chemistry, causing occasional alarms when experiments did not always go as planned. While he was distilling some methylated spirits in the kitchen, using a large flask with a reflux condenser, the flask cracked and the spirit caught fire. 'I had the presence of mind to unclamp the condenser, take it out to the scullery still burning brightly with a beautiful blue flame.'[65] Brigid Murphy, the red-headed housemaid, enjoyed practical jokes and was 'in fits of laughter'. Her friend the cook, Kate O'Meara, had a more sedate disposition and stayed in a 'blue funk' for several hours. The next morning, Desmond was banished to the fields to shoot crows. No doubt he received emphatic instructions from his father because a previous shooting outing had resulted in tragedy, when the only bird that sat still enough for Des to hit it was Kevin's tame magpie.

Kevin never entirely forgave him for this.
Desmond took with him to the hide a piece o
problem of finding an expression for the numb
I did not get very far however. Some crows appea
and missed them.' A month later, back at school, Bern.
had set himself and devised a notation for isomeric hydr

Desmond's last term at school was blighted by news of .
health. At the beginning of July, he and Kevin received a telegram   them
to return home at once, but then their father rallied and they stayed in
Bedford. When they set foot on Irish soil again at the end of July, Desmond
noticed for the first time the extreme poverty of Dublin, where 'the contrast
with England is striking. The dirty streets, the idlers and bare legged raga-
muffins all wanting to do something for you.'[66] It was as though the anxiety
about his father had sensitized him to the misfortunes of others. With his
father so ill, Desmond, as the eldest son, had to become involved in the
business of the farm. On 2nd August, an auction of the standing fields of
oats and wheat was held, and the lack of enthusiasm shown for the crops
dismayed the naïve young man – 'the bids came slowly and sullenly as if each
shilling involved much heart wrenching, and there was not a bit of competition. I had no idea that the Irish farmer was so apathetic, miserly.'[67] Perhaps
the farmers of Tipperary were simply unable to shake off the habit of the
'boycott' at auctions, first taught them by Parnell during the Land War of the
1880s. Then any tenant who bid for a farm from which his neighbour had
been evicted was to expect isolation 'from the rest of his kind as if he were a
leper of old'.[68]

For the rest of the summer, Sam Bernal remained jaundiced, and he was
mostly confined to bed. Desmond spent many hours reading to him and a
great closeness developed between them. In mid-September, Desmond had to
travel to London to take one final set of scholarship examinations. His father,
who had been in and out of consciousness for the preceding fortnight, died
while he was away. Desmond returned for the funeral and was humbled by the
loss. The sight of his dead father 'swept away in a moment all my philosophy
and elaborate reasonings and made me weaker and more human than I have
ever been before'.[69]

2

━━━◆◆◆◆◆━━━

Cambridge Undergraduate

The Great War changed Cambridge from a vibrant university town to a dark, cheerless place, where army divisions camped and drilled before going to fight in the trenches. Their officers spent a last few civilized weeks living in the colleges. Tens of thousands of soldiers returned to Cambridge from the front after being blinded, maimed or gassed, for treatment at the First Eastern General Hospital (a medical campground spread over the gardens and backs behind King's and Clare Colleges). About sixteen thousand Cambridge undergraduates and recent graduates went to war, of whom a third were either killed or seriously wounded.[1] Teaching did not stop altogether, but the undergraduate numbers for the last three years of the conflict averaged about one fifth of the pre-war level. At Emmanuel College, the photograph of the 1916 freshmen contained just five, solemn, young men – three of oriental appearance. At the end of a war that had lasted a year longer than the usual degree course, the new Master of Trinity College, Sir J.J. Thomson, was concerned that the hiatus might result in a permanent loss of traditional ways and customs. He soon realized that his worries were groundless. Within two months of the Armistice, a record number of new students matriculated, the largest contingent comprising four hundred naval officers sent by the Admiralty to complete their scientific studies. Although there was no time to organize the Boat Race in the spring, the annual cricket match against Oxford took place in the summer of 1919. Then most of the naval officers left, and Bernal was among the first regular intake of undergraduates that October, one of eighty freshmen to come up to Emmanuel.

The routine for Bernal was established on his first morning, when his 'bedder' woke him with the words, 'Twenty minutes to eight, Sir.'[2] Later in the day, he met his supervisor, Mr Herman, who gave him his timetable. There would be twelve lectures scheduled each week on electricity, optics, pure geometry, calculus and particle dynamics. In addition there would be two mathematics tutorials with Herman. The first lecture, on geometry, was given in Peterhouse College by Mr Grace. Bernal was one of the first students to arrive, and the dark-beamed room with its narrow arched windows reminded him of the schoolroom in Nenagh. He sat watching the other students arrive, and at length 'Mr Grace turned up, sharp blue eyes, lank grey hair and dry thin lips, harmonizing wonderfully with the general aspect of the place. His lecture was not a long one, he made some drily witty general remarks on examinations, set us some easy looking problems and dismissed us after ten minutes.'[3] So ended his first encounter with John Hilton Grace FRS, a wayward don whose deep love of geometry was conveyed by his teaching in such a way that an interested and talented student, like Bernal, would sometimes follow him far beyond the boundaries of the undergraduate course.

For the first few weekends at Emmanuel, Bernal gravitated towards the familiar company of his old schoolmate, Broughton Twamley. On a Sunday afternoon walk together, 'the conversation was as usual mostly of girls'[4] with Twam bemoaning the lack of female company – for Bernal it was a case of not missing what he did not know, but he could imagine the pleasures of which Twam boasted. Twam, in turn, was distressed because every time he opened a book he would soon fall asleep. Bernal was already revelling in the cavernous stacks of the University Library, and filled the end pages of his diary with lists of books read (including two books on Assyriology on 29th October, for example). Bernal's circle of friends soon widened and he found himself in the company of more intense conversationalists, who shared at least some of his interests. The experience was liberating, and made him think that he knew relatively little outside mathematics and science. He did his best to rectify this by reading and talking with renewed energy. Bernal found himself more drawn towards the company of 'socialistically inclined economists or historians'[5] rather than to his fellow scientists. 'Night after night, sitting over a fire and drinking more and more diluted coffee or strolling around moonlit courts, we talked politics, religion and sex.'[6] It was difficult to meet members of the opposite sex: women were a small minority of students and were closely chaperoned at social events. Still Bernal's days were fully occupied and he seemed to manage quite easily with five or six hours sleep a night. In addition to his intellectual pursuits, he rowed with more enthusiasm than technique, but was powerful enough to occupy the number three seat in a college eight.

Although the recent war remained the dominant backdrop to life in Great Britain, wartime experiences were almost the one taboo subject for Bernal's contemporaries. Those who served had no wish to rekindle the horrors witnessed, and their younger contemporaries, many of whom had lost brothers or cousins, understood and respected their reticence. The destabilizing political and social effects of the war were, by contrast, exciting, divisive, and fascinating subjects for debate. While Cambridge University managed, to a large extent, to preserve its pre-war institutional style, the country as a whole was undergoing radical changes, and even Cambridge students could not afford to be complacent about the future. The Bolshevik revolution in Russia was the great, unresolved event in 1919. British troops were fighting in a bitter civil war alongside White Russians, and in June the Royal Navy had sunk several capital ships of the Red Navy. It was all part of an attempt led by Winston Churchill, Secretary of State for War in Lloyd George's Coalition Government, to 'strangle at birth' the Bolshevik state. Churchill was convinced that 'of all the tyrannies in history, the Bolshevik tyranny is the worst, the most destructive, the most degrading'.[7] Ultimately he could not persuade the rest of the Cabinet to support his anti-Bolshevik crusade, and he was derided in the popular press for wanting a new war with Russia. There was widespread disgust in Britain with wartime profiteers and an unprecedented level of unrest amongst the labour force (despite the introduction of an eight hour working day and weekly wages more than double what they were in 1914).[8] Nearly two-and-a-half million British workers went on strike in 1919, and there was strife in the shipyards of Clydeside and Belfast. When looting took place in Liverpool during a policemen's strike, Lloyd George feared 'anarchist conspiracy' and sent a cruiser to the Mersey and troops to the city.[9]

The political balance within the University was not out of kilter with that in the country at large, but what made Cambridge different was the intellectual ferment and youthful idealism of the debates inside its stonewalls. The most influential voice belonged to John Maynard Keynes, a don at King's College and member of the secret Apostles society. He wrote *The Economic Consequences of the Peace* in 1919, arguing against harsh reparations being imposed on Germany, partly on moral grounds and also because he feared that a weakened Germany would fall prey to Bolshevism.[10] It was one of the few books that Bernal actually bought, and he was moved by it. Kingsley Martin, an undergraduate at Magdalene whom Bernal would soon meet through socialist circles, believed that Keynes' monograph gave 'enormous encouragement to a generation of idealistic undergraduates',[11] who were nearly all pacifists at this stage of their lives.

Martin had been a conscientious objector in the war and served as a medical orderly in France, before entering Magdalene College in January 1919. On his first night in Magdalene, he befriended Patrick Blackett, one of the naval officers who had been sent for six months of general studies, and during the course of an all-night conversation converted him to socialist beliefs.[12] Bernal's socialist epiphany was the result of an almost identical encounter, although in his case the proselytizer was not Martin but a fellow Emmanuel freshman, H. Douglas Dickinson. Dickinson's father was a curator of the Science Museum in London and an expert on the Industrial Revolution. The young Douglas had learned to appreciate the significance of the

history of science and engineering, but came to Cambridge to read economics. Bernal's conversion to socialism took place in Dickinson's rooms on the
night of 7th November, as a result of a conversation, which lasted until two
o'clock in the morning and left Bernal feeling ecstatic. The next morning
Bernal awoke 'not very tired and perfectly happy', and felt as though 'my old
life was broken to bits and the new lay in front of me'.[13] He was inclined to
melodrama in some of his diary entries so that the day before, for example, his
elevation to Emmanuel's first rowing eight was also noted as 'a turning point
in my life'.[14] But the thrill of his political awakening endured and a few years
later, Bernal reflected: 'This socialism was a marvellous thing. Why had no
one told me about it before? And Dick knew it all, explained it so simply in a
few hours. The theory of Marxism, the great Russian experiment, what we
could do here and now, it was all so clear, so compelling, so universal.'[15]

Dickinson was not slow to exploit the new convert's zeal. He called into
Bernal's rooms the following afternoon to ask him to speak in a Labour debate
he was organizing. One of the speakers had dropped out, and Bernal saw it as
an opportunity not to be thrown away so that 'after a minute of hesitation',[16]
he accepted. Three days later, at the eleventh hour of the eleventh day of the
eleventh month, Dickinson caused him two minutes of acute discomfort. The
pair were walking back from a lecture when Bernal 'realized that it was
Armistice Day and that the two minutes silence was going to begin. It was
an impressive sight, the silence and the people standing with the white snow
gently falling. Dickinson and I walked resolutely on. I confess that left to
myself I would have bowed to authority.'[17]

Bernal and Dickinson cast themselves as Emmanuel's leading radicals and
as such risked occasional physical retribution from the abundant ranks of
hearty, conservative students. The pair posted red notices around the college
advertising future socialist meetings, knowing that this could provoke
trouble, which they half expected and welcomed. Bernal was physically strong
from daily rowing and, after Bedford school, no stranger to ragging. Several
years later, C.P. Snow, then an undergraduate with an interest in crystallography, was told about a famous raid by five or six naval officers on Bernal's
rooms.[18] Bernal heard a commotion outside his door and turned off all his
lights so that his eyes became dark-adapted. His assailants burst into the pitch
darkness, betraying their own positions by lighted cigarettes. Bernal collared
several of them, banging their heads together, and then quietly slipped out as
the attackers exchanged blows with each other.

Dickinson, also a prominent target as Secretary of the University Socialist
Society (CUSS), received his come-uppance one cold evening in February
1920, when a group of naval officers ducked him in a trough in the market
square. The following week a meeting of the Union of Democratic Control,

being addressed by the pacifist, Norman Angell, ended in uproar as a group of ex-servicemen tried to carry off the speaker and throw him into the river. Bernal and Dickinson got wind of the fact that the same group intended to kidnap Noel Brailsford, the speaker they had arranged for CUSS a few days later. Brailsford was a socialist journalist, who in 1914 wrote a scathing and perspicacious attack on the international arms industry, *The War of Steel and Gold*. Bernal had just read the book and enjoyed organizing a 'protective force'[19] to keep Brailsford safe during his visit.

While their politics earned them a degree of notoriety, Bernal and Dickinson were certainly not outside the mainstream of university life. Indeed the theories of socialism flourished in the generally permissive atmosphere of privilege. A pink-cheeked, nineteen-year-old dandy, Maurice Dobb, gave a tea party at Pembroke College, where his guests consumed éclairs, while earnestly discussing workers' ownership and other socialist issues. Dobb, whose family owned a small draper's business in London, had become interested in socialism during his last year at Charterhouse school. He won an Exhibition to Pembroke, and spent the months between school and university attending as many Labour and socialist meetings as he could in London; like Dickinson, he arrived in Cambridge with some knowledge of the works of Marx and other socialist thinkers.[20] On first meeting him, Dickinson in his capacity as Secretary of CUSS, interrogated Dobb briskly 'under the impression that so spruce and conventional-looking a young man must be a provocateur'.[21] Dobb read Economics and joined Keynes' Political Economy Club; he joined forces with Dickinson as one of the most active socialists amongst the student body. One small incident from the end of the first term serves to illustrate the limits of Bernal's non-conformity and a bourgeois talent of Dobb's that might have atrophied come the revolution. Preparing for the Christmas dinner at Emmanuel College, Bernal was in despair about tying his bow tie, and Dobb was happy to oblige his friend.

The only region of the British Isles close to revolution in 1919 was Ireland, where there was a new militancy amongst the Irish Volunteers (soon to be renamed the Irish Republican Army) under the leadership of Michael Collins. Collins was also a leading figure in de Valera's Sinn Fein party, which had made stunning gains in the post-Armistice General Election of 1918 and was now assembled in Dublin as Dail Eireann (the Irish Parliament) – declaring Ireland to be a sovereign, independent state and defying the might of the British Empire. The sparks kindled by the Easter uprising of 1916 burst into flame in Tipperary in January 1919, when a pair of masked Volunteers murdered two popular Irish constables, who were guarding a shipment of gelignite being delivered to a quarry. Although these Volunteers were acting on their own volition and not under instructions from Collins, he made plain his support of such violent action a few weeks later, when addressing a meeting of the Sinn Fein executive: 'The sooner fighting is forced and a general state of disorder created throughout the country, the better it will be for the country. Ireland is likely to get more out of a general state of disorder than from a continuance of the situation as it now stands.'[22]

Collins had built up a widespread intelligence network and organized the Volunteers in Tipperary and elsewhere into strictly run military units with a primary aim of murdering those members of the Royal Irish Constabulary not sympathetic to their stated intention of ending British oppression. About a dozen policemen were killed by the end of 1919, and Ireland was headed for insurrection. Driven by Collins, Sinn Fein's aim was to obtain freedom on its own terms and not be beholden to the British government for the grant of Home Rule.

As Bernal was preparing to leave Cambridge for Christmas in the now lawless County Tipperary, he was asked by his college tutor, P.W. Wood, if he were a Home Ruler. Bernal replied, 'No, Sir, I am a Sinn Feiner', and recorded in his diary that this was the first time that he had dared to admit as much to a superior. He also noted Wood's matter-of-fact, but nonetheless perceptive reply that 'things had gone too far for any solution to be workable'.[23] Back home, he found less tolerance for his new opinions. Mary Waller, an old friend from his days at Nenagh school, came to visit the Bernal family and remarked that 'the Irish ought to be strafed'. Desmond rose to their defence but ran into a withering rebuke from his aunt, Cuddie, who argued that 'the Irish were ignorant, changeable, dissatisfied and vindictive', a point of view that 'for lack of knowledge I can not deny convincingly'.[24] The social highlight of his vacation was a fancy dress party, for which he decided to appear as a Bolshevik. A parcel arrived from Gamages department store, just after Christmas, containing a flowing beard and a wig – an outfit he found to be ferocious but uncomfortable. He and Kevin decided to play a prank on one of the farm labourers. After dark, Desmond donned the disguise and took an old revolver from the house, meaning to scare the worker. The two brothers, hiding behind a stone wall, heard voices – a group of soldiers talking to some local girls. The soldiers were on patrol to protect the neighbourhood against the Volunteers, and it occurred to Desmond that in his present costume he could be shot on sight. He imagined the newspaper headlines, 'Regrettable Accident' or 'Practical Joker's Fate', and waited with his heart thumping. Eventually the soldiers moved off, and Desmond attacked the labourer's cottage, thrusting his gun through a broken windowpane with a crash. Kevin later told him that the whole incident had been witnessed by one of the soldiers, lingering behind with a local girl. Instead of challenging the armed revolutionary, the soldier turned tail and ran back to town with the young woman following.[25]

Desmond's stupid prank would have been even more dangerous had he staged it in his next vacation. The level of IRA violence against the police continued to escalate and inevitably led to reprisals by the police. Even Desmond, a notional party supporter, was appalled by the spate of Sinn Fein inspired murders because they 'seem such a waste, and done in so cruel and cowardly a manner'. The police retaliation in kind began on 15th March 1920 with the assassination of the Lord Mayor of Cork, Thomas MacCurtain, who was also a well-known Sinn Feiner. His death was greeted with some joy in the Bernal household, where the general attitude towards Sinn Fein was 'hang the lot of them'; Desmond sensed this was based on a fear that it might otherwise be their turn to be killed first.[26] MacCurtain was shot by a gang of masked men, some of whom spoke with English accents.[27] The Royal Irish Constabulary was now recruiting men from England, often ex-servicemen, to replace those Irish policemen killed and the growing number who had resigned from the force because of Sinn Fein threats. The overall strength of the police force needed to be increased since they were to bear the brunt of the struggle with the IRA. Lloyd George was not prepared to commit troops and accept that there was a civil war in Ireland, but he encouraged 'unauthorized' reprisals.[28] There were not enough bottle-green uniforms for the new recruits, who were instead issued with khaki trousers or tunics. Many members of the new force were British Army veterans of the Great War and when they first appeared in County Tipperary, they were nicknamed the Black and Tans, after a local pack of hounds. The Black and Tans acted as an autonomous mercenary force, matching the IRA for viciousness, and thereby solidifying anti-British sentiment in many quarters. Not at Brookwatson though, where Cuddie continued to believe that the Irish were about the worst nation on the face of the earth; by the end of the Easter vacation, she and Desmond had got beyond arguing and 'into quarrelling'.

In his academic studies, if not in other areas of his life, Bernal was already beginning to show a level of maturity and a depth of interest, which para-doxically interfered with his mastery of the undergraduate courses. At the beginning of the Lent Term, he switched courses in order to attend Grace's lectures on analytical geometry, which he soon liked 'more and more, every-thing is so symmetrical and neat'.[29] Analytical geometry is the bridge between algebra and geometry: it brings numerical values to points in space (e.g. latitude and longitude) and also allows an algebraic function to be repre-sented graphically by points on a plane. The basic examples using two-dimensional coordinates at right angles (x- and y-axes) were already very familiar territory for Bernal, as were conic sections comprising the equations of circles, ellipses and hyperbolas. From his study of astronomy, Bernal also had a good working knowledge of *polar coordinates* where the position of a point is determined by its distance from a fixed origin or pole and the angle between a fixed polar axis and the line joining the pole to the point. Polar coordinates are particularly useful for studying spirals, symmetrical forms often found in architecture and nature. Grace's mathematical treatment of different spiral forms, such as the logarithmic spiral of the snail's shell, delighted Bernal.

Grace was at the top of his form as a teacher during that academic year. In 1918, while deputizing at Aberdeen University for a professor away on war service, he published half a dozen notes and papers – the highest total of a career, in which consistently 'he tackled a problem simply because he found it interesting'.[30] It seems that the pressures of teaching at Cambridge blunted his aptitude for original work, and a few years after returning from Aberdeen, he withdrew from academic life permanently. One of his major papers in 1918, 'Tetrahedra in relation to spheres and quadrics', concerned three-dimensional shapes, and another short note, 'An analogue in space of a case of Poncelet's porism', involved projective geometry (the study of transforming three-dimensional objects into flat, two-dimensional configurations). Projective geometry has a long history in that it was unwittingly applied by the architects of the ancient world and by Renaissance painters, but it was not until after the Napoleonic Wars that a French mathematician and engineer, Jean Victor Poncelet, published a textbook, *A Treatment of the Projection of Figures*, that set out the basic laws of perspective and projection.[31]

Grace divulged his particular enthusiasms in his lectures, as on 13th February 1920, 'Mr Grace is more and more interesting – a lot of beautiful mathematics about Poncelet's porism and 22 symmetric relations.'[32] Aside from the beauty of his ideas, there was a fragility about Grace himself that was attractive. In 1895, he had been in the running for Senior Wrangler, the most prestigious prize for the Mathematical Tripos examination, but according to legend celebrated a day too early and came in second. Bernal learned that Grace's subsequent career had been blighted by drink and 'now he walks about the town in his disreputable old clothes with some old crony... leading a miserable existence only enlivened by maths or visits to the Blue Boar'.[33] Grace would continue to publish short, ingenious, papers for many years after leaving Cambridge in 1922, always with the pure spirit of an amateur, and only because he found the topic inherently worthy.[34] Bernal, while appreciating the elegance of the mathematics, was always far more interested in what he could do with the techniques. What Grace gave him was an invaluable set of tools with which to attack the intricacies of crystalline structure.

Bernal's attraction to Grace's teachings meant that he ignored some of the core content of the curriculum, and of course there were plenty of other distractions outside the curriculum. In the Lent Term of 1920, he was still a sexual innocent, while Twam enjoyed the status of a man of the world. He told Bernal that he would be bringing two sisters, Joan and Jose Kingsley, family friends from Bedford, to Emmanuel for a visit. He suggested that they might take tea in Bernal's rooms. Desmond expended considerable energy clearing the general debris in his sitting room for the occasion, and then spent an equal amount of time rearranging furniture and placing books in just the positions to create the ambience of a distracted but creative young genius. Bernal was bewitched by Jose, the smaller of the two young women. At tea, he held forth about the laziness and aimlessness of Cambridge life. Twam became annoyed by his friend's affected pose and said that Desmond only held these attitudes because he was a socialist. Jose was intrigued, and Bernal needed no extra prompting to launch into a diatribe, talking of 'capital and labour, of control and nationalization and entered into eulogies of the Bolsheviks'.[35] Jose attacked his ideas, defending capitalism 'with all the old fallacies'. Bernal, finding that he could not easily counter all her arguments, switched to abstract ideals, and then 'brought in pure science and my discursiveness led me to talk about Einstein and hormones and what not'.[36] Twam and he walked the sisters to the station to catch their train back to Bedford. Bernal wanted to ask Jose if he might write to her, but his courage failed him. As the train pulled out of the station, Twam told Desmond that he was an ass, for although Jose was the smaller of the two sisters, she was twenty-three years old and engaged to be married. This news made no difference to Bernal, who was convinced that he was in love, and he wrote to his mother two days later, describing Jose's soft brown eyes and lovely teeth.[37]

At the start of the Easter vacation, Bernal invited himself to stay with the Twamley family in Bedford in order to see Jose again. He found her even more adorable than she seemed six weeks earlier, and during Mass on the Sunday felt a 'higher pitch of emotion' than he had experienced for a long time. After church he met some boys from the school, who told him that Mr Tearle had warned the House to beware of socialism and of Bernal in particular. The previous day, while watching the annual cross country race with Jose, Bernal had handed out some socialist leaflets. Now Bernal went back to his old House, and was set upon by a gang 'with coats off and sleeves rolled up'. They challenged him to sing *God Save the King*, and when he refused, set upon him. Just as Bernal thought he could hold out no longer, the lookout warned that Mr Tearle was approaching, and Bernal was left to stagger to his feet. Tearle asked accusingly, 'Are you at the bottom of all this row?' to which Bernal replied, 'I am, Sir, very much at the bottom of it.' While his wit delighted his assailants, Bernal regretted the 'almost irreparable' breach with the master who had shown him such kindness.

During his short stay in Bedford, Bernal was relentless in his efforts to impress Jose, and talked continuously, without ever thinking that she might have things to say to him. After telling her of his conception of God and the Trinity, he 'dropped into psychology, palming off my garbled second-hand knowledge culled from McDougall or Freud about various instincts which I called emotions'.[38] Jose seems to have treated him kindly, perhaps unaware that she was being wooed, but Bernal worried later that he was 'a selfish windbag' who talked incessantly to satisfy his own vanity.

The Freudian emphasis on sexual drives gave lustful young males the opportunity at least to talk about some of their frustrations, and to claim an intellectual basis for doing so. No doubt this liberating influence was largely responsible for the cult status that Freud enjoyed in post-war Cambridge. Freud's reputation was also enhanced by the success of psychoanalysis in aiding some sufferers of shell shock or war neurosis. In Vienna, Freud listened to the terrible dreams of soldiers in German, while a military psychiatrist, W.H.R. Rivers, at Craiglockhart Hospital near Edinburgh undertook the same psychological analysis of British soldiers. Before his wartime clinical work, Rivers had followed a varied career as a physiologist and anthropologist. In 1919 he returned to Cambridge and was given the free-ranging position of Praelector of Natural Science Studies, which he used as an opportunity to get to know as many undergraduates as possible and to introduce them to friends of his like H.G. Wells, Bertrand Russell, Robert Graves and his ex-patient, Siegfried Sassoon. His rooms at St. John's College, were according to the novelist Arnold Bennett, 'like a market square', with undergraduates coming 'at nearly all hours to discuss the intellectual news of the day'.[39] Bernal would not get around to reading any works of Freud for another year or so, but when he did they made such an impression on him that he wrote 'the laying bare of the unconscious basis for human desire and action will rank with that of the cosmologies of Copernicus and Newton and of the process of Evolution as one of the greatest liberating discoveries of mankind'.[40]

Apart from Rivers' rooms, there was another lively forum where discussion often turned to psychology. This was the Heretics, an elite gathering of iconoclasts, where the spirit was open, vigorous and heterosexual, (in contrast to the secret, precious and predominantly homosexual society of the Cambridge Apostles). The Heretics had been founded before the Great War, initially to question the religious orthodoxy of university life when attendance at chapel was still compulsory; the original object was 'to promote discussion on problems of religion, philosophy and art'.[41] Membership of the Heretics implied 'the rejection of all appeal to Authority in the discussion of religious questions', or as Bertrand Russell quipped, the Ten Commandments should carry the same rubric as a term examination paper, where 'only six need be attempted'.[42] In his first year, Bernal listened to the querulous, squeaky-voiced, Lytton Strachey address the Heretics on the proper attitude to sex.[43] Strachey's *Eminent Victorians*, his caustic debunking of such revered figures as Florence Nightingale and General Gordon of Khartoum, had appeared in 1918: there was no one better qualified to appeal to the irreverent audience. The certainties of Victorian times were in tatters as a result of the Great War and the civil wars in Europe that supplanted it; any remnants of the old order were now being dissected in Cambridge by intellectuals using the varied instruments of humanist philosophy, anthropology, economics, politics and psychology. The same forces that undermined rigid social mores could corrode an individual's religious faith, unless he or she took determined measures to repel them. Bernal, for one, found them irresistible.

Bernal had arrived in Cambridge as a devout Catholic and on his first Sunday went to a solemn High Mass, where he was struck by the smallness of the congregation and its homogeneity: 'not two hundred souls all told and mostly well off. The absence of the poor is a distressing sign.'[44] Their absence may have been just as well since Bernal had neglected to bring any money with him and so suffered 'the usual tortures at the collection'. He continued to attend Mass regularly, in Cambridge and at home, for the first two years of his university life. As his political views hardened, the Church's emphasis on the individual's redemption and such moral entreaties as 'thou shalt love thy neighbour as thyself' seemed to him to become increasingly irrelevant. On rare occasions, there seemed to be some common ground between his religion and his politics – notably, a fiery sermon in Nenagh at Easter 1920, when the priest used the resurrection as a metaphor for Ireland's struggle for independence, predicting that the country would rise from the darkness of oppression by the will of God to become the leader of the civilized world.[45] More usual was the sense of growing exasperation, as when Bernal 'sat in church crushed by the weight of an appallingly dull and empty sermon... [wondering] what force of inertia was preventing the congregation from rising and slaughtering the preacher on the spot'.[46]

The weather in Ireland over Easter 1920 was wet and windy, in keeping with Bernal's low spirits. On his return to Emmanuel, he had 'a short and rather terrifying interview' with his tutor P.W. Wood, who admonished him to concentrate on revision for the end-of-year exams. Bernal was feeling dejected and even seemed depressed about his appearance: 'my pallid haggard face, my shock of hair, my podgy dirty hands, my bent shoulders, my untidy clothes and my slovenly walk.'[47] He cheered up after a long walk with Dickinson, who had been to a University Socialist Federation meeting during the vacation, where there had been a split between the reformers and the revolutionaries.

Dickinson supported the reformers and Bernal agreed with him implicitly, although he was in awe of Dickinson's grasp of the facts and his lucid exposition of them – when it came to politics he still felt that he had 'the status of a disciple'.[48] It is difficult, based on the evidence of Bernal's diaries, to avoid the conclusion that his political beliefs at this stage were shallow. Together, Bernal and Dickinson attended the usual round of Heretics, socialist, and Union meetings, including a speech by Ernest Bevin, the transport union leader, at the Guildhall on the aims of Labour. Bernal was impressed by Bevin: 'an enormous man with a fine voice – immensely inspiring.'[49]

For a few days, Bernal seemed to heed the warnings of his college tutor and worked hard on revision, but this was too boring to capture his full attention. He constructed a billiard table in his sitting room, using library books as the cushions, and a poker and a tennis racket as the cues. Such a simple invention brought a stream of visitors to his room, and led to hours of idle amusement and chatter that were far more enjoyable than time spent learning formal theorems. Inevitably, the first week of June arrived, and the weather was beautiful as he took the Part I Tripos examinations. At the end of the week, he felt no sense of relief that the exams were over because he felt that he had not done himself justice; but with luck, he hoped that he might still gain first-class honours. The results reached him by letter at Brookwatson a fortnight later and were bitterly disappointing. He was awarded Class II, causing the 'hardest blow my self-esteem has ever had to bear'. He had always been confident that his 'scholarship could surmount all obstacles in its path' but now, 'baulked by the first ditch which [he] had scorned and thought to take in stride', Bernal felt a failure, and could not imagine facing his friends, family or tutor.[50]

His family was sympathetic, knowing how much academic success meant to Desmond, but over the summer became increasingly impatient with his self-indulgent moods and political posturing. He would help out in the cowshed and with other jobs around the farm, but could not hide his resentment for such menial work. The family was worried about the escalation of violence in Tipperary, which apart from threatening their physical safety was also undermining the local economy. The standard form of reprisal by the police and the Black and Tans had been to raze the homes of suspected IRA members and sympathizers, but now they were also destroying cooperative dairies or creameries, causing devastation to the milk trade.[51] While, as Michael Collins correctly predicted, this policy stoked anti-British sentiment in the population as a whole, middle-class dairy farmers like the Bernals felt their way of life threatened from both sides and saw no reassurance in the prospect of Irish independence. Desmond, who spent most of the year in England and was not inclined to bother himself with the business of the farm, was oblivious to the daily pressures and as a matter of principle supported the concept of an Irish Republic. At tea one afternoon, there was 'such an acrid argument on the Irish situation that Cuddie was driven to say "If you have got views like that I can't see why you do not join the Sinn Feiners".[52] Her contemptuous shaft struck home as he later reflected, 'What had I done for Ireland – nothing at all.' His first direct encounter with the Black and Tans came while biking to Tullaheady to play tennis one afternoon in late August. He was searched by soldiers, picketed at the roadside, and noticed that they had one prisoner in their lorry, who wore 'an expression of sheepish embarrassment' as if to say 'this is not quite the place I expected to find myself'.[53]

On 1st September, recorded by Bernal as 'a hateful day', there was a much more disturbing occurrence when a neighbour, Dr Galway Foley, was shot in his home by raiding Sinn Feiners. The violent attack carried out in the name of the Irish Republic led to bitter denunciations at the Bernal dinner table: 'Sinn Fein was called many dreadful names and I was fool enough to object and to try and justify things, pointing to parallel cases on the other side. I was not only quarrelling violently with the lot of them, but they were eyeing me with absolute loathing. I felt like doing something desperate, joining the Volunteers, but I am much too much of a sensible coward. After this, of course, I could not possibly go and meet all the people at the tennis and was rude to Eva in refusing. Instead I worked at reaping which settled my mind…'[54] There were repercussions the next day when he had a 'fierce row' with Cuddie, who criticized him for not helping the family more and for avoiding his responsibilities as the eldest son. Desmond candidly admitted that he cared more about his education and scientific work than the immediate 'bread and butter for the family which is secured amply even without my assistance'.[55] Privately, he regretted that he did not do more to help around the farm, but his main misery remained that his work was going badly.

Adding to his unsettled mood that summer were two guests at Brookwatson – his American second cousin, Virginia Crawford, and her mother, Aunt Sarah. Although Bernal had originally thought Virginia rather plain, he grew to like her spirit and even allowed her into his private study, where she persuaded him to tidy his books. With Kevin and Gigi, they took trips in the horse-drawn milk wagon to visit local places of interest. One of these was Handley's Mill, where they watched the process of producing tweed from wool. Desmond's attention was caught by an emaciated young girl of twelve, whose job it was to load the raw wool into the carding machine: she had 'a pallid face shining with grease out of which shone two deep eyes looking at us… with an indescribable expression that had misery in it and yet pride'. He was also moved by the contrast of the noisy, dusty, slavish conditions of the mill and the joyous freedom of the surrounding countryside. At the hand-looms, there were rows of bent-backed men, sitting on narrow benches, pedalling fiercely, and pulling threads back and forth with each hand, while 'behind each man was a window that looked out on the gurgling river below and away over the sunbathed country to the blue mountains beyond'.[56] He concluded that Ireland would be better without such cottage industries.

By the end of the summer, Desmond was spending every minute of the day with Virginia, causing his sister to become quite jealous. As Virginia was packing to leave, he finally confided his feelings to her and there was a histrionic build-up to their first kiss. After a period of sobbing, Virginia yielded to his request. The kiss was emunctory rather than erotic because he noticed that she had not blown her nose. Desmond did not feel emotionally involved – in fact, he imagined himself to be a character from a novel. He thought he should pledge his love to Virginia, and suggested that they should become engaged. She accepted, and they spent the next day kissing more passionately in his laboratory, where they were almost caught by Biddy, the housemaid, who instead found them 'intent over a copy of Bell's *Solid Geometry*'.[57] Bernal thought that Biddy suspected something.

When he returned to Emmanuel College in October, he was advised by his college tutor to switch to Natural Sciences in the light of his disappointing showing in the Part I of the Mathematics tripos. The science curriculum – physics, chemistry, geology and mineralogy – was a far better match for his broad interests. He soon began to regain some of his self-confidence through verbal sparring with his contemporaries. His diary for 27th October was triumphal after a commanding display to Dickinson and other members of CUSS: 'I surpassed myself in arriving at rapid and novel conclusions. I shall never be afraid of philosophers again, it takes them years to arrive at a truth that I take a minute to reach and it is just as liable to be quite wrong.'[58] He wondered if his mind was capable of originality or 'merely an undigested mass of Einstein and Freud with a top dressing of Wilde and Shaw'.

The originality of Bernal's mind soon emerged, fertilized by the work of an Irish genius – not Wilde or Shaw, but Sir William Hamilton. Hamilton* was perhaps the most remarkable Irish prodigy of the nineteenth century: he knew at least a dozen languages including Greek, Latin, Hebrew, Persian and Hindustani, and at the age of eighteen was hailed by the Royal Astronomer of Ireland as the first mathematician of the age.[59] His greatest contribution to mathematics was his investigation of *complex numbers*, culminating in his invention of *Quaternions* in 1843. Complex or *imaginary* numbers involve

---

* William Rowan Hamilton (1805–65) married Helen Bayly of Nenagh in 1833, and they spent their honeymoon at the family farm, which Bernal visited as a schoolboy to look at diatoms.

the concept of the square root of minus one, $\sqrt{-1}$, usually represented by the symbol, i. *Real numbers,* such as the familiar integers 1, 2, 3, etc., can be located on a number line running from left to right, with negative numbers being to the left of the central point, 0, and positive numbers to the right. The product of multiplying any two real numbers that have the same sign ($+$ or $-$) is always positive (if we ignore zero). The square of any real number is therefore always positive and lies on the number line to the right of 0. The square root of a negative number cannot be expressed as a real number, and cannot be located on the real number line running from west to east on a page. Complex numbers can take the form $a + b$i, where a and b are real numbers and i is the imaginary unit defined as: $i^2 = -1$. It had been accepted since the late seventeenth century that a complex number, such as $z = a + b$i, can be represented on a plane surface by locating its real part a along the west–east number line or axis, and the imaginary part b along an orthogonal north–south axis. The complex number will then appear as a point (a, b) in the coordinate plane.

Thus a two-dimensional plane can be represented by complex numbers; Hamilton's ambition was to develop an algebraic system that would account for three-dimensional space, since this would have great utility in physics and mechanics. If one imagines the west–east number line as an axle for a cycle wheel, while there will be spokes running in the north–south line, there are many spokes lying out of the page, as it were, representing alternative planes all perpendicular to the original west–east axis. After fifteen years of trying to devise a method, Hamilton had a momentary flash of inspiration and realized that a four-dimensional algebra would provide the necessary tools for the job – the *quaternion.* A quaternion consists of an ordered set of four terms, $a + b$i $+ c$j $+ d$k, three of which involve imaginary parts defined by the relationships: $i^2 = j^2 = k^2 = ijk = -1$.

The quaternion system expresses all lines in space by a distinct square root of minus one, and if the three symbols, i, k, and j represent mutually perpendicular square roots of minus one, they can serve as a mathematical device to rotate a line through ninety degrees. The fourth term in the quaternion allows the treatment of lines not mutually perpendicular. Hamilton extended his ideas in a book, *Lectures on Quaternions,* which was incomprehensible even to many mathematicians, but was notable for the first use of the term *vector* to describe quantities such as force, velocity or acceleration that have direction as well as magnitude. He established that vectors when multiplied together as *vector products,* are *anti-commutative:* that is to say, the product of vector a multiplied by vector b will have exactly the opposite direction to the product of vector b times vector a (written as $a \times b = -\{b \times a\}$).

As we have seen, as a result of Grace's lectures Bernal was particularly imbued with the concepts of symmetry, and now he was studying crystals in geology and mineralogy naturally applied his mind to their three-dimensional symmetries. Geometers divide symmetry into two broad classes: *point groups* or *space groups*. Point-group symmetry depends on one unique point in a symmetrical figure that is unique and not repeated elsewhere in the pattern – think of the bulls-eye on a dartboard. Space groups consist of symmetrical patterns that lack a unique point; they are created by the repetition of a certain element in one, two or three dimensions. An example of a one-dimensional space group would be a row of identical columns or a single file of soldiers of the same height. The pattern results from *translation* or the shifting of the motif by regular intervals along a line. If the repetition of the pattern is then extended in two directions (e.g. multiple rows of soldiers standing at attention), a planar pattern of two-dimensional symmetry is obtained. Other common examples of planar patterns include tiles on a roof or patterns printed on fabric. Such planar patterns can be generated from the elemental motif of one soldier or one tile, by a variety of operations such as translation, rotation about an axis perpendicular to the plane or the use of a mirror to produce reflections. For any motif, there are only seventeen symmetry variations, or ways of manipulating it into different, two-dimensional, repeating patterns.[60]

When one comes to three-dimensional symmetry, the permutations are of course much more complicated. As mentioned in Chapter 1, the nineteenth-century geometers had recognized that there were thirty-two possible crystal shapes, and that the facets shown on the exterior of a crystal were an embodiment of the internal planes created by the regular arrangement of molecules within the crystal. The operations of translation, rotation and reflection still apply to three-dimensional space groups, and there are the additional complexities of glide planes and screw axes. All these operations are applied to bring the crystal into congruence with itself: that is to say, if an observer leaves the room while a crystal undergoes one of these symmetry operations, the crystal would look exactly the same when he returns to the room. As a simple example, consider a six-sided, unsharpened pencil. If it is cut in half and a mirror held perpendicular to the cut end, the whole pencil will be restored by the mirror image. Now imagine the whole pencil being rotated around an axis passing down the centre of the lead. This is a six-fold axis of rotation because the pencil comes into congruence with itself every sixty degrees of turn. In crystals, there are two-, three-, four- and six-fold axes of symmetry,[61] but not five-fold axes so commonly seen in the petal arrangements of blossoms, as well as in many starfish.

The basic building block or motif that is repeated to build up the three-dimensional structure of a crystal is called the *unit cell*. That there are 230 space groups, or different symmetric arrangements of unit cells, in crystal lattices was first shown by a German mathematician, Artur Schoenflies, and a Russian crystallographer, E.S. Federov, in 1891. Employing different methods, they reached this final total after several years of independent work.[62] It seems that Bernal became seriously interested in this complex subject in the spring of 1921. His diary entry for 4th April contains the following statement: 'An idea has blossomed in my mind on the connection between the atomic structure of crystals and their elastic and thermal constants. I attempted to attack the problem mathematically with a certain success.' The idea, which he developed over the next few months, was to treat the unit cell of a crystal lattice as three vectors, **a, b, c** that intersect at a common point or origin, and then to develop the symmetrical possibilities using Hamiltonian quaternions. This was a completely original approach to the daunting set of 230 space groups that had previously been solved only in a qualitative geometrical way, which allowed one crystal structure to be distinguished from another. Bernal's aim was to develop a quantitative theory so that every crystal structure could be represented by a formula and the analysis of that structure could be reduced to solving a number of equations.

Beyond the mediaeval walls of Cambridge, a springtide of socialism seemed about to engulf the British Isles in April 1921. The post-war economic boom was over and unemployment began to rise rapidly. Coal miners were on strike after refusing to accept wage cuts, and were trying to persuade the transport workers to join them in a Triple Alliance. Bernal followed events by reading the London newspapers everyday at Brookwatson, and felt that a negotiated settlement 'seems impossible. The crash must come. Yet like butterflies we sport in the sunshine.'[63] He was certainly enjoying the rustic pleasures of Ireland, spending idyllic afternoons in High Wood – 'a wood of dreams. Green moss with anenomies and hyacinths and primroses, big ivy grown trees and saplings circled with honeysuckle' – when not engrossed in his work. On 9th April the newspapers announced that the Triple Alliance would strike and army reserves were called in. Bernal thought that civil conflict on the mainland was almost inevitable, and in turn might force the withdrawal of auxiliary troops from Ireland. He remained worried though by 'the Government's deep laid plans [that] almost make me despair of victory and that means another century of slavery'. Not that he was intending to join the Volunteers or IRA, but would continue to watch and wait. Two days later, the papers reported negotiations and compromises that angered the armchair socialist: 'it's all going to fizzle out, bluff on both sides. I am furious.'[64] The next day he went to a dance in Nenagh, where there were 'tales of raids by the auxiliaries and atrocities of the "Shinnies"'. Surrounded by mostly Protestant young farmers, Bernal held his tongue 'out of prudence'.

As the level of violence in Ireland escalated, it appears that Desmond also decided to restrain his political comments at home. He had become accustomed to quarrelling with Cuddie, which he did not enjoy, but recent criticisms from his mother and his sister, Gigi, had stung him. His mother, annoyed that he would spend all day reading or playing instead of helping around the farm, accused him of selfishness. He increased her annoyance by replying that his selfishness was a deliberate policy. Privately he did express some remorse, noting in his diary that selfishness seemed to be his one constant trait and that he needed to look over his morals. He decided to write to his cousin Virginia and break off their engagement. Gigi, a rebellious and breezy character, thought him conceited. She had little time for his personal introspections and when he showed her his diary, she 'rocked with laughter' over the passages that he had taken the most trouble over. Desmond conceded that 'I am a joke especially on paper, but if I don't take myself seriously, who will?'[65] Desmond and Gigi never remained at odds for long, and he also enjoyed an affectionate relationship with Gofty, their youngest brother, who was now at school in Cambridge. Desmond would spend Sundays entertaining Gofty in his rooms or in a punt on the river.

Bernal now decided that physics was going to be his subject because 'my mind delights in taking readings. Chemistry is too full of smells and Geology of names.'[66] He would soon be faced with examinations again, this time in Natural Sciences. First came the geology examination in which he did 'rather badly' and then a physics paper he spoiled, but at last a triumph: 'A beautiful chemistry paper, I walked over it, trampled over it and jumped on it.'[67] He remained in Cambridge during the summer of 1921 and made the acquaintance of the crystallographer, Arthur Hutchinson, whom he described as 'a very gentlemanly don at Pemmer [Pembroke College]'. Hutchinson encouraged him to continue with four subjects on the basis of his examination results, to Bernal's delight. He continued to read extensively and in July came across a paper by W.L. Bragg on the arrangement of atoms in crystals. Bragg had just become Professor of Physics at Manchester University; he had shared the 1915 Nobel Prize for Physics with his father, W.H. Bragg, for the development of X-ray crystallography. In this paper,[68] Bragg presented some empirical results on the inter-atomic distances in simple crystals, and then discussed these findings in the light of theories of atomic structure proposed independently by two American chemists, G.N. Lewis and I. Langmuir. This was the first Bernal had heard of Langmuir's theory, and he felt exultant after reading Bragg's paper. Two days later, he spent ten hours studying the ideas of Langmuir and found 'the scope of the theory leaves me dazed. A slight imagination and plenty of donkey-work, and chemistry will emerge as a branch of physics. I had not dared hope that the clue would come into my hands so soon.'[69] The following week he found time between his other activities to read more of Langmuir's 'beautiful theory of atoms with wobbly tails and fat, insoluble heads'. He felt satisfied that 'in this glorious new world of science, there may be some paths left for me to walk'.[70]

He left Cambridge in mid-August 1921 for a truncated summer vacation in Ireland and took books on vector analysis with him. On 2nd September, 'the morning I spent rapt in geometry and complex vector algebra. It is all new and my method of attack is both haphazard and roundabout; however, I gained a few positions and consolidated them. It was with great reluctance that I left my new set of points to go to help with the threshing.'[71] By the next week there had been substantial progress: 'I have cleared up simple space lattices pretty thoroughly and I have fifty pages of manuscript to copy out. Not so bad for a week's very interrupted work.'[72] His private research continued during the Michaelmas Term, and by November he felt emboldened to make some remarks about vector analysis after a lecture by the physicist, Charles Darwin, on X-ray crystallography.

This sequence of small academic successes did a lot to restore Bernal's self-confidence. He continued to devour books on science, history, art, and politics, and to be a prominent figure in the Union, the Heretics and the Emmanuel Science Club. His readings had by now led him to embrace communism and he was one of the leading figures of that faction in the CUSS.[73] His range and brilliance were encapsulated in his new nickname of 'Sage'. The name came not from one of Bernal's fellow students, who had seen him surrounded by obscure tomes in the library, but from Dora Grey, who had witnessed his mesmeric performances at the Heretics and CUSS. She lived in Cambridge with her brother, and worked in a second-hand bookshop owned by C.K. Ogden, the creator and president of the Heretics. On May Day 1921, Bernal went to a Labour Party rally addressed by Hugh Dalton, the economist, who was standing for parliament. Bernal found himself 'packed in a crowd of well dressed proletarians ... [to] listen to insipidities and party lies for two hours'.[74] He had the luck to run into Dora Grey, and they went for tea in Allen Hutt's room in Downing College. Hutt was a good friend of Bernal's from the first-year mathematics course and was also a communist active in CUSS. Bernal would sometimes join Hutt at meetings of a small communist group, the Spillikins,[75] along with Maurice Dobb and Ivor Montagu. The quaint name was adopted to avoid the unwelcome interest that the 'Young Communist League' might have earned from Scotland Yard's Special Branch.

Hutt knew Dora Grey through the Cambridge Trades Council and introduced her to Bernal.[76] The sobriquet of 'Sage' secretly pleased Bernal; she in return was known as 'Goblin'. On that long May evening, Bernal and Dickinson idly amused themselves by sliding Dora from one end of Hutt's table to the other. Bernal thought she was 'a funny little thing but she has a fine mind'.[77] Whatever her attributes, 'Grey's shop' became a regular rendez-vous for Bernal, Hutt and Dickinson. At the end of the month, Bernal had to take the first-year science exams, and Grey was on hand to cheer him up, after the first paper seemed to go badly. By now he was convinced that he was in love with her, but she and Hutt were already lovers. Bernal admired them as a thoroughly modern pair, disillusioned with the conventions of life, and with no expectations of the future. Free love had spread from Bloomsbury to Cambridge and Freudianism, in Bernal's phrase, was 'the new religion'.[78] To emphasize the free nature of their association, Hutt challenged Grey to fall in love with Bernal. Bernal on hearing this idea was 'almost alarmed by the prospects it opened up' and viewed it as a dangerous experiment, unlikely to succeed. On 22nd July, the day he spent ten hours reading Langmuir's atomic theory, Bernal invited Grey to his room for supper. She sat in his armchair talking of her affair with Hutt, while Sage sat on a cushion at her feet, growing more and more impressed with her independent attitude. As both of them had been encouraged to experiment by Hutt, they exchanged 'a white hot kiss that drew the fire from our souls' before she left to go to a socialist meeting. An ecstatic Sage 'walked light footed to Hutt's' to give the news. He then resumed work on the atomic theory until 2 am, signing off 'a record day, a new theory of the universe and new love though really they are both second-hand'.[79]

A week later, Sage diagnosed himself as suffering from 'sex repression' after Dora Grey had spent the afternoon sitting in his lap. He began to think 'there are more difficulties in our experiment than the first analysis showed'. After a night of tumultuous dreams, and not feeling as fit as he would have liked, Bernal walked to Dora Grey's house with Hutt. Hutt had a more elaborate Freudian theory about their amorous connections: Grey's 'erotic energy first manifested towards him was inhibited and that the overflow went into the first suitable channel which happened to be the sympathetic and not unwilling Sage'.[80] The arrangement was ended by Dora, a few days later, when she told Sage that she loved him 'mainly from pity' and because Hutt had suggested it. Bernal readily conceded that he had a great gift for self-pity and announced that he would exaggerate the love he had for Dora so that he could feel more miserable at having lost so much! In fact, his misery was short-lived because he soon found himself a new female companion, Eileen Sprague. She was a friend of Dora's, also politically active and like her worked in Cambridge – at Miss Pate's secretarial agency, where she had transcribed Keynes' *The Economic Consequences of the Peace* in preparation for its publi-cation. Bernal had first spotted Eileen at a CUSS meeting at Emmanuel at the end of his first year. Then he sat on the floor with a college friend,

Lucas, and 'looked at a girl in a yellow jumper and pale bobbed hair whom we both found very attractive. We learned afterwards that it was a certain Miss Sprague.'[81]

Bernal met Eileen Sprague on a casual basis at several other meetings, including one where they heard a talk on sex by 'the stupendous Jonty Hanaghan'.[82] Hanaghan was a self-proclaimed Freudian psychoanalyst, who was instrumental in setting up Hutt's relationship with Dora Grey. Bernal decided that Eileen was also likely to be a free-spirited woman and invited her to tea in his rooms. Again she looked very pleasant but 'her conversation for the most part is gush but it is affected so that does not matter'.[83] Hutt was also there and they talked about religion. As usual, Bernal did most of the talking, but did discover that Eileen was agnostic. Agnosticism was, in fact, a Sprague family tradition – her grandfather, Thomas Bond Sprague, had been Senior Wrangler in the 1850s and was a fellow of St John's College, Cambridge before leaving the academic life to become an actuary. He rejected the Bible as nothing more than a human creation and saw no evidence for divine providence in the world so that religion held no meaning for him.[84] The afternoon conversation with Eileen finally pushed Bernal into action, and after Hall that evening, he went to see Father Marshall to announce his 'gradual and inevitable descent from religion'.[85] Bernal appreciated the priest's 'gentlemanly restraint and delicacy'; on leaving, 'I wanted badly to go into the familiar chapel to pray to his God and mine, but I passed the door and stepped down the stairs . . . The God of my childhood is long departed from me.'

Bernal soon came to realize that Eileen Sprague was a formidable opponent in an argument, and also backed up her political beliefs with action. In a debate the following week, Bernal was arguing for moral relativism, denying the existence of an objective good. Eileen took him on in a spirited dispute, and he eventually backed down. Later that evening, the two of them wandered through the streets of Cambridge and she talked of 'the hopeless monotony of most peoples' lives'.[86] There had been municipal elections in November 1920, and Eileen canvassed on behalf of the Labour Party. She 'spoke of what she had seen in the Central Ward. Being a coward and an idler I have no arguments with people who dare and do things. I can only admire them and agree with them.' They parted after four hours of talking with a handshake and Bernal felt he was 'in love with Sprague but not enough to make me miserable'.[87]

Bernal and Eileen exchanged letters while he was in Ireland later that summer, but when he returned to Cambridge there was another suitor in her life. By taking her out on the river and walking in Grantchester meadows, Bernal soon ousted his rival. Their relationship was tempestuous though, with Eileen the dominant partner, now quite capable of making him miserable. She started to type his space lattice paper, but every few days, work seems to have been interrupted by a quarrel or by Eileen losing her temper. The Freudian seminars by Jonty Hanaghan continued, promoting the virtues of sex, but when Sage confessed that he was attracted to Sylvia, Dickinson's girlfriend, Eileen threatened to leave him.

During the Christmas vacation, Bernal told his family that he was planning to marry Eileen. There was outright opposition from Gigi and Cuddie, but his mother, recognizing that this was a futile tactic, made the enlightened suggestion that since 'all these advanced girls believed in free love. Why can't you do what you talk about, live together without marrying and make a success of it.'[88] According to Sage, Hanaghan managed to weave a tangled web amongst his followers where 'triangles have given place to the most complexly joined polygons and jealousy is by no means absent'.[89] Sage and Eileen were the nexus for several of these relationships. After a week of mounting jealousy, Eileen came to Bernal's room wearing a brown cloak and muffler. She challenged him to undress her and 'perform the final rites'. Sage replied it would be like unveiling a statue and wished there was a brass band playing *God Save the King*, but gently slipped open the big buttons one after the other until 'with a sharp turn of the wrist ... all fell apart'.[90]

Despite the intensification of their affair, desultory intrigues continued on both sides. In March 1922, Bernal went with Sylvia to visit a friend, a bewitching blonde named Dorothy, in hospital. After a while, Sylvia left and Sage made overtures to Dorothy. Eileen apparently was very amused by this, and in turn flirted openly with his friends Lucas and Twam. When Sage visited Dorothy back at Newnham College, Eileen responded by going off with Hutt. After a few days, Sage was reconciled with Eileen, but could only think of Sylvia! Not the least surprising aspect of this tortuous story is that it appears in a letter to his mother, who was already suspicious of Eileen as 'an experienced husband hunting woman'. The engagement was now a matter of public knowledge, and they decided to marry at the end of the academic year. Bernal wrote to his mother informing her of the plan, although he knew that she disapproved strongly, 'partly for my sake, partly for the family's, partly for your own'.[91] If her objections that a wife would be a burden at the beginning of his career and that he was too young for the responsibility proved true, he would 'find a way out, not so difficult in spite of abominable divorce laws'. He reminded her that his life was his work – science. To be successful he had certain minimum requirements: 'food, clothing and to be left alone. If I am not happy, if I cannot do my best work without a mate, I must have one. For these ends I take what I can, not greedily, my wants are few, but what I take I feel is my right and I am not ashamed to have it gathered from the pennies of the poor by my own mother's labour. What I give to the world is my own work's worth, however poor it may be, I cannot give more.' He feared that his mother saw only obstinacy, folly, and selfishness, where he felt determination, insight, purpose.

Reflecting on the eve of his twenty-first birthday, Bernal felt ambivalence towards his fast approaching marriage, about which he was 'apathetic'. He was far more concerned about the Tripos Part I examinations, which started in two weeks and for which he felt unprepared, although he was desperate to get a first. Eileen was also harbouring doubts and shared them with Barbara Wootton,[92] a young economics don at Girton and friend from CUSS. Sage felt 'at the threshold of adulthood' but thought his character remained childish and vacillating. While he felt no emotion about marriage, he believed that if he were in love at all, it was with Sylvia, although she would bore him in a week. Having experienced the excitement of sex with Eileen, he nurtured an ambition to have all that and more with many other women. Before the wedding, they pledged that each would still be free to take other partners,[93] a vow which both upheld in the years to come. On midsummer's morning, Lucas gave them a wedding breakfast in his rooms at Emmanuel,[94] and following the civil ceremony, the happy couple spent the afternoon punting on the river with Hutt and Grey.[95] Punting was always a favourite activity of Sage's: he took 'great pleasure in the swing of the pole as it springs dripping from hand to hand, the hard crunch of the gravel and then the straight steady push ... while the others loll on their cushions and the water laps under the bows'.[96]

Bernal was awarded first-class honours in the Part I Natural Sciences Tripos. During his final year, as a married man, he had to live outside Emmanuel. He and Eileen found a flat to rent, where his youngest brother, Gofty, and friends like Hutt, Twam, Sylvia Barnes and Dickinson were frequent visitors. Eileen busied herself with decorating and furnishing the flat, but there was a general economic slump and little secretarial work available.[97] Fortunately for Sage this meant that she was free to type new drafts of his mammoth derivation of the 230 space groups; their only income came from Bernal's scholarship and his personal allowance from home. In January 1921, just as the post-war economic boom was cresting, Bernal noted in his diary that his income 'from trusts and dividends was only 500 pounds'.[98] This was about four times the income of a farm labourer.[99] By 1923 agricultural prices had halved,[100] and his mother, Bessie Bernal, worried about the dairy at Brookwatson closing down. Her eldest son, as usual, had no time for such worldly 'trivialities' and she was finally moved to write him a reproachful letter.[101] After pointing out that some sons write to their mothers 'unbidden', Bessie castigated him: 'If you prefer me never to mention our economic and labour difficulties here, I'll do so. I have never interfered in your affairs. I supposed you took some interest in our efforts to keep things going here. It is our one preoccupation.'

Sage's one preoccupation was to finish the space lattice paper, which he did at the end of February 1923. He had discussed the manuscript with Hutchinson, the mineralogist, and with H.F. Baker, a mathematics professor. The manuscript consists of eighty or so pages densely covered with mathematical formulae.[102] In a short preface, even its author seemed to recognize the work's inaccessibility since the theory 'is given in extremely condensed form, and the absence of examples and diagrams may make it difficult to follow the geometric meaning of the various expressions ... As the theoretical part has been written independently the absence of references will be understood.'[103]

The Cambridge Philosophical Society expressed some interest in publishing it, but decided that even a shortened sixty-page version was unprintable, on account of the expense involved in setting large numbers of tables containing unusual symbols. The work attests to Bernal's mathematical powers as well as his extraordinary ability to think, in abstract, about three-dimensional patterns. Arthur Hutchinson, the Professor of Mineralogy, encouraged him to submit the paper for a prize at Emmanuel. The Herculean labours of Sage were rewarded with a half-share* of the Sudbury Hardyman prize and £30.[104]

---

* The prize was shared with a graduate student at Emmanuel, R.G.W. Norrish (1897–1978), later a Nobel Laureate for Chemistry.

3

Bohemian Crystallographer

While his two-year effort to develop a quantitative analysis of the 230 space groups cost Bernal the first-class honours degree he coveted, the resulting thesis, 'On the analytic theory of point group systems', launched his career as a scientist. Without a first-class degree in physics, there was little prospect of being taken on as a research student in the Cavendish Laboratory, and even if Sage had managed to take a first, it is difficult to see how he would have satisfied Sir Ernest Rutherford's edict that no communist propaganda would be tolerated in the laboratory.[1] Nor would Bernal's interest in the physics of crystals and his idea to use discoveries in that field as the keys to unlock the secrets of chemical structure have met with any degree of comprehension or sympathy in Rutherford's department, where the major goal was to advance understanding about the atomic nucleus. In Rutherford's robust view, scientific work aiming to establish the relative positions of atoms in space rather than to dissect the miniscule aggregation of electric charge and mass at each atom's core would probably have been regarded as a branch of geography rather than physics.

Fortunately for Bernal, there were other, lesser, Cambridge scientists who lacked Rutherford's single-mindedness, but who were shrewd enough to recognize the young graduate's outstanding ability. One was the 'very gentlemanly don at Pemmer', Arthur Hutchinson, who wrote to W.H. Bragg in London in June 1923, saying that in his opinion Bernal was a remarkable person:

He is a shy, diffident, retiring kind of creature, but something of a genius. He attended my course on Elementary Crystallography and I realized that he was interested and was taking things in quickly. I did not however realize (and he never let on) that he had got so keen that he spent the whole of his next vacation in developing a method of dealing with point systems in the hope it might be useful in X-ray work! When therefore, he suddenly appeared and deposited on my table a thick type-written MS, rather with the air of a dog bringing a poached rabbit to his master's feet, I was quite amazed – of course I make no pretence of being able to appraise its merit or even its usefulness – still it seemed to me a remarkable effort for an undergraduate in his third year – and Professor H.F. Baker was much interested in it and I believe thinks well of it.[2]

Bragg replied that he had already heard about Bernal from Alexander Wood, the physics tutor at Emmanuel, who had sent him the space group dissertation. He was happy to take Bernal on as a research student, but had no funds available at that time to support him. Emmanuel College generously stepped into the breach by offering Bernal a research grant that would cover his first few months in London.

A man of equable temperament in his early sixties, Sir William Henry Bragg was about to take over as Director of the Royal Institution. Established in a grand Mayfair house in 1799, the Royal Institution (RI) from its inception had been concerned with harnessing science for the public good, both through research and education. Bragg was well qualified to oversee such efforts, since he was an experienced teacher and a natural communicator, in addition to being a Nobel Laureate. After graduating as one of the top mathematicians of his year at Cambridge, at the age of twenty-three years Bragg had taken the post as professor of mathematics and physics at the fledgling Adelaide University;[3] from this flying start, strangely Bragg did not attempt any original research for nearly twenty years. His first published work in 1904 was a major contribution to the field of radioactivity and led to a regular exchange of ideas with Rutherford. Bragg's initial research was concerned with the properties of alpha (α) particles, which he showed have a characteristic range in air that depends on their initial energy.[4] He thought of the α-particles travelling through air in a straight line, like a bullet passing through a block of wood. Soon he convinced himself that the uncharged gamma radiation from radioactive sources also consisted of high-speed particles and not waves. He expressed this opinion confidently in a letter to Rutherford in December 1907: 'I have got the decisive experimental proof that the gamma rays are not pulses, but corpuscular...'[5] Other physicists, for example Charles Barkla in Liverpool, working with lower energy X-rays, found equally compelling evidence for wave properties of radiation, and a lively debate ensued.

Decisive evidence for the wave school came from Max Laue's department at Munich University in June 1912, when it was demonstrated that X-rays could be diffracted by crystals. Bullets do not bend around objects – they cannot be diffracted – but waves can, providing that the object is comparable in size to the wavelength. Think of Bernal watching the waves bouncing off the hull of the ferry as he crossed the Irish Sea, and the subsequent interference patterns of the secondary wavelets in the ship's wake, before the original wavefront would be restored. A lifeboat from the ferry would not have produced such a wave interference pattern because its size would have been so much smaller than the wavelength – the distance between successive crests. Similar constraints apply to the diffraction of light: the process depends on the wavelength of light* being comparable to the size of the diffracting object. Laue, after talking to his doctoral student, Paul Ewald, formed the idea that some kind of diffraction effect might be obtained from crystals, if they were subjected to incident radiations of wavelengths similar in magnitude to the inter-atomic distances in the crystal lattice. Ewald had explained to Laue that the atoms in crystals were thought to have internal regularity or periodicity of structure, and although the distances between neighbouring atoms were not known accurately, they were estimated to be perhaps 1/1,000th of the wavelength of visible light.[6] Crystals could not serve to diffract light, but Laue thought that perhaps X-rays would have short enough wavelengths to be affected by their internal atomic framework.

The crucial series of experiments was carried out by two junior assistants in Laue's department, who constructed a lead box to hold the crystal and a photographic plate. One side of the box had a 3 mm diameter hole drilled through it to admit a narrow beam from an X-ray tube; the X-ray beam was further narrowed to about a 1 mm pencil by passing through a series of apertures. The first crystal studied was copper sulphate, which was irradiated for about twenty hours, with interruptions every so often to let the X-ray tube cool down. The photographic plate on the far side of the crystal showed a large central dark blob with a pattern of smaller spots surrounding it. The copper sulphate crystal was then ground into a powder and the experiment repeated. This resulted in just a central circular spot from the primary beam with no peripheral spots, suggesting that indeed the first pattern was due to diffraction of the X-ray beam by the intact crystal. Convincing evidence came when they next used a crystal of zinc sulphide, which has a more symmetrical form than copper sulphate. This time the cubic crystal was carefully mounted so that the X-ray beam intersected one face of the crystal at ninety degrees. Now the dark spot on the plate due to the primary beam passing straight through the crystal was enclosed by a regular pattern of smaller elliptical spots. The most prominent feature was a diamond shaped ring of these subsidiary spots, showing four-fold symmetry as one would expect from a cube.

Word of these revolutionary findings quickly reached England and were discussed by William Bragg with his son, Willie,[†] during his summer vacation from Cambridge. At the time, the younger Bragg was 'an ardent supporter' of

---

* The wavelength of visible light ranges from 400 to 700 nanometres ($1\,nm = 10^{-9}$ $m = 0.000\,000\,001$ *metre*). One Ångström unit (Å) $= 10^{-10}$ m.

† Although William Lawrence Bragg (1890–1971) was familiarly known as Willie, I will refer to him henceforth as Lawrence. The confusion caused by sharing his father's first name was one reason that his remarkable contributions as a very young man were underestimated for many years, even though he was a Nobel Laureate.

his father's view that X-rays consisted of a stream of high velocity particles, and made some unsuccessful experiments to see if he 'could get evidence of "X-ray corpuscles" shooting down the avenues between the rows of atoms in the crystal'.[7] When he returned to Cambridge after the summer vacation, Lawrence Bragg continued to ponder Laue's results and became convinced that the observed effect was due to the X-rays having a wave nature and being diffracted by the crystal's atomic lattice. Bragg realized though that Laue's analysis of the process was incorrect. Laue had interpreted the pattern of spots seen on the exposed photographic plate as being due to X-rays of a few discrete wavelengths produced by resonating atoms in the crystal lattice, but struggle as he might, he was not able to account for all the spots in the diffraction pattern. Lawrence Bragg, a 22-year-old research student in J.J. Thomson's Cavendish Laboratory, considered the problem from several aspects before proposing a simpler and more complete explanation that required one supreme flash of intuition. Bragg's crucial insight was that successive planes in the crystal lattice effectively acted like mirrors, and reflected a fraction of the incident X-rays so that each spot on the photographic plate represented a parallel set of these atomic planes.

Visible light is reflected from the facet of a crystal in a continuous way so that the surface still looks shiny as the crystal is turned in the light. X-rays are oblivious to the crystal facets, but can be scattered by the array of atoms within. The atoms scatter the X-rays into wavelets that retain the ability to interact with one another to produce interference patterns. At some angles, the wavelets are in phase and reinforce each other so that diffraction occurs. At other angles, the wavelets are out of phase and cancel each other out so that nothing is detected on a photographic film. The spotted pattern that results on the film gives the clue to the internal structure of the crystal and is the key to X-ray diffraction as an investigative technique.

Bragg found that he could account for all the spots in Laue's zinc sulphide pattern if he assumed that the atoms were arranged in a face-centred cube (with atoms not only at the corner of adjoining cubes, but at the centre of each face). The pair of figures below shows a face-centred cubic lattice on the left and its corresponding X-ray diffraction pattern on the right. The diagrams are for common salt, another face-centred cubic lattice, with the sodium atoms shown as light spheres and the chlorine atoms dark. The spots or reflections found in the diffraction pattern show four-fold symmetry: the pattern is identical when rotated through ninety degrees. The crystal and its diffraction pattern share the same symmetry, but there is not a direct correlation between the position of the molecules in the crystal lattice and the reflections on the X-ray photograph (note, too, that the intensity of the reflections varies).

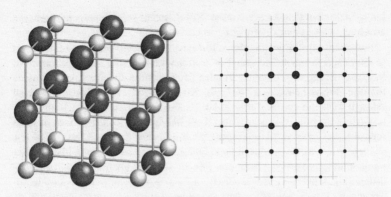

Idealized crystal lattice structure of common salt (left) with the sodium atoms shown as light and the chlorine atoms dark. The corresponding X-ray diffraction pattern (right) showing the same four-fold symmetry. © Jeremy Karl Cockcroft

Once Bragg had made the momentous assumption that the primary mechanism was like reflection from successive atomic planes, it was easy for him to formulate Bragg's Law:

$$n\lambda = 2d \sin \theta$$

where n is an integer, λ is the wavelength of the X-ray, θ is the glancing angle at which the radiation falls on the atomic plane, and d is the distance at which the diffracting planes are spaced. The most exciting implication of this to Lawrence Bragg was that 'X-ray diffraction could be used to get information about the nature of the crystal pattern',[8] and before the First World War interrupted his research, he had analysed the structures of rock salt (NaCl), fluorspar (CaF$_2$), pyrites (FeS$_2$), calcite (CaCO$_3$) and simple potassium salts in addition to zincblende (ZnS). Bragg was thereby able to confirm the long-held belief that the internal atomic structure of crystals displays a periodicity or repeating pattern – what the nineteenth-century French crystallographers had called 'la molécule intégrante'.

W.H. Bragg soon reconciled himself to the fact that X-rays could not be regarded solely as particles, but in some circumstances appeared to behave as waves. This duality, which would be at the heart of quantum theory in the 1920s, he internalized by thinking of X-rays as waves on Mondays, Wednesdays and Fridays, as particles on Tuesdays, Thursdays and Saturdays, and nothing at all on Sundays! While his son concentrated on analysing diffraction patterns to establish the atomic structures of various crystals, Bragg senior was more interested at first in the other side of his son's equation – the wavelengths of X-rays.

Bragg senior invented an instrument called the X-ray spectrometer that was as important to the development of crystallography and to the exploration of the X-ray spectra of different elements, as the telescope was to astronomy or the microscope to biology. Having carried out no original work until well after his fortieth birthday, W.H. Bragg made a series of spectacular contributions over the next decade. During the enforced hiatus of the Great War he turned his hand to acoustic methods for submarine detection, but could not wait to return to X-ray crystallography research. Eschewing the highly symmetrical inorganic crystals that his son had begun to analyse so brilliantly, he decided to attack the much less symmetrical, soft, organic molecules, whose main atomic constituents are carbon, oxygen and hydrogen. His first results for naphthalene and anthracene were published in 1921, and that same year he gave his Presidential Address to the Physical Society on 'The structure of organic crystals'.[9] While recognizing the daunting complexity of studying such large molecules, Bragg predicted that if methods could be developed, it seemed likely that 'they would quickly be fruitful'. As a start, he presented diffraction data to show that the benzene ring of six carbon atoms and the double naphthalene ring were real entities and have 'a definite size and form, preserved with little or perhaps no alteration from crystal to crystal'.[10] The multifarious duties that came with the chiefship of the Royal Institution, not to mention the other distractions that accrete to the great and the good, inevitably limited Bragg's opportunities to work in his own laboratory. Instead he would prove himself as an inspirational and open-minded mentor of a young research group, without ever seeming intent on directing them.

When Sage arrived at the Royal Institution in October 1923, he joined a group of about a dozen research workers. Most were in their twenties like him, and new arrivals were put under the general supervision of Alexander Müller, a Swiss physicist in his mid-thirties. Müller had been Bragg's research assistant for a year before moving to the RI, and together with George Shearer had carried pioneering work on the structure of long-chain organic compounds, such as the fatty acids and paraffins. Both men were talented instrument makers, and when confronted by the clumsy, talkative, new recruit, who had a habit of breaking equipment, Müller tended to become 'extremely abusive'.[11] Closer to Bernal in age and perhaps in their general view of the world were Bill Astbury and Kathleen Yardley (one of three young women in the group). Both were from poor backgrounds – Astbury's father was a potter's turner in the Potteries of Staffordshire, and Yardley was the last of ten children, in a family where four of her brothers died in infancy. Both had succeeded through winning scholarships, as they mounted each rung of the educational ladder.

Astbury[12] took first-class honours in both parts of the Natural Sciences Tripos at Cambridge, and had been recommended to Bragg by Arthur Hutchinson, two years before he set Bernal on his way. Kathleen Yardley[13] was a diminutive young woman, whose fiercely independent mother moved her surviving children from the poverty of rural Ireland to a slightly better life just beyond the East End of London. She was rewarded by seeing her youngest daughter, Kathleen, gain admission to Bedford College for Women in London, where she graduated in 1922 at the top of the London University list in physics, with the highest marks recorded for ten years. W.H. Bragg, who was one of her examiners, needed no outside referral in her case and sent for her immediately to offer her a research studentship and a government grant of £180 a year. Almost certainly, Sage would have regarded Astbury and Yardley not as examples of how the British system could identify and promote men and woman of exceptional ability, but as shining reminders of the untold thousands, kept in poverty, who would never be able to express their talents.

Astbury and Yardley were both skilled users of the Bragg X-ray spectrometer, but Bernal gave up after a few days of instruction from Kathleen Yardley, recognizing that he did not have the level of patience required to master the exacting technique. Instead he was attracted to a new method of photographic analysis, which gave far less accurate estimates of the intensities of diffracted X-rays but could measure many more reflected spots. Bragg's longstanding laboratory steward, who had built the first X-ray spectrometer, gave Sage 'a few pieces of brass . . . some miner's lamp glasses, a little aluminium foil for the window, plenty of sealing wax to stick everything together . . . some glass tubing and a little mercury to make a diffusion pump, some copper and iron wires for a transformer and as an essential ingredient an aluminium hot-water-bottle and a small piece of platinum to make the interrupter'.[14] Even with assistance of Müller and Shearer, Sage could not get things to work, and after three months of endlessly burning himself and breaking things, there was not even 'the trace of an X-ray out of the apparatus'.[15] At this point he approached Sir William and pleaded to be allowed to return to the *theory* of crystallography. Although Bragg had seen the young man with his thick shock of fair hair almost daily at teatime in the library, this was the first time that they had spoken since Bernal was taken on. When Sir William seemed nonplussed by his request, Sage reminded him of the space group dissertation. Bragg, raising his tufted eyebrows a little, retorted 'You don't think I *read* your paper', which perversely cheered Sage up.

Now the ice was broken between the Director of the Royal Institution and his most loquacious research student, their relationship flourished, and over time Sage came to regard W.H. Bragg as a sort of scientific father.[16] With Bragg's unobtrusive support, Bernal persisted in the laboratory and made some significant experimental discoveries. At the same time, he invented new techniques for interpreting the complex data that were emerging and was always seeking a theoretical framework to tie things together. The first scientific problem that Bragg passed on to Bernal was the unresolved structure of graphite. In 1913, Bragg had been the first to demonstrate the arrangement of carbon atoms in diamond (each atom being surrounded by four others in a regular tetrahedron), but to date there had been no satisfactory model for the humbler isomer of carbon, graphite. There had been previous X-ray diffraction studies on graphite, but they were not in accord. Single crystals of graphite are difficult to obtain, and in fact the two published reports employed a new technique of diffraction by powder, in which X-rays are diffracted by thousands of microscopic crystals orientated at random in all directions. The powder method was invented independently during World War I by Debye and Scherrer in Germany and by an American, Albert Hull, working in the General Electric Research Laboratory. Both of those groups soon applied the technique to graphite powder. Bernal read their papers and also the older mineralogical literature, and decided that there was still no satisfactory solution to the structure of graphite, although it did appear to have hexagonal symmetry. The most compelling evidence for this was provided by Ewald, who had taken a Laue photograph of a single graphite crystal in 1914.

Bernal decided that the X-ray analysis of single crystals would be more informative than the powder method, even though such specimens were difficult to obtain. He was given a piece of Ceylon graphite 'from which, by careful dissection and picking out, I obtained a few crystalline fragments which, though very far from perfect, were sufficiently so for my purpose'.[17] As if the acquisition of a suitable crystal were not trying enough, Bernal had to contend with the unwanted zeal of the Royal Institution charwoman, Mrs Dyke, who 'had an extreme and quite unnecessary interest in laboratory cleanliness'.[18] Sage had selected some potential crystals by looking at them under a microscope and carefully placed them on a clean sheet of paper. He then went to eat his sandwich lunch and play ping-pong (a Royal Institution ritual); on his return to the laboratory, the crystals had vanished. After searching unsuccessfully, he asked Mrs Dyke whether she had seen them. She exclaimed: 'Them smuts? I swep' 'em up.' Bernal admitted that he was 'not entirely upset when very shortly after that she tried to clean the X-ray apparatus while it was going'. The terminals always collected an enormous amount of dust, and she received a jolting electric shock for her efforts!

The apparatus used for the graphite work had to be constructed from scratch and included a cylindrical camera made out of a piece of brass tubing about one inch in diameter. The film lining the brass cylinder was held in place with bicycle clips, and Sage used 'an old alarm-clock and a nail to mount and turn the crystal'.[19] Crude though it was, the setup worked and others in the laboratory helped Bernal to build more stable and refined equipment with which he was able to confirm the hexagonal symmetry of graphite and also to make the first accurate determination of the dimensions of its unit cell. The crystal was rotated about two axes at right angles to one another and this enabled him to draw a stereographic projection of the reflecting planes, thereby obtaining indices or spatial coordinates for every reflection. Astbury took Laue photographs of several crystals with their cleavage planes perpendicular to the X-ray beam, and Miss Yardley provided some spectrometry measurements enabling Bernal to establish the complete structure for the first time. He concluded that the carbon atoms in graphite 'lie in planes in which they form nets of hexagons'[20] and he provided details of the inter-planar and inter-atomic distances. Now Sage could explain that 'the great difference between the mechanical properties of graphite and diamond (hardness, flexibility, etc.) is due to the fact that the atoms are linked closely in a two-dimensional net in the former and in a three-dimensional lattice in the latter'. In the plane of a hexagonal net, the carbon atoms in graphite are strongly bonded together, 2.45 Å (Ångström units) apart, but successive cleavage planes are 6.82 Å apart and can slip over one another, accounting for the material's flaky property.

The experimental method employed by Bernal of a small crystal mounted on a rotating spindle, positioned inside a cylindrical camera, had been devised in Germany a year or so earlier, but Bernal was the first to develop the full mathematical analysis of the system. The crystal lies on the axis of the cylindrical film and the diffracted X-rays make a complex pattern of spots on the film. In addition to the Bragg's Law equation relating the distance between atomic planes in the crystal to the wavelength and glancing angle of the X-ray beam, in this method it is also necessary to allow for the angle between the reflecting plane and the axis of rotation about which the crystal revolves. Even a geometer as talented as Sage found the necessary calculations 'rather laborious'[21] and he devised a much simpler graphical method by which the spots on the film could be projected onto a standard family of curves so that values for the important angles could be read off directly.

While this method was sufficient for a simple crystal like graphite, Bernal realized that it would not be able to handle the X-ray diffractions from the more complex and less symmetrical organic crystals that the Royal Institution workers were beginning to tackle. For these crystals he devised other ready-made tables based on the general concept of the *reciprocal lattice*. The reciprocal lattice is a mathematical abstraction – the looking-glass world of crystallography – and while its definition is abstruse, it affords the crystallographer a convenient way of analysing the diffracted beams from all sets of parallel planes in the crystalline lattice. While the concept of the reciprocal lattice was first published by Paul Ewald in 1921, the same idea had occurred to Bernal, while still an undergraduate: his diary for 23 April 1920 contains a brief mention of some 'very interesting investigations on three-dimensional reciprocation' in which he 'brought in some new surfaces, also reciprocation w[ith] r[espect] t[o] a circle of complex radius, and on various mesh systems'.[22]

Having completed the experimental work on graphite, Sage now set out to prepare charts that would be of practical use and enable crystallographers to establish directly coordinates in the reciprocal lattice for the diffractions appearing as spots on X-ray photographs. He wanted charts that worked for both flat plates and cylindrical films and this required a prodigious amount of calculation. In an important refinement of technique, he pointed out that even the very complicated patterns obtained from crystals with large unit cells could be resolved if instead of a complete rotation, they were subjected to a series of much smaller oscillations. At one point he asked Sir William Bragg if he could have £20 for the hire of an adding machine, but 'as this was apparently beyond the capacity of the Institution, [he] had to do the whole thing by hand and eye using seven-figure logarithm tables'.[23] The number crunching took him about two months – a degree of effort easy to overlook when reading the paper.[24] The whole was an in-depth mathematical treatment of the methods he was using and also contained many practical tips to others on how to deal with crystals of different symmetry and complexity. He assured his readers that 'these methods have all been tested in practice and it has been found that even for complex organic crystals, some of which give over 500 measurable planes, they are sufficient in themselves to do this. References would be given, but so far none of the work has had time to be published.' The manuscript of Bernal's paper was available to others at the RI for a year or so before it appeared in print, and it was extensively studied by Astbury and a research fellow from Canada, A.L. Patterson, in connection with their own experiments. During their reworking of the paper, Patterson and Astbury sometimes arrived at different answers from one another and from Bernal.[25] Patterson made a list of minor corrections, which he gave to Sage, but the original version of the paper was the one that duly appeared, giving some sport to future researchers, who could correct Bernal's mathematics in margin jottings.[26]

With the publication of this landmark paper with its 'Bernal charts', Sage established himself as one of the leading exponents of the burgeoning subject of X-ray crystallography. While there were some frustrations working in the cramped, dingy, rooms of the Royal Institution, for someone steeped in the history of science like Bernal, it was also immensely satisfying to occupy the basement 'still festooned with flasks full of Dewar's rare gases,'[27] where Faraday himself had worked. With his contemporaries, Bernal was establishing the fundamental techniques of X-ray crystallography, and young though they were, they all believed that their efforts would pave the way for important future discoveries. Bernal looked back on the RI as a place where one's wits were sharpened, where all the scientists 'shared in common a lively enthusiasm for the discovery of the new world of crystal structure which they were privileged to share. It was a very happy time: there was no real rivalry because that world was quite big enough for all their work. They were effectively and actually a *band* of research workers, dropping into each other's rooms, discussing informally over lunch and ping-pong and formally at Bragg's colloquia every week.'[28] There was a youthful, irreverent atmosphere, where Sage felt he was accomplishing a lot of research just by wandering from room to room and chatting with his friends.

The weekly colloquia were held in the study of Sir William's flat at the top of the Royal Institution and, according to Bernal, tended to be dominated by Astbury, who 'was always brimful of ideas but often these were rather difficult to understand. When he spoke, most people thought he was talking nonsense. I found out fairly early that when Astbury was talking, it might appear nonsense, but it always contained a valuable and new idea and I did my best at these meetings to interpret them and, what was much more difficult, to get Astbury's agreement that I had interpreted him correctly.'[29] Astbury was a buoyant, provocative figure, who referred to all his RI colleagues as Bill (regardless of their sex); he even gingered up the lunchtime table tennis matches by placing objects such as matchboxes at strategic points on the table.[30] In addition to the in-house talent at the RI, a constant stream of distinguished scientists came to give lectures; there was also a library well-stocked with books and periodicals, thanks to more than a century of members' annual subscriptions.

During the 1920s, Sage and Eileen lived, appropriately, in London's two most Bohemian quarters – Soho and Bloomsbury. Their credentials and Cambridge connections gained them ready access to left-wing intellectual circles.[31] They would often go to the 1917 Club in Gerrard Street, where they could rub shoulders with other young admirers of the Russian Revolution. They were fringe members of the Bloomsbury group of artists and writers, and shared the same creative spark. The Bernals seemed intent on proving that the sex life of a scientist could be as variegated and piquant as that of any painter or novelist. An inkling of the open nature of the Bernal's marriage surfaced when they had another couple, Peter and Aimee, to stay in their Soho flat. Lying in bed with Eileen, Sage wanted to kiss Aimee good night, but his courage failed him. He thought of his countryman, Oscar Wilde, who could resist everything except temptation. Eventually Eileen egged him on and he ventured into the adjoining room where Aimee kissed him with an OPEN AND WET mouth [Sage's ecstatic capitals], and 'wonder of wonders, her tongue peeped out'. Peter then reciprocated with Eileen, before Sage and Eileen enjoyed 'a perfect fuck'.[32] On leaving the next morning, Aimee promised Sage future favours.

A few days before Aimee and Peter's visit, Sage had been 'indiscreet' with another woman, identified only as Pearl, and had spent the night with her 'on the Canterbury road'.[33] In the spring of 1925, Sage reflected that while at Cambridge just three years earlier, he had been finding out about life and sharing common experiences, he was now moving beyond the conventions of society. Such is the mark of a Bohemian, but to live by their own lights, Sage and Eileen were finding there were penalties to be paid: 'Today Eileen has her lover and I have my loves and we live together but it is difficult... I cannot be jealous of E. or indifferent to her... Is it all worthwhile? What is gained by exchanging the secure bliss of conjugal fidelity for this feverish, dangerous life, a life that may... wreck all our happiness.' Later that year, on a visit to Cambridge where they saw old friends who seemed to have lost their former lustre (Dickinson was 'cowed', Sylvia 'insipid' and Dorothy, the bewitching blonde, 'miserable'), Sage took the 'cowardly' step of writing his diary after Eileen had fallen asleep. He reflected that they were 'too close in marriage' and as a result of knowing each other so well, were adept at hurting each other when the occasion arose and suffered the consequences. He also wrote he was in love with Pearl, 'the devil is in the woman', who combined charm, intellect, beauty and inaccessibility.[34]

For Sage, the opportunity to be a social rebel and to explore the boundaries of personal behaviour was as irresistible as the chance to be at the leading edge of science. At times he appeared distracted in both arenas, seeking new excitements, but he thought of himself as a serious pioneer, who could help those following on 'to avoid the snares' in their private or scientific lives. In fact his hectic schedule, both in and out of the laboratory, was not given to imitation. He was able to concentrate for long hours on abstruse scientific problems and then seek sexual adventure in the evenings. January 1926 was a particularly full month. The night of the 8th found him in bed with the inaccessible Pearl, his hand on her 'unexpectedly lovely breast', while Magda's warm body curved round his naked back – 'with infinite pains we all turned round in the narrow bed... then by magic we all slept.'[35] The next week he had lunch with Molly at her club and then she came home to dinner. Over the ensuing fortnight, there were separate assignations with Magda, Pearl, and Naomi. Not surprisingly he sometimes got into trouble by making too many appointments; quite remarkably, he still found time to finish the paper on single-crystal rotation techniques. By the end of the month, even Eileen had had enough of his energetic philanderings, and they discussed separation; Sage was miserable for the next day until they made up. No sooner was harmony restored than he embarked on an affair with a married woman, named Ivy, who lived in Hampstead. Ivy's young daughter, who became immensely fond of the entertaining Sage, had her first introduction to him when her mother opened the bedroom door one morning, and she saw the enormous head of a man fast asleep. Ivy said to her, 'This is my new lover and he's the most fascinating, brilliant man I've ever met.'[36]

At the time of these shenanigans, Eileen was six-months pregnant, but probably not with Sage's child. As her confinement approached at the end of April, Sage was moved to write: 'And now she lies in child bed fighting out life ... This is her great moment because with the child she justifies all the difficult year behind and our struggle for freedom ... For the child don't imagine anything, he seems incidental now, I doubt any less than if he were mine. Love may things go well with you.'[37] Eileen was admitted to a nursing home on 29th April and Sage spent an anxious night. A son arrived the next day and Sage was there to see the first bath. During Eileen's pregnancy, her mother-in-law, Bessie Bernal, had often sent new-laid eggs and other farm produce from Ireland; in return, Bessie felt that Desmond had been ignoring her. 'I think', she wrote, 'I am not unreasonable in asking you to devote ten minutes per week in writing to Brookwatson; the letters you write could not take much longer than that.'[38] She had no idea of her son's unconventional domestic life and wrote anxious for information 'about how Eileen and the boy are, what he is to be called and many other interesting facts that you must supply'.[39] She was also concerned that the General Strike would stop all mail and although she hoped the strike would be short-lived, did not know where Desmond's 'sympathies lie, so will say no more'.[40]

Sage's sympathies of course were completely with the strikers, and he was as exultant in making street speeches against the evils of capitalism as any undergraduate taking a turn as a stand-in bus driver or docker. On 6th May, towards the end of the first week of the General Strike, he walked eight miles through the City of London to Leather Lane in the East End to give a speech, and noted with satisfaction that there was a complete stoppage everywhere. The Government printed a newssheet, the *British Gazette*, under the direction of Winston Churchill, to make the case for the authority of Parliament and to offer the prospect of negotiation about the crisis in the coal mines that had pushed the Trades Union Congress (TUC) to call the General Strike in the first place.[41] The Prime Minister, Stanley Baldwin, made a conciliatory BBC broadcast on 8th May, and forty-eight hours later, Bernal felt that the tide was turning against the strikers. He wrote in his diary: 'A gloomy day. Government propaganda telling. I go to work and do not speak.'[42] On 12th May, the TUC drew back from the precipice and decided that it could no longer support a continuation of the strike, since there seemed to be willingness on both sides to negotiate a 'fair deal' for the miners.[43] Sage found consolation the week after it ended, when Vera, a friend of Eileen's, invited him 'to distract her from the strike'.[44]

Occasionally Bernal would escape from the multifarious demands of his London life by visiting Cambridge for a day or two. In January 1926, he had dinner there with Nathan and Susan Isaacs. Their other guest was J.B.S. Haldane, the geneticist, with whom Sage argued about the philosophy of science.[45] Susan, a woman her early forties, had made a reputation as a psychologist before being recruited to run Malting House – a progressive school which aimed to educate the young children of Cambridge dons in an environment that would encourage curiosity and self-reliance. The school was conceived by Geoffrey Pyke, a flamboyant and disorganized eccentric, who financed the enterprise by nerveless speculation in the London commodities market. Bernal was introduced to him a few weeks later at a Bloomsbury gathering, where Pyke stood out amongst the self-conscious crowd. Geoffrey Pyke was very tall and gaunt; he talked with the conviction of a man entirely reliant on his own ideas. Sage for once was the beguiled party, and was fascinated by Pyke's incongruous appearance. In particular, he could not understand why Pyke was wearing a pair of highly coloured spats – the insignia of a city slicker – at a radical soirée. When he chided Pyke about them, Pyke explained that they were very sensible items, and reaching down to his ankle, said: 'You see, they can be worn for weeks – *and* they obviate socks which I'd have to change much more often!'[46] Shortly after this first encounter, Sage and Eileen invited Pyke to dinner, and he stayed the night. Somewhat to Sage's discomfiture, Pyke and Eileen spent hours discussing his affair with Ivy.[47]

Both Sage and Eileen had joined the Communist Party of Great Britain (CPGB) soon after moving to London, but were still entitled to membership of the Holborn Labour Party, which was a particularly active, left-wing constituency.[48] Just as the General Strike polarized the country at large and left a legacy of bitterness that endured much longer than the strike itself, the Holborn Labour Party was riven by factional disputes. In the summer of 1926, it appeared to Bernal that the Left-Wing Group within the branch might dissolve, but it survived and he subsequently emerged as its leader. The position did not bring him much joy, and in November he complained that 'The Labour Party saddle me with many unpleasant jobs.'[49] The coal miners had remained on strike through the summer, desperately surviving on 'home-grown lettuce and mutton stolen from the hills',[50] but eventually gave up. Many pits closed, throwing hundreds of thousands out of work, and those who did return were forced to accept lower wages – the original grievance that had sparked the strike. The Communist Party in the 1920s provided no specific role for intellectuals in its ranks,[51] and Sage found himself instead at the Holborn Labour Party offices 'addressing letters for the belated Miners' Appeal'.[52] In February 1927, Sage carried the Holborn banner during a march to Trafalgar Square,[53] but even his patience and conciliatory nature could not hold the Left-Wing Group together; he soon resigned the leadership, one senses, with little regret.

After solving the structure of graphite, Bernal was preoccupied with general improvements in the practice and theory of crystallography and attempted little more experimental work at the Royal Institution. He was stimulated by a talk given by A.J. Bradley, a young research student from Lawrence Bragg's department in Manchester. Bradley was establishing himself as the most brilliant crystallographer in the field of metals, especially alloys, and he had just employed the powder method, with unrivalled virtuosity, to establish the structure of brass (Cu_5Zn_8). Emboldened by his previous success with graphite, Sage decided that the single crystal method would be superior to the powder technique and set out to study bronze, an alloy of copper and tin. He succeeded in taking the first cylindrical diffraction photograph in February 1926, and the following month began to measure the spacings between the atoms of copper and tin in a crystal of bronze. He needed to ascertain the density of the crystal, which was less than half a millimetre in size, and decided to use a very delicate flotation technique:

I sat all day in the cellar next to where Faraday worked. All around were great globes, which held the first of the rare gases, on the table a trough of water and in the middle my beaker of heavy yellow liquid. I had six floats of aluminium wire and six small counter weights and then I had my crystal, very precious crystal, which I hung in a small cage, a cage the size of a breadcrumb. One by one I had put the floats in with their counter weights, and then gradually, with the most delicate touch, I cut with a razor a mere shaving off the ends of the fine wires so that in the liquid they hung steadily suspended neither rising nor falling. Each time I cut I weighed them again on a fine balance made of quartz fibre. A thousandth of a milligramme more or less, that is what I must know. All were out, and weighed and balanced, and last of all the crystal in its cage was in the liquid and floated. I took the aluminium wire and shaved and shaved at it until the whole stood irresolutely in the liquid, moving still upwards. So imperceptibly upward, that I seemed at the end of my task. I waited, then cut again, and now it sank. I lifted the wire and the cage from the liquid, carefully, delicately and then without knowing, my hand shook, it had disappeared, gone. The crystal had gone. Crystal that I had worked on for months. Crystal about which I knew everything, but that one final weighing, and now it was gone, and all those months of work with it. 'Stupid', I thought, and as I gathered patiently all the dust of that room, looking through it grain for grain, for my crystal, 'If you had thought more, this could not have happened.' It was stupid to arrange things so that any weakness or wavering may lose everything.[54]

Sage did recover from this setback, and a year or so later published a letter in *Nature*[55] in which he announced that the structures of bronze were much more complex than metallurgists had previously believed. The single crystal of δ-bronze, the type he first studied at the Royal Institution, he demonstrated was closely related to γ-brass and had a cubic structure. The δ-bronze crystal had a very large unit cell probably containing 328 atoms of copper and 88 of tin: instead of the currently used formula of Cu_4Sn, Bernal suggested that the simplest formula could be $Cu_{41}Sn_{11}$. Displaying generosity and also a fluidity of purpose that would be repeated many times in his career as a scientist, Bernal chose not to carry his investigations further and instead gave his δ-bronze data to Bradley (who had published the structure of γ-brass in 1926), and the beautiful needle crystals of ε-bronze to Linus Pauling, when he visited England from the US in 1930.[56]

For the year or so that Bernal remained at the RI, he concentrated on designing an accurate and serviceable crystal rotation X-ray camera that could be used in any laboratory. The result was the universal X-ray photogonio-meter, a solid and versatile instrument, which could take single-crystal rotation and oscillation photographs as well as Laue and powder photo-graphs. It would be the mainstay of many crystallography laboratories for years; details of its construction, as well as notes for its use under various conditions with different types of crystals, were contained in a series of four papers that appeared over the next four years. Bernal approached the Cam-bridge firm of W.G. Pye and Company to manufacture the photogoniometer; by the spring of 1928, they were able to offer the 'spectrogoniometer' for the basic cost of £50, plus £26 12s for extras such as the goniometer head and powder attachment.[57]

In 1926, Bernal was earning an annual salary of £300 as a research assistant in Bragg's department. To supplement this, his mother sent him a quarterly allowance of an extra £50, sometimes in the form of dividend cheques from investments (that he always cashed but rarely acknowledged). Although he was much better off than most of his contemporaries at the Royal Institution, Sage's expenditure was in excess of his income. He was always unworldly about financial matters, and his mother tried to inject some degree of discipline. As usual, the farm was not going well and dairy revenue was falling due to oversupply. Desmond's younger brother, Kevin, had gone to work in the United States as an engineer for Chevrolet in Detroit, and Bessie was con-cerned about the prospects for her youngest son, Gofty, at Brookwatson –

a place she had come to loathe as a stagnant backwater. She encouraged Desmond to write to her brother Jack, the physician in California, to see whether there would be any openings for him there. Sage did receive a list of crystallography departments from a professor at the University of California in Los Angeles, but was warned that there would be a lot of competition for jobs and some teaching would be required.[58] This was not an appealing prospect, and he stayed put.

While Bessie Bernal may have tried to love her children equally, she always lavished the most attention on her eldest, Des. Her devotion was ensured by his precociousness – she was the first woman to be infatuated by his charm and intelligence. Desmond unwittingly placed more and more demands on her time as he grew through his childhood, and the only way she could satisfy him was to hand over the rearing of her two youngest children, Gigi and Gofty, to the maids and staff at Brookwatson. They became native Irish children, relaxed and happy, unconcerned by any British connections that in different ways troubled both Desmond and Kevin.

As a young woman, Gigi was lively and headstrong, and much to her mother's annoyance Desmond tended to egg Gigi on, rather than attempt to restrain her. In a postscript to the letter in which she had already upbraided Des for not paying any attention to the family at Brookwatson, Bessie beseeched him to: 'Write Gigi; God knows I wish you had not encouraged her in "self-expression"'.[59] Gigi, who was then twenty years old, wrote to Des about a dance at Brookwatson, which had been a 'roaring success',[60] and listed all the men she had kissed, including Commander Bennett – 'ripping, about 38, fair and quite exciting' – whose attractiveness in her eyes was enhanced because he was married to a pretty American. It was unrealistic for Bessie to expect Desmond to take on the role of a disapproving father figure, but by the following year the rift between mother and daughter had widened. Bessie wrote to Desmond setting out conditions for Gigi to be allowed to return to Brookwatson to live: she should cease being insolent and sneering, behave with modesty and decency, wear proper and decent underwear, do her share of the work (milk cows in the evening), and must not make confidantes of the servants.[61] Bessie remained furious that Desmond had encouraged Gigi 'to cut loose' and to 'find herself . . . although the worst of it is you do not suggest how'.[62]

Since Desmond had not followed her advice to emigrate to the United States, Bessie wanted to know whether he was still on the same salary and what the prospects for the laboratory were. Fortunately, Bernal would soon be able to tell her that he 'had been appointed the first lecturer in Structural Crystallography to the University of Cambridge'.[63] The post had been created on the initiative of the new Professor of Mineralogy at the University, Arthur

Hutchinson. It was an exciting position which, if the successful applicant had enough drive and talent, might lead to the creation of a new school of crystallography that would rank with those already established by the Braggs, in London and Manchester. The two most likely candidates were Astbury and Bernal, who had both been supported by Hutchinson in the past and who had more than repaid his faith in them already by their accomplishments at the Royal Institution. While Bernal had been developing the equipment, theory and practice of single crystal rotation photographs, Astbury had been launched on his life's interest by the most casual push from 'Bill' Bragg.

One of Bragg's delights was to give a series of Christmas lectures for schoolchildren, and he decided the theme of the 1926 talks would be 'The imperfect crystallization of common things'. In connection with this, he asked Astbury to prepare some photographs of materials such as wool. There was work going on in Germany on the X-ray patterns of textiles such as silk and cotton, but no one in England had so far taken up their lead. Astbury was not put off by the rather imprecise and sparse X-ray diffractions obtained from fibres, and saw that in fact they offered the first glimpse of the three-dimensional structure of biologically important molecules. By the time the interviews were held in Cambridge in the summer of 1927, Astbury was just beginning his work and had not published anything to suggest that the field would be as fruitful as it eventually proved to be. There was a risk, no doubt, in the minds of his interviewers that he might be doggedly navigating his way into a cul de sac, and his answer to the question of how he viewed the prospect of collaboration did nothing to reassure them. In his bluntest Potteries accent, Astbury told the committee, 'I am not prepared to be anybody's lackey.'[64]

In the face of this, Bernal probably just needed to be affable and to talk about his body of published work to land the position, especially as the committee already had a letter of recommendation from Sir William Bragg describing him as a 'good and loyal colleague' who 'willingly and efficiently... has helped other workers whose experience was less than his own'.[65] Instead when his turn came, Sage sat with his chin buried in his chest and seemed completely uninterested in the matter at hand. Hutchinson, who was in despair at the sight of his second candidate self-destructing, finally asked him what he would do with the job if he were appointed. 'At which,' according to C.P. Snow, 'Bernal threw his head back, hair streaming like an oriflamme, began with the word No... and gave an address, eloquent, passionate, masterly, prophetic, which lasted forty-five minutes.'[66] After such a virtuoso performance, 'There was nothing for it but to elect him', said Hutchinson.

A few months later, Desmond was in his mother's bad books again because he had written to the family's solicitor about his inheritance. The problem was that his father's estate was all tied into Brookwatson. In the lawyer's opinion, it could not be divided until the youngest child reached the age of majority (Gofty was not yet 17 years old), and 'in any event, it is not an estate which easily lends itself to division, because the bulk of it consists of land, at present of very uncertain value'.[67] Bessie brought a dowry of £1,600 to Brookwatson at the time of her marriage in 1900, and was now dependent on the farm for her livelihood, as were her children to various degrees. Although times had been especially difficult during the years after Samuel Bernal's death, Bessie, aided by her sister Cuddie, had become a shrewd manager, and farmed the 120 acres of prime grassland very competently. Her costs were low, largely because labour was cheap: she employed 15 labourers at minimum wage.[68] She was not prepared to sell the farm at a gross undervaluation to ease Desmond's financial straits. His salary at the Royal Institution had been modest and the lecturer's salary at Cambridge was not much higher. He had to provide for Eileen and the infant Michael, but the immediate problem confronting him was that he owed £100 in tax on the unearned income from investments that his mother sent him every quarter. Once he explained this, his mother was sympathetic and wrote him a cheque, delivered with the admonishment: 'For God's sake get away from the money lender's clutches.'[69] So despite a high degree of freedom in his academic and personal life, Desmond was still mindful of his mother. She would continue to write letters to him, covering every inch of the paper in her spidery hand, dispensing advice and news in a mixture of French and English. Even though she did not always understand or even approve of his activities, Bessie's loyalty to Des was unwavering.

4

Science Fantasy

While at the Royal Institution, Bernal began to write his memoir. He might perhaps have chosen the title, *A Portrait of the Scientist as a Young Man*, as a nod to his countryman James Joyce (a writer whom he admired), but instead settled on the duller but less pretentious, *Microcosm*. Although clearly intended for publication, *Microcosm* was never finished and survives only as a collection of mostly undated manuscripts (some typed) and notebooks.[1] The writings begin with the following statement: 'At the age of twenty-five I have set myself the task of writing down the results of my life, the sum of all the influences that have borne on me, and what my mind makes of these in its knowledge and action.' Realizing that such an undertaking at his tender age might be regarded as impertinent, Bernal quickly acknowledged that he did not 'despise the wisdom of age or prefer that of youth' but thought that 'they are different wisdoms'. He worried, though, if he waited till old age before attempting such a book, something would be lost: 'There is a lack of adaptability in old men, the ideas they acquired in their youth tend to become fixed and new ones are absorbed with more and more difficulty so that they become out of touch with the times they are living in. Their ideas become also in a sense part of themselves, they are less conscious of the influences which formed them and thus less judges of the effect of these influences.'

Bernal supposed that young people were generally too busy assimilating their environment and too anxious about the troubles that confronted them to commit their impressions to paper. The outpouring of Great War literature at the end of the twenties would disprove his theory, but at a time when those works were being written and their deep impact was yet to be felt, Bernal saw an abundance of youthful novels, poems and plays that seemed shallow, being 'replete with influences and occupied, almost preoccupied, with problems'. These literary attempts were depictive rather than interpretative, dealing with the universe as it presented itself to the authors, whereas with his mainly scientific education, he was seeking to 'violate nature so that she be understandable'. Such an analytical approach seemed to him to be as valid as any synthetic work of fiction: the two forms might appeal to different minds but had an equal right to appear. The ambitious aim of his book was 'to put down the conscious dynamic content of a mind reaching its maturity in the first half of the twentieth century'. By conscious dynamic content, he meant 'that part of knowledge and experience that appears to urge us to further thought and action'. His analytical method was a throwback to the armchair psychology of the nineteenth century, relying heavily on introspection. Mindful of Freudianism, he acknowledged the importance of unconscious pressures, but as he had no special training to articulate them, he disregarded them.

Even though he restricted himself to conscious events, he faced an immediate difficulty: 'In the whole field of thought I have no one supreme interest but am fascinated wherever I look.' He prided himself on possessing an integrated mind, where every new piece of information was worked into his existing knowledge and thereby stood a chance of modifying his future judgments. He did not concern himself with the question of heredity, although he was well aware of the continuing influence of his family and other individuals who played a role in shaping his childhood. Apart from such personal relationships with their chronic and subtle effects, Bernal noticed that even more discrete ideas and experiences still tend to register as blurred impressions in the mind, after being filtered through culture, the physical environment and learning. 'A single day will introduce us to a new way of cooking asparagus, a new political situation, a new passage of Herodotus, a new form of cement conveyer, new that is to us.' There were, it appears, some necessary limits even to Sage's brain or spheres of interest: 'we cannot, as in our childhood, afford hours of study to the various sizes, shapes and colours of stones on the gravel beach, or the intimate habits of crabs, unless we are professed petrologists or zoologists.' But even a single subject could give rise to protean connections, for example his thoughts about mathematics 'which began with some crude attempts at a theory of numbers twenty years ago and [go] on to the appreciation of tensor calculus, mixed inextricably in my mind with associations of mistresses and books and professors, money sums and physics and crystallography'. In retrospect, it is easy to see that while Sage's attempts to dissect out the formative strands of his existence are skilful and fascinating to watch, the exercise was bound to end in a tangle rather than in a recognizable pattern. The youthful memoirs did not materialize into a book.

Some of the more developed themes in *Microcosm* became an exaggeration of features that Bernal wished to possess. His profile as a radical comes across as strong and unwavering, and he is especially eager to establish his credentials as an Irish revolutionary from a tender age. Recalling that at the Protestant school that he and Kevin attended in Nenagh, history was taught from a British imperialist perspective, Desmond mentions that he countered the bias by reading the history of Ireland for himself at home: 'the long oppressions, the repeated failures, moved me to self-pitying resentment, a determination to be myself the instrument of delivery.' Casting himself as 'a singularly closed-in child' who was fascinated with the possibility of inventing new things, he claims to have conceived a revelatory scheme in his pre-teen years that would dominate the next ten years of his life: 'I would use science and apply it to war to liberate Ireland. But why stop at Ireland?... My phantasy occupied half my reflective thought. Everything I did, learning and growing, was with reference to it. Science, and Engineering, school would give me; for the art of war I would join the British Army to betray it. It would be a hard and unpleasant life, dangerous but worth the reward.' There is no record of such an exciting and grandiose strategy in his teenage diaries, which give such unselfconscious accounts of his other preoccupations.

His recollections of Bedford School in *Microcosm* were bitter and again revealed anti-English sentiments, missing from his earlier diaries: 'There I could be tortured, humiliated, waste my time and my interest on dully repetitive games and military drill, but I could learn everything I wanted. I lived like a hostage in an enemy land. My companions were cheerful thieves and liars, and furtive sexual perverts. I merely thought they were English and kept my hatred of the race closer to myself. The war raged taking in turn all my seniors for Military Crosses or glorious deaths.' For his own part, he gloried in an 'obstinate insistence on being different' and quietly rejoiced at the great struggle that Germany was making against the world, hoping it would lead to the destruction of England's power.

When considering the modern world, Bernal thought many people had not realized that the nineteenth century was over, and that the Russian Revolution, in particular, meant that the future development of society would not be a continuation of past trends. He was convinced that he was witnessing the last days of capitalism, a system doomed because it could not engender the loyalty of the majority of citizens, even though it commanded the services of the most intelligent. His analysis of money and wealth is full of idealism and remains aloof from any marketplace, where buyers and sellers might be active: 'Instead of taking wealth as a good, in which case there is no halting in the pursuit of it, or an evil to be avoided at all costs, let us suppose for each individual, at each stage in his life, there is an optimum income.' Optimum income he defined, on an individual and subjective basis, as enabling the citizen to be most effective in his or her contribution to society and to be happy. Once attained, no more effort should be spent in generating more income, for once bodily discomfort has been avoided, extra income leads to 'the heavy comfort of the bourgeoisie, an excess of over-eating, over-dressing, over-furnishing, gross and sensual pleasures. The comfort that comes with increasing income comes so subtly that it is difficult to resist. It enervates by continued satiety and wastes endless time over the mere bodily business of living.' He allowed that a certain amount of disposable money can enhance social pleasures but again favoured the concept of optimal limits. For example, travel was an endeavour that in Sage's opinion should be undertaken on a limited budget because those who go first class shield themselves from any intense, local experience. He suggested that 'snobbery can be just as great a destroyer of independence as poverty', since people consumed by reputation or status are as constrained in their behaviour just as much as the poor are. The ultimate motivation for the pursuit of riches, in his view, was to obtain power over others. He concerned himself very much with the behaviour of the individual rather than considering the aggregate picture of an economy.

Industrialization seemed to Bernal to have brought near equality in the sphere of popular entertainment, where both rich and poor bought their amusement. The quality available to the millionaire, though uniformly bad in his opinion, was hardly different from that 'available through film, wireless and the dancing hall to any honest workman'. Truly to enjoy oneself it was essential to have 'friends who know you well enough to pick up allusions' so that 'you can laugh at the world together'. There was no such equality or frivolity in human sexuality, which Sage considered to be 'a complex and delicate art' for men and women. It was also the one activity that seems to be exempt from his law of optimal economics, in that 'money can and does buy...the opportunity of practising it. The working man, or even more the working woman, has neither the time nor energy to develop it adequately... [it is] essentially the prerogative of people of leisure.' Writing in the mid-1920s, Bernal had no doubt that a sexual revolution was already under way: 'The successful use of birth control for over fifty years and its increasing dissemination is in an irresistible manner forcing a new sexual ethic based on the separation of intercourse and procreation. The effect is the surer because it partakes of the nature not of opinion or propaganda but of a material change of environment. Separated from its previous consequences, the sexual act becomes like a kiss, merely a demonstration of affection, more violent, more pleasurable but essentially of the same nature. It ceases to concern society and concerns only the parties involved and then only for the occasion. This is no moral doctrine but the physiological logic that can be seen in the increasing number of young people every year, beginning with the cleverest.' But he still admitted that even the pre-eminent are 'obliged to make some outward gestures to conformity'. In addition to effective contraception, the other powerful factor he identified as changing sexual mores was the 'influence of Freudian psychology which gives scientific sanction to this behaviour'. He credited Freud with releasing him from the 'phantasies of religion and rationalism' so that he could fulfill his own desires.

Microcosm contains a cryptic list of his own sexual encounters with some of their salient features. Helen, for example, brought 'friendly copulation and companionship' whereas with Phyllis it was infatuation and copulation without intimacy, and a partner identified only as R. brought 'high spirits and sexual technique'. *Microcosm* is more than a black book of conquests, and Bernal reflected on the stages of love with all their varying emotions. He referred to adultery as 'a division of love' and portrayed his own jealousy and marital torment in a passage of dialogue he entitled 'Incomprehensibility'. The conversation takes place between a man and a young woman waiting at a bus stop. The man is feeling miserable and strikes up a conversation with the woman, telling her that he is married, but that night his wife is sleeping with another man. The woman, initially affronted by this salacious information from a stranger, cannot curb her curiosity. She chides him for taking 'another man's leavings'. The man protests that he loves his wife and, because he loves her, does not want to deny her the pleasure she derives from her lover. The woman tries to torment him. 'You know that he is not just sleeping with her, that he is fondling her, caressing her. And you will go back to her after that.' He did not expect the woman to understand, but is eager to keep the conversation until her bus comes. As she is about to board the bus, she suddenly gives him her address and suggests that they might meet again. His transitory misery is dispelled.

There is also a lyrical story about a couple who rendezvous in Avignon, after the man has travelled from London and the woman from the south of France. (Bernal recorded taking the night train to Avignon on 3rd September 1926 in his diary.)

Now they could breathe again, shake gradually free from unendurable hope. How they were melting. Ease could come, and joy, and ecstasy. This was a time snatched out of their lives. London was very far behind, work, prospects, duties, confusions. She had left the hermitage by the lake, d'Annunzio's villa and his fantastic warship. In the afternoon they came into the sun and warm life…the sunlight was yellow coming down through the ilexes. She lay on the rampart of the stairs, stretched out like a lizard. He protested gently. 'But what does it matter,' she answered, 'here nothing and no one matters. For once I can do what I like, be what I like.' They came down the steep side to the bridge. The bridge which is like no other bridge in the world. The bridge that leads nowhere. The bridge that they dance on, through the town wall, past the church to the last arch. There they sat looking down on the river and on the other bank that could never be reached.

While *Microcosm* was never developed into a book, Bernal soon published his first monograph – *The World, the Flesh & the Devil*.[2] The title was chosen to reflect the three enemies of the rational soul – the obstacles of the physical environment, the limitations of our cellular fabric and the darker aspects of our characters. It is essentially a treatise on the future. The writer Arthur C. Clarke has called the small book 'the most brilliant attempt at scientific prediction ever made',[3] and credited Bernal with being the well-spring of many of his own ideas. In the book, Bernal set out two aspects of the future – man's desire, 'itself all future', and destiny, 'that which will inevitably happen'.[4] In asking the question 'how is it possible to examine scientifically the future', Bernal soon came up against the problem that prediction is a limited technique when it is not soon followed by verification. He identified twin hazards to be avoided – hopeful illusions and the ingrained tendency to see the future as a continuation of the present – and cautioned that 'even the more enlightened prophets let their imagination stop in some static Utopia…despite…all evidence pointing to ever increasing acceleration of change'.[5] There were, it seemed to him, three disciplines of thought that might help in unravelling the complexities of the future – history ('a storehouse of illustrative facts'), the physical sciences (as a way of comprehending the whole universe of space and time) and our knowledge of human desires. The third of these, he warned, was such a murky area in the underdeveloped subject of psychology that it made predictions from physical, chemical and biological laws seem inevitable, even though knowledge of those sciences was minimal.

To Bernal then, it seemed that prediction about the material world was on the surest ground, although as he pointed out in *Microcosm*, the brilliant discoveries of twentieth-century physicists 'looked at from the commonsense and metaphysical points of view…seem definitely negative. The practical man finds that the matter that we have been investigating for the last 30 years has all melted away in our hands, has become probabilities, imaginary amplitudes and such like, while the metaphysicist, searching for reality finds that with us it has lost all meaning it ever possessed.'[6] The problem with commonsense and metaphysics, according to Sage, was that they are anthropocentric, and the modern physicist had gained an immense amount of mathematical knowledge for which everyday logic and our power of visualization were inadequate. He returned to this theme in the chapter on 'The World', stating: 'So far we have been living on the discoveries of the early and mid-nineteenth century, a macro-mechanical age of power and metal.'[7] These discoveries tipped the balance in favour of man against the forces of nature by substituting steam and electrical power in place of muscle energy. Bernal believed that the new discoveries in 'the micro-mechanics of the Quantum Theory which touch on the nature of matter itself, are far more fundamental and must in time produce far more important results'.[8] In the years immediately before he wrote this, there had been rapid advances made in quantum mechanics with Pauli's Exclusion Principle (1925), Schrödinger's Equation

(1926), and Heisenberg's Uncertainty Principle (1927); but these were abstractions exchanged by a charmed circle of theoretical physicists. Sage's bold prediction that such recent and abstruse ideas would prove to have fundamental significance and change man's environment is testimony to his faith in the power of science. Our reliance on computer chips, with their digital operations, would not have surprised him.

The other major topic discussed in relation to the physical universe is space travel and colonization. Bernal identified the need to acquire sufficient acceleration to escape the earth's gravitational field as the major barrier to extraplanetary travel, and surmised that 'the most effective method is based on the principle of the rocket'.[9] Recognizing that the momentum acquired by a rocket is equal and opposite to the momentum of the gas expelled from it, he was troubled that the mass of gas required as fuel would be 'of the same order as the weight of the rocket itself, so that it is difficult to imagine how the rocket could contain enough material to maintain its propulsion for any length of time'.[10] Although he could not see an immediate answer to this problem, he never doubted (unlike other eminent scientists then and later) that it would be solved and that space travel would become feasible. In unpublished notes probably written in 1930,[11] Bernal contemplated the prospects for manned travel to the moon, and divided the project into three stages. The first would be the development of an efficient and reliable rocket, which would include a gyroscopic stabilizer to prevent it turning end over end like a Catherine wheel. Next would follow an initial space shot out of the earth's atmosphere with successful return. Finally there would be a voyage in which a rocket was allowed to gravitate around the moon, fairly close to its surface without attempting to land, before an actual journey to the moon could be 'anything but a suicidal venture'.

Bernal considered using an aeroplane as an alternative to rocket power to escape the earth's gravitational pull; he calculated that if a body can attain a horizontal velocity of three-and-one-half miles per second, it will move off the earth in an ellipse. While this was impossible in the lower atmosphere, Sage reckoned that it could be done at an altitude of 50–60 miles above the earth. He adumbrated the space shuttle when concluding: 'There is nothing of course to prevent a combination of the aeroplane and rocket method, and it is very possible that some combination will be found most effective.'[12]

Now that space travel has entered history in ways similar to those predicted by Bernal decades earlier, his ideas on the subject do not strike us as outlandish. By contrast, his musings on space colonization and the transformation of the human form in *The World, the Flesh & the Devil* are as startling now as when he wrote them. If nothing else, they reinforce his strictures about taking the present for granted and only being able to see the future as a continuation of the present. For man to live in space, Bernal argued, he would need to build a permanent, large sphere or 'celestial station'. The model he suggested involves a small spaceship attaching itself to an asteroid, which would then be hollowed out to provide a large, life-supporting, shell. He imagined it as 'an enormously complicated single-celled plant', with an outer protective wall that would be protective and rigid, as well as allowing the free access of radiant energy and preventing the escape of its internal atmosphere. He thought that man in adjusting to a three-dimensional, weightless way of living, would change radically in this environment. After contrasting the almost impercept-ible slowness of changes due to natural evolution with the speed at which man alters his physical surroundings, Bernal suggested that in the future 'man himself must actively interfere in his own making and interfere in a highly unnatural manner',[13] if he is to succeed in inhabiting new worlds, where oxygen and water are not freely available. Although biologists were apt to regard the mechanism of evolution as sacred, to Bernal it was 'only nature's way of achieving a shifting equilibrium with an environment'[14] and if the process could be speeded up by the use of intelligence, then the natural way would be superseded. To change the human species by direct action, one 'must alter either the germ plasm or the living structure of the body, or both together'.[15]

Altering the germ plasm would nowadays be referred to as genetic engin-eering or modification; in the 1920s, as Bernal pointed out, its most notable adherent was J.B.S. Haldane. John Burdon Sanderson Haldane, the son of an eminent Oxford physiologist, was nearly ten years Bernal's senior, and his equal as an intellectual. He was an uncompromising, menacing, bulldog of a Scotsman, who had served with such ferocity in the Black Watch regiment during the war that the British Commander-in-Chief, Sir Douglas Haig, described him as 'the bravest and dirtiest officer in my Army'.[16] After the war, even though his undergraduate degree was in Classics, Haldane took up his father's trade of physiology before switching from Oxford to Cambridge in 1923 to be reader in biochemistry. It was there that Bernal first got to know him, through meetings of the Heretics. The war had made Haldane ever distrustful of authority, whether human or divine, and he made no secret of his atheism (to do so, in his view, would be cowardly). His first book, *Daedalus*, grew from a talk given to the Heretics, and in it he lustily tackled a number of taboo subjects in biology, notably the potential benefits of 'ectogenesis' – the manufacture of babies to specified designs, outside the human body. The book sold in unexpectedly large numbers and established Haldane as a gifted and provocative popularizer of science. Haldane's pungent literary style, coupled with such controversial subject matter exploded the convention that scientists could not or should not write entertainingly for the general public. *Daedalus* also provided Bernal with a text, as Haldane wrote that science 'is man's gradual conquest, first of space and time, then of matter as such, then of his own body and those of other living beings, and finally the subjugation of the dark and evil elements in his own soul'.[17]

The limitation of Haldane's hypothetical alteration of the human species through ectogenesis, in Bernal's opinion, was that the end product would still be limited by 'the possibilities of flesh and blood'.[18] Ever since 'the ape-ancestor first used a stone he was modifying his bodily structure by the inclusion of a foreign substance',[19] and Bernal was now proposing that through the use of surgery and other medical techniques, it might be possible to introduce useful tools into the living tissues of the body. Assuming that man would live in increasingly complex environments, where the level of mental activity would be the supreme function, Bernal thought that the limbs could be replaced by more energy-efficient, artificial devices, and new sense organs (e.g. to detect infrared radiation and X-rays) might be incorporated. Admitting that his examples were far-fetched and cautioning that his account should be taken as a fable, Bernal elaborated on the existence of a transform-able human being, pointing out that the operations themselves would soon come under the control of transformed individuals, and suggesting that the process would not result in one static or identical final form.

The one organ preserved in Bernal's schema was the brain, although it was no longer to be housed in a skull but in a rigid lightweight cylinder, under optimal conditions. If new sense organs could be wired into the brain's circuitry, then Bernal saw no reason why a direct connection could not be made with the brain of another 'person', setting up neural networks that permit the perfect transference of thought. 'The minds would always preserve a certain individuality, the network of cells inside a single brain being more dense than that existing between brains; each brain would be chiefly occupied with its individual mental development and only communicate with the others for some common purpose.'[20] Sage pointed out that the new life-form would be more plastic and adaptable so that over time the human heritage would dwindle; finally, he wondered whether 'consciousness itself may end or vanish in a humanity that has become completely etherealized, losing the close-knit organism, becoming masses of atoms in space commu-nicating by radiation, and ultimately perhaps resolving itself entirely into light'.[21]

Before we can abandon the world and subdue the flesh, according to Sage we first have to expel the devil, or those unseen, internal demons of our existence that confuse and hinder us. The obstacles that he saw to future progress were 'a failure in the capacity for maintaining creative intellectual thinking' and 'the lack of desire to apply such thinking to the progress of humanity'.[22] One of the leading threats to creative thinking, in Sage's opinion, was the tendency towards specialization as scientific knowledge expanded. At the current stage of development, Sage regarded the modern scientist as 'a primitive savage' who hunted on his own or in small packs, and built success by his own talent but also depended on the richness of nature and the paucity of his own companions. With the expansion of science and the increased complexity of research, Sage predicted that 'good hunting will not last much longer' and foresaw a transition from food gathering to a food producing society, where there would be a far greater degree of planning and control of scientists' activities. Recognizing that this change would risk the loss of independence and originality, he saw the need for an intelligent system of communication that would keep the individual scientist abreast of work in other fields and also allow every research worker potentially to sway the direction of any programme in which he or she is engaged. Sage still envisaged hierarchical organizations because 'it is certain that originality, organizing power and industriousness will continue as now to be very unevenly distributed'.[23] The obstacles to such an open system are 'pedantry and bureaucracy – symptoms of an unintelligent respect for the past'[24] which could be made to vanish, in Sage's view, once their root causes were understood.

Important though intellectual capacity is, in Bernal's estimation, the success of an age or an individual depends far more on desire. As a framework for analysing individual motivation, Bernal suggested a hybrid psychology, based on Freudianism, which would bring the aspirations and ideals of the super ego into line with external reality, while yet 'rendering innocuous the power of the id'.[25] Unlike most followers of Freud, Sage did not accept that human instincts and motivations were necessarily immutable. Under the influence of this fresh approach, whether through psychoanalysis or education, he speculated that art and science, and even religion, might coalesce. Although not cited in the book, Bernal always had Leonardo da Vinci in mind as the model of pure curiosity, searching for understanding and beauty in the whole universe. Leonardo's observations were scientific and aesthetic at the same time; to Sage, he represented beauty in science, 'a beauty unexpressed since his day from the tragic divorce of art and science'.[26]

In *Microcosm*, Bernal showed that he was conscious of the deep antipathy engendered by revolutionary change in society. He admired the eighteenth-century French aristocracy for their learning, wit and aesthetic sensibilities, but deplored their ignorance of the cruelty and misery that surrounded them. When the unstoppable terror of the masses was unleashed, it not only swept away their mannered way of life, it also led to a reaction against all liberal ideas. Unlike the 'gentlemanly' American Revolution, the French Revolution carried a lasting effect due to its spontaneity and the ruthlessness of its attempt to break with the past. History spoke vividly to Bernal: 'The fall of the Bastille and Valmy are still exhilarating, the execution of Louis XVI and the assassination of Marat are still horrifying events.'[27] Despite this ambivalent legacy, he embraced the concept of revolution and admired Lenin for recognizing the need to work with 'ruthless intelligence' for mankind. Indeed he believed that Marxism offered the only solution to the world's political problems, although he recognized that the implications of such an approach were 'difficult and uncomfortable'. In *The World, the Flesh & the Devil*, Bernal stated that any desire for future progress needed to be strong enough to overcome the residual 'distaste and hatred which mechanization has already brought into being'.[28] He readily admitted that his readers may have already felt that distaste, particularly in relation to the bodily changes he outlined in 'The Flesh', because he had felt distaste himself in imagining them. While progress to date had meant that the power of those effecting changes such as industrialization had outweighed the emotional reactions of the masses, it was quite possible, in Bernal's opinion, for the pendulum to swing in the other direction so that society reverted to an earlier stage. He believed that the writings of Aldous Huxley and D.H. Lawrence were straws in a wind blowing in that reverse direction. Bernal was probably thinking of the novel *Antic Hay*, published a few years before, in which Huxley sharply satirized both Haldane and the idea of altering the germ plasm.

In his own book, Bernal examined the possibility that mankind would divide into progressive and unprogressive factions, but unlike the aristocracies of history, the progressive class would gain its position from scientific intelligence. In a modern nation, he believed that the scientists would have a dual function: 'to keep the world going as an efficient food and comfort machine, and to worry out the secrets of nature for themselves.'[29] If these conditions for a progressive society led by scientists were met, and mankind as a whole was given peace, plenty and freedom, the masses 'might well be content to let alone the fanatical but useful people who chose to distort their bodies or blow themselves into space'.[30] But in the end, Sage discounted the development of a permanent human dimorphism because of the emotional conservatism of scientists themselves, who in 'every respect, save their work... resemble their non-scientific brothers, and no one would be more shocked than they at the suggestion that they were raising up a new species and abandoning the bulk of mankind'.[31] The safeguard of scientists' collective emotional identification with the rest of humanity would not, in his view, protect the world against the unforeseen or unintended consequences of their research. For example, Sage foresaw the possibility that 'scientific corporations might well become almost independent states and be enabled to undertake their largest experiments without consulting the outside world'.[32] In that setting, the emotional allegiance of scientists might switch from humanity at large to the progress of science itself, reversing the existing balance against the splitting of mankind. Sage explored this possibility and arrived at his final, chilling, fancy that 'the world might, in fact, be transformed into a human zoo, a zoo so intelligently managed [by the new species of scientists living in space] that its inhabitants are not aware that they are there merely for the purposes of observation and experiment'.[33] Lest it be thought that Bernal was completely besotted by the beneficence of science and its practitioners, it is worth remembering his statement that 'the scientists are not masters of the destiny of science; the changes they bring about may, without their knowing it, force them into positions which they would never have chosen. Their curiosity and its effects may be stronger than their humanity.'[34]

The World, the Flesh & the Devil was written with extraordinary imagination, and the predictions about the material world reveal Bernal to be an estimable prophet. Apart from imagination, such a book required great audacity, since the author could expect to receive ridicule or just quiet disapproval from senior colleagues. Although J.B.S. Haldane had blazed the trial when writing *Daedalus*, he was regarded by many as a dangerous character; the tradition that academics should remain cloistered and not debase themselves by communicating with the general public was still strong. One of those most likely to disapprove of *The World, the Flesh & the Devil* was Sir Ernest Rutherford, a loyal subject of the British Empire and a man of conventional beliefs and Christian morals, whose distaste for speculation in science was the foundation on which experimental physics at the Cavendish was built – he was fond of reminding his juniors that endless theorizing without the hard work of experimental verification was like 'drawing a blank cheque on eternity'. Sage, of course, did work hard in the laboratory and like Rutherford was a prolific source of ideas for others to test; but *The World, the Flesh & the Devil* taken together with his communist politics and sexual promiscuity made him 'one of the two men whom Rutherford loathed'.[35]

In *The World, the Flesh & the Devil*, there was little direct reference to Marxism, although as we have seen, Bernal did explore various potential class struggles for power, especially that between a scientific elite and a non-progressive majority. In *Microcosm*, Bernal repeatedly pledged his allegiance to Marxism as the way to order society and yet he retained a concern for the individual citizen that puts into question his level of ideological commitment at that time. Having abandoned his Catholic faith, he had not yet apparently come to the realization that Marxism also has to be swallowed whole. Its modernity and quasi-scientific form appealed to him enormously, still he had reservations: 'Ever since Marx, the chief scientific basis of communism has lain in economics. Economics has seemed the only basis on which communist theory could rest; but I think it is safe to predict that in future the place of economics will be taken by psychology.' In reality, Marx's original theories sclerosed into absolutist dogma, and the only applications of psychology in communist systems were in the production of propaganda or, even more crudely, in the inculcation of mass fear; there was certainly no inclination to understand individual human differences. Indeed, the historian, Robert Conquest, has identified the assumption 'that our knowledge of the workings of human behaviour is now so scientific that we can shape society according to scientific, or rational, blueprints' as Marxism's 'most persistent fault, and the hardest to be rid of'.[36] Bernal, for all his protestations in his chapter 'The Devil' about the rudimentary understanding of what makes men tick, would not avoid this fallacy.

In an essay, '*Unholy alliance*',[37] that first appeared a year after *The World, the Flesh & the Devil*, Bernal mounted a vigorous attack on the Church as a conservative force protecting wealth and property, while denying the poor material improvements in their lives. Science, which had exposed the basic beliefs of religion such as the creation, Adam and Eve and 'the whole crop of miracles' as just 'plain lies', now offered the prospect of a much more secure and comfortable world. 'If science were used properly there would be no need for anyone in the world to go hungry',[38] and this alone justified the destruction of the present 'tottering social order' which was supported by religion. To Sage in 1930, the outcome seemed inevitable since the new Soviet state had denounced religion as 'unnecessary and harmful, while science was to be the basis of the reconstruction of material and social life'.[39]

At the time Bernal wrote '*Unholy alliance*', Stalin was ordering the liquidation of the kulaks, or smallholders, and the collectivization of farms. The utter desolation that soon followed dwarfed any biblical famine, yet was blithely denied by visiting Western intellectuals like George Bernard Shaw and the Webbs. That Bernal felt able to publish this essay in a collection nearly twenty years later, with no apparent embarrassment, while tipping his hat to 'the enormously increased control over environment that has come with the full-scale and conscious application of science and ... the development of the social forms of the organised working class capable of utilising that science on a large scale, first in the Soviet Union'[40] showed that he had still not tumbled to the big lie. Bernal always insisted on portraying Marx as a scientist, but in assessing Marxism he failed to heed Rutherford's wise dictum about the dangers of endless theorizing in the absence of supporting evidence.

5

The New Kingdom

The Cavendish Laboratory in 1927 was passing through a quiet period. Patrick Blackett's bright star was already shining in the firmament, but the other young men in Rutherford's department were engaged in painstaking preparatory work – refining experimental techniques and building new equipment – not yet making fundamental discoveries of their own. Rutherford was steadfast in his intent to reveal the structure of the atomic nucleus, relying for the most part on the trusty α-particle as his major tool of interrogation. Unlike Bernal, Rutherford was sceptical of the new quantum theory, and did not disguise his mistrust – for example, thanking Heisenberg, who had just delivered an invited lecture to the Cavendish Physical Society in perfect English, for 'a lot of interesting nonsense'.[1] Rutherford's research programme was not seen as having any possible practical applications and did not attract much outside funding. The entire annual budget during the late 1920s for the Cavendish, including salaries and wages, apparatus and materials, heating, water, gas and electricity, averaged between £10,000 and £15,000, with nearly all the money coming from students' fees.[2] The Victorian building could not be extended and space was already at a premium; Bernal would have to be content with four, dimly lit, rooms for his X-ray crystallography group.

Arthur Hutchinson, the Professor of Mineralogy, did his best to make this limited accommodation ready for his new lecturer. He wrote to Bernal to tell him that the water supply had been connected and that there would soon be electricity from the main in Free School Lane.[3] He could not have shown more consideration in planning Bernal's work schedule: 'I have only put you down for a single course of lectures (eight) in the Easter Term – my idea was that you would be fully occupied for the next six months in installing apparatus and getting it going, and in starting research and that a single course of lectures of rather more than an elementary character was all that we ought to expect of you.'[4] A series of twelve introductory lectures would be given by W.A. (Peter) Wooster, the demonstrator in crystal physics, who had been one of Rutherford's most promising research students. The only other original member of staff in structural crystallography was Arthur Lanham, a young technician, who taught himself to become an accomplished instrument maker; he would be just as crucial to the success of Bernal's laboratory as the technicians in the main Cavendish department were to the revolutionary discoveries in nuclear physics. His first task with Bernal was to set up an X-ray tube brought from the Davy Faraday laboratory of the Royal Institution. At one point, they had disconnected it from the mains supply but neglected to discharge the condenser; Bernal held the earth wire and told Lanham to cut it, forgetting there was a potential of 40,000 volts across it: 'Sage gave a tremendous yell and went half way across the room, and I went down on my backside about 6 yards away.'[5]

In general, Sage was very happy to be back in Cambridge and to be mixing with the great men of science. Rutherford and Sir William Pope, the Professor of Chemistry, invited him to tea. He heard Rutherford lecture on the nucleus at the Cavendish Physical Society, but this was surpassed by Niels Bohr's visit in early November 1927 and his talk on the 'Quantum of action'. Bohr had just come from a Solvay Congress in Brussels, where he had spent most of his time countering Einstein's criticisms of quantum mechanics.[6] Rutherford, in contrast to his rude treatment of Heisenberg, always accorded Bohr the greatest respect, and the occasion struck Bernal as an historic scene.[7] After the lecture, Bernal dashed off to London by train and spent the night with Kitty 'very happily'.[8] Two weeks later, he had breakfast with Kitty and was then pleased to return to 'Cambridge and away from women'![9] Bernal also recorded in his diary that he was 'V. happy with E[ileen]', although on 13 November Eileen threatened to divorce him because he was late for tea.[10] He and Eileen and the toddler Michael were living in an old rented house in Hildersham, a village outside Cambridge, which Bernal loved.

As Professor Hutchinson expected, the first year in the new department was a very busy one for Bernal. He continued his research on single crystals of bronze, but otherwise his time was largely taken up with organizing work for others in the laboratory. As soon as the academic year was over, at the suggestion of Sir William Bragg, Bernal undertook a European tour to survey different schools of crystallography. Sage was in many ways the ideal choice for such a role because, apart from being an acknowledged expert on the single crystal rotation technique, he was well versed in crystallography's published literature. He took a round view of how the subject related to the other sciences, and would be just as interested in work that promised to spill over into biology or quantum physics as in direct structural analysis. He was easy to talk to and his genuine enthusiasm for others' efforts encouraged them to share their thoughts and aspirations.

Bernal was away for two months and visited 14 institutions, mostly in Germany. In his handwritten report, he first defined the English school with its 'emphasis on the actual atomic positions [in the crystal] from accurate intensity determinations, and the chief instrument is the ionization spectrometer. Photographic methods are considered definitely subsidiary and are only used where the ionization method cannot be profitably employed. Even where the intensities are not sufficient, owing to the complexity of the substance, to determine the actual atomic positions, some plausible model is usually suggested.'[11] The German crystallographers, by contrast, were sceptical about the British emphasis on establishing atomic positions, and restricted themselves largely to considerations of symmetry so that they were satisfied with 'finding the [unit] cell and space group of any crystal'.[12] Although the Germans seemed prepared to spend more on equipment, Bernal found that the ionization spectrometer was an almost unknown instrument there. He assessed the individual schools by criteria which included leadership, equipment and experimental techniques.

While he was in Berlin, Sage met up with Helen Kapp, a young English artist who was then studying in Berlin. At his urging, they visited the Museum of Primitive Chinese Art, which had just reopened in new premises. The collection was disorganized after the move and was unlabelled. Sage wandered round talking freely about all the exhibits – bronzes, frescoes of Mongolian horses, and pots of various types and dynasties. After a while they were shadowed by a man, who was clearly listening to Sage's commentary. Eventually he came up to them and bowed. 'Herr Professor,' he said to Sage, 'I think you must come from the British Museum.' Sage was taken aback. 'But you know everything – everything you have said about all the exhibits is absolutely correct.' The man was the Director of the Museum.[13] On another evening, he was with Helen at the Romanisches Café, when a group of Hitler's brownshirts came stomping through, giving Sage his first sight of the Nazis.

The scientific leader who impressed him most during his summer visit was Hermann Mark, an Austrian of great charm and energy, who was only a few years older than Bernal. Mark did not work in one of the ancient German universities, but was running an X-ray diffraction laboratory for the industrial giant I.G. Farben in Ludwigshafen on the Rhine. He had moved there in 1927 from the Institute of Fibre Chemistry at Dahlem on the outskirts of Berlin. That institute was founded in 1920 under the auspices of the Kaiser Wilhelm-Gesellschaft as a centre of applied research to bring fresh ideas to Germany's moribund textile industry. At the Institute of Fibre Chemistry, a team of exceptionally talented research workers assembled, and they made a start by subjecting crushed natural fibres to X-ray analysis.[14] Materials like silk and cotton had previously been assumed to have an amorphous gel-like structure, but X-ray diffraction photographs revealed a repeating pattern of small crystalline segments, termed crystallites, embedded along the fibre axis. So far from an amorphous structure, insoluble fibrous proteins, at least in places, resembled crystalline material. Research was then extended to whole fibres of materials like rubber and cellulose, where according to one of his colleagues, Mark showed 'manipulative skill bordering on genius'.[15] Mark, more modestly recalled how the group subjected the fibres to 'swelling, stretching, relaxing and drying. We established changes in their crystalline-amorphous system and explored how the macromolecules react to changes in their physical and chemical environment.'[16]

During his 1928 summer visit, Bernal found Mark's research team at the I.G. Farben laboratory working on structural models for natural polymers like silk, rubber, and cellulose. Together with a Swiss chemist in the laboratory, Kurt Meyer, Mark published what would become a very influential model of cellulose, based on its X-ray pattern but also consistent with the known chemical data. Cellulose, a polysaccharide not a protein, is the primary structural component in the cell walls of plants and gives them their toughness. Meyer and Mark proposed that cellulose comprised a long chain of glucose rings each linked to the next in line through an oxygen atom. Cellulose fibres were built up by a number of these long chains running parallel to the axis of the fibre with secondary forces sticking the chains together.[17] Although cellulose gave X-ray diffraction patterns that were far from clear-cut, when taken together with other chemical and physical data, Mark showed how a detailed structural model could be assembled that began to explain crucial properties of such an important natural substance. Bernal was entranced.

There was one important similarity between cellulose and proteins that had been known since the mid-nineteenth century. The English chemist, Thomas Graham, noticed that starches, proteins and cellulose formed sticky solutions that would not easily pass through fine filters. He called them *colloids* and contrasted them with the *crystalloid* solutions of inorganic salts and simple sugars that readily cross filters and membranes. Graham also suggested that colloids were in fact aggregates of crystalloids – a theory that was still popularly applied to proteins in the early 1920s, and which seemed to be supported by the X-ray diffraction results being obtained at the Institute of Fibre Chemistry in Dahlem. But by 1928, several lines of enquiry in Germany and elsewhere had effectively demolished the aggregate theory, and it was generally accepted that proteins were true macromolecules whose primary structures were long chains of amino acids linked together.[18]

The characteristic way in which amino acids join together, *the peptide bond*, had been established as early as 1902. Although this provided the clue to how long peptide chains might form, a group of chemists persisted in believing that there was a limit of about 30 amino acid residues or links per chain, and that these threads then stuck to each other in some non-specified fashion to form proteins. The fatal blow to the aggregate theory of the colloid chemists was administered by one of their own ranks, Theodor 'The' Svedberg. He was the Professor of Physical Chemistry in Uppsala and in the early twenties invented a new machine, the ultracentrifuge, which remains an invaluable tool for separating proteins, nucleic acids and sub-cellular particles by sedimentation. The ultracentrifuge relies on the simple principle that if an emulsion containing dispersed colloidal particles is subject to rapid rotation, the heavier colloidal particles will be separated from the lighter molecules of the solvent. This is exactly the way a milk separator works, where skimmed milk migrates to the periphery and lighter cream accumulates at the centre. Whereas the centrifugal force necessary to separate cream can be achieved at manual speeds, Svedberg's ultracentrifuge could rotate at over 40,000 revolutions per minute and generate a field of force 100,000 times stronger than gravity.

Amongst other colloids, Svedberg examined very dilute solutions of haemoglobin, the oxygen carrying protein present in red blood cells. He expected to find multiple red boundaries corresponding to the constituent peptides of haemoglobin, but instead observed a single line. The sedimentation pattern produced in the ultracentrifuge proved that haemoglobin consisted of individual molecules of a weight of 68,000. He studied other proteins such as egg albumin, again with precise molecular weights emerging, suggesting strongly that proteins 'must be regarded as substantially uniform chemical individuals' and not aggregates of smaller peptides.[19]

While Svedberg was busy spinning protein solutions at unprecedented speeds in Sweden, a determined lecturer, James B. Sumner, at Cornell University in upstate New York was finishing a series of intricate experiments that provided the first unequivocal proof that enzymes were proteins. Working with the Jack bean, he painstakingly separated out a metabolically active substance, the enzyme *urease*, in such a pure form that he was able to crystallize it. Sumner had no assistants and worked with a paralysed arm, the legacy of a boyhood shooting accident; the research took nine years before he published his results in a short paper in 1926. He carefully demonstrated the urease crystals had catalytic activity that was destroyed (as was their protein structure) when they were digested by other proteolytic enzymes. A biochemist at Cambridge, Frederick Gowland Hopkins, had already concluded that 'all metabolic tissue reactions are catalysed by enzymes', but Sumner brought the first proof that an enzyme corresponded to a protein molecule and was not some extrinsic factor absorbed by the protein.[20]

By the summer of 1928, it is likely that all of the above information had gelled in Sage's mind. Enzymes, the molecules that governed every chemical reaction inside cells, were proteins. Proteins were true macromolecules, not aggregates of smaller molecules, and could in many instances be crystallized so that they could be studied by X-ray diffraction. Mark and his group had made a start at modelling macromolecules with cellulose, and even though cellulose was a monotonous chain of glucose residues, Sage was unperturbed by the bewildering variety of protein structures. He might not be able to achieve a full analysis, but even a partial understanding of proteins would revolutionize our understanding of the nature of life and transform physiology and medicine.

The only scientist in England in 1928 to have made an X-ray analysis of natural protein fibres was Bill Astbury, at the Davy–Faraday Laboratory of the Royal Institution. In September, he wrote to Bernal in gloomy tones: 'I don't know whether you have heard the sad news, but it seems possible that I have abandoned crystallography. I have accepted the new lectureship in Textile Physics at Leeds University and am leaving the Davy Faraday at the end of the present month. I am making one last despairing effort to keep in touch with crystallography by attempting to do some X-ray work on wool etc. and I want to get some apparatus together.'[21] He asked Bernal for advice on setting up a new crystallography department, and for recommendations on the best X-ray tube for general photographic research and the best microscope for studying the structure of fibres. The textile industry department was in fact the largest department at Leeds University, and thanks to the support of the Worshipful Company of Clothworkers, Astbury's new endeavours were going to be quite generously supported, certainly with far more resources in terms of research manpower and money than Bernal would ever be offered at Cambridge.[22]

It was fitting that Astbury should turn to Bernal for expert opinion; after his fact-finding visit to the Continent, Sage possessed an unrivalled grasp of the whole subject of X-ray crystallography. Sir William Bragg wrote to thank him for his 'interesting and helpful' report on the European laboratories, and asked permission to circulate it to his son, Lawrence, in Manchester and to Henry Tizard, the senior government scientist at the Department of Science and Industrial Research (DSIR), who had responsibility for supporting university research likely to bring benefits to the country as a whole. Bernal persuaded Bragg that the time was ripe to impose some shape on the burgeoning subject, and Bragg arranged a one-day conference for interested parties at the Royal Institution on 15 March 1929 to follow a meeting of the Faraday Society. The Faraday Society meeting was on 'Crystal structures and chemical constitution' and was expected to attract all the leading workers from Europe as well as from England.

In the months leading up to these events at the Royal Institution, there was a flurry of correspondence between London, Cambridge, Leeds and Manchester about producing a comprehensive multi-author textbook of crystallography to be edited by Sir William. Bernal was to write about the space groups and other topics in conjunction with Astbury and Kathleen Lonsdale

(Yardley). In answer to an enquiry from Astbury about the division of labour, Bernal indicated that he wished to deal with 'the vector theory of space groups, including the recent work of Ewald on lattices and Hermann's derivation of the space groups. I would also unless you are keen on doing it yourself, like to deal more or less critically with the structural theories of Weissenberg and the topological ideas of Niggli.'[23] Sensing that Bernal's contribution might be too theoretical, Astbury emphasized that the section on space groups should be of practical use to crystallographers on a daily basis in their laboratories, and while elegant methods of deduction were fine for illustrative purposes, it would be 'the things which we deduce that are going to count in the end'.[24] Bernal accepted Astbury's views, but was 'so busy now over this metal business and the general organisation of the Conference'[25] that he had no time to write anything for their chapter.

The metal business was a paper on 'The problem of the metallic state'[26] that he was to deliver at the Faraday Society meeting. In this paper, Bernal pointed out that the usual definition of a metal was in terms of a material transmitting electricity by flow of electrons. By considering other properties of metals and their alloys, he attempted to uncover new ways of classifying the metallic state that would be scientifically fruitful. Naturally he started with X-ray crystallography data that showed all metallic substances examined to date contained atoms packed very close together. From this he deduced that the atomic diameter, or atomic volume, of any given element in the metallic state is constant: 'one of the primary facts to be taken into account in any theory of the metallic state.' It had been well known for thousands of years that pure metals tend to be soft and are easily bent, whereas alloys, formed by melting two metals together and allowing them to cool into a solid solution, are much harder. To Bernal, this mechanical property was as fundamental as electrical conductivity but it had been largely ignored by scientists. The major clue to this age-old puzzle, again came from the young science of X-ray crystallography, and Bernal reminded his audience that in an impure metal crystal, the reflection of X-rays by a crystal plane, instead of being extremely sharp is noticeably diffuse. This was an indication that the atoms no longer lie in absolutely parallel planes: the crystal lattice is distorted so that smooth gliding of one plane over another is no longer possible and malleability is lost. He went to discuss how such distortion might also affect the electrical conductivity of metals and its bearing on the pioneering work being carried out at the Cavendish Laboratory on superconductivity by Peter Kapitza.

Bernal's paper was packed with detailed information in chart form and what he modestly described as 'rather hazardous speculation'. In a conclusion that would have earned Rutherford's approval, Bernal stated that 'the confusion which exists in this field is quite as much due to lack of systematic experimentation as to the intrinsic difficulties of theory'. He called for an organized research effort because 'without such a framework of experimental fact, the quantum theory on which we rely ultimately to explain the nature of the metallic state, will be working in the dark and will pile up useless formulae with immense labour'. Although he published nothing more on metals, Bernal encouraged many researchers in this field, which has proved so important in solid state physics and metallurgy, and he continued to contribute generously to their work without accepting any formal acknowledgement. Linus Pauling credited Bernal's extensive 1929 review of the metallic state with stimulating his own research into the electronic structure of metals such as iron, copper, nickel and gallium.[27]

There was one technique that Bernal discovered that was not picked up by anyone else, but was rediscovered twenty years later and became one of the essential foundations of the semiconductor industry. Kapitza asked him to prepare a very pure crystal of the metal bismuth because he wanted to study its electrical resistance in strong magnetic fields at very low temperatures.[28] Bernal found that by passing a hot wire through the bismuth he could draw all the impurities to one end of the crystal – a technique that would become known years later as zone refining. Kapitza gave no acknowledgement to Bernal for his help,[29] but it seems clear that the Cambridge crystallographers used the technique of zone-refining to prepare pure organic and metallic single crystals for X-ray analysis.[30]

At the Royal Institution conference that followed on from the Faraday Society meeting, three committees were formed to look into various aspects of crystallography, and Bernal was a member and secretary of all three. The various national schools of crystallography had adopted different conventions to describe the atomic structures of crystals revealed by X-ray diffraction, and published tables of data contained significant discrepancies. A proposal from Bernal served as the basis for discussion: 'At present the results of structural crystallography, being published in a great diversity of journals and in a variety of technical terms and symbols, are neither (a) generally accessible nor (b) easily comparable.'[31]

He suggested that future publication should be restricted to journals with wide circulation and employ unified nomenclature and standardized tables.

Six months after the conference, Astbury wrote to ask about Bernal's progress with their textbook chapter ('Has <u>anybody</u> written anything yet?'[32]) and to complain that he and Kathleen Lonsdale were still held up by the lack of an agreed nomenclature or even any accepted convention on how axes of symmetry should be labelled. Bernal was working hard to resolve these issues with Paul Ewald and visited him in Stuttgart in September 1929. They failed to untangle the mess resulting from having at least three published and disparate sets of tables for the space groups, but the following summer managed to convene a working conference, which brought all the leading figures together in Zürich. The host for the conference was Paul Niggli, the Professor of Mineralogy and the editor-in-chief of the world's most prestigious crystallography journal, *Zeitschrift für Kristallographie*. Niggli himself had published an influential textbook in 1919, in which he proposed one method of representing the space groups. Ewald and Bernal prepared an agenda for the meeting, which the Tables Committee worked through, with growing agreement. Ewald, who was chairing the committee, noticed that Niggli took little part and sat tight-lipped. On the third day, he suddenly exclaimed: 'Gentlemen, you are stealing my book.'[33] It seemed that the progress the Committee had been making towards a unified set of *International Tables* would be blocked by the immovable Niggli, and there was general despair. The project was saved by Bill Astbury who talked to Niggli on his own and, in Bernal's words, used his 'transparent honesty and disinterestedness'[34] to persuade Niggli to withdraw his objection.

Another of Astbury's qualities – his irresistible enthusiasm – had already advanced the state of knowledge about fibrous proteins. He expressed almost a reverence for the properties of wool, writing to Bernal, for instance: 'The wool is very exciting.'[35] One of his new colleagues at Leeds, J.B. Speakman, had been studying the physical and chemical properties of wool for some years, and in particular had amassed data on the elasticity of wool fibre. Starting in the summer of 1929, Astbury took over a hundred X-ray diffraction photographs of wool in its unextended and stretched states. In his report for the Clothworkers Department of the University, Astbury wrote that these photographs had convinced him that keratin, the protein matter of wool, showed a reversible change in its molecular structure on stretching. He labelled the unstretched protein, α-keratin, and the stretched form, β-keratin, and recorded the different periodicities of X-ray diffraction along the fibres. He also soon realized 'that natural silk finds its counterpart, not in normal wool, but in *stretched* wool. There is a close similarity between the X-ray photograph of silk and of β-wool, from which we may make the deduction that silk does not show the long-range elastic properties of wool *because it is already in the extended state...*'[36] His former colleague at the RI, A.L. Patterson captured the essence of Astbury's discoveries in the following verse:

> *Amino acids in chains*
> *Are the cause, so the X-ray explains,*
> *Of the stretching of wool*
> *And its strength when you pull,*
> *And show why it shrinks when it rains*

Apart from stretched wool and silk, Astbury soon found surprising similarities in his X-ray photographs of other natural materials. He wrote to Bernal again: '...let me tell you at once of the really exciting discovery I have made. Last Saturday I took a photo of a common fishing float, and it is identical with that of wool and hair, however fine!!! The fishing float is, of course, the quill of a porcupine, but isn't it staggering that such a large epidermal structure – anything up to a foot long – should give an indistinguishable X-ray photo? The implications seem to me very great.'[37] Astbury, through his ingenious interpretation of rather vague X-ray diffraction photographs, was beginning to realize that the mechanically durable and chemically unreactive protein, keratin, formed the animal appendages of hair, nails, horn and hoof, and he would soon find that it was the common supportive element in tissues like tendon.

Astbury presented this work at a Royal Society meeting in November 1930, and its subsequent publication, in Bernal's opinion, represented 'the key paper of all Astbury's work.'[38] In the paper, Astbury advanced a structural model for α-keratin that was analogous to the Meyer and Mark model for cellulose, but instead of calling for glucose rings to be linked together in a chain, he proposed that the repeating ring in keratin results from two amino acid molecules condensing (fusing together), and that this ring was broken open when the fibre was stretched into the β-form. To arrive at this model, Astbury and his associates had made some chemical investigations, hydrolysing the keratin of wool into its constituent amino acids. They knew that the elastic properties of hair and wool 'are intimately bound up with the state of combination of the sulphur atoms'[39] and therefore had concentrated their efforts on cystine, the only amino acid which contains a sulphur atom, and the most abundant amino acid by weight in wool. Although they had not been able to obtain large crystals of cystine, they found that 'a micro-crystalline specimen of pure *l*-cystine gave a remarkably fine powder photograph.'[40] If single crystals of amino acids could be grown and studied, they would give far more complete and detailed maps of atomic structure than the rather smeared images that Astbury was obtaining from fibres.

Astbury recognized that Bernal was the master of the single crystal technique, and by the spring of 1930 the two had made an arrangement for the division of work along these lines. In the same letter where he disclosed his excitement about the porcupine quill, Astbury wrote: 'I have already collected specimens of most of the important amino-acids found in hair proteins and, as I told you, have got some sort of structure out for cystine . . . But if I send these amino-acids on to you, will you harden your ridiculously soft heart and stop doing odd jobs for other people? That would be an essential condition, of course, if we are to keep this job in our hands and out of reach of those damned

Germans (God bless 'em!). By the way, I suppose you know that these protein amino-acids are all <u>alpha</u>-amino-acids. You ask me if I am going to stick to the proteins of animal fibres, but, of course, in a job like this it is impossible to stick to anything. It is not crystallography, but a kind of higher detective work, searching for clues, however faint, day after day.... I feel considerably safer with you on my side, so long as you are not developing my photos!'[41]

The work on amino acids soon gathered momentum. In October 1930, Astbury sent Bernal 'pure specimens of L-cystine, leucine and glutamic acid. The cystine is in the form of a crystalline powder, and if you can grow big crystals, I believe you will be the first to do it. It may not be impossible... These three acids, together with glycine and alanine (and I should say arginine) are very important biologically, and, of course, the three I am sending are the most important constituents of hair... I shall look forward to getting some really authentic information from you about these amino-acids. It is a job worthy of your steel, and should prove extremely valuable from the biological point of view.'[42] Bernal obtained other single crystals from the Biochemical Laboratory in Cambridge and made great inroads in just three short months: he was able to suggest, for example, why certain amino acids were soluble and others insoluble. From a single crystal of cystine, he took the most beautiful series of X-ray photographs revealing the symmetry of the molecule. Following Astbury's hypothesis that α-keratin contained ring forms of amino acids linked together in a chain, Bernal made the first pass at the structure of the diketopiperazine ring that is formed from the condensation of two glycine molecules and was already known to occur in intact proteins. He wrote to Astbury that: 'Diketopiperazine is fairly simple. It seems to consist of fairly flat hexagonal rings attached to each other sideways by electro-static forces and lying nearly parallel in fairly close sheets. When I get the intensity measurements I'll be able to measure the dimensions of the ring fairly accurately. All these structures give the possibility of polymer linkages such as you suggest with the keratins, particularly the di-acid substances. Both cystine and diketopiperazine yield horny substances which I am trying to get for investigation.'[43]

As soon as Astbury heard this news, he congratulated Bernal effusively, but could not quite conceal his chagrin at Sage's virtuosity: 'Your letter was great news, and I can only hope you found my letter to *Nature* on the structure of keratin equally plausible. I have only one grumble to make, and that is that you have done the diketo-piperazine after all, and just as I was meditating an attack on it. I have had the crystals of this extremely fundamental substance quite a year now, and since my structure of wool is more or less based on an indefinite repetition of this ring, I had come, in a way, to regard it as my own private property, to be analysed simply and solely by myself. However, I suppose I must not be selfish, especially as the structure which you have got out of it is so thrilling. You undertook to examine all the a.[mino] a.[cid]s with the exception of dkpip., so I shan't forgive you now until you carry out the investigation to the bitter end, <u>and tell me the exact dimensions of the molecule</u> and everything about it . . . I cannot rest now until I know the exact dimensions of the molecule itself. The important fact is that the main periodicity of alpha-hair is about 5.15 Å. I shall now also continue to urge you, night and day, to get me the dimensions of the <u>molecules</u> of glycine, alanine, leucine, glutamic acid and arginine.'[44]

Faced with such a brilliant collaborator, Astbury was anxious to reserve proteins for himself and wished to relegate Sage to a supporting role:

It is a fine bit of work which you have done, and I feel that together, me at the proteins, and you at their constituents, we should be able to knock a considerable hole in the subject. But I insist that you stick to the constituents, and don't 'snaffle' any proteins. I am not sure whether you ought to take any poly-peptides, because the amino-acids have simply got to be worked out with all the intensity details. You have the apparatus and 'flair' for that sort of thing, while I have not.

With regard to cystine, I regret to say that I have a paper in press with the Roy. Soc. in which I have put forward a [unit] cell, from the powder photo only, which is not the same as yours . . . it seems that I am wrong – which is a pity, damn it! I argue that cystine, being the chief constituent of hair, supplies the 'rungs' of a polypeptide ladder into which it is incorporated. I shall be glad to learn all about cystine, as I have a lot of cunning theories as to how it functions in the structure of hair.

I should like to know what you think of my solution of the terrific mass of facts that constitute the problem of the structure of keratin . . . still a number of points which my conscience tells me are a little hazy, but for all that . . . I am convinced that structures quite analogous to that of hair are the basis of <u>all</u> proteins.[45]

Exactly one month later, Bernal, showing no irritation with Astbury's attempt to limit his activities, replied that he had 'finished alanine quite plausibly . . . I have also done aspartic acid and phenylalanine, both of which show molecules associated in pairs'.[46] A month after that he had submitted a paper to *Zeitschrift für Kristallographie* giving his results on the crystal structures of eight natural amino acids as well as diketopiperazine and some peptides. He included details of the crystals' optical properties as well as the unit cell and space group symmetry derived from X-ray oscillation photographs. By considering ancillary chemical evidence, he attempted 'to fit plausible molecular structures to the cells and symmetry conditions found'.[47] Bernal emphasized that these findings were preliminary, and alluded to the difficulty of obtaining precise structures because of the variability of the crystals and the limits to the resolving power of the available X-rays, amongst other problems. He urged anyone else 'possessing such crystals of a magnitude of 0.1 mm or over' to send a few milligrams of them to him for examination.

Bernal's concentration on the X-ray analysis of organic substances was established within a year or two of his return to Cambridge, and was bolstered by an affinity with the researchers in the new Dunn Institute of Biochemistry at the University. The inspirational head of the Dunn Laboratory was Sir Frederick Gowland Hopkins, who, as was mentioned earlier, had been the first to state publicly in 1913 that enzymes were vital to all metabolic processes in living tissues. He went on to share the 1929 Nobel Prize for Physiology or Medicine in recognition of his discovery of the 'accessory food factors' or vitamins. Known inevitably as 'Hoppy', Hopkins was a slightly built, elegant, man of Edwardian demeanour and deep tolerance; he gathered a team around him who could stand comparison with Rutherford's physics department as scientists, but who were far more active on the political left. Prominent amongst them were J.B.S. Haldane, Reader in Biochemistry, Joseph and Dorothy Needham, Conrad 'Hal' Waddington, as well as Bill Pirie and R.L.M. Synge. They were natural allies for Sage, and his close interactions with them over the next few years led to many mutual benefits, as well as a profound effect on the tenor of British science over the coming decades.

If the Cavendish and Dunn Laboratories were the two powerhouses of Cambridge science, with Hopkins succeeding Rutherford as President of the Royal Society in 1930, Bernal had the status of an urchin living on the street between them. As a married man, now with two young boys, Bernal could not live in college, but nor was he made a Fellow of Emmanuel. Many believe that this was a deliberate snub, a disapprobation of his libertine sex life and radical politics. C.P. Snow tried to get him elected to a Fellowship at Christ's, but the cause was lost when an elderly don remarked: 'No one with hair like that can be *sound*.'[48] Even Bernal's department, the Department of Mineralogy, lacked a secure place within the University. When Hutchinson was appointed in 1926, the chair of mineralogy had become vacant on the death of the previous incumbent in his eightieth year, after an unproductive 45-year tenure. The statutes were changed so that Hutchinson would retire at the age of 65 years, after a term of just five years, but the Council to Senate also set up a syndicate to plan the future of mineralogy in the University.

The syndicate included Rutherford, but not Hutchinson, who complained that he found out about it only 'from the casual conversation of friends in London.'[49] The syndicate recommended splitting mineralogy into two departments: one for crystallography and one for mineralogy and petrology, each with its own chair. To Bernal's horror, the crystallography department was to remain true to its Victorian geological foundations and not be primarily an X-ray based enterprise. When the report came up for discussion in January 1930, he, Hutchinson, Wooster and Sir William Bragg argued strongly for the 'new' crystallography. Bernal tried to persuade the authorities that it would be folly to maintain an emphasis on the superficial, descriptive approach to crystallography at the expense of X-ray methods, which were not only more revealing about molecular structure, but also predictive in the sense that 'there were now means of saying *a priori* that such and such an arrangement of atoms was possible and would produce a crystal of such and such properties'.[50] The Council to Senate announced that they could not afford to create two chairs, but merely agreed that the teaching of crystallography should be separated from that of mineralogy and petrology.

It is not hard to imagine Bernal's frustration and despondency at this turn of events. He viewed X-ray crystallography as fundamentally a branch of modern physics, but one that had enormous implications for chemistry and biology, as well as offering the promise of practical advances in the textile industry and metallurgy. Indeed he wrote a review article for an American medical journal at that time which concluded with the prediction that the chief utility of X-ray crystallography 'will always be the fundamental assistance it gives to the process of knitting together all physical science into a harmonious whole'.[51] Yet here he was at the epicentre of physical science in Great Britain, and he could not convince those in charge that this endeavour was worth supporting other than in the most dilatory and begrudging fashion. He did have at least one influential ally, Lawrence Bragg, who was moved to write the following letter[52] from Manchester, dated 5th March 1931.

Dear Rutherford,

I have just had a letter from Bernal enclosing the report of the Council on Mineralogy, Petrology and Crystallography. He is very distressed at the subsidiary role assigned to crystallography and its prospective severance from Physics and Chemistry.

I cannot say or write anything publicly about the report, because if a Chair were founded and offered to him in the future I would be very glad to hear it. But I gathered that there was no immediate prospect of that for two years or so. Quite apart from that, as regards Bernal's own position, is there no chance of giving him more independence? Universities over all attach the greatest importance to X-ray laboratories. They give them very fair facilities, and I have been very much impressed by the new lines which are being worked out in the ones I have seen. I do think the work has a tremendous future, and all the more so because it lies on the borderline between Physics and Chemistry, and so is often not directly backed up by either.

Bernal is extraordinarily good, though he talks rather much sometimes, and he keeps himself aware of the latest ideas in crystal work better than anyone else I know. He seems utterly discouraged by this report, and I think the best way I can help him is to appeal to you, and tell you how very good I think he is in his own line.

Yours very sincerely,
W.L. Bragg

Bragg's letter had no immediate effect. The University did identify a bequest that they used to establish a chair in mineralogy and petrology, leaving the crystallography research group to fend for themselves in their four-room hut, which was not even weatherproof. The one advantage afforded to the crystallography group was their central position, only a few minutes' walk from the Cavendish or the departments of zoology, chemistry and anatomy; as a new subject which needed to interlope onto the territories of older scientific disciplines, the topography could hardly have been better. Sage had acquired a colourful reputation that made him a much more prominent figure, in Cambridge and beyond, than if he had just been an extremely talented and productive scientist. There was really no range to his interests – everything put to him was likely to be considered as grist for the mill, and he was perpetually open for the cross-pollination of ideas. Other scientists faced with a new problem, especially involving a question of molecular structure, would naturally think of Sage and have no hesitation in asking him for help, even about a topic on which he had not previously worked.

So it was, over a matter of a few days in the spring of 1931, that Sage was approached about two apparently separate questions that would eventually turn out to be closely related. One enquiry came from J.B.S. Haldane and concerned vitamin D, the remedy for rickets. The 1928 Nobel Prize in Chemistry had been awarded to Adolf Windaus, a German professor, who had proposed structures for a family of compounds known as the sterols (cholesterol being the best known example); Windaus had also shown that vitamin D is produced by the action of ultraviolet light on ergosterol, a sterol found in yeast and many fungi. More recently, four different substances, each having antirachitic properties, had been crystallized. There was some argument amongst the chemists involved as to whether the different crystals really represented alternative forms of vitamin D or just resulted from one or more impurities. Haldane put Bernal in touch with the research group at the National Institute for Health in London, who were working on the problem, and they provided Bernal with some tiny, needle-like crystals of the different vitamin D candidates to study by X-ray.

The second challenge was also delivered to Bernal by an intermediary, Solly Zuckerman. Zuckerman, who was a year or two younger than Bernal, came to London as a medical student from his native South Africa, but after qualifying quickly disavowed clinical practice and embarked on a research career, building on his talents as an anatomist and anthropologist. He was an ambitious young man of limited means, who used his personal charm to enter many social circles, centred in both Bloomsbury and the Home Counties. One weekend he crossed paths with Bernal, who was probably the only active scientist he had ever encountered outside laboratory walls. The two struck up a friendship, and Zuckerman quickly came to respect Sage's probing intellect. Indeed, he decided that Bernal was such an entertaining figure that he should be exposed to a wider audience. Zuckerman arranged for him to be invited to some country house weekends and London dinner parties. Bernal, who never let his political principles interfere with having a good time, was used to travelling light, and arrived for one weekend 'with just the clothes he was wearing, carrying a briefcase which, in addition to papers contained only a razor and a slide rule'.[53] The maid who unpacked his bag was flummoxed. Bernal did not disappoint the other guests at dinner, who included the novelist Evelyn Waugh, as he ranged over a number of topics with fluency. Waugh at the time was aspiring to join the Catholic Church, and he and Bernal held forth over the development of Christianity, while the port circulated. The argument went on until midnight, and Bernal, no doubt emboldened by the return of the ladies from the drawing room, seemed the more convincing of the two protagonists, to Zuckerman at least.

On graduating from medical school, Zuckerman had been appointed as the Prosector of London Zoo, where his main interest was the behaviour of apes and monkeys. He naturally spoke to Bernal about this, and also told him that a colleague at University College Hospital (UCH), Guy Marrian, had discovered what appeared to be a female sex hormone in the serum and urine of pregnant women. Marrian had obtained the substance, then known as oestrin, in the form of crystals measuring about $1 \text{ mm} \times 0.1 \text{ mm} \times 0.005 \text{ mm}$. Several laboratories other than UCH were attempting to define this new hormone, and Bernal told Zuckerman that he was sure he would be able to help if Marrian gave him some of the miniscule crystals to study. Confronted by the persuasive Sage, Marrian reluctantly parted with a few crystals, and Bernal carefully carried them back to Cambridge on the train.

If Marrian realized what a tall order it was to make any sense of the molecular structure of oestrin by X-ray crystallography, he might well have refused to hand over any crystals. The diffraction of X-rays is not a nuclear phenomenon, but is rather due to the interaction of the waves of radiation with the negatively charged cloud of electrons around each atom in the crystal. As Bernal himself pointed out in 1930: 'It has, up until now, proved impossible to determine atomic positions [in a crystal] by direct calculation from the intensities of diffracted beams of X-rays. The inverse process is, however, straightforward: from a known distribution of atoms it is possible to calculate exactly these intensities, and the problem reduces itself to finding by any means whatever a plausible structure and then establishing it accurately by means of numerical correspondences between observed and calculated intensities.'[54]

The crystallographer typically started with some idea of molecular structure from the known chemical formula of the substance. In the case of relatively simple compounds such as the amino acids, there were few arrangements of the atoms possible, and by looking at and mathematically analysing the diffraction pattern, often one proposed structure would emerge as the most likely. Even with amino acids, the diffraction spots were not that sharply defined because of the limited intensity of the X-rays available, and their interpretation was further confounded by the *phase problem* – there was no way of telling whether a spot on the film represented a maximum (crest) or minimum (trough).

A large organic molecule like oestrin would seem to be a most unpromising problem because there were no good pre-existing ideas about its structure, and its diffraction pattern would be indistinct and ambiguous. It was on 10th June that Zuckerman[55] had written to Bernal suggesting that Marrian might provide some material for X-ray crystallography, and despite all the inherent difficulties it appears that Bernal arrived at an answer before the end of the month. He wrote to Astbury: 'I have done a hormone, oestrine, and a compound related to uric acid, but I am having awful difficulties with the people here and may resign at any moment. They have completely let me down over giving me apparatus.'[56] Astbury advised him not to let 'those villains at Cambridge beat you down'.[57] Working under far from ideal conditions and with his usual number of competing distractions, Sage was able to deduce the size of the oestrin molecule, and ventured that its structure involved a number of condensed rings with small atomic groups (O and OH) attached at either end of the molecule.

That same month, he began to analyse the crystals of vitamin D and other sterol compounds supplied to him by the group at the National Institute for Medical Research. He subsequently wrote a letter to *Nature*[58] summarizing his preliminary results. The five compounds included cholesterol and ergosterol as well as the antirachitic substance, calciferol, that had been prepared by the action of ultraviolet light on ergosterol. Bernal's main conclusions were that calciferol comprised a single molecular entity that was virtually identical in size and shape to the parent ergosterol molecule. But after considering the X-ray data, he suggested that the dimensions that he had measured 'are difficult to reconcile with the usually accepted sterol formula'. In other words, Bernal was politely disputing Windaus' model and his intervention forced a radical change of thinking amongst sterol chemists. Rosenheim, who was the head of the group at the National Institute for Medical Research, wrote to Bernal in April 1932 to let him know that he had been led 'to a modified constitutional formula for sterols and bile acids, which seems in better harmony with your results than the old formula'.[59] Rosenheim kept Bernal supplied with a steady stream of crystallized sterol derivatives to study, as did Windaus. Thus both the British and German schools relied on Bernal's laboratory, while they were involved in a sharp public debate about the structure of cholesterol. He was happy to provide data to both and was not tempted to take sides.

What Bernal failed to see, despite the fact that he was studying both at the same time, were the shared features of the sex hormones and the sterol molecules. His model for the sterols was a four-ringed head with a long tail of carbon atoms attached. He had correctly deduced that oestrogens also contained condensed carbon rings, but failed to consider that they were in essence the sterol ring system less the long tail. It was a surprising oversight since the evidence was literally under his nose – in his laboratory notebook there were observations for cholesterol and pregnandiol (a metabolite or chemical product derived from cholesterol and the sex hormones) on the same page.[60] Had he only made this connection, it seems certain that he would have shared the 1939 Nobel Prize for Chemistry; as it was, there were those like Solly Zuckerman who believed that Bernal and Marrian were unfairly overlooked by the Nobel committee.

For Bernal the work on sterols and sex hormones, while satisfying, was only a small piece in an increasingly ambitious scheme that was taking shape in his generously sized cranium. He rehearsed his ideas in front of the select group of philosophically minded biologists and biochemists at the Dunn Laboratory. Foremost amongst these was Joseph Needham, who in 1931 had just completed a monumental three-volume work, *Chemical Embryology*. Like much of Needham's output this was a wide-ranging book, encyclopedic in its treatment of the developing egg, but nevertheless subject to parody in the Dunn Laboratory magazine as *Eggs; From Aristotle to the Present* (in 27 volumes).[61] The tomes of *Chemical Embryology* did in fact contain a good deal of history, and appropriately Needham was one of the organizers of the Second International Congress of the History of Science and Technology held in London during June and July 1931. As we shall see, the Congress had a lasting influence on Bernal and on the politics of British science. In the lecture he prepared for the meeting, Bernal was intent on making the case for modern physics holding the key to the solution of fundamental biological problems.

Bernal believed that from the physical point of view, the two central puzzles of life were that of activity, (e.g. muscle contraction or nerve conduction), and growth, which included both the building up of organized elements in the cell and the reproduction of cells. He stated that X-ray crystallography, for the first time, was allowing direct study of the structure of organic molecules, and he felt that scientists like him were 'beginning to grasp the chemical and physical nature of the protein molecule'.[62] He referred to Astbury's demonstration that stretched and unstretched wool depended on two different forms of protein – α- and β-keratin. He thought that two different protein states would also account for the extension and contraction in muscle, where X-ray pictures looked very similar to those of hair. Bernal was convinced that the structure of proteins was the key to understanding the secret of life.

In 1931, genes were known to reside along chromosomes and were thought to consist of proteins – only the almost limitless variety of proteins with their vast number of possible amino acid sequences seemed to offer a physical basis for the biological specificity of cell function. When a cell divides into two identical daughters, Bernal stated: 'The facts of genetics demand, as J.B.S. Haldane has pointed out, that... the individual [protein] molecules in a chromosome must be exactly duplicated.'[63] In Bernal's opinion, 'only a supernatural agency, a divine copyist', could exactly duplicate a three-dimensional solid molecule by entering its inner complexity. 'If we prefer a natural solution,' he continued, 'we must imagine the molecule stretched out either in a plane or along a line. In either case the simpler constituent molecules have only to arrange themselves one by one on their identical partners in the original molecule, and then become linked to each other.'[64]

The analogy he had in mind was of a lacemaker's frame, on which simple organic molecules would settle before being joined into larger aggregates. He then rejected the idea of two-dimensional replication because while each amino acid can exist in a right-handed or left-handed form (a classification based on the rotation of polarized light), only the left-handed form is found in nature: two-dimensional reproduction would lead to mirror image molecules which do not occur. 'There remains then,' he continued, 'only one-dimensional reproduction. At the moment of reproduction, but not necessarily at any other time, the molecule of a protein must be imagined as pseudolinear, associating itself element by element with identical groups, related by an axis instead of a plane of symmetry...'[65] He ended on a note that was at once cautionary and optimistic: 'It is impossible to claim that these ideas are anything but preliminary guesses, but they have the advantage of being susceptible to experimental test.'[66] Two decades later Crick and Watson would show that the genetic material in cells is the double helix of DNA (not a protein), and that the exact replication of genes depends on the linear sequence of bases along the DNA molecule. It is ironic that the Second International Congress was regarded by its delegates, especially Sage, as a political rather than a scientific milestone, for buried amongst all the bombast was the essence of the most powerful idea in twentieth-century biology.*

---

* Francis Crick made the following comment when shown Bernal's 1931 notes: 'What an interesting quotation. How perceptive of Sage. I myself did not consider the 2-D case. But of course I know a lot more about proteins than they knew in 1931.' (Letter to the author 14/12/01.)

Another speaker at the Congress who would have been impressed by Bernal's thesis that understanding the reproduction of protein molecules was a necessary first step to a complete description of the behaviour of whole organisms was Joseph Henry Woodger, Reader in Biology at the Middlesex Hospital Medical School. Woodger's ambition as a philosopher of science was to invent a symbolic logic for biology, which would allow diverse phenomena to be integrated into an ordered theory. He and Needham had been corresponding about this question for some years, and after the Second International Congress they felt that the time had come to expand the discussion to include other original scientists in a 'Biotheoretical Gathering' or informal club. Needham proposed Sage as a member, referring to him as 'perhaps the most acute mind of my acquaintances here and particularly interested in biological problems'.[67] So it was, paying six shillings a day to his hosts to defray the cost of food, that Bernal found himself staying at Woodger's house on Epsom Down for three days in August 1932, with about half-a-dozen others.

The meeting meandered through Woodger's house and out into the garden; meals were served but did not interrupt the flow of ideas. Some attempt was made to keep embryology in mind as the centre ground; it was a field that was energetically ploughed with a variety of tools from mathematics and logic as well as chemistry and biology. Bernal's set contribution was an exploration of the junction between biology and chemistry, beginning at the sub-atomic level of quantum mechanics, passing through his own territory of crystals, colloids and polymers, and on to life forms such as viruses and protozoa before arriving at multi-cellular organisms. Of all the speakers, Bernal had the strongest background in the physical sciences, but he was not inhibited in joining arguments about embryology with the biologists present. Needham left an image of how Bernal typically reacted to a setback or a perplexing scientific problem: 'He would long look down and away from you while discussing it, but then would suddenly turn and look you straight in the eye, propounding with his dazzling smile some remedy for the trouble, some unseen aspect of the facts, some unimaginable new theory, or some amusingly paradoxical truth.'[68]

Shortly after the inaugural Biotheoretical Gathering, Bernal left Cambridge for a lecture tour to Russia in the company of a number of other scientists and physicians, led by Lawrence Bragg. The main purpose of the trip was a meeting with Russian scientists at the School of Physical Chemistry in Moscow. After the meeting, the British party was supposed to fly out from the new Moscow airport and assembled there at 4 o'clock in the morning only to find that the countryside was enveloped by a thick autumn fog. Facilities at the airport were non-existent, and all Bernal could do to pass the time was to pace up and down. He was joined by Ralph Fowler, a Cambridge mathematician and Rutherford's son-in-law, who limped as a result of wounds sustained in the war, but managed to keep pace with the voluble, long-haired Sage. Naturally the fog became the major topic of conversation. Bernal began to muse on the water droplets, about 1 micron in diameter, that comprised the mist. He wondered why they did not coalesce to form rain-drops. Fowler asked him what his ideas were on the structure of water, and in doing so unleashed a flood.

The first mystery to Bernal was why water existed at all – other heavier molecules such as hydrogen sulphide were gases and yet here was 'the lightest of small molecules, which was sufficiently held together at ordinary temper-atures to form a liquid'.[69] There were other anomalies too, notably the fact that ice is less dense than water, and while these were commonplace observa-tions, Bernal found the conventional explanations to be vague and unsatis-factory. And while the phenomena were commonplace, they were of immense significance for the Earth (where lakes and seas would be permanently frozen if ice were heavier than water and therefore unexposed to the warming of the sun) and for the evolution of life in an aqueous environment. As he was talking to Fowler, Bernal thought about the molecular structure of water and began to consider novel solutions such as the two hydrogen atoms being buried inside the oxygen atom. He came to the realization that just as with a crystal, the physical properties of a liquid must depend on the geometrical and physical relations between its constituent molecules, atoms or ions. The conversation lasted about twelve hours until the fog lifted, and on the aeroplane Fowler suggested to Sage that he write up the new theory.

Bernal and Fowler both worked on the problem after returning to Cam-bridge, and in April 1933 presented their results at a conference on 'Liquid crystals and anisotropic melts' that Bernal helped to organize at the Royal Institution. Bernal had obtained X-ray diffraction curves for water that showed that it differed from the close atomic packing of an ideal liquid. They also stated that water is not a linear molecule, H–O–H, but shaped like a boomerang, with oxygen at its centre and hydrogen atoms at the tips. The oxygen atom has a far higher affinity for electrons than the hydrogen atoms do so that each O–H bond has a small negative charge at one end and a positive at the other – it is a *dipole*. In the paper, they made the first accurate estimate of the distance along an O–H bond, 0.96 Å. The dipolar nature means that there is a weak attraction, a hydrogen bond, between adjacent molecules, and Bernal and Fowler deduced that the molecules would orientate themselves so that each limb of a boomerang molecule would point towards the negatively charged oxygen atom at the centre of an adjacent molecule. This meant that the molecules would be arranged in a tetrahedral pattern. In ice, the tetrahedral pattern is regular and gives an open structure of low density: the key hypothesis forwarded by Bernal and Fowler was that to a large extent the hydrogen bonding between molecules largely persists in liquid water providing its remarkable internal cohesiveness. At low temperatures, the X-ray diffraction curve of water 'approaches the ice-like arrangement' while at high temperatures it resembles that of an ideal liquid: 'the nature of water is determined by different geometrical arrangements of the same molecules in small regions of the liquid due to different amounts of molecular movement imposed by the temperature. In each small region, containing a few hundreds to a few tens of molecules at different temperatures, the arrangement is pseudo-crystalline.'[70] This was not only a landmark paper in the history of physical chemistry, it would have a huge bearing on the subsequent understanding of living systems, whose cellular components exist in an aqueous environment.

The presentation on the pseudo-crystalline nature of water at the Royal Insitution was the second paper at the meeting with Bernal's name on it. The first was given by his new doctoral student – a shy, dreamy, twenty-two year old Oxford chemistry graduate, Dorothy Crowfoot. She had spent her fourth year as an undergraduate working on X-ray crystallography and had arrived in Cambridge in October 1932 to work with Sage. Although Miss Crowfoot presented the paper[71] on organic liquid crystals and undoubtedly did the lion's share of the experimentation, the work bore Bernal's unmistakable style. First, great stress was laid on the optical properties of the crystals as well as the results of X-ray photographs. Bernal always made a point of carefully examining any new crystal under a polarizing microscope before subjecting it to X-ray analysis. The second feature was the confident tone of the conclusion, where the authors enquired 'as to the nature of the molecules required to form liquid crystals' and made some suggestions which were both detailed and comprehensive. There were 150 scientists at the meeting, with a strong international contingent, but the name Mr Bernal (*Cambridge*) dominated the discussion after nearly every paper, with penetrating and often lengthy comments. Although many of his remarks addressed arcane physical theory, Bernal was particularly excited by the role that liquid crystals might play in cellular components such as the myelin sheaths around nerves.

Dorothy Crowfoot's background was quite exotic – she was born in Cairo, where her father worked in the Egyptian Education Service – but in many ways she was a very innocent young woman. Apart from science, her major passion was archaeology (her father later became Director of the British School of Archaeology in Jerusalem), and although it was never difficult to find a topic for conversation with Sage, this interest provided an instant connection between them. Dorothy blossomed in the informal atmosphere of Bernal's small, dilapidated department, where her skill and determination soon won her the admiration of all. She particularly looked forward to lunchtimes when, with coffee percolating on a gas ring on a laboratory bench, Sage would initiate conversations that one day might be 'about anaerobic bacteria at the bottom of a lake in Russia and the origin of life, another, about Romanesque architecture in French villages, or Leonardo da Vinci's engines of war or about poetry or painting. We never knew to what enchanted land we would next be taken.'[72] Dorothy joined two other women, Helen Megaw and Nora Wooster, who were already carrying out research under Bernal's supervision. They had both studied mineralogy as undergraduates at Cambridge and were working on inorganic crystals. Nora married Peter Wooster shortly after arriving in the laboratory. Unlike Dorothy, Helen and Nora believed that Sage was fallible, and one lunchtime they jointly decided to test his erudition. They asked him to talk about Mexican architecture, believing that he would not be prepared. He merely paused to ask whether they were interested in periods before or after the Spanish conquest and then launched into an enthralling account.[73]

Helen Megaw, a young woman from Belfast, began her PhD research under Professor Hutchinson in 1930. Bernal suggested to her that she should measure the thermal expansion of ice crystals along different axes. This was technically very demanding work which Megaw undertook with a modified gas X-ray tube, in which she could change the anti-cathode easily in order to obtain X-rays of different wavelengths. The tube needed to have its gas leak carefully controlled or otherwise it would blow a fuse or stop working. Helen had to sit by the tube, hour after hour, with one ear cocked, making the necessary valve adjustments in order to obtain any data.[74]

In 1934, Rutherford accepted administrative responsibility for the crystallography group under the aegis of the Cavendish, and Bernal was appointed the Assistant Director of Research. Perhaps as a goodwill gesture, Rutherford gave Bernal a small sample of heavy water, from which Megaw was able to grow crystals and compare their structure with that of ordinary ice. For her next project, Bernal suggested that she make a detailed X-ray analysis of hydrargillite crystals, an hydroxide of aluminium, for which the American Linus Pauling had already suggested an octahedral structure. Megaw broadly confirmed Pauling's structure, but found an interesting irregularity in that the OH groups were drawn closely together. This finding was analogous to the observations made by Bernal and Fowler for water, and lead to a comprehensive review article by Bernal and Megaw on 'The function of hydrogen in intermolecular forces'.[75]

Sage, preoccupied with the structure of proteins, believed that a revolution in biology was at hand, a feeling he likened to 'looking through a hole in a wall at a new kingdom beyond'.[76] In 1934, Bernal and Crowfoot joined forces on a piece of research that would breach the wall. Their achievement involved the interplay of serendipity and mental preparedness that characterizes so many great scientific discoveries. The accidental starting point of this story involved a visit by a friend of Bernal's, Glenn Millikan, to a laboratory in Sweden. Millikan, the son of the 1923 Nobel Laureate in Physics, was a peripatetic physiologist, based at Trinity College, who loved to travel around Europe with a small rucksack as his only luggage. During the spring of 1934 he had been on an expedition to Lapland and on his way back to England, Millikan visited Svedberg's laboratory in Uppsala. There he found John Philpot, an English biochemist who was learning the ultracentrifuge techniques in order to work on proteins. Philpot had left a beaker of pepsin in solution standing while he had gone away on a skiing trip for two weeks. Pepsin is an enzyme secreted by glands in the stomach to digest protein. On his return, Philpot found that some unusually large pepsin crystals, up to 2 mm in length, had appeared in the beaker. He showed these to Millikan who thought of Sage, always on the lookout for interesting crystals, and Millikan said 'I know a man in Cambridge who would give his eyes for those crystals.'[77] Philpot knew Bernal because he had been on the team at the National Institute for Medical Research in London working on vitamin D, and he was happy to send some crystals to him.

Millikan carried the tube with the pepsin crystals bathed in their acidic, mother liquor back to Cambridge, in his pocket. As Millikan expected, Sage was delighted with the present for these were the best protein crystals he had ever seen. He immediately took one crystal from the tube, mounted it on his X-ray camera and photographed it. To his enormous disappointment, there was no diffraction pattern. Bernal then took another crystal and examined it under the polarizing light microscope. It showed *birefringence* – a double refraction pattern characteristic of crystals that results from polarized light travelling at different speeds as it passes through the crystal in different directions. Then came the crucial realization – as the pepsin crystal dried out, it lost its birefringence which told Bernal that it had become disordered. He needed to take X-ray photographs of the crystal in its wet state. He sucked a single crystal into a thin walled glass capillary with a few drops of its mother liquor and sealed the end with a flame. Now the X-ray analysis yielded a rich pattern of slightly blurred spots that extended all over the films. Sage was ecstatic and spent the night wandering about the streets of Cambridge, imagining how much information about the structure of proteins and about their functions would be unlocked if only these photographs could be interpreted in every detail.

Dorothy Crowfoot had been experiencing stiffness and pain in her fingers, the first symptoms of rheumatoid arthritis, and was away from the laboratory for a few days. As soon as she returned to Cambridge, Bernal asked her to take more X-ray photographs of the pepsin crystals and together they began to derive the space group and unit cell dimensions of the protein. A letter was sent to Astbury, who had carried out his own study of pepsin over a year earlier. He had obtained some pure but small crystals from the American laboratory of John H. Northrop, and took powder photographs in the dry state. At the time, he informed Bernal that the pepsin gave 'a good X-ray photo, consisting chiefly of two broad rings'[78] from which he deduced that pepsin consisted of essentially straight peptide chains. Now confronted by the much more convincing X-ray diffraction patterns from Bernal's laboratory suggesting a globular or spherical shape for the molecule, Astbury immediately wrote to congratulate Sage on the 'fine news about the pepsin crystal. I think it must be right too.'[79] Quickly Bernal and Crowfoot sent a letter to Nature[80] announcing the first X-ray photographs of a soluble protein.

Gowland Hopkins had shown that the biochemical reactions that sustain life in cells are made possible by enzymes, which are soluble proteins. Now Bernal and Crowfoot had proved that one of these enzymes, pepsin, was not just an amorphous colloid but had a definite three-dimensional shape. It was not possible at that time to be more precise about the arrangement of atoms in the pepsin molecule, but surely the structure might hold the key to how pepsin exerted its enzymatic effect. Taken together with Astbury's work on the fibrous proteins, these were two crucial pillars on which the edifice of molecular biology could be constructed. In the same month that Bernal and Crowfoot's findings were published, Astbury, in a letter to Sage, wrote what was probably the first job description for a molecular biologist: 'perhaps a physiologist would be best, but he must not be the romantic biologist, but one who thinks or wants to think, in terms of molecular structure, and is not likely to wreck my apparatus, and will not ask me too often what *cos theta* is.'[81] He was excited about the future, and recognized that Bernal, whom he affectionately regarded as 'the most unreliable fellow in the whole of crystaldom' was likely to play a crucial role. Knowing only too well Sage's wayward nature, Astbury made the following plea: 'I feel if you and I do not make the most of biological crystallography, we should have our respective bottoms kicked – and if we do make the most of it, then I think things are bound to work out well in the end, in spite of the machinations of nuclear physicists. Please let me know if you discover anything more exciting, and if not for my sake, then for the sake of the proteins and structure analysis, do make an effort to answer this letter, or at least attend in some way to what I am asking you to do.'[82]

6

Soviet Pilgrims

Sage and Eileen were a politically active couple during their London years, but when they returned to Cambridge in the autumn of 1927, Eileen could not easily resume her Labour Party work and Sage's first priority was to organize his new department. Although most of his political comrades from undergraduate days such as Dickinson, Hutt and Montagu had moved to start careers in other places, Maurice Dobb was an economics don at Trinity College and poised to become the most influential communist in the University. While Sage may have let his CPGB membership lapse, his affiliation was never in doubt or concealed. One can speculate that having renounced the Catholic Church, which once offered him such comfort, Bernal was eager for any alternative system of beliefs that would bring a comparable level of certainty to his life. In *Microcosm*, Bernal recognized the integrative nature of his own mind, and it is not surprising that all-encompassing philosophies like Freudianism and Marxism appealed to him. The combination of the two *isms*, each with its closed ideology irrefutable by discordant facts and each undermining the bourgeoisie, was fashionable in intellectual circles of the day.[1]

There was another, more direct, threat to the stability of British society in the late twenties. The economy, already limping from the self-inflicted wound of returning to the gold standard in 1925, was knocked to the ground by the repercussions of the Wall Street crash of 1929. British exports fell by more than half, and unemployment, starting from a relatively high level of one million, rose on a monthly basis to reach almost three million by the end of 1931 – one in five workers.[2] The resultant misery and widespread hardships were enough to make even seasoned politicians doubt the future of a system that had failed its people so lamentably. Ramsay MacDonald, the Prime Minister, addressing the annual Labour Party Conference in October 1930 was driven to state: 'It is not the Labour Government that is on trial; it is Capitalism that is being tried...It has broken down, not only in this little island, it has broken down in Europe, in Asia, in America; it has broken down everywhere, as it was bound to break down. And the cure, the new path, the new idea is organization – organization which will protect life not property... organization which will see to it that when science discovers and inventors invent, the class that will be crushed down by reason of knowledge shall not be the working class, but the loafing class.'[3]

The reference to science and organization in the same breath by the Prime Minister was a notable conjunction, and no doubt encouraged any scientists listening to believe that they would in future have more political influence. Stimulated by this prospect and the prevailing economic depression, Solly Zuckerman decided to assemble an informal club of lively young academics to explore how their expertise might be useful to society at large.[4] The founding members were mostly scientists, (Bernal, Haldane, Needham, Lancelot Hogben, Julian Huxley), or economists (including Bernal's old friend Dickinson, and two Oxford men Hugh Gaitskell and Roy Harrod). The club was soon christened the Tots and Quots, after a Latin tag provided by Haldane (*quot homines, tot sententiae*), and met on an irregular basis at various Soho restaurants selected by Zuckerman. Club membership was limited to twenty and lived up to the essence of its name: 'so many men, so many opinions'. At an early meeting, Gaitskell made the point that scientific research resulted in improved technology, more efficient production, and ultimately transformed social values. In his view, the fact that scientific research was supported both by private capital and public funding confirmed its implicit social value. His ideas did not find favour with Bernal, Haldane or Hogben, who were not impressed with the notion of willingness to pay as a yardstick for social worth. Although the discussions were always lively and generally free from cant, the scientists tended to argue as a block and Zuckerman recorded his concerns about, what seemed to him, their uncritical belief in Marxist theory: 'Marxism, as expounded particularly by Dickinson, [is] likely to end in illiberalism and rigid dogma because of a failure to recognise the psychological inequality of people.'[5]

The deteriorating economic conditions also led to a political awakening in the undergraduates arriving at the British universities from the late 1920s onwards. Blessed with the clarity of youthful vision, the solution seemed obvious to many of them – the Soviet Union. It was a propitious time for Bolshevism: the chaotic violence spawned by the 1917 Revolution had abated and its replacement by the systematic violence of the state was not yet apparent. Where MacDonald in 1930 was calling for central organization, Stalin had already set the first Five Year Plan in motion in 1928 and was promising to leapfrog the world's trading nations by establishing the world's most industrialized and egalitarian state. While the radical undergraduates typically came from solid middle-class backgrounds or from well-known liberal families and had attended public schools, they were not abashed to support communism and Russia. A disproportionate number of them came to Cambridge, and Trinity College was their epicentre.[6] Once there, they would come to the attention of Maurice Dobb, the *eminence rouge*, as well as the less obtrusive figure of Anthony Blunt, a Fellow in Art History. Trinity's senior scientists were the apolitical knights, J.J. Thomson and Ernest Rutherford; but Peter Kapitza, the Russian physicist, held regular meetings in his rooms (the Kapitza Club) that were attended by many politically active young physicists. Glenn Millikan, descended from old New England stock, represented the same anti-establishment strain amongst Trinity's biological scientists.

The 1929 intake of Trinity freshmen included Harold (Kim) Philby, a reticent young man who came to read history, joined the CUSS, became its secretary, and at the beginning of his third year decided to switch to economics after being impressed by the ideas of Dobb. Another Trinity freshman of 1929 who made a more immediate splash was David Haden Guest, the brash son of a Labour MP. He came to study mathematics and became deeply interested in logic and the philosophy of mathematics (taught by the newly arrived Ludwig Wittgenstein). He decided to spend his second year at the University of Göttingen. While there, he witnessed several street fights and became alarmed by the nascent threat of the Nazis; he took part in a communist-led protest march and was arrested. After two weeks in solitary confinement, he was finally released after going on a hunger strike. He returned to Trinity in the summer of 1931, firmly committed to revolutionary Marxism as the only way to beat fascism and avoid war.[7]

That summer also marked an important turning point for Bernal. His epiphany came at the Second International Congress of the History of Science and Technology in London. What might have been a jejune affair, held in a lecture hall of the Science Museum, was galvanized by the unexpected arrival of a delegation from the Soviet Union. The group of eight was led by Nikolai Bukharin, a perennial favourite of Lenin's, who as a leading member of the Politburo had devised most Bolshevik policy from 1925–7, with Stalin as head of the party Secretariat providing the 'organizational muscle'.[8] In 1929, Bukharin succumbed to Stalin's drive for absolute power and lost his place on the Politburo as well as the editorship of *Pravda*. By 1931 he was relegated to the minor post of director of research under the Supreme Economic Council, and although vilified as a 'Right deviationist' by the paranoid Stalin, his credentials as a leading intellectual figure of the Russian Revolution and a staunch opponent of capitalism were enough to endear him to enthusiastic socialists in London. The same reputation was sufficient grounds for the *Daily Mail* to mount a Red Scare story in an attempt to embarrass Ramsay MacDonald and the Labour Government, already tottering under the pressure of a run on the pound that threatened the solvency of the Bank of England. Under

a headline 'Moscow Hater of Britain now in London', the paper portrayed
Bukharin as 'a red revolutionary politician' who was intent on 'world revolution in general and the overthrow of the British Empire in particular'.[9]

Bukharin brought with him a seven-man group that included N.I. Vavilov,
the plant geneticist, who was President of the Lenin Academy of Agricultural
Sciences, A.F. Joffe, the leading Soviet physicist, B.M Zavadowsky and Boris
Hessen, two philosophers of science. Since the Russians were last minute
attendees at the Congress, (they had dramatically flown from Moscow two
days before the meeting started), no time had been allotted to them to speak.
Although a Saturday-morning session was added to accommodate them,
there was a cultural impasse: they had come prepared to speak for several
hours, but the English moderator vigorously rang a ship's bell to restrict them
to twenty minutes each. To ensure that their material reached its intended
audience, it was suggested to Bukharin that a collection of their translated
papers be made available. With the resources of the Soviet Embassy, what the
Manchester Guardian christened 'The Five Days' Plan' swung into operation
and a bound volume, *Science at the Cross Roads*, appeared within two weeks.
The foreword to this work was intended to leave the bourgeois scientist in no
doubt that he was trapped in an inferior system:

In Soviet Russia absolutely new prospects are opening before science. The planned
economy of socialism, the enormous extent of the constructive activity... demand
that science should advance at an exceptional pace... In the capitalist world the
profound economic decline is reflected in the paralysing crisis of scientific thought
and philosophy generally.[10]

The single paper that made the greatest impression on Bernal, Needham
and Crowther was Hessen's 'The social and economic roots of Newton's
Principia'. Until then, Newton had been regarded by most as the model of a
scientific genius, who pushed forward the bounds of understanding, certainly
by standing on the shoulders of others, but in the main as a result of his own
creativity. Hessen's thesis was an audacious one – that Newton, far from living
his life in a vacuum, was responding to the needs of seventeenth-century
entrepreneurs so that while he was drawn to the stars and the planets, the
roots of his work were nourished by the practical needs to understand
navigation, ballistics, mechanics, metallurgy and so forth.[11]

Readers of the Conservative weekly, *The Spectator*, might have been surprised to read a two-page report of the Congress the following week, penned
by Mr J.D. Bernal[12] who, they were reminded, had previously contributed to a
series on 'The challenge to religious orthodoxy'. The reason Sage was able to
slip the occasional essay into such an unlikely magazine was that Celia
Simpson, (a friend from the 1917 club and an ardent socialist), worked

there, nominally as a secretary: she was fired a few months later for being too left-wing.[13] Describing the Congress as 'the most important meeting of ideas that has occurred since the Revolution', Bernal relayed some progressive remarks from the English contributors (e.g. that the history of ideas was traditionally ignored in favour of kings, parliaments, battles and treaties that are but proof of the collective stupidity of man), but when it came to the history of science compared to the Russians, in his opinion, the English were 'essentially amateurs'. His immediate sense was that the meeting had been a failure:

The time was too short, the gulf between the points of view too great, for there to be any real understanding. The Russians came in a phalanx uniformly armed with Marxian dialectic, but they met no ordered opposition, but instead with an undisciplined host, unprepared and armed with ill-assorted individual philosophies. [The Russians'] appeal to the dialectic, to the writings of Marx and Engels, instead of impressing their audience, disposed them not to listen to the arguments that followed, with the feeling that anything so ungentlemanly and doctrinaire had best be politely ignored.[14]

Bernal was certain that it would be unwise to ignore the Soviet ideas in the long run, for the present system of bourgeois science 'tied as it is to academic and impoverished universities and to secretive and competitive industries and national governments' was appallingly inefficient and not worth preserving.

Although the British Home Office regarded Bukharin as a 'back number', they did take the precaution of intercepting telegraph messages from the Soviet Embassy during his stay. Like Bernal, the Soviet delegation did not feel as though much was achieved in terms of exchanging ideas at the meeting, but they regarded its chief success as 'getting in touch with the progressive left wing' and forcing dialectical materialism to the attention of young scientists like Hogben, Needham and Guest.[15] Curiously, Bernal was not once mentioned by name.

Any *Spectator* readers who persevered to the end of Bernal's article were faced with the rhetorical question: 'Is it better to be intellectually free but socially totally ineffective or to become part of a system where knowledge and action are joined for one common social purpose?'[16] For his own part, Sage had come to the conclusion that the notion of intellectual freedom was an illusion, and thought it high time that intellectuals abandoned their 'dreamland of art and science'.[17] He recognized that intellectuals as a group were more likely to indulge in entertaining debate than to agree on a common basis for effective action, so that he was prepared to accept the loss of status demanded by the Communist Party in the pursuit of supporting the workers in their struggle. He did not expect the subjugation to Party doctrine at the expense of free thought to be an enjoyable exchange, and was not heartened by the existing Party memberships: 'The Russian members are admittedly heroic but ruthless in politics and muddled and inefficient in economics, while those in bourgeois countries are both fanatical and neurotic. The policy of the party is unnecessarily violent, the emphasis throughout is on hate not love . . . The propaganda is virulent and overstated . . . the communists invoke revolution, the very prospect of which with its attendant civil wars and famine is too horrible to be borne.'[18] The brutish nature of class warfare was, though, inevitable since 'the effective human driving force must be composed of those who have nothing to lose and know it'.[19]

Bernal's membership of the CPGB lapsed around the time that he returned to Cambridge in 1927, and apparently was not renewed until prompted by one of his many lovers, Magda Phillips, in 1933.[20] The lack of a Party card meant little, and in June 1931 it seems that Sage was at least an interested bystander when a communist cell was established at Trinity College.[21] The lead was taken by David Guest and his fellow philosophy student, Maurice Cornforth; apart from holding meetings in the College, the two sought to recruit workers from the town into communist cells. The Master of Trinity, J.J. Thomson, then in his 75th year, was fully aware that the world was changing, but was far too involved with trying to keep up with the latest discoveries at the Cavendish Laboratory and thinking about his memoirs to be concerned with a few idealistic students starting a Bolshevik club. Guest's tutor at Trinity showed a humorous indulgence of Guest's politics when he wrote to congratulate him on his brilliant first-class honours degree: 'I suppose you will celebrate your success in the usual way by attacking the "lackeys of the Bourgeoisie", and being locked up for it.'[22]

Public criticism of the Soviet system was generally muted in those days. Winston Churchill would occasionally flare with a grandiloquent warning of the dangers of communism, and the rabid Fleet Street attacks from the *Daily Mail* and the *Morning Post* were all easily dismissed by Bernal as 'mendacious accounts'[23] of the great Russian experiment. Far more common, at least amongst progressive thinkers, was a fair-minded attitude to give the new system the benefit of the doubt, and in many cases a determination to see for oneself by making a visit to Russia. Such was the outlook of many readers of the *Manchester Guardian*, whose science correspondent, J.G. Crowther, was a communist and member of the Tots and Quots. In the summer of 1931, Crowther organized two short visits through the auspices of the Society for Cultural Relations. The majority of Crowther's tourists were physicians, but there were also about twenty scientists. Bernal's name appears in both the July and August lists, although his papers give details only about the second trip. The July visit was recorded by the zoologist, Julian Huxley, who went along with his wife and his brother, Aldous. Julian Huxley explained that it was necessary for the visitor to Russia 'to discard some of his bourgeois ideas about democracy, religion, and traditional morality, his romantic individualism, his class feelings, his judgements of what constitutes success, and pick up what he can of the atmosphere in which the Russians live immersed'.[24]

Huxley regarded Russia as being in 'a transition between a mediaeval past and a communist future'[25] and as functioning like a nation on a war footing. He tried to go beyond the restraints imposed by the careful hospitality of the officials and consequently observed the overcrowded living conditions and food queues in Moscow. But on the whole, he believed 'the level of physique and general health rather above that to be seen in England'.[26] Although some of the surgeons in the party were shocked to witness women undergoing abortions at the official clinic in Moscow with no anaesthesia, Huxley was convinced by the official statistics that health care was steadily improving. Like Bernal, Huxley thought that Britain cared little for science, whereas it was the essential ingredient of Stalin's plan; he believed that the Soviet authorities were 'preparing to increase expenditure on pure scientific research to a scale far beyond that attempted in any capitalist country'.[27] The head of the British Embassy in Leningrad, Reader Bullard, who was becoming all too aware of the grinding repressions of Stalin's regime, wrote in his diary on 26th July 1931: 'A party of English doctors and scientists passed through – mostly much impressed by what they had seen, and as they had been taken to all the showplaces and nothing else this is perhaps not remarkable.'[28]

The second group eagerly set sail from England on 8th August, and was dominated by Cambridge scientists. During the visit, Crowther became aware of 'the uniformity of outlook of Cambridge scientists, in spite of wide variations in personality and political beliefs'.[29] In addition to Sage, there were John Cockcroft and a young Canadian, W.L. Webster, from the Cavendish; the Piries (Bill and his wife, 'Tony'), both biochemists from the Dunn Laboratory, and Glenn Millikan. The voyage to Leningrad took five days; the anticipation of arriving in the promised land overcame any disappointment at the cramped, unsanitary conditions on the boat. Malcolm Muggeridge, another *Manchester Guardian* journalist, made the same voyage the following year in the company of a group of academics and writers. He was struck by the festive mood on board ship and sensed that each of his fellow passengers harboured some special hope like 'meeting Stalin, or alternatively falling in with a Komsomolka, sparkling eyed, red scarf and jet black hair dancing the *carmagnole*'.[30]

Soon after arriving, Sage and his party met up with Academician Nikolai Vavilov, who of course had just been in England at the History of Science Congress. Vavilov, then in his mid-forties, was President of the Lenin

Academy of Agriculture. He spoke excellent English, as a result of working with W. Bateson in England before the Great War, and was one of the world's most knowledgeable botanists and plant geneticists. Although his family background was distinctly bourgeois (his father had been a successful merchant in Moscow before the Revolution), Vavilov had come to embrace the socialist model of scientific research. At his Institute's field station twenty miles outside the city, there were large-scale trials in progress. These were aimed at improving the efficiency of Soviet agriculture by studying which of the huge collection of grains that he had collected from all over the globe would be best suited to grow in the climactically varying regions of the Soviet Union, and whether rice could be sown from airplanes. Vavilov's smiling, open manner, his extensive travels through Central Europe and the Americas, and of course his family background, all made him a target of suspicion under the dour Soviet regime. Earlier in 1931, he had been publicly denounced by a jealous subordinate, who accused him of the Marxist sin of 'a reactionary separation of theory and practice and advised him to stop collecting exotica and to concentrate on plants that could be introduced directly into farm production'.[31] While he survived this unwarranted attack with little consequence, there would be far worse to follow.

The three-day programme in Leningrad was packed. Apart from Vavilov's Institute, the group also went to the Pavlov Laboratory, met the President of the Academy of Science, A.P. Karpinsky, and spent a morning touring the geology, mineralogy and zoology museums, before going to the Hermitage Museum for the afternoon. Sage was in his element as the unofficial guide at all sites. They took the night express train to Moscow, and it may have been on this journey that Millikan awoke to find that his rucksack had disappeared. He found the guard and together they searched the entire train, rousing unappreciative passengers from their sleep. There was no sign of the rucksack, but Millikan was not inclined to accept his loss philosophically. He announced, to the amusement of his companions, that 'if it is not in the train it must be on the train'.[32] Not to be outdone, Millikan, a keen mountaineer, then climbed out of a window on to the roof of the speeding express and found the rucksack, together with a certain amount of other stolen property, tied to the ventilator on the carriage roof. Sage marvelled at Millikan's sense of adventure and his blithe ability to pull off unlikely stunts – when they got to Moscow, he managed to get into the Kremlin without a pass.

Bernal recalled that Millikan was 'very difficult to keep under control and would wander off on his own, but then would always turn up at the critical moment'.[33] Bill Pirie, on the other hand, remembered that Bernal disappeared on his own private tour of Kiev and only rejoined his companions many hours later. They asked him what he had been up to, and 'he replied that he had been meditating in Kiev Cathedral on the meaning of socialism'.[34] Crowther's July party had been a more orderly group and were given VIP treatment during their stay in Moscow. On behalf of the Soviet Government, Bukharin hosted a sumptuous banquet for them at the Dynamo Sports Stadium, 'where the most lavish variety and quantity of food any of us had ever seen was piled up' and they were entertained by the massed band of the OGPU (secret police), whose 'soft music . . . floated to us on the warm evening air'.[35] The authorities did not repeat this level of hospitality for the August visitors – perhaps there was not enough food left in Moscow or the OGPU foot-soldiers had less pleasant duties to undertake. By travelling hard, the August group saw more of the country, and it certainly made an indelible impression on Sage:

I went round the Soviet Union in those rough, primitive and casual days when one saw very much of the difficulties as well as of [the] achievements. I saw the construction camps for the Dneiper dam, and at the same time saw something of the hard times that were produced in the period of early collectivization – a consequence of the concentration of all efforts for the building of heavy industry, very remote from immediate enjoyments . . . And yet there was no mistaking the sense of purpose and achievement in the Soviet Union in those days of trial. It was grim but great. Our hardships in England were less; theirs were deliberate and undergone in an assurance of building a better future. Their hardships were compensated by a reasonable hope.[36]

To Pirie, there seemed to be a religiose quality to Bernal's belief in the Soviet system.[37]

No doubt Eileen Bernal would have liked to visit Russia with her husband that summer. It was not practical for her to go because she now had two young children – a second son Egan was born in March 1930. It was also a time when Sage's personal life was more complicated than usual. He was having a passionate affair with his American cousin, Persis, and also trying to support his ex-lover, Ivy, who had contracted tuberculosis and was admitted to a sanatorium.[38] The start of a new academic year at Cambridge helped to restrict his activities to a more manageable level again. He had completed the analysis of oestrin crystals immediately before the International Congress at the end of June and now took up work on the sterol problem again. In October 1931, Bernal addressed the Kapitza Club on 'Methods of x-ray crystal analysis', and his audience would have included fellow members Blackett, Cockcroft, Dirac, Fowler, Gray, Kapitza, Massey, Mott, Oliphant, Snow, Walton and Wooster amongst others.[39] By attending these informal evening seminars at Trinity College, Bernal could keep himself abreast of all the latest advances in nuclear and theoretical physics: the 1931–2 session was destined to be the most dramatic in the Club's history, largely because of research coming to fruition at the Cavendish. In February 1932, Chadwick announced his discovery of the neutron to a spellbound group in Kapitza's rooms, and Cockcroft followed in June with news of the first disintegration of an atomic nucleus by artificially accelerated particles.

About the time that Bernal returned from Russia in August 1931, the Labour Government found itself facing unacceptable cuts in public expenditure in order to stem the sterling crisis. Over a few days, Prime Minister MacDonald was persuaded to form a Government of National Unity, with Conservative and Liberal politicians displacing the socialists from the Cabinet. For this betrayal, he was despised by the Left, but in a General Election that followed in October, the coalition candidates swept the country with only 46 Labour MPs being returned to Westminster. One MP who lost his seat was John Strachey, a friend of Bernal's from the 1917 Club, who stood as a communist in all but name and then set about writing his first book on Marxism.[40] Strachey was far from alone in believing the Labour Party had grossly betrayed the workers, and it now seemed to many that a fair deal could only be obtained by extra-parliamentary means. The desolation of England's industrial heartland was caught by the young poet, W.H. Auden:

> *Smokeless chimneys, damaged bridges, rotting wharves and choked canals,*
> *Tramlines buckled, smashed trucks lying on their side across the rails;*
> *Power-stations locked, deserted, since they drew the boiler fires;*
> *Pylons fallen or subsiding, trailing dead high-tension wires...*[41]

The sense of the coming class struggle was most keenly anticipated amongst the comfortable intelligentsia rather than by the downtrodden unemployed. Recruitment to the Communist Party swelled in Cambridge, thanks especially to the efforts of Guest and Cornforth. A series of plentiful harvests in the early 1930s gathered in Burgess, Philby, Maclean and May, all destined to achieve notoriety as spies, as well as many other men of true conscience. David Guest made a commitment unique amongst the British intellectuals – he took a teaching job in Moscow. He left behind him a flourishing organization in Cambridge, and his natural successor, John Cornford, appeared at Trinity College as a history scholar that autumn. Cornford, the son of a classics don and great-grandson of Charles Darwin, was a tall, gaunt, curly-headed firebrand, who within weeks of his arrival was a contender for 'the title of Cambridge's best-known revolutionary'.[42]

In January 1933, Adolf Hitler was invited to become Chancellor of Germany and lost no time in consolidating power by suppressing any potential opposition to his Nazi Party. Prominent amongst Hitler's internal foes were the socialists and communists, and their comrades in Britain now had another powerful reason to believe in the necessity of their cause. That winter, Bernal, in an annotated piece 'The scientist and the world today'[43] sounded a clear alarm about the immediate dangers posed by the Nazi regime. He was especially concerned about the prospect of war and the passive acquiescence of scientists in national preparations for war, as well as the threat to the tradition of liberalism. In his view 'as most of the practical expressions of liberalism in human welfare and education are due to the influence of science, those most affected after the immediate victims are the scientists who see the efforts of centuries purposely destroyed.' He saw the doctrine of anti-Semitism as a direct threat to science and intellectual life. To Bernal, fascism seemed a pathological reaction to the chronic instability and impending failure of capitalism: salvation lay in the example of the USSR – the only nation showing both economic and cultural progress. He held up the USSR as providing 'the antithesis to the whole catalogue of cultural reaction represented by Fascism. In science, in education, in religion, in the family, in the prisons, the USSR gives practical embodiment to the progressive ideas of the nineteenth and twentieth centuries. The Communists are the heirs and the only defenders of the liberal tradition.'[44]

Although Bernal did not actively recruit young people to the cause in the way that student leaders like Guest and Cornford did, he was a notable figure on the University scene; his 1933 warning of the dangers of fascism was printed in the pamphlet *Cambridge Left*, a local staple of fenland intellectuals on their way to man the barricades. According to the historian, Herbert Butterfield, Bernal managed to influence 'hundreds of undergraduates' while 'showing a cavalier disregard for ascertainable historical facts'.[45] In his wide-ranging piece for *Cambridge Left*, Bernal had attacked organized religion for 'showing its compatibility with fascism' and the law for its 'hypocrisy of impartial justice'. He was proposing a classless community free from inequalities and cultural superstitions. Whatever the influence of his writings and speeches, Sage's brazen promiscuity was slyly regarded by many young men as an encouraging foretaste of life in the classless society. The lean and handsome John Cornford did not share Bernal's penchant for affairs with more than one woman at a time and felt a little embarrassed by his own conventional attitude, jokingly describing himself as 'a monopoly capitalist in love if not in politics'.[46] Others like Blunt and Burgess, whose homosexual activities were illegal, surely regarded Sage's free and easy sexuality as an example that they could happily follow after the revolution.

London's *Izvestiya* correspondent had reported to Moscow after the 1931 Congress that 'it provided tremendous impetus [to] study dialectical materialism...among growing generation [of] scientific workers':[47] this opinion was confirmed by the publication of *Aspects of Dialectical Materialism*[48] three years later. The book was a collection of talks given under the auspices of the Society for Cultural Relations; the first in the series was by Hyman Levy, an applied mathematician at Imperial College, London and longtime member of the 1917 Club, who once memorably described his friend Sage as 'that sink of ubiquity'.[49] Levy made a rather circumspect beginning, contrasting the precise language in which he conducted his academic work with 'the vague phraseology of much that passes for philosophy' and in particular with 'the terminology of Dialectical Materialism, with its "unity of opposites", its "contradiction of contradictions", its "quantity changing into quality", and so on'.[50] Indeed it was only because 'certain individuals, for whose intellectual capacity and integrity' Levy held a 'profound regard' and who 'appear to have satisfied themselves of the validity of it all that I have personally striven to overcome my initial abhorrence of the language'.

The identity of one of those individuals is clear from the longest and most strident essay in the book. Bernal's contribution has an uncharacteristically forceful opening paragraph:

Dialectical Materialism is the most powerful factor in the thought and action of the present day. Even its most bitter enemies are forced to recognize its analysis and ape its methods. It is all the more essential that it should be correctly understood by all those who want to play a conscious part in the world and not be carried away by events they can neither understand nor control.[51]

Bernal took the orthodox Marxist position that Dialectical Materialism (DM) is more than a philosophy, it is also a blueprint for revolutionary politics: 'from the dialectical point of view thought and action form an inseparable unity.' The central idea in DM, Bernal stated, was that of transformation both in the physical and social universe and how transformations can be brought about. He considered some of the concepts such as 'the unity of opposites' and 'the change from quantity and quality' that bothered Levy and assured his audience that they were 'from the Marxist point of view, universal modes of behaviour of matter, modes of the same generality as the conservation of energy'.[52] This was all too much for Michael Oakeshott, the conservative philosopher of Gonville and Caius College, who accused Bernal of a 'primitive passion for analogy [that was] almost unchecked and the result is a mystical and esoteric philosophy which can be paralleled perhaps only in the writing of the alchemists'.[53] Where Bernal tried to make the case that DM 'cuts away at one blow the whole set of idealistic, mythological, and mystical views of the universe that are expressed in all religions and all other philosophies',[54] Oakeshott observed acidly that among its followers 'DM is like a theology turned into a gospel and a gospel turned into a dogma.'[55]

Bernal's fame was burnished in the summer of 1934 by the publication of a novel, *The Search*, by C.P. Snow. The narrator of the story is engaged in X-ray crystallography research at Cambridge, and Bernal appears in the guise of

Constantine, 'the most original, the wildest mind in England'.[56] While the book makes the standard disclaimer that all the characters are drawn from the author's imagination, the descriptions of Constantine bear more than a coincidental resemblance to Sage. After Constantine treated the narrator to a disquisition on sanitation in ancient civilizations, he feels magnified by Constantine's assumption that they were equally knowledgeable on the subject. And when describing his revolutionary discoveries about proteins, Constantine is 'inexhaustible, full of facts and speculations... happy, exuberantly at home, overflowing with a sort of scientific wit'.[57] Constantine makes a fundamental discovery – a method for synthesizing proteins – and is a member of a Royal Society committee looking into the possibility of a National Institute for Biophysical Research. At the first committee meeting, he makes a plea for a purpose-built Institute with multi-disciplinary teams of scientists. Surrounded by staid academic figures, Constantine, throwing back his unruly hair, launches into a passionate, undiplomatic, argument for the rejection of a traditional university model 'which will keep our scientific organisation mediaeval'. To him the universities are: 'Accidental agglomerations for the study of Christian theology with Latin and Greek appended. And they didn't even do that well. And in their later days, they called what they had been doing humanism – which meant that it was chittered up with superstitions and religion and morals and social barriers, and that they lived monastically while they were doing it and added on a little science as patronisingly as they dared.'[58]

In the autumn of 1934, Bernal was invited to the USSR to give a series of lectures. He decided to go with his new lover, Margaret Gardiner, who thought it would be a good opportunity to see the November celebrations in Red Square. A spirited and perceptive young woman, Gardiner had been introduced to Sage at a party in London. During their first conversation she said to him: 'Everybody tells me that you're so wonderful and so intelligent, and I haven't noticed it yet.'[59] He replied, 'That's because you don't really know me.' Their relationship did not develop immediately because she was in love with Solly Zuckerman, but in 1933 decided not to follow him to the United States, and at some point her friendship with Bernal melted into a love affair. Her father was a well-known Egyptologist and she had private means, which allowed her to pursue her interests in a spontaneous fashion. After graduating from Cambridge in the mid-1920s, where she was a regular member of the Heretics and friendly with Ivor Montagu and Patrick Blackett, she taught for a time in a village school. She met and became a close friend of W.H. Auden, and although not overtly political, her sensibilities led her towards the Left, and she was always concerned for those less fortunate than herself.

So on a blustery grey morning, Margaret Gardiner found herself anxiously looking down from the deck of a dowdy Russian ship at Tilbury docks as the crew pulled up the gangway. Standing on the quayside below was Bernal 'wild-haired and shouting to me against the wind. "I haven't got my visa", he yelled. "They haven't given me a visa . . . I'll fly out as soon as I can." '[60] It was a remarkable reflection of Gardiner's self-confidence and generous nature that she neither asked to get off the ship nor blamed Sage for the muddle. Instead she got to know her fellow passengers (mostly from a trade-union delegation, 'excited at the prospect of visiting the workers' paradise') and settled down to a routine of caviar for breakfast every morning, followed by a bitterly cold walk on deck. On her arrival at the Intourist hotel in Leningrad, she was greeted by Peter Kapitza, who was disappointed but not surprised by Sage's non-arrival. A few weeks earlier, Kapitza, who had been making his annual summer visit to Russia to see his mother, was refused an exit visa by the authorities so that he could not return to Cambridge. The Soviets had decided that he was too important a scientist not to have under their direct control. Kapitza was outraged by the decision and told Gardiner that he felt 'like a woman who has been raped when she would have given herself for love'.[61]

Bernal arrived in Moscow in time for the November celebrations, which he and Margaret watched from their hotel. She was bored by 'column after marching column, gun carriages, tanks, all the grisly paraphernalia of power and war, with that row of grey men sitting there hour after hour to take the salute and acknowledge the applause'.[62] Gardiner managed to have her visa extended, and she and Bernal moved into a hostel for visiting university teachers. The weather was as cold as any Muscovites could remember, but while Bernal was lecturing, Gardiner would risk frostbite while wandering the streets to watch the people. Her 'general impression was drab, a pervasive sort of shabby greyness: people wrapped shapelessly in their padded jackets and heavy fur coats, shops poorly stocked with goods of poor quality, long queues quickly forming when anything new appeared. Nevertheless, there was a feeling of hope.'[63] She was a good linguist and was able to talk to ordinary members of the public, she thought, without being watched. She encountered a depth and breadth of bureaucracy that were in striking contrast to the happy-go-lucky tendencies of the Russian character.

Gardiner and Bernal were often invited to the Moscow flat of Ivy Litvinov, the English-born wife of Maxim Litvinov, Stalin's Commissar for Foreign Affairs. The Commissar, it seems, was determined not to meet the British visitors: they were never invited when he was in residence, and although he did once come home while they were there, he turned and fled as soon as he saw them. Maxim Litvinov was a leading Bolshevik revolutionary from the opening decade of the century, when, like so many, he was exiled from his

Russian homeland. He came to London in 1908 and was adopted by the Fabians of the Bloomsbury set (which is likely where he first met Ivy). They married in London in 1916 and, after the Revolution, he became Lenin's envoy in London. Ivy, who was ten years Bernal's senior, was an affectionate woman who was 'unfaithful almost on principle'.[64] Sage had enjoyed her faithless favours during the summer of 1924, when she had been in England without Maxim, and their affair may have been briefly rekindled when he was in Moscow in 1931. Ivy now accepted that she had no further claim to Sage and was very friendly towards Margaret Gardiner. The Litvinovs had a sixteen-year-old daughter, Tanya, dark and demure, who delighted in talking to Sage about history. One weekend, when Maxim was away, they went to the family's dacha outside Moscow. While walking through the countryside, Sage spotted a tall building, standing on its own. He asked Tanya what it was, and she replied that it had been built by a rich landowner whose wife had borne seven daughters in succession. The landowner longed for a son and had built this tower so that on the arrival of each new daughter, he seized her in fury, climbed to the top of the tower and flung the baby off. Desmond, utterly convinced of the wickedness of the Tsarist landowners, was mortified and took some moments to realize that Tanya was pulling his leg. The tower was, in fact, a granary.[65]

Sage's gullibility again became apparent to Gardiner when they reached Leningrad, where he was to give some lectures in December. While the city looked splendid in the snow, Gardiner thought the grandiose socialist statues threatened to disfigure the landscape, and in particular she 'disliked the ubiquitous, inescapable, huge portraits of Stalin'.[66] She confessed to Sage that she hated Stalin because he had such a horrible face; Sage mildly rebuked her for her irrationality and observed that 'It's just a nice, simple Georgian peasant face.' On the morning of 2nd December, Bernal went off to the university to lecture and Gardiner took her customary walk. She was immediately aware of something different – the posters of Stalin in the shop windows had been replaced by portraits of a different man, surrounded by black ribbon and laurel leaves. The whole city seemed hushed, and the few people on the streets were wearing black armbands. Gardiner asked a shopkeeper what was going on, and he told her that Kirov had been assassinated. She met Bernal for lunch and he explained that Kirov was the Party leader in Leningrad and a member of the Politburo. She remembers Bernal being very perturbed. Later in the day, she told Sage that there were strong rumours that the killing had been ordered by Stalin because Kirov was too popular. Bernal dismissed this idea as malicious gossip.

Bernal and Gardiner returned to Moscow, where Kirov's body lay in state for three days before a lavish funeral that seemed to plunge the whole city into mourning. Tanya Litvinov was distressed and told her mother that several older boys at her school had stopped attending; no one dared ask what had happened to them. To Gardiner there seemed to be 'caution and unease on every side'.[67] She asked Bernal: 'Isn't it horrible? Don't you feel it?' He answered 'No I don't.' Sage took a train to Vienna, where he had a conference to attend. Gardiner remained in Moscow for another few weeks, and nothing changed her impression that the nascent optimism of Russia had been snuffed out with Kirov's life, to be replaced by a heavy pall of suspicion and fear.

7

The Shadow of the Hawk's Wings

About the time Hitler was grasping control of Germany in 1933, students in an Oxford Union debate passed what Churchill later described as 'their ever-shameful resolution' that 'This House refuses in any circumstances to fight for King and Country.' Yet those Oxford undergraduates were more in tune with the national mood than was Churchill, a brooding backbencher. Peace and national security were not seen by most as mutually exclusive goals, and there was no appetite for militarism in a country still trying to expunge the raw memories of the previous war. The Prime Minister himself was putting the final touches to 'The MacDonald Plan' to be presented to the Geneva Disarmament Conference. There was a widespread feeling, artfully exploited by the Nazi Party, that the Versailles Peace Treaty of 1919 had been unfair to the extent that it was now threatening the stability of Europe, and that the restitution of equal rights to Germany would enhance the prospects of security for all nations. To this end, Ramsay MacDonald proposed, amongst other measures, that the deliberate imbalance between the French and German militaries should be removed by reductions in the size and firepower of the French Army and Air Force. Churchill had just visited Germany and was distressed by what he saw there: 'the tumultuous insurgence of ferocity and war spirit, the pitiless ill-treatment of minorities, the denial of the normal protections of civilised society, the persecution of large numbers of individuals solely on the grounds of race.' He reminded parliament in March 1933 that they should 'Thank God for the French Army.'[1] This heartfelt and reasoned plea was greeted with 'looks of pain and aversion' in all parts of the House.

If Churchill could not convince more than a handful of his cronies that a strong French Army was the best guarantor of a belt of small countries stretching from the Balkans to Belgium, and that parity between the French and German Armies would increase the risk of a general European war, it is not surprising that he was regarded as a baleful figure by those seeking peaceful coexistence. Even Ramsay MacDonald, the unspeakable traitor of socialism, could see that disarmament was essential. Aside from any political considerations, the moral imperative for avoiding war was unanswerable and had been powerfully restated a decade after the end of the Great War by the publication of books like *All Quiet on the Western Front, Goodbye to All That* and *Journey's End.*

While Oxford students grabbed the headlines with their ostentatious debate, Cambridge scientists were quietly forming grassroots organizations. The first of these was the Cambridge Anti-War Council, set up with the encouragement of the Communist Party (CPGB) in 1932. Membership was not confined to communists and its first public meeting was chaired by Joseph Needham, a devout Christian and loyal supporter of the Labour Party. The Cambridge pacifists soon moved beyond debate and pamphlet distribution, staging a public demonstration on Armistice Day in November 1933. They marched in the procession to the town War Memorial, where they were planning to lay a wreath, 'To the Victims of a War They Did Not Make, from Those Who are Determined to Prevent All Similar Crimes of Imperialism.' One of the marchers was Eric Burhop, who had recently arrived from Australia on an Exhibition of 1851 Scholarship, and was just starting research in physics at the Cavendish Laboratory. Burhop, the son of two Salvation Army officers, wore a lapel badge which read 'Christ Claims You for Peace'. The procession was waylaid by a group of Conservative students, 'fascists... [who] attacked and seized the banner'. Burhop, tall and well built, had his Sunday-best suit spoiled by eggs and tomatoes, and was then insulted by the coverage in the evening paper under the headline: 'Hooligans at Cambridge'. On reading the article, Burhop discovered that 'we were the hooligans, and not the fascists who had attacked us. I think this was the first thing that brought home the realities of the political situation...in Great Britain.'[2] From that day, Burhop was committed to the socialist cause. Nearly forty years later, he still described the students who disrupted the march as fascists – it never seemed to occur to him that some of them probably lost fathers or uncles in the First World War and that many of them subsequently fought against Hitler – so deep were the impressions formed as a young man in 1933.

Burhop was readily convinced by Bernal's argument that fascism was a symptom of the failure of capitalism, and for the first time he stopped to consider what the social responsibilities of a scientist should include. In his wide-ranging polemic, 'The scientist and the world today',[3] Bernal pointed out that scientists could exert a powerful influence in modern states only by organizing into cohesive groups. He saw the opportunity to display their implacable opposition to war and fascism as the rallying cry around which scientists could unite. Sage quickly emerged as the movement's most important strategist.

Prior to 1933, there was no general issue on which scientists could campaign, and trade union entities such as the Association of Scientific Workers

(AScW) were poorly supported. With such a preponderance of left-wing scientists, the Dunn and Cavendish Laboratories were the perfect recruiting grounds, providing the AScW with a rush of new members to replace those lost in other parts of the country. Bernal, Wooster and Pirie became prominent local organizers of the Association's liveliest branch. They were fortunate that Hopkins, the head of the Dunn Laboratory and President of the Royal Society, was using his status to promote closer contact between science and society at large, and the editor of *Nature*, Sir Richard Gregory, was a long term supporter of increasing state funding for scientific research.[4] This confluence of forces resulted in a *Nature* editorial at the end of 1933 announcing the setting up of the Parliamentary Science Committee. In the words of the editorial, the aims and aspirations of the Committee were

to promote discussions in both Houses of Parliament on scientific matters in their application to economic policy and national well-being; to arrange periodical addresses by scientific authorities to the chief Parliamentary committees and groups; to consider Bills before Parliament which involve the application of scientific method; and to urge the proper representation of science on public committees ... In the very forefront of the programme will be the modernisation of the system of financing scientific research, with the view of ensuring that State aid to science should either take the form of block grants or outright endowment. It is felt that the present system of fluctuation in annual grants alternating between foresighted vision and nervous gusts of parsimony must be relegated to the limbo of oblivion if wise and prudent progress is to characterise national policy.[5]

Realizing that the AScW could now become a significant force in the shaping of national science policy and could also serve as a means to imprint socialist philosophy on British scientists in the universities and in industry, Bernal stood, successfully, for election to the National Executive. What had been until recently a moribund body was revitalized by his arrival; within two years he had rewritten the AScW's policies and had engineered the appointment of the dogmatic Peter Wooster as its Honorary General Secretary.[6]

Wooster, with his wife Nora, was also the organizer of the Cambridge Scientists Anti-War Group, (CSAWG), which met most lunchtimes in a basement room on King's Parade. Sage was an irregular presence, but would always energize the small group on the days he attended. Although he saw war as the worst perversion of science, he thought there was a dangerous tendency 'to deplore war while admitting its inevitability and doing nothing to prevent it'.[7] In his opinion, scientists could play a role by obstructing the material preparations for war – refusing to undertake any research on armaments – but what was required ultimately to remove the antecedents of war was opposition to 'the state, particularly one's own state, in so far as it is an organ for war'.[8] Sensing the depth of pacifist feeling in the country in 1934, the British Government introduced the Incitement to Disaffection Bill. This prompted letters to the *News Chronicle* and *Cambridge Review* from the CSAWG, protesting that the Bill threatened to restrict their civil liberties by hindering them from dissuading fellow scientists from conducting research for the military. The letters were signed by 79 faculty members, researchers and post-graduate students, representing nearly 40% of the combined staff of the Cavendish and Dunn and about 10% of the pure scientists from other laboratories.[9] Another vigorous letter-writing campaign was undertaken by CSAWG in October 1935, urging the University to refuse a gift from Sir John Siddeley, the founder of the Armstrong–Siddeley Company, to fund aeronautical research that could obviously have military applications. This protest came during the same month that Churchill urged the Government to make up for lost ground by making 'a renewed effort' to establish air parity with Germany, and the month that the Italian Air Force started to bomb defenceless Abyssinia.

The CSAWG by no means restricted itself to letter writing and philosophical arguments. In Cambridge, it rented advertising hoardings to display posters calling attention to the increasing risk of war: one poster which read 'Fascism means mass murder and war' was disallowed by the hoarding's owner on the grounds that it might be libellous to Fascism![10] In July 1935, the group produced an *Air Display Special* newspaper to be distributed at Duxford air-field near Cambridge. The King was coming to take the fly-past, and the Cambridgeshire police decided to confiscate all copies of the *Special* in case he saw one. Wooster, as chairman of CSAWG sued the Chief Constable and won – he was awarded £1 in damages.

Bernal's summer vacation in 1935 was largely taken up with meetings of politically minded scientists. In August, he went to Oxford for a symposium on academic freedom: other committee members included Patrick Blackett, Bertrand Russell, Sir Frederick Hopkins, Needham and Hal Waddington, the geneticist. The committee saw the preservation of free speech as its main task; Bernal seconded a motion that the justification for scientific work lay in the possibility it offered for a general and progressive increase in welfare and culture for all. He proposed that another representative committee should be elected to coordinate such efforts, because scientists had to do it for themselves – bodies such as the Department of Scientific and Industrial Research (DSIR), the Royal Society, the British Association for the Advancement of Science (BAAS) had taken no action to further scientific research to meet human needs.[11] The resolution was carried but in the wider world there were already notable figures registering their disagreement with Bernal's repeated calls for central planning of scientific research. The first and most weighty dissenter was Professor A.V. Hill, Nobel Laureate and Secretary of the Royal

Society, in his 1933 Huxley Memorial Lecture. He made curt reference to the Russian delegates, whom Bernal and his friends so admired at the 1931 International Congress in London. In Hill's words, they wanted science to be regarded 'simply as the handmaiden of social and economic policy' whereas he argued that, in a sense, science was above the State. He proposed that 'science should remain aloof and detached, not from any sense of superiority, not from any indifference to the common welfare, but as a condition of complete intellectual honesty. Emotion, entirely necessary in ordinary life, is utterly out of place in any scientific decisions. If science loses its intellectual honesty and its political independence, if – under Communism or Fascism – it becomes tied to emotion, to propaganda, to advertisement, to particular social or economic theories, it will cease altogether to have its general appeal, and its political immunity will be lost. If science is to continue to make progress, it must insist on keeping its traditional position of independence, it must refuse to meddle with, or to be dominated by, divinity, morals, politics or rhetoric.'[12] Like the rest of the British scientific establishment, Hill abhorred what was taking place in Germany, where he said: 'The facts are not in dispute.' He was generally gloomy about the future, but insisted that those dismissed or persecuted should be offered opportunities to continue their work in England and other countries.

A few days after the Oxford meeting, Bernal was a leading figure at an East Anglian Peace Conference organized by Wooster; there were well over one hundred delegates from the CSAWG, peace groups, the TUC, the churches, the CPGB and the Labour Party. Bernal addressed the meeting, holding up two test tubes – one containing a liquid and the other a powder. The liquid, he informed them, was Phosgene under pressure and would kill everyone in the room if he dropped the tube. The powder was even more poisonous and had been developed to penetrate gas masks. One of the lingering memories of the Great War was the horror of poison-gas attacks in the trenches, and the prospect of civilian populations being gassed from aerial attacks was the cause of more fear in the early thirties than the threat of explosive bombs. In 1927, Bernal, writing under the pseudonym 'X-ray' had written an article in *The Communist*, entitled 'The great poison-gas plot'.[13] In the article, he suggested that the British Government, with the aid of university chemists, were constructing a formidable chemical warfare machine and that in the next war, it would be the innocent masses who were gassed from aeroplanes, unless capitalism was smashed and replaced by communism. In 1935, the Home Office's Air-Raid Precautions (ARP) Department started issuing handbooks for householders who wished to reinforce their homes and make them gasproof.[14] Sage thought that this was a disingenuous attempt to reassure the public and he criticized the National Government for being 'deliberately

deceptive about air defence'.[15] Bernal pointed out to his audience at the
conference, some of whom were no doubt wondering whether he was being
careful enough with the two deadly test tubes, the inherent unfairness of such
a self-help policy that depended on property ownership and called for expenditure that was beyond the reach of many.

The economic crisis and now the advent of fascism had led Bernal to
become a more serious student of Marxism, and he read and wrote about
Engels' philosophy as well as the history of Marxism. By 1933 he was a card-
carrying member of the CPGB again, although the official party line still made
no special dispensation for those from the bourgeois intellectual stratum.
Palme Dutt, the chairman of the CPGB, writing in *The Communist* in
September 1932 advised the intellectual who joined the Party 'first and
foremost ... [to] forget that he is an intellectual ... and remember only that
he is a Communist' so that he would concentrate on the paramount concern –
the workers' struggle. Bernal was able to accommodate this stricture by
recognizing 'Scientists are in an anomalous position. Socially they belong to
the capitalists, culturally to the workers. The workers' state needs science
more than any other. The transition would be easier and progress more rapid
if the bond between worker and scientist was already effective before it is
achieved. Cooperation by the scientist in working-class movements removes
his isolation and provides a firm basis of political support. In this way, and
only in this way, can the scientist come to understand the full reality of the
present situation and the practicability of the means of altering it.'[16] Bernal
saw himself as fulfilling this duty by resuscitating the AScW and making it a
vital component of the British Trades Union Congress. On a personal level, he
was prepared to submit to the revolutionary class movement and to forgo
pleasures such as 'comfort, work, sexual relations' expecting instead the
unpleasantness of 'persecution, loss of work, imprisonment'.[17] Fortunately
for Sage, no such sacrifices would be necessary.

Like many European communists in the early thirties, Bernal thought that
the Soviet Union represented the closest to an ideal, progressive society, and
that the power of capitalism would soon be broken in Western Europe. While
the pulse of England seemed imperturbable, the heartbeat of France positively
raced at the prospect of revolution. During the time that MacDonald's
National Government had been in power, France had seen half a dozen
administrations come and go. There was increasing industrial strife in Northern France; the advent of Hitler emboldened anti-Semitic and anti-communist
factions, as well as activating left-wing groups, who perceived the immediate
threat of fascism. Tensions increased in a series of fascist demonstrations and
communist counter-demonstrations. They came to a head in February 1934,
when another weak government tottered under the weight of a major

financial scandal, the Stavisky affair. Right wing opponents of the government took to the streets of Paris, where they clashed with the socialists; the police lost control and opened fire, killing fourteen and injuring hundreds. Neither side drew back in the wake of the violence, and the French Communist Party (PCF) became a major political force for the first time.

Bernal made a visit to Paris in the spring of 1934 to assess the state of strife for himself. The French communists had no objections to intellectuals taking high-profile positions and listened especially to Paul Langevin, a leading physicist, intimate friend of Mme. Curie's and party member since 1920. Langevin was supported in his political activities by his protégé, Frédéric Joliot-Curie. Joliot-Curie and Bernal could have been brothers – not only did they have similar faces with bright smiles and long, pointed noses, but each was a brilliant talker, at ease in any company – and both belonged in the first echelon of scientists of their generation. Joliot-Curie with his wife, Irène (Mme. Curie's daughter), as recently as January 1934 had discovered the phenomenon of *artificial radioactivity* and identified the first artificial (man-made) radioactive isotope. Langevin and Joliot-Curie, once they had adjusted to Bernal's French, which still bore the New Orleans dialect from his mother's early tuition, found him to be a sincere and energetic comrade. For his part, Bernal was especially struck by Langevin's personal example of putting the ideals of social justice as a citizen ahead of his brilliant achievements as a scientist. This quality first became evident when Langevin was a research student under J.J. Thomson at the Cavendish in 1898, and he signed a public letter protesting about the Dreyfus affair. He told Bernal, wistfully, 'Those were happy times when the fate of a single man was so valuable that it could excite the whole of mankind.'[18] Now that the fascists in France were emboldened by Hitler's regime in Germany and Mussolini's in Italy, Langevin was outspoken in pointing out the threat to the French Republic and to human liberty. He founded the Comité de Vigilence des Intellectuels Anti-Fascistes and inspired Bernal. The words he used to justify his extensive political activities were often quoted by Bernal in later years, when he was challenged about the amount of time he was spending away from his laboratory: 'The scientific work which I can do, can be done, and will be done, by others, possibly soon, possibly not for some years; but unless the political work is done there will be no science at all.'[19] Langevin was instrumental in forming the Front Populaire, in which the PCF were encouraged by Moscow to affiliate with organized labour and socialist groups in a unified movement against the fascist menace. This ultimately resulted in the election of Léon Blum's Popular Front government in June 1936.[20]

Fired by Langevin's example, Bernal campaigned for an English equivalent to the Comité de Vigilence. The organization, which became known as For

Intellectual Liberty (FIL), held its first meeting on 5th December 1935 in the Gordon Square rooms of Dr Adrian Stephen, Virginia Woolf's psychiatrist brother. Virginia Woolf wrote to her nephew, Julian Bell, about the gathering: 'We had such a meeting at Adrian's last night to form a group to encourage the French... There were dear old Peter and Aldous and Auden; besides a mass of vociferous nonentities, chiefly journalists and scrubby men with rough hair – you know the sort.'[21] Bell also heard from his mother, Vanessa, about the meeting: 'a most peculiar assembly... the meeting argued and argued, mostly as to whether to form a new society... I think in the end they just elected a committee... everyone was asked to subscribe ten shillings. I daresay it's really a very good thing to get people to commit themselves to being anti-fascist while it's still a very remote danger in England...'[22] Bernal, Margaret Gardiner and Kingsley Martin formed the FIL delegation to an international anti-fascist rally in Paris in early January 1936. At the second meeting of FIL in March 1936, there was a noticeably larger contingent of scientists present (Blackett, Dorothy Crowfoot, Waddington, Dorothy Wrinch and Zuckerman), who were presumably brought along by Sage. The literary members were still dominant and Aldous Huxley was elected FIL's first president, with Leonard Woolf as vice-president; Margaret Gardiner became honorary secretary. Bernal proposed a resolution, which was discussed at some length, amended and passed by the meeting. It stated that: 'This meeting of members of the learned and liberal professions resolves to set up a council broadly representative of those who feel the need for united action in defence of peace, liberty and culture.'[23]

FIL set out initially to oppose the government's rearmament policy, and together with the Comité de Vigilence published a letter in the *New Statesman* (Kingsley Martin, editor) calling for general disarmament, a reconsideration of Germany's economic difficulties and a universal treaty of peace. The signatories included Langevin and the Joliot-Curies for the Comité de Vigilence, and Huxley, E.M. Forster, and Gowland Hopkins for FIL. Curiously Bernal never signed any of the numerous FIL letters to the press, but as they were all typed and circulated by Margaret Gardiner, it seems likely that he had a role in drafting many of them. In April 1936, FIL took up the cause of Carl von Ossietzky, the German journalist and pacifist, who was interned without trial by the Nazis in 1933. They wrote a letter supporting him for the Nobel Peace Prize, which he was awarded in November 1936. Bernal and Margaret attended FIL meetings assiduously, as noted by Virginia Woolf in a lament to Julian Bell in June 1936: 'Societies seem wrong for me, as I do nothing; with Leonard meeting a dozen times a week and filling the drawing room with Bernal and Miss Gardiner and Ha [Margary Fry, the social reformer and Principal of Somerville College, Oxford] and Aldous we do our bit for liberty... I assure you, never a day passes but we don't get asked to sign a protest, telegraph a message, or join a new group.'[24] Virginia's study was next to the drawing room and she complained to Ethel Smyth, the composer and suffragette, 'Still though I withdraw, Leonard doesn't. Last winter the bray and drone of those tortured voices almost sent me crazy – meetings in the next room.'[25]

Within the Woolf's drawing room, there was a more meditative tension between Aldous Huxley and Bernal. In *The World, the Flesh & the Devil*, Bernal had identified Huxley as a writer opposed to the march of technology and to the potential of science to change the human condition. Since then, Huxley had published *Brave New World* in which he depicted a dehumanized utopia, where individual differences are eroded through biological and psychological manipulation. *Brave New World* contrasted starkly with Bernal's optimism about the social benefits of science. But Huxley was a powerful advocate for liberty and peace and a nationally known figure, so that Bernal was quite happy to have him as the FIL president.

Although the destruction of academic liberty and traditional tolerance in Germany was plain to many by 1933, the more harrowing facts about the Soviet Union, while available, were generally disbelieved by British intellectuals. Muggeridge wrote accurate first-hand reports in the *Manchester Guardian* of the politically driven famine in the Ukraine, where 5 million or so died in 1932–3, but such horrors could not be accepted by those, like Bernal, who had made an emotional commitment to socialism. They were comforted by their own memories of the Soviet Union, overlooking just how limited their experiences were, and their faith was reinforced by the good opinion of others. Muggeridge was no match for his wife's relatives, Sidney and Beatrice Webb, who wrote of their visits to the Soviet Union in 1932 and 1933 that the government had no option but to drive out 'the universally hated kulaks' who had sabotaged the grain harvest out of spite. Bernard Shaw, a writer whom Sage read avidly as an undergraduate, wrote a flippant letter to *The Times* after a chauffeur-driven tour of the USSR saying that 'tales of a half-starved population dwelling under the lash of a ruthless tyrant' were nonsense[26] – a reassuring riposte to any scare stories appearing in the *Guardian*. The politically active Cambridge scientists, like Bernal and Blackett, forgot their customary scepticism and embraced the full Soviet mythology, adding their voices to the chorus of propaganda.

The first, and almost the only scientist in Great Britain to bring his critical faculties to bear on the divergent information emerging from the USSR was Michael Polanyi, a man who 'in a flock of black sheep... shocked many by seeming almost white'.[27] A Hungarian Jew by birth, he had worked at the Institute of Fibre Chemistry in Dahlem after the Great War, where he made seminal contributions to X-ray crystallography including, with Mark and Weissenberg, the rotating crystal technique. After a few years, Polanyi returned to his first scientific love, the kinetics of chemical reactions, and became a professor of chemistry at Berlin University. In 1933 he resigned his life membership of the Kaiser Wilhelm Society in protest against the Nazis expulsion of Jewish scientists from their posts, and with considerable reluctance accepted a chair in Physical Chemistry at Manchester University. His first non-scientific writing was an essay on Soviet economics, in which he combined evidence that he had gathered during repeated visits to the USSR with a detailed analysis of official Soviet documents. Even without realizing that these documents were fabricated to conceal the disastrous failures of Stalin's first Five Year Plan, Polanyi concluded that the nutritional value of food per head was considerably worse than it had been in pre-1914 Russia, and the housing of the workers (which had been described by a Soviet writer in 1928 as being more terrible than Engels had seen during the Industrial Revolution in England) 'suffered a drastic deterioration during the following four years'.[28] Polanyi also made an astute deduction about the state of public health − not surprising in the light of the two previous points − that the standardized death-rate (i.e. death-rate corrected for the population's age profile) was more than double those of Western countries.

A second essay, 'Truth and propaganda', showed a deep understanding of the workings of a totalitarian state and contained a devastating critique of the Webb's adulatory new book, *Soviet Communism*. He described how the modern dictators subvert 'the machinery of democracy... to let the people show their enthusiasm for the reigning party' a tactic which can only work if it is backed up by 'swift and merciless' police action at the behest of determined party members. To Polanyi, the technique of engineering public displays of support while ruthlessly eliminating any potential opposition should be plain to anyone 'who is out of sympathy with the reigning party. If he cares little for either Communism or Fascism, the similarity of the various Party dictatorships will seem equally obvious to him.'[29] He found the most unnerving aspect of the Webbs' writings was their disregard for truth, a trait they shared with numerous other intellectuals. Until this failing was reversed and thinkers became inspired by 'unflinching veracity', they would forfeit 'their right to restrain governments in the name of truth... [and] truth will remain powerless against propaganda'.[30]

Whether Polanyi considered Bernal's politics as reprehensible as the Webbs' is not clear, but he would remain a trenchant critic of Bernal's ideas about the nature of science, as we shall see. As practising scientists, however, the two showed mutual respect and were always cordial. Polanyi had read Bernal's papers on the structure of water and wrote to him soon after arriving in

Manchester asking for further details: 'Could you give me a short list of characteristic distances between oxygen atoms linked together by a hydrogen atom between them? I am writing up a paper of reaction kinetics for which this information would be of great value to me.'[31] Bernal replied: 'The question you ask is rather a difficult one. The actual distances between oxygen atoms, as you have probably seen from the copy of my paper, vary according to the polarizing power of the neighbouring atom.'[32] He supplied Polanyi with a list of the varying oxygen radii for the hydroxides of various metals (e.g. lithium, calcium, magnesium, zinc, aluminium, iron and boron).

The year that Polanyi wrote 'Truth and propaganda', 1936, saw the start of the Spanish Civil War – a conflict so complicated that propagandists on all sides had little to fear from the truth. It was not a civil war in the style of English-speaking countries, with the fighting confined to opposing armies, but involved vicious street-gangs indulging in fratricide and the grisly killings of neighbours and priests. In England, where the regional and religious aspects of the war were easy to ignore, it came to be viewed as a fight between the democratically elected Popular Front government, the Republicans, and the fascist rebels, the Nationalists, led by General Franco.[33] The immediate reaction of the British Government, now headed by Stanley Baldwin, was to sign a Non-Intervention Pact in August 1936 with France, Germany, Italy and the USSR, but the last three had no intention of staying out of the war. Hitler and Mussolini took the opportunity to try out their armies and their burgeoning air power on essentially defenceless targets, while the Soviets enjoyed plaudits from the American and European press for its moral stance on Spain and sent 'advisers' there to organize the demise of the non-communist Left.[34]

For British intellectuals, the Spanish Civil War was the defining event of the decade: it allowed them to display passionate support for the Republican cause, and disgust for the craven neutrality of the Baldwin administration. Leonard Woolf wrote to Margaret Gardiner on 1st August 1936 about a proposed FIL letter on the Spanish Civil War, which he thought would do no harm but could not possibly do any good: 'It is too vague and mushy; it is the twitter of sparrows under the shadow falling on them from the hawk's wings. I admit I am impotent and a sparrow; but even a sparrow should refuse to twitter.'[35] The FIL letter was sent to *The Times* and subsequently carried prominently in the Madrid press as a message of sympathy, sent to the Spanish nation by 29 English intellectuals from H.G. Wells to Virginia Woolf.

For some intellectuals, messages of sympathy were no longer enough and they chose the courageous course of direct action. A handful of Cambridge graduates, most notably the communists David Guest and John Cornford, went to fight for the International Brigades and were killed. Very few in the Cambridge Scientists Anti-War Group now held to their pacifist principles, and the group became a Popular Front, anti-fascist organization in all but name, with Bernal as its first formal president. The CSAWG produced numerous leaflets, supporting the Republican cause in Spain, and Sage was an unreserved partisan, as one would expect. In their opinion, the Spanish working-man, 'standing up to the fascist tanks and aeroplanes',[36] was fighting for more than his own liberty: if fascism triumphed in Spain, France and England would not be safe – yet Bernal was frustrated by 'a general attitude of apathy and withdrawal' amongst the majority of people.[37] He also found himself at odds with Aldous Huxley, still resolute in his pacifism. Huxley upbraided him for using the word 'force' in an abstract sense without ever specifying its nature. Huxley wrote: 'To speak of "the use of force in a just cause", or "a just war" is altogether too vague. One should say "the use of thermite, high explosives and vesicants in a just cause"'. He also criticized Sage for being 'completely self-contradictory' on moral issues, speaking of 'just' wars and 'noble' purposes, while denying that there are any absolute moral standards.[38]

The CSAWG provided Bernal with the complete answer to Huxley's charge of relying on abstract words to avoid consideration of the unpalatable physical damage of modern warfare. In what Bernal came to regard as the advent of operational research (OR), the Cambridge scientists were spurred by the Spanish Civil War to undertake experiments that directly examined the likely consequences of aerial attacks on the public. Bernal suggested to the CSAWG that they should carry out some studies on poison gases and the efficacy of government-issue gas-masks. One of the main experimenters was a physics research student, John Fremlin, aided by his fiancée, Reinet. The laboratories were in the basement room in Kings Parade and the Woosters' home. Reinet, a graduate of Newnham, lived in lodgings and was therefore able to spend nights taking readings. John had to be in his college rooms at night, and on one occasion carried out his own experiment on tear gas there. He thought he had cleared the room of the heavy gas by leaving his windows open, but wore a respirator mask in bed, just in case. He woke in the morning 'feeling a bit odd' and was greeted by his 'bedder', who was 'weeping copiously. She was very concerned about what was happening to me. But she very nobly went down the stairs, wiping her eyes, and prevented one of the college porters coming up, because this might lead to trouble ... As it happened, the gas still had two or three days to evaporate.'[39]

The CSAWG also examined high explosives and incendiary bombs. One of the few undergraduate members, Maurice Wilkins, 'was asked to verify by experiment a report from the war in Spain that incendiary bombs, landing on the top floors of high buildings, could burn their way to the bottom. I made incendiary bombs and set up some flooring in the garden of W.A. Wooster, one of my lecturers. However hard I tried, I could not get the bombs to burn through the floorboards. I was very disappointed because we were keen to show that the Spanish report was right. Wooster took such a grave view of my failure that he advised me that, whatever I did after graduating, I must *not* do experimental science.'[40] Wilkins spent so much time on anti-war activities that he managed to take only a low second-class physics degree and could not therefore obtain a research post in Cambridge (none of which stopped him sharing the Nobel Prize with Watson and Crick in 1962).

Sage's main contribution to the CASWG was as a generator of ideas – an inspirational figure to the predominantly young group, and an effective public spokesman. He was very good at presenting information to lay audiences and often dramatized his talks with demonstrations. A favourite trick of his was to breathe out a mouthful of tobacco smoke through a gas mask which had its valve removed and to illuminate the wreath of smoke curling out of the snout by means of a spotlight. This led to a modification of millions of stockpiled masks.[41] The greatest public impact of the CSAWG research came with the promotion of their book *The Protection of the Public from Aerial Attack* by the Left Book Club in the spring of 1937. Among its major charges were:

1. 'Gas-proof' rooms prepared according to the instruction given on the ARP handbooks are not gas-tight, and in any case millions of people live in accommodation where they could not set aside a room as a gas shelter.
2. Incendiary bombs would be used in such numbers that the present fire brigade system would be inadequate to deal with the resulting fires.
3. No protection for children under five years of age has been proposed.

Bernal led two delegations to the House of Commons to speak to interested MPs. He met complacent Conservatives and Labour MPs, still banking on the League of Nations. As Churchill wrote in a letter to the press baron, Lord Rothermere in March: 'Parliament is as dead as mutton and the Tory party feel that everything is being done for the best and the country is perfectly safe.'[42] A Government spokesman, Geoffrey Lloyd MP, tried to play down the significance of the CSAWG book, stating that the experiments depended on academic assumptions and that the deductions made from them were open to grave criticisms.

A hostile review of the book appeared in *Nature* from General C.H. Foulkes,[43] a former commander of the British Army's chemical warfare section. He conceded that 'in many of the poorer homes completely gas-proof shelters can only be provided with great difficulty; but that is no reason why the remainder should not be protected'. He also thought that the Home Office's recommendations 'are generally sound and reasonable, and it is important that public confidence in these measures shall not be shaken unnecessarily'. He saved his most damning remarks for the final paragraph: 'This book can do nothing but harm. It suggests no better defensive measures than those recommended by the Home Office, while it is calculated to destroy confidence in them and to create panic.' Predictably, there was a vigorous rejoinder from the CSAWG, three weeks later.[44] After defending their methodologies and assumptions, the scientists replied to what they saw as the chief burden of Foulkes' argument, namely that their experiments were academic exercises with little relevance to actual war conditions:

He considers the measures proposed by the Government as adequate to deal with the kinds of attack which are probable and points to the experience of the Great War. We believe, however, that with the immensely increased potential force of modern air fleets, attacks of a different order of intensity are now possible, and that against such attack the measures are hopelessly inadequate... We have no desire to create panic, but those who persuade the people of Great Britain to believe that they are safe when they are not are inviting panic and worse than panic in the case of war. We would be lacking in our duty as scientists and citizens if we were to accept, without question, assurances of the validity of which we have not been convinced... Experiments are to be believed, not on account of the authority or bias of the experimenters, but because they can or cannot be repeated by anyone who chooses to do so. We would accordingly urge that the whole question of the protection of the population from aerial attack should be studied openly by representative scientists; then a rational estimate can be made of the probable efficiency of any measures which are finally adopted.

There was some mild concern in the press about the official ARP recommendations, but the Government was not disposed to take any advice from the CSAWG. In November 1937, Mr Lloyd, the junior minister for civil defence, attacked their motivation. He scornfully warned the House of Commons that 'this group was quite distinct from the general body of Cambridge scientists, and their using a name which was liable to be taken as investing them with a certain authority was gravely resented by the senior members of the faculty. This group, to say the least, has a political tinge. [Ministerial cheers.]'[45] Bernal, undaunted, immediately hit back in the *New Statesman*: 'Once the Government, by their own propaganda, have roused the country to a realisation of the air danger, the public will demand that it should not be paid for by the people who can least afford it.'[46]

There was a large and successful meeting of the British Association in Cambridge in the summer of 1938. Aside from a full and high-quality science programme, there were sessions on the relationship between science and society at which Bernal was a prominent speaker. He also spoke at a conversazione organized by the AScW and at packed meetings put on by the CSAWG at Trinity College and FIL at St. John's.[47] The summer drew to a close with

Hitler's troops massing on the border with Czechoslovakia, (Austria having been annexed earlier in the year). The threat of impending war caused Kingsley Martin to write an editorial in the *New Statesman* (which he soon regretted) suggesting that the existing 'Bohemian frontier should not be made the occasion of a world war'.[48] The softening of the magazine's anti-Nazi stance at a crucial time seemed an inexplicable betrayal to many of its readers, and Martin was inundated with letters of protest, 'the bitterest from Professors Lancelot Hogben and J.D. Bernal'.[49]

Sage also took part in a large demonstration in Trafalgar Square, protesting against the German menace. It was suggested that the crowd take its protest to the German embassy, situated nearby. The embassy was protected by a double cordon of policemen, and seeing them, the urbane British crowd turned back, with the solitary exception of J.B.S. Haldane. He was, in Sage's words, a man who 'preferred to express himself in clear and possibly violent ways' and he made a solitary charge at the police cordon. Their truncheons beat him senseless and he was dragged away by his friends. When he recovered, he said 'This peace movement is no good, it won't fight!'[50]

Haldane had made several visits to Spain and seen the effects of German aerial bombing on undefended towns. Based on this experience and his own war record, he considered himself to be an authority on ARP and entered the debate with characteristic vigour. He was convinced that high explosive bombs represented more of a threat to the civilian population than gas attacks. He argued powerfully for the construction of communal deep shelters in a book that he hastily wrote, and Bernal credited him with making it 'impossible for the Government to continue with a policy of providing only brown paper refuge rooms'.[51] The two men, together with John Strachey, undertook a national campaign, organized by the Left Book Club, to spread the word about the need for purpose-built shelters. Even senior Cabinet ministers were finally realizing that these communist scientists had a point: Sir Samuel Hoare, the Home Secretary, wrote confidentially to Sir John Simon, the Chancellor of the Exchequer:

We are dangerously backward in protection against the consequences of high explosives, especially in the vulnerable areas represented by important industrial cities with crowded populations . . . It is clear that the country is anxious for large developments in the shelter policy, and the government must adopt measures which will secure vigorous and quick progress with all practicable schemes for providing such protection.[52]

The date of this confidential memo was 26th October 1938 less than a month after Prime Minister Chamberlain's triumphant return from Munich, promising 'Peace for our time'. Hoare and Simon had been two of the leading appeasers of Hitler and Mussolini, although even they were beginning to worry a little. FIL members wrote letters to the press, denouncing the Munich Agreement. Bernal, worried about the lack of resolve that the *New Statesman* had recently shown over Czechoslovakia, immediately went to see Kingsley Martin and persuaded him that they should organize an anti-Chamberlain meeting.[53] He also wrote an editorial for *Nature* on 'Science and National Service'[54] in mid-October. Bernal saw the post-Munich period as no more than a breathing space – 'there are clear signs that the peace obtained by consultation is not of a character which will permit of any relaxation of military preparations.' In order to face the risk of war realistically, Bernal thought that certain immediate steps needed to be taken in the organization and use of science, 'while others of a more drastic character will be needed only if and when war breaks out'. He identified five principal needs of a modern community under war conditions:

1. maintenance of the military and civilian populations;
2. maintenance of war production;
3. defence against aerial attack;
4. the carrying on of military, naval and air operations;
5. care of casualties.

To each of these scientists could make important contributions, but they must be allowed to criticize and not be treated as military subordinates 'whose business is to obey orders and not to think'. He concluded by warning:

The full utilization of scientific workers requires the use of their ingenuity far more than of their routine service, and this can only be secured by giving them opportunities and liberty of initiative. The degree to which this is done may be a decisive factor; and its neglect might mean defeat in which the prospects of reconstruction afterwards would be irretrievably damaged. It is for the citizens and scientific men in the democratic States to see that this does not happen on their side.

This plea was fully heeded by Sir John Anderson, a crusty, career civil servant, who had been persuaded to accept a safe Parliamentary seat and was now in Chamberlain's Cabinet as Lord Privy Seal. Anderson was the only senior politician with any scientific background and was put in charge of civil defence. In January 1939, Sir Arthur Salter, the sitting MP for Oxford University, invited Anderson to a luncheon party at All Souls College. Salter knew Sage from the 1931 trip to the Soviet Union, and although they had political differences, he thought it would be stimulating to expose Anderson to the Government's most vociferous and informed, civil defence critic. Bernal was therefore invited, along with Solly Zuckerman, who had just woken up to the imminent risk of war, to meet the man whose name would soon be indivisibly linked to a corrugated shelter. Sage, always courteous, never short of quantitative data, and masterly in capturing complicated pictures with a few bold strokes, decimated the Government's provisions or lack thereof. Anderson, a taciturn but shrewd man, recognized the sincerity and depth of Bernal's opinions. On his return to Whitehall, he mentioned to his Chief Scientific Officer, Dr Reginald Stradling, that they must make use of this man's extraordinary talents. Stradling not used to such enthusiasm from Anderson warned him that Bernal was a well-known 'red'. Anderson replied, with conviction, 'Even if he is as red as the flames of hell, I want him.'[55]

Stradling arranged to meet Bernal in London, and at the appointed time found Sage already in his office reading Stradling's official papers.[56] This minor breach of protocol did not stop Sage being appointed to the Civil Defence Research Committee, along with a small number of engineering professors and physical scientists, to advise the Lord Privy Seal and 'to secure the fullest possible co-ordination over the wide field of work now comprised in civil defence'.[57] Even after Bernal's name was officially put forward there were concerns about his fitness to serve. A senior Home Office civil servant, while endorsing the rest of the committee, wrote that he was 'not quite sure about Professor Bernal. Last year he was less reliable owing to his rather extreme political affiliations. But, this apart, he would be a reasonable addition.'[58] Anderson replied with a pencil-written note on the Home Office minute: 'Get on with it quickly. I don't think in present circs. we need object to Prof Bernal.'

Sage attended the first meeting in London on 12th May and like other members of the committee signed the Official Secrets Act, apparently with no qualms. He was immediately appointed to Sub-Committee A, which was constituted 'to study the physics of explosion, blast and penetration'.[59] Amongst the most urgent problems identified by Stradling for the Sub-Committee to consider were blast measurements, the design specifications of air-raid shelters and the question of whether the tube tunnels passing under the Thames needed to be reinforced against possible bomb damage.

The British Government managed to preserve the traditional freedoms of scientific research to a remarkable degree in World War II and were rewarded for their trust with a string of ingenious inventions and discoveries that not only changed the course of the war, but still have a beneficial impact on our lives. Bernal in 'Science and National Service' emphasized that both citizens and scientists needed to keep in mind the ultimate aim of science, which, in his opinion, was to improve human welfare in times of peace. While it would be fatuous to suggest that events turned out to some extent as he hoped because of what he wrote in that 1938 editorial, he undoubtedly raised the scientists' own awareness of their roles in society and added to their collective confidence to challenge authority, when it seemed necessary.

Bernal's opposition to fascism in the thirties was public, relentless and right. Yet he completely ignored the growing evidence of even worse atrocities from the Soviet Union. He was far from alone in this, and the Spanish Civil War with the open involvement of Hitler's and Mussolini's forces, gave Stalin the most effective cover for his unspeakable terror. The twin evils were conjoined in the Nazi–Soviet Pact of August 1939, which came as no surprise to Polanyi and Muggeridge, but which so contorted the collective thoughts of progressive British intellectuals that, almost to a man and woman, they ignored it at the time and then forgot about it altogether.

One event widely covered in the British press that must have caught Bernal's attention was the great Moscow show trial of 1938, in which Bukharin was one of the famous defendants. In addition to the blanket accusations of espionage, wrecking, undermining Soviet military power and supporting overthrow of the socialist system to return to capitalism, Bukharin faced the extra charge of plotting to seize power after the 1917 Revolution through the assassinations of Lenin and Stalin.[60] Here was a man that Bernal admired, had talked to at length about science, socialism and the future, facing an appalling fate. After being tortured, and to prevent the execution of his young wife, Bukharin made a partial confession and was shot. Although Bernal could not have been expected to imagine the grotesque cruelty of Bukharin's tormentors, did he just accept the confession at face value? Or did he make the sad reconciliation that innocent blood must be spilled to achieve the ultimate goals? Margaret Gardiner does not believe that Bernal subscribed to the ruthless principle of the end justifying the means, but rather that his political stance was grounded in emotion and this allowed psychological defences that resulted in him making excuses for or denying unpleasant facts. Margaret thought that he did have doubts about communism, but never mentioned them to her. She said to him at one point, 'I suppose if you were ordered to kill me, you would.' To which Bernal replied, 'Yes I would – but very reluctantly.'[61]

8

The Entertainment of the Scientist

Dorothy Crowfoot spent the summer of 1934 in Cambridge taking more X-ray photographs of pepsin, but then returned to Oxford to take up a fellowship at Somerville College.[1] At the same time, Bernal lost his other PhD researcher, Helen Megaw, who went to Vienna to spend a year working as a post-doctoral student with Hermann Mark, now professor of physical chemistry there. The loss of these two hard-working and talented young women resulted in a temporary drying-up of the stream of new data from Bernal's laboratory. His growing involvement with the Association of Scientific Workers, FIL and the Cambridge Scientists Anti-War Group precluded him from spending the long hours necessary to generate and interpret X-ray photographs, and he could no longer summon the solitariness of purpose necessary to undertake such demanding work himself. He spent almost as much time in London as he did in Cambridge and was often out of the country. At the end of 1934, he spent two months in the USSR with Margaret Gardiner, coming home via Vienna. At the beginning of 1935, he returned to Paris and stayed with his cousin, Persis: his attempt to rekindle their affair was rebuffed so that the week was 'rather miserable though wonderful food'.[2] When he was in Cambridge, he continued to live with Eileen and their two sons, and although he was quite open about his divided affections, he experienced some 'difficulties with Margaret in London'.[3]

Soon after the week in Paris, Bernal became ill with a fever and jaundice. Word of his illness reached Dorothy Crowfoot in Oxford just as she had made the first X-ray photograph of a crystal of insulin. She was bursting to tell Sage the news, but hesitated and instead wrote to Eileen asking her to tell him about the unit cell measurements of the rhombohedral-shaped crystals, 'if he is well enough'.[4] He was not all well, but nothing could stop him from responding to this exciting breakthrough. He made cryptic suggestions to Dorothy about how she might proceed and also urged her to write up her preliminary results. So she wrote a letter to *Nature*, but having posted it, started to get cold feet. This was her first independent research and she had grown the crystals herself, adding a dash of zinc to the insulin in solution so that the metal would be incorporated into the crystal. Unlike the pepsin crystals she had worked on in Sage's laboratory, the insulin crystals did not disintegrate on drying so that she mounted them in the dry state for the ten-hour X-ray exposure. Her main concern was that the crystallization process and then the long period of radiation might have altered the chemical structure in some way, so that the diffraction pattern she obtained was not truly that of active insulin. She confided as much to Sage in a letter, dated 7th March: 'I'm rather worried about the "insulin"... I wish really I'd waited the *Nature* letter till the biological tests were made. It'll serve me absolutely right if the thing is all wrong.'[5] To set her mind at rest, Bernal arranged for some of the zinc insulin crystals to be sent to Sir Henry Dale, the leading physiologist, for assay. Dale wrote to Dorothy, on 19th March, assuring her that the crystalline zinc insulin that she had been using for spectroscopy retained its biological activity and therefore the radiation exposure 'did not significantly change the structure of the crystalline compound'.[6]

At Oxford, Dorothy continued to study the structure of sterols, a subject to which she had been introduced by Sage soon after she arrived in his laboratory, and which now formed the basis of her PhD thesis. She once described the hectic pace of working with Bernal in a Christmas letter to her parents. She had brought fresh photographs of ergosterol to Bernal in London, which he analysed on his way to give a paper at the Chemical Society: 'It was simply marvellous. Sage was working out structures all the way there – in the bus, in the tube and in the station waiting for the next train – to say nothing of during the meeting while everyone else was speaking. And then it all came out beautifully arranged and ordered as though he had known it all weeks ago!'[7] Sterol structures remained the subject of controversy between British and German chemists, and Sage continued to supply expert opinion to both camps. In June 1935, Windaus wrote to him from Göttingen with a surprising new structure for calciferol (vitamin D). Bernal studied it for some months and concluded that for both Windaus' formula and his own crystallographic data to be correct, the molecule would have to be curled up in an improbable way. He wrote back to Windaus in September admitting that he was still uncertain about the formula and found 'it almost equally difficult to agree with your formula'[8] or an alternative proposed by Rosenheim at the National Medical Laboratory in London. Bernal asked Windaus to send more crystals of different vitamin D compounds, no doubt intending to send them to Oxford for Dorothy to photograph.

Now that she was working in her own laboratory, Dorothy, in addition to generating new data on insulin, subjected some of her previous photographs of sterols to more rigorous analysis than the rather impressionistic review they had received from Bernal. She made use of a new mathematical tool developed by Lindo Patterson, who had worked at the Royal Institution with

Astbury and Bernal. The Patterson map, derived from a Fourier analysis of X-ray diffraction waves (a technique that breaks complex waveforms down into constituent sine waves), is like a contour map; it can be used to define the distances between atoms in a crystal lattice. The calculations had to be made by hand and were laborious, often involving hundreds of trigonometric functions for each spot on the X-ray photograph. Dorothy, from the first, was a gifted exponent of the Patterson, and wrote to Bernal in June 1936 about her 'first attempt at a Fourier of cholesteryl bromide' – given the residual phase uncertainties with such a complex molecule and the limitations of the Patterson technique, she was pleased that 'the whole thing does look rather surprisingly like a sterol.'[9]

Dorothy was in her mid-twenties, nine years younger than Sage, her PhD supervisor and scientific mentor. She had fair hair which, 'when caught by the sun, stood around her head like the halo of a stained-glass window mediaeval saint'[10] and she possessed a slow, captivating, smile, which only added to her air of innocence. Sage, despite his worldly experience, retained a youthful appearance with dimples and his trademark shock of thick, fair hair. In addition to introducing her to many of the leading biochemists and crystallographers in Britain and Europe, Bernal, through his example and conversations, persuaded Dorothy to take an interest in some of the political activities that consumed him. Although she knew about his ongoing affair with Margaret Gardiner and his marriage to Eileen, Dorothy was infatuated with Sage, and inevitably the two became lovers. There was not much opportunity for them to spend time together, but in November 1936 they travelled to the Netherlands, where Bernal had been invited to lecture on sterols to the Dutch Biochemical Society and to visit some university departments. Sage made a bargain with Dorothy that 'he would give all the lectures and that I should write up a lecture text, which should be published . . . every morning in Holland we hurried down to breakfast to get the first news on the radio, of whether Madrid had fallen or not. All that time it held out.'[11]

On their return from Holland, as one of her PhD examiners, Bernal had to write a report on her 300-page thesis, 'X-ray crystallography and the chemistry of sterols'. It was a monumental piece of work, which he described as 'the first comprehensive attempt at a joint crystallographic and chemical study of a group of substances of great intrinsic interest as well as of critical biological importance.'[12] Bernal was careful to emphasize the impossibility of arriving at complete solutions for sterol structures because of their complexity and the absence of 'centres or axes of symmetry in the molecules' but was genuinely impressed by the style and depth of Dorothy's research. For once, Sage was discreet about their short affair and several reasons can be advanced for his uncharacteristic reticence. First, Dorothy was his PhD student and while he did not want to provoke the attention of the University authorities by his open immorality, he wanted even less to be responsible for any stain on Dorothy's academic reputation. Second, Margaret Gardiner was pregnant and already posing 'complications'; indeed he was 'converted to trial monogamy with one spectacular failure'.[13]

Margaret's son, Martin Bernal, was born in March 1937. That same month Dorothy was introduced to Thomas Hodgkin, a scion of the Quaker family of distinguished intellectuals. He had recently joined the CPGB and was training, unhappily, to be a teacher. Hodgkin was Dorothy's age, classically handsome, and entertaining – despite a current period of depression. That summer, Dorothy wrote to 'Sage dear' expressing happy memories of time they had spent together, but suggesting a disentanglement of their physical relationship: 'Do you think it would be very stupid to stay with you only for walking and talking?'[14] A less tentative letter followed a few weeks later with Dorothy telling Sage that she felt 'perfectly happy and oddly virtuous'. She said that she expected to marry Thomas, but could not 'bear to think of you miserable and want to keep you somehow deeply in my life'.[15] Absurdly for such a practiced Lothario, Bernal did seem to mind when Dorothy became engaged to Thomas, but was soon mollified. He always tried to stay friends with his ex-lovers, and in Dorothy's case the depth of their shared passion for crystallography made it inconceivable that they would not remain on the closest personal terms.

A replacement for Dorothy in Bernal's laboratory appeared towards the end of 1935. He was Isidore Fankuchen, the atheist son of a Brooklyn rabbi. After graduating in physics from Cornell University and working in various departments in the USA, Fankuchen came to Manchester in 1934 to work with Lawrence Bragg. Bragg wrote to Bernal about him in October 1935, asking if Bernal would mind him taking up work on the sterols.[16] The request was prompted by a chemistry professor in Manchester, Heilbron, who thought the sterol formula proposed by Rosenheim from the National Medical Laboratory was wrong. Bernal replied that he shared Heilbron's concern and would welcome active cooperation with Fankuchen, who should visit Cambridge. The visit was soon arranged and 'Fan' never returned to Manchester. He was the perfect addition to Bernal's meagre staff – technically accomplished, inquisitive, good-natured, politically radical and tactless. The research tradition in Bragg's department was to study inorganic substances, especially metals and alloys, which was why Bragg felt obliged to write to Bernal rather than just let Fan trespass into the organic world of sterols. For a short period after arriving in Cambridge, Fan worked on the structure of uranium compounds, and although he remained at heart a physicist, he soon became involved in the study of proteins. The protein was in a new guise – a virus.

Tobacco mosaic virus (TMV) causes tobacco leaves to become variegated, dark and light green, and the plants to be stunted. It is the most stable of viruses and was the first to be discovered at the end of the nineteenth century, when it was shown that sap from an infected plant remained infectious after being passed through filters that retained all known bacteria. Other viruses were identified over the years, some of which cause serious diseases like polio and smallpox in humans, but detailed knowledge about their structure remained elusive. They were known to be extremely small; unlike bacteria they could not be cultured on inert media, but needed host cells in which to reproduce, and they could not be made visible under the light microscope by staining procedures. In 1935, Wendell Stanley working at the Rockefeller Institute succeeded in preparing TMV as a crystalline protein – the first virus to be isolated. He showed that all the virus activity present in infectious sap was retained in the crystalline material, and that one billionth of a gram of the material was enough to cause infection. Stanley's research was the biggest breakthrough in virology in over thirty years, and was immediately taken up in Cambridge by the biochemist Bill Pirie and Fred Bawden, (a plant virologist who had recently taken a position at the Rothamsted Experimental Station in Hertfordshire). Pirie and Bawden had been studying viruses that attack potato plants, a more important crop in England than tobacco. Now Bawden switched to growing tobacco plants infected with TMV, and 'in a few weeks, using methods that had been standard in protein chemistry for 50 years'[17] (clarifying the sap in a centrifuge), they succeeded in preparing gram quantities of liquid crystalline TMV material. Stanley had reported his crystalline material as pure protein, but Pirie and Bawden detected 0.5% phosphorus and 2.5% carbohydrate. They concluded that in addition to protein, there was 'nucleic acid of the pentose type'[18] (i.e. RNA) present.

It was natural that Pirie should bring some crystalline material to Sage for X-ray study. It was equally natural for him to give the task to his new assistant Fankuchen. Fan immediately rose to the challenge, impressing Bernal: 'Fankuchen threw himself into this examination. He excelled in the devising of apparatus specially tailored for the purpose. One problem was that of examining the liquid crystals at very low angles, and for this monochromatic X-rays were essential. He devised an X-ray monochromator made of a pentaerythritol crystal sliced in such a way that it could give a very narrow beam of strictly monochromatic radiation [X-rays of a single wavelength] of high intensity.'[19] Bernal and his group observed that TMV in aqueous solution forms two layers. The bottom layer is a gel in which all the rod-like particles are aligned. In the less-dense top layer, there is no orderly arrangement and the particles are pointing in all directions (*isotropic*). Bernal thought of them as tumbling in the solution, with each particle sweeping a sphere. As the concentration of the solution is carefully increased, there comes a point where those spheres touch, the particles are no longer free and instead form a liquid crystal phase. If, at that critical concentration, the solution is gently agitated, the long rod-like particles become linearly orientated and, when viewed in polarized light, give a beautiful shimmering effect, known as *anisotropy of flow*. The Cambridge scientists demonstrated this at a Royal Society soirée, where instead of using mechanical stirrers, they let a goldfish and seahorse swim through the dilute solution. According to Pirie, the demonstration was more popular with fish physiologists than with plant pathologists, and their discovery of the first nucleoprotein 'excited no interest at all'.[20]

Nucleic acids, in Pirie's words, were not fashionable at that date, and Wendell Stanley was one of many who initially refused to believe that RNA was present in the virus. Even Bernal underestimated the significance of Pirie and Bawden's discovery, and he needed to be persuaded by Pirie to accept the last paragraph of the letter sent to *Nature*,[21] which stated that while their results had a certain intrinsic interest, if it could be shown that the rods in their solution were in fact TMV particles, the interest would be greatly enhanced. 'This conclusion seems to us both reasonable and probable, but we feel it is still not proved, nor is there any evidence that the particles we have observed exist as such in infected sap.'

Bernal was fascinated by the way the long rod-like particles were packed in a regular arrangement, parallel to each other, in solution: did this mean that there were long-range intermolecular forces between them? The X-ray photographs showed some consistent details whether the virus was in a wet gel or dried in air, suggesting that there was a high degree of structural order within the viral protein – it appeared to him 'to have about the same order of complexity as that produced by feather keratin'.[22] Fankuchen used his ingenious new apparatus to study other viruses prepared by Bawden and Pirie. These included potato virus X and a bacteriophage (a virus that attacks bacteria). Bernal wrote to his old friend Astbury in Leeds about the work and also mentioned 'the most interesting thing... nucleic acid which I have got in fibre form and which shows very strong negative birefringence and rather a peculiar photograph with a particularly strong line at 11 Å and another at 4.5 Å with a fibre spacing at some multiples of 3.3 Å'.[23] Bernal also thought he could see some evidence for the nucleic acid line on the bacteriophage photograph.

Research into the structure of viruses started by Bernal would flourish in his department at Birkbeck College in the 1950s, as we shall see. Two categories of virus structure would be identified, in ever-greater detail: *helical* and *spherical*. TMV is the prototypical helical virus in which the *capsid* or protein coat forms helical tubes through which the viral RNA is threaded. The other main class of viruses, spherical viruses, have icosahedral capsids – their protein coats form a symmetrical, twenty-faced, polyhedron that approximates to a sphere – that enclose their viral nucleic acid, protecting it from a hostile environment. Bawden and Pirie were the first to prepare crystals of a spherical virus – the tomato bushy stunt virus (TBSV) – although when they brought the tiny (0.01 mm) crystals to Bernal, they had no idea about the importance of their latest preparation. The crystals were too small for single crystal photographs and Fankuchen, working with Dennis Riley (a research student of Dorothy Hodgkin's spending a few weeks in Bernal's laboratory), took powder photographs of the crystals suspended in their mother liquor. Bernal, working with a pair of dividers, carefully measured the two very faint diffraction lines obtained after the long X-ray exposures and working from Federov's Law deduced that the virus particle had a diameter of 340 Å and was probably a body-centred cubic lattice. He sent a draft of a letter to *Nature*[24] to Pirie, who was unimpressed and commented, 'I still feel that you haven't much to say and not even anything to contradict.'[25]

Bernal and Fan continued the virus work over the next few years, but their initial optimism that they would be able to solve the detailed structure of viruses faded. They attempted to use Patterson analysis for the diffraction patterns, but the better the narrow-angle X-ray photographs became, the more reflection spots were obtained that could not be made to fit any symmetrical model they tried. Eventually they admitted defeat: 'It appeared that it was quite impossible to explain the pattern on the existing theory of X-ray diffraction from a crystal, for any [unit] cell large enough to give the observed spots was found to be larger than the size of the particle as inferred from all the intermolecular measurements.'[26] They were the first to discern repeated subunits in TMV protein, but were ultimately frustrated that 'the crystalline nature of the viruses that we have studied cannot in itself be given a biological significance nor [can it] give an answer to the question as to whether they are or are not the infective agents, nor to the far more metaphysical question as to whether they are to be considered living organisms'.[27] It would not be until the mid-1950s that virologists would finally realize that infectivity of TMV depended on its RNA core and indeed the RNA, not the protein, was the repository of its genome.

Within days of receiving Bragg's letter introducing Fankuchen, Bernal received another from his friend Hermann Mark recommending a young Viennese student, Max Perutz, to come to Cambridge to study X-ray crystallography. Mark had been in Cambridge, at a meeting of the Faraday Society devoted to macromolecules, at the end of September 1935. Before coming, he had been asked by Perutz to make enquiries about a research position in Hopkins' biochemistry department. The Faraday meeting was attended by all the world's leading researchers in polymer chemistry, and Mark completely forgot to ask Hopkins about Perutz. Mark also missed Bernal at the meeting, but heard that he was looking for a research student. On his return to Vienna, he strongly suggested to Perutz that he should go to Cambridge to work with Sage instead of with the more renowned Hopkins. Perutz pointed out that he did not know the first thing about crystallography, and Mark replied 'Never mind my boy, you'll learn it.'[28]

Max Ferdinand Perutz, as his middle name might suggest, was the product of a family that had prospered under the Austro-Hungarian Empire. He was born in 1914, one month before the Archduke Franz Ferdinand was assassinated, and both his parents came from families of textile manufacturers, who had made fortunes from introducing mechanical spinning and weaving into Austria. His father, Hugo, had been sent as a young man to Liverpool to learn the trade and was an unrestrained Anglophile. He coached his son in the ways of the English gentleman, emphasizing personal reserve and mode of dress. So it was the smartly dressed Perutz who presented himself at the Department of Mineralogy at the beginning of the 1936–7 academic year. As he entered the cramped and chaotic laboratory, not at all as he had imagined, he found himself being looked at suspiciously by three men working at one of the benches. The silence was broken by one of them barking at him in a thick New York accent: 'What religion are you?' Perutz said as calmly as he could 'Roman Catholic', to which came the immediate rejoinder 'Don't you know the Pope's a bloody murderer.'[29] Perutz understood this to refer to the Pope's support for General Franco and soon came to the conclusion that the department was staffed entirely by communists. A few days later, Sage blew into the laboratory, sat on a table and talked with enthusiasm and charm about a bewildering range of subjects before suddenly looking at his watch and rushing off 'with the air of somebody having to do something much more important'. At once, Perutz was fascinated by Sage, and readily imbibed his core belief that protein structure was the key to the understanding of living matter and that X-ray crystallography was the only method that could solve it. He asked to work on a biological problem, but Bernal had no crystals of biological interest available and instead gave him 'some horrible chips of silicate from a slag heap' to get started on.

Perutz inherited the gas-filled X-ray tube, originally built at the Royal Institution, that Helen Megaw had used. Like her, he had to master the tube's idiosyncrasies, learning to adjust the valve to the vacuum pump so that the correct current was set up in the tube and the resultant X-rays would not be too hard (energetic) or too soft. He was taught experimental technique by Fankuchen, whose aggression was but a cloak for his essential good nature, and he received lessons in interpreting X-ray photographs from Bernal, who also instilled in him the importance of examining each crystal under the polarizing microscope first. At the end of his first year, Perutz returned to Europe for the summer and made a visit to Prague to see a cousin who was married to Felix Haurowitz, a biochemist. Haurowitz, who was working with crystals of horse haemoglobin,[30] showed Perutz under the microscope how the purple plate-like crystals of deoxyhaemoglobin transform into scarlet needles of oxyhaemoglobin as oxygen is taken up by the haemoglobin molecule. Perutz decided that this would be his crystal of biological interest and Haurowitz suggested he should approach Gilbert Adair, the Cambridge physiologist, for some specimens. Adair gave him some beautiful single crystals of horse haemoglobin, 0.5 mm in diameter, and within months Perutz was able to obtain rich X-ray diffraction photographs. The work was tiresome because the exposure times were so long, and Perutz had to resist the claims of others in the laboratory, who wished to use some of his apparatus. Excitedly, he wrote to Sage, who was staying in London, 'Dear Mr Bernal, There are [*sic*] lots of news' and asked whether there were any special photographs Bernal wanted to have taken because 'I cannot hold back the 4 cameras very much longer against the claims of Wells and Knott.'[31] Perutz proudly showed his photographs to his friends in Cambridge, but when they asked him what the photographs meant, he changed the subject because he had no idea![32]

Perutz's difficulty was essentially the one that confronted Bernal and Fankuchen in the interpretation of the X-ray data from viruses – there was no information about the phases (relative peaks and troughs) of the diffracted X-rays that is necessary to determine the electron densities of the molecule in question. Perutz was able to deduce the size and space group of the unit cell, which contained two haemoglobin molecules and possessed a two-fold axis of symmetry. By combining this information with the optical properties of the wet crystal, Perutz was able to define the orientation of the iron-containing, haem part of the molecule – by itself a new important detail about such a complex substance. He took photographs of wet and dry haemoglobin and showed that the intensity patterns were similar, suggesting that the protein molecules were not extensively altered by the loss of water around them. Bernal emphasized this point in the letter they wrote to *Nature* and believed it might offer 'an opportunity of separating the effects of intermolecular and intramolecular scattering. This may make possible the direct Fourier [Patterson] analysis of the molecular structure once complete sets of reflections are available in different states of hydration.'[33]

Perutz had taken to heart Bernal's advice about carefully examining crystals under the polarizing microscope, and as a result had noticed that his haemoglobin crystals acted like sponges: 'They shrank and lost most of their X-ray diffraction pattern on complete drying, but I found that I could dry them in discrete stages, each of which still gave detailed diffraction patterns from which I could derive Patterson projections. These projections all showed the same pattern of vector peaks as that of the fully wet crystals, indicating that the interior of the haemoglobin molecules was rigid and impenetrable to water, which must therefore be filling the interstices between them.'[34] Bernal's idea was, both for proteins like haemoglobin and for viruses, that if they were studied in different states of hydration (where they might be swollen or shrunk), variations in the spacing and intensity of the diffraction patterns would be due to differences in the way the molecules were packed together, but any constancy would be due to the molecular structure itself. As a theory, it was correct, but in practice it did not lead to a foolproof way of separating the wheat from the chaff.

When Bernal accepted the position of Assistant Director of Research in 1934, he was not accorded life tenure under the new University Statutes, although he previously held tenure as a lecturer in mineralogy. Rutherford accepted administrative responsibility for X-ray crystallography through the Cavendish Laboratory, as long as its activities were satisfactorily financed and 'the reasonable development of the subject' was assured.[35] Thus the department as a whole was adopted under sufferance, and Bernal especially so. J.G. Crowther, the science correspondent of the *Manchester Guardian*, witnessed the clash of temperaments between Rutherford and Sage during one visit to the Cavendish. Rutherford had little patience with any of his researchers, not because of personal intolerance but because his appetite for new data was insatiable, and he could be particularly harsh with those who did not approach a problem directly. Sage was much more discursive and could always see complications ahead that Rutherford would rather not be warned about. On the occasion that Crowther was interviewing Lord Rutherford, Bernal came in to the room to talk to Rutherford, who was 'explosively critical' of Bernal's points of view. Bernal showed submission, 'hanging his head', but was 'still unable to forget the complications' that Rutherford did not want to be bothered with.[36]

In 1935, the Jacksonian Chair in Natural Philosophy fell vacant through the retirement of C.T.R. Wilson. Joseph Needham waged a one-man campaign to have the Chair 'occupied by a crystal physicist ... one deeply interested in the biological implications of his subject'.[37] He gently stated that perhaps 'the biological importance of crystal physics is not yet as widely appreciated as would be desirable' within the University, before summarizing the central role of molecular fibres in living organisms – linking the linearity of the chromosome and of the muscle fibre with the linearity of 'crystalline' protein molecules. He also referred to the liquid crystal as 'not merely a model for what goes on in the living cell... [but] a state of organization actually found in the living cell'. Without mentioning him by name, Needham provided one further example where Bernal's work had made a valuable contribution – the structure of the sterols, which could not have been solved by chemistry alone. It was a well-intentioned effort to seat Sage in the Jacksonian Chair, but Rutherford was still riding the crest of the nuclear physics wave that he had created and saw no reason to diversify the department. Indeed he had just lost three of his most valued juniors in quick succession – Kapitza, Chadwick and Oliphant – and was therefore especially eager to appoint another nuclear physicist. In the event, Needham's memorandum may have been useful to those who thought the Cavendish had become too narrow in its focus, and Edward Appleton, the radiowave expert, was appointed. Many years later, Sage told Helen Megaw that he believed Rutherford had not wanted him appointed to the Chair because of his age, not because of his politics.[38]

Aside from the Jacksonian Chair, Needham was at the heart of another attempt to establish inter-disciplinary research in Cambridge in 1935. The tandem scheme involved approaching the Rockefeller Foundation (RF) to fund an Insitute of Mathematico-physico-chemical Morphology at the University, with five division chiefs, all of whom had been founder members of the Biotheoretical Gathering that had first met at Woodger's house in the summer of 1932.[39] The RF had begun to foster the application of physical sciences to aid biological research, and were, for example, already supporting Astbury's department in Leeds. The idea for the Biotheoretical Gathering to put itself on a more formal footing, as an institute funded by the RF, was Dorothy Wrinch's, and she persuaded Needham to join her in approaching the Foundation. As part of their proposal they included a five page memorandum from Bernal, outlining a programme for the application of crystal physics to biology. He suggested a systematic survey of 'typical proteins' such as albumens and globulins, to determine their characteristic architectures as well as a more detailed structural analysis of those proteins that seemed the most likely to yield information about their molecular structures. He lamented the difficulty of obtaining suitable crystals to study in Cambridge, now that Miss Crowfoot was back in Oxford, and sought to assure the RF that if it 'could see its way to providing this assistance' it would be 'coming to the help of research in what I am convinced is a most promising junction between biology and physics at a critical stage in its development'.[40]

The whole scheme was remarkably similar to the fictional National Institute for Biophysical Research that had featured in C.P. Snow's novel, *The Search*. In the novel, Constantine, the character based on Bernal, calls for *ad hoc* teams of scientists to be formed to attack whatever problem seems the most promising, 'all the workers having a share in deciding the programme to be followed. It may take years, you would want biochemists, a zoologist or two, an organic chemist, a crystallographer and so on.'[41] Needham, who with his wife had written a favourable review of *The Search*, wrote to the RF about the ideal of 'achieving institutional freedom for a small body of picked investigators... enabled by adequate endowments to work for certain periods on whatever may seem best'[42] – words that were almost identical to those used by Constantine in the novel. Needham met high-level officers of the RF who were well disposed towards the revolutionary science embodied in his grand scheme, but alarmed by the absence of administrative details (an aspect not ignored in *The Search*). After visiting Cambridge, the RF officers decided to start small by giving out a few individual grants, and stated that the 'large plan was not under active consideration'[43] until they became convinced of its viability within the university system. Over the next few years, any residual hopes still harboured by Needham and Bernal were dashed by the University hierarchy, reflecting both academic conservatism and personal antipathies.

The first to receive RF funding was Dorothy Wrinch, who was awarded a grant for five years to study theoretical biology. Wrinch, then in her early forties, was an applied mathematician of the highest pedigree. She had studied at Cambridge in the Great War and graduated as a Wrangler. While still an undergraduate, she sought out Bertrand Russell becoming an acolyte and a friend. She published influential mathematical papers, including one on seismic waves, before marrying an Oxford physics don in 1923. She then moved to Oxford and tutored mathematics in all five women's colleges. Her husband was an alcoholic and after a few years they separated, leaving Dorothy with a young daughter to look after. Whether or not she was embittered by her failed marriage, Dorothy was combative and sharp-tongued, but found herself welcomed into the avant-garde Biotheoretical Gathering for her originality of thought and not handicapped by her lack of biological training. At the group's summer meeting in Cambridge in 1934, she advanced the idea that there was a direct link between the sequence of amino acids assumed to be present in the genetic material of chromosomes and the sequence of amino acids in proteins. This was the same basis for gene specificity that Bernal had adduced in his talk for the International Congress on the History of Science in London three years before, but unlike Bernal, Wrinch committed her ideas to paper in a subsequent note to *Nature*.[44]

Within six months of receiving her RF grant, Wrinch had a second paper in *Nature*[45] – one which sought to make a fundamental change in the way scientists thought about protein structure. What she suggested was an extension of an idea of Astbury's about how molecules of α-keratin were folded in unstretched wool. Astbury had put forward a model of α-keratin that included regular hexagonal folds, which the Oxford chemist, F.C. Frank, had validated by suggesting a novel chemical bond between amino acids in the polypeptide chain or protein molecule. This transformed peptide bond had been brought to Wrinch's attention, as she acknowledged in her *Nature* paper, by Bernal. She now applied the transformation to all manner of globular proteins, suggesting that they existed in regular hexagonal arrays, rather like those of a honeycomb. Instead of globular proteins comprising long polypeptide chains, folded in some arbitrary pattern, portions of them consisted of closed hexagonal 'cyclols'. She considered the cyclols as essentially two-dimensional structures that were one amino acid thick, and then explained how these layers might be built up into three-dimensional aggregates. Very pleasing to her as a mathematician was the existence of geometrical series of cyclols, in which different orders of symmetry were associated with predictable numbers of amino acid residues.

While she put the cyclol theory forward as a 'working hypothesis', Wrinch was convinced that such an elegant, logical theory explaining the known facts about native, globular proteins must be true. Astbury, always enthusiastic about ideas that echoed his own, saw the cyclol hypothesis as a way of treating the soluble globular proteins and the fibrous proteins under a unifying theory: 'Wrinch has attempted to build up a consistent molecular system for the globular proteins by folding back, theoretically, these liberated polypeptide chains into series of folds that are none other than those first postulated to explain the X-ray diagrams and properties of keratin.'[46]

Wrinch undertook a vigorous campaign to persuade the world that her cyclol hypothesis was correct, both by writing papers to journals and letters to leading scientists. She managed to convert one very distinguished American chemist, Irving Langmuir, who had won the 1932 Nobel Prize for his many investigations of surface chemistry. Indeed it was probably the prospect of protein films, one molecule thick, which attracted Langmuir to Wrinch's theory. As a mathematician, she had no laboratory expertise and no way of testing her own hypothesis, but was entirely dependent on the data of others. In 1937, her theory received a tremendous boost when two chemists published their analysis of egg albumin suggesting that the molecule contained 288 amino acid residues – 288 being a number that was found in one of her geometric series. Such was the attention her ideas were receiving that Sir William Bragg decided that they should be aired at a Royal Society meeting. Before the meeting he wrote to Bernal asking his opinion and received the following response: 'The present position of our knowledge of the structure of the protein molecule is one where our only method of advancing is by guesswork. If a structure is proposed it can be tested, but the difficulty is to get the leading ideas. It may be, of course, that these will be arrived at by orthodox analytical methods, but in the meantime I think speculation is legitimate.'[47] Bernal thought that Dr Wrinch was proceeding along the right lines.

The Royal Society meeting did not take place until November 1938, by which time there had been a polarization of views between Wrinch and Langmuir, still vigorously supporting the cyclol hypothesis, and the rest of the biochemical world. Wrinch immersed herself in the mathematical techniques of Patterson analysis, and lacking her own crystal data, had reworked Dorothy Crowfoot's published results on insulin to show that they were compatible with a cyclol model for the molecule. This had understandably infuriated Crowfoot, who did not believe that her data supported any particular theoretical model and certainly not the cyclol hypothesis; she turned to Sage for support. His original support for Wrinch's ideas had largely dissipated by this stage as more discordant experimental findings were made, and perhaps because he knew that Linus Pauling had launched a devastating attack on the cyclol theory. Bernal wrote to Wrinch in the weeks before the meeting, trying to explain why her insulin model was invalid. Wrinch was impervious to argument, and the correspondence finished just four days before the meeting in London with Bernal saying he did not think it would be profitable for him to list all his reservations about her method of Patterson analysis. He did say that one objection but not the main one was 'that you don't take nearly enough account of the physical character of the molecules'.[48]

At the meeting, Wrinch gave a spirited presentation of her 'geometrical attack on the problem of protein structure', claiming that the cyclol hypothesis explained a number of disparate facts about proteins. In a nod to her ally, Langmuir, she predicted that 'surface methods will enable us to investigate the nature of the bonds maintaining the specific structure of proteins'.[49] Neither Crowfoot, who was heavily pregnant and giving her first lecture at the Royal Society, nor Sage wanted to challenge Wrinch directly at such an auspicious venue; neither of them even mentioned the cyclol hypothesis, while both were careful to stress the preliminary nature of all protein crystallography. Bernal's forbearance was too much for Bill Pirie, who wrote to complain: 'The ignorant people from this laboratory [William Dunn Institute, Cambridge] who went [to the meeting] came away with the impression that everyone, including you, now agreed with her. I wish you would develop the art of being rude.'[50] Nor did Bernal's restraint earn any thanks from Wrinch, who now viewed him as 'jealous, brutal and treacherous'.[51]

The continued, energetic promotion of an increasingly suspect theory was becoming damaging to the nascent subject of protein crystallography. Bernal and Lawrence Bragg decided that they needed to make a concerted effort to discredit the cyclol hypothesis. Bernal told Bragg that he had had a long talk with Langmuir, in which he did not succeed in 'getting across the crystallographic point of view'.[52] At the same time, Bernal wrote to Langmuir, sending him a copy of a letter which he was proposing to send to *Nature*, saying 'I very much regret having to do so because it must produce open controversy on a subject which I should prefer settled in private conversations.'[53] For his part, Bragg promised 'to thresh [*sic*] the whole thing out'[54] with Langmuir when he visited Manchester. Bernal objected both to the tone of the Wrinch school, which was far too certain, and to their misuse of the Patterson vector diagrams which 'needs to be pointed out because the ultimate effect would be very bad for crystallographers' credibility among chemists when the fallacies eventually came out'.[55]

In January 1939, Lawrence Bragg wrote a long, patient letter to *Nature*, explaining why Langmuir and Wrinch's theory was unsubstantiated and less than it seemed to its propagators. His letter was followed in the same issue by Bernal's, which while not rude, was certainly blunt by his standards. Bernal characterized the additional assumptions made by Wrinch in her application of Patterson maps as being of 'extremely dubious validity', he repeated the objections of the chemists to the idea of amino acid residues being linked to four others (rather than to two others by peptide bonds), and demolished any notion that the 'vector maps of Dr Wrinch's hypothetical cyclol structure bear [any] resemblance to those which have been derived by Miss [*sic*] Crowfoot from her observations'. In rejecting the cyclol hypothesis, which failed completely to account for the X-ray scattering results for insulin, Bernal thought 'it is not necessary, however desirable, to put forward another model – the problem remains an open one'.[56]

Within weeks of writing those words, Bernal was putting forward another model, which would eventually prove invaluable. At Sir William Bragg's invitation, he gave a Friday evening discourse at the Royal Institution on the structure of proteins. After a very complete, polished, review of the subject, referring to recent findings by Astbury, Crowfoot and Perutz, Bernal suggested 'working hypotheses' of his own as a guide to future work. One idea he put forward was that large protein molecules are not unitary but consist of subunits: his objection to a single long chain molecule was that it was difficult 'to imagine any kind of fold or coil by which a single chain can occupy the observable space and at the same time not be so intricate that its formation by any natural process would be enormously improbable'.[57] By invoking subunits, 'the improbabilities of the coiling become much less', and while the sub-units themselves might be non-symmetrical, they might be arranged together in a symmetrical way, explaining why 'the symmetry of protein crystals is much higher than would be expected statistically from compounds of such great complexity'. There was, he thought, good experimental evidence for such subunits, and the next question was how they were linked together.

Whatever the means of attraction between the subunits, it had to hold the protein molecule together in water. The mechanism that most appealed to Sage was one suggested, in a different guise, by none other than Langmuir at a lecture in London the previous month. It is a reflection of Bernal's open-mindedness and acute perspicacity that he would still pay attention to a man whose theory he was actively discrediting and be able to hear one inspirational note against a background of noise. Langmuir's original insight was that in aqueous solution, the hydrophobic side chains of amino acid residues would become buried on the inside of the folded protein molecule away from the surrounding water – a profound variant on the old adage that oil and water do not mix. Although Langmuir presented this as part of a rearguard defence of the cyclol theory, Bernal realized that the hydrophobic interaction between water and protein molecules was an idea that could stand alone. After crediting Langmuir, Bernal stated: 'In this way a force of association is provided which is not so much that of attraction between the hydrophobe groups, which is always weak, but that of repulsion of the groups out of the water medium.'[58] The overwhelming influence of the hydrophobic forces in determining the way proteins fold into their native configurations was not generally appreciated by protein scientists until the mid-1950s. Even Perutz, who was struggling with the tortuous folding of haemoglobin, was unaware of it until then.[59] The clinching piece of evidence for the mechanism came from thermodynamic considerations of the hydrogen bonds in water – a subject that Bernal had initiated with Fowler in 1933.

In *The Search*, when Constantine is proposed for Fellowship of the Royal Society, he is 'put up' not by his own professor but one from Manchester. About a year after the novel appeared, the real-life Sage received a letter from a professor in Manchester, who had 'been thinking for sometime that you should be put up for the Royal'.[60] Bragg told Bernal that he had sounded one or two people out and he thought there would be good support. This might have spared Bernal the anxiety experienced by his *doppelgänger*, Constantine, who took the pessimistic view that 'the physicists won't like me because I'm a renegade from physics . . . and the chemists won't like me because I'm a physicist. And the biologists won't like me because I do biology. And the mathematicians won't like me because I don't do mathematics.'[61] Sage was elected FRS in March 1937, at the remarkably young age of 35 years. His 'proud and loving mother' wrote from Florence[62] to congratulate him; she and her sister, Cuddie, were recapitulating the grand tour of their youth, having handed over the running of Brookwatson to Desmond's younger brother, Kevin.

Desmond was now living, most of the time, with Margaret and the new-born Martin in her house in Hampstead. Margaret was still secretary to FIL and was spearheading their efforts to rouse public opinion on the dangers posed by the growth of fascism in Europe. She was finding it a struggle to keep the momentum of the organization going. Aldous Huxley resigned as President at the end of 1936, followed shortly afterwards by Leonard Woolf, the Vice-President, who succumbed to his wife Virginia's growing irritation with 'dirty, unkempt, ardent, ugly, entirely unpractical but no doubt well-meaning philanthropists at whom I should throw the coal scuttle after ten minutes if I were in his place'.[63] When Bessie Bernal returned from her European trip, she asked to visit Hampstead so that she could see Martin, but was embarrassed about meeting Margaret.[64] Margaret took no offence, and the house was left in charge of Agnes, her pretty brunette, cook general; Martin was presented by Ully (his youthful, German, communist nanny). Bessie came away impressed by the cleanliness of the house, but no doubt bewildered by Desmond's living arrangements. It is said in the Bernal family that she devoted herself to raising gentlemen and scholars, but could never get the two to coincide!

Life with Margaret expanded Sage's already wide social horizons beyond scientists and radical intellectuals and brought him into contact with many of her artist friends. W.H. Auden would come to stay in Hampstead and talk to Margaret for hours as they smoked their way through a packet of cigarettes. Sage was a non-smoker and suspected it was an unhealthy habit. On occasion, Sage would express surprise at Margaret's comparative ignorance about a topic. She once asked him, 'What do you expect me to know?' He replied: 'Well, more or less, what happened everywhere at any time.' And Margaret retorted, 'Do you know that?' Sage thought for a minute or two and said: 'I know nothing at all about the fourth century in Romania.'

The friend of Margaret's whom Bernal really latched onto was Barbara Hepworth, whose abstract sculptures fascinated him. In October 1937, Hepworth held a show of her work at a Mayfair gallery and asked Bernal to write the preface to the catalogue. Her work reminded him very strongly of Neolithic stone monuments – just as those monuments employed extremely limited symbolic forms that could be seen as reaction to the living representations in the art of the Cave painters, so Hepworth had reduced her sculptures to the barest elements as a reaction to the representational art of the nineteenth century. Her use of bare, unadorned shapes made it possible 'to see the geometry which underlies it and which is so obscure in more elaborate work'. To Bernal's eye, 'the elements used are extremely simple: the sphere and the ellipsoid, the hollow cylinder and the hollow hemisphere. All the effects are gained either by slightly modulating these forms without breaking their continuity, or by compositions combining two or three of them in different significant ways.'[65] Barbara Hepworth enjoyed Bernal's analytical approach to her work: 'When you criticised my carving, you were quite right, sculpturally, spatially and constructively... you always seem to me to be searching for, discovering and applying basic laws and principles.'[66] Hepworth regarded Bernal as 'the most inspiring person ever to come into my workshop as he had the amazing capacity for comprehending in an instant the nature (and even the formula) of every sculpture, and hours were spent in exciting discussion and drawing'.[67]

Hepworth encouraged Bernal to write a chapter on 'Art and the scientist' in a book, *Circle*, that was being compiled by her husband, Ben Nicolson, and a number of other artists in the Constructivist movement. This gave Bernal the chance to lament the separation of art and science – 'the last official link was the annual reviews of the Royal Academy which used to be given in *Nature*, and in which the academicians were chided for putting the moon the wrong way up in the sky or for painting a flower with too many petals ... In the great creative periods of science the artists and the scientists worked very closely together and were in many cases the same people ... Leonardo da Vinci, though the greatest, was only typical of whole schools of artist-scientists. Gradually, however, with the development of bourgeois culture the useful and the ornamental were piously separated. Science was used to make the money, art simply as a means of spending it. The result of this separation has been the most incredible mutual ignorance.'[68]

As a crystallographer, Bernal constantly thought in three dimensions and his remarkable facility in doing so may explain why sculpture and architecture were the two arts that appealed to him the most. He gave a talk to the Royal Institute of British Architects in 1937, which included a wonderful exposition of symmetry:

'The only aspects of symmetry that are formally considered in architecture are those of mirror symmetry in elevation, and, to a minor extent, radial symmetry in plan, but there are far more symmetries than these. Any type of repeatable operation, whether it is a reflection, a turning or merely a translation in space, gives rise to a symmetrical structure ... An equal-spaced arcade, for instance, is a particularly simple example of translation symmetry.' He explained that there were only a limited number of possible symmetrical modes: 'In surface repetitions, for instance, such as those for pavements or walls, there are actually only seventeen different rhythms, all of which have been used unconsciously in art, but many more of the subtle ones only in the textile work of primitive tribes. In three dimensions the complexities are naturally greater. Here there are no fewer than 230 modes, most of which have certainly not been used up till now in architecture, but which might be made to produce new and significant effects ... the architect is no longer tied to the massive piling of rectangular blocks and can place his elements almost where he likes in three dimensions.'

This was followed by an equally engaging discourse on topology, which Sage informed his audience was a branch of modern mathematics that derived from town planning: 'It arose from the problem proposed in the eighteenth century at the Russian Academy of Science as to how to cross all the bridges in St. Petersburg without crossing any of them twice.'[69] *

At times, Sage might have wondered whether there was a topological solution to crossing North London without encountering one of his lovers. Eileen moved to Clifton Hill, well within walking distance from Margaret's house in Hampstead. Sage would see her and the boys regularly and still go on summer holidays together – once to a holiday camp in Wales with the Malleson family. Joan Malleson was a gynaecologist and family planning pioneer who was Eileen's closest friend. Her husband, Miles, a playwright and comic film actor, was also a good friend of Sage's. While on a walk, the holiday party came to a derelict bridge over a muddy estuary; the iron support pillars of the bridge were full of eels, which could be seen only by precariously crawling along some railway ties. The Bernal boys were ecstatic about the adventure, but Joan felt that her eight-year old son, Andrew, was too small to be allowed to go. He was mortified and had a temper tantrum, which left him too exhausted to walk. Sage carried Andrew all the way back to the camp on his shoulders. He always felt an affinity with children and could talk to them with ease and mutual enjoyment. That summer of 1938, Bernal also spent time in Cornwall with Margaret, who had taken a house there for several months. He told her that he could not live with Eileen, but nor could he make a complete break from her. Margaret asked him about the boys and he stated, 'I don't believe in all this nonsense about paternity.' She pointed out to him, 'Well, you do seem to have a rather special sort of feeling about Martin.' He replied, 'That's different, he's a personal friend of mine.'[70]

Tensions grew between the two North London households. Eileen threatened to write to their friends saying that Sage had abandoned her. Joan Malleson wrote to him about Eileen's profound emotional distress, saying that Eileen 'feels your silence to be flippant and your attitude casual... you are deserting her and slighting her'.[71] Joan suggested that he might try psychoanalysis, which he did with no success. There were also inevitable difficulties with Margaret, not to mention the irresistible attractions of her nubile domestic staff. At one stage, his presence at either house became unwelcome and he went to stay for a while with his sister Gigi, also living in London, before returning to Margaret.

If Sage was affected by emotional turmoil, it never seemed to interfere with his work. He was invited to give a series of evening lectures by Sir William Bragg at the Royal Institution on the 'Molecular architecture of biological

---

* Alan Mackay informs me that Euler reported to the Academy in St Petersburg in 1735 on the problem of the seven bridges of Koenigsberg, which started the mathematics of topology.

Systems'. In the first talk on 25th January 1938, he concentrated on the
problem of scale: 'The microscope cannot effectively study anything smaller
than one hundred-thousandth of a centimetre, and chemical analysis anything larger than one ten-millionth. Unfortunately the structures of the
greatest significance for the maintenance and the very existence of life lie
precisely in this gap. The molecules of proteins, which are never formed
except by living organisms, and without which life processes are impossible,
have dimensions of the order of a millionth of a centimeter.'[72] He then
explained how X-ray crystallography was such a valuable technique for
bridging that gap between chemistry and light microscopy. The crystallographer could build on the chemist's knowledge of constituent amino acids
and the chemical bonds that linked them and, by determining the symmetry
of protein molecules, propose three-dimensional structures that were in
accordance with all the known facts. He held up Crowfoot's recent work on
insulin as an outstanding example of this approach. Over the next four weeks,
Sage treated his audience to a comprehensive survey of the field, taking in
Astbury's work on fibrous proteins, his own work on plant viruses, the
importance of protein in muscle contraction and his ideas on enzymes.

Bernal moved to London permanently in 1938, when he took up the chair
in physics at Birkbeck College. He succeeded Patrick Blackett, who had taken
the Langworthy Chair at Manchester University, recently vacated by Lawrence
Bragg. Birkbeck had been founded as the London Mechanics' Institute and
functioned for the best part of a century as a night school for intellectually
curious young workers from modest social backgrounds. It was formally
admitted as a School of London University in the 1920s, but its charter still
required that its undergraduate students be 'engaged in earning their livelihood'.[73] The idea of a college catering to unprivileged students, who were bent
on self-improvement, appealed to Blackett, a committed Fabian; his move
there in 1933, when he was already the most highly regarded experimental
physicist of his generation, surprised many of his colleagues. In the short
period of his tenure, Blackett turned the Birkbeck department into one of the
best in the country: a leading centre for cosmic ray research and a haven for
emigré scientists from Europe. Sage was invited to apply for the post and sent
in a curriculum vitae, which described his duties as the Assistant Director for
Research and his major research interests in proteins and the structure of
liquids. He felt obliged to point out that he had never taught a regular
elementary course in physics, but in his teaching 'tried to avoid stereotype
and have attempted to bring into the course all material, however lately
discovered, which will conduce to a greater interest and appreciation of
essential principles. I have paid particular attention to practical work with
the idea of developing a really experimental attitude towards scientific

problems.'[74] Bernal, like Blackett, was attracted by the radical tradition of Birkbeck, and the restriction of teaching to the evenings meant that the whole day was free for research.

On the day, 19th Ocotber 1937, that Bernal indicated that he was prepared to let his name go forward as a candidate for the Chair in Physics at Birkbeck, Lord Rutherford died unexpectedly, leaving a gaping hole in the fabric of British science. Lawrence Bragg, who had only just moved from Manchester to the National Physics Laboratory, was soon elected as the new Cavendish Professor, and naturally brought some of his crystallography team with him to Cambridge. Bernal took Fankuchen with him to Birkbeck, but Perutz remained in Cambridge. He sent Bernal regular progress reports on his haemoglobin work, but became increasingly concerned about his lack of university status and the question of financial support. Bernal sought to reassure him, saying that he would talk to Bragg, who already 'gave me an undertaking that you would be looked after and I am sure that he will'.[75] Months passed without Bragg visiting Perutz in the laboratory and eventually Perutz decided to make a direct approach, taking some of his haemoglobin photographs for Bragg to see. The impact was immediate and Bragg from that day became Perutz's staunchest advocate. He wrote to Bernal: 'I had a talk with Perutz this morning. He told me about his work on haemoglobin which interested me very much. I should like this line to continue at Cambridge if it does not interfere with what you are doing, and I gather from Perutz that there is no clash.'[76] Bernal of course had no objection to Perutz continuing the haemoglobin research and told Bragg that 'Perutz is an extremely capable worker, particularly on the experimental side, and his protein pictures are certainly the best that have been taken by anybody so far.'[77] This was the dawn of the new era of molecular biology at the Cavendish Laboratory.

By moving from Cambridge to London, Bernal exchanged a lowly, leaking, hut in the courtyard of the Cavendish for Breams Buildings, a Dickensian thoroughfare between Chancery and Fetter Lanes, lined by dilapidated, tall, Victorian buildings. There were two laboratories given over to research, one in the basement and the other at the top of the building, which in Blackett's time housed the large cloud chamber and Geiger counters that he used to capture cosmic ray tracks. Blackett moved all this equipment to Manchester, along with a handful of researchers. Bernal, in turn, transferred his X-ray equipment and cameras down from Cambridge. Just as the physical layout of Breams Buildings was awkward, the attitude towards research equipment had been penny-wise with the chief technician, Mr Dobb, begrudgingly parting with bits of apparatus, much in the style of his counterparts at the Royal Institution or the Cavendish. At Birkbeck, he had hung up a large paper sign, which read 'PLEASE RETURN TOOLS AFTER USE'. Blackett's 'League of

Nations' scientists had added their own translations underneath, and after the first years of Bernal's tenure, the list included several dozen languages, including Urdu and Arabic.[78] Blackett also left behind one or two researchers, including Werner Ehrenberg, a German refugee physicist, who walked with a severe limp as a result of childhood polio. The extrovert Fankuchen had no difficulties fitting into the cosmopolitan group, which soon expanded with the addition of an MSc Student, Harry Carlisle, (originally from Burma) and Käthe Schiff, already an accomplished crystallographer, who had fled her native Vienna.

As with any new professor, Bernal was expected to give an inaugural lecture. The title he chose was 'The structure of solids as a link between physics and chemistry' for which he scrawled some key terms in pencil but gave little thought until the appointed day, 1st December 1938. The chair was to be taken by Sir William Bragg, and that afternoon Sage decided to go to the Royal Institution to borrow some slides. While there, he bumped into Langmuir and spent the next several hours trying, unsuccessfully, to explain the deficiencies of the cyclol theory to him. Time was therefore tight when he returned to Breams Buildings, and instead of being able to rehearse his lecture he was swept off to a sherry reception in his honour by the Master of Birkbeck. He did manage to hand over his collection of slides to Fankuchen, who was to act as projectionist. According to Fan, 'The whole way through the lecture the poor guy never knew which slide was coming next.'[79] It seems unlikely that anyone else in the audience realized that Bernal's lucid thoughts were being marshalled on the spot, and the following week he received a postcard from the editor of *Nature* asking for the non-existent transcript of the lecture.

Now that Bernal had achieved a certain standing in the scientific community, he decided that he would write a book exploring the role of science in contemporary society and seeking ways to remove those impediments that prevented science from fulfilling its enormous potential to benefit mankind. As a first step, he hired a part-time secretary to help with the book. He heard from Magda Phillips that a friend of hers, Brenda Ryerson, was looking for work. Brenda was a fellow communist, who had married a man wounded in the International Brigades in Spain. She had a newborn baby and, although she badly needed some money, was concerned that her husband could not cope without her at home. Sage was immediately sympathetic to her plight and suggested that her working hours could be quite flexible. So Brenda started on what would become *The Social Function of Science*,[80] working erratic hours at Birkbeck or in Hampstead, with secretarial duties soon spilling over into the Association of Scientific Workers, and, after the Munich crisis, typing memoranda dictated by Bernal on science and national defence.

She also found herself dealing with phone calls from various women anxious to talk to Sage, and in time would join the ranks of his lovers.[81]

When *The Social Function of Science* reached the galley-proof stage, Sage added references. He did this by telling Brenda the author, the name of the book or journal article and the date of publication: she found that he was seldom wrong by more than a year. The book was published in January 1939 and was divided into two main parts. The first 'What science does' is Bernal's personal opinion and experience, buttressed by original economic data. The second 'What science can do' is his prescription for the future and relies on his imagination and politics. In the preface to the book, he gave clues to his motivation for writing it, noting a contemporary disillusion with science as a method of procuring continuous improvement in the condition of life. He attributed this to the psychological damage wreaked by the Great War and the later economic depression. Bernal started with an historical survey, which was not overtly Marxist in its language, but soon led to a rejection of the traditional view of science as a contemplative activity in which knowledge is sought for its own sake, in favour of one where science is driven by the material needs of society. Essential economic progress depended on improved technology, resulting from the application of science. Where the Victorian historian Macaulay had celebrated the success of science in multiplying human enjoyments and mitigating human suffering, Bernal was concerned that modern physical science had no more solved the problems of universal wealth and happiness than the moral sciences of the ancients. Bernal counted modern warfare, financial chaos and general undernourishment among the bitter fruits of science – ignoring the role of corrupt and inadequate political systems.

The sweep and detail of his treatise were unprecedented. He managed to create statistical data for some aspects, and, where quantification was impossible, relied on his own experience and judgement. Relative to its wealth and importance as a country, he noted, England 'spends very little on science and makes less use of its potential scientists than do any other of the great Powers'. There was also a tradition in England 'that science is felt rather than thought' that had fared well in 'the easy bits of science', but which Bernal thought would be less successful in the future, when the problems would be less straightforward and would demand the use of systematic theory. He portrayed Rutherford exploring the structure of the atom 'as if it were a kind of coconut shy at a village fair, [when he] throws particles at it and looks to see what bits fall out'.

The Americans possessed the English empirical character and had invented most of the world's most useful devices. Where Great Britain spent about 0.1% of its national income on scientific research, the relative US figure was probably eight times higher, at around $300 million. Still, he did not believe that the American scientists were contributing proportionally more to the advancement of science, partly because of the higher costs in the US, and more subtly, because of the individual scientist's need to promote himself in a society driven by worldly success: 'American publications are if anything slightly more bulky than corresponding German ones, but, whereas in Germany one feels that it is just thoroughness for thoroughness' sake, in America there is a suspicion that the position of a man may depend on the bulk of his published work.'

Concentrating on Britain, Bernal considered science research by the government and industry as well as in the universities. The two per cent of science graduates who escaped careers as school teachers or solitary, secretive work in industry or government and became academic researchers 'have rather painfully to unlearn much of the inaccurate and out of date information acquired in the universities and to forget the rest'. While constructing the case for the inefficiencies and poor organization of science, Bernal recognized that it is extraordinarily difficult to impose discipline without snuffing out the originality and spontaneity on which scientific progress depends. He thought there were three main aims to be satisfied:

1. the entertainment of the scientist;
2. new understanding of the external world;
3. the application of that understanding to human welfare.

None of these was being widely achieved under the present haphazard arrangements, where development was driven by the need to make profits rather than by the needs of the great mass of the population. Many scientists were bitterly frustrated by lack of funding or lack of opportunity to cooperate with one another, and, for example, 'the condition of medical research in this country is not only a disgrace but a crime'. Readers were reminded periodically that things were much better in the USSR, where for the past two decades science had been subjected to central planning and was integrated into the productive processes in order to meet human needs.

Bernal thus set the stage for the second part of the book: 'What science could do'. There must be a comprehensive reorganization of science, which 'presupposes therefore a change in society itself'. He thought 'the inadequacy of the scale of science is more immediately important than its inefficiency' so that the prime requirement under any new system was 'a very large expansion' in activity. Sage's expansionist mode leads him at one point to propose 'unlimited sums for scientific research, that is, sums limited only by the ability of existing scientists to spend them'. Since the funds would not be used to increase scientists' salaries and there was a limit to how much apparatus an individual could use, there would be an inherent limit on expenditure in practice. Whatever the overall budget set by society, the internal distribution of that budget between different subjects should be decided by consultations between representatives of science and national economists 'as is already occurring in the Soviet Union'. Even if countries like Britain did not adopt a central command economy, Bernal thought that the financing of science could be placed on a better footing by publicizing the benefits that science could bring and by making more use of scientific and industrial councils to apportion funds. Once the role of science in advancing society became clear, there should be no difficulty in raising the modest sums necessary to maintain a flourishing level of research. Although Bernal acknowledged that, historically, the advent of capitalism led to an acceleration in early scientific development, he believed ultimately that the transformation needed to direct science towards the good of humanity 'is incompatible with the continuance of capitalism'.

Bernal next set out to show how science could be organized without killing its necessary freedom and flexibility. He did not accept that science could not be planned because it 'is in its very essence unforeseeable'. It was plain that there had always been an element of short-term planning in scientific research, while the longer term had depended on a mixture of tradition and opportunism. The challenge was to put in place an explicit long-term strategy that allowed for 'the unpredictable nature of scientific discovery'. At any time, there might be subjects where advance was easy and rapid, while other areas of ignorance were left fallow. By allocating talented scientists to those neglected areas, the overall front of advancement could be broadened to the benefit of all. Central planning could also ensure a proper balance between fundamental and applied research. Disillusion with the destructive consequences of science in capitalist society would be overcome with the realization that science is the chief agent for social change. It offered not only the promise of a minimum level of well-being for all mankind, but beyond that the greatest possibilities for social and intellectual development. Science could transform society indirectly through the technical changes it brings about and directly through the force of its ideas: 'The association of scientists in times of crisis with other positive and progressive forces is not a new phenomenon; it occurred in the age of Bruno and Galileo and again in the French Revolution.' It seemed to Bernal that the task which the scientists had undertaken – 'the understanding and control of nature and of man himself – is merely the conscious expression of the task of human society. The methods by which this task is attempted, however imperfectly they are realized, are the methods by which humanity is most likely to secure its own future. In this endeavour, science is communism.'

The Social Function of Science was original, lively and topical: there had been several editorials in *Nature* over the previous year or two on the social relations and responsibilities of science, and the ideas in the book reflected a view increasingly held in the science world that scientists should not be content to pursue their intellectual vocation in isolation. The book found immediate favour with Bernal's contemporaries like Blackett, Needham and Zuckerman. At Caltech, 'Pauling devoured the book, made it a topic of discussion in his seminar classes . . . and sympathized with most of its message.'[82] The book also reached a wider audience, and a review in *The Spectator* stated: 'No other book of this range and vision is going to appear for many years. It is the testament of one of the few minds of genius of our time . . . It is a unique book and contains an accumulation of knowledge and a passion for ideas that are not likely to be combined again in one man for a long time to come.' Less effusively, the *New York Times* called it 'a provocative and valuable book which is badly needed'.

There were a few critics, however, and none more pointed than Michael Polanyi. Describing the book as an 'able and powerful treatise', Polanyi identified its central theme as 'the passionate desire to put science into the consciously organized service of human welfare'.[83] While Polanyi granted that Bernal was not following an orthodox Marxist line, he remained suspicious of Bernal's apparent defence of the freedom of science. Polanyi found Bernal lacking on the crucial point of how science can be directed in order to benefit human welfare. He cited the development of the electric discharge lamp as an example of the defect in Bernal's thesis. This humble street lamp was, in Polanyi's opinion, the only practical invention to follow directly from the quantum theory developed between 1900 and 1912, by such luminaries as Planck, Einstein, Rutherford and Bohr. He posed the question as to how Bernal's central planning authority, if it existed in 1900, would have guided those men to discover the atomic theory in order to improve street lighting to the level required twenty years later in connection with the popular use of motor cars. 'And then the crucial question: Supposing the likely case that the scientific world controllers had *not* performed this miracle of foresight, would they then have had to reduce their support of the investigations which were leading to the discovery of atomic structure?'[84] By skirting the central point in his own thesis, Bernal was, in Polanyi's opinion, succumbing to use of Marxist propaganda, rather than relying on the power of truth, and this behaviour could only result in the 'merciless oppression of intellectual liberty'.

Polanyi objected strongly to Bernal's relentless criticism of capitalist institutions and constant praising of Soviet Russia. It seemed to Polanyi that nowhere was scientific thought oppressed so comprehensively as in the USSR because 'the thrust of violence is guided here by Marxism, which is a more intelligent and more complete philosophy of oppression than is either Italian or German fascism'.[85] As a result, 'many well-known young [Soviet] scientists have been imprisoned in the course of the last year, no one knows why or for how long. Their names can be mentioned only in a whisper.' That Bernal did not even mention their plight as a whisper in his book, drew a withering rebuke from Polanyi: 'Dragooned into the lip service of a preposterous orthodoxy, harried by the crazy suspicions of omnipotent officials, arbitrarily imprisoned or in constant danger of such imprisonment, the scientist in Soviet Russia is told, from England, that the liberty which he enjoys can only be appreciated by living it. Since the terms of this liberty prevent him from answering his British colleagues, I have taken it upon me to point out the anomaly of the situation.'

By the time *The Social Function of Science* appeared in 1939 there were already the unmistakable beginnings of 'big science' in the USA. There were gigantic hydro-electric schemes to bring energy to the Western states, Du Pont was transforming nylon from a laboratory specimen into a commercial product through a huge industrial research project, and, within the University of California, Ernest Lawrence at Berkeley was building cyclotrons for high energy physics research. All these large-scale endeavours would be brought together in the wartime Manhattan Project – a military engineering project of unprecedented complexity and size. After the war, the model of large teams of scientists and engineers became the dominant fashion in particle physics, defence research and the electronics industry (e.g. Silicon Valley). Writing twenty-five years after the publication of *The Social Function of Science,* Bernal stated that the scientific revolution had entered a new phase – it had become self-conscious: 'This is now recognized not only among scientists or among men of general education but in the world of private business and of state finance: research itself is the new gold field.' The scale of big science in terms of its financing, its multifaceted complexity and its demands for specialized personnel forced scientists 'to confront the world outside their disciplines';[86] not exactly in the way Bernal prescribed, but nonetheless resulting in a social consciousness he surely welcomed.

The historic advances made in biological sciences after the war, especially under Bragg's avuncular eye at the Cavendish Laboratory were, by contrast, achieved by determined individuals like Perutz or by small groups, most famously the Watson–Crick duo. The twenty year period after 1945 likewise saw revolutionary changes in medicine, such as effective anti-tuberculosis drugs, open-heart surgery, kidney transplantation, all of which were developed through the single-minded efforts of a few dedicated individual scientists and doctors.[87] None involved central planning or large collaborative teams. The Human Genome Project was certainly big biology, and fulfilled many of the notions promoted in *The Social Function of Science*. Sage would have been even more enthusiastic about human proteomics, which has the goal of cataloguing all the body's proteins, describing their three-dimensional structures and the way they interact with one another. X-ray crystallography will remain a key tool in this present day exploration of Bernal's original dream, but it will be done by robots, who will not first squint at crystals under a microscope and imagine how the atoms might be arranged.

9

Scientist at War

In the summer of 1939, Bernal returned to the United States for the first time since he had been taken there as a small boy by his mother. As before, California was his main destination, but now he was invited to give a series of lectures at Stanford University. These were part of the celebrations organized by the University to mark the centenary of the theory that all living things, plant and animal, are composed of cells. At the end of June, Bernal gave lectures on successive days to the Pacific Division of the American Academy of the Advancement of Science on the structure of proteins, and to the American Physical Society on the X-ray studies of plant virus particles. After the fourth-of-July holiday, he took part in a four-day meeting at Stanford on colloids.[1] On the first day of the conference, Sage presented a theory in which he attempted to relate the dynamic process of cell division, *mitosis*, to the physical mechanism of the protein molecule that formed the characteristic cell structure known as the *mitotic spindle*. His talk was reported the next day in the *New York Times* under the cryptic headline 'Links cell splits to protein crystal' and the subsequent account gave readers the impression that Bernal was making an original and significant contribution to cell biology.

Following the Stanford conference, Bernal undertook a tour for the Progressive Education Association, talking to teachers at workshops in Chicago, Ohio and New York. He wrote to Fankuchen at the end of July[2] complaining about the one hundred degree weather and 100% humidity, and mentioned that, except for four days, he had given two lectures a day since arriving in the country. During his educational workshops, Bernal was elaborating proposals that he had originally made in *The Social Function of Science*. He was concerned with the need for science to become a central component of general education and at the same time addressed the question of how the humanities could be brought to bear on the teaching of science. Keeping science and the humanities rigidly separate, stifled intelligence and criticism, and resulted in citizens who understood so little of the major influences on their lives. In his view, there were two main, overlapping objectives in science education:

1. 'to provide enough understanding of the place of science in society to enable the great majority that will not be actively engaged in scientific pursuits to collaborate intelligently with those who are, and to be able to criticise or appreciate the effect of science on society.

2. to give a practical understanding of scientific method, sufficient to be applicable to the problems which the citizen has to face in his individual and social life.'[3]

Bernal thought the inability to transmit to students the scientific method had been the greatest defect in traditional teaching and in order to rectify this, 'every science teacher and every science pupil must be to some extent a research worker'. The scientific method could be appreciated only by using it. Science now offered the prospect of improved material living conditions, but the world needed to develop more advanced social and economic policies: 'the confusion and struggle of our own times is largely the result of the inability of an economic and political system which grew up in an era of small trading and handicraft industry to deal with the new possibilities of large-scale mechanised industry and transport, which by their very nature imply a far more highly organised and planned society... If we fail to educate people to think about this, our present difficulties will grow worse, until they culminate in the miserable serfdom of fascism, and the wars which are fascism's only answer to the difficulties they cannot cope with. Science and education are still powerful weapons for the defence of democracy, and for making possible the extension and development of democracy in the direction of an ordered, yet free, co-operative community.'[4]

Sage spent most of August in New York sharing an apartment with 'L'.[5] He also met Jean and Iris again – Iris was Iris Barry,[6] a diminutive woman with black hair and striking blue eyes. In her Bloomsbury years, she had been the painter Wyndham Lewis' ill-used lover, and she moved to the USA in 1930. She was now the curator of the film library at the Museum of Modern Art. Iris and Sage had many friends in common – Ivor Montagu and John Strachey for example – and she also shared his love of conversation. Bernal's engagements as an educational consultant were over by mid-August and he was then able to enjoy upper New York State, visiting the Finger Lakes and Ticonderoga. He returned to the city at the end of the month, in preparation for another series of lectures to be given to the International Congress on Microbiology and then at the Rockefeller Institute. His trip was meant to end in Boston on September 12th with a talk to the American Chemical Society on protein structure, but with the declaration of war now seeming inevitable, he cut short his visit and dashed back to England. He wrote a letter to Edwin Cohn, the Harvard biochemist, who would have been his host in Boston, regretting that:

Events seem to have decided things and any co-operation in the protein field will have to count out most if not all Europe from now on. I am sorry because it seemed as if we might have contributed something to the solution of the main problems. I shall not be able to touch it for a long time, and I do not think anyone else here will either. My only hope is that it may be possible to get it well started in the States through Fankuchen, who I am sending over with all my materials to carry on if he can find some means of doing so.[7]

By the time Bernal returned to London, blackout precautions were already in place in anticipation of German air raids. He transferred from his office at Birkbeck to the ARP Technical Department, a new research unit that had taken over the Forest Products Research Station, Princes Risborough in Buckinghamshire. The Thames Valley would become an important locus of wartime activity, offering good access to the capital without providing any obvious targets for enemy bombing. For this very reason, Margaret Gardiner, at the time of the Munich crisis, had rented a two-bedroomed cottage at Maidensgrove,* near Henley-on-Thames. In the summer of 1939, her duties with FIL came to an end because the spirit of the country was now anti-fascist; she decamped from London with her young son, Martin, and domestic staff, Agnes and Ully. In September they were joined at Maidensgrove, for a short time, by Brenda Ryerson and her son. On the third weekend of the war, all were reunited with Sage. Under the terms of the recent Nazi–Soviet Pact, once the Germans invaded Poland from the west, the Red Army soon advanced from the east to a pre-arranged demarcation line. This was one of the leading stories that weekend, and when she heard about it, Margaret commented, 'Russia is as bad as Germany.' Sage did not argue with her openly, but quietly explained to Brenda that it was just the Soviets reclaiming territory that they had lost at the end of the Great War.[8]

The British Government had used the period following the Munich Agreement to step up its civil defence measures, in particular issuing gas masks to the public and constructing steel bomb shelters. As a *Nature* editorial had remarked in May, 'Great Britain is now alive to the risk of being unprepared to meet attack from the air'[9] and it was obvious that effective protection would need to be provided for the civilian population both at home and at their places of work. To make such provisions, basic data were required on the effects of explosion on different types of structures. Information was lacking on the physics of shock waves – the nature of the pressure changes and how they were transmitted through buildings or through the ground. The state of

---

* Some years later, Bernal was joking with friends about what titles they might take in the House of Lords. Lord Bernal of Maidensgrove was suggested, but Waddington suggested Maidensgrave would be more apt.

ignorance on the physiological effects of blast was, if possible, even more complete. About the only scientist to have pronounced on these matters was Haldane, on the basis of his informal observations in Spain. Writing in biblical style, he likened the shock waves from the explosion of a big bomb to the blast 'of the last trumpet which literally flattens out everything in front of it . . . It is the last sound which many people ever hear, even if they are not killed, because their ear-drums are burst in and they are deafened for life. It occasionally kills people outright without any obvious wound.'[10]

The formation of the Civil Defence Research Committee, under Anderson's driving, in May 1939 was intended to correct the prevailing ignorance about explosions, starting with the physical aspects. At the first wartime meeting at the end of September, Reginald Stradling was able to announce that five committee members (including Bernal) were working at the Research and Experimental Headquarters at Princes Risborough. Much work was already in hand, and two of the engineering professors had shown that framed buildings needed 'surprisingly little strengthening to resist debris loading' – the shortage of timber and steel, however, meant that there would be little chance of reinforcing existing buildings.

Bernal's own work was presented as a paper to Sub-Committee A on the physics of explosions. He had been thinking about the novel problems of how to measure temperature, pressure and velocity at the centre of an explosion. At the very centre, the temperature would exceed the melting points and even the boiling points of most substances so that spectroscopy from a distance would have to be used, but within a few centimetres the temperature would fall to between 3,000 and 1,000°C.

By placing a number of small pieces of select material near the charge, it should be possible to see on recovery and subsequent microscopic examination the maximum temperature to which they had been exposed, and by the thickness of altered material the time during which they were exposed to this temperature. The method is essentially similar to that of measuring meteorites' temperature in the upper atmosphere by the thickness of the layer of fine crystal iron melt surrounding them.

His idea for measuring pressure was to detonate explosives in evacuated copper spheres and then make comparisons with the pressure of air that would cause the spheres to burst. This notion received short shrift from Sir Geoffrey Taylor, the Cambridge mathematician and expert on fluid mechanics, who chaired Sub-Committee A: 'I do not think that pressures can be estimated using copper cylinders in the way suggested by Bernal. If you pump up air into a copper cylinder the cylinder will expand in radius till at a certain radius it will burst. If you try to introduce air at higher pressures you cannot do it because the container has already burst'![11] Taylor then presented his own mathematical treatment of the way shock waves are reflected by and also bend around a wall – he used Fourier analysis in a way that would have been very familiar to Sage from X-ray crystallography. Two months later, Sage wrote to Paul Ewald, now working in Belfast, and offered him 'a nice problem', which G.I. Taylor thought insoluble, about the events subsequent to placing a sphere containing gas at 3,000°C and 10,000 atmospheres pressure in an infinite ocean of elastic solid. Sage ended the letter with the hope that 'Belfast is sufficiently peaceful for you to treat this as a piece of abstract physics, without any immediate application in your neighbourhood.'[12]

When the Civil Defence Research Committee was set up, it was intended that a physiologist should be appointed to complement the engineers and physicists. Now that the fighting had started, Bernal decided that there should be urgent consideration of the likely damage to humans, and he approached his friend Solly Zuckerman, at the Anatomy Department of Oxford University, to take charge of compiling evidence on the biological effects of explosions. He invited Zuckerman to come to Princes Risborough, only about twenty miles from Oxford, to meet Stradling and to give advice on the question of whether people in underground shelters might be harmed by shock waves passing through the earth from a bomb exploding nearby. Zuckerman suggested that the situation be simulated by placing some monkeys in a concrete-lined shelter and then detonating a bomb buried near the concrete wall. The test was carried out on Salisbury Plain in October 1939, with the monkeys being restrained against the concrete wall of a trench while a bomb was detonated. Zuckerman recalled 'about two minutes after the explosion, Des and I were in the trench. The wall closest to the bomb had been fractured, but none of the monkeys seemed at all affected. Against the advice [of the Home Office Inspector of Explosions], Des and I then sat in another trench while a second bomb was fired. I do not think we were as close as the monkeys had been, but to the surprise of the others who were stationed much further away, neither of us was aware that a second bomb had been exploded before anxious faces peered in to see if we were safe. In those days no-one seemed to know anything about the precise effects of bombs.'[13] By the end of the year, Zuckerman was effectively working fulltime for the Ministry of Home Security.

Birkbeck College had shut its doors to students on the outbreak of war. Several of the physics staff wrote to Bernal, offering their services for civil defence research. Carlisle asked to join the services, but Bernal refused to endorse his application form, telling him, 'Wait until you hear from me.'[14] In late September, he told Carlisle that he had made arrangements for him to work in Dorothy Hodgkin's department in Oxford and he was to take the Birkbeck X-ray equipment with him. The equipment was new and not paid for – Bernal had been counting on a large grant from the Rockefeller Foundation (RF) to cover the costs. The transfer to Oxford was effected, with Sage for once concerned about money and complaining about the carriage fee of £17 10s charged. Carlisle fitted into the new surroundings easily, continuing his novel structural investigation of the synthetic sex hormone, stilboestrol. Sage was fearful of the future of X-ray crystallography and wrote a long letter to the Rockefeller Foundation:

The position of X-ray research on proteins and viruses in this country is at present in a promising but critical state. I have myself been forced to drop it almost entirely by having taken up work in connection with National Defence. However, the work which was carried out in my laboratory is still continuing. Dr Fankuchen, as an American Citizen, has returned to the States... there he intends to carry on with X-ray work on proteins, though not for the moment with virus work. My other assistant, Mr Carlisle has been transferred to Oxford where with Mr Riley he is working under the direction of Miss Crowfoot. He has taken with him part of the Birkbeck apparatus. Dr Perutz is still working in my old lab in Cambridge and is receiving as you know a Rockefeller grant. Very interesting results are being obtained, notably... wet insulin and haemoglobin. If this work can be maintained there now seems a direct way to attack the fundamental problem of protein structure, namely that of the effect of the variation of water and salt content on the X-ray photographs. The position however is precarious. All research work which has no immediate bearing on the present military struggle is being carried on somewhat on sufferance, and funds for its continuation may be stopped at any moment. Even now it is difficult to find money to pay for apparatus and supplies already in use, and unless some support can come from the outside the whole work on this side of the water may come to an end in a few months time... I would like, therefore, to put the following suggestions... to the Foundation. That a sum of £1,000 should be granted to Dr Crowfoot... for researches on proteins and viruses, with the object of carrying out more general and fundamental investigations which I proposed in my original application of 12 December 1938... A grant of this size would enable the work to be carried out in a satisfactory way for another year or two. There is little serious risk of destruction by war as Oxford is not considered to be a military target.[15]

Sage also wrote to Fan in New York asking him to 'get Cohn or somebody important to get Rockefeller to send Dorothy £1,000 at once. The apparatus will have to be pawned otherwise and about the only piece of good pure research on proteins stopped.'[16] Dorothy learned within weeks that the RF approved her grant so that she was able to pay for the Birkbeck apparatus and for two research assistants.[17]

Bernal's reassurance to the RF that Oxford was unlikely to be bombed because it was not a military target was, in the early months of the war, the received opinion. Indeed, Churchill circulated a note in November 1939 suggesting that the blackout restrictions should be relaxed because 'we know it is not the present policy of the German Government to indulge in indiscriminate bombing in England or France'.[18] It was the period of the Phoney War, when the British population began to adjust to the shortages and restrictions of wartime and was anxious about possible air-raids, but was not yet exposed to lethal dangers of the *Luftwaffe*. Sage was billeted in the small Oxfordshire village of Chinnor, at the foot of the Chiltern escarpment. The winter was a very cold one, and his life was complicated by 'landlady difficulties'.[19] At weekends he would either drive the short distance to Maidensgrove or into London to stay with Eileen. One evening they were invited to a dinner party at the flat of Cyril Connolly, the essayist and literary critic, who had just launched the magazine *Horizon*. Before Sage arrived, Connolly had confided to his other guests that he had discovered the true religion, Taoism. He asked them not to tell Sage about it because he did not want to have his cherished, new belief undermined. His guests kept quiet, but Connolly, an arch poseur, could not resist announcing at the dinner, 'Sage – I *must* tell you – I have found the true religion! It has already given me great happiness and peace of mind. But knowing your scorn as a scientist for everything beyond the natural world, I've no intention of telling you what the religion is.'

'Oh, but Cyril,' Sage remarked, 'I'm afraid you've gone too far already.'

'What do you mean?'

'If one knows a man really well, that must be enough to tell one what religion he is going to take up.'

'Tell me then – what is it in my case? Go on – tell us.'

Relishing the challenge, Sage laid down his knife and fork and took a drink. 'In the first place, Cyril, it has to be something unusual, something nobody else has thought of yet – I don't imagine you've suddenly discovered the underlying truths of Protestantism. Nor do I suppose you've decided to follow your friend Evelyn Waugh into the Catholic Church . . . seeing that he's got there first. Nor do I fancy you'll have been attracted into a warlike religion such as Shintoism. And I don't even think you've become a Muslim – despite the attraction of four wives. Buddhism – that could be tempting . . . Except, of course, for one difficulty.'

'What's that, Sage?'

'You'd have to look on the whole material world as an illusion – *maya*. I can't imagine you doing that. Food, drink, even claret like this – an illusion? Not the religion for you, I'll fancy, Cyril.'

By now, Connolly was looking uneasy, sensing that Sage was not going to lose the scent.

'The really important thing for you, Cyril, in choosing a religion, must be that it makes absolutely no demands on you. You won't want to attend temples or churches, give up a lot of your income to the poor, be obliged to say prayers at all odd hours...that's not *your* religious cup of tea. And certainly you won't want a spiritual programme that tries to turn you into an ascetic...So if you've *really* discovered the religion that suits you, Cyril – plenty of quiet contemplation, vague in character, with no demands for a change of any kind in your way of life – I can only suppose you've become a Taoist.'[20]

Sage's wit and supreme intelligence also adorned a less frivolous dinner group – Zuckerman decided to resurrect the Tots and Quots club. He and Bernal felt strongly that those running the war had no real understanding of the potential offered by the application of the scientific method to novel operational problems and did not recognize the untapped resources embodied in experimental scientists. The original members formed the nucleus for the reincarnated Tots and Quots, although not without some misgivings – Lancelot Hogben wrote to Zuckerman saying, 'I'd like to meet Needham and yourself again, but can't say that meeting Haldane and other popular fronters again thrills me. I think the shameless inconsistencies of and servile subservience to Stalin of such people as Haldane has put back the social influence of men of science for a whole generation.'[21] The club structure was looser, reflecting the exigencies of wartime – Blackett, for example, declined to become a member but frequently attended the dinners. Zuckerman also made a point of inviting influential guests, who invariably came away impressed by the quality of the discussants, if not the food. The club reconvened in November 1939 at the *Jardin des Gourmets* in Soho, where the menu sounded enticing (Truite Gastronomme, Longe de Veau aux Primeurs, Poire Hélène), but was 'not too good' according to Zuckerman. The subject for discussion, appropriately, was the present state of science in England; after the recent success of *The Social Function of Science*, Sage was regarded as an expert, even in this company.

In his remarks, Bernal was pessimistic about the state of science and saw little evidence that it was being reorganized to meet the war needs. One reason was the war was being run by politicians and civil servants, who did not understand science, and this shortcoming was compounded by senior scientists, who did not want to disturb the equanimity of their masters. He observed that: 'In the general view, scientists who want to get things done are meddlesome and troublesome.'[22] Given that no initiative could be expected from the scientific societies, Sage thought that the impetus would have to come from the scientists themselves. It would be an uphill task because the Government was unprepared to support science, indeed the drastic lack of funding now threatened the future of any academic research in Britain, not to mention the supply of new scientists.

In February 1940, Zuckerman invited a representative of the French Embassy to a Tots and Quots dinner to explore what might be done to foster closer links between French and British scientists. By the end of the evening, it was decided that Crowther, the science journalist, should fly to France to see if it would be possible to found an Anglo-French Society of Sciences.[23] Thanks to decisive support from Frédéric Joliot-Curie and Pierre Auger, the nuclear physicist, French ministerial consent was secured within days and an impressive committee was assembled. The British side was organized with no formality as a result of just one meeting in Zuckerman's laboratory in Oxford. Joliot had been made the French president and it was decided that Paul Dirac, the Cambridge theoretical physicist, should be his British counterpart. The executive committee would comprise Bernal, Blackett, Cockcroft, Darlington, Waddington and Zuckerman, with Crowther as secretary.[24]

Even before Crowther's trip to France in early April, Bernal had held some discussions with Colonel Paul Libessart, the Chief Engineer of French Artillery. As Bernal reported to Stradling, Libessart had studied the early phases of an explosion wave by the 'ingenious method of spark photography', which enabled him to show that the process was more complicated than had been thought, preliminary detonation giving rise not to carbon monoxide, as had been supposed, but to carbon dioxide and carbon, which later reacted to form CO as a secondary explosion process'.[25] Libessart had also established that an explosion produced a small central zone, only about twice the diameter of the charge, of very high pressure, beyond this a zone of gas burning and beyond that only the effect of the shock wave. In addition to his detailed studies of the mechanisms of explosion, Libessart had tested the resistance of certain materials such as reinforced concrete to high explosives in air. More important tests on bomb-proof shelters were going to be carried out at the end of the month in France, which Sage thought it would be useful to witness. Finally, the French had done far more experiments on animals than the British had, and 'demonstrated that there is very little harmful effect upon animals outside the zone of re-inflammation of gases, i.e. about 30 feet from a 500 lb. bomb'.[26] He suggested to Stradling that Zuckerman should be present for the animal experiments also scheduled for the end of April.

Sage and Zuckerman, together with a civil servant Mr R.C. Blyth, took the early morning boat train from Victoria station to Paris on Sunday 21st April. Their mission, in addition to witnessing the French explosives tests, was to learn about French civil defence measures and to act as ambassadors for the new Anglo-French Society of Scientists. They stayed at the Hotel Scribe, close to the Opera House. Monday was taken up with meetings every hour with different representatives of the French civil defence organizations. They met General Daudain at the Department of Passive Defence, and then

Commandant Benier of the Sapeurs-Pompiers, who told them about the deficiency of trained firemen, especially in provincial towns. Zuckerman formed the opinion that the French expected that he and Sage should be in uniform. At the end of the afternoon, they went to *L'Institut d'Optique*, the largest optics research group in Europe. The institute was founded by Charles Fabry, who counted among his many contributions the discovery of the ozone layer in the upper atmosphere. Professor Fabry, now in his early seventies, described to the British visitors a new infrared radiation device designed in his laboratory that could detect a human being or a heat-generating object at a distance of several miles. Blyth noted in his diary that 'Professor Bernal secured details'.[27]

Libessart gave them dinner at the Gare de Lyon before they boarded the night train for Savoy and the Alps. Their destination was Modane, a small border town, from where they could visit forts in the alpine segment of the Maginot Line that were intended to close off any invasion routes from Italy. About fifteen minutes after leaving the station, Zuckerman realized that he had left his briefcase of documents at the station restaurant. He informed Libessart, who was accompanying them on their tour, but he seemed unperturbed. The colonel arranged for the train to make an unscheduled stop and Zuckerman was soon reunited with his briefcase, which had been collected by the secret policemen who had been tailing them![28] They arrived in Modane at 7.30 the next morning, and found a lorry at the station to take them up to Fort Sapey, the largest of the Maginot emplacements. It had originally been built in 1885, but had undergone extensive modification as part of the Maginot policy of the previous decade and now boasted huge subterranean chambers and caverns. Zuckerman was far more impressed with the lunch, served underground with great ceremony, than he was with the explosives tests. In the afternoon they drove to the smaller Fort Le Lavoir, positioned at an altitude of seven thousand feet, south of Modane. There they witnessed more animal tests with dogs and rabbits being exposed to explosions in wire cages. Again the animals 'seemed to be entirely unaffected by the blast'.[29]

They broke their journey back to Paris at Laroche Migennes in Burgundy, where they spent Thursday watching artillery tests; Bernal took particular interest in the effects of shell-fire on steel plates and concrete. He had an opportunity to discuss his observations with two professors at the Sorbonne the next morning, before visiting Libessart's laboratory near Versailles for a demonstration of the spark photography method used to capture the trajectory of small projectiles. After touring the school of camouflage in the afternoon, Bernal gave an evening lecture, in French, at the Quai d'Orsay to an audience that included four Nobel Laureates and Emile Borel, the distinguished mathematician and current Minister of the French Navy. A dinner was then given in Bernal's honour, where he and Zuckerman were introduced to the Earl of Suffolk, a tall dark-haired man about forty years old. He was the British Government's Scientific Liaison Officer in Paris, but no ordinary functionary. He lived at the Ritz Hotel, now crowded with wealthy Frenchmen who had abandoned their country estates because their servants had been called up for military service; he was a most cavalier nobleman, always in the company of beautiful women and often sporting a pair of pistols in his belt. He took Sage and Zuckerman to a number of parties over the weekend, before they flew back to England.

The Phoney War ended abruptly on 10th May, Sage's thirty-ninth birthday, with the German invasion of Holland and Belgium. Bernal spent the day chairing a meeting of an explosives committee at Woolwich, attempting to coordinate research being carried out by the Army with that of the Ministry of Home Security.[30] He was especially concerned that the Army should be aware of the French work that he had just learned about. He told them about a French method for measuring the velocities of shell fragments, and arranged to forward a report of French trials on the penetration of concrete by projectiles. His particular concern here was the time taken for a bomb to penetrate to its fullest depth in a concrete target so that the timing of the fuse could be set accordingly. Bernal's scientific expertise was no longer confined to the passive protection of civilians, but was now being applied to the effectiveness of weapons. He learned about research going on at Woolwich into the detonation of explosives, the power of explosives, the measurement of pressure at the boundary of a detonating explosive, the rate of change of pressure in air surrounding an exploding charge, the conditions immediately preceding and immediately following the bursting of a bomb case, the effect of the thickness of charge-case on the blast produced by a bomb and on the fragmentation pattern. All this work, which the Army had generated in order to maximize lethality, had some bearing on civil defence issues. That evening, Bernal celebrated his birthday at the Players' Theatre, where his sister Gigi was a cook. A few hundred yards away, on the other side of Trafalgar Square, Winston Churchill returned to Admiralty House from Buckingham Palace as the new Prime Minister.

Within days, a new spirit of determination radiated from London. Churchill's pugnacious resilience was fully tested over the next few weeks as the wave of the Nazi invasion rolled into France and threatened the catastrophic loss of the British Expeditionary Force, miraculously avoided at Dunkirk. Two weeks after Dunkirk, the Tots and Quots held their June dinner in Soho with Kenneth Clark, the art historian now at the Ministry of Information, and Allen Lane, publisher of Penguin Books, as the guests. The general opinion amongst the Tots and Quots was that although Britain would soon be facing

Hitler's war-machine alone and then the prospect of an invasion, fewer than half of her scientists were engaged in active war work. Bernal thought that this was partly the fault of the scientists, who were not initiators but 'yes' men. A lengthy debate ensued about the need to galvanize the scientific community and also to raise the public's awareness that this was going to be a war in which technology would be a key component. Suggestions were made about encouraging questions in parliament and for club members to write articles for the press. At the end of the evening, Allen Lane said how much he had enjoyed the discussion and it was a pity that no record had been kept because it would have been good to publish it as a special Penguin paperback. Zuckerman immediately suggested that each participant should write down his contribution and this could form the basis of such a book. A deal was struck there and then: the deadline for the production was to be four weeks – half the time devoted to writing and editing and half to production. Zuckerman functioned as the editor-in-chief, assisted by Bernal, Crowther, the science journalist, and Edward Carter, Librarian to the British Institute of Architects.

The book, *Science in War*, duly appeared a month later, an 'abbreviated gestation', as Julian Huxley remarked, 'more characteristic of a rodent than of a human being or a book'.[31] The book had twenty-five anonymous contributors, who apart from giving numerous suggestions of how science could be used in the war effort, were insistent that a scientific approach was needed in all facets of the war – military strategy and tactics, the supply of materials and food, even questions of propaganda and morale. There was an ignorance and mistrust of science in many important quarters – business, farming, the Civil Service and the military authorities – which meant that scientists were usually relegated to a lowly advisory role, 'on tap but not on top', providing answers to whatever questions were put to them. But as Huxley pointed out 'as every research worker knows, half the battle in science consists in asking new questions which the non-scientist cannot be expected to think of'. Huxley's was one of many, generally favourable reviews, and the book certainly succeeded in raising the level of awareness in many quarters of the role that science could play in the war. The same issue of *Nature* that carried Huxley's review led off with a battle cry, 'Men of science and the war', encouraging scientists to 'Go to it' and to 'force on an unscientific administration their reading of the dangers and of the means for counteracting them'.

In the wake of *Science in War* and the public debate it spurred, the membership of the Association of Scientific Workers expanded rapidly, and Brenda Ryerson, by now Sage's London lover, became its organizing secretary. Sage would still attend weekend meetings, when he was able, but when he was unavailable Brenda would often go to Blackett for advice. On one occasion, Blackett became irritated and said to her, 'It's no good, I'm not like Bernal,

I can't switch my mind about from one thing to the other, I need to concentrate.'[32]

One of the many problems confronting Sir John Anderson as Minister for Home Security at the outbreak of war was what should be done with German and Austrian aliens living in Britain. Anderson, an imperturbable and fair-minded man, understood that the great majority of these aliens were refugees from Nazi oppression and were implacable opponents of fascism. He did, however, take the precaution of having each alien appear before a one-man legal tribunal, as a result of which 569 were interned out of a total of over seventy thousand interviewed. Anderson sought to balance the need for national security against the private rights of the individual, and was concerned not to 'be stampeded into an unnecessarily oppressive policy'.[33] As the disasters of 1940 unfolded, especially an invasion of Norway aided by 'Quislings' and stories of German spies disguised as priests and housemaids plotting the collapse of Holland, Anderson's principled position became untenable. Public calls to intern all aliens intensified, and on 11th May, as the new Home Secretary in Churchill's Coalition, Anderson was approached by the military authorities who recommended to him that 'in view of the imminent risk of invasion, it was ... of the utmost importance that every male alien between 16 and 70 should be removed forthwith from the coastal strip'.[34] Anderson accepted the logic of their argument; once he ordered the first three thousand men from coastal areas to be interned, the pressure to round up the rest became irresistible.

Max Perutz's name was amongst the next three thousand in category B (absolute reliability uncertain). He was arrested by a solitary policeman, in Cambridge, one 'cloudless Sunday morning in May'.[35] After being herded together with several hundred other men in the same predicament, including many Jews and a surprising number of scientists, Perutz embarked on a harrowing sea voyage from Liverpool, which took him to Canada, where he was treated as a civilian prisoner of war. The week after Perutz's arrest there was an editorial in *Nature* stating that 'It seems impossible that any man of science, no matter what his political or other views may be, could, in the extremely grave circumstances and in view of the amazing revelations concerning the activities of "fifth columnists" in other countries, take exception to the internment of alien scientific workers and students.'[36]

One man of science who did take exception was Sage. As soon as he found out where Perutz was, he started to write letters trying to get him a position in the United States. He wrote to Pauling, saying that Perutz had been 'sent over to Canada with a batch of anti-fascist internees'. He thought Pauling would find him a very useful addition to his lab 'as he is particularly adept in preparing, mounting, and photographing protein crystals, as well as being a good all-round chemist'. Sage pointed out that in addition to having a very large amount of unpublished material on haemoglobin, Perutz, as a sideline, had 'probably settled the problem of the transformation of snow into glacier ice' from work he had carried out at the Jungfraujoch. After regretting that such ability should be wasted when Perutz could help 'real experimental protein crystallography take root in the States', Sage told Pauling that he had 'left the field myself for the duration and spend my time being an engineer, architect, and explosives expert. Ce n'est pas magnifique mais c'est la guerre'.[37]

As the *Luftwaffe*'s offensive intensified that summer, Sage devoted more time to becoming an expert on bombs. At an early meeting of the Civil Defence Research Sub-Committee A in June 1939, Wing Commander Craw-ford from the Air Ministry stated it was probable that the most bombs likely to be dropped on England 'would not be fitted with delayed-action fuses of any appreciable duration (longer than 1/40th sec)'.[38] The Air Ministry's opinion was optimistic in the light of German patents on electric time-fuses from the early 1930s and would have been disputed by witnesses of the devastating effect of delayed-action bombs dropped by the *Luftwaffe* on Madrid and Barcelona. As soon as a few German bombs were found on the east coast in the opening months of the war, it became plain that the clearance of unexploded bombs (UXBs) was to be a major task. The German electrical condenser resistance (ECR) fuses were set to arm the bomb only after it had been released from the bomb-rack.[39] A bomb dropped from an altitude over one thousand feet would detonate instantaneously on impact, whereas those dropped from a lesser height would not be fully charged on hitting the ground and would lie buried in a dormant state until a subsequent jolt caused them to explode. An unexploded bomb (UXB) committee was set up by the Ministry of Supply in February 1940, with Stradling as one of its original members, to coordinate efforts and to develop new techniques. The Research and Experi-mental Branch at Princes Risborough designed a prototype apparatus for neutralizing the fuse without activating the sensitive trembler-contact that would cause the bomb to explode. Unfortunately, changes in bomb design rendered the apparatus obsolete very quickly.

The alternative to disarming unexploded bombs was to blow them up where they lay, but of course this would be equivalent, in many instances, to doing the *Luftwaffe*'s work for them – causing damage to industrial plants and to arteries of transportation and communication. By the early summer of 1940, twenty-five small bomb disposal sections were formed, with most men being drawn from the Royal Engineers, and although the number of bombs they had to deal with at that stage was relatively small, their casualty rates were 'shockingly high'.[40] Stradling was all too aware of this through his membership of the UXB Committee and encouraged as much research into

1. Desmond's father, Samuel Bernal, and mother Elizabeth 'Bessie' Bernal (née Miller)

2. The Bernal children (Kevin, Gigi, and Desmond l. to r.) with their nurse, Daisy, and either Bessie or Aunt Cuddie in 1908

3. The eighty freshmen of Emmanuel College Cambridge, October 1919. Bernal is seated on the Senior Tutor's left

4. Sage and his wife, Eileen Bernal (née Sprague)

5. Patrick Blackett as an Acting Lieutenant in the First World War. He arrived at Cambridge in 1919 in uniform

6. Sage, Sylvia Dickinson, Isidore Fankuchen (Fan), and H. D. Dickinson (l. to r.) at a British Association Meeting, Nottingham 1937. Sylvia married Dickinson, Sage's Emmanuel friend, and worked as a Rockefeller research assistant in Astbury's Leeds department

7. W. T. 'Bill' Astbury (1898–1961), the man Sage credited with coining the term 'molecular biology'

8. Max Perutz (1914–2002) who joined Bernal's lab in 1936 and determined the structure of haemoglobin

9. Bernal with Margaret Gardiner in the Alps, 1936

10. Dorothy Hodgkin looks on as Sage demonstrates Tobacco Mosaic Virus gel to Irving Langmuir at the British Association Meeting, Nottingham 1937

11. Dorothy Wrinch (1894–1976) whose cyclol theory of protein structure Bernal patiently discredited

12. Geoffrey Nathaniel Pyke (1894–1948) the begetter of Habbakuk, described by Sage as 'one of the greatest and certainly the most unrecognized geniuses of the time'

13. A subdued Solly Zuckerman surveys damage in Tobruk harbour in February 1943, when he felt Sage had abandoned him

14. Photo-reconnaissance of a D-Day beach. The cap on the stake in the right foreground is a Teller anti-tank mine

15. Beach on D-Day+1 with vehicles stuck 'like flies in amber'

possible solutions at Princes Risborough. Naturally, Sage was drawn into these discussions and 'hit in a few minutes on a solution derived from schoolboy egg-blowing. It consisted simply of emptying the explosives out of the bomb with steam from a safe distance and thus making it harmless regardless of the fuse.'[41] There may have been some previous attempts to boil out the explosive by heating the whole bomb, but Bernal's new idea was communicated to the UXB Committee by one of his colleagues at the Research and Experimental Branch, suggesting 'a Mark 2 drilling and steaming apparatus which should result in considerable saving of time re Mark 1 apparatus for boiling out the main filling'.[42] This Mark 2 apparatus became known as the steam-sterilizer and, as Bernal recalled, under wartime conditions was adopted very quickly – the first production order was made in June 1940.[43]

A less subtle technique for dealing with delayed-action bombs was promoted by the Earl of Suffolk. He had returned to England after the fall of France in June on a commandeered ship from Bordeaux, bringing with him some of France's leading physicists, canisters of heavy water and a cache of industrial diamonds (stolen by him at pistol-point). Once back in England, he had inserted himself into the ramshackle bomb disposal services as an expert in unexploded bombs – especially those with novel features. He would arrive at the scene of the UXB having been driven through blacked-out streets by Mr Harts, his chauffeur. He preferred to work with a blacksmith's leather apron covering his otherwise bare chest and would call out details of the device to be dealt with to Miss Morden, his glamorous blonde secretary, taking notes a few yards away. The trio quickly became legendary throughout the bomb disposal sections and was known as 'The Holy Trinity'.[44] Suffolk's original technique for disarming many bombs was to fire a bullet through the fuse-head to disrupt the electric circuitry and stop the timer; it was a method which did not attract many followers and which even Suffolk had to abandon when the Germans changed the design so that the clock was no longer uppermost.

As German bombing of the airfields in the Home Counties intensified during the Battle of Britain, the organization of bomb disposal and the collection of information about bomb sizes, fuses and safe disposal techniques became a matter of supreme urgency. By early September, when the Blitz of London itself started, there were already 2,500 UXBs waiting to be dealt with in south-east England.[45] It soon became apparent that not all these were delayed-action bombs and many were just duds. In terms of the allocation of skilled disposal teams and to avoid unnecessary disruption, it was extremely important to be able to distinguish between the two. Lord Suffolk undertook many field trials to this end, in a remote area of Richmond Park, where he was often joined by Sage. Sage saw these explosions as a good opportunity to test the resistance of various shelter designs. Before the war, an inter-service

committee had made an arbitrary decision that for brick shelters, the walls
should be two to three times thicker than the roof.[46] In Richmond Park, Sage
came to the conclusion that the concrete roof should be reinforced to reduce
the chance of a bomb penetrating into the shelter. On one occasion, Sage took
along the Bomb Disposal Officer to the Port of London, Peter Danckwerts, a
recent Oxford chemistry graduate. It seemed to Danckwerts that the purpose
of the trial was 'to show that air-raid shelters built to government specifications were death-traps' because when the German UXB was detonated the
shelter duly collapsed. What impressed him more was that 'there was a
perceptible interval between the explosion and the time at which Bernal
ducked down into our shelter trench. He explained that he knew the velocity
of the bomb-fragments and could calculate their time of arrival in his head.'[47]
It should be noted that Danckwerts himself was an extremely cool-headed and
courageous young man. He was later awarded the George Cross for neutralizing many magnetic mines dropped on London in the Blitz, using his own
improvised technique that depended on having a good ball of string available
to yank the fuse out of its mounting.[48]

Daylight bombing of London started on 7th September, and one of the early
raids took place while Bernal was at Civil Defence Headquarters in Whitehall,
with Zuckerman and Stradling. News reached them that St. Pancras Station
had been closed because of an unexploded bomb, and Bernal said to Zuckerman, 'That's for us.'[49] Sage set off with Zuckerman and after negotiating many
blocked streets arrived to find a great throng outside the station. They were
people who had been trying to leave the city and now found their way blocked
by huge iron gates. Sage mused that whoever 'put up the gates had forgotten
the Mediaeval requirement that if you want to let only one person in you must
have a small postern gate in the big gate'.[50] He and Zuckerman fought their way
to the front and identified themselves to the policemen inside, who then
pushed the gates open just enough to let them through. Sage asked to be
taken to the stationmaster, who had sensibly taken cover with other station
workers in a deep shelter. He told Sage that the bomb was on Number One
platform, 'so I went along, and sure enough at the end of the platform there
was a large hole where the bomb had gone in. But that hole had suspicious
blackening around it and a few fragments, and I was very soon able to identify
the thing as not a bomb at all; it was a shell from the anti-aircraft batteries . . . so
I came back very cheerful and I had the pleasure of telling the Stationmaster,
"You can start all your trains again . . .".'[51]

Such identification problems became more critical as the bombs rained
down heavily, and Bernal began touring the London boroughs, especially in
the East End, to give lectures to Air Raid Wardens 'on how to tell a dud from
an unexploded delayed-action bomb, or how to tell whether a bomb, which

had penetrated deep into the ground, had exploded. These lectures used to be illustrated by practical examples which could be found all around at the time.'[52] As a teacher, he was inordinately pleased when visiting a bombed building in central London, and the warden recognized him and asked 'Are you the Professor who gives those lectures?' Sage confirmed that he was and was even more delighted when the warden had remembered the content of his lecture correctly. The warden had found a UXB in one of the rooms still standing and said to himself, 'What did the Professor say?' It was the kind of bomb that did not normally carry a delayed-action fuse and so the warden had already moved it down below. When Sage went down, he could see 'the bomb was lying on a small handcart, and a violent argument was going on between my photographer and the officer in charge. They belonged to two different departments – Bomb Disposal and Home Security – and naturally each of us considered that we had a right to information about the bomb. In the end I decided that the argument was not a very healthy one, we were both standing by the bomb, and I was not as sure as the warden had been that my estimate about its non-explodability was correct. So in the end, I got my photograph surreptitiously and departed.'[53]

Sage regarded it as his business to go round looking for all kinds of unexploded bombs. It was dangerous work, not just because of the risk of explosion, but because many of the evacuated buildings he entered to survey were on the point of collapse. He seemed fearless – C.P. Snow described him as 'by long odds'[54] the bravest man he had ever known. Zuckerman, the anatomist who was engaged in some grisly experiments with human cadavers to understand the pathology of explosions and penetrating wounds, remembered going with Bernal to see his first real bomb damage. A factory in Luton had been hit and 'a few men had been blown to bits, and some pieces of human flesh – I particularly remember a piece of brain – had not been completely cleared from the fallen masonry. I was deeply impressed both by the incident and by Bernal's objectivity as he tried to reconstruct exactly what had happened when the bomb burst.'[55]

The daily German bombing raids that hot September stretched the RAF fighters to their limits and caused severe damage to London. In the early hours of the 25th, Birkbeck College was hit by a number of incendiary bombs so that the lecture rooms were open to the sky. Civilian deaths climbed to one thousand per week and the War Cabinet started to meet in reinforced rooms below ground. The Tots and Quots decided that it would be foolish to risk meeting in London: their August dinner had been disturbed by a stray stick of bombs falling on Soho, causing their guest of honour, H.G. Wells, to make his one memorable contribution as he looked at his glass and then at the ceiling and announced: 'At the last I could say I was drinking good old Empire.'[56] The most prescient opinions expressed at that dinner had come from Haldane, who was concerned that no attention was being paid to the brutal Japanese occupation of China, and predicted that 'further disaster could not be prevented while the eastern and western conflicts remained separate'.[57]

At the September dinner, moved to the peaceful surroundings of Magdalen College, Oxford, Haldane was operating 'on a London ration of sleep and an Oxford ration of port'.[58] He scribbled this clerihew on the back of his menu and passed it to Sage.

> Desmond Bernal
> Is not eternal
> He may not escape from
> The next bomb

In early December, Bernal made the first public disclosure of what he and others had learned about the physics of air raids, at a special afternoon lecture at the Royal Institution. He warned his audience that his would be no more than a broad outline of the work, both because of 'its intricate nature and even more because of the requirements of secrecy'.[59] He illustrated how an explosion gives rise to an initial shock wave, with a steep rise in pressure, and this is followed by a longer phase of sub-atmospheric pressure or suction. His work with Zuckerman had shown that people were directly injured by blast when the peak pressures rise to about one hundred lb per square inch (through blunt trauma to the lungs) and the suction phase did no direct harm. Such high pressures only occurred very close to explosions and because the shock wave was of short wavelength, it could not pass around even quite small objects. So 'to have even a small garden wall between oneself and the bomb is practically to be secure from direct effects of blast. On the other hand, an open doorway is a danger and the necessity of putting baffles in front of Anderson shelter entrances applies to the blast as much as it does to the splinters.'[60]

He explained how shock waves could be reflected from tall buildings and how in narrow streets, the reflected suction wave might be much stronger than the original suction wave of the bomb and 'may produce violent effects on windows and doors in lower stories, drawing them out towards the street'. Reminding his listeners that the great majority of bombs explode either underground or inside buildings, he explored the consequences in these situations with his customary clarity. Such an authoritative lecture from a man, who could calmly separate the underlying processes from the all too familiar instant violence of explosions, was a rare example of informed discourse in the siege conditions of London. His remarks were picked up by the press, and one reporter described Sage as 'young, with a shock of yellow hair, and a collar that followed no scientific law'.[61]

The year ended with a huge *Luftwaffe* raid centred on St Paul's Cathedral, on the night of 29th December. Hundreds of incendiary bombs were dropped and although several landed on St. Paul's, it did not burn, unlike the Guildhall and eight other Wren churches in the city. Bernal watched the great fires, fanned by high winds, wandering around Lincoln's Inn Fields on the very edge of the inferno.[62] The Blitz brought disorder and danger, but also excitement that dispelled social restraints and dignity. Tom Hopkinson, the editor of *Picture Post* who had witnessed Sage's disquisition on Cyril Connolly's new religion, on another occasion asked Sage for simple precautions to increase the chances of surviving an air raid. He was told to lie face down in the gutter: 'gutters give good protection – blast and splinters will almost certainly fly over you.'[63]

Sage himself, on at least one night during the Blitz, took shelter in the basement of a flat owned by Lord Rothschild at 5 Bentnick Street, just off Oxford Street. Two of Rothschild's tenants were the Cambridge communists, Anthony Blunt and Guy Burgess, who gave the premises 'the air of a rather high-class disorderly house, in which one could not distinguish between the staff, the management and the clients'.[64] Burgess was working at the War Office and Blunt in MI5, alongside Rothschild who had recruited him. Malcolm Muggeridge, also working as a wartime intelligence officer, was taken to the flat once and found 'John Strachey, J.D. Bernal, Anthony Blunt and Guy Burgess, a whole revolutionary *Who's Who*'.[65] Muggeridge, ever the sharp-eyed moralist, felt a visceral repulsion for this millionaire's nest, 'Sheltering so distinguished a company – Cabinet Minister-to-be, honoured Guru of the Extreme Left-to-be, Connoisseur Extraordinary-to-be, and other notabilities, all in a sense grouped round Burgess; Etonian mudlark and sick toast of a sick society, as beloved along the Foreign Office corridors, in the quads and the clubs, as in the pubs among the pimps and ponces and street pick-ups, with their high voices and peroxide hair.'[66] He did not sense conspiracy in the room as much as 'decay and dissolution'.

The irresistible question arises as to whether there was any intrigue going on between Sage and Blunt and Burgess, who were later exposed as spies and were passing information to the Soviets during the war. Sage had known Rothschild since the latter became a Fellow of Trinity in 1935. Rothschild was a member of the Apostles, and he, Burgess and Blunt would all have been aware of Sage as one of Cambridge's leading communists. The flat was therefore a natural meeting place for like-minded Cambridge men, and there were even two left-wing Cambridge women living there, who might have been responsible for Sage's presence. It seems improbable that the Soviets during their recruitment drive of the 1930s in Cambridge would have overlooked Bernal, and his fervent communism, emotional detachment and ability to compartmentalize life would all seem to be good qualities for a spy.

Recent publication of the *Venona* decrypts has exposed both J.B.S. Haldane and Ivor Montagu as secret agents, who actively passed information to the Soviets early in the war, but there has been no suggestion that Sage was involved.[67] He had detailed knowledge of civil defence and bomb disposal, which would have been useful to the Nazis, to whom it could have been passed via the Soviets, if he had divulged any information to Blunt or Burgess in 1940 or early 1941. The circumstantial evidence for such indiscretions is non-specific, but colourful. Goronwy Rees, a journalist friend of Burgess who had joined the Army in 1939, recalled that visitors to Bentinck Street 'all appeared to be employed in jobs of varying importance, some of the highest, at various ministries; some were communists or ex-communists; all were a fount of gossip about the progress of the war, and the political machine responsible for conducting it ... to spend an evening at Guy's flat was rather like watching a French farce which has been injected with all the elements of political drama. Bedroom doors opened and shut; strange faces appeared and disappeared down the stairs where they passed some new visitor on his way up; civil servants, politicians, visitors to London, friends and colleagues of Guy's, popped in and out of bed and then continued some absorbing discussion of political intrigue, the progress of the war and the future possibilities of the peace.'[68]

For most of his life, Sage championed the Soviet Union and, with the possible exception of the period of the Hitler–Stalin pact, would have vigorously supported the unchecked flow of information from London to Moscow. As we shall see after the war, his pro-Soviet stance led him to become an increasingly controversial figure, despised by some, but his return to England in 1939 should be to his eternal credit. As a citizen of the Irish Free State, especially one with an American mother, he could have easily stayed in New York or California and secured a prestigious, well-financed, university post. But that would have been to miss the excitement and the endless diversity of the wartime challenges, which suited him so well.

10

Bombing Strategy

Although the crucial Battle of Britain was won by the magnificent few of Fighter Command, the RAF from its inception had been intended as an offensive bomber force. Sir Hugh Trenchard, the first Chief of Air Staff, pointed out to his fellow chiefs in 1929 that an air force held an advantage over an army or navy in being able to take the fight directly to the enemy nation, without needing to defeat its armed forces first. It could therefore 'attack direct the centres of production, transportation and communication from which the enemy war effort is maintained'.[1] Even more than the physical damage that an air force could wreak, Trenchard was aware of the fear that would be induced by heavy bombing and estimated that 'the moral effect of bombing stands undoubtedly to the material effect in a proportion of twenty to one'. Although the RAF's strategists preferred to avoid the unpalatable truth that the undermining of enemy morale by bombing required the indiscriminate killing of civilians, one of their political masters, Stanley Baldwin, made no bones about his vision of future warfare in a House of Commons debate in 1932. Baldwin's speech is famous for the phrase 'the bomber will always get through', a conclusion that was based on the impossibility of intercepting more than the odd plane flying through the vast volume of the skies, and led him to the terrible prophecy that to save your country, 'you have to kill more women and children more quickly than the enemy'.[2]

While Baldwin's words were heartfelt, they projected a mood of defeatism and fed an unrealistic hope for international disarmament. Churchill's riposte at the time that as soon as the disarmament negotiations in Geneva failed, the National Government should take 'measures necessary to place our Air Force in such a condition of power and efficiency that it will not be worth anyone's while to come here and kill our women and children in the hope that they may blackmail us into surrender'[3] served only to reinforce his reputation as a warmonger. Instead, Ramsay MacDonald and Baldwin showed their faith in the ideal of European disarmament by reducing the RAF and quickly losing air parity with Germany.

A vigorous challenge to Baldwin's fatalistic attitude appeared in a letter to *The Times* in August 1934. The writer disapproved of the prevailing assumption that there could be no defence against the bombing of cities. While agreeing that there was no present means of 'preventing hostile bombers from depositing their loads of explosives, incendiary materials, gases or bacteria upon their objectives ... [to suppose] that no method can be devised to safeguard great centres of population from such a fate appears to be profoundly improbable ... It seems not too much to say that bombing aeroplanes in the hands of gangster Governments might jeopardize the whole future of our Western civilization. To adopt a defeatist attitude in the face of such a threat is inexcusable until it has been definitely shown that all the resources of science and invention have been exhausted.' The letter was signed F.A. Lindemann, Professor of Experimental Philosophy, University of Oxford.

Frederick Lindemann was a prickly man, whose cynicism and cutting manner did not encourage easy friendship. Tall and athletic, he was a forbidding figure, habitually dressed in a dark suit with a bowler hat and tightly rolled umbrella to complete a most unlikely uniform for an English physicist of the interwar period. Indeed it was as though he needed to establish his Englishness through his appearance. His family was from Alsace, and his father emigrated to Devon after the Franco-Prussian War. His mother was American, but was at Baden-Baden taking the waters when Frederick was born in 1886. The family was very wealthy and not hidebound by any long-standing traditions. His father decided that the best scientific education for his sons would be in Germany and after attending schools in Darmstadt, Frederick became a doctoral student of Walter Nernst at the University of Berlin in 1908. While there, he got to know the giants of quantum theory such as Max Planck and Albert Einstein.

Lindemann was refused a commission in the British Army in 1914, his strong German connections being the unspoken reason, but was accepted the following year into a group of extremely talented young scientists at the Royal Aircraft Factory, Farnborough: 'It was the first time since leaving prep school that he had lived with his British contemporaries and he seems to have been uneasy, initially, lest he should not be fully accepted.'[4] Lindemann made his name at Farnborough by first his theoretical analysis and then his practical demonstration of the problem of a spinning aircraft. In order to test his theory, Lindemann took flying lessons and then proceeded, with reckless courage, to put a small biplane into a deliberate tailspin and to extricate it before it crashed. In the particular plane he used, with canvas-covered wings supported by wire struts, the ground below would have appeared to rotate every four seconds or so, and Lindemann would have experienced a force of $2.5g$ as the plane fell about 430 feet per turn.[5]

After the war, Lindemann was elected Dr Lee's Professor of Experimental Philosophy and became the head of the Clarendon Laboratory at Oxford – 'a magnificent mausoleum',[6] which could boast none of the pioneering research accomplishments nor the depth of talent that Rutherford found when he took over the Cavendish Laboratory the same year. Just as Lindemann felt himself rootless as an Englishman, so he was an outsider in the world of British physics. He shared with Bernal the distinction of being one of the two men that Rutherford actively disliked. Lindemann did not possess the creativeness of either Rutherford or Bernal as a scientist, but he did succeed in guiding the Oxford physics department into the first rank through his astute leadership. His most important hiring of research staff was done after travelling to Germany in his chauffeur-driven Rolls Royce to see Nernst. That was in May 1933, and he simply asked Nernst, 'Have you got anyone for me?'[7]

The fastidious, teetotal, vegetarian, non-smoking Lindemann did make one friend in the 1920s, who turned out to be even more powerful than Rutherford – Winston Churchill. He shared Churchill's Conservative politics, but what brought them together was Lindemann's broad knowledge of science (Einstein once described him as 'the last of the great Florentines' to emphasize his Renaissance quality), and his ability to explain the applications of science to the famously impatient statesman. Churchill described Lindemann, whom he invariably referred to as 'the Prof', as his 'chief adviser on the scientific aspects of modern war and particularly of air defence, and also on questions involving statistics of all kinds'.[8] Churchill's daughter, Sarah, remembered the Prof as being a constant part of their lives at Chartwell, at a time when Churchill was in the political wilderness. On one occasion after dinner, Churchill challenged the Prof to explain the quantum theory 'in words of one syllable and in no longer than five minutes . . . without any hesitation, like quicksilver, he explained the principle and held us all spellbound. When he had finished, we all spontaneously burst into applause.'[9]

Churchill and Lindemann kept up a ceaseless two-man campaign to rectify what they saw as official complacency in the face of the growing threat from German air power; they were especially distrustful of the British Air Ministry. In the summer of 1934, they went on holiday together in France and called in on the hapless Baldwin to remind him again of the need for a more active air defence policy. Lindemann wrote to Baldwin in November calling for a non-departmental committee with a chairman of Cabinet rank to be set up 'to find some method of defence against air bombing other than counter-attack and reprisals'.[10] On 28th November 1934, Churchill made a powerful speech, embarrassing the Government as he pointed out that the *Luftwaffe* was rapidly approaching parity with the RAF (a fact that was denied by Baldwin when winding up the debate). Churchill said that while not accepting the 'sweeping claims' of some alarmists, he believed that in a week or ten days' intensive bombing of London no less than '30,000 or 40,000 people would be killed or maimed' and in the subsequent panic three or four million people would be 'driven out into the open country'.[11] In December, Lindemann wrote again to Lord Londonderry, the Secretary of State for Air, still lobbying for a non-departmental committee. Londonderry, feeling the political heat from Churchill and one or two others, was relieved to be able to tell Lindemann that an Air Ministry Committee was being set up under the chairmanship of 'Mr Tizard' and Lindemann should get in touch with him.

Londonderry's letter was the first that Lindemann had heard about what quickly became known as the Tizard Committee, and may have sown the first seeds of distrust between two old but wary friends. Lindemann and Henry Tizard had first met in Nernst's department in Berlin, where Tizard, an impoverished Oxford chemistry graduate was in Lindemann's shadow academically and socially. Their subsequent war experiences were remarkably similar – Tizard was a scientific adviser to the Royal Flying Corps and also learned to fly himself (again managing to survive a tailspin). He was instrumental in setting up the first programmes to test flying equipment and a pioneer in quantifying the accuracy, or inaccuracy, of aerial bombardment. After the First World War, Tizard became an Oxford don and it was he who first put forward Lindemann's name for the Clarendon appointment.[12] The two men met at the Royal Society in November 1934 and Lindemann told Tizard of his proposal for a high-level committee on air defence; Tizard apparently offered his support, but did not mention to Lindemann that plans were already well advanced inside the Air Ministry for a Committee for the Scientific Survey of Air Defence. Tizard's reticence is understandable – his name was already being proposed as the chairman but he had not decided whether to accept – and he did not want to complicate matters or to make himself appear indiscreet by inviting Lindemann's interest. Although Lindemann still thought of Tizard as 'a good man', he implied to Churchill that he might have been tainted by his contact with the Air Ministry; nor was he reassured by the fact that the leading physicist on the Tizard Committee was to be Patrick Blackett, an inveterate socialist.

With Churchill's support, Lindemann set about securing a position for himself on the Tizard Committee, while continuing to push for the creation of a rival board under the Committee of Imperial Defence. In the words of Tizard's biographer, the Tizard Committee eventually became 'the custodian of the country's safety' through its successful adoption of the radar early warning system. The origin of radar was a memorandum on 'The detection and location of aircraft by radio methods' presented to the Committee at its first meeting in February 1935. The author was Robert Watson-Watt, a persuasive Scot, who was the head of the government's Radio Research Station in Slough. By the time Lindemann attended his first meeting in the summer of 1935, Watson-Watt had successfully demonstrated his prototype apparatus to Air Chief Marshal Dowding, and further experiments had confirmed the inventor's initial conviction of its worth. The harmony of the Tizard Committee was rudely shattered by Lindemann's first input in July 1935. He failed to grasp the overwhelming significance of the radar work and instead pressed his own ideas on Tizard – ideas, which the latter wryly commented, 'depend largely on two pre-conceived notions, both wrong'.[13] Following this inauspicious start, relations between Lindemann and the rest of the Committee worsened to the extent that the following summer the three original independent members, Blackett, A.V. Hill and Tizard himself, all resigned rather than continue to work with the Prof.

Although the Tizard Committee was immediately reconstituted, with Sir Edward Appleton taking Lindemman's place, and succeeded in integrating radar defence into Fighter Command, a bitter legacy remained between Lindemann and Tizard. In addition to the many coincidences already noted, both men were almost blind in one eye. Lindemann became a pilot after instantly memorizing the letters on the vision-testing chart and fooling the examiner; Tizard simply asked for permission to wear glasses under his flying goggles. Their outlooks on life were very different: Lindemann possessed a grasp of power politics that Tizard found distasteful. Tizard had a common touch and collegial manner that Lindemann completely lacked. Their inability to work together, apparent so soon in committee, would have major repercussions during the war to come.

At the outbreak of war, Churchill immediately installed Lindemann and a team of statisticians and economists at the Admiralty to supply him with data on all aspects of shipping and to scrutinize all the departmental papers that were circulated to the War Cabinet. Churchill used Lindemann's group to present him with a continuous stream of information on the war effort – he preferred it to be in diagram or chart form and any numbers had to be interpreted by Lindemann. The Prof was a member of his closest circle and, as Churchill explained to Lord Gort, the Commander-in-Chief of the British Expeditionary Force in 1940, 'in all my secrets'.[14] Churchill later gave a revealing assessment of his wartime relationship with Lindemann: 'There were no doubt greater scientists than Frederick Lindemann, although his credentials and genius command respect. But he had two qualifications of vital consequence to me. First... he was my trusted friend and confidant of twenty years. Together we had watched the advance and onset of world disaster. Together we had done our best to sound the alarm. And now we were in it, and I had the power to guide and arm our effort. How could I have the knowledge? Here came the second of his qualities. Lindemann could decipher the signals from the experts on the far horizons and explain to me in lucid, homely terms what the issues were.'[15]

Hard-working and productive though Lindemann's statistical department was, the cream of Britain's statisticians in 1940 were working on civil defence research at Princes Risborough, where they had been brought by Stradling and Bernal. They included Bradford Hill, the medical statistician from the London School of Hygiene and Tropical Medicine and Frank Yates, who had carried out important studies of crop production at the Rothamsted Experimental Station. Bernal may have met Yates through his plant virus work with Pirie and Bawden, and he subsequently introduced him to Zuckerman, starting an important collaboration on the quantification of bomb damage.

Less illustrious than Bradford Hill or Yates was Dr F. Garwood, and it was with him that Bernal worked on a remarkable theoretical exercise in the spring of 1940. Their intention was to make a realistic assessment of the damage that would result from an intensive air raid on a city. We have seen how Churchill in 1934 predicted tens of thousands of deaths in London from a week of bombing, and if anything, government estimates in the intervening years had become more apocalyptic. The basis for these calculations rested on the limited experience of German bombing in World War One, when about 300 tons of bombs had produced almost 5,000 casualties, of which about one third were fatal. The casualty rate in two daylight raids on London had been high, and the Air Staff assumed a casualty rate of about 50 per ton of bombs dropped on a city. In 1938, the Committee of Imperial Defence predicted that the *Luftwaffe* could maintain a daily rate of 600 tons on London alone and the Ministry of Health were projecting 600,000 deaths and twice that number wounded in the first six months of such a campaign.[16] These dire predictions took no account of the details of any raid, nor of any protection from shelters, and were crude linear extrapolations from meagre World War One data.

Bernal and Garwood set out to make a more realistic analysis and for verisimilitude chose the city of Coventry as 'an attractive target on account of its numerous aircraft factories'.[17] They worked from Ordnance Survey Maps and marked points on the maps where bombs might fall, and then assessed the likely damage and casualties from the explosion of 250 kg bombs. Bernal thought that even if Coventry were targeted because of its aircraft and engineering factories, *Luftwaffe* pilots would need an unmistakable aiming point. The analysis was run with two different bull's-eyes: Coventry Cathedral and the Humber car factory about one mile from the Cathedral. He and Garwood also allowed for probable error by drawing circles of different radii (one mile and 1/2-mile) to define areas in which there was a 50% chance of a bomb falling, when it was aimed at a conspicuous landmark at the centre. In this way they were able to build up spatial distributions of the bombs dropped on the city. The number of casualties caused by each bomb was then estimated, assuming people to be in their houses or in Anderson shelters or in factories, where they might be unsheltered or in trenches. Exact figures for total and factory populations were unavailable so Bernal and Garwood made estimates depending on whether the raid took place in daylight or at night. They ran their statistical model for different-sized raids (500 or 1,000 bombs), with two different aiming points, and for sheltered and unsheltered populations, with location varying depending on day or night attack. This was a much more meticulous analysis than any previously attempted and showed that 'the great majority of bombs do no damage at all, but that the greatest number of casualties are produced by direct hits on single shelters'.[18] For a one-thousand-bomb raid, the number of predicted casualties varied between 630 (at night with everyone sheltered) and 7,350 (daytime raid with no one sheltered). It appeared to them that 'in industrial towns a great saving of life could be brought about by improving the standard of factory shelter'.[19]

Bernal and Garwood's report appeared in June 1940 at a time before there had been any heavy bombing of British (or German) cities. On the night of 14th November, Coventry suffered the heaviest raid on any British city to date and the bombing was particularly destructive because the *Luftwaffe* were guided by *X-gerät*, a radio navigational aid which was accurate to about 100 yards at a range of up to 200 miles.[20] Bernal's assumption that the Cathedral would be the aiming point seems correct in that it was completely destroyed, and it is estimated that 500 tons of high explosive (HE) plus incendiary bombs were dropped during the night-long attack. More than five hundred people were killed, out of total casualties of just under two thousand. This was about twice the quantity of HE bombs used by Bernal and Garwood in their model, and if one doubles their estimates to reflect this, their closest figure of 2,260 casualties was based on a night raid, where the population took shelter and the probable error in dropping the bombs on the Cathedral was one mile. Even in what Churchill described as 'the most devastating raid which we sustained'[21] the casualty rate was about four per ton in comparison to the pre-war estimate of fifty per ton, and 'the all-important aero-engine and machine-tool factories were not brought to a standstill; nor was the population, hitherto untried in the ordeal of bombing, put out of action. In less than a week an emergency reconstruction committee did wonderful work in restoring the life of the city'.[22]

Once the German bombing started in earnest, it became clear to Bernal that the type of evidence that he and Zuckerman had collected on a sporadic basis needed to be compiled more systematically in order to build an accurate picture of the damage being caused. Zuckerman took the lead in establishing a

Casualty Survey, which had its London headquarters at Guy's Hospital. Most of the surveyors were young women like Renée Brittan, a student at Birkbeck College, who was recruited for the work by Brenda Ryerson and Bernal. Birkbeck had reopened for classes at weekends (instead of nights), and Renée fitted in the bomb survey work with her studies. She wandered around small streets 'in Bermondsey and Southwark, particularly in Bermondsey docklands and got a list of the "incidents" that happened the previous night. We went around the sites of the "incidents" as they were known, and measured the bomb holes, and drew maps of the surrounding physical damage and interviewed as many people as we could who had been involved, and took the information back to Guy's where we did our homework. Then I went home and did Birkbeck homework, which was due before the weekend lectures and started work again on Monday.' After collecting figures from the health department of the local Bermondsey Council on the dead and injured, she tried to plot the places where the casualties occurred: 'It was a mapping job: people, places, effects and of course the size of the bomb – a 25 pounder or a 50 pounder, no 25 kilos or 50 kilos – it was my first introduction to kilos I think.'[23]

The information collected and plotted by Renée and other field workers was sent to Oxford for analysis. Zuckerman wanted to know whether his experimental estimates about the effects of direct blast were valid and would give a reasonable estimate of what to expect in the field; he also wanted to find out to what extent bomb splinters or small fragments caused serious injuries to people during air raids. Frank Yates, the statistician introduced to the work by Bernal, quickly saw that the types of observations that Zuckerman had been making could be generalized into 'standardized casualty rates' that could be adjusted for the proportion of the population in shelters or in the open. As a result, Zuckerman was able to write a report on air-raid casualties that became 'the standard work on the subject'.[24]

Margaret Gardiner moved from her tiny cottage in Maidensgrove to a slightly bigger one in the Buckinghamshire village of Fingest. The arrangement suited Sage admirably since it was close to both Princes Risborough and the headquarters of Bomber Command in High Wycombe, where he was spending an increasing amount of time. His life was organized as much as it could be by another capable young woman Kathleen Watkins. She was a graduate and a Wren, who had been appointed as assistant secretary to the Civil Defence Research Committee in July 1940. After committee meetings, Sage always seemed to leave some of his belongings behind and it became her task to return them to him. He then would ask her to take some dictation for him and soon she became his personal assistant, working at Princes Risborough. Dictation proved a challenge because he would often not bother to finish one sentence before rushing on to the next. Miss Watkins subsequently wrote a guide for future secretaries, assuring them that there was 'no need to be afraid of him although many are. In spite of all appearances to the contrary, he is really good-tempered, kind-hearted and exceptionally reasonable. He expects you not so much to do what he tells you to do as to do what he meant to tell you to do, or what he would have told you to do if he'd thought it out more carefully. Do not mistake impatience for ill-humour; his time estimates are usually between 33–50% of time required (applies to his own work as well).'[25]

Margaret's son, Martin, now 'a most ill-disciplined small boy' according to one acquaintance, adored having regular visits from his father. Kathleen Watkins was struck by the likeness of father and son. She used to bicycle to Fingest on Sunday evenings to deliver papers to Sage for him to take up to London the next day. One summer's evening she arrived at the cottage, which appeared deserted. She called out and went upstairs to find Sage in bed with Martin reading *How the Leopard Got his Spots* – their faces looked identical.[26]

Bernal and Zuckerman's bomb survey findings were noticed at the highest level, and although the research was initially motivated by a desire to improve civil defence, their results were seen to have immediate application in weapon design. Churchill sent the following note to the Secretary of State for Air on 16th July 1941: 'Investigations by the Ministry of Home Security into the effect of German high-explosive bombs has shown that a far greater amount of damage is done by blast, which destroys building, etc., than by splinters, which find very few useful targets, especially at night, when most people are under cover. The higher the proportion of high explosive to bomb-case the greater the blast. If the weight of the metal case is increased we get more splinters. Our general purpose bombs have a charge-weight ratio of about 30–70. The Germans work with a larger ratio, about 50–50. These are not only more efficient for destroying cities; they are also cheaper.'[27] Churchill had a renewed interest in the effects of bombing because the Soviet Union had been invaded by the German army the previous month and, as he wrote to 'Monsieur Stalin', the RAF would continue to bomb German towns heavily 'to force Hitler to bring back some of his air-power to the West and gradually take some of the strain off you'.[28]

Like all British communists, Sage rejoiced at having the Soviets as anti-fascist allies after their period of appeasement. He was an enthusiastic contributor to a two-day symposium on 'Science and Marxist philosophy' held in London in August 1941. His account of the meeting was published in *Nature*, and was followed three weeks later by his review of present-day science and technology in the USSR. In this second article, Sage returned to a familiar theme of planning science to meet the needs of society, something which he thought the Soviets had been doing successfully for twenty years and which the British were finding difficult to manage even in wartime. He hoped that 'fighting together in a common cause, scientific workers in Great Britain will come to understand, far better than from any description, the new spirit and method which characterize science in the USSR, and that, in turn, we may be able to provide some of the advantages of a long tradition of discovery and criticism. The new world for which we are all fighting and working will need every contribution that science can bring.'[29]

After some heavy losses on daylight bombing raids, the RAF had confined itself to night flights over Germany from the spring of 1940. The primary objectives had been to bomb oil installations and aircraft factories, but with the continuing Blitz of London and other British cities, it was made clear in a series of directives to Bomber Command that incendiary bombing of areas surrounding the primary targets was encouraged to undermine German morale: thus began the area bombing of industrial German cities.[30] By the start of 1941, Bomber Command was steadily losing crews and planes, with no indication that their sacrifice was bringing about any worthwhile damage to the German war machine. The RAF remained, however, the only force that could attack the enemy, which was still trying to strangle Great Britain. Early in 1941, Sage became officially attached to Bomber Command in order to assist in the assessment of its operational performance. He spent most of his time in the photographic room, where the results of raids were charted, and quickly became aware that the accuracy of bombing at night, after journeys of several hundred miles with uncertain navigation in unpredictable winds and weather, was lamentable. This was well understood by the flight crews themselves. One pilot said to him: 'You can think it damn lucky, old boy, that we drop the bombs in the right country.'[31]

A senior officer at High Wycombe told Bernal that 'Bomber Command is not concerned with the results of bombing'[32] as long as their planes flew over Germany and as many as possible got back. But at the 'lowly level' of the photographic room, the Canadian officer in charge was 'unaccountably interested in the actual conduct of the war with the Germans rather than inter-service and inter-command politics'.[33] Sage promised him that he would see what he could do to improve matters, and the next time he spoke to Lindemann, he mentioned the unsatisfactory state of affairs at Bomber Command. Lindemann's response was dismissive – he was a regular visitor to High Wycombe on his journeys between Oxford and London, and received a steady supply of photographs showing the successes of the Bomber Command. Sage knew about this, because every time Lindemann came, he arrived with great ceremony in his Ministerial limousine and was received at the front entrance by the Air Marshal. There was also a standing instruction that

'Whenever a photograph could be obtained in which a British bomb could be seen exploding on any kind of target in Germany, it was blown up and sent to the PM.'[34] When this was explained to Lindemann, his initial reaction was one of 'blank incredulity', but Bernal insisted that he was being given a biased impression, and after repeated pleading, the Prof agreed to visit High Wycombe incognito.

So it was that the Prof and Sage drove from Princes Risborough in the latter's 1938 Austin 10 to 'a postern at the back' of the HQ from where they could make their way, unannounced, to the photographic room. Once the Prof saw the unglossed evidence, 'he was immediately convinced and horrified'. He turned to Bernal and said: 'You realize that I have not seen anything.' Sage replied diplomatically that he quite understood and thought that Lindemann would find the right way to deal with the situation. The consequence was that at the next meeting of the Air Council, the Prof, 'with characteristic suavity' congratulated Bomber Command on its performance, but recommended that a little more statistical analysis should be performed. He went on to propose that, Mr David Butt, an economist from his 'circus', should be seconded to Bomber Command for this purpose.[35]

Butt soon set about analysing photographs from one hundred different raids to determine the accuracy of RAF bombing around the stated aiming points. His results were available within weeks, and represented a stunning indictment of the existing bombing programme. Butt concentrated on the two-thirds of returning air-crews, who claimed to have reached their targets, and found that in fact only about one third of them came within a radius of five miles of the aiming point. In raids on the Ruhr valley, which was always covered by industrial haze, the proportion fell to one-in-ten. On moonless nights or in the face of active German fighter planes, the figures were even worse. Butt's sobering conclusions were met with disbelief by some in the higher reaches of Bomber Command; they were a complete repudiation of the idea of precision bombing.

The Butt Report would prove a major stimulus to the introduction of new navigational aids and the Pathfinder squadrons; it made a deep impression on Churchill, who now realized that the claims made by Bomber Command were exaggerated. His memorandum to the Chief of the Air Staff, dated 7th October 1941, while expressing hope that 'the air offensive against Germany will realise the expectations of the Air Staff' warned against 'placing unbounded confidence in this means of attack'.[36] He cautioned that even 'if all the towns of Germany were rendered largely uninhabitable it does not follow that the military control would be weakened or even that war industry could not be carried on . . . It may well be that German morale will crack, and that our bombing will play a very important part in bringing the result about. But all things are always on the move simultaneously, and it is quite possible that the Nazi war-making power in 1943 will be so widely spread throughout Europe as to be to a large extent independent of the actual buildings in the homeland.' The memorandum mildly admonished the Air Staff for its pre-war assessments of the destruction that would be wrought by air raids, the prospect of which paralysed statesmen of the day, contributed to the desertion of Czechoslovakia in 1938 and 'after the war had begun, taught us sedulously to believe that if the enemy acquired the Low Countries, to say nothing of France, our position would be impossible owing to the air attacks'. In this penetrating note, Churchill was thinking subtly about complex issues and reached, what with hindsight, appears to be a balanced position. It also demonstrated that he had assimilated Bernal and Zuckerman's major findings, no doubt with the benefit of Lindemann's explanation, as well as the Butt Report.

Before the war, Bernal and Lindemann had known each other by reputation, an arrangement more likely to produce mutual repulsion than attraction. It is possible that they might have crossed paths at the country house of Lord Melchett, who was friendly with both men, but their first recorded meeting was when the Prof came as a guest, with Melchett, to a Tots and Quots dinner in March 1940. Zuckerman's minutes of the occasion recorded Sage as making his characteristic plea for the effective planning of science, when the Prof intervened to point out that the war first had to be won before the future of science could be considered – the minutes do not record whether the Prof's remark was delivered with his characteristic sneer.[37] Undaunted, Sage replied that unless the role of scientist was greatly expanded, the war would not be won. Zuckerman, a more emollient and flexible character than Bernal, contented himself with the observation that 'the Prof could always be relied upon to stir dissent, even when he stated the obvious'.[38]

Zuckerman knew the Prof well – they were both Fellows of Christ Church, Oxford and often conversed in the Common Room after dinner. They met there one evening late in August 1941 and naturally talked about the progress of the war. It did not take long for the subject of bombing to come up, since Zuckerman was in the midst of analysing the data collected by the Casualty Survey and was writing papers on blast injury and the wounding mechanism of high-velocity missiles. Lindemann, who had been given a barony in June, was now Lord Cherwell of Oxford. He had just returned from Newfoundland with Churchill on the battleship *Prince of Wales* after the first meeting with President Roosevelt. One of the first documents Cherwell received on his return to London was the Butt Report, and its unhappy findings were at the forefront of his mind as he talked to Zuckerman. While not disclosing the contents of the report to Zuckerman, Cherwell was 'much concerned about the hostile reaction in official and unofficial quarters to our bomber offensive'.[39] There was a growing feeling in the face of the shipping losses to U-boats in the North Atlantic that Bomber Command's attention should be turned to anti-submarine measures and more new planes should be diverted to Coastal Command. Cherwell thought that it would be a mistake to ease up on the offensive against the German homeland, since it was possible that the performance of Bomber Command could be improved, and he asked about ways of assessing the overall damage done in heavy raids.

Zuckerman thought that some measure of what could be achieved 'as a result of a "unit attack" of, say, a thousand tons of bombs against a German city by deriving a corresponding measure from German attacks against selected British cities'.[40] The cities he had in mind were Birmingham (an engineering and munitions center) and Hull (a port). The Ministry of Home Security had initiated a Bomb Census in 1940 so that a record was made of every bomb dropped on the United Kingdom, with estimates by local observers of the resulting damage and casualties. Zuckerman knew from Bernal that the bomb tallies were accurate for Birmingham and Hull. Cherwell told Zuckerman that he was interested in such questions as 'how many tons of bombs does it take to break a town' and 'how should the bombs be delivered – should it be in one sharp attack, or in what ratios should the total load be distributed and over how many nights'.[41]

The request to survey Birmingham and Hull soon arrived at Princes Risborough. Stradling selected Bernal and Zuckerman to carry out the work, with Zuckerman in charge of casualty and social aspects, and Sage in charge of everything else. Two teams of about forty members each were assembled over the next two months, and they mounted the most detailed day-to-day analysis of the economies and wartime stresses of the two cities, recording 'everything in great detail from the number of pints drunk to the number of aspirins bought'.[42] There were three major raids on Birmingham between June 1940 and July 1941, while Hull experienced four in the shorter period March to November 1941. The Bomb Census showed that for an area with a radius of about twenty miles around Hull, a total of 960 tons of bombs were dropped, of which one third fell within five miles of the city centre. To study the effects on the cities' populations and general way of life, seven thousand questionnaires were completed and analysed. Several thousand essays were collected from schoolchildren, giving their impressions of life in the air raid shelters, and how the bombings affected them and their families. Production figures for over six hundred factories were obtained for the periods in question, and detailed structural studies were made for some one hundred factories, mills and storehouses.

Results began to emerge early in 1942 and a short final report was delivered on 8th April.[43] At the centres of the cities the calculated density of high explosive (HE) bombs was forty tons per square mile, and at that intensity there was no evidence of breakdown of morale: 'In neither town was there any evidence of panic resulting from a series of raids or from a single raid.'[44] The destruction of homes (typically by HE bombs and not by fire) caused the most public distress, and thirty-five people were de-housed for every one killed. But a large city like Birmingham could absorb the bombed-out population easily, and temporary evacuation did little to disrupt work patterns. When it came to the local economy, it was found that the direct loss of production in Birmingham due to raids was only about five per cent. What losses there were resulted almost entirely from direct damage to factories, which in distinction to dwellings, proved very susceptible to fire. Crucial machine tools were extensively damaged by fire (which in most cases could have been prevented by adequate water supplies and better fire services), but overall only two per cent of factories were seriously damaged by high explosive. Transportation was only interrupted temporarily in the absence of continuous attacks. In conclusion, the authors wrote that they were not yet in a position 'to state what intensity of raiding would result in the complete breakdown of the life and work of a town, but it is probably of the order of 5 times greater than any that has been experienced in this country up till now'.[45]

Bernal's pocket diary[46] for 1942 shows that he had multiple meetings early in the year with the three protagonists in what became the most infamous dispute involving WW II scientists. In its first iteration, it was essentially an argument about Bomber Command's operational performance, although there were also personal differences adding some acidity to the mix. Two decades later with two of the principals dead, the debate was revived by C.P. Snow, essentially as a morality play. On both occasions, Bernal was a peripheral figure, but his role was influential.

On 29th January, Sage had lunch with Lord Cherwell. Despite the recent entry of the United States, the war was going badly with the Japanese overrunning South-East Asia, and Rommel's tank forces rampant in the desert of North Africa. Churchill that day wound up a three-day Vote of Confidence debate, in which he had warned the House that 'worse is to come'.[47] There is no record of the conversation between Bernal and Cherwell, but the lunch would have been at the latter's behest, and the main reason surely was to glean information from the surveys of Birmingham and Hull. On 10th and 13th of February, Sage had meetings with Tizard, who was still prominent as an unofficial scientific adviser to the government and service chiefs, although operating always in Cherwell's shadow. Bernal gave Tizard a summary paper on the Birmingham and Hull surveys, which Tizard noted as showing, on the whole, that 'the effect on production and morale has been surprisingly small'.[48] The week after his meetings with Bernal, Tizard wrote to the Secretary of State for Air stating that 'the present policy of bombing Germany is wrong' and much the same effect of tying up German resources on home defence 'could be achieved by steady bombing on a much smaller scale than is at present contemplated by the Air Staff.[49] Tizard thought that far more effort should be put into using long-range bombers to attack the German U-boats and to protect North Atlantic convoys. At the same time, Tizard wrote to the Deputy Chief of the Air Staff pointing out that during the previous nine months Bomber Command had lost more than seven hundred planes and, with them, probably as many crew members as Germans killed by the bombs dropped. The Air Marshal's immediate reaction was that Tizard had 'been seeing too much of Professor Blackett . . . [who was, in turn,] biting the hand that fed him'.[50]

The Bernal diary shows that he had been seeing plenty of Professor Blackett, newly appointed as the Admiralty's Chief Adviser on Operational Research, having already pioneered operational research (OR) in the Anti-Aircraft and Coastal Commands. Blackett was a Navy man, having served as a gunnery officer and then lieutenant in World War One; he held to the ethical principle that wars should be fought between opposing armed forces and that the enemy's civilian population should not be made a deliberate target.[51] In early 1942, he made his own estimates of the casualties that Bomber Command were likely to be inflicting on German citizens. The method he chose was to base his calculations on the known effectiveness of German bombing of England between August 1940 to June 1941, and after making allowances for bomb types and navigational errors to project the outcome of the RAF bombing raids for 1941. His estimate of 400 civilian deaths per month was shown to be remarkably accurate after the war,[52] and it seems very probable that he would have discussed his calculations with Bernal (and to have relied on him for data on bomb detonation and tonnage dropped on Britain). Whatever degree of collaboration there was between Sage and Blackett, they both delivered their notes to Tizard at the same time.

Aside from his briefing by Bernal in January, Cherwell was also being fed information by Zuckerman, who received a letter from D.M. Butt, dated 24th February, saying 'Lord Cherwell has quoted in conversation some figures you gave him relating air-raid casualties to the tonnage of bombs and the density of housing, and has asked me to do certain calculations which involve them. He did not seem, however, entirely clear about the definitions and . . . you could perhaps let me have a note of them. What I am particularly anxious to get is the casualties per ton in areas with different housing densities.'[53] Butt's letter closed with the assurance that 'We do not want to anticipate any results of the Birmingham–Hull survey, but these figures are rather essential to an argument on quite different matters.'

Butt was plainly doing his master's bidding, and because he did not know why the Ministry of Home Security survey was commissioned in the first place, the study he was now working on must have seemed quite different to the survey. Lord Cherwell, however, was pursuing his original intention of assembling evidence to support the devastation of Germany from the air. Cherwell started to construct his own argument from the Hull–Birmingham statistics, using simple logic (which appealed to the politicians and airforce chiefs) to reach false conclusions. Like any minute to Churchill, Cherwell's had to be kept to one side of paper and was delivered on 30th March, before circulation to the Defence Committee on 9th April. It read in part:

Careful analysis of the effects of raids on Birmingham, Hull and elsewhere have shown that, on the average, 1 ton of bombs dropped on a built-up area demolishes 20–40 dwellings and turns 100–200 people out of house and home... We know from our experiences that we can count on nearly 14 operational sorties per bomber produced. The average lift of the bombers we are going to produce over the next 15 months will be about 3 tons. It follows that each of the bombers will in its lifetime drop about 40 tons of bombs. If these are dropped on built-up areas they will make 4,000–8,000 people homeless.

In 1938 over 22 million Germans lived in 58 towns of over 100,000 inhabitants, which, with modern equipment, should be easy to find and hit. Our forecast output of heavy bombers (including Wellingtons) between now and the middle of 1943 is about 10,000. If even half the load of 10,000 bombers were dropped on the built-up areas of these 58 German towns the great majority of their inhabitants (about one-third of the German population) would be turned out of house and home.

Investigation seems to show that having one's house demolished is most damaging to morale. People seem to mind it more than having their friends or even relatives killed. At Hull signs of strain were evident, although only one-tenth of the houses were demolished. On the above figures we should be able to do ten times as much harm to each of the principal 58 German towns. There seems little doubt that this would break the spirit of the people.[54]

This statement was regarded by Zuckerman as a misrepresentation, since he and Bernal had concluded that there was no breakdown of morale in either Hull or Birmingham, but Cherwell could have pointed to the following passage in their report:

The situation in Hull has been somewhat obscured... by the occurrence of trekking [people leaving the town at night to take shelter in surrounding countryside], which was made possible by the availability of road transport and which was much publicized as a sign of breaking morale, but which in fact can be fairly regarded as a considered response to the situation. In both towns actual raids were, of course, associated with a degree of alarm and anxiety, which cannot in the circumstances be regarded as abnormal, and which in no instance was sufficient to provoke mass anti-social behaviour.[55]

While Cherwell was selective in his reading of the Bernal–Zuckerman report, the greatest fallacies in his own minute resulted from false assumptions that were immediately obvious to Tizard and Blackett. Bernal and Zuckerman were not privy to its contents, although it is possible that Bernal learned of them from Blackett. Cherwell's paramount error in Blackett's eyes was to assume that all the bombers to be delivered from the factories in the next eighteen months, would, during the same period, drop their full quota of bombs on Germany. As a result, Blackett thought 'Lord Cherwell's estimate of what can be achieved is at least six hundred per cent too high.'[56]

Tizard challenged nearly every statistic given by Cherwell, and told him that 'the way you put the facts as they appear to you is extremely misleading and may lead to entirely wrong decisions being reached, with a consequent disastrous effect on the war.'[57] The Tizard view would be confirmed in the official post-war history, which observed that the policy of area bombing 'could not be justified by the probability calculations themselves because the calculations seemed probable only to those who, in any case, believed in the policy'.[58] At the end of April, Tizard combined his criticisms with Blackett's in a detailed memorandum to Cherwell and the Air Minister in order to show that 'a policy of bombing German towns wholesale in order to destroy dwellings cannot have a decisive effect by the middle of 1943'. In an accompanying letter, he also attempted conciliation with Cherwell, saying that he did not 'really disagree with you fundamentally, but only as a matter of timing . . . [because] we must preserve command of the seas, and it is difficult for me to see how we are going to do this without strong support of the Navy by long-range bombers'.[59]

Blackett and Tizard were correct about the shortcomings in Cherwell's proposal, but they were seeking to be objective and he was not. Tizard knew this and 'was never prepared to accept any opinion emanating from Cherwell as an honest one'.[60] Soon after Churchill became Premier in 1940, Tizard had contributed to a scathing memorandum 'On the making of technical decisions by HM Government' deploring Churchill's exclusive reliance on the Prof for technical advice. In the words of the memorandum:

Professor Lindemann . . . is completely out of touch with his scientific colleagues. He does not consult with them, he refuses to co-operate or to discuss matters with them, and . . . his judgement is too often unsound . . . He has no special knowledge of many of the matters in which he takes a hand . . . Most serious of all is the fact that he is unable to take criticism or to discuss matters frankly with and easily with those who are intellectually and technically at least his equals.[61]

Despite all that he had achieved at the Clarendon Laboratory, the Prof was still not accepted by the British scientific community; when he was elevated to the peerage in 1941, Churchill's private secretary predicted it would 'cause anger in many quarters and especially at Oxford, but not as much as when it is learned that he proposes to call himself Lord Cherwell of Oxford'.[62] On hearing of the title, Tizard's only comment was 'the Cherwell is a small and rather muddy stream'.[63] But Tizard knew that he could never match Cherwell in influence once Churchill became Prime Minister, and for all Tizard's own great contributions, Cherwell had an annoying habit of wrong-footing him. Tizard was not as tough as Cherwell and lacked his visceral hatred of the Germans.

Churchill's promise of 'worse is to come' made at the end of January 1942 was amply fulfilled by March. Singapore had fallen, and the Japanese had invaded Java and Burma; the US Navy proved completely unready to defend its Atlantic coastal waters and U-boats were sinking an increasing tonnage of shipping. Closer to home, the two battle-cruisers *Scharnhorst* and *Gneisenau* were able to pass through the English Channel, to the dismay of the British public. Stalin was pressing for an Allied amphibious landing in northern Europe that would create a Second Front to draw German troops away from the Eastern Front. Roosevelt made it clear to Churchill that this would not be practicable for at least two years, and in the meanwhile British Intelligence decrypts of Enigma signals were suggesting a renewed German offensive against Russia in the summer. Under 'the continuous crushing pressure of events' as his daughter put it, it was not surprising that Churchill was at a low ebb.[64]

Against these disasters, Bomber Command was the only way to demonstrate a continued will to fight. Churchill remarked to Sir Charles Portal, the Chief of Air Staff on 13th March, that while the raids on Germany were 'not decisive' they were 'better than doing nothing, and indeed a formidable method of injuring the enemy'.[65] With the foreknowledge of German plans, Churchill wanted to mount the heaviest British air offensive against Germany possible to take 'the weight off Russia'.[66] Cherwell was aware of all these factors and his most important role was to give Churchill continued encouragement. It was a time when any call for restraint would have seemed like defeatism. Even if Bernal and Zuckerman had been allowed to present their own findings directly to Churchill and the Defence Committee, it is doubtful whether the outcome would have been different. Their one-page summary of conclusions could easily have been accepted at face value, but the rejoinder would have been that if the present level of bombing was ineffective, it needed to be stepped up. Indeed, this was the nub of the Air Ministry's response in early May to the Ministry of Home Security report. It dismissed the raids on Birmingham as 'light' and suggested that Bernal and Zuckerman's data collected from a year earlier were no longer relevant: 'what was true of England then is not true of England now, still less of Germany.'[67] As the official history of the RAF offensive against Germany concluded, 'The Air Staff... had already devised this theme [of area bombing] towards the end of 1941 and Lord Cherwell had added little that was new. All the same because of the position which he occupied and the time at which he submitted the minute, Lord Cherwell's intervention was of great importance. It did much to insure the concept of strategic bombing in its hour of crisis.'[68]

Later in 1942, following some success for the allies, Sir Charles Portal the Commander-in-Chief of Bomber Command turned his mind to the question of what scale of bombing would be required to undermine the Nazi industrial and economic war machine, so that Germany could be conquered by relatively small land forces. He persuaded his fellow Chiefs of Staff to the view that 'the heavy bomber will be the main weapon' in this endeavour and should therefore have 'absolute priority of Anglo-American production'.[69] The Chiefs of Staff (COS) also expressed confidence that with the technical improvements now in place, the performance of Bomber Command would be far superior to the limited results attained since 1940. These statements represented a notable endorsement of the Air Staff, but after two weeks of harmony the Admiral of the Fleet, Sir Dudley Pound, began to have second thoughts. On reflection, he was unconvinced by some of Portal's estimates of what Bomber Command could achieve and suggested that an 'objective scientific analysis' be carried out by a committee which would include Cherwell, Tizard, Bernal and Blackett amongst its membership. Portal disagreed on the basis that the proposed members of the committee 'would probably roam about over a very wide field' and he doubted 'whether they would agree with one another or we with them'.[70] If the COS really wanted further scientific advice, 'Lord Cherwell should be asked to give or obtain an authoritative opinion.'

Bernal wrote a perceptive note to Blackett on area bombing soon after the war: 'I think', he said, 'it might be stressed that air staffs on neither side had really worked out the quantitative aspects of strategic bombing: the Germans possibly because they did not intend to use it, ourselves because the then level of staff thinking had not got around to quantitative aspects. I still remember being told that the high level of Bomber Command was not interested in the results of bombing. The tragedy is that this excuse will not hold for the policy on German cities which was adopted later in the war. We had ample and numerical information from the Bomb Survey in R. and E. [Ministry of Home Security]. The fact is the policy was decided for three closely interrelated reasons: (a) it was an RAF policy: the old Trenchard policy justifying the separation of the RAF from the Army; (b) the attitude of Churchill and Cherwell, who felt that little could be done with the Army and that they must concentrate on the RAF and consequently on strategic bombing; (c) the desire to provide an alternative for the Second Front.'[71]

Bernal felt that Cherwell 'twisted the results' of the Ministry of Home Security survey to suit his purposes, by arguing that since the degree of bombing by Germany had a negligible effect on production in the English cities, 'much heavier bombing of German cities was bound to have an enormous effect'. He thought Cherwell's worst fault was 'his deliberate and dishonest neglect of what we came to call the operational factor: the ratio found between what happens in the field and what happens in trials under the best possible conditions or even worse what is supposed to happen.'[72] It was Cherwell's betrayal of scientific truth that Bernal, Blackett and Tizard found unforgivable. In the wartime disputes, Bernal thought Tizard was at a great disadvantage because he could never promise such returns as Cherwell did and 'had much less appeal to the totally unquantitative and romantic mind of Churchill'.[73]

11

Combined Operations

In 1941 the BBC began a weekly radio programme called the *Brains Trust*. It was to prove popular and uplifting to a nation straining to resist the Nazis. The undoubted star was 'Professor' Cyril Joad, the head of Birkbeck's philosophy department, but not in fact a professor of the University. To give himself time to answer a question, he would invariably start with the gambit, 'It all depends what you mean by...' Bernal was another regular member of the Trust, and was valued, amongst other qualities, as being a match for the populist Joad. The *Brains Trust* on 7th December 1941 comprised Joad, Bernal, Cyril Connolly (the essayist), a clergyman and a naval commander.[1] Sage was in his element. The first question about the Aurora Borealis, from a twelve-year-old boy, was naturally his to answer. The next, 'What service does the speculator on the Stock Exchange render to the community?' found no takers and so Bernal offered an opinion. After giving a textbook economics answer on competitive markets arriving at the ideal value of a security 'by a mystical concourse of wills', he went on to say that he did not believe a word of it: the speculator was either gambling or attempting to corner the market.

He apologized to his fellow panelists when the next question was 'What do scientists mean by an expanding universe?' before discussing the Milky Way, red shift, and the idea he credited to Abbé Lemaître that 'the whole universe started as just one atom that just exploded and went in all directions'. More philosophical questions followed, such as 'What is the nature of evil?' which Joad and the clergyman clearly regarded as their bailiwick. Sage chimed in at the end with a relativist view that must have unsettled an audience who thought the answer was probably 'Hitler'. He said, 'I don't think evil has any objective existence at all. I think the reason behind the myth is that in society, when people started living together, they didn't always suit each other. Out of that grew the harmonious thing we call *good*, and the disharmonious or conflict-producing thing which we call *evil*. And there is no need to invoke myths or any remoter explanations for a very simple sociological fact.'

The final question was on a subject dear to Bernal's heart – should there be a temporary ban on applied science research to allow humanity to recover from the devastation of war. While understanding the sentiment behind the question, Bernal took the opposite tack of calling for more research. He said 'we haven't begun to see what science could do for human beings' and blamed scientists for staying in their ivory towers, believing that it was their job to find things out but no concern of theirs what was done with their discoveries afterwards. During the broadcast, Bernal displayed a breadth of knowledge and an ability to talk brilliantly that none of the other panelists could match.

Cyril Connolly came to stay at Fingest that Christmas. Prompted perhaps by his dazzling performances on the *Brains Trust*, Connolly asked Sage to write an essay for his new magazine, *Horizon*, setting out his thoughts on man and the world at that pivotal moment in history. The result was 'The freedom of necessity'[2] – Bernal's reaction to the precarious international situation. The tone he adopted was that of a secular prophet, who saw the present conflict as 'the most terrible and at the same time the most hopeful of wars' which marked a change in human affairs 'more important than any that has happened for many thousands of years'. The great social transformation taking place was, in his view, the culmination of four centuries of increased power over nature through the use of science that had brought humans to the point where they could begin to control the conditions of their lives. With this new freedom brought by knowledge, came new responsibilities greater than those borne by any previous generations, and the realization that human cooperation was a necessity because it was the only alternative to increasing poverty, insecurity and death. The possibility for human unity was again the result of scientific progress leading to increased communication and economic interdependence.

It appeared to Sage that the whole world was becoming Marxist because 'in wartime, we are coming naturally to think and act in terms of directed economic and social organisation... In every industrial region of the world today – and non-industrial countries can have no effective say in world affairs – there exists a form of planned economy determining the quantity and quality of production, fixing the movements and the occupations of the population. More and more the capitalist states are showing an external similarity, in their means of control of production and distribution, to the planned socialist economy of the Soviet Union.'[3]

Sage credited Hitler with understanding the nature of the historical social transformation to communism and reasoned that Hitler's appeal to aggressive nationalist feelings was an attempt to thwart the ultimate establishment of a democratically organized or socialist 'world order'. Sage was anxious to avoid the pitfalls of seeking utopia, and, rather than set out ideals for society, suggested what was needed was a greater understanding of the process of transforming society, 'sufficient to enable us to see which things are worth attempting and which are doomed because of the inherent contradictions which they contain'.[4] The inherent contradiction that could never endure was a society where 'one class has a definite advantage over others [because] that class is bound either to sweep away or to evade its constitutional limitations and to generate among the rest of the population an antagonism that sooner or later comes to revolution or war'. While a new society should address the universal demand for justice, it was more important to establish the right social and economic conditions and assume that individual human rights would follow. This was what had happened in the Soviet Union where the 'constitution not only guarantees the liberal rights of equality before the law, but also the new rights of employment, of education and of security in illness and in old age'. Such a constitution could be drawn up only 'after the achievement of a socially operated and controlled productive system'. The USA, by contrast, lacked 'the economic and political basis that could secure and guarantee' President Roosevelt's promise of freedom of speech, freedom of worship, freedom from want and freedom from fear.

Sage's faith in the Soviet system as the model for the post-war world was unshakeable when he wrote 'The freedom of necessity'. The quotes above praising the Soviet Union are but a few examples of the many contained in the essay, which ran to nearly sixty pages. The sting in the tail was reserved for 'the ruling class of this country [who] did not go into the war to save democracy; they do not know what democracy is and if they did they would not like it. They went into the war to save their status, their pockets and their skins, and even in the war they have not forgotten that their position has to be secure, not only against the enemy, but against each other and against the Common people... Class-vested interests in the civil service and the fighting services have resulted in our slow and unadaptable response to modern fighting conditions on land, sea and in the air... We have failed for eighteen months to assist the only ally that can resist and has resisted the Nazis. Ostensibly this is for tactical reasons; we are told we have been unprepared and we are still unprepared for a second front in Europe. The way things are going, and with the people we have directing them, there is no guarantee that we will not always be in this state.' Nor did Sage spare the Trade Unions and the Labour Party who had allowed themselves to be bought off by marginal increases in real goods for the working class, and would not face up to the need for violent action on occasion to produce the necessary disruption of the existing system. 'Neither the people nor their leaders had any social philosophy, and the latter were even proud of the fact and spent what little intellectual energy they had in attacking Marxism, which presented the only coherent account of society and its changes.'[5]

The Association of Scientific Workers (AScW) held a two-day conference on science and the war effort in January 1942. The speakers were mostly rank-and-file scientists engaged in practical work in factories as well as in research laboratories. Discussion ranged over issues of training and efficiency, and covered a wide variety of subjects such as agriculture and food, building and housing, and air-raid precautions (ARP). There were many grievances of a general nature, and in particular the perceived lack of contact between the Services and scientific workers. In his summary of the proceedings, Bernal 'stated that if the truth could be told, the situation would seem to be even worse than that described by the speakers from their first-hand experience'; in his view, 'the opposition to scientific workers in the last few months is equivalent to sabotage, and perhaps something rather stronger'.[6]

In 'The freedom of necessity', Sage seemed to exclude Churchill from his strictures about the ruling class; although not naming him, he did remark that 'it is not enough to have a great leader'.[7] In general though, he felt that the ruling class, while not active traitors, 'will not press things unduly, they will not take risks, they will not demand the impossible'. These concerns do not seem to have given Sage any pause when, in April 1942, he was approached by Lord Louis Mountbatten to join Combined Operations (CO). Mountbatten was one of Queen Victoria's great-grandchildren, and for two decades had combined a playboy existence with a career in the Royal Navy. At the outbreak of war, he held the rank of captain, and after a period commanding destroyers, which demonstrated both his courage and his questionable judgement, he was suddenly appointed by Churchill as Chief of Combined Operations (CCO). In his new role, he became a junior member of the Chiefs of Staff Committee, and in order to carry the necessary authority in any discussions about Commando activity, Churchill promoted him Vice-Admiral with the honorary ranks of General and Air Marshal. Without question a member of the ruling class, Mountbatten loved risk-taking and would prove to have quite a taste for the impossible.

An unlikely affection developed between the royal sailor and the communist scientist. Sage thought Mountbatten 'had the habit that great commanders have of acting first and thinking afterwards',[8] a judgement fondly meant, but one which could provide ammunition to those modern historians who have come to view him as a vainglorious and reckless commander. On his appointment as CCO, Mountbatten's first move was to bring along some of his own courtiers such as the Marquis de Casa Maury, a Cuban who shared his love for speed in cars and polo ponies, whom he appointed as head of intelligence, and Sir Harold Wernher, one of the richest men in England, as his chief of procurement. In March 1942, Mountbatten received a letter from Leo Amery, a member of the War Cabinet, recommending the services of Geoffrey Pyke, the spat-wearing eccentric, whom Sage had first met at a Bloomsbury soirée in the 1920s. Pyke had pursued a characteristically wayward course in the darkening European scene before the war. He set up the Voluntary Industrial Aid society during the Spanish Civil War, which amongst other contributions, sent Harley-Davidson motorcycles modified with side-cars to serve as field ambulances. Just before Germany invaded Poland in the summer of 1939, Pyke had been in Germany with a group of researchers, in the guise of visiting English golfers carrying out surveys of public opinion towards the Nazis and their prospects for military success.[9] Pyke, in fact, would have been turned away at the door of most English golf clubs: his already spare frame had become emaciated as a result of chronic lung disease, his dark beard was untrimmed and he did not possess a tie. Pyke arrived at the ducal townhouse that served as Combined Operations Headquarters (COHQ) in a particularly scruffy pair of trousers – 'flannels that had no turn-ups and were inches above his battered crepe-soled shoes'. He was shown in to see the immaculately dressed Rear-Admiral and lost no time in presenting his credentials, announcing, 'Lord Mountbatten you need me on your staff because I am a man who thinks.'[10]

Mountbatten had been given the task of harrying the Nazis in occupied Europe by staging dramatic raids, with the ultimate objective of launching the largest ever sea-borne invasion across the Channel. He decided that he needed unorthodox thinkers like Pyke to supplement the input of more conventional minds schooled in the military staff colleges. He discussed his plans with Henry Tizard, saying that he 'wanted to get two first-rate scientists who would be put on to the operational analysis of devices and equipment and techniques for the landing that was to come'.[11] Tizard suggested the names of Bernal and Zuckerman, who were fast becoming the boffin equivalent of Gilbert and Sullivan. Mountbatten wrote to them both. Sage replied that he would accept as long as Zuckerman came too. When they arrived at COHQ in Richmond Terrace close by Scotland Yard, morale was buoyant as a result of the brilliantly executed Bruneval Raid at the end of February. RAF reconnaissance planes had gathered photo-reconnaissance evidence of a German *Wuerzburg* radar installation at Bruneval, near Le Havre. A company of men from the 1st Parachute Brigade was dropped on a moonlit night, inland of the target, and succeeded in overrunning the installation, removing vital parts of the equipment and capturing its operator before being picked up on a nearby beach by navy boats. The time spent on French soil was about two hours, and the British casualties and missing were fifteen in total.[12]

The Bruneval Raid was a small but spectacular success, made even more notable by the losses that the Allies were experiencing in more far-flung places. In the first few months of Mountbatten's period in charge, the staff at COHQ grew from two dozen to over 350 and they seemed immune from the penny-pinching controls that restricted other Whitehall departments.

After recruiting Bernal and Zuckerman, Mountbatten sent a memorandum introducing them to his military planning staff, saying that they should be involved in operational planning from the very beginning so that 'when their scientific knowledge is required, they may be completely in the picture'.[13] Both Scientific Liaison Officers reported to a retired naval captain, Tom Hussey, who was called CXD – Coordinator of Experiments and Development – Mountbatten had a passion for crisp, meaningless, initials. He also managed to weld together the first, true, inter-services force, which shed traditional loyalties completely and developed its own style of combat. A junior Army officer seconded to Combined Operations found Mountbatten's headquarters 'bursting with young soldiers, sailors and airmen who had not only been elaborately trained in the technique of combined operations but had both planned them and carried them out in person... They all talked learnedly about tides and wind and moon and weather, of navigation by sea and air, of beach gradients and landing craft... To join this fish–flesh–fowl company was to find oneself almost literally at sea or up in the air; one felt oneself hopelessly earthbound, a clumsy and ignorant landlubber.'[14]

Zuckerman's first task was to calculate the number of nights per month that the weather, the moon and tides would be suitable for small commando raids across the Channel: his conclusion was that there would never be such a night. Zuckerman was also asked to make an assessment of the aerial attack that would be necessary to silence the gun batteries on the Channel Island of Alderney so that it could be captured by commandos. He found that the military officers he spoke to could not articulate the objective in a meaningful way. Zuckerman produced a grid map of the island and superimposed actual bomb plots from German bombing of British towns, calculating that at least one in five of the bombs dropped would miss the island altogether. Churchill was impatient for some small territorial victory, but the Chief of the Imperial General Staff, Sir Alan Brooke, on 6th May, rejected any attack on Alderney

Despite his written instructions, Mountbatten, to his disappointment, found the Combined Operations military staff were reluctant to take the scientists into their confidence and tried to use them as purely technical advisers. This state of affairs lasted until one young naval officer asked Bernal about the problem of making a portable echo-sounder to measure shallow depths accurately. Sage asked why he wanted to be able to sound depths in this way, and the officer refused to tell him, saying the matter was too secret, and more or less ordered Bernal to provide an answer. Bernal refused, saying that Mountbatten had given clear instructions that he was to be to given full details so that he could decide whether the correct question was being asked. The officer rather reluctantly divulged that it was his idea for measuring the gradients of beaches on which assaults might be mounted, work which was very much within Bernal's sphere of interest at COHQ. Bernal said 'You've asked the wrong question, you should have said "How do we measure the beach gradients and runnels, without the Germans knowing?".'[15] Sage's solution was to take aerial photographs of the beach at different stages of the tide and to include wide stretches of territory on either side so that attention was not drawn by frequent flights just over the beach in question. The uniformed staff soon came to realize that Sage would not help unless he was brought fully into the picture, and when he was, the solutions he put forward were completely novel.

The beach in question was at Dieppe, and the first plans for a major amphibious landing at the port were made in April.[16] Zuckerman recalled that he and Bernal shared an office for a short period at COHQ until Bernal became much busier than he, and was given his own room. Zuckerman also said that he and Bernal did not work on the same projects and often he 'did not know where [Bernal] was or what he was doing'.[17] This may explain Zuckerman's statement that neither 'Bernal nor I took part in the planning of the big raid on Dieppe' for Bernal's own cryptic notes for 1942 include 'Plans for raids, including Dieppe raid'.[18] Dieppe was not going to be another smash-and-grab raid like Bruneval, but an opposed landing of a division of troops at a heavily defended port. The original plans involved a preliminary aerial bombardment, flanking attacks to neutralize gun emplacements covering the beach, and a frontal assault by troops and tanks under supporting naval artillery fire. The beach at Dieppe is shingle, and there was no experience with landing tanks on such a surface. According to Goronwy Rees who had been seconded to Combined Operations, COHQ at this time 'lived in an atmosphere of continuous improvisation, of meetings and conferences hurriedly called and as hurriedly cancelled, of brilliant and unorthodox ideas adopted with enthusiasm and abandoned when found to be impracticable'.[19]

Although the military staff at COHQ came to accept Bernal and Zuckerman quite quickly, working with Pyke remained an unequal contest. Pyke was not really interested in anybody else's ideas because he was overflowing with his own. Mountbatten was fascinated by these 'pykeries', as he called them, and was always ready to listen to him. The COHQ officers, collectively referred to as the 'numbskullery' by Pyke, became so frustrated with the time that Pyke would spend in the CCO's office that they disabled a magnetic lock that Mountbatten had installed so that he would not be disturbed when closeted with a visitor. Pyke's leading idea in the spring of 1942 was that a small marauding force could be landed in Norway and travel around with unprecedented speed by using a novel type of snow tractor that would be propelled by Archimedean screws. The presence of this force would mean that the Germans would have to commit a far larger army to Norway to protect the

power stations and communications links. Pyke was incapable of summarizing any of his ideas because new details would constantly intrude, and Bernal
was charged with writing a one-page proposal that Mountbatten could take to
Churchill. It was presented at Chequers, on 11th April, at a meeting that had
been arranged to examine the ongoing question of a Second Front. Harry
Hopkins was at Chequers representing Roosevelt and had General Marshall
with him. Churchill, who had been hankering for action in northern Norway
ever since the failed campaign of 1940 was favourably impressed and noted in
his minutes, 'Never in the history of human conflict will so few immobilize so
many.'[20] He suggested that Pyke, with one or two assistants, should fly to the
United States and try to build the revolutionary snow vehicles. Churchill's
suggestion was enthusiastically supported by the officers at Combined Operations, and Pyke was in the USA by the end of the month.

Within a matter of two weeks, Pyke's mission was in disarray. He felt as
though the Americans were not taking his requests seriously; the Americans
for their part found Pyke to be irksome. He also managed to fall out with the
Army officer from CO nominally in charge of the visit, and found himself
excluded from most discussions and site visits. He therefore submitted his
resignation to London, which produced a cable from Mountbatten to the CO
Liaison Officer in Washington urging him to smooth things out and as 'I hope
to visit you personally within a month please ask Pyke to carry on . . . until
I arrive.'[21] Another cable arrived for Pyke at the same time from Sage. It read:
'Don't be a bloody fool. Your resignation disastrous not only to scheme but to
whole of scientific collaboration in war effort. Will be possible to clear up
difficulties if you reconsider resignation and discuss matter with CCO. I can
help on scientific side if you let me know what problems are. Writing.'[22]

Vice-Admiral the Lord Louis Mountbatten occupied a unique position in
the British realm in 1942. He brought youthful vigour to Combined Operations. The promise of their irregular operations, involving derring-do and
the use of lethal technical gadgets, was the only bright spot that Churchill
could discern against the dark background of defensive struggles and military
setbacks. Lord Mountbatten's royal charm had disarmed Roosevelt in
Washington the previous year, and he was the British officer that Americans
in London most wanted to meet. Indeed, although Mountbatten had only just
had time to be fitted for his new ceremonial uniform, with its broad rings of
gold braid at the cuffs, it seemed as though he was in line for even greater
advancement. General Eisenhower visiting London that summer suggested to
Sir Alan Brooke that Mountbatten might be put in command of the major
cross-Channel invasion that the Americans expected to take place in 1943.
Eisenhower had not previously met Mountbatten, and was basing his recommendation on what he had heard about the CCO in America. Brooke

responded calmly, but he and his fellow chiefs of staff retained a deep scepticism about Mountbatten's lack of strategic experience and the way he had been thrust into their company. Mountbatten would enhance his standing with all these powerful figures if Combined Operations could deliver some successful raids.

The proposed raid on Alderney was cancelled in early May, and Zuckerman had predicted that opportunities for cross-Channel raids would be extremely sparse. Better then to throw all Combined Operations resources into one spectacular major raid on Dieppe. The planning for operation Rutter, as it became known, was headed by a naval captain at Combined Operations, John Hughes-Hallett. It was decided that the bulk of the invasion force would comprise the 2nd Canadian Division, and that their inexperienced commanders would be advised by General Montgomery. It quickly became apparent that the logistics for such a large-scale assault were prodigiously difficult, and any chance of success would depend on surprise, precise timing and the flawless coordination of forces. In retrospect, there was an obvious contradiction in the planning: the element of surprise was incompatible with a heavy preliminary bombardment, yet without effective destruction of defensive machine-gun positions, a frontal assault would be doomed.

A full-scale training exercise was carried out in the West Bay area of the Dorset coast on 11th June. Mountbatten arrived back from a high-level diplomatic trip to Washington two days earlier. Churchill had sent him to douse the Americans' enthusiasm for an early Second Front and to promote the alternative of guerilla activity in northern Norway, which meant that Mountbatten had to reinvigorate the Pyke mission during his short visit. Zuckerman and Bernal both attended the practice landing in Dorset, and what they saw was a shambles. Far from split-second timing, the landing craft had trouble with the currents and poor visibility, so that hundreds of soldiers were delivered to the wrong beaches at sporadic intervals. A second exercise, ten days later, was successful enough that Montgomery judged that the attack could go forward in early July with a good chance of success given 'a) favourable weather, b) average luck, c) that the Navy put us ashore roughly in the right places, and at the right time.'[23] But the weather was not favourable, and the *Luftwaffe* spotted the armada of landing craft near the Isle of Wight and bombed them. Operation Rutter was called off on 7th July 1942.

Montgomery, concerned by the security risks, recommended that Rutter should be cancelled 'for all time',[24] yet within two weeks Hughes-Hallett and Mountbatten were colluding on an emergency operation 'to be carried out during August to fill the gap caused by the cancellation of Rutter'.[25] Knowledge of the replacement operation, known as Jubilee, was to be restricted to the Rutter Force Commanders, the Canadian General McNaughton and

CO intelligence chief, the Marquis de Casa Maury. Mountbatten received no written authority from the Chiefs of Staff to remount a raid on Dieppe, and it seems that he neglected to tell Churchill about it. Despite the surreptitious and flawed planning, the Dieppe raid was launched in the pre-dawn hours of 19th August. Mountbatten, ever mindful of image and the power of publicity, had arranged for members of the press to sail with the troops. Zuckerman and Bernal asked to go as observers in one of the naval support ships, but Mountbatten refused them and was unmoved by Bernal's comment that it was 'surprising that room could be found for war correspondents, but not for his two scientific advisers'.[26]

There was no preliminary bombing of the port, a portion of the attacking armada was disrupted by a passing German convoy, and the initial attempts to capture the gun positions flanking the beach were unsuccessful. The consequence was that the Canadian troops put onto the beach were cut down by raking machine-gun fire, and the slow-moving Churchill tanks were easily destroyed by anti-tank guns. Despite the fearful events on the beach, some Canadian soldiers managed to fight their way into the town. When the order to withdraw was given in mid-morning, about two thousand of them were left stranded on the beach. Armed only with rifles and Tommy guns they fought tenaciously and attacked the flanking German batteries with fixed bayonets. They surrendered only when their ammunition ran out.[27] About four thousand young Canadian soldiers went ashore at Dieppe: about one thousand were killed that morning and nearly two thousand taken prisoner, many with terrible wounds. It was obvious to those on the ships sailing back to England that operation Jubilee had been a disaster. Mountbatten attempted to maintain his air of breezy optimism, but Zuckerman and Bernal were immediately dispatched to Newhaven to attempt some accounting of the human casualties, and the damage to naval ships and landing craft. After seeing and interviewing the exhausted, demoralized infantry, Sage was moved to anger for perhaps the only time in his life. He said to Kathleen Watkins, his personal assistant at Princes Risborough, 'The planning of that Operation was appalling – I would have planned a fortnight's holiday with more care.'[28]

Within two weeks, a summary document was circulated which contained important points for future planners of amphibious landings: 'The chief lesson learned is that although vertical air photos supply the great bulk of knowledge, they are incomplete. Final details must be supplied by low oblique photos or preferably good ground sources, otherwise many defences are not seen.'[29] Reliance on aerial photos taken from high above Dieppe meant that the planners had missed the machine guns placed in caves in the high cliffs. They had also not seen anti-tank guns that were kept in houses during the day and wheeled out at night. Troops were told that the gradient of the beach was

1-in-20, but few realized how steep this was. Eye-witnesses saw that the tanks had great difficulty moving up the shingle beach and then were unable to mount the promenade. The overall impression was that the British 'had not taken into consideration the character of the land and the defence positions of the Germans on the coast, either from lack of knowledge or for tactical reasons'.[30] Sage kept a list of work priorities in his diary, and the analysis of what went wrong at Dieppe appeared as one of the most consistent items during the next few months. John Cockroft, now Chief Superintendent of the Air Defence Research and Development Establishment at Malvern investigated what might have been learned from radar surveillance of shipping movements in the Channel and sent Bernal a report later in December 1942, which Bernal failed to acknowledge,[31] but all these errors of omission were indelibly stamped into his memory so that they would not be repeated, if he had any say in the matter.

At the Tots and Quots dinner in October,[32] the subject for discussion was the application of science to naval problems. Sage repeated a favourite idea of his that in all war research the crucial factor was speed in the application of science to problems as they arose and speed in implementation, once the solutions had been found. Blackett, the ex-navy lieutenant now in charge of operational research (OR) at the Admiralty, was pessimistic about the potential impact of science on the navy because all naval officers are imbued with naval history – an enormous obstacle to fresh thinking.

During his June visit to North America, Mountbatten was extremely conciliatory towards the querulous Pyke, introducing him to Eisenhower and recommending him warmly to Roosevelt. Just before Mountbatten flew back to England, Pyke mentioned that he was working on a new and bigger scheme with an eminent scientist at the Brooklyn Polytechnic Institute, 'in whom Professor Bernal had full confidence'.[33] He would not disclose any details to Mountbatten until the professor in Brooklyn had completed some preliminary experimental research, but wanted Mountbatten to promise to read the proposal that he would soon submit. The mystery professor was Hermann Mark, Perutz's old chemistry professor from Vienna, who was now at the Brooklyn Polytechnic Institute working alongside Fankuchen. Mark had come to New York via Montreal, where he had spent two years reorganizing the research department of the Canadian International Pulp and Paper Company, concentrating on new uses for wood pulp.[34] Bernal had contacted him to say that Pyke was on a military mission in Washington and asked him to visit Pyke when he could.

At their first meeting, Pyke was preoccupied with the U-boat threat to North Atlantic convoys and told Mark what was urgently needed: more landing strips for planes between Newfoundland and Northern Europe so

that planes could hunt and destroy the U-boats. Steel was in critically short
supply so that building aircraft carriers was not a solution. Pyke though had a
characteristically original answer: to use flat icebergs as 'unsinkable landing
fields' for allied planes.[35] The main drawback was that ice is brittle and Pyke
had realized that a bomb hitting such an ice landing strip would cause it to
shatter. He asked Mark if the brittleness of ice could be substantially reduced.
Mark instantly supplied an idea based on his recent work in Canada – the
addition of a few per cent of wood pulp should greatly increase the strength of
a layer of ice. As soon as he returned to New York, Mark began to investigate
the question in more detail. He and his group quickly confirmed that the
addition of a small amount of sawdust or wood pulp increased the tensile
strength of a sheet of ice and its impact strength, so that it would no longer
shatter. The wood pulp also made the mix much more resistant to melting
than pure ice.

Pyke sent a typed memorandum that was 232 pages of foolscap in a
diplomatic bag to Mountbatten in London. He implored the COC to 'read
only the first 33 pages. If you find it no good, so be it. Chuck it away.'[36] He
pleaded with Mountbatten to navigate the shoals of officialdom so that this
grand project might be realized and told him it should be known as HABBA-
KUK. There is some mystery about this title – whether it referred to the Old
Testament Book of Habakkuk (*'I will work a work in your days, which ye will
not believe though it be told to you'*) or a character in Voltaire's *Candide* who
was, like Mountbatten, capable of anything. Mountbatten passed the weighty
parcel to his Chief of Staff, Brigadier Wildman-Lushington, (referred to in
Pyke's covering note as 'that damned fool Lushington'). The Brigadier called
for Bernal and asked him to prepare a one-page summary of the document.
Pyke's writings were wondrous and included every conceivable application of
ice warfare, no matter how fantastic. Sage at first thought he would not be
able to reduce them to one page, but on reflection the essential idea was very
simple and the summary easily written.

Bernal's list of priorities for October 1942 was as follows:

> New ops.
> Habbakuk
> block ships
> landing support
> synoptic picture of bombing and bombing policy
> Dieppe analysis
> army–air force cooperation.[37]

Mountbatten's priorities that autumn were rather different: they were headed
by the need to protect his own reputation after the catastrophe of Dieppe.

He was attacked by General Sir Alan Brooke, Chief of the Imperial General Staff, at a dinner party given by Churchill, and Admiral Ramsay rebuked him for the poor discipline and incompetence of his organization.[38] Mountbatten realized the best method of disarming his critics, and especially of avoiding the wrath of Churchill, was to involve his cousin, King George VI, in his affairs as much as possible. One of the ways to do this was to entertain the King with stories of the eccentrics he had surrounded himself with at COHQ. The two favourites were a long-haired Irishman and a bearded Jew; indeed so familiar did these characters become that the King would refer to them by gesture – either sweeping his hand through his hair or stroking an imaginary beard – as his cousin regaled him with their latest madcap activities.[39] On the 28th September 1942, the King paid a visit to COHQ. Sage, typically, was not present when he should have been, and Mountbatten was worried that he might have gone to get his hair cut for the occasion. Zuckerman recalled that Sage eventually turned up 'with his hair in its pristine state, and the King, who had been told what to expect, was not disappointed'.[40] The culmination of months of self-promotion took place two weeks later at Buckingham Palace with the premier of Noel Coward's film, *In Which We Serve*, in which the hero was based on Mountbatten, the dashing naval officer.

Max Perutz had been released from internment in Canada and returned to Cambridge at the beginning of 1941; since he did not seem to be required for war work, he quietly took up his researches on haemoglobin again, with the enthusiastic support of Lawrence Bragg. In October 1942, he was summoned to London by Pyke who told him 'with the air of one great man confiding in another, that he needed [his] help for the most important project of the war'.[41] Perutz left the meeting excited but not much wiser about what he was supposed to do; a few days later he heard from Bernal that he 'should find ways of making ice stronger and freezing it faster, never mind what for'.[42] Neither Pyke nor Bernal thought to mention to Perutz that Hermann Mark had already made considerable inroads into this question, and Perutz wasted the next week or so trying to find non-existent data in the published literature, while mounting some unsuccessful experiments of his own. As soon as Pyke thought to hand him Mark's report, which he said he had found hard to understand, Perutz knew what should be done and made recommendations to Pyke and Bernal. As a result, 'Combined Operations requisitioned a large meat store five floors beneath Smithfield Market' and with a small team Perutz began to manufacture and test reinforced ice.

We built a big wind tunnel to freeze the mush of wet wood pulp, and sawed the reinforced ice into blocks. Our tests soon confirmed Mark and Hohenstein's results. Blocks of ice containing as little as four per cent wood pulp were weight for weight as strong as concrete; in honour of the originator of the project, we called the reinforced ice 'pykrete'. When we fired a rifle bullet into an upright block of pure ice two feet square and one foot thick, the block shattered; in pykrete the bullet made a little crater and was embedded without doing any damage. My stock rose, but no one would tell me what pykrete was needed for, except that it was for Habakkuk [sic].

Lord Mountbatten was an early visitor to the freezing laboratory. According to legend, he took away a piece of Pykrete that he then demonstrated to Churchill, while the latter was in his bath at Chequers. A more formal presentation of the Habbakuk idea was made to the Prime Minister through Lord Cherwell in December and elicited an enthusiastic minute for the Chiefs of Staff Committee.[43] After telling them that he attached 'the greatest importance to the prompt examination of these ideas', Churchill told the COS that Mountbatten should be given 'every facility' and that he would be reporting to him weekly. Churchill's imagination was captured by the grandeur and originality of the scheme: 'I do not of course know anything about the physical properties of a lozenge of ice 5,000 feet by 2,000 feet by 100 feet,' he wrote, 'or how it resists particular stresses, or what would happen to an iceberg of this size in rough Atlantic weather, or how soon it would melt... The advantages of a floating island or islands, even if only used as refuelling depots for aircraft, are so dazzling that they do not need at the moment to be discussed. There would be no difficulty in finding a place to put such a "stepping-stone" in any of the plans of war now under consideration.' The beauty of the project in Churchill's eyes was the promise that Nature would do nearly all the work and he thought the downfall of the scheme would be moving 'very large numbers of men and a heavy tonnage of steel or concrete to the remote recesses of the Arctic night'.

Churchill could not resist adding his own ideas about how a berg ship might be extracted from the Arctic icefield and then equipped, but the research and development aspects of Habbakuk were Bernal's responsibility. Sage spent Christmas Day at Fingest with Margaret and Martin, and the next day drew up the following headings:[44]

A. Materials: mechanical properties re gravity, wave strain and attack.
   2. improved properties (best reinforcement).
   3. speed of preparation.
B. Study of natural conditions: wind, current etc. N. Atlantic; temperature/depth relationship.
C. Design problems: Hull/insulation and refrigeration/engines and steering/aircraft storage and runways.
D. Construction problems.
E. Supply and costs.

On New Year's Eve, Sage circulated some general conclusions, which were of course labelled 'most secret'. He thought that the tests in America and Perutz's work had already shown that a vessel could be constructed out of Pykrete and it would be possible for fighter aircraft to take off from it. He also listed what he saw as the outstanding problems and thought they were soluble 'if they are given sufficient priority'.[45] Of paramount importance would be full-scale manufacturing trials, which must be carried out in Canada and needed to start that winter if the project was going to be realized before 1945.

The first meeting of the Habbakuk committee took place under Mountbatten's chairmanship at COHQ on 7 January 1943. Pyke and Sage were both there, as was Lord Cherwell, who expressed scepticism about the use of natural materials, commenting that everything was known about concrete, very little about ice. Bernal explained how the ice would be reinforced against shearing stress with steel rods as for concrete, but Cherwell was unconvinced and brought up a second problem – how would it be prevented from melting. Bernal tried to reassure him that with the slow melting rate of Pykrete, the refrigeration plant needed would be similar to any Ministry of Supply Food Store! At this point, the CCO took Cherwell's side and thought concrete might be better than ice. Sage disagreed flatly and Pyke remained silent. Sage thought that the UK was singularly ill-equipped for the necessary research and development, and that the USA and Russia could offer better facilities. The CCO replied that the PM wished to confine the project to Britain and Canada for security reasons, but he would recommend informing the USA and Russia.

The day after the meeting, Sage wrote a formal note on the practicability of Habbakuk.[46] He listed the advantages: costless fabrication of material; gravity placing of ice blocks that could be slid into position and never need to be lifted; self-welding of 100 ton blocks by letting them stick together with a little water between. The whole construction process would require far less labour and be at least ten times quicker than the building of large conventional vessels, so that Sage believed a vessel should be available in 1944. He also listed two major disadvantages: lack of knowledge as to mechanical strength and reliability; the need for insulation and permanent refrigeration. With the collaboration of Canadian scientists, Sage thought 'we should know by the summer whether the scheme is technically feasible or not'. He pointed out that 'we', meaning COHQ, had no brief for the Habbakuk scheme and that any alternative which could provide fighter cover at an earlier date and at equal or less cost 'is clearly to be preferred'. Sage thought such an alternative to be not very likely, and it seemed to him that in the emergency of war, it was worth running 'some quite big risks' to bring Habbakuk to fruition: 'Even if the Bergship is not perfectly unbreakable in exceptional storms or to concentrated enemy attack, and one or two are put out of action, this happens to the best of His Majesty's Ships now.' The ultimate decision must rest with the Chiefs of Staff, 'but it seems to us that the main value of this scheme is in its furnishing an early solution, and it is worthwhile pushing forward either full out or not at all'.

Sage spent the next few days preparing a detailed programme of research to be undertaken in Canada, but this was to be his last input into Habbakuk for a couple of months – he and Zuckerman were to go to the Middle East. The lowest subject on Bernal's list of priorities in September and October, Army–Air Force cooperation, had now risen to top following the battles in the Western Desert of North Africa. Whereas the Germans had employed a devastating combination of dive-bombers in close support of mechanized armies during their *Blitzkrieg* of so many European countries, the fighting in the Western Desert gave the RAF its first experience as an attack force in concert with ground troops – in this case, Montgomery's Eighth Army, as they pounded Rommel's Panzer Divisions. During the fighting, operational research reports were sent back to the War Office in London concerning the relative effectiveness of Hurricane fighters as tank-busters flying at low levels and using their cannons versus the dropping of 250 pound bombs by Boston light bombers.[47] After being defeated at El Alamein in early November, Rommel still managed to escape with large numbers of his Afrika Korps, and this raised questions about why the RAF had not been able to cut the retreating columns of men to ribbons.

Tizard, who was still retained as a semi-official adviser by the Ministry of Aircraft Production, had initiated a series of 'Informal meetings of Independent Scientific Advisers' in June 1942 to facilitate the exchange of information between those directing operational research for the different services.[48] He was concerned that they were working on overlapping problems, but had no forum in which to discuss their efforts. The regular attendees were Bernal, Blackett, Cockcroft, Fowler and Sir Charles Darwin, another Rutherford-trained physicist and grandson of the biologist. Darwin was in charge of OR at the War Office and monitored the reports coming from the Middle East. At the ninth meeting of the informal committee on 15th December, Tizard announced that as Bernal and Zuckerman were likely to go out to the Middle East in the near future those present had an opportunity to request any information they needed.[49] The first to respond was Darwin who wanted information on four points:

1. An estimate of the weight of explosives per square yard (shells or bombs) required to 'soften' an area for assault within say half-an-hour of the assault.

2. What tactical collaboration exists between the Army and the Air Force in the Middle East?
3. Was the bombing used for direct Army support?
4. Any information on anti-tank mines.

Sage immediately replied that he thought the second item was beyond his terms of reference because 'he could not undertake to make an investigation of the efficiency of, for instance, communications'.[50] On Tizard's suggestion, he did agree to make enquiries as to whether a report on communications efficiency was in preparation.

Bernal gave a general outline of what he and Zuckerman hoped to achieve. They would concentrate on major problems such as the tactics of Army–Air Force cooperation, and hoped to make some comparison of the relative efficiency of German and British weapons in causing casualties and damage to towns, docks and ships. Blackett chipped in to mention the apparent indestructibility of the Benghazi fuel store. Sage went on to say that he would also be looking at attacks on aerodromes since it appeared that more aircraft had been destroyed on the ground than in the air. This would be done using photographic records, and he commented that photographs that he had recently seen in the Admiralty Topographical Section were unfortunately all undated. In a similar vein, he was concerned about the scarcity of reliable maps. Bernal summarized the work that Zuckerman would be doing, most importantly a detailed study of the causes of casualties in tanks. Zuckerman was present at the meeting, but apparently did not speak – there was no doubt that Sage was to be in charge of the mission.

At the mid-December meeting, Bernal alluded to 'administrative difficulties', which put the Middle East visit in doubt, but by the end of the year, after Tizard's intervention, these were sorted out. The Vice-Chief of the Air Staff informed RAF Middle East HQ that 'Professors B. and Z. are leaving by air... early in January.' They would travel as civilians, but in the event of accident or death would be regarded as Group Captains RAF for benefits purposes. According to the Vice-Chief, 'they are being sent out to study at first hand the effect of British bombs on various types of targets'.[51] The visit was expected to last up to six weeks, and it was requested that they be provided with what facilities they required, especially in areas where recent operations had taken place. The extent of disagreement between the services at the time is underscored in another cable sent by the Under-Secretary of State at the War Office: the up-coming enquiry was described as 'of the greatest importance since it is meant to discover that information which alone can determine whether direct air support is unprofitable – a view to which the RAF have in the past been attached – or, as the Army believe, essential'.[52]

The two scientists left Bournemouth on 15th January 1943, 'tightly packed with two other passengers in a small Catalina flying-boat'.[53] Zuckerman was embarking on a tour that would establish his reputation as a military scientist and lead to ever-greater responsibilities in the defence sphere. For Sage it would be an odyssey that touched four continents. A sudden parting of the ways would rupture their friendship. The trip started out very pleasantly – they were marooned by fog on the west coast of Ireland for a week. Zuckerman thought that Bernal was all but overcome with sentiment to be back in his own country; he turned to Zuckerman and said, 'I feel like taking off my shoes, tying the laces together, slinging them round my neck and just walking off into the mist.'[54] They were free from blackout restrictions for the first time in three years; fresh food was plentiful, though Sage did record at one point that there was 'no more drink at Dunraven Arms'.[55] They went for long walks through the countryside, 'where Bernal was at his very best, discoursing on the differences between the various ruined abbeys... and much else about the history of Ireland'.[56] After a week of waiting around, they flew off to Lisbon and then down the west coast of Africa, touching down in the Gambia before reaching Lagos on 24th January. It was now Zuckerman's turn to be flooded by childhood memories of his native Africa. He wrote to his wife from Lagos describing 'everyone smiling and showing their teeth, women in vast shawls and strange coiffures, poorer women in rags and babies on their backs, and flat breasts. Our own people, almost all in uniform, and very superior.'[57]

From Lagos they made a long and spectacular flight, mainly over desert, to Khartoum. They spent three days of intensive sightseeing, visiting the Mahdi's tomb and the museum, where Sage naturally overflowed with enthusiasm and knowledge about the local artifacts. He was especially fascinated by the camel drivers and the spears which they carried. Bernal and Zuckerman made a detour to Omdurman, where less than half-a-century before, thousands of dervishes armed with spears had been massacred by the Maxim guns of the Anglo-Egyptian Army to avenge the Mahdi's siege of Khartoum. Flying north up the Nile Valley, they landed in Cairo after skimming over the pyramids. It was springtime, and arrangements had been made for the two scientists to stay at the Mena House, a hotel with beautiful patios and gardens next to the great pyramids at Giza. The splendid setting reminded Zuckerman 'of glorious pre-war luxury [but] where one now eats out of the tinned rations one brings in'.[58]

They spent four very busy days meeting the local Army and RAF officers and their small, field OR teams. One Squadron Leader, only in his mid-twenties, made a particular impression on Sage. His name was John Kendrew and he had been in Cairo for just over a year. Curly-haired and bespectacled, he was a Cambridge chemistry graduate who had worked on radar development in England, before being posted to the Middle East. The new arrivals absorbed as much information as they could about armaments, bombing tactics, photo-reconnaissance and a host of other subjects. A cable had been sent from the Air Ministry in London to Middle East HQ saying that 'Professors B. and Z. feel that some sort of uniform should be worn when in operational areas.'[59] They were not commissioned and therefore could not wear service uniforms, and it was left to those in Cairo to 'suggest something suitable' for them to use when in battle zones. The quasi-military uniform eventually provided in Zuckerman's view made them look 'less like airmen than like commissionaires of some seedy back-street hotel'.[60] They wore neither unit nor rank badges, but 'some wit in Cairo had thought it fun to fix a large brass crown' to their caps.

There was another cable waiting for Bernal in Cairo. It was from Mountbatten instructing him to make his way to Canada as soon as possible to oversee the Habbakuk tests that were about to start; enclosed with the cable was a travel permit that gave Sage 'stratospheric priority' for his journey. Clearly the CCO had persuaded his fellow Chiefs of Staff to move ahead with the programme that Bernal had outlined in his various reports. Their acquiescence had come despite a demonstration at COHQ by a naval officer, who fired bullets into a large block of ice and a block of Pykrete prepared for the occasion by Perutz.[61] The ice duly shattered, but the bullet fired at the block of Pykrete rebounded and hit Sir Alan Brooke in the shoulder, fortunately without causing any injury. Sage was in a quandary – there was an enormous amount of work to be done in North Africa and everyone was relying on him to organize it, yet he could hardly ignore the wishes of the CCO on a project that he knew had Churchill's support. He put the cable and travel warrant in his pocket and said nothing for the moment.

After five days of briefings in Cairo, it was time for Bernal and Zuckerman to move closer to the front. They took off for Libya, but after an hour in the air had to turn back to Cairo because of engine trouble.[62] The engine was repaired and they flew over one thousand miles west following the coastal road that Rommel's troops had used to flee, three months before. They spent the night at a camp known as Marble Arch, where Sage, in unknown circumstances, lost his pyjamas![63] The next day they flew a further six hundred miles or so west, before landing at the heavily damaged Tripoli airfield of Castel Benito. Rommel had ceded the port of Tripoli two weeks before and only after sinking as many blockships as possible to make the harbour unusable. Prior to that the port had been bombarded for two years, first by the Royal Navy and then by the RAF. Bernal was supposed to assess the extensive damage to ships, docks and harbour and apportion the blame – like an insurance loss adjuster under arms.

Before starting their work, Bernal and Zuckerman established contact with the senior Army and RAF officers, who now controlled Tripoli, and also met the Italian Prefect, who had been encouraged to retain some authority over the civilian population. After a few days, they had won over the military chiefs, one or two of whom had been unimpressed by their arrival in the middle of such chaos: 'Oh, you're the two fellows who've been sent out to see what's in a bomb hole'[64] was their greeting from the head of the Desert Air Force. Once they had been recognized as making a serious contribution and the initial plans were in place, Sage decided it was time to break the news to Solly about his impending departure. Zuckerman was devastated. In a letter written thirty years later, he admitted to Kendrew that he was 'terrified to be left to do what I had taken would be his job'.[65] In his memoirs, Zuckerman described the ensuing scene:

I spent hours that evening, pleading with him by candlelight – there was no electricity in the hotel – not to go, saying *Habbakuk* was nonsense, and rattling off a list of his many ideas and projects about which he had got people excited in the past, and where he had reversed his judgement at the last moment ... Des became more and more silent as, in desperation, I added accusation to accusation. But all to no avail.[66]

The next morning, Zuckerman accompanied Sage in their staff car back to Castel Benito and sadly watched him wade through a desert flood to reach the plane that was to return him to Cairo. In the middle of the desert, miles from anywhere, was a small unit from the Royal Signal Corps headed by Capt. Norman Waddleton. Waddleton was a Cambridge physics graduate, who had taken the course in X-ray crystallography taught by Bernal. He was astounded when his old tutor suddenly walked into the encampment, alone, dressed in an ill-fitting RAF uniform.[67] No explanation was offered, and Waddleton took the view that Bernal was on a secret mission, so asked no questions. Bernal shared his tent for the night, and the next day Waddleton drove him the remaining miles to Cairo in his jeep.

Back in Cairo, Sage took the opportunity to visit mosques and museums. He found Kendrew, whose mother was a distinguished art historian, to be an amiable companion, and Kendrew for his part was amazed by Sage's erudition.[68] Bernal spent one night by the Nilometer – a stone column standing inside a large cistern that is connected to the river by three tunnels. It was used from the ninth century to measure and predict the annual flood of the Nile, and so to set taxes on that year's harvest – a perfect example for the Marxist view of science and society. He flew out from Cairo under a full moon, headed for the Gold Coast. Before leaving, he scrawled a hurried and apologetic letter to Zuckerman to wish him luck. He gave him names of some new contacts he had made, including Army experts on the clearing of minefields and a Paramount studio cameraman who had 'good ideas for better use of cine cameras'. He also told Zuckerman that Kendrew was now in charge of OR for the RAF in the Middle East, and that he was 'more and more impressed with his ability'.[69]

The only accommodation Sage could find on his arrival in Accra was a stable, which he shared with a shipwrecked sailor.[70] He made friends with a local boy, who asked him if he was American. Sage said 'No' to which the boy responded 'Then you are British like me.' This spontaneous, friendly remark caused Bernal to reflect on how deep the imprint of colonization was – in the boy's eyes, they were equal subjects of the British Empire. There were some American airmen in town, and after showing them his travel warrant, Bernal was able to hitch a ride on their 'inferior plane'. They flew to Ascension Island, a barren mountain covered with volcanic lava in the mid-Atlantic, just south of the equator. The Americans had built an airbase there the previous summer, as a staging post for flights to North Africa and as a base from which bombers could hunt U-boats. They stopped just long enough to eat a meal and to refuel before setting off, but within a short time they had turned back because of engine failure. This time there was no quick repair and Sage found himself marooned. He persuaded the American pilot to explore the island with him on foot. They found a beautiful white-sand beach and took the 'best bathe ever'. Only afterwards did Sage learn that no one swims there because of sharks. He saw the sharks, but reasoned that they did not see him; he also saw some of the indigenous giant turtles and learned that they formed the chief ingredient for the soup traditionally served at the Lord Mayor of London's banquet.[71] His afternoon was crowned by meeting the District Nurse, who invited him to tea.

Back at the airbase, he found that the Americans had 'no gas and more whiskey than water'. He attempted to board the first plane out, but was thrown off by a senior American officer and lost his travel permit. After about a week, he managed to get a ride on a Canadian plane, which took him to Recife on the Brazilian coast. From there, they set off for Trinidad, but had to make a forced landing in the forest of Guyana, where he spent a sober night in torrential rain. When they arrived in Trinidad, he made the mistake of taking the pilot to a cricket match and only just avoided being thrown off the plane as a consequence. The next leg of the journey involved flying 'over the track of Columbus to Nassau and Miami'.[72] He arrived in New York on 28th February to find a patriotic parade taking place, with drum majoresses marching in sub-zero temperatures. He had lunch with Hermann Mark and then toured Brooklyn Polytechnic, reunited with Fan.

Geoffrey Pyke had also arrived in New York, and the next day he and Bernal flew up to Ottawa, where they had meetings with Dean Mackenzie and the staff of the National Research Council of Canada. They then took a train west to Saskatoon; it might have been spring in Cairo a month earlier, in Saskatoon the thermometer showed minus 30°C (−22°F).[73] They found a team of engineers and scientists at work on problems such as the rate of freezing of Pykrete, bonding together of blocks, and the use of steel beams as reinforcement. A major issue was emerging over the plastic flow of ice – evident in glaciers under the effect of gravity. Perutz in London was also studying this phenomenon and came to the conclusion that a large ice-ship would sag under its own weight amidships. He believed that 'a ship of pykrete would sag more slowly [than pure ice], but not slowly enough, unless it were to be cooled to a temperature as low as 4°F'.[74]

Bernal and Pyke now journeyed to the Canadian Rockies, which, although still cold, were more temperate that Saskatoon. In Jasper National Park, a large-scale model was being built to examine techniques of insulation and refrigeration and to see how it would stand up to ballistics tests and explosives. Sage was as excited by the explosions in the ice as he was to walk past moose and bears. Their final destination was the stunningly beautiful Lake Louise, surrounded by mountains, where they studied the deformation of large steel beams and the construction of large ice blocks; there were more explosions. On the 13th March Bernal sent a generally optimistic progress report[75] to COHQ, which concluded: 'The general view is that the construction of the vessel as such will not offer any particular difficulties.' He informed London that the Canadians were building a 1,000 ton model, which they expected to complete in fourteen days with the labour of just eight men. The CCO responded with a cable on 21st March saying that the Prime Minister had invited the Chiefs of Staff Committee to arrange for an order to be placed for one complete ship at once with the highest priority, and for further ships without delay if it appeared the scheme was certain of success. Churchill also wanted Pyke and Bernal to go and tell him the whole story, when they returned to England.[76]

This was perhaps the high-water mark for Operation Habbakuk. The Canadians were confident about constructing a vessel for 1944: the necessary materials were readily available to them (300,000 tons wood pulp, 25,000 tons fibre-board insulation, 35,000 tons timber and 10,000 tons steel). The estimated cost was £700,000. Now that the order had come to move ahead, the project was subjected to wider scrutiny. An Admiralty committee headed by the Chief of Naval Construction sent a critical memorandum to the CCO, who passed their reservations onto Pyke. This led to a return cable labelled 'HUSH MOST SECRET. CIRCULATION RESTRICTED TO CHIEF OF COMBINED OPERATIONS ONLY.' The cable read: 'CHIEF OF NAVAL CONSTRUCTION IS AN OLD WOMAN. SIGNED PYKE.'[77] The message was much too funny for the CCO to keep it hushed, and it quickly reached the ears of the Admiral himself, who was furious.

Perutz and his Smithfield Market team kept testing different mixtures of ice and pulp, before deciding that 14% pulp: 86% water gave the best structural properties. Although Perutz rarely left the cold store for meetings at COHQ, he recognized the daunting pitfalls that Operation Habbakuk needed to avoid, and also the time constraints, given that even Canadian winters do not last for ever. He wrote to Pyke in early April pointing out that if certain tests were not completed in May, there would be no chance of delivering a berg ship in 1944. He also expressed some frustration with Bernal, who evidently had suggested that alternatives to wood pulp such as cotton, straw and sawdust might be tried.[78]

By May the problem of plastic flow or creep, first identified by Perutz, was becoming more serious. Bernal sent back a series of technical reports giving details of the Canadian research findings. The need to use more steel reinforcement, combined with a more effective insulating skin around the vessel's hull, as well as more elaborate refrigeration soon led to a revised cost estimate of two-and-a-half million pounds. Gloomier news followed in a cable from Bernal and Pyke to the CCO informing him that the Canadians had decided it was impractical to attempt the project 'this coming season'.[79] Despite 'tactful pressure' from them, there had been a marked lack of quantitative investigations. The Canadians were not conscious of the urgent strategic need for Habbakuk and therefore displayed a natural reluctance to use unusual methods and to depart widely from customary procedures. In short, whereas Bernal had persuaded those at COHQ that the vital need was to press ahead with Habbakuk and be prepared to abandon the scheme if it ran into insurmountable obstacles, the Canadians were not willing to accept a greater risk of failure than would be usual in a large commercial engineering project. In these circumstances, Bernal and Pyke had both come to the conclusion that no Habbakuk vessel would be ready in 1944.

Sage was now back in New York where he took a few days to visit his cousin Persis and other old friends. It was time for him to return to London and again it was a question of a makeshift flight with considerable hazard. He crossed the North Atlantic in an unheated bomb bay shared with Alexander Korda, the film director.[80] After a 'nightmare journey' he was relieved to see the dawn over Ireland on 16th May. The following week the *Evening Standard*, which in early February had announced Bernal's arrival in North Africa, ran a small news item under the heading 'Sealed Lips'.[81] No doubt fed by the COHQ publicity department, the newspaper informed its readers that Professor Bernal 'who is a scientific adviser to Lord Louis Mountbatten has returned to this country. The task which took him to North Africa and North America is secret.' Sage was quoted as saying, 'I wish I could tell you, but I can't.'

12

Overlord

The headquarters of Combined Operations (COHQ) occupied what was formerly the town house of the Dukes of Buccleuch, in Richmond Terrace. One of the more volatile and cantankerous characters in residence during 1942–3 was Evelyn Waugh, the novelist. He was there as Liaison Officer representing the Special Service Brigade, until he was forced out by his senior officers for constantly causing trouble. He was often drunk. The week after Bernal returned from his travels, Waugh arrived for lunch with Mountbatten 'rather tipsy' and 'found the house a nest of Communists',[1] suggesting that Sage was back at work. Habbakuk remained the highest priority for Bernal, although the Canadians were not pressing ahead with a large-scale model and there seemed no prospect of an operational berg ship until 1945. A meeting was held at COHQ to review the situation at the end of May; Bernal stated that he still believed a berg ship was feasible and that Pykrete was the best material to use. Perutz indicated that 1.7 million tons of Pykrete in block form would need to be produced during the next Canadian winter to construct one berg ship ready for use in 1945.[2]

When Churchill appointed Mountbatten as Chief of Combined Operations in November 1941, he emphasized that COHQ was to think offensively, and that its primary object would be to prepare for the great invasion of the Continent. It was natural, therefore, that the CCO should be a member of the Combined Commanders, a group of senior officers assembled in May 1942, to plan the invasion. From the first, Mountbatten favoured a landing on the wide beaches of Normandy, rather than the closer, but more heavily defended, Pas de Calais. In discussions at COHQ, it was pointed out to Mountbatten by Hughes-Hallett, his naval adviser, that if the landing was going to take place on relatively undefended beaches, the invading force would have to bring harbours with them to provide protection from rough seas and to allow mechanized equipment and heavy supplies to be offloaded.[3] Soon after the first meeting of the Combined Commanders, Mountbatten sent the Prime Minister a minute on 'Piers for use on beaches'. This considered the relative merits of piers constructed from scaffolding versus pontoon piers. Churchill wrote a reply on the bottom of his copy, dated 31st May 1942, addressed to the CCO or deputy: 'They <u>must</u> float up and down with the tide...Let me have the best solution worked out. Don't argue the matter. The difficulties will argue for themselves.'[4] A prototype, the Spud Pontoon Pier, had already been designed in the Transportation Department of the War Office. At Combined Operations, Captain Tom Hussey, to whom Bernal reported, was the head of a committee that had been looking into 'certain alternatives for forming sheltered anchorages by means of blockships'[5] since 1941. Bernal's diary in October 1942 showed that work on blockships (old vessels sunk to form breakwaters) was his second priority to Habbakuk.

Uncoordinated work on providing artificial harbours continued at both the Admiralty and the War Office, but in March 1943 Churchill reminded Mountbatten of the lack of real progress with the floating piers: 'Dilatory experiments with varying types and patterns have resulted in our having nothing...I was hoping to reduce the strain on landing-craft by the rapid building of these piers. I am very much disappointed.'[6] Churchill arranged that an engineer from the War Office, Major Steer-Webster, would report to him frequently on the latest developments, and in May rebuked the Chiefs of Staff for their lack of attention to the problem. They responded by calling on Steer-Webster to give his opinion about the rival schemes. He felt confident in his answers to such senior officers because he had already checked his 'mathematics and engineering principles' with many experts, including Cherwell and Bernal.[7] In his opinion, the best option was the one from the War Office, which involved the construction of huge concrete caissons or cubes that would be towed across the Channel and form the floating inner harbour wall. These caissons, known as Phoenixes, would have a flexible steel roadway – a Whale – laid over the top of them. The whole became known as a Mulberry harbour. Steer-Webster built scale models and relied heavily on guidance given to him by Sage on wave formation. In later years, he told Bernal that 'but for your practical and theoretical advice there would have been no Mulberry harbours'.[8]

Mountbatten had been convinced by Steer-Webster's arguments and felt it was important to establish a unanimous acceptance of the War Office's Mulberry design. Apart from needing a consensus on the Mulberry harbours, the CCO was also determined to set a coherent planning strategy for the whole invasion. At the Casablanca Conference in January 1943, which he had attended, it was agreed between Churchill and Roosevelt that a Supreme Allied Commander (SAC) should be appointed to be in charge of the allied invasion of Western Europe. It was further agreed that the SAC should be British, and Churchill gave the nod to Sir Alan Brooke, Chief of the Imperial General Staff. Mountbatten realized that his own role would be diminished once the SAC was formally appointed, but by the summer this had still not happened. In June, Mountbatten sensing that his influence on planning for the invasion was about to be curtailed, called a conference, codename 'Rattle', in Largs – a small seaside town on the Clyde estuary.[9] The Allied top brass at 'Rattle' resolved that the assault landing beaches would be somewhere between Cherbourg, on the Cotentin peninsula to the west, and Dieppe, to the east.

During the early summer, naval architects and engineers continued to work on Habbakuk in close cooperation with Bernal and Perutz. The requirements for the vessel became ever more demanding: it had to have a range of seven thousand miles and be able to withstand the biggest waves ever recorded in the world's oceans. The Admiralty wanted it to be torpedo-proof, which meant a hull at least forty feet thick. The Fleet Air Arm decided that not just fighters but heavy bombers should be able to take off from its deck, which had to be fifty feet above water and two thousand feet long. Perutz recalled that 'steering presented the most difficult problem. At first, we thought that the ship could be steered simply by varying the relative speed of the motors on either side, like a plane taxiing along the ground, but the Navy decided a

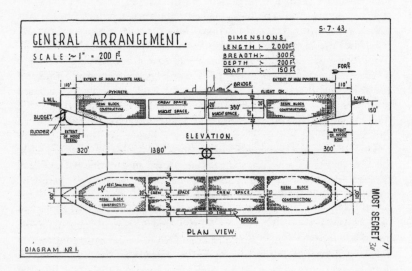

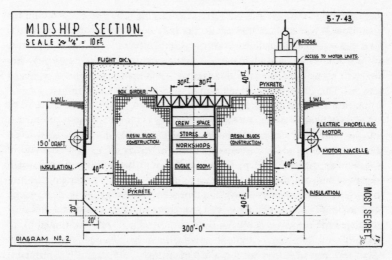

1943 Admiiralty blueprints for Habbakuk, the giant aircraft carrier to be constructed from Pylrete. Public Record Office (ADM 1/15236)

rudder was essential to keep it on course. The problem of suspending and controlling a rudder the height of a fifteen-story building was never solved.'[10] Early in July 1943, detailed drawings for the ice Leviathan appeared and are reproduced above.

At COHQ, Pyke was no longer satisfied with the original function of a berg ship as a landing strip, and now advocated a more direct offensive role for the unsinkable vessels: the occupation of enemy harbours. Egged on by Pyke, Sage called for a change in existing strategy to suit Habbakuk, rather than trying to fit Habbakuk into existing strategy. The Royal Navy captain chairing a Habbakuk committee meeting in July was unmoved by their fantastic schemes.[11] Mountbatten was meant to have said, jokingly, that 'COHQ is the only lunatic asylum in the world run by its own inmates', but it seems that now he was perturbed by the wildness of Pyke's and Bernal's latest ideas. A week or so after the meeting, the CCO sent for Perutz, whose technical reports always conveyed a sense of urgency and realism; he asked him one question: 'Who should represent Habbakuk at a high-level meeting?' Without hesitation, Perutz replied, 'Bernal' as 'the only man who possessed the technical knowledge, the intellectual stature, and the persuasiveness to stand up to the war leaders.'[12] Mountbatten took Perutz at his word, and told Sage he ought to go to Canada again. Sage replied, 'I suppose you must have your reasons.' The CCO said: 'I think you should go fairly soon. In fact, I have arranged for you to go this afternoon.'[13]

Following the invasion of Sicily in July 1943, Italy appeared poised to collapse. Churchill was intent on the immediate invasion of Italy, as well as attacking other points in the 'soft underbelly of the Axis'. The Americans were by now adamant that the primary focus should be on the cross-Channel landing. Churchill therefore proposed another Anglo-American Conference to discuss the progress of the war, and Quebec was soon agreed as the meeting place for what became known as the Quadrant Conference. Mountbatten was instructed to bring a small contingent from Combined Operations with him. Bernal would find himself the only civilian scientist included (Cherwell, for once, was not at Churchill's side). The British entourage of about two hundred 'captains and kings'[14] included several Cabinet ministers and the chiefs of staff (COS). They sailed from the Clyde aboard the *Queen Mary* on 5th August. Amongst them were two inspirational war heroes – Brigadier Orde Wingate and Wing Commander Guy Gibson – whom Churchill wished to present to Roosevelt. On the first day at sea, Mountbatten ordered Sage to get a haircut so that he might cut a respectable figure in front of the Chiefs of Staff and told him to stay out of the way until he was called upon.

Sage was not kept skulking around the ship for long. On Saturday 7th August, the COS Committee met, and the provision of artificial harbours was one of the main items on the agenda. They heard from Captain Hussey of COHQ on proposed modifications to merchant ships for launching amphibious vehicles and on ways of getting tanks ashore. Mountbatten, with his usual touch of theatricality, then informed his fellow chiefs that 'the greatest expert in the world' on artificial harbours happened to be on board. Bernal was produced from below decks and spoke for a short time on two of the Admiralty's proposals for making temporary breakwaters.[15] Sensing that these senior men of action would prefer a demonstration to a lecture, Bernal suggested that they should move to an adjacent bathroom. The tub was filled with water, and he made a flotilla of about twenty boats from newspaper. He invited his audience, which had grown considerably from the original five chiefs, to imagine the boats at one end of the bath were just off the coast of France, and asked a naval lieutenant to make waves at the other end of the bath with a back brush. The fleet became waterlogged and sank; Bernal said: 'That, gentlemen, is what will happen without an artificial harbour.'[16] He then took a Mae West lifebelt and laid it across the bath close to a second fleet. Calling for more waves, they all watched as the lifebelt damped the vigorous motion of the water and his newspaper boats stayed afloat. In the words of Lord Mountbatten: 'There was no doubt that Bernal's demonstration, together with his extremely able exposition of the subject, helped tip the scale with the Chiefs of Staff and made Mr Churchill more enthusiastic than ever.'[17]

The Prime Minister was not one of the onlookers in the bathroom, but heard about it from the COS. He soon sent for the professor to ask him some questions. They sat at either end of a long table. Churchill had difficulty hearing Sage's rather high-pitched, reedy voice, and growled: 'I can't hear a word you are saying. Come and sit up here, Bernal.'[18] Following this comical day of 'bathroom and bedroom scenes',[19] Sage retired to his bunk, a stowaway no longer. Mountbatten sent a cable to COHQ reporting that 'the Prime Minister has taken the most enormous personal interest in the artificial harbours'.[20]

Sage was back in front of the COS two days later to discuss Habbakuk. The naval architects had expressed Pyke's original concept of a floating airstrip in three alternative versions. Habbakuk I (soon discarded) would have been made of wood. Habbakuk II was closest to the COHQ model and would be a very large, slow, self-propelled vessel built of Pykrete reinforced by steel. Habbakuk III was a smaller, faster version of Habbakuk II. Air Chief Marshal Portal asked about potential bomb damage to Habbakuk III. Bernal suggested a certain amount of deck covering would be forced off, but could be repaired by some kind of flexible mat. It would be more difficult to deal with bomb holes in the centre portion, though the roof over the hangers would be made proof against 1,000 kilo bombs.[21] With regard to the bigger Habbakuk II, Bernal thought no one could say whether it would prove a practical proposition, until a large-scale model was built and tested in Canada in the spring of 1944. He had no doubt about the suitability of Pykrete, but constructional and navigational difficulties remained to be overcome.[22] The COS seemed satisfied with Bernal's answers, and agreed that Habbakuk should remain a high priority – the Prime Minister to be informed accordingly. They agreed that the CCO would write a memorandum on the subject to be tabled at Quadrant.

During the historic voyage on the *Queen Mary*, the COS apprised Churchill of the plan to land the allied armies on the Calvados coast of Normandy, during the early summer of 1944, to establish the long-awaited Second Front. Named Operation Overlord, this would be the greatest invasion from the sea in military history. Churchill saw the provision of artificial harbours and air superiority as the keys to success. The Mulberry harbours and some type of floating airstrip seemed to him to be vital engineering projects that would underpin Overlord. He was finally convinced that a cross-Channel invasion would be feasible in the next year.

When the ship docked at Halifax, Nova Scotia, Churchill noted with surprise, in spite of all attempts at secrecy, large crowds were assembled on the quayside to greet the British arrivals. The scenes were repeated at every station that their train passed through on the journey to Quebec. Before the formal start of the Quadrant Conference, Churchill travelled with his daughter to Hyde Park, the Roosevelt family home in upper New York State, to spend a few days in private with the President.[23] The two leaders discussed many weighty policy matters, including a secret, bilateral agreement (the Quebec Agreement) for the 'full and effective' interchange of information and collaboration on atomic weapons. Their talks also resulted in key decisions about supreme military commands. Despite his previous promise to Brooke, Churchill recognized that the Americans would be providing the bulk of the invasion force for Overlord so that the Supreme Allied Commander should be American – General Eisenhower would be the eventual choice. Fired by his conversations with Wingate on board ship, Churchill wanted to intensify the war in South-East Asia; Roosevelt took little persuading that this command should be given to Lord Mountbatten, who was soon appointed Supreme Allied Commander South-East Asia (SACSEA).

The venue for Quadrant was the Chateau Frontenac – a luxurious hotel that towers above Old Quebec and has magnificent views of the St Lawrence River. Sage was delighted to find 'everything on the house'![24] As the conference progressed, he wrote cryptic notes to himself in pencil – essentially lists of daily priorities. He first discussed Overlord with Mountbatten on 11th August, and on the 15th was studying the plans for Overlord and preparing remarks on certain aspects.[25] At the same time, he was working on a report on waves and looking into questions about the three possible versions of Habbakuk, such as the wood needed for H[abbakuk] I.

The first official discussion of Overlord took place in a closed session between the American and British COS on 17th August, during which they refined their strategic plans for defeating the Axis forces in Europe. They reported to Churchill and Roosevelt at the first plenary meeting two days later and that afternoon, Bernal was admitted to the inner sanctum for a presentation of Habbakuk by Mountbatten. According to the official record, 'Professor Bernal demonstrated with the aid of samples of pykrete, the various qualities of this material.'[26] The unofficial versions depict scenes of near mayhem, with Churchill's account being typical:

On receiving permission one of his [Mountbatten's] staff wheeled in on a large dumb-waiter two blocks of ice about three feet high, one common-or-garden ice, the other

Pykrete. He invited the strongest man present to chop each block of ice in half with a special chopper he had brought. All present voted General Arnold into the job of 'strong man'. He took off his coat, rolled up his sleeves, and swung the chopper, splitting the ordinary ice with one blow. He turned round, smiling, and clasping his hands, seized the chopper again and advanced upon the block of Pykrete. He swung the chopper, and as he brought it down let go with a cry of pain, for the Pykrete had suffered little damage and his elbows had been badly jarred.

Mountbatten then capped matters by drawing a pistol from his pocket to demonstrate the strength of Pykrete against gunfire. He first fired at the ordinary ice, which was shattered. He then fired at the Pykrete, which was so strong that the bullet ricocheted, narrowly missing Portal.

The waiting officers outside, who had been worried enough by the sound of blows and the scream of pain from General Arnold, were horrified at the revolver shots, one of them crying out, 'My God! They've now started shooting.'[27]

The next day, Bernal attended a meeting on the docks and artificial harbours, and intended to take his first look at the charts of the Normandy coast. While immersing himself in preparations for Overlord he was also being drawn into the operational planning for South-East Asia, by Mountbatten; Sage talked to Wingate several times about the realities of fighting in the jungles. Mountbatten was intent on appointing a senior scientific adviser to his new command and no doubt wanted to retain both Sage and Zuckerman. On the last day of Quadrant, Bernal received a summons to come to the Citadel, where Roosevelt was staying. Churchill wanted a repeat demonstration of the thermal properties of Pykrete.

No one else was there when Professor Bernal was ushered in, followed by a waiter who carried a silver pitcher of boiling water and two large silver punch bowls.

'Wait till you see this!' the Prime Minister said excitedly as Bernal placed a small block of ice in one of the bowls and added the water.

'See!' smiled Churchill after a few minutes. 'The ice melted!'

Roosevelt nodded and watched Bernal put a cube of Pykrete in the other punch bowl and pour on some more scalding water.

Churchill waited several minutes, then sat back in his chair and said quite happily, 'Hasn't melted at all!'[28]

No doubt, Sage then explained to the two statesmen that the wood pulp in Pykrete formed a soggy, insulating layer on the surface so that heat was not conducted to the interior of the block.

By the end of Quadrant, the combined Chiefs of Staff rejected Habbakuks I and III, but agreed that a research and development programme for the huge Habbakuk II should move ahead, under the direction of an Anglo-American-Canadian Habbakuk Board, with Dean Mackenzie of the Canadian National Research Council as its head. The COS cabled their deputies in London suggesting that Rivett of COHQ should be involved and that he should come over immediately with Perutz. Bernal and Lieutenant Commander Grant RN from the CCO's staff were to remain in North America, but should be transferred from Combined Operations to the Admiralty.[29] It was soon made clear that Geoffrey Pyke, Habbakuk's begetter, would not be welcome. Mountbatten sent a telegram to COHQ saying: 'Dean Mackenzie has just sent me a message to say that it is his considered opinion that if Pyke came out it would have a disastrous effect on American participation in this scheme, and he would have to advise his government accordingly. In the light of this uncompromising attitude, I am afraid Pyke will have to stand down for the good of his own scheme. Consulted Bernal who entirely agrees. We are both so sorry.'[30] Just a few days before, Pyke had been elated as word reached COHQ that Habbakuk was being supported at Quadrant, and he was preparing to return to Canada. Now he was devastated and blamed Bernal for hijacking his project.

Although Roosevelt had given his assent to Habbakuk in principle, there were members of his COS, notably Admiral King, Chief of the US Navy, who had grave doubts about its practicality. His reservations were shared by many in the British Admiralty. King ordered his staff to prepare a critical review to be presented to the new Habbakuk Board. Sage travelled down to Washington by train as soon as Quadrant was over, and was staying happily in the 'negro district' of Georgetown.[31] Jon Rivett had joined him from COHQ and was preparing to go before the Habbakuk Board with Sage. A cable was sent from London to Washington stating that Rivett and Bernal were not qualified to represent the Admiralty's views.[32] Sage seemed to sense the growing hostility to Habbakuk, judging by the letter he wrote to Mountbatten, who had returned to London to organize staff for his new posting to South-East Asia. The letter also indicates that Churchill at Quadrant raised the possibility of a hybrid between his beloved floating piers and Habbakuk:

BRITISH JOINT STAFF MISSION OFFICES OF THE
COMBINED CHIEFS OF STAFF WASHINGTON

6th September 1943

MOST SECRET AND PERSONAL

Dear C.C.O. and S.A.C.S.E.A.,

A number of points have arisen since you left here that may be of interest to you.

We have had very rough weather over the Prime Minister's Floating Airfields, the Americans much preferring carriers. I am being sent to a Committee of four American Admirals in order to be sunk without a trace.

There does seem to be some point in these airfields, however, if we can make them light enough and readily unpackable from one or two ships. This I am convinced can be done in either of two ways; using the American Naval Pontoon equipment in an expanded form, carrying a light landing platform, or by re-designing larger pontoons and joining them together in a way which has been worked out most ingeniously by Major Steer-Webster. By now Lochner will have seen you and given the details. I think he is well worth listening to and has got something in using ingenuity rather than brute force in dealing with waves.

Whether we have these fields or not would depend almost entirely on your wanting them. That is, if you are finding sheltered harbours or lees of islands where you could use them in your operations [in S. E. Asia] . . .

As you have seen from my cable and possibly heard from Lochner, I have been somewhat distressed at the prospect of being attached here for the duration on Habbakuk II. I realise quite well it was because it is so hard to find anybody that they put me on to the Committee, but I feel very strongly, especially after the work started in Quebec for OVERLORD and the Far East area, that I would be much more use, once the thing has got started, back in England. I hope you will be able to represent this fairly strongly before you leave, particularly in regard to any plans that you may have for organising a separate technical service in your command.

. . . I hope that you have been able to provide satisfactorily for Pyke, so that he can be most use to you and to the Habbakuk scheme.

Yours sincerely,
J.D. Bernal[33]

At the board meeting, Bernal gave his progress report on Habbakuk, and then listened to Admiral King's team attack the project. Bernal thought they had not made the best of their case, and with typical impartiality and eloquence, put forward the arguments against on their behalf. When word of this Jesuitical performance reached Churchill, he sent a telegram to Mountbatten saying: 'The next time you come to a Combined Chiefs of Staff Conference, you must not bring your scientific advisers with you.'[34]

A day or so later, Perutz arrived in Washington and was surprised to be greeted at Union Station by the whole British Habbakuk team, who 'seemed in no hurry to get back to their desks'.[35] He imagined they would be 'busy sixteen hours a day with the planning of the bergship's construction' but soon learned that work was at a standstill until the US naval engineers issued their final report. The tide was ebbing fast for Habbakuk. Mountbatten listed several reasons[36] – the great demand for steel; permission from Portugal to use airfields in the Azores which facilitated the hunting of U-boats in the Atlantic; long-range fuel tanks that allowed British fighters extra time to operate over France; and the American preference for conventional aircraft carriers. To these should be added Mountbatten's own withdrawal from the project. The final Habbakuk Board meeting took place in December 1943, and Pyke's unsinkable vessel was melted down in a few tepid words: 'The large Habbakuk

II made of Pykrete has been found to be impracticable because of the enormous production resources required and technical difficulties involved.'[37]

Mountbatten succeeded in bringing Bernal back to London, after he had spent about one month in Washington. Although Sage had expressed some interest in joining the SE Asia command, he was soon fully committed to Overlord or more precisely to Operation Neptune, which was the codename for the maritime part of the invasion. Never before had such a huge seaborne force been assembled, and the problems of landing thousands of troops with their equipment on defended beaches were completely novel. The most infamous amphibious landing in military history, at Gallipoli in the First World War, was the only precedent for attempting to put large numbers of troops ashore without first capturing a port. The long shadow of that tragic debacle, apart from causing Churchill continual nightmares, had provided the impetus for the inter-service collaboration that culminated in the formation of Combined Operations. There must never again be such amateurish preparation, tactical dithering, lack of troop protection and lack of proper equipment when putting an attacking force ashore. To make Overlord successful, there needed to be detailed knowledge about the nature of the Normandy shore – safe approaches for the ships and landing craft that were free from mines or rocks, the range of the tides, mean high and low water marks, underwater obstacles and fortifications on the beach, beach gradients and dimensions, exit routes from the beaches that would support tanks and heavy equipment, the topography of the hinterland. To preserve the vital element of surprise, all this intelligence needed to be collected without alerting the enemy.

When Sage returned to COHQ in late September, there was no specific information available on any of the above issues. How he came to be in charge of providing the necessary data is not clear, but having been the only scientist present at Quadrant, he was perhaps the obvious choice. He certainly had Mountbatten's full confidence and had made a positive impression on the Chiefs of Staff. Pyke was fond of quoting Chesterton's Father Brown stories to the CCO, especially the saying: 'It isn't that they can't see the solution. It is that they can't see the problem.' Faced with numerous imponderables in the planning of Overlord, who better than Sage to define and elucidate the problems? His strength as a scientist was always to have the first word on a subject, before handing it over to someone else with more doggedness, for the ultimate solution. Here was a role that would test his multi-faceted brilliance, where it was vital that no potential pitfall should go undiscovered, and where every dimension of each problem needed to be examined and related to one another. By 9th October, Bernal was able to report to Mountbatten that 'good progress is being made on the provision of harbours, information as to swell etc.'[38]

Mountbatten's departure from COHQ in October brought the opportunity to review the structure and function of Combined Operations. The COS appointed Air Marshal Bottomley to carry out the assessment, which he quickly did. To the annoyance of the Admiralty, he recommended that, with minor pruning, COHQ should continue much as before. The new CCO, Major-General Sir Robert Laycock, arrived in December. In the light of Bottomley's report, Laycock decided that Pyke should be transferred to the Admiralty, and that he would make do with Bernal as his sole scientific adviser (Zuckerman was still in the Mediterranean, where he had proved himself indispensable to the American and British airforce chiefs in the invasion of Sicily). In fact, the Admiralty had no work for Pyke, and he was to sit, ever more despondently at his desk, before quitting COHQ a few months later.[39] Sage's central role at COHQ was not diminished by the change in leadership; for example, when the Graham Report to the COS on 'all existing means of providing fire support when landing forces on a heavily defended coast' surfaced just before Christmas, he was one of two members of the Assault Warfare Committee at COHQ charged with gauging its impact and making sure its findings were being incorporated into planning for Overlord.[40]

When Bernal took his first glance at the charts for the Overlord landings in Washington at the end of August, his immediate reaction was to recall a holiday visit he had made to Arromanches, ten years earlier. He remembered swimming in turbid water, due, he thought, to a suspension of peat. Starting his research in the obvious place (one previously overlooked by British Naval Intelligence), Sage consulted *Le Guide Bleu* where he read: 'The beach at Arromanches is very sloping, indeed the sea goes out a long way and at extreme low tides the peasants go out to the end of the beach and pick up a material they call "gourban" which they use to manure their fields.'[41] Sage asked a geologist in London whether any British beaches were laid on peat, and was told that Brancaster, on the north Norfolk coast, was certainly one example.

Bernal quickly came to realize that virtually nothing was known about the interaction of waves and beaches, and was fortunate to enlist the help of Brigadier Ralph Bagnold, who had recently returned from service in North Africa. In the 1930s, Bagnold had planned and carried out a number of expeditions through the great deserts of the Middle East, and in 1941 published a book, *The Physics of Blown Sand and Desert Dunes*. Recalled to the Army at the outbreak of war, Bagnold had set up the Long Range Desert Group in 1940, which operated behind enemy lines in the Libyan Desert providing intelligence on Rommel's Afrika Corps as well as engaging in sabotage.[42] It is probable that Bernal heard about the exploits of Bagnold's Long Range Desert Group when he was in Cairo. Now that Bagnold was back in England, Bernal approached him to carry out experiments on the action of waves on the formation and erosion of beaches. The work was carried out at the Hydraulics Laboratory of Imperial College, London and resulted in Bagnold showing, as Bernal explained:

...on a normal gentle day the waves coming on to the beach do not produce simple circular movements of the water but have a residual progressive movement. In other words the water at the top moves forward and so does the water at the bottom. The excess water is carried away by a current flowing between the top and bottom – the undertow which is often fatal to swimmers.

In gentle weather, the current along the bottom carries grains of sand and builds up the beach and normally a beach will continually grow or, windblown, form dunes. However, in a storm, an entirely opposite phenomenon occurs. The sand is stirred up by the waves and lifted into the returning stream, to be carried right out to sea and deposited in deep water. A beach may be built up as much as three to four metres in a season and then swept clean in a single night of storm in winter. Fishermen know this very well and so do people living by the sea, but the ordinary seaside visitor only sees the beach at its best, when it is fully built up in the summer.[43]

The critical unknown factor about the beaches chosen for the landings was whether they would support the weight of armed vehicles, and in particular whether trucks and tanks would be able to drive across them without getting stuck. Opportunities to take direct samplings from the beaches around Arromanches were obviously going to be limited, and so Bernal decided that he would do his best to infer the beach structure by studying its geological and recent history. To do this he needed to read obscure volumes in the British Museum and in Oxford. An arrangement was made with the Principal Keeper of Printed Books at the Museum that Sage would have unfettered access to all their books and take away whatever he wanted, without any ticket being issued, on the understanding that he would eventually return the volumes to their correct places.

Sage read every volume of the Proceedings of the Linnaean Society of Caen, starting in the 1840s. He 'paid particular attention to the accounts of the summer excursions, which were usually made to a part of the seaside. It's true that much of the material was concerned with the dinner and with the speeches made there, but in the daytime there were excursions of geologists, of botanists, of zoologists, who brought back information very valuable to me: the character of a snail or of a plant would indicate the nature – marshy or otherwise – of the particular piece of country.'[44] While reading these prosaic descriptions of the naturalists' rambles, in his mind's eye Sage was picturing tanks and army lorries making their way over the land.

One of the most significant contributors to the Linnaen Society of Caen was Abbé Huc, a local priest, who achieved fame as a missionary to the Far

East. He was fascinated by the geology of the Bay of Calvados, and described in one article how he awoke after a tremendous winter's storm to find that all the sand had been stripped off the underlying peat. The Abbé wandered around at low tide and found 'a coin which bore the distinct imprint of the features of the Empress Crispina, thereby dating a period at which this had been farmland as no later than 230 AD'.[45] From this account, Sage pictured the Calvados reef as marking the headland of a pleasant wooded valley, rocky only at the edges and marshy in the middle. Much of the beach and shoreline was laid down on a base of clay and peat, the residues of an ice-age forest. The land was likely to be treacherous and Bernal's notes show that 'soft ground' and 'beach tests' were his top concerns in November 1943.[46]

There were other unlikely sources of recent shoreline history. The *Roman de Rou*, a twelfth century Norman epic by Maistre Wace, Sage regarded as a 'somewhat propagandist account of the escape of William the Conqueror, before he had earned that name, from a castle near Cherbourg to a friend of his at Ries'.[47] The journey was carried out at night and alone, and Sage was impressed by the detailed knowledge of the local countryside shown by the author. William 'crossed, at low tide, what the writer calls Le Grand Gué, and which is now called La Baie des Ryes. The writer indicated that a ridge of rock and gravel crosses this muddy bay, and enables one at extreme low tides to avoid a detour of some forty kilometres.'[48] Bernal was able to arrange for the RAF to take reconnaissance photographs of the bay at low tide 'which amply confirmed the existence of the submerged causeway that William took'.[49]

As he looked at old maps, Sage was puzzled by the name given to a small low-lying promontory – Hable de Heurtot. Thinking that this name should indicate a harbour, he investigated further and came across a fourteenth century lawsuit between the Le Sieur de Courseulles and the King, who claimed the Hable de Heurtot was being used to evade the tax levied at royal harbours. Bernal then found a report of a great storm in the sixteenth century that had completely silted up the mouth of the harbour so that it could never be cleared.[50] This ground was clearly unfit for tanks.

While the military planners were no doubt impressed by Sage's erudition and scholarship, with so much at stake they wanted some direct evidence from the Normandy coast. If the ground were too soft to support wheeled vehicles, miles of metal tracking would have to be manufactured in the USA and shipped in time for the planned summer invasion. In early November, Sir Bertram Ramsay, the Scottish admiral in charge of Neptune, issued a memo setting out the urgent need for a survey of the proposed positions of the Mulberry harbours.[51] He thought reconnaissance should be carried out during the moonless nights at the end of the month by naval force J, with Combined Operations providing suitable cover. Data should be recorded on the depths of water and nature of bottom, with samples and borings taken at frequent intervals if possible. The strength of tidal stream, any corrections to the silhouette of the coastline, any information about the nature of the beach and its rocky outcrops should be noted.

One of the men picked for this crucial and dangerous reconnaissance was Logan Scott-Bowden, a 24-year-old major in the Royal Engineers. He went to COHQ to be briefed by Professor Bernal, who struck him as a venerable professor.[52] On his overflowing desk were some Latin documents. Bernal explained to the observant young officer that they were reports on fuel reserves for the Roman Empire. The Romans used peat as a fuel and had carried detailed surveys of where it could be found in northern Europe. Secrecy about Overlord was imperative and Churchill would not authorize any reconnaissance of the French shore until the exercise had been tested in England first. Bernal was skeptical that commandos like Scott-Bowden could swim ashore and carry out a meaningful beach survey without detection by sentries. It was decided to hold a trial on Brancaster beach with Sage as one of the sentries.

Scott-Bowden and his sergeant, Bruce Ogden-Smith, were brought offshore by a landing craft and swam a mile or so to the beach in freezing conditions. They wore primitive wetsuits made of canvas-like material, which covered their heads and were sealed at the ankles. They saw Bernal standing guard next to an Army truck, and 'crawled around him, making notes on what he was doing and collecting soil samples'.[53] As the night wore on, both soldiers felt admiration for the professor who was prepared to endure the cold, windswept beach. After about four hours, they stood up and shouted at Sage, who had not seen them at all; they were able to tell him what he had been doing, with great precision. Exhausted, they all climbed into the Army truck and drove down to London, dropping Bernal off at 6 am. He reported to Churchill, through Cherwell, that the Brancaster rehearsal had been a success and Churchill decided that the Normandy beach reconnaissance could go ahead. He also instructed that it should take place on New Year's Eve, even though this was not a completely moonless night, because the Germans would be celebrating.

One of Mountbatten's personal appointments to COHQ was Sir Malcolm Campbell, the land-speed record holder. In Sage's opinion, he was an inspired amateur with unrivalled knowledge of beach surfaces, as a result of his speed trials on sand and salt flats. Campbell had devised various formulae and reckoned that a depth of fourteen inches of sand was sufficient to support wheeled vehicles, even if there was soft clay underlying. Campbell was a talented mechanical engineer with his own private workshop, and he constructed various gadgets for the raiders to use. One difficulty was that

Campbell thought he should go on the reconnaissance and took some persuading by Scott-Bowden that he would probably not make it to the beach swimming in the frigid water.[54]

After crossing the Channel in a Motor Torpedo Boat (MTB), Scott-Bowden and Ogden-Smith swam ashore. Both men carried 'a dozen long tubes, numbered in phosphorous on the top, in a bandolier on our backs, and the idea was to make a sample from various parts of the beach, noting on the underwater writing tablets which were strapped to our arms approximately where each sample had been taken'.[55] After crawling along the beach below the high water mark so as to leave no tracks, and avoiding detection in the sweeping beam from a lighthouse, they found the area where they were due to carry out a detailed survey. Scott-Bowden described the data collection:

We came across a large outcrop of peat, which had been suspected from aerial photographs, but by and large we thought the area would turn out all right from the point of view of bearing capacity. When we had each filled about eight tubes I reckoned we had got enough and so I said 'Let's go.' That's when the trouble really started, because the breakers were quite heavy and we were positively bogged down with our bandoliers and all our other kit.[56]

After struggling to break through the incoming breakers, the two soldiers swam out and managed to rendezvous with the MTB; they were pulled on board, cold and exhausted, with their precious samples. The samples confirmed what Bernal had been saying about the subsoil of peat and clay.

Writing to Mountbatten a week later to explain why he could not visit the new HQ in Delhi, Bernal mentioned 'the necessity to attend personally to detailed briefings of recce parties which depend on moon and tides'.[57] For the next operation, at the end of January 1944, the Combined Operations Pilotage Party arrived off the French coast in a midget submarine that had been towed about a third of the way across the Channel by a trawler. For several days, detailed observations of the cliffs at Pointe du Hoc that would be such a deadly obstacle for the Americans on Omaha beach were made through the submarine's thin periscope. Their eel's-eye view was used to supplement information from aerial photographs. At night, further beach samples were taken, following which Scott-Bowden had to struggle out of his wetsuit in the battery compartment of the submarine, where there was only eighteen inches of headroom.

Bernal's 1944 desk dairy lists 'trials at Brancaster' beginning on 11th January.[58] The trials confirmed that as long as there was a layer of sand 18 inches deep covering the *gourban*, vehicles would not get stuck, providing that they did not follow in each others' tracks.[59] It would be necessary, therefore, to clear mines over a wide front, and not just be content to provide a narrow passage. It was concluded, nevertheless, that the beaches at Arromanches would support tanks, providing the mines were cleared successfully and the tank drivers carefully briefed.

Further data were obtained by an RAF sortie over the Normandy beaches by a single plane that was burning excess oil, so that from the ground it looked in trouble. It dropped its load of bombs causing craters in the beach that could be measured by subsequent aerial photography. As a bonus, one of the bombs landed in the sea and set off a pattern of plumes, suggesting explosions at a distance and indicating that the waters were heavily mined.[60] To the alarm of Brancastrians, the RAF bombed their Norfolk beach for comparative purposes! In addition to supervising the large-scale tests at Brancaster, Bernal met representatives from Montgomery's 21st Army group and briefed the American military about the beaches near the Cotentin peninsula. By the end of January, the reports on the Neptune beaches received final approval.[61]

With the basic topology of the beaches established, Sage now became more concerned with the waters of La Baie de la Seine. The Calvados and Bernières reefs had broken many hulls over the years, and the coastline had a fearsome reputation. As he began to look at charts, Sage realized that the main purpose of showing a rocky coastline was to warn sailors to stay away.[62] The coastal chart that he was provided with by the Admiralty was based on the *pilote francais* chart of 1823. It had been reproduced by the Admiralty hydrographer in 1902, with additions and corrections in 1911. Bernal had the most up-to-date edition from March 1920.[63] He now immersed himself in antiquarian maps and found that the earliest maps of this coast had been prepared on royal orders by 'the great French hydrographer Beautemps Beaupré'[64] in 1776. As he studied successive editions of the charts, Bernal noticed that errors seemed to creep in, and most seriously, submerged rocks present on Beaupré's chart were omitted over time. It occurred to Sage that this was because the copyists were paid according to the number of charts they copied, not the number of rocks they plotted. During February and March, Bernal made frequent visits to Norfolk House, St James' Square, the headquarters of the Chiefs of Staff Supreme Allied Command (COSSAC). There he worked on maps and liaised with the Theatre Intelligence Section (TIS), who were responsible for organizing and distributing intelligence needed for Overlord.

Just as the existing charts were unreliable, there were no up-to-date tide-tables available for Courseulles, for example. So Sage decided to generate his own. Soon after Dunkirk, advertisements had been placed in newspapers asking members of the public to send in postcards and snapshots of any seaside holidays they had spent in France. COHQ now obtained this collection of tens of thousands of pictures of the coast 'from Calais to Nice'.[65] Careful sorting left Bernal and his assistants with 'an almost complete photographic record of Arromanches, taken from every angle'. Photographs with people in them, especially children paddling or wading, were very helpful in showing the depth of water at particular states of the tide, allowing some estimate of the beach gradient. The snapshot approach was reinforced with more systematic data obtained from aerial reconnaissance. Bernal explained why precise estimates of the gradient of the gently sloping beach and the tidal depths were vital.

If you take the fact that the slope of the beach was often as low as 1 part in 200, you can easily see that an error of even only five centimetres [in the depth of the tide] could mean an error of as much as ten metres along [up or down the slope of] the beach – and for beaches which are defended by mines and obstacles the precise point of [dis]embarkation can mean the vital difference, not only between life and death, but between victory and failure.

The tides, too, proved a way of measuring the depth of water down to low-watermark. For deeper waters, of course, one had to rely on indications given by the refraction of the waves – a wave travels more slowly in shallow water, and by using appropriate formulae, it is possible from an air-photograph alone to calculate the depth of water.[66]

Bernal's diary entry for 31st January, in addition to recording the final approval of reports on Neptune beaches, shows that he was preparing to brief the CCO on 'Gooseberry'.[67] Gooseberry was the codename given to the breakwaters to be created by blockships. Churchill had held a meeting the previous week when it was decided there would be a total of five Gooseberries, one in each divisional assault area, two of which would form the outer protection of Mulberry artificial harbours.[68] Churchill had also called for a weekly committee, under his own chairmanship, to keep the preparations for Overlord under constant survey.[69] The Bernal diary for 1st February records that he had been appointed to the 'Attack on defended beaches' subcommittee. It is clear that Sage was a key figure in planning Overlord – especially in defining the crucial subjects of the tides, shallows, shoals, beaches, cliffs and marshes. Although he lacked formal qualifications as an engineer, geologist or geographer, who but Sage would have had the ability to make sense of clues buried in mediaeval French literature, combine them with casual observations from nineteenth-century French natural scientists and from pre-war holiday-makers in order to produce lucid, predictive reports for the military that were backed by fresh empirical data?

It is not surprising in view of the intense and unremitting nature of the task he was undertaking that Bernal should be out 'sick' from 23rd to 27th March. He probably spent the time with Margaret Gardiner and Martin, who had returned to her house in Hampstead. She remembered that 'Desmond was, rightly, very careful about what he told me. I remember at one point . . . I had decided that we were going to invade France. I had decided entirely on my own, and mentioned it to Desmond. He said, "You mustn't say things like that, people will think I told you." And he hadn't told me, but I had deduced it myself from what was going on, what I knew. I remember that he was horrified when I mentioned this."[70]

One of the lessons learned from the Dieppe raid was that exclusive reliance on vertical aerial photographs meant that vital details would be missed that might be visible on low-level oblique photographs. From mid-February, obstacles on the Arromanches beaches were identified by aerial reconnaissance. Their positions were plotted on 1/12,500 scale maps from vertical photos, with the identification of obstacle type being made from oblique photos. The number of mapped obstacles increased quickly as each successive sortie produced information at different states of the tide. More detailed 1/5000 scale maps were then produced showing the beach contour lines capable of being related directly to the position of the water line at any time of tide on any particular day. These maps also showed accurate beach profiles at frequent intervals along the beach and portions of rock outcrops and clay patches on the beaches.[71] During the three months before D-Day, 200,000 sorties were flown over enemy-occupied territory,[72] many simply to mislead the Germans about the Allies' intended landing place, but the handful of photo-reconnaissance missions over the Normandy beaches provided information that prevented thousands of casualties.

The Bernal diary for April shows him concerned with underwater explosions, craters in beaches, surf, swell, weather, beach gradients, tides and underwater obstacles, beach obstacles, and beach mines.[73] Small armed Combined Operations reconnaissance parties were sent to the Pas de Calais area in May. They found Teller [anti-tank] mines on stakes that would be detonated by any movement of the stake. This led to increased concern that earlier photographs from Arromanches were not detailed enough and might have missed this type of hazard. On 19th May, an RAF sortie flown at an altitude of just 50 feet gave precise identification and showed that a high percentage of the Arromanches beach obstacles were mined with Teller mines or adapted shells.[74] While all the information was coming in on underwater mines, mines and shells on stakes, concrete tetrahedra and steel hedgehogs on the beaches, others at COHQ were undertaking trials to find the most rapid way of dealing with obstacles, and the probable damage they would cause at different states of the tides. At the end of April, Bernal was plotting the positions of known beach mines, and also working out their charges and fusing.[75] The results of these endeavours were incorporated into the detailed orders for the landing.[76]

As the build-up to D-Day intensified, Bernal naturally became anxious about the quality of the charts he had produced. He worried that his new maps were still not detailed enough and requested new hydrographic sound-ings.[77] In particular, he was concerned that opposite Bernières landing craft would be in danger of grounding on the rocks. Once again the unlikely figure of Abbé Huc came to his aid. Huc's geological interests extended to the distribution of glacial erratic rocks.[78] He had explored the Bay of Calvados with local fishermen, whose intimate knowledge of the waters owed nothing to charts and who knew the rocks by individual names, such as Dos de L'Ane and La Vieille Femme. The abbot took cross-bearings on the rocks at low and high tides to plot a safe passage through them. The work of Abbé Huc was recapitulated by plotting the positions of the rocks from aerial photographs at known states of the tide so that safe passages could be identified.[79]

On 23rd May, Bernal travelled down to Southwick House, north of Portsmouth, where Eisenhower had established his operational headquarters. There he briefed Admiral Ramsay and Rear Admiral Vian, who was to command the naval task force that would transport the British 2nd Army, on the accuracy of his rock maps. He then had meetings with the navy hydrographer, and the following day they continued to work on beach maps using aerial reconnaissance photographs. Bernal was still studying 'Huc's monograph'.[80] On 25th May, those holding naval orders for Operation Neptune were ordered to open them, and Bernal discussed the forthcoming assault with Blackett, who was at Southwick House in his capacity as head of Operational Research for the Admiralty. Sage attended a final meeting on underwater obstacles; his last map revision was completed on 31st May.

The timing of D-Day was predicated on the tides and, of course, the weather. The landing on the beaches was intended to take place at dawn on the half-tide with the tide rising. This was so that the landing craft would be grounded to seaward of the densest obstacles on the beach, and would float off easily after discharging their human and mechanical cargoes. If the craft landed at high tide, many would detonate mined underwater obstacles, and landing at low tide would expose the attacking troops for too long on open ground. Peter Danckwerts, who had started the war as the Bomb Disposal Officer for the Port of London, had been nominally sharing an office with Sage since the beginning of 1944, although Sage 'had so many irons in the fire that he was seldom there'. Danckwerts recalled: 'There was nearly a breach of security because of Bernal's desire to be on the beaches by D+1. His lank locks had to be shorn and he had to be kitted-out with battle-dress and ammunition boots. All this took some time and he was not a particularly military figure at the end of it.'[81]

Bernal was driven back to Southwick House on 5th June, the day originally set for the invasion. The weather was poor and so the operation was put on hold. On reaching Portsmouth, Sage noticed empty parking strips that 'had

been so full of tanks and guns two days before'.[82] He sought out Blackett, and
the pair went for a walk through the maze of tents and huts surrounding the
main building; they emerged on the Downs and 'looked out on the sea where
the whole Expedition lay just about to start . . . It was an immense assembly of
ships but against the cloud and the sea, it looked very small'.[83] Blackett
thought it was silly of Sage to go, as did Sage to some extent. He knew that
there was nothing he could do now to influence events, but felt that he had to
be there and would never forgive himself if the operation went ahead and he
missed the opportunity to observe what actually happened. He went to bed at
midnight, after preparing 'all my heads of enquiries', knowing that the fleet
had sailed. Waking at 4 am, he 'carefully dressed in the very doubtful disguise
of a naval officer'.[84] The weather was bad and Sage was worried that this
would diminish the effectiveness of the air bombardment on the far shore, but
there was the compensating advantage of genuine surprise, suggested by early
reports of German coastal batteries 'firing very feebly'. After a three-course
breakfast, Bernal listened to the early news trickling in; it did seem as though
things were going better than predicted. Footholds had been gained on several
beaches, although there were still no reports from the Americans.

On the afternoon of D-Day, Bernal sailed across the rough English Channel
in a fast MTB.

The boat was alive. It swung from side to side and leaped up over the waves to
come crashing down and sending up sheets of foam. It was no use trying to keep dry
but it was so exhilarating that it did not matter. We began to pass the convoys of the
second wave: hundreds of LCTs [Landing Crafts for Tanks] and all kinds of other craft
wallowing along in the waves while we shot past. The wind rose as we got towards the
centre of the Channel and the seas were high . . . Then the sky began to clear . . . [and] the
whole journey became altogether a joyous one. The crew were all young, I suppose the
oldest was twenty two; we were all excited but we could not talk except to point, between
the roar of the engine and the crash of the waves. We began to pass returning convoys
and to look for signs of action; a few were on tow, others showed holes made by mines –
but their return at all meant success. This was not going to be a second Dieppe. How
well I remembered those battered and scarred LCTs – the few that got home.

The sky was now all blue except that a pile of clouds lay on the southern horizon
and clouds over France. Then I saw a very thin grey line. France that I had not seen for
four years. Then the shapes began to appear. All around cruisers, battleships, merchant ships and LSTs [Landing Ships for Tanks] and hundreds of other ships. We
could see the coast clearly now – the coast already burnt into my memory, having
poured over so many maps and photographs. I knew every bit of it. The distant
steeples of Langrune and Luc: the noble steeple of Bernières rising above its woods: the
water tower above Courseulles: the hill of Mont Fleury and the lighthouse of Vire. The
village of Rivière with the children's sanatorium: and then, beyond it in the next dip –
Arromanches. Arromanches where I had been ten years before, such a failure and sad

turning point in my life. They were fighting still in Arromanches: you could see occasional little flashes. The lower part of the coast was covered with smoke from fires. The big ships were booming out – but a desultory bombardment. Shells seemed to be falling beyond Cap Montvieux: the sky clouded again and the sea stayed rough.

The MTB swung alongside a large naval ship – Sage managed to time his jump onto the rope ladder and scrambled aboard. Once inside, he realized how cold and wet he was, but he was soon standing at the bar downing 'excellent and unobtainable' drinks with some naval officers he had known at Cambridge, who were amused to see him in uniform. They sat down together in the wardroom for dinner, and Sage listened to the latest news on how the beaches had been secured by the British, but there was still no news at all from the Americans. At nine o'clock, they all listened to a speech on the radio by the King – 'a strange, halting speech' – followed by the playing of the national anthem with the officers standing to attention rather casually. Later the ship's siren sounded and Sage came on deck to witness the ships firing flak at some distant planes, producing 'beautiful streams of red fire: fountains rising and falling, swaying and twisting in the sky'. Then the bombs started to fall and he found to his surprise that his teeth were chattering. He was not 'rationally scared but somehow the isolation of being in a ship was worse than any raid on land'.[85] Lines from John Donne's Elegy *Love's War* came into his head.

> To mew me in a ship, is to enthral
> Me in a prison, that were like to fall.

He slept uneasily for a few hours lying on a bench in the Commodore's cabin. Very early the next morning, he and the Commodore decided that they would try to go to the beaches. Just as Sage was gathering his things together, the ship shuddered and there was a loud crash.

We had been hit forward about thirty feet from where I was. In a few seconds flames were rising to the height of the mast. The wind was throwing them through the companionway and along back towards me. I worked it out: it was a bad conjunction. The ship lay head to the wind and the fire would be driven along and have most chance to spread. The sea was rough and the chance of getting out the boats, which were almost certainly too few, would not be great. I was probably the only man on board without a Mae West. I had procured an excellent one, but had left it behind at H.Q. I remembered studying the statistics of the bombing of ships, how one in three caught fire, and remembered the burnt out hulks in Tripoli harbour. But all this was not frightening, it was simply irrevocable fact. The fire parties started running up with the hose... the whole anchorage was alive with flak... everyone was on edge... any plane in sight [Spitfires included] would have been fired on. Then, in practically no time the flames began to die down a little. I moved forward. At the edge of the deck I could see the body of one of the A.A. gunners lying up against a rail, clearly dead, already pale and distorted and it was less than ten minutes since the bomb had fallen.[86]

Bernal and the Commander decided to try to go ashore but the heavy swell and strong onshore wind made it impossible to land. The weather on D-Day+ 1 was even worse than it had been on D-Day.

There was nothing for it but to turn back. Now we were moving in the teeth of the wind, very slowly and much beaten by the waves. We got depressed. In weather like this it would be practically impossible to land supplies or reinforcements for the assault troops. After two hours we got back to the dispatch boat. It was more difficult to get on board than ever: both vessels were pitching: there was nothing for it but to judge one's time and jump. Both of us were feeling pretty sick, wet and cold but revived in a little time, enough for coffee and sausages.[87]

Before long, Sage was playing poker with a group of senior officers, who were all aware that the fate of the whole expedition depended on the weather. Bernal had talked to the two meteorological officers at Southwick House the night before D-Day, discussing how the accuracy of forecasts could be measured. He remembered how they had predicted a complicated series of depressions such as had not been seen in living memory. It was now noon Wednesday, when they had said there might be a slight improvement.

And then almost miraculously the change came. The clouds flew away, the wind dropped, the sea quieted almost at once. The strong, bright sun shone over all the ships and the woods and the fields of the coast. The whole anchorage seemed to shake itself and stir into activity.[88]

With an American major, Bernal now made another attempt to reach the shore – this time successfully. He jumped out of the landing craft at 'one of the precise spots that [he] had studied so often and whose history and geography were more familiar [to him] than any place on earth... It was an incredible scene: the confused row of stranded craft: the queue of vehicles coming off the beach, some broken down or bombed, derelict tanks here or there.'[89] The assault the day before had taken place on a spring tide with a strong onshore wind that had made the tide two feet higher than expected. Sage saw what had happened: as each wave of landing craft grounded, a number failed to clear because of enemy action or because they were holed by underwater obstacles. In addition, 'many undamaged craft broached to, were washed up by the tide and neaped'.[90] There were repair and salvage parties trying to clear the beach, the Military Police were directing the traffic, and bodies were laid out in rows under blankets awaiting burial. Bernal and the major walked off the beach up a dusty road, observing considerable damage from bombs and shells as they went.

Then we saw our first civilians, blue-bloused peasants, quiet and almost surly, none of the enthusiasm of the Arabs or even the Italians in Tripoli. A woman passed by and smiled but ever so slightly. Further up the houses were not so knocked about, their doors were wreathed in roses but the roses were dusty and dust, road dust and bomb dust, gathered everywhere. I saw a middle-aged man and his wife passing along the street: he looked intellectual, I think he was the village schoolmaster. I said 'Bonjour, monsieur.' We talked for a few minutes... Later I addressed some nuns very politely, but was received with frozen and taciturn virtue.[91]

Sage and the major split up, and he continued to meander through the village, where he saw a large group of bewildered-looking prisoners being watched by just a pair of armed guards. He met some soldiers who immediately began to press him for local information about minefields and for any broader news on how the invasion was going. He began to feel too warm in the afternoon sun, but dare not remove any part of his uniform in case he lowered 'the dignity of the officer caste'.[92] Hearing bangs that were very familiar to him from all the bomb trials he had attended, Sage returned to the beach and found gangs hard at work trying to clear the hedgehogs and mined posts.

The willing ones were shinning up the posts and defusing the mines and shells. They complained that it was dangerous work: they did not mind defusing, they said, but it was unfair to make blast waves whilst they were at work. I took their photos not feeling too happy about it myself, as I was effectively just as close to the shells as they were. However, I did not think that they were sensitive enough to matter. From time to time, there would be a somewhat feeble whistle which made us take cover but usually we only took cover after the explosion so as to keep clear of the bits and pieces falling from the sky.[93]

The clearance gang had been working for thirty-six hours with hardly a break, and Bernal could see that there were far too few of them for the enormous task. Their spirit was indefatigable and they made suggestions for improving the methods and for better equipment. They were led by a tough, young lieutenant, who had been wounded in the shoulder during the assault, but kept working.

More obstacles were being blown up [and] rather heavy pieces of steel were being thrown into the air; we took cover behind stranded craft. The men were drinking soup out of tins; they offered me some energy tablets which were very good, and asked for news eagerly, but not anxiously... Everything was quiet again, no gunfire or planes.[94]

Sage went to take a close look at the German gun emplacement, and found himself 'very irritated at the stupid and slipshod construction of this work and felt like sending a note to the Todt organization, telling them to sack the people responsible'. He wandered along the beach to the area where he had predicted peat and clay, and was dismayed by what he found. Sure enough the ground was soft, with the peat laid down in the Neolithic Period on top of the clay of the last ice-age.

In it, like flies in amber, were stuck every kind of vehicle except the jeep: tanks, lorries and even DUKWs. Some were being pulled out, but others were getting bogged down again. I thought – it is always the same way: I may be right, I may even know that I am right, but I am never sufficiently ruthless and effective to force other people to believe that I am right and to act accordingly. All this was so unnecessary: it all could have been avoided. If people had not thought that my objections were just theoretical and statistical, and that they were practical people [who] need pay no attention to them.[95]

At nightfall he managed to get back to the dispatch boat and felt uplifted by the sappers he had met on the beach – so cheerful, kind and energetic. In the wardroom, he discussed his observations with four other officers, one of whom had managed to cover the entire front, walking and hitch-hiking rides in jeeps. He reported the beginnings of a small counter-attack, north of Caen. Sage thought that this small group 'knew more about what was going on, on the second day of the second front than anyone in the world'. D-Day+2 dawned peacefully, with the water glassy smooth. Bernal and a colonel transferred to a control ship opposite Bernières. After a while they hailed a passing LCM (Landing Craft Motors) with a heavy lorry on board. They soon approached the rocks, 'the charting of which had caused such a flurry a fortnight before'.

A number of ships were stranded on the rocks – I could see them now, vast, ill-defined, patches of seaweed. A man in the bows was taking soundings with a pole . . . we were aground. The boat swung round and managed to back out. I said to the coxswain, 'I think I know something about these rocks. You will never get in at this stage of the tide; better wait for it to rise a foot or two and then I think I can show you the way in.' We drew out further and waited. I was impatient . . . After twenty minutes we started again . . . I said 'Steer for the church, but then, to allow for the wind, you had better bear a little to the right.' . . . there was a grating sound and when the coxswain tried to reverse one of the propellers went. We drifted clear again and tried to edge forward but it got more and more difficult. The wind was freshening and catching in the large hood of the lorry and kept swinging the boat away from its course and there was a strong tide running as well. It took us the best part of two hours to get in that mile, but at last we landed on a firm sand beach and the lorry, with us in it, rolled out.[96]

While waiting for the tide, they had heard some sporadic firing and seen flashes of fire coming from the village. Now on land, they were told the battle of Bernières was over, but that there were snipers in the great tower of the church, which dominated the whole countryside. Sage badly wanted to see the church, but felt that it would be foolish to be shot 'for the love of Norman architecture'. So he stuck to the beach defences, where he was again disappointed by the quality of the German construction. There was a rumour that eight captured snipers were Frenchwomen in German uniforms: they had been summarily shot. Sage wondered whether the story was true, and if so whether the women were motivated by affection or politics. He walked west along the beach and was intrigued by the range of activities taking place in what was such a pretty setting, if one removed the trappings of war.

... in the water meadows between the church and the dunes, the tank machines were clearing mines, looking for all the world like hay-tedders, but which belied this by suddenly becoming enveloped in a pall of black smoke from an exploded mine.... The tide was up and the beach was in full activity. Enormous pontoon rafts, every inch loaded with vehicles and men, were coming in and discharging ... Men just ashore were looking around them; the older hands were digging in against expected air-raids, or hanging out their clothes to dry or cooking meals. Sitting against a telegraph post of a little railway, a midshipman was writing his first letter home. Behind, the clearance of mines went on punctuated by explosions and smoke.[97]

Sage reached the small port of Courseulles, famous for its oysters, which was so peaceful it reminded him of Ireland. Most of the houses were punctured by shell fragments, not destroyed like the bombed houses in England. A gaping hole in the recently vacated German HQ allowed access straight into the officers' mess, its walls covered with Nazi slogans. On the bar, there was an empty champagne bottle and a full glass of milk; the piano had its strings torn to pieces by shell splinters.

Still accompanied by the colonel, Bernal set off next for the marshes inland, which they found full of bomb craters. They came upon a tank stuck in a ditch; the tank commander told them his story:

'We had a tough time getting through', he said. 'There were a lot of defences in the dunes which we could not see and mortar fire from the hills behind. When we did get through we found the floods, or rather the first tank found them when it disappeared in the blown up culvert across the stream. The local people were specially helpful. They showed us the sluice to let the water out. Then we bulldozed some rubble over the tank and went on ahead. I got stuck in the ditch because I could not see it under the water.'[98]

The late afternoon and early evening was taken up with waiting for the next bus, as Bernal had come to regard the landing craft, plying their way to and from the larger ships. He spent some of this time writing up his notes, but found it hard to stay awake. He had to go back to England that night, but did not want to: 'I had got attached to the place and its strange inconsequent life, its near peacefulness and its distant dangers.' He returned to Portsmouth on the same MTB that had brought him across on D-Day, and watched as the young navigator plotted their course in a lane through the minefields – one of ten approximately parallel routes that had guided the invasion force to La Baie de la Seine.

Sage could be pleased with the preparatory work done over the previous eight months at COHQ. The obstacles encountered on the beaches corresponded 'in almost every detail to expectations' from the charts issued for the landings. 'The methods for dealing with them were adequate if allowances are made for the extra difficulties introduced by the weather.'[99] Among the lessons learned were that mechanical removal of obstacles by armoured bulldozers, at low tide, was more successful than destruction by explosives, and that some of the landing craft were overloaded and should have been reinforced so that they could force their way through underwater obstacles. The engineering feat that was the Mulberry harbour would prove its worth in protecting ships and other vessels during the great midsummer's storm to come. COHQ issued a series of bulletins on the planning of Overlord in November 1944. Three conclusions stood out:

1. The element of surprise offset the rough weather.
2. Heavy preliminary bombardment, although it did not effect a lot of material damage, achieved the desired effect of neutralizing enemy batteries by its effects on the defenders.
3. Although uncleared and causing considerable damage to incoming craft, the underwater obstacles were not sufficiently dense or effective to jeopardize the operation.[100]

In short, Overlord was a 'planning triumph'.[101]

13

Lessons of War

The complexities of South-East Asia Command (SEAC) were such that they would have overwhelmed a leader without Mountbatten's ineffable self-confidence. By 1943, most of South-East Asia was firmly under Japanese control, following the unstoppable advances they had made through thick jungles, which the British had long regarded as impenetrable. To the British soldier, the Japanese had taken on the aura of invincibility, and morale was further depressed by the debilitating tropical conditions that bred mosquitoes and malaria. Mountbatten's approach to raising spirits was direct and simple.[1] Relying on his royal pedigree, he cheerfully informed the troops that they were not the Forgotten Army: no one had ever heard of them, but this was all going to change under his leadership. His absurd optimism and ironic humour proved irresistible.

Mountbatten's background naturally predisposed him towards amphibious operations in the new theatre; as soon as he was appointed SACSEA at Quadrant, he asked Bernal to think about the prospects for landings on the peninsulas and islands of the Indian Ocean. Sage's early impressions were not encouraging:

I have been chasing up information on swell and weather on your coasts with Hussey. Extraordinarily little quantitative data is available. The best we can hope for is the statement of sailors on their experiences, which, even if all were true, are not always representative. I am hoping to get much better information from cinema films, which would give some indications of the height and period of surf, and also from air photographs.

The whole thing wants to be organised rapidly and scientifically as part of intelligence. I strongly urge you to ask for a Scientific Advisor who is up in the M.W.D. work, to be sent out to Colombo immediately. You will want this information, not only for ports, but for landings. They should be able to match the conditions pretty well on the Southern coasts of India for practice purposes. I gather that the best Dutch intelligence as to the island coasts is also to be had from the Dutch representative in Colombo.[2]

Aside from the lack of intelligence and the operational problems to be faced, there were delicate political balances to be struck. The Americans were distrustful of renewed British imperialism in Asia, while being benevolent towards Generalissimo Chiang Kai-shek and the Nationalist Chinese. The American paradox was personified in General 'Vinegar' Joe Stilwell, Mountbatten's limey-loathing Deputy Supreme Commander, who also served as Chief of Staff to Chiang Kai-shek and commanded his Chinese troops in Burma. Stilwell's first experience with these men in battle against the Japanese was dismal. He was alarmed by the almost total lack of medical services in the Chinese Army to deal with casualties, and by the poor health of the men due to malaria, dysentery and malnutrition – all of which greatly reduced their fighting power. Finally, SEAC was bound to take second place to the planning of Overlord, as Bernal warned Mountbatten in September 1943.

There was marked unwillingness to make any attempt at covering your area, here in Washington. Wernher quite rightly wanted to get back to OVERLORD, which will need every bit of effort we can put into it, and I think it would be advisable to appoint an entirely fresh committee to deal with your harbours. I doubt if the Americans are likely to be of much use, although if the committee could work to cover very similar West Pacific areas, they would be more keen on it and could contribute more experience.[3]

Sage recommended that if Mountbatten found himself in Chungking, Chiang Kai-shek's capital, he should 'look up my great friend Dr Joseph Needham, British Council Scientific Representative in China, who should be able to give you a very complete picture of what the technical, as well as scientific, possibilities are there'. Writing one month later from COHQ, Bernal informed Mountbatten of a proposed Royal Army Medical Corps mission to China to report on what medical assistance and supplies were needed by Chiang Kai-shek's army.[4] The sending of such a mission appeared to Bernal 'to be one of the few ways in which it is open to Britain to give concrete and impressive assistance to China in the military sphere'. He suggested that it would be important for the RAMC mission to make contact with SEAC's own medical advisers so that a uniform health plan might be adopted for the whole area. Mountbatten was in agreement: the statistics for the 1943 monsoon season showed that for every wounded man admitted to hospital there were 120 admissions for dysentery and malaria.[5]

When he left COHQ in October, Mountbatten took with him the last, fantastic scheme hatched by the dejected Geoffrey Pyke to overcome the lack of suitable ports in South-East Asia. Pyke's preliminary 'Note on the Military Significance of Power-Driven Rivers' began in his finest orotund style ('In pursuant of your instructions of September 1943... to submit to you personally any suggestions, particularly those relevant to the war in the Far East') and continued for another fifty pages.[6] As with Habbakuk, Pyke's wonderful idea was crisply summarized for Mountbatten by Sage. Power-Driven Rivers were 'essentially for the use of pipelines to carry military and other stores in cylindrical containers travelling along with the oil or other liquid in the pipe'.[7] Ships at anchor would send large-bore pipes ashore, and all manner of supplies would then be pushed along the pipes by hydraulic force. Once a secure lodgment was established, the pipes could be extended inland, through swamps and over mountains, to overcome the lack of conventional roads. To Pyke, Power-Driven Rivers was a solution of 'intellectually abnormally elementary nature', but Sage, for once, was cautious saying that the idea would need a lot of investigation. He agreed with Pyke that the scheme should be technically possible, but could foresee problems in the production of such lengths of pipe and the pumping gear necessary.

Mountbatten was looking forward to a visit from Bernal and Zuckerman in December, but, as we have seen, this proved impossible because of their commitment to Overlord. Sage instead wrote a long apologetic letter to Mountbatten saying that he did not want his unavailability 'to deprive you of scientific advice and research until some problematical date'.[8] As on previous occasions, he suggested the name of G.I. Taylor as an alternative adviser; Bernal knew Taylor was in Washington but did not know that he was an indispensable member of the Manhattan Project team. He was encouraged that John Kendrew, whose company he enjoyed in Cairo, was transferring to Delhi to take charge of operational research for the RAF. Bernal was also hoping 'to establish better liaison with Needham in China' and was sorry to hear that he had been stuck in the Gobi Desert, while Mountbatten was in Chungking. He suggested flying Needham to Delhi, when Chinese matters were being discussed. With the handwritten letter, Bernal sent 'a longer and more official document on some topics that seem from this end to need attention on the spot'.

The formal memo on OR organization in South-East Asia was just over two pages long and contained five headings:

1. Physiological effects of tropical conditions, including disease.
2. Physical effects of tropical conditions on equipment, etc.
3. Transport. Land, sea and air.
4. Sea conditions.
5. Topographical and anthropological intelligence.[9]

It was a typically wide-ranging effort by Sage (who at the same time was supervising the survey work for the Overlord beaches); he was particularly concerned to relate these subjects to conditions that Mountbatten's forces would encounter. So, for example, while acknowledging that there was a medical section at SEAC interested in malaria, he was worried that they were not thinking about 'actual conditions that face armies in the field, and . . . their requirements for insect fighting and the treatment of malaria and other diseases'. Bernal recommended that small local research stations should be established for each of the five subject areas, manned jointly by American and British scientists and including Indian colleagues where possible. In the case of sea conditions, which the Admiralty acknowledged were largely unknown, Bernal suggested 'a sea and swell station, run in connection with the meteorological station . . . initially situated in Ceylon and later at advanced bases'. Their role would be 'to predict swell and surf at places and times required for operations, and to work in conjunction with the landing craft experimental station to find what conditions of sea were admissible for operations'.

Bernal was so preoccupied with work on Neptune and Overlord that it was impossible for him to take these ideas any further for the moment. He did have a discussion with Blackett and Ralph Fowler in early February on operational research in South-East Asia and air attacks on Japan.[10] A short time later, he received a letter from Kendrew in Delhi, giving his impressions of the state of operational research at SEAC. After expressing his great disappointment that Bernal would not be able to visit soon, Kendrew reported that 'research at the Supreme Command level is going very much at half-cock at the moment'.[11]

What Kendrew would have found on taking up his new posting was that aerial reconnaissance was still a fledgling activity. Prior to April 1943, the RAF had no planes of their own available and made do with a few Tiger Moths chartered from Indian Air Survey and Transport Ltd.[12] Even though a more concerted effort was now being undertaken, the distances involved were enormous – they were trying to survey an area equivalent in size to 'France, Germany, the Low Countries and Italy'.[13] The monsoon meant that reconnaissance was impossible between April and October. In his letter, Kendrew listed the work in progress – mainly on the corruption of signals traffic, and the problems of supply drops and air transportation in mountainous tropical forests. Perhaps as a result of what he had learned in North Africa, he was concerned about the correct selection of weapons for particular purposes. He gave as an example the fact that '4,000 and 1,000 lb. bombs are being used for attacking dispersal areas on airfields; and I am told by the Army O[perational]R[esearch]G[roup] that the Army in the forward area made a written statement to the effect that "for the attack of ground close-support objectives, the larger the bomb the better, under all circumstances".' Kendrew intended to carry out a fact finding survey of the present use of weapons in the South-East Asia theatre so that he could see where 'education is necessary'.[14]

While Kendrew's plans were exactly the sort of thing that Bernal supported, he had no time to reply to the letter and seems not to have thought seriously about SEAC again until after D-Day. Even then his major concern was to collect as much information as possible to analyse the D-Day landings; he was worried that the commanders at SHAEF (the Supreme Headquarters Allied Expeditionary Force) were pressing on with future plans without incorporating any recent results. On 23rd June, Bernal visited Bentley Priory (where much of the D-Day planning was done), with Blackett and Zuckerman to lobby for the establishment of a SHAEF Operational Research Group; they were not successful.[15] That morning, he and Pyke had appeared before the Chiefs of Staff to present the Power-Driven Rivers scheme, which had now been augmented by Pyke to include the movement of soldiers, enclosed in cylinders with oxygen tanks, through large-bore pipes. Even Pyke admitted that the 'idea of transporting human beings inside the pipe has a slightly imaginative and speculative quality about it',[16] and the Chiefs discarded it rather quickly.

Bernal recorded in his diary for 7th September, 'need to proceed directly to S.E. Asia'.[17] Mountbatten was in London in August to press the case for an amphibious attack (Operation Dracula) across the Bay of Bengal to take Rangoon. Churchill managed to persuade his doubtful Chiefs of Staff that enough men and landing craft could be transferred to SEAC from Europe to make this feasible; after a year of inactivity, Mountbatten was desperate to break out of the military doldrums. Some rapid planning advice would be needed, and there was no one better qualified than Sage to provide it. Mountbatten's headquarters were now in Kandy on the island of Ceylon, close to the Fleet, but many hundreds of miles away from the fighting in Burma. Just as his earlier appointment as CCO had been soon followed by an inexplicable expansion in staff numbers, so Mountbatten's new HQ took on the trappings of a royal court and attracted some powerful criticism. Writing to the Admiral of the Fleet, the naval chief in Ceylon, Sir Charles Layton, wondered 'if it is right that one Commander should collect together 7,000 able-bodied men and women to plan and supervise operations the scale of which is not settled'.[18]

Untroubled by such considerations, Bernal travelled to Oxford to discover what he could about sources of intelligence on tropical forests and swamps. He talked to forestry experts at Princes Risborough, where he was also putting the finishing touches to reports on Overlord for the Ministry of Home Security. In early October he took off, landing first in Gibraltar, and then flying on over the Algerian desert. He made an unscheduled stop on the island of Djerba, off the coast of Tunisia, because of mechanical problems with the plane. By chance, a party of senior Indian scientists was also marooned there, and Bernal had long conversations with them about the possibilities for science in India after the war.[19] He met some local sponge fishermen and hired a 'very expensive dhow'[20] from which he enjoyed the sun and sea breezes. After a pleasant few days on Djerba, he reached Cairo, where he stayed long enough to contract food poisoning, before heading over the Dead Sea and Arabian Desert to Mesopotamia. He visited Babylon and Ur on 14th October, and the next day flew down the Persian coast of the Gulf, over the mountains of Oman, landing in Karachi. Following a one-day break for sightseeing, October 17th was a long day during which he flew down over the Western Ghats, refueling at Bangalore and Madras before finally arriving at Colombo. Then he took a slow night train up to Kandy, where he was installed in the Queen's Hotel, overlooking a lake and very close to the holy Tooth Temple that is said to house Lord Buddha's tooth.

Mountbatten's headquarters were in the Peradeniya Botanical Gardens, an incongruously beautiful and sedate setting for planning warfare. It was there, during a long afternoon meeting, that Sage learned Operation Dracula had been postponed by Churchill for at least six months because 'the German resistance in France and Italy has turned out to be far more formidable than we had hoped. We must clean them out first.'[21] Relieved of a definite object-ive, Sage now became an itinerant OR consultant and could roam wherever he wished over the subcontinent. He stayed for a few days in Ceylon, holding meetings with Kendrew and representatives from the Army and Navy oper-ational research groups. He then flew up to Bombay for a conference, where he took part in a discussion on using Weasels to cross mangrove swamps; (Weasels had their origin in Pyke's recommendation for a fast track-vehicle to transport troops across snow and ice in Norway). While in Bombay, Bernal was able to visit the Hindu temples cut into the rock on Elephanta Island – his 'first impression of Indian sculpture'.[22]

From Bombay he made his way north to Delhi, delighting in the sunrise over the Ghats and the chance to see Indian villages at dawn. Delhi was cooler and he spent a day at the Maharajah of Bikaner's palace, which was 'entirely decorated with tiger skins'. The atmosphere of unreality extended to the staff: 'five servants and a bearer – a groom with no horse, a cook with no food, a gardener with no garden, a boy to look after the other servants, most of the time sleeping outside my door.'[23] Returning to Kandy on the 4th November, he was asked to involve himself in the research Kendrew had initiated into the best type of bomb for jungle use. Kendrew gave the following exposition:

The problem under study in the bombing trials concerned methods of bombing troops in the jungle, because the RAF having run out of the proper fragmentation bombs was using naval depth charges instead. These made a much louder bang than fragmentation bombs and therefore the Army thought them tremendously effective; in fact they were more or less completely useless (having only a very thin casing). Mountbatten was subjected to enormous pressure from the Army to continue using depth charges even after new supplies of fragmentation bombs arrived, so he asked Bernal and myself to arrange trials in the jungle.[24]

Bernal suggested a small-scale trial of the effect of depth charges in the jungle. The Army representatives resented him as a 'high-powered bod throwing his weight around without any experience of local conditions'.[25] Kendrew contacted the official rat catcher of Kandy, who deposited a writhing sack containing about a hundred rats on his desk one morning. On the 9th November they drove about 35 miles down the valley from Kandy to the jungle. For Kendrew, it was a day that changed his life. Sage was 'interested and expert in everything around him – the war, Buddhist religion and art, the geological specimens he would retrieve from every ditch, the properties of mud, luminous insects, the ancestry of cycads, but his recurrent theme was the fundamentals of biology and of the enormous developments just becoming possible through the advances in the physical and chemical techniques of the 1930s'.[26] His message came through very clearly to Kendrew, a young scientist removed from the laboratory by the war and uncertain what to do next. Like Perutz before him, he understood from Sage that the 'central challenge was to apply the methods of physics to gain a deeper understanding of the complexity and the beauty of life and, more specifically, that the key problem then becoming ripe for a solution was to understand the architecture of proteins, those enormously complex molecules whose versatility of function lay behind every activity of every living organism'.[27]

The depth charges were carried into the jungle by elephants, to be detonated at chosen places. The rats were placed into cages and suspended at varying distances from the explosions; even those very close were totally unharmed, as predicted. Just 'before one of the bombs was detonated Bernal pulled his slide rule out of his pocket and calculated that he and [Kendrew] were at a safe distance; there followed the most enormous explosion and we rapidly dived into the nearest ditch with rocks and earth flying overhead. Bernal emerged brushing earth out of his hair and looking very puzzled, saying that he thought he must have got the decimal point in the wrong place.'[28]

With the postponement of Dracula, the liberation of Rangoon in the south of Burma would have to be left to the Army divisions, now under the brilliant command of General Slim. Mountbatten decided that Sage should visit the frontline on the Arakan peninsula. His first view of Burma was on 18th November; after camping in a mountain forest, he saw wild elephants come to the river at dawn to bathe. The next few days were spent with Army planners at their HQ on the Naf River, and travelling around the narrow coastal plain mostly by boat. He took walks in the jungle covering the Mayu hills and saw enormous spiders, leeches, shrieking monkeys and brilliantly coloured birds. He also found the time to write a paper over the course of three days.[29] After five days in Burma and one last meeting with Army planners, Bernal took his seat on an overloaded plane that struggled to take off in heavy rain. After a short hop, he breakfasted on two fried eggs and transferred to another plane for Calcutta. In Calcutta, he was offered two more eggs, as he was at every stop made that day, so that by the time he finally landed in Ceylon, he had consumed sixteen eggs![30] Undaunted, he drove to Kandy from Colombo and had dinner with Hal Waddington, the geneticist. The next day was spent talking 'infinite shop' with Kendrew, Waddington and other operational research scientists.

On 27th November, Bernal was involved with staff meetings with Mountbatten and his commanders. They discussed a limited amphibious attack to secure the island of Akyab, about halfway down the long Arakan peninsula. An overland attack on Rangoon would need air cover, and possession of Akyab would give vital airfields to the RAF, less than 350 miles from Rangoon.[31] After what Bernal described as a 'Council of War at HQ preparing for landing at Akyab'[32] he left Kandy on 1st December and returned to Army HQ in north Burma. He wrote to Mountbatten ('Dear Supremo') from there to say that he had accomplished all the important things he had to do.[33] Bernal advised that the landing force should aim to take the 'fairly hard southern beach' on Akyab because 'the bomb evidence seemed conclusive that there was deep mud over most of the other beaches'. An unusual note of irritation then crept in, as Sage explained that the bombing trials had been unnecessary because Intelligence had unearthed 'rather at the 11th hour a BOAC man who knew all the beaches, had built the pier, and possessed a detailed chart of the beach, which Intelligence had not considered it worthwhile to bring. I am sorry to harp,' he continued, 'but it would have saved enormous time and labour if the information which has been available for three years had been produced earlier. Could it be made clear that we are interested in *all* charts and beach information for ports along the coast.'[34]

The man who had led the Cambridge Scientists Anti-War Group just a decade earlier and who had fulminated against the prostitution of science in the pursuit of military advantage was now so deeply immersed in the push for victory that he wrote the following passage without apparent hesitation.

With the bombardment plan I am also in general agreement. We have less and less to do it with and I have been convinced by the operational research workers here that the Napalm fire bombs represent the most efficient use of our heavy bomber effort. Even on a very conservative view they should be three times as effective as H.E. against Japs in pill boxes or foxholes.[35]

Sage closed by saying how much he had enjoyed his prolonged and varied visit, and hoped that he had been of some use. He should not have had any doubts after receiving Mountbatten's affectionate reply.

PERSONAL & SECRET   23rd December 1944

My dear Bernal,

Thank you so much for your letter of the 11th December, which I found on my arrival at Calcutta.

Wherever I went I found you were being quoted as the Bible on beach Intelligence, and several senior officers remarked that they did not know what they would have done if you had not come out to help on this aspect . . . Do not forget that we want to see you out here again yourself in the near future.

I am investigating the possibility of using Commando raids to obtain beach and airfield construction Intelligence where we at present lack this.

It was so nice seeing you again; I always find discussion with you stimulating and refreshing.

Yours very sincerely,

LOUIS MOUNTBATTEN

Bernal flew out of Calcutta on 12th December, and after 'ambling' back via Cairo, he spent the week before Christmas catching up with developments at COHQ. He reported to various groups on his recent findings, and held several meetings with Blackett to discuss the operational research needs of SEAC and the Pacific theatre.[36] On the day Bernal left India, General Slim commenced his historic Arakan offensive. Akyab was recaptured in early January without a shot being fired because the Japanese had withdrawn; the landing on the southern beach became a flawless technical exercise. Slim, with guaranteed air cover and some measure of mosquito control thanks to DDT spraying, executed a masterly campaign that culminated in the liberation of Mandalay in March and Rangoon in April 1945, just before the monsoon broke.

Soon after the New Year, Bernal, as one of four principal scientific advisers to the Services, was appointed to a sub-committee to be chaired by Tizard. Like Bernal, the other scientists were Cambridge men (Blackett representing the Admiralty, Charles Ellis now at the War Office and Sir George Thomson for the Air Ministry). The sub-committee was to report to the Joint Technical Warfare Committee (JTWC) which had been established under the aegis of the Chiefs of Staff in November 1943 to 'co-ordinate and direct the technical study of . . . operational projects and problems'.[37] Bernal had attended JTWC meetings irregularly, depending on his whereabouts and availability, as he conducted his preparatory research for Overlord. The new sub-committee, confusingly known as another Tizard Committee, was instructed by the Chiefs of Staff 'to review the position and to forecast to the best of their ability developments in weapons and methods in each important field of warfare during the next 10 years, having regard both to the theoretical possibilities and also to the practical limitations at present foreseeable'.[38] The members of the Tizard Committee were free to consult other technical experts of their choosing, and were also to receive submissions from the Services about the defence needs and 'industrial war making capacity of the country against aggression' before issuing their report.

Solly Zuckerman had become the most influential scientific adviser to the Allied Expeditionary Air Force; before D-Day, he had been an outspoken dissenter from suggestions on bombing policy promoted within the JTWC.[39] Against the opposition of such weighty figures as 'Bomber' Harris and Lord Cherwell, Zuckerman persuaded the top decision-makers that the strategic bombing of the French railway system to prevent German reinforcements flooding into Normandy was more vital than the continued destruction of targets in Germany.[40] When Paris was liberated in August 1944, Zuckerman was installed there by Air Marshal Tedder to carry out frontline analysis of bombing damage through his Bombing Analysis Unit. Zuckerman also took the opportunity to examine the records of the French railway system, which showed that the disruption caused by the bombing campaign before D-Day had been more complete than anyone had predicted.

Bernal and Zuckerman had met two or three times in the weeks after D-Day, mostly to discuss the latest threat posed by German flying bombs.[41] Now that he was on the new Tizard Committee, Sage wanted to talk to Zuckerman and to learn as much as possible of the observations made by the Bombing Analysis Unit on the targets hit in France. In early April, Zuckerman 'arranged a splendid tour of which the first four days were spent in Paris, where Desmond had some business of his own to conduct'.[42] There was an Anglo-French Scientists dinner with old friends such as the Joliot-Curies, whom Sage had not seen for five years. Through Solly, there were introductions to new acquaintances like Air Marshal Tedder, and the Duff Coopers, who gave an Easter dinner for Bernal and Zuckerman at the British Embassy. Since they were going into the war zone, both scientists were in uniform. Sage wore his naval lieutenant's uniform from D-Day, and Zuckerman's staff pointed out that he had far too much hair sprouting from under the outsized cap. At their insistence he had a haircut before driving north-east with Zuckerman past Arnhem and up the Rhine to Cologne. There, Bernal was astounded by the degree to which the allied air raids had levelled the city. The Cathedral seemed to be the only structure left standing, and Sage was of course eager to examine its architectural features at close quarters. He and Zuckerman were prevented from approaching it by a platoon of American rangers, who politely told them that it was structurally unsafe and that there were still German guns trained on it from the east side of the river. Later that day they visited the collapsed Remagen Bridge, which had been the only bridge on the Rhine captured intact by the advancing American army the previous month, and which was now blocking traffic on the river.

In early 1945, Churchill was increasingly concerned that the French and the Russians were attempting to find out about the Manhattan Project.[43] All the scientists on the Tizard Committee except Bernal had been closely involved, at various stages, with the British wartime atomic energy programme. When Churchill, in January 1945, agreed with Sir John Anderson that the Chiefs of Staff should finally be let into the secret of the Manhattan Project, he stated specifically that he did not want Tizard told. By that time so many British scientists were in North America that it was common knowledge amongst senior physicists that a major attempt was in hand to build an atomic weapon. Tizard made an approach to the COS to include atomic weapons in his Committee's remit, but again Churchill forbade it.

Sir Henry Tizard ... surely has lots of things to get on with without plunging into this exceptionally secret matter. It may be that in a few years or even months that this secret can no longer be kept. One must always realise that for every one of these scientists who is informed there is a little group around him who also hears the news.[44]

Even with no up-to-date evidence on the development of the atomic bomb, when the Tizard Committee released its report on the 16th June, there was reference to this horrendous new possibility. Even if the population were to be subjected to a 'troglodyte existence' underground, with whatever comforts modern engineers could provide, the members of the Committee doubted that there would be 'any defence on which a country could rely'.

The only answer that we can see to the atomic bomb [they wrote] is to be prepared to use it ourselves in retaliation. A knowledge that we were prepared, in the last resort, to do this might well deter an aggressive nation. Duelling was a recognised method of settling quarrels between men of high social standing so long as the duellists stood twenty paces apart and fired at each other with pistols of a primitive type. If the rule had been that they should stand a yard apart with pistols at each other's hearts, we doubt whether it would long have remained a recognised method of settling affairs of honour.[45]

One of the Tizard Committee's firm conclusions was that the close liaison between scientists and the Services that had developed in wartime should be continued in peacetime. Their prescription was:

to concentrate much of the scientific effort available for defence on to basic research into the physical principles underlying the design of weapons of war, and not on improvements in detail for which there is naturally always a persistent demand from the Service departments...in the effort to provide for the immediate needs of everyone we run the risk of grasping at the shadow of things of the past and losing the substance of things to come.[46]

Among the things to come that they foresaw were supersonic jet fighters, nuclear-powered submarines, guided missiles and torpedoes, anti-ship weapons that would home in on radar transmitters (and counter-measures against the same), and great refinement in radar communications. The Navy would rely increasingly on submarines, and battleships would be obsolete because surface ships had to be large enough only to carry their complement of guided missiles. While the Navy would remain central to the protection of the British Isles, 'alone [it] is no longer our sure defence and the scientific development that we foresee forces us to the conclusion that the air and sea war are indivisible'.[47]

Two days before the Tizard report was presented to the Chiefs of Staff, Bernal was meant to have flown to Moscow in a group of thirty scientists invited to celebrate the 220th Anniversary of the founding of the Russian Academy of Sciences. Hours before their planned departure, Bernal, Blackett and six others had their exit visas cancelled; a press release was issued saying that they could not go because they 'were engaged on work of the greatest importance in the production of war materials and research'.[48] There seems little doubt that Churchill and Cherwell were concerned with possible security breaches about atomic energy, even though none of those prevented from going had worked directly on the Manhattan Project. The scientists were furious and saw it as an unwarranted restriction on their freedom of speech and movement. Blackett staged a magnificent, one-man walkout from the Admiralty in protest. Sage with two others wrote to Lord Woolton, the Lord President of the Council, seeking an assurance that participation in government research would not limit their freedom of contact with scientists in other countries. Woolton replied that he and all his colleagues owed a debt to British scientists for 'the great and indispensable contribution' made in the war. He recognized that progress in science ultimately depended on the freest possible interchange of ideas between scientists and hoped 'this wartime restriction will be brought to an end with all speed'.[49]

Sir John Anderson, the Home Secretary, wrote an apologetic note to Bernal the following month. He said that 'the decision was the Prime Minister's in his capacity as Minister of Defence and the reason publicly given was his reason'. He also revealed that Churchill had instructed that 'the names of those excluded [from the visit] should be so jumbled up as to make it as difficult as possible to draw any inference about any particular individual'.[50] While admitting that he had been influenced by 'the probable attitude of America', Anderson gave his personal assurance that there had been no loss of confidence in any particular individual, 'nor any consideration of the political views of any individual'. This last claim seems preposterous. The fact that Anderson wrote to Bernal personally suggests that he was one of the scientists the government did not want to risk in Moscow, and Blackett was surely another, given that he was a nuclear physicist with intimate knowledge of the bomb. It is also likely that their membership of the Tizard Committee weighed in the balance.

The Tizard Report was withdrawn from circulation in Whitehall a few days after its release in June 1945, probably because of the references to atomic weapons; but within two months the bombs at Hiroshima and Nagasaki had jolted the world into the atomic age. Although British scientists had been actively working on nuclear research for five years, the unprecedented level of secrecy meant that there had been no debate about the implications for the country's own defence. Attlee had replaced Churchill as Prime Minister less than two weeks before the Hiroshima bomb was dropped; he was just as much a neophyte in nuclear affairs as the new US President, Harry Truman. On the day after the bombing of Nagasaki, General 'Pug' Ismay (Chief of Staff at the Ministry of Defence) suggested to Attlee that Tizard be asked to revise his recent report in an attempt to provide information about the production and potential use of the bomb and about possible counter-measures because such knowledge was 'almost completely lacking'.[51]

Many scientists spoke out in the weeks after Hiroshima and Nagasaki, and as one would expect, Sage was one of the first in print. While accepting that the use of the atomic bombs had been decisive in ending the war, he shared the common opinion that the actuality of the bomb 'implicitly changed the whole existence of man in this universe'.[52] The fears of further destruction were stronger in the public mind than the hopes of untold benefits because 'though the people may have little experience of the behaviour of atoms, they have considerable experience of the behaviour of men, corporately and individually. They remember in the past, science has only been fully deployed in human destruction, and this gives a poor augury for the beneficent use of these more powerful forces.'[53] Although the benefits of harnessing atomic energy were not yet clear, Sage was optimistic that its most immediate impact might be on undeveloped nations which lacked fossil fuels: 'such energy can be used to pump water and to make fertilizer . . . to extend and to intensify agricultural exploitation . . . in effect, that the basic limitation of food supply, already being felt acutely in the world, will be removed.' He insisted that the responsibility for controlling atomic energy from the first should be fully international and under the aegis of the United Nations. 'The maintaining of secrecy on the principles and processes involved and the limitations of their application to the use of particular nations would be doubly disastrous, partly in slowing down the rate of useful progress, but, far more seriously, in withholding the utilisation of atomic energy on account of mutual suspicion.' The enormous scale of the Manhattan Project, and the collaboration required to achieve its goal made it plain to Sage that science needed to be organized on a world-wide basis; it could no longer be 'done in holes and corners'.

Bernal covered several of the same themes on a BBC overseas broadcast on 3rd September. He thought atomic power would have great possibilities in countries like India with poor natural fuel sources: 'in tropical countries, power means water, water means food, and food means people.'[54] His sceptical opponent, A.V. Hill, said that there had been a similar enthusiasm for science at the end of the First World War, 'but only a very small fraction of the plans came to anything'. Sage disagreed saying that he thought there had been a much bigger kick this time to start things off. It was imperative that the country took the right approach to science research and unless scientists were given a say in public policy decisions, 'the decisions will be nonsense'. Countries without a solid science base would be like savages of the eighteenth century were in relation to Western Europe – unable to affect the civilized world.

At the end of September, Sage shared a platform with Blackett, the Joliot-Curies, Sir George Thomson, Marcus Oliphant and others at a meeting on 'The social implications of the atomic bomb'. It was resolved that British scientists 'should continue to make very strong representations, as a body, to influence the use of the weapon; that it was a matter in which there could be no more secrecy. It was agreed also that for Great Britain this was not an offensive weapon, for we are far more vulnerable than almost any other country to attack by atomic weapons, but that the peacetime applications might prove more important to the Empire than to any other nation.'[55] In private conversation, Blackett was the most outspoken, railing against 'the incompetence and sheer stupidity' of the British atomic effort to date, and describing the Quebec Agreement (the secret 1943 agreement that atomic weapons would be developed as an Anglo-American collaboration and only used against third parties with joint consent) as 'a degrading document'.[56]

On 16th October, Blackett and Bernal took their seats as two members of the reconfigured Joint Technical Warfare Committee to revise the Tizard Report. They now had access to official information on atomic energy through the Tube Alloys Directorate (Tube Alloys was the meaningless title given to the British wartime atomic research programme) and from Sir James

Chadwick, still in Washington as head of the British scientific team. The original Tizard Committee was dissuaded from identifying any specific country as a potential foe, and its report was criticized subsequently as a technical document written in a strategic vacuum. The new JTWC included senior military representatives, and they were determined to link the revised findings to the world as the Chiefs of Staff saw it. The COS had for some time been convinced, to the discomfort of the Foreign Office, that the possibility of a hostile Soviet Union in the post-war period should be seriously considered. The scientists from the original Tizard Committee must, therefore, have been surprised when Major-General Gordon MacMillan circulated the following, hypothetical queries.

What scale of effort would be required *on the target* to knock out all cities of (a) over 100,000 or (b) over 50,000 in, for example, the U.S.S.R. assuming that there were no other targets worthy of attack? What then would be the total number of atomic weapons we should have to produce?[57]

He also asked what nuclear arsenals the Russians would need to mount similar attacks against the major cities in the United Kingdom, the Dominions and the USA. The JTWC met frequently over the next few weeks, and while atomic weapons remained its main priority, it also heard evidence from leading experts on chemical and biological warfare. By mid-November, MacMillan concluded that given the projected ranges of bombers and rockets over the next decade, it was improbable that either the USA or the USSR could target the other's major cities for nuclear attack. The general problem of an attack using atomic bombs, therefore, 'may conveniently be reduced to the particular case of a war between the UK and the USSR, not because such a war is likely, but because it presents a suitable example of different vulnerability in each country'.[58] He asked Bernal and Dr Henry Hulme, who had succeeded Blackett at the Admiralty, to compile a report on the weight of attack required 'to knock out for practical purposes' target cities in the UK and USSR, the best modes of delivering such attacks, and the resulting losses.[59]

Bernal and Hulme gave a progress report on 22nd January.[60] They had identified 84 Soviet cities with populations over 100,000, and calculated their distances from three hypothetical British bases: the English city of Norwich, Nicosia on the island of Cyprus, and Peshawar then in north-west India. They had made the reciprocal calculations for 49 large British cities in terms of their distances from bases in Soviet-controlled Germany and Latvia. The pair was authorized to continue their work. That month, Sage gave a lecture to the Fabian Society on 'Atomic energy and international security'.[61] Quoting General Groves on the advent of far more powerful atom bombs, Sage urged his audience not to think of the present weapons as the last word in destructiveness, rather the first word of the atomic age which should be stopped 'at the very beginning of its career'. There was, he warned, no defence against an atom bomb – 'there is only retaliation'. It was essentially a weapon of terror because it was most effective against populations concentrated in cities; and of course about half of the most beautiful cities in Europe had been destroyed in the war just ended. That war did not 'destroy civilization, but it is not the kind of thing we want to repeat on a larger scale'. The bomb was only a new technical device and as such would not prevent war: 'the only way in which a new technical device can bring an end to war is if it stirs people into effective political action against war.' It could not be used in war 'unless a previous state of mind has grown up in which the governments of large countries, or...the people of large countries, are capable of thinking that the inhabitants of other large countries belong to a different species, are subhuman...The one sure protection against the atom bomb is the prevention of any kind of international and inter-racial attitude of contempt, fear or hatred. We must begin by outlawing the bomb because once we decide that human beings are not to be bombed and slaughtered in hundreds of thousands totally indiscriminately, we shall begin to see that slaughtering them by tens of thousands more or less discriminately is not a particularly good idea either.'

Although Bernal seemed not to understand it, the behaviour of the Soviet Union in Eastern Europe was giving rise to deep distrust and alarm in the United Kingdom and the United States. Far from honouring the promises made at Yalta in 1945 that liberated peoples should exercise choice in 'the form of government under which they will live' through free elections, the Soviets were imposing their despotic rule across a block of countries. In March 1946, Churchill made his 'Iron Curtain' speech in Fulton, Missouri, which provoked a furious response from Stalin. On 2nd April, the Warner Memorandum[62] setting out 'The Soviet campaign against this country and our response to it' circulated in the Foreign Office. Reflecting on recent speeches by Stalin, Molotov and other members of the Politburo, Warner identified three major trends in Soviet policy:

1. the return to the 'pure doctrine of Marx–Lenin–Stalinism';
2. the intense build-up of industrial and military strength;
3. the revival of 'the bogey of external danger to the Soviet Union'.

Accepting that the Soviet Union was war-weary and the British COS view that the Russians 'do not wish to get involved in another war for at least the next five years', Warner still thought the Soviets were 'practising the most vicious power politics' and seemed 'determined to stick at nothing, short of war, to obtain [their] objectives'. In his opinion, it would be 'in the highest degree rash' to assume that the Russians would not continue to attack Great Britain 'which they must regard as the leader of Social Democracy and the more vulnerable of the two great Western powers'. He concluded that:

The Soviet Government makes coordinated use of military, economic, propaganda and political weapons and also of the Communist 'religion'. It is submitted, therefore, that we must at once organise and coordinate our defences against all these and that we should not stop short of a defensive-offensive policy.

British diplomats and military chiefs were beginning to think as one.

On 13th April 1946, Hulme (who by this time was also Scientific Adviser to the Air Ministry) presented a twenty-page 'Preliminary note', summarizing the work he and Bernal had undertaken over the previous six months. Their simple model was intended 'to provide a very tentative estimate of the situation ten years hence'.[63] They grouped cities together into targets suitable for individual bomber raids. Realizing that the attacks on Russia would be deep into defended territory, so that the chances of a single bomber reaching a target in the presence of radar-controlled fighters would be virtually nil, the chosen tactic was to send large protective forces to accompany a relatively small number of planes carrying atom bombs. This large force would peel off close to the target cities in each defined group, and the bombs would be dropped. There were fifteen Soviet groups and a further eleven cities that would need to be attacked individually, (26 raids), in order to demolish those centres housing 88 per cent of the urban Russian population. For this wholesale destruction, 242 atom bombs would need to hit their target, and so about 370 would have to be dispatched. An equivalent degree of devastation could be visited on the largest 42 British cities by just seven large Russian raids, needing 159 atom bombs to hit their target.

Hulme's paper was considered at the JTWC meeting on 16th April and formed an important component of their final revision of the Tizard Report, which was delivered to the Chiefs of Staff in May. The revised report also included data, collected in Hiroshima and Nagasaki, on fatalities and material damage. The JTWC pointed out that the United Kingdom, mainly for reasons of geography, was far more vulnerable to nuclear attack than the USA or the USSR. As few as 30 atom bombs dropped on British cities 'with the promise of more to follow' could produce national collapse. By contrast, the collapse of Russia 'would require the rapid delivery of several hundred bombs on target'.[64] If an attack on Russia was not well coordinated, the spread of terror could be controlled by an authoritarian government and the remaining cities evacuated. Atom bombs would need to be stockpiled in peacetime because wartime production would be negligible. Within the projected defence budget over the next decade, the cost of producing several hundred atomic bombs would be relatively small; the JTWC also pointed out that although there was no operational experience, the use of biological warfare might be just as devastating and cheaper.

It is hard to imagine more sensational or dangerous official documents than the revised Tizard report and Hulme's Preliminary Note. There were 'severe repercussions at COS level' when one JTWC paper that identified 'a particular Power' as a potential enemy and another that contained ' "Top Secret" material vital to the security' of the UK were allowed 'a dangerously wide circulation' in the revision of the Tizard Report.[65] Leaving aside the moral and historical issues raised by these documents, there are two obvious questions concerning Sage's role in their preparation. First, why was a man recognized as being as 'red as the flames of hell' at the start of the war, allowed to take part in such a sensitive strategic exercise? Second, why did Sage agree to do it? As we shall see later, Zuckerman maintained vehemently that by the end of the war, Bernal was a recognized security risk. There are reasons to doubt Zuckerman's memory on this, but it is incontestable that in June 1945 Sage was prevented by the British Government from visiting the USSR. If one looks at the eight who were refused permission to travel, only one, Sir Charles Darwin, had any recent connection with the Manhattan Project; but Blackett and Bernal were probably thought to be communist sympathizers with knowledge of sensitive military information.

Julian Lewis, the historian, suggests: 'The involvement of Bernal in the revision of the Tizard Report, notwithstanding his co-authorship of the original version, would appear to have been an early instance of the implications of the change in potential enemies not being fully thought through in terms of governmental personnel recruited during the war.'[66] Sage never sought, and never declined, any job that was offered to him as part of the war effort. He became one of a handful of scientists to gain direct access to military and political leaders, who in turn came to recognize his exceptional abilities and to trust him. He was also very agreeable company, as Mountbatten found. He did make some political statements during the war, mostly at scientific gatherings, but once the war was over his opinions on the state of the world were readily available in print and through the BBC's home and overseas services. It would still have needed a sharp-eyed security service to identify Sage as a potential misfit within the defence establishment, although the arrest of the first atomic spy, Alan Nunn May, in the spring of 1946 should have triggered a systematic review of scientists in government service.

The May case came too late to affect Bernal's role in the revision of the Tizard Report, as did a sharp denunciation of his morals, his totalitarian outlook and his 'pompous and slovenly' prose by George Orwell. Taking as his text an essay on 'Belief and action'[67] that Bernal had written as 'an attempt to set down briefly and logically the canons of a modern faith, one essentially as humanistic as it is scientific', Orwell reduced Bernal's message to the following propositions:

Apart from 'truthfulness and good fellowship', no quality can be definitely labelled good or bad. Any action which serves the cause of progress is virtuous.

Progress means moving towards a classless and scientifically planned society.

The quickest way to get there is to co-operate with the Soviet Union.

Cooperation with the Soviet Union means not criticising the Stalin regime.

To put it even more shortly: anything is right which furthers the aims of Russian foreign policy.[68]

One can imagine the looks of dismay on the faces of any Foreign Office or military chiefs connected with the revised Tizard Report, who happened to read the May issue of *Polemic*.

As to the second question of why Sage would undertake such a distasteful task, several reasons come to mind. The obvious one would be to inform the Soviet Union of these sinister plans. No evidence for this has ever come to light, and for him to do so might run the risk of escalating a theoretical military contingency into a genuine conflict with incalculable consequences (that potential transition had certainly troubled the Foreign Office). Just as there was some inertia on the side of the Establishment, it would have taken a deliberate step by Sage to exclude himself from the process. He regarded the discovery of atomic energy as a revolutionary event in human history: he told the Fabians in his January 1946 talk that the advent of agriculture was the only previous discovery of the same magnitude. He was convinced that scientists needed to play a central role in guiding governments towards an international system of control that would banish the use of atomic bombs, while maximizing the benefits of the civil use of atomic energy. This was no time for Sage to withdraw from the debate – rather he needed to immerse himself in the challenge. A logical analysis of the insane deployment of atomic bombs might persuade the British Government to repudiate them forever.

14

Rebuilding

Bernal's wartime contact with Birkbeck College was slight and somewhat peevish. Breams Buildings had closed after being hit by incendiary bombs in September 1940, but reopened the following month, with lectures being given at weekends rather than in the evenings. Lewis Simons became acting head of the Physics Department, and in March 1941 word reached Sage that he had sacked Mr Reggie Dobb, the senior laboratory technician. Bernal immediately wrote a letter of protest, but the dismissal was upheld on the basis that staff numbers needed to be reduced. Sage then decided that since the College was in operation at weekends only, he should take up the reins again (this was at the time he was starting to work at Bomber Command). After several Faculty meetings, a compromise was reached whereby Mr Dobb would be re-employed, perhaps on a part time basis, when conditions improved. Eventually, he was rehired for four days per week, and Sage asked the College to pay him for a full week 'to lay the last ghosts of a controversy'.[1] H. Gordon Jackson, the Acting Master, complained to Sage, asking 'Where is this to stop?' Sage's response was judged by the College administration to be 'a complete travesty of the facts'.[2]

Gordon Jackson explained that he was much more concerned about welfare of the Physics Department as a whole and Bernal's inability to spend more than a few hours per month at Birkbeck, although he understood that he was carrying out work of paramount importance. Gordon Jackson was therefore going to recommend to the Governors that Simons be reappointed as acting head. Sage was 'extremely surprised' by Gordon Jackson's letter and in his own defence stated: 'As far as I am aware there have been no difficulties in the running of the Department of Physics in the present year, in marked contrast to the previous year.'[3] He could not countenance the appointment of any deputy in whom he did not have full confidence and wished to put his views to the Governors in person. At this point, the Acting Master relented and explained that he was not unsympathetic to Bernal's difficulties and suggested that they should meet for lunch. At the lunch, he seems to have persuaded Bernal that he could not run the Physics Department himself and that Simons was not such a bad deputy. He also suggested that Bernal's original five-year appointment should be suspended for the duration of the war, with four years left to run after hostilities ceased. At the end of the four years, Sage could decide whether he wanted to stay and would be offered a lifetime appointment. This was mutually agreed in October 1942.[4]

After that, Bernal's thoughts did not return to Birkbeck until early in 1945. In February of that year, he drew up a 'Draft Scheme for a Biomolecular Centre'.[5] This would be a multi-disciplinary department that would seek to exploit all of the available physical techniques to investigate the structure and biological functions of proteins. His proposals echoed those of the fictional Constantine in *The Search* for a National Institute of Biophysical Research. Sage would still be honouring the gentlemen's agreement he made with Astbury before the war, that he would concentrate on crystalline proteins and leave the long-fibre structures to Astbury in Leeds: the Centre 'would not be concerned with the high polymer molecules either natural or synthetic, the structure of which has been so ably elucidated by Professor Astbury and his co-workers. It would include both extensive study of the largest number of proteins readily available in a pure form, particularly those of agricultural or medical interest', besides taking up work on viruses again and making 'a particular drive' to examine the protein constituent of chromosomes. He foresaw the laboratories being divided into six sections: biological (to prepare and assay the proteins to be analysed); biochemical (mainly for protein purification); physico-chemical (to measure the electrical and surface characteristics of the biological molecules. A good ultracentrifuge would be an essential piece of equipment); optical (ultraviolet and polarizing microscopy as well as the best light microscopes available); electronic (for the use and development of the newly invented electron microscope); X-ray (with diffraction apparatus suitable for examining structures such as viruses with very large unit cells, and for liquids. Improved X-ray tubes more suitable for biological work would be developed in this lab).

Bernal's stock was at its zenith at the end of the war. With Blackett, Waddington and Zuckerman, he was a founding father and leading exponent of operational research. The Royal Society gave him the Royal Medal in recognition for his X-ray analysis of the structure of proteins and other substances. One month after drawing up his scheme for a Biomolecular Centre, Sage received a letter from Tizard informing him that the Nuffield Foundation, of which he was a trustee, would buy the necessary equipment and support the salaries of senior research staff; Tizard also mentioned that since there was no viable laboratory space at Birkbeck, Sage might be given temporary accommodation at the Royal Institution.[6]

While others rightly saw Sage as the country's leading exponent of structural analysis of biomolecules, he was acutely aware of his six-year enforced absence from the field. He admitted this concern in a lecture to a conference at the Institute of Physics, but knowing little of recent work, he thought he would 'not fail to see the wood for the trees'.[7] The one piece of current work that he had followed closely was Dorothy Hodgkin's Oxford project on the structure of penicillin. He referred to this obliquely in his talk 'as one of the triumphs of crystallography' resulting in 'the complete determination of the structure of one extremely important compound before the chemists had unravelled its structural formula'.[8] When Dorothy told him about the β-lactam structure of penicillin, sitting on the steps of the Royal Society, Sage said to her, 'You will get the Nobel Prize for this.' She replied that she would rather be elected a Fellow of the Royal Society, and he commented, 'That's more difficult.'[9]

Bernal wrote back to Tizard in the summer of 1945 to say that although the Royal Institution was prepared to put five rooms at his disposal from 1st September until 31st July 1946, it could not guarantee the space for any longer than that. He asked the Nuffield Foundation for £1,000 to buy equipment and £8,000 annually for five years towards running costs.[10] In the meantime Bernal set about assembling his research team. He would have loved to bring Fan back from Brooklyn, but in his absence approached Harry Carlisle (who had taken the Birkbeck cameras to Oxford during the war) to head the crystallography section that would work on proteins and viruses. Helen Megaw, who had spent several years teaching science in a girl's grammar school and the last two years of the war in industry, needed little persuasion to return to academic life; she was to be in charge of a group studying the structure of cement and other building materials (an area in which Bernal held official responsibilities). Werner Ehrenberg, who had been brought to Birkbeck by Blackett, would be in charge of developing new apparatus – especially fine-focus, high-intensity X-ray tubes that would cut down on the exposure times and give much better resolution. The final section chief was to be Andrew Donald Booth, a self-confident man in his late twenties, with a recent PhD in crystallography from the University of Birmingham. Sage was not particularly interested in his abilities as a crystallographer, but wanted him for his mathematical and engineering talents. Booth was a computer pioneer. At Birmingham, he had already built an analogue computer, which he used to calculate the reciprocal spacings for a crystal X-ray diffraction pattern. Dorothy Hodgkin had begun to explore the use of computers for Fourier analysis, and no doubt Sage had seen how they speeded up the painstaking calculations. Booth found Sage 'as interested in computing as I was'.[11]

Although Booth was an inventor at heart, he had to do his share of teaching. In the autumn of 1945, the evening physics classes were still held in the bomb-damaged Breams Buildings. Booth was assigned to give a 'modern physics' course (relativity and quantum theory). For the first lecture, he was shown up several flights of stairs to a room containing a demonstration table, some chairs and a large blackboard. One of the seasoned lecturers gave him some tips on how to keep the class awake and then advised him not to lean on the blackboard. When he asked why not, he was invited to look through a gap in the wall and saw that there was a forty-foot drop to a heap of rubble below.

Sage wrote to Fan giving a progress report that reflected the shortages and skimping, which were such a feature of post-war life in England.

I am afraid, however, that at present my new Institute is definitely embryonic. The organisers are there but there is very little to organise. I am back where I started, on the top floor of the Davy–Faraday [Laboratory of the Royal Institution], with one X-ray tube which works about one day a fortnight between breakdowns, and vague prospects of getting three more and a few of my old cameras. Beside [Sam] Levine, I have Helen Megaw, Carlisle and a very bright Fourier merchant called Booth, an electronics man called Ehrenberg, whom you probably remember at Birkbeck, Katie Schiff and a number of small fry.

Our proposed programme is to pick up more or less where we left off plus all the experience we can get from published material in the interval. Bill Pirie is going to supply us with viruses and I hope also to do some work on antigens and antibodies. The main idea is to link the long range forces with the biological systems. . . . Another line I am running is on the apparatus side. I want to improve the type of X-ray tubes by using electron lens methods in the way Goldsztaub has done in Paris. We are going to work together on this. As a side-show, mostly from Ehrenberg, I am going to work on semi-conductors, both X-ray and electronically. Besides all this, I have a general plan of work for the building industry on the shrinkage of cements, which is going to be Helen's particular field as it is mostly hydroxides.

The chief snag at the moment is apparatus and information. What I need, of course, is an electron microscope but there is faint chance of that now that Lease/Lend has come to an end, so I will probably have to make one . . . My chief trouble, however, is X-ray tubes. There is some hope of getting back to Dutch made Philips tubes but the RAF seems to have done their work there too thoroughly.

How are you getting on with encouraging American manufacturers? Has anything come of your idea about the X-ray flash bulb? I thought it very practical but more use to radiologists than to us. The real trouble is that I have not really got into the picture on X-ray work and other work on proteins and high polymers. Could you possibly get me some kind of critical bibliography of papers that have appeared in the last five years in the States and any reprints you can lay your hands on? We have very little to show here except for Max's work which is extremely exciting but I expect he sends you reprints. As a matter of fact I have never seen a copy of my own paper to the Cell Congress in 1939 which I believe has been published in a book, but I don't even know its title. If you can trace it I should be very grateful to have it.

I am very puzzled about what your hot idea on phase determination is. It is worth putting everything into it if it really works, because, short of that, I rather despair of doing anything serious with the proteins.[12]

In 1946, Bernal arranged for Booth to go to the inaugural meeting of the American Society for X-ray and Electron Diffraction at Lake George, New York and to carry out a tour of the nascent American computer centres. He visited Harvard, the Massachusetts Institute of Technology, the Moore School in Philadelphia, and the Bell Labs in New Jersey, but the project that excited him most, although it was not as developed as some of the others, was von Neumann's at Princeton. Bernal had persuaded Warren Weaver of the Rockefeller Foundation to contribute $400 towards Booth's expenses for the short visit, and once Booth had returned to London, with Sage's backing, he was able to obtain a Rockefeller Fellowship to return to the Institute of Advanced Study (IAS) at Princeton in 1947. Von Neumann's idea for the IAS computer was to store information on a cathode-ray tube, a notion lavishly supported by the RCA record company. Booth thought that this approach would not work, and even if it did, it would be unaffordable at Birkbeck. He decided that magnetism could provide the solution to the problem of a reliable data storage device, and bought ten discs coated with an oxide, which were components of a well-known voice-recording machine. His idea was to have a rotating floppy disc, on to which a magnetic record would be imparted. Booth waited until he got back to London to try out his new invention, and through his own contacts was able to use the laboratories of the British Rubber Producers' Association, there being no suitable equipment at Birkbeck. He later described his failure to produce what would have been the world's first floppy disc:

I would spin the 10-inch Mail-a-Voice disc at about 3,000 RPM at which speed it would stay flat, and then move a rigidly mounted read–write head close to the surface. The theory was that the Bernoulli effect would draw the disc to a fixed distance from the head and maintain a very small air gap. Unhappily this did not occur, the attraction was perfect but the distortion of the disc surface resulted in unstable 'flapping' which led to eventual disintegration.[13]

His next attempt was much more successful: a two-inch diameter cylindrical drum coated with permanent magnetic material (nickel). The cylinder rotated under a series of read–write heads, each about the size of a matchstick, and with the associated magnetic circuitry it provided a compact and permanent way of storing digital data – the forerunner of modern hard drives. Booth gave the first demonstrations of his system in May 1948 and it was incorporated into many early computers. One of these was the All Purpose Electronic X-ray (APEX) Computer for the Birkbeck crystallography department of the early 1950s: this computer model was manufactured commercially by the International Computers and Tabulators company and outsold the combined output of all other British manufacturers (more than 120 machines).[14] Much of Booth's research was in the new field of machine translation – the use of computers to translate natural languages. This was a direct consequence of his 1947 trip to the USA, when Weaver (who was the instigator of the subject) mentioned to Booth that while the Rockefeller Foundation would not support the development of computing in London for numerical analysis, they might grant funds for non-numerical uses such as translation.[15]

Although Booth continued to work on mathematical problems in crystallography, his prototype computers were never of much practical use to the Birkbeck crystallographers because they did not have data storage capacity adequate for protein work. In consequence, some were inclined to take a rather jaundiced view of Booth, but Bernal, recognizing his originality and imagination, remained supportive and was instrumental in creating a new Department of Numerical Automation at the College. In 1998, Booth had the pleasure of telling an audience at Birkbeck that a precise structural determination that in the early 1940s had taken a team of two or three people three years to complete, and for which he had subsequently written a computer program, could now be run on an Intel P2 400 MHz personal computer in less than 0.1 second!

Astbury had warned Sage in 1931 not to attempt to 'snaffle' protein structure, but to restrict himself to the exacting analysis of the constituent amino acids and leave the overall protein molecule to him.[16] In setting up his new institute, Bernal made it clear that he would not trespass into Astbury's territory of long polymers, and he told Carlisle that they would confine themselves to small molecules of biological interest.[17] In the years before the war, there had been new interest in nucleic acids, particularly DNA, which was recognized to be an active component of chromosomes. It had been established by chemists that DNA and other nucleic acids were linear polymers – long chains of *nucleotides* linked together. A nucleotide is a complex unit of a sugar, a base and a phosphate group. In 1938, Astbury had announced that DNA was a single-chain molecule, with the nucleotides sitting on one another like a pile of pennies.[18] The nucleotides in DNA consist of a deoxyribose sugar coupled with one of four bases, plus the phosphate. Astbury and his assistant Florence Bell decided that the sugar residues and the bases (which were all ringed-structures) lay in the same plane and that like a pile of pennies or stack of plates, each nucleotide was perpendicular to the primary axis of the chain molecule.

Just as Sage had made the first determination of the shapes of individual amino acid molecules, he now thought it would be valuable to make X-ray studies of nucleotides and their component parts. The first work at Birkbeck was done by a doctoral student, Geoffrey Pitt, supervised by Carlisle. Pitt confirmed Astbury's assumption that the pyrimidine type of base found in DNA was a flat, six-carbon-atom ring. He was the first to provide accurate data on bond lengths and angles for pyrimidine bases. A second PhD candidate, Sven Furberg, soon arrived to build on Pitt's success. Furberg was encouraged by his chemistry professors in Oslo to spend time in Bernal's laboratory and came to Birkbeck in 1947 on a two-year British Council scholarship. He was quiet, courteous and clever. Carlisle managed to obtain some crystals of *cytidine* (which is formed by the pyrimidine base, *cytosine*, linking to a deoxyribose sugar ring), and gave this material to Furberg to make the first X-ray study.

The cytidine crystals were prism-shaped, about 3 mm in length and 0.08 × 0.08 mm in cross-section. After X-ray exposures averaging 130 hours, Furberg managed to define the unit cell of the crystal and amassed photographs, which were exceedingly difficult to interpret. Years later, Francis Crick commented that Furberg's was 'a very remarkable piece of work. It was in fact such a difficult problem that if he had asked advice he would have been told that it was not possible to solve it.'[19] Drawing on the established chemical data and showing great physical insight, Furberg combined two-dimensional Fourier projections into a three-dimensional structure that has stood the test of time. His main conclusions were that Pitt's flat ring for the pyrimidine base was correct, but the five-membered sugar ring (deoxyribose) was puckered with one of its five carbon atoms lying out of the plane of the other four. He provided detailed data on bond angles and bond lengths and concluded that, far from being parallel to each other, the rings of the base and the sugar were virtually at right angles.[20] Was DNA like a pile of bent pennies?

The use of rooms at the Royal Institution lasted less than a year, and in the summer of 1946 Bernal's department was scattered to the four winds. Pitt went to Birmingham to carry out his work on pyrimidine structure, while Carlisle and his organic group made do with two rooms of a suburban house in Hendon. On one occasion, Sage arranged to drive Carlisle and his researchers from Hendon to Cambridge for a meeting. They packed into his small car and of course Bernal was bursting with ideas for what their next research might be. To illustrate them, he drew diagrams on a sheet of paper balanced on the steering wheel, as he drove.

Ehrenberg's physics group returned to the bomb-damaged Breams Buildings. Booth did continue to work at the RI and came to Birkbeck to lecture in the evenings. That summer, a cheerful young man from Manchester, recently demobbed from the Army, answered a newspaper advert to become Technical Supervisor to the Crystallography Department. Tall with wavy hair, he had joined the Royal Signals Corps in 1939 and saw action in North Africa, the Middle East and Italy. His name was Stan Lenton: he would become indispensable as Bernal's chauffeur, mechanic, and occasional butler, in addition to his paid job overseeing the laboratory staff and equipment. Bernal soon entrusted to him the role of departmental accountant. When he first arrived at Birkbeck, he asked about the whereabouts of the crystallographers, and was told, 'that lot, you won't see them for months'.[21]

Sage still drove his pre-war Austin 10, which had spent much of the war parked at various airfields, while he was overseas. Apart from gross mechanical neglect, the car's back doors remained integral components of the vehicle only by being tied together with rope across the backseat. Lenton, who had no car of his own, offered to look after it if he could make use of it while Sage was away – a bargain that was accepted with alacrity. Even though the streets of London were not crowded in those days, Sage would sometimes arrive at work late, looking sheepish and admit to a driving mishap. It was Lenton's job to retrieve the car. On one occasion, there had been a collision with a London taxi. When Lenton arrived at the scene, he found the cabbie studying geometrical patterns drawn in the dirt on his taxi. Sage had demonstrated, using angles of incidence and deflection and Newton's laws of motion, how the accident had not been his fault: not only was the cabbie satisfied, he told Lenton he was never going to clean his taxi.

A second incident required quick thinking from Lenton. Sage had broken down at Piccadilly Circus and simply abandoned the car. Lenton arrived to find two cross policemen directing the traffic around the obstacle. After Lenton explained that the car was not his, but belonged to a distinguished university professor, the police were not impressed. One of them said, 'He is going to get done anyway.' But, said Lenton, this professor had been Lord Louis Mountbatten's chief scientific adviser in the war and had been responsible for D-Day planning. He was sure that Mountbatten would have to be informed if the police were going to take any action. The policemen helped Lenton push the car out of the way, and watched as he got it started with a bent paper clip in the ignition – Sage having lost the key.[22]

In 1947 London University granted Birkbeck the use of two Georgian houses that, prior to the Blitz, were part of a terrace just north of the Senate House. Numbers 21 and 22 Torrington Square would house Birkbeck's Crystallography Department for the next twenty years. Number 22 was propped up by large timbers; there was a gaping hole in the back wall, and the builders were in the middle of making repairs when the first scientists moved in. The apparatus moved back from the RI had to be kept under tarpaulins to protect it from brick dust and rain. Each house had four storeys plus a basement. The rooms, arranged around the staircases, were fairly small but would serve as laboratories. The top two floors of No. 21 were taken by the chemistry department, who would not prove to be ideal co-tenants. The original servants' quarters right at the top of No. 22 became Bernal's flat.

The provision of living accommodation for Sage came at a useful time. Margaret Gardiner was aware enough of his philandering to decide that she would no longer have him living with her. They remained fond of each other, and Margaret accepted that it was impossible for him to love only one woman: she continued to believe that 'in his curious way, Desmond was a very faithful person'.[23] For Martin, who had seen more of his father during wartime than was the norm, there came a realization that his father was unusual in not coming home every night. Sage went back to his old haunts and found himself the main attraction to a circle of women, who were as open about sharing their favours with him as they were in sharing their politics. Successive young research workers were warned that if they heard footsteps on the wooden staircase going up to the professor's flat, they should cover their ears. At social gatherings, some of the young wives or girlfriends of his research team would sense lasciviousness in the professor's attitude towards them.

Sir Lawrence Bragg performed the grand opening of the Biomolecular Research Laboratory, 21–22 Torrington Square, on 1st July 1948. A booklet was produced by Birkbeck College to mark the occasion, with an introduction from the director, J.D. Bernal. The four assistant directors were listed with their research teams (15 individuals). The support staff numbered nine, headed by Miss Anita Rimel, who had replaced Brenda Ryerson as Bernal's secretary at Birkbeck during the war. Anita was a dogged communist, with advanced views on women's rights.[24] One of eleven children of a Jewish food merchant, she was stocky and had frizzy dark hair. She was devoted to Sage and eager to make herself known to his wide circle of colleagues – which she did, by adding postscripts of her own to his dictated correspondence. One name that might well have appeared as a researcher on the X-ray analysis team, but did not thanks to Anita, was Francis Crick. He had decided that he wanted to make the transition from physics to biology, following a wartime career designing acoustic and magnetic mines. After a little preliminary investigation, including reading *The Search*, Crick decided that Professor Bernal at Birkbeck would be the best mentor for him. He paid a visit but got no further than Miss Rimel, who struck him as 'an amiable dragon'. 'Do you realize', she asked Crick, 'that people from all over the world want to come to work with the professor. Why do you think he would take you on?'[25]

While Anita Rimel would become the dominant, some would say domineering, personal assistant in Bernal's life, she was but one of a trio of women trying to keep tabs on him at the end of the war. He still needed a secretary at

COHQ and there was Kathleen Watkins at the Ministry of Home Security at Princes Risborough, who would soon move to London to help Sage run the Scientific Advisory Committee at the Ministry of Works. Sir Reginald Stradling, the wartime head of the Ministry of Home Security, was now the chief scientific adviser to the Ministry of Works and appointed Bernal to the new position at the end of 1944. Sage's brief was to take charge of research on how best to meet the urgent need for new housing in Britain. The new role would enable him to indulge his love for architecture within a state-controlled programme devoted to improving the lives of ordinary citizens. There would also be an opportunity to carry out the first systematic scientific analysis of conventional and novel building materials at Birkbeck.

In June 1941, at a time when he was preoccupied by analysing various aspects of bomb damage, Sage composed a long note on 'Research organisation in the building industry'.[26] Writing as a member of the 1940 Council (a self-appointed body to promote planning of the social environment), he called for the setting up of a Building Research Council so that the post-war need for construction could be met as well and speedily as possible. Assuming it was 'axiomatic that structural truthfulness is as essential to great architecture as it has ever been', he argued that:

It is a common mistake to assume that the introduction of the scientific method into the field of design tends to cramp the imaginative powers of the designer. The reverse is true, for it is the supreme characteristic of the scientific outlook that it forever looks forward.[27]

It was natural, therefore, that the Building Research Station (BRS) should consult Bernal about their post-war plans. While generally impressed with their forward-looking and comprehensive approach, Sage suggested that the techniques of operational research should be used to examine the utilization of existing buildings, so that better designs and improved domestic equipment could be incorporated into the new houses. Again and again he would stress the functionality of buildings: their designs should match the uses to which they would be put, but before that could be achieved, much more needed to be known about the ways people actually behaved at home, in school or at work. In his comments to the BRS director, Bernal also urged consideration of fundamental physical properties of silicates (cement, brick and glass), fibres (wood, fibre board) and metals. There was a need 'to develop crystal structure and phase diagrams for silicates in various states', and for the detailed study of the setting process in cement, (including accelerating and retarding agents). Sage made an initial visit to the Building Research Station at Watford in September 1944, when he was in the middle of preparing the final reports on Overlord and getting ready for his trip to South-East Asia.

Among the topics he discussed with the staff were the temperature effects, shrinkage, creep, and plasticity of cement, the use of porous materials, soil mechanics, stress in large masses, design of complex structures, and the problem of vibrations.[28]

Sage made promises at the Ministry of Works soon after his appointment that he would discover why cement sets and why it is subject to shrinkage and creeping. The cracking of concrete was a common and unpredictable occurrence that vexed the construction industry. Partly to educate himself, but more importantly to raise the level of interest in these rather mundane-sounding matters, Sage suggested that a meeting be held to discuss the fundamental scientific problems associated with building. The result was a one-day symposium at the Royal Institution in May 1946 on 'Shrinkage and cracking of cementive materials'. One of the speakers described recent electron microscopy studies suggesting that cement, in its hydrated form, consisted of 'a matrix of interlaced fibrous crystals'[29] that gives concrete its cohesive properties. Water is held in the capillary-like spaces between the crystals and depending on the moisture content, the volume of the concrete is altered giving rise to internal stress and, eventually, to cracking. In 'a short contribution to the afternoon session, Prof. Bernal commented that the fibrillar material revealed by electron microscope studies of set cement suggests an analogy with certain other fibrillar materials such as tobacco mosaic virus, and with the behaviour they show when the concentration of their solutions is changed.'[30]

This connection is very unlikely to have occurred to anyone else, but prompted Sage to think more deeply about the fundamental properties of gels, and how there might be similarities between hydrated cement and the structure of living cells, for example. In September he was back at the Royal Institution, giving the general introduction to a three-day international meeting on 'Swelling and shrinking' held by the Faraday Society. Modestly describing himself as a newcomer to the field of colloid science, he pointed out that the definition of a gel was still a very loose one: 'It has been taken to cover any fluid-containing system showing mechanical rigidity, with a structure which cannot be elucidated by the optical microscope. It is extremely difficult to draw a line between a weak gel and an anomalous fluid showing viscous elasticity, or between a gel and a paste of microscopically visible particles.'[31] He referred to his work with Fankuchen with the gels of TMV that 'demonstrated conclusively regular hexagonal two-dimensional associations of elongated particles with distances apart ranging from contact up to at least 500 Å.'[32] He went on to tease out the question that he thought should be explored in many colloids.

The regularity of the structures showed that we are here dealing with energy systems possessing minima at these distances, or to put it another way, with attractive and repulsive forces in equilibrium, this equilibrium itself being determined by the ionic constitutions of the medium. Other work has shown that also in soaps, clays and inside the crystals of proteins, long-range forces, leading to equilibria are involved. One of the most interesting features of this conference should be the discussion of the physical nature of these long-range forces.

I am myself somewhat uncertain whether we are dealing here with a single or a complex phenomenon. It may well be that the forces working over a distance of the order of 10–30 Å, such as occur in clays, soaps and proteins, may be of a different kind from the longer range forces observed in the virus and hydroxide tactoids; and that the first may in fact be fairly normal association through water or solvent molecules held in fixed positions. But whether this is so or not, the longer range forces need a different type of explanation.[33]

Bernal's introduction set the stage for a stimulating meeting of the Faraday Society, one which he had conceived as a result of the earlier meeting for the building industries, and it demonstrated his subtlety and fluency of thought. One can trace in his remarks strands of previous research including the thermodynamics of water and liquid structure that he initiated with Fowler, the virus work with Fan, Perutz's observations about haemoglobin crystals acting as a sponge, and his own ideas on protein folding due to hydrophobic forces.

Many of the topics he mentioned were under investigation at Birkbeck. He continued to work on crystalline plant viruses with Carlisle, and the Cement Section were beginning to examine the structure of tricalcium silicate and related compounds, using powder and single crystal X-ray crystallography. Helen Megaw left in 1946 to become Director of Scientific Studies at Girton College, Cambridge. After a short hiatus, her role as assistant director for the Cement Section was taken over by Dr Jim Jeffery, who knew Sage slightly from the political scene in Cambridge before the war. Confronted with the task of studying crystals of tricalcium silicate, Jeffery found them to be impossible to orientate correctly for X-ray photographs. Sage informed him, somewhat impatiently, that similar problems confronted the crystallographers at the RI in the old days and 'had been solved as a routine matter'.[34] He gave Jeffery some clues, which enabled him to get the crystals properly set and soon led to his first research paper.

In his progress report for the opening of the Biomolecular Research Laboratory, Jeffery remarked that work in his section was being held back by a lack of available research workers. He would soon acquire a research student, Alan Mackay, who came with the perfect credentials for Birkbeck: a Cambridge physics degree and socialist convictions. Even before arriving, Mackay had come under Sage's influence, at a distance. He had chosen *The Social Function of Science* for a prize won at Trinity College; his introduction to crystallography had been provided both by a course of lectures given by Peter Wooster and at a summer school set up by Helen Megaw in Cambridge. After graduating, he took a job with Philips, the electrical company. At the Philips Laboratory he became involved in research on calcium phosphate, one of the materials used in fluorescent tubes. He decided to study its structure by X-ray crystallography and to do this as a part-time PhD student at Birkbeck. Sage was his nominal supervisor, but immediately handed him on to Jim Jeffery. Mackay soon discovered that 'supervision was rather slight. But the atmosphere was very cooperative and people just got on with things.'[35]

With his Birkbeck teams making the best of their limited resources to address fundamental questions, their professor continued to play an innovative role in government service. The post-war need for the efficient and rapid expansion in housing seemed to Bernal to provide an ideal opportunity for science to transform a rather backward industry. In a 1946 radio broadcast, Sage informed his audience that the really astonishing thing was how little building had changed over the preceding four or five thousand years: 'the bricks, the mortar, the scaffolding, the trowels, the hods and most of the building appliances including the plans of the architect and the estimates of the contractor are all known from the times of ancient Egypt and Babylon.'[36] Amongst major industries, building was the least mechanized, which was absurd when one considered that building a traditional house involved transporting about one hundred tons of materials and then lifting them against gravity. Building was a slow process because of the conditions faced by the workers – cold, damp, dust, poor food – which despite the labour-intensive nature of the industry had been largely ignored. Equally overlooked were the requirements of the eventual users of a home. As Sage pointed out in an earlier broadcast: 'It is probable we know far more about the domestic habits in the Trobriand Islands than in the London suburbs.'[37]

The solution to many architects, engineers and politicians seemed to lie with the use of novel materials and the provision of prefabricated homes. Indeed so many new prototypes were being suggested that the Minister of Health (who had ultimate responsibility for housing) suggested that Bernal should study 'every kind of the 1,300 varieties of prefabricated house which have been put forward, deciding which seem the best, and pulling all the ideas together': a terrible task, thought Sage, which was 'certain to get me down.'[38] As usual, he found some solace in science.

For instance, if instead of prefabricated houses we were dealing with insects, we should find that ordinary people, looking at insects, would say, 'There are an awful lot of them, you cannot make sense out of them.' In the course of time, however, scientists have found classificatory methods of dealing with something like 20,000,000 species of insects, so that a mere 1,300 prefabricated houses is a comparatively simple business.[39]

To attempt an answer, Bernal together with the BRS launched a bold experiment in the summer of 1945. A dozen developments, each comprising fifty houses, were to be put up using standard methods in various parts of the UK. The contractors' work at each site would be carefully timed and costed. At the same time, twenty-one groups of fifty prefabs would also be constructed and compared to the conventional buildings. Adjunctive studies would be made at the BRS and at Birkbeck of individual trades such as plastering, plumbing etc. in an effort to analyse the individual skills required so that selection, training and safety could be improved.[40] The exigencies of the times did not lend themselves to such methodical planning. The pre-war labour force of one million in the building industry had shrunk by about two-thirds; apart from the loss of housing stock due to bomb damage, families were being created at an unprecedented rate as men returned from military service, leading to extra demand.[41]

The Minister of Health, Aneurin Bevan, while holding firm views on the quality of public housing the country needed to produce, was necessarily more involved with planning the National Health Service. While Attlee would have been better advised to move the housing problem to another ministry, there would still have been the inherent drawbacks for any central attempt to plan in detail and undertake such an important enterprise. These were sharply pointed up by *Picture Post* in September 1946.

Mr Dalton, the Chancellor of the Exchequer, is responsible for providing the capital required to pay out the housing subsidies. Mr Arthur Greenwood, the Lord Privy Seal, has certain, vague, overruling functions. No one quite knows what he does do. Mr Tomlinson, the Minister of Works, directs the building industry, licensing private builders, controlling building materials, and providing temporary and prefabricated permanent homes. Mr Isaacs, the Minister of Labour, has to provide the manpower. The Minister of Town and Country Planning can decide against house building on any site. The Minister of Agriculture must be consulted about rural housing. The Minister of Supply deals with materials, and especially with the provision of house components, of which there is a serious shortage. Mr Bevan's writ does not run north of the border, where the Secretary of State for Scotland controls housing. The tenth cook is Sir Stafford Cripps, who, as President of the Board of Trade, is now calling upon all builders employing more than fifty men to reply to ninety questions. Everyone in this industry considers that the issue of these forms will add to the delays and costs of housebuilding.[42]

Against a backdrop of bureaucratic muddles, shortage of labour and materials, the freezing winter and sterling crisis of 1947, the Attlee government managed to oversee the construction of about 100,000 prefabs during its first two and a half years in office. Sage later regretted that the best examples of prefabs tested, 'beautiful and suitable in every respect', were never built because they were too expensive (the typical post-war unit cost about £1,000). He said ruefully: 'To get anything that could actually be built by prefabrication and did not cost too much was beyond the wit of man, and so we went back to the bricklayer.'[43] The post-war prefabs proved popular with their occupants because of their simple but liveable design; they often lasted decades longer than originally intended. In the opinion of one architect and town planner, looking back half a century, 'Time has shown that their construction and space-for-living standards were soundly conceived and carried through, both within the "units" and in their gardens and neighbourliness; being put down often on inner-city sites after war damage, they made homes where they were wanted.'[44]

The third aspect of Sage's post-war rebuilding effort, in addition to Birkbeck and public housing, was to help repair the edifice of science. The first public manifestation came at the United Nations Educational and Cultural Conference in London in November 1945. The Americans had wanted a UN agency devoted to educational and cultural reconstruction in those parts of Asia and Europe blighted by the Axis Powers, but British scientists, in the words of Julian Huxley, considered it 'essential that the word "Science" or "Scientific" should occur in the title of the Organization...the Conference should put the S in UNESCO'.[45] In his address to the Conference, Bernal endorsed this idea saying that an international scientific commission had long been needed and 'never more than in the present period of rehabilitation and reconstruction'.[46] Nor should it be confined to physical sciences because 'one of the main lessons of the War was that mixed research teams, ranging from mathematicians and physicists to economists and psychologists, were needed to cope with regional problems in their entirety'. The war had seen a complete pooling of American and British Commonwealth resources in science and demonstrated that the effects of science transcended national boundaries. He referred to work carried out by Kendrew and others in Cairo who examined 'all the related problems of the region – of agriculture, industry and health – from Morocco to Baluchistan'. He sensed an appetite for science in many undeveloped countries of the world, and the 'history of the Soviet Republics of Central Asia shows how rapidly science can be built up and how eagerly it is seized on by a population starting from a medieval standard of culture'.[47] In the aftermath of the atomic bomb, the Americans soon accepted the political necessity for having the S in UNESCO, and Huxley would become its first Director General.

In February 1946, the Association of Scientific Workers organized a conference on 'Science and the Welfare of Mankind'. It provided an opportunity for leading British scientists to expound their views on the social and ethical responsibilities of science and to listen to opinions from a number of foreign delegates. During the conference a resolution was passed that a World Federation of Scientific Workers (WFSW) should be formed, and its inaugural meeting was held in London that July. The prime mover of the federation, Frédéric Joliot-Curie, was elected its first president with Bernal and Nikolai Semenov, a Soviet chemist, as vice-presidents. The meeting was attended by observers and delegates from eighteen associations in fourteen countries. Joseph Needham, now the director of the natural sciences division of UNESCO, sent a message of goodwill. Part of the reason for the strong turnout from overseas was the Newton Tercentenary celebrations organized by the Royal Society. The Federation's lofty goals were reported in the *Manchester Guardian* by J.G. Crowther, who would soon find himself its Secretary-General. He was most impressed by Bernal's speech: 'it was a brief, condensed, deep but transparently clear description of the aims of the new organization.'[48]

Earlier in July, the crystallography world had reunited happily at the RI under the genial presidency of Lawrence Bragg. To Bernal's delight, Fan was one of a number of Americans who came, and despite the travel restrictions, it was also possible for von Laue and two others to come from Germany. A Russian delegation arrived a few days late, and the meeting resulted not only in the creation of an international journal, *Acta Crystallographica*, but the founding of the International Union of Crystallography (IUCr). Sage of course played a prominent role in planning all of this and was as energetic outside the meetings, entertaining the visitors. He and Fan threw a party for the American contingent at his sister Gigi's flat. This was a high-spirited event, momentarily interrupted by the discovery of 'a dead rat under the davenport in front of the fireplace', whose presence was explained away on the spurious grounds that Gigi's husband was a taxidermist![49]

The crammed summer schedule of meetings, coming just after he had completed his work for the Joint Technical Warfare Committee, and the demands of administering his fragmented physics department left Bernal himself little opportunity for travel. In November, he did manage to go to Paris for a meeting to honour the fiftieth anniversary of the death of Louis Pasteur. For his lecture, Sage chose to talk about Pasteur's first great discovery of the *chirality* or handedness of molecules.[50] This experiment took place in 1848, a year after Pasteur gained his doctorate, and established the concept of asymmetrical molecules which, through association with fermentation and other living processes, became the key to Pasteur's later work with microbes. Sage traced the genesis of Pasteur's breakthrough from previous knowledge of crystals and chemistry, and ascribed his singular success to an ability to combine physical and chemical methods of analysis. In a Marxist aside, he also pointed out that Pasteur's discoveries and their enormous consequences depended on him choosing to work with tartar, ('a by-product of the greatest chemical industry of antiquity and the Middle Ages – the fermentation of grapes') which had been well-studied because of its economic importance.

Bernal's lecture was not just an entertaining and humble genuflection to the great Pasteur. It had spontaneity and excitement not customarily heard at august, historic meetings. For once, his preparation had been diligent before coming to Paris, and he had reached his own conclusions about why Pasteur had successfully found a solution to a problem that 'had occupied the best brains of European science for the best part of twenty years'. Then, the day before he was due to speak, Sage was given access to Pasteur's original notebooks at the Sorbonne. No one but Pasteur had looked at them for nearly a century and they revealed 'another story, no less an achievement but far more illuminating', which caused Sage to recast his lecture. He delivered it in French and showed the audience pages of Pasteur's handwritten notebook. He marvelled at the detail and accuracy of Pasteur's observations, his familiarity with precedent and his grasp of crystallography.

The puzzle confronting Pasteur was that a small proportion of tartaric acid seemed to consist of a chemically identical, but physically distinct substance he knew as paratartaric acid. It was established by Pasteur's day that the predominant natural tartaric acid rotated polarized light to the right, whereas paratartaric acid was optically inactive. The two acids had different melting points and their salts differed in solubility. Pasteur prepared double salts of both acids and crystallized them out. He examined 'a very great number' of crystals of the tartrate double salt and found that they were all asymmetric in the same way, with small facets presenting to the left (hemihedral-to-the-left). When he came to the paratartrate crystals he expected them not to show any asymmetry, but in fact found that 'all the crystals bore the facets of asymmetry'. At this point, an emotional Sage reported to the audience that Pasteur's heart missed a beat (*j'eus un instant un serrement de coeur*). The paratartrate crystals were of two distinct types, twins or mirror images, with their asymmetries to the right or left. Pasteur then meticulously separated out the two types of crystal and dissolved them again into separate solutions. The solution from the crystals hemihedral-to-the-left rotated polarized light to the right, just like the common form of tartrate crystals. Those crystals that were hemihedral-to-the-right caused polarized light to rotate to the left. If he took an equal measure of both, the mixed solution was again optically inactive – the two forms cancelled each other out. As Bernal put it in Paris: 'That is all – the page is complete – molecular asymmetry is established.'

Pasteur spent the best part of the next decade studying *la dissymétrie moléculaire*, and this lead him to cross over into the virgin territory of microbiology. His work on asymmetry led him to believe that there was a 'profound line of demarcation between the mineral and organic worlds' defined by some cosmic asymmetric force that in biomolecules produced either right-handed or left-handed molecules. 'Almost imperceptibly he modified this idea in the course of his biological work, replacing it with that of life as a unique chain of beings, each one being asymmetric and each one passing its asymmetry to the next.'[51] Sage, while recognizing that Pasteur 'was absolutely correct in saying that the molecular complexity of living things or even of the products of life were of a completely different order from anything reached by non-living matter', reminded his audience that Pasteur had slightly overstated his case. He had predicted, for example, that a crystal of albumen could not exist because its structure would be so complicated that it could not crystallize. 'We know now that in this he went too far; proteins do crystallize.' Sage used one of his favourite diagrammatic forms, that of a branching tree, to illustrate how early nineteenth-century science provided the tap root of Pasteur's discovery, which then grew branches into twentieth-century science, with its widespread ramifications. One of the branches was labelled crystal chemistry, and carried the names of the Braggs and Kathleen Lonsdale amongst others. Yet the branch was severely pruned: the name Bernal, and the first structural pictures of proteins and viruses, is missing.

Bernal remarked in his lecture that Pasteur's great discovery, unlike say Röntgen's later discovery of X-rays, was not immediately taken up by other scientists. In part this was because only Pasteur had the chemical and crystallographic knowledge to develop further ideas, but also because scientists of the day tended to communicate sporadically by letters or through personal visits. As he wrote in *The Social Function of Science*, in those days the number of workers was so small that there was a reasonable possibility of acquiring knowledge from one's contemporaries, but by the Second World War the very quantity of scientific information had made its diffusion an enormous problem, with which existing machinery had utterly failed to cope. Even though in his opinion, three-quarters of the material did not deserve to be published at all, there was still the need to ensure that 'every scientific worker, and for that matter every member of the general public, receives just that information that can be of the greatest use to him in his work and no more'.[52] He thought the present system of journals of lengthy papers was cumbersome and inefficient and while the full details should be available on demand, what was required was a wider distribution of short abstracts or summaries.

The war had subsequently shown that efficient information services were vital, when dealing with novel subjects and a rapidly broadening front of knowledge. The traditional, passive role of libraries as repositories of knowledge was no longer adequate to meet the needs of active researchers. Bernal conveyed these thoughts to a conference of the Association of Specialist

Libraries and Information Bureaux in September 1945. He thought the twin aims of a modern information service should be to send the right information in the right form to the right people, and secondly to arrange that facts of whatever diverse origin, bearing on any particular topic, should be integrated for those studying that topic. This would represent a great improvement over the current position where 'the research worker receives in journals and books a very large number of facts that are of no use to him at all but which have to be ploughed through'.[53] He thought that the primary unit in scientific communication should be the individual scientific paper dealing with a particular subject: it should certainly not be the scientific journal of a learned society that 'consists essentially of a number of papers which have in common only the fact that they were submitted at the same time'.[54]

The Association of Scientific Workers, responding to suggestions from Bill Pirie, had come up with its own proposals for a radical overhaul of information services.

In the proposed scheme, each country would have a centre of scientific publication and exchange which would receive from societies papers already passed by referees as suitable for publication and lists of members to whom papers from any part of the world on specified subjects or groups of subjects, should be sent. The national centres would act as clearing-houses for these papers, arranging for their internal distribution and sending others in blocks in appropriate numbers to the clearing-houses in other countries for distribution to the scientists there. Payment of a subscription to one society would entitle the subscriber to the services of the whole organization.[55]

Over the next year or so, there were sporadic papers from various organizations and individuals on the themes of a national information service and the distribution and use of scientific information. At Bernal's suggestion, Kendrew, now a doctoral student in Cambridge working with Perutz, conducted the first survey of the use of scientific literature at British universities. He found that there were severe delays in publication due to paper shortages, a lack of typesetters in the printing industry and the energy crisis of 1947.[56] These delays, coupled with the enormous number of papers submitted for publication, meant that there was wasteful duplication as scientists attempted to make pre-announcements of their work through preliminary notes and letters, while the definitive papers were held up. Towards the end of 1947, the Royal Society decided to air the whole issue at a conference and appointed Bernal as a member of the organizing committee.

The winter of 1947–8 was another dreary period, with food rationing and energy shortages still prevailing. Geoffrey Pyke, the inventor of Habbakuk, had turned his mind to the coming National Health Service. The elusiveness of public health policy exasperated him; he had come to a fundamental conclusion that no one knew the correct time for making future economic plans – should it be five years, a decade or fifty years? He felt abandoned by Bernal at the end of the war and was depressed. Pyke stored boxes of documents in Margaret Gardiner's garden shed and on one occasion threatened to commit suicide there to punish Sage. Margaret changed the padlock on the shed.[57] In February 1948, Pyke took a fatal overdose in his rented rooms in Hampstead. Sage wrote obituaries for the *Guardian* and *The Times*. Describing Pyke as 'one of the greatest and certainly the most unrecognized geniuses of the time', Sage defined his personal tragedy as the possession of 'abilities of such an order that they could only be expressed in action on the vastest scale and yet he was constitutionally incapable of directing the action of others'.[58] Pyke's despair about the inertia of the world was summed up in his motto 'nothing must ever be done for the first time'.

The Royal Society Scientific Information Conference was held in the summer of 1948 with over two hundred scientists and librarians from Britain, the Commonwealth and the USA in attendance. About 45 papers were received from delegates and circulated in advance so that the discussions would be informed. One, from Bernal on a 'Provisional scheme for central distribution of scientific publications' caused a furore. It extended the ideas put forward by the AScW and was intended to 'overcome the major disadvantages of the present system of publication and provide a more rapid, cheaper and more rational system of distribution'. What Sage's paper did was to threaten the role of the learned societies in producing the majority of scientific journals, and they were outraged. A consortium that ran the gamut from the Anatomical to Zoological Societies sent a memorandum 'to place on record that for the fields of science which we represent we consider that the proposed scheme of central publication and distribution of scientific papers is undesirable and would also interfere with the statutory and accepted aims of individual societies as free centres of interest and encouragement of research'.[59]

It was not just the learned societies attacking Bernal's ideas: John Baker and Sir Arthur Tansley, two founding members of the Society for Freedom in Science, were quoted in *The Times*, describing Bernal's proposed scheme as 'totalitarianism'.[60] Pirie had previously dismissed their objections as those of 'reactionary biologists saying they wanted their chaotic publications left alone',[61] and there is no doubt that the bitterness of their criticism was occasioned by personal dislike of Sage. Baker had been a trenchant critic of his ever since the publication of *The Social Function of Science* and had written a 'Counter-blast to Bernalism' in the *New Statesman* in the summer of 1939. It was this piece that led to the formation of the Society for Freedom in Science in 1940. Sage replied to Baker and Tansley, accusing them of spreading undue alarm. He stated that the 'real object of my own scheme was not centralization but better service to scientific readers'.[62] He thought that the two biologists did not realize that 'the object of scientific communications is not merely to publish scientific papers, but to see that they are read by those who might profit from them. The present chaotic abundance of scientific publication ensures, as effectively as any imaginary system of control, that a large number of papers should not be read'.[63]

Sage was unable to convince the press that he meant no harm to scientific discourse. Several weekly publications, such as *The Economist* and the *Observer*, worried about the infringement of the tradition of free scientific enquiry. A *Times* leader denounced Professor Bernal's 'insidious and cavalier proposals', and printed a letter describing his scheme as 'contrary to all which British scientists have always held sacred. It appears to embrace many of those fundamental principles upon which the Nazi scientific information service was based and which were developed during the Hitler régime'.[64]

The Royal Society's President, Sir Robert Robinson, deplored the 'premature propaganda in the popular Press' and the relish with which it anticipated 'a clash of ideologies and the probable conflict between the planners and those who don't want to be planned'.[65] Bernal's paper had been pre-circulated and was printed in the conference proceedings, but he withdrew it from discussion 'on account of the misunderstandings about the status, nature and scope of these proposals'.[66] While this may have been partly to avoid unproductive argument on the conference floor, it was mainly because the results of Kendrew's questionnaire (presented by Bernal) showed that the mode of distribution of papers to individuals played such a small part in scientific communication that it would be a waste of time at the moment to attempt reform. As the physicist, Neville Mott, had pointed out in committee weeks earlier, physicists relied almost exclusively on library journals; Sage realized that the major effort needed to be directed towards improving library services, not on the distribution of papers to individual subscribers. At the opening of the conference, Bernal, as he had in his letter to *The Times*, explained that he was not wedded to any particular system but just wanted to ensure 'the satisfaction of the user and the advance of science'.[67] These two objectives were not independent but neither were they synonymous: an individual reader might be satisfied with a slow and incomplete service, but the confusion and inefficiencies of the present system acted 'as a continuous brake to the progress of science'. In a humorous plea for planning rather than trusting slow evolution, Sage reminded his audience:

Many races of animal have died out as the effect of overmuch evolution in some particular direction. The horns of the Irish elk, admirable as weapons for mutual slaughter, turned out in the long run to be a disadvantage when the animal was pursued by enemies against which they were of little value. At the present moment the confusion and multiplicity of scientific publication is being met by the creation of new journals and the multiplication of papers containing substantially the same facts in order to achieve adequate circulation.[68]

Bernal's various suggestions had little immediate impact in Britain, but they were read with interest by a young American, Eugene Garfield, who was just embarking on a career that would transform scientific communication and the exchange of information. For him the 1948 Royal Society's conference proceedings became 'a bible', and in particular Sage's 'idea of a centralized reprint center was in my thoughts when I first wrote about the yet nonexistent *S[cience] C[itation] I[ndex]* in *Science* in 1955'.[69] One of Bernal's insights was that scientists are not trained to retrieve published information that might be useful to them, and that an ideal system should deliver that information with minimal effort on the consumer's part. Garfield sensed that such a result could be best approached by using computers to generate indexing terms that effectively described the contents of a paper, avoiding the duplication, cost, confusion and tardiness of human indexers. During the decade from the mid-fifties, he brought his ideas to fruition in a series of ever more ambitious information tools culminating in the *SCI*. He found Bernal to be encouraging during its infancy, while 'others found all the reasons that it couldn't work',[70] and Sage was a member of its editorial advisory board for the first few years. Apart from recognizing Garfield's monumental achievement in producing an information retrieval system that was multi-disciplinary, comprehensive, easy to use and up-to-date, Sage was the first to draw attention to its sociological implications as a way to monitor trends in science, whether on a national, institutional, or disciplinary basis. In 1975, Garfield dedicated the first large-scale statistical analysis of journals 'to the memory of the late John Desmond Bernal, whose insight into the societal origins and impact of science inspired an interest that became a career'.[71]

Bernal's fundamental contributions to X-ray crystallography were generously recognized by Sir Lawrence Bragg, in his presidential address to the British Association for the Advancement of Science in the summer of 1948.[72] Reminding his audience that no one had done more than Bernal as an explorer and pioneer, Bragg said:

Time and again, when reviewing some branch of X-ray analysis which is now very active, we have to acknowledge that the first critical experiment was due to his inspiration. Settlers have moved in to farm the land, but he has been the pioneer who pushed the frontier forward; one may add that, like all true pioneers, he becomes impatient and restless when the new country is developed and moves to fresh fields! ... In the early days we painstakingly examined X-ray diffracted beams one by one with an ionization chamber. Highly accurate analyses are now made by the far more rapid method of recording all the beams on a photograph plate. The method itself was not new but it was Bernal who showed us how to systematize and docket the observations and draw logical and far-reaching conclusions from them about the architecture of complex compounds.... It was he who first obtained a regular diffracted pattern from a protein crystal ... and he advanced further to study the scattering by the very large-scale regularities in virus preparations ... his work only gave an indication in each case of what might be discovered, but it made the first steps possible.

While this was a kind tribute from Bragg, Bernal had no intention of resting on his laurels and was still energetically plotting the future of crystallography. At the Royal Society meeting on scientific information in 1948, Sage approached Olga Kennard with an idea for systematically logging new crystal structures as they were solved by X-ray analysis. Olga studied as a research student with Perutz in Cambridge and had just moved to London to work for the Medical Research Council. Bernal saw the limitations of single scientific papers that asked and answered one or two questions about one or two crystal structures, and he thought that by integrating the data from individual studies in a systematic way, radically new information would emerge. Until such combinatory analysis became possible by computer, Olga devised an index card system where structural characteristics were denoted by having holes punched at certain positions. When she wished to retrieve structures with common features, such as hydrogen bonding, she could do so by the simple device of inserting a knitting needle through the holes in the cards. A few years later, Bernal suggested that the three hundred or so structures that Olga had registered should be published in a book. From such simple beginnings, the Cambridge Crystallographic Data Centre would slowly grow.[73]

The Nuffield Foundation gave £5,000 annually to Bernal's department for the five years after the war, (which does not sound much, but was double the MRC annual grant to Bragg's new research unit at the Cavendish). By 1949, Bernal was writing to the Master of Birkbeck about the impossible congestion of research and teaching activities in Torrington Square. He was given permission to make use of a static water tank (used in the war for fire fighting) at No. 23. This was a cubic space with sides about 60 feet long that became the lab for Booth's computer group. Bernal's fiftieth birthday in May 1951 gave his staff an opportunity to celebrate his leadership and to reflect on their achievements over the first quinquennium. From the electronics department of the Biomolecular Research Laboratory, Werner Ehrenberg remembered how they all pretended that they had to work under difficult conditions, at first with no fixed home, and then with the move into bomb-damaged accommodation with 'floors half burned, windows blasted out, water only available next door, electricity from a point in the cellar'.[74] While he had joined the chorus of complainers, he secretly thought their situation offered supreme advantages, not least because of a ' "boss" who always pretended to know so much less of the matter in hand than you did, but always knew enough to see the tremendous importance of your projects'.

A map on the front of the staff report showed that the Birkbeck scientists came from eighteen countries around the globe. There were reports from the physics groups still working at the Breams Buildings site on Theoretical Physics (Furth), Nuclear Physics (Siday), and the Cosmic Ray Group (George) who had been chasing new sub-atomic particles in venues as varied as Holborn underground station, a colliery in Somerset, the Jungfraujoch and at Dakar, near the equator. There were of course summaries from Carlisle on the Organic Section, Jeffery (Cement Section) and Booth (The Computer Project). The Nuffield Foundation had agreed to increase its funding to £8,000 per annum for a further four years, but by 1951 Bernal was seriously concerned about keeping such a varied and expanding department on the rails. He wrote to the new Master, John Lockwood, in February that 'the situation in the teaching of crystallography for the degrees of MSc and PhD will be extremely serious unless steps can be taken in the near future to provide more space and some equipment'.[75] In September, Bernal proposed that crystallography be established as a separate sub-department. Although it was called a physics department, Kendrew came to regard Bernal's post-war Birkbeck unit as the prototype for all Institutes of Molecular Biology, with its computing department, and its electronics group dedicated to improving X-ray tubes for the structural study of proteins and nucleic acids.[76]

15

Central Dogma

In the 1930s, the Rockefeller Foundation supported several small European meetings where physicists were invited to pollinate the debate about fundamental problems in biology. One of these gatherings took place at Klampenborg, about ten kilometres from Copenhagen, early in April 1938. A mixed British contingent of scientists, with Astbury and Bernal representing X-ray crystallography, attended. The crossing from Harwich to the Hook of Holland was distinctly rough, and while most of the party attempted to sleep despite the rolling of the ship, Bernal sat up in the second-class lounge deep in conversation with a tall, rather sleek, young man. His companion was Cyril Darlington, Director of the John Innes Horticultural Institute – a geneticist who had recently written on the coiling of chromosomes. Darlington had proposed that this observable alteration in chromosomal form might be due to an invisible *molecular* spiral in the constituent nucleoprotein. During the night, Darlington taught Sage 'all the genetics and cytology anyone needs to know'.[1]

The main focus of the Klampenborg meeting was on the physical mechanics of changes in chromosomes that had been observed under the light microscope at different stages of the cell cycle. Darlington's ideas on 'relational coiling', the term he used to describe two chromosomal threads coiling around each other, were central to the discussions, and suggested to Hal Waddington that 'the internal genes have some spiral arrangement' that produced this effect. It was still believed that the ultimate genetic structure was protein, although the nucleic acid DNA was now accepted to be a constituent of chromosomes. Bernal offered some ideas on what physical forces might bring pairs of homologous chromosomes together during the development of sex cells (sperm or ova) and also prevent other chromosomes from becoming entwined. This process in which genetic material can cross over from one chromosome to its homologue, or matching partner, results in the assortment of genes during sexual reproduction so that offspring are not genetically identical to their parents or to their siblings.

Sage returned to this subject on his pre-war lecture tour of the USA, elaborating on ideas he had first considered at the Klampenborg meeting.

He predicted, incorrectly as it would turn out, that the 'fundamental question of the molecular structure of the chromosomes must necessarily wait for its full elucidation on the knowledge of protein structure'. His next statement would be borne out in time, however, that the chromosomes' molecular structure bore a 'marked similarity of chemical composition to the viruses of the tobacco-mosaic type [suggesting] that it is also a long-moleculed nucleoprotein with internal crystalline structure'.[2] In his American talk, he proposed the novel 'zipper hypothesis' of chromosome pairing. He based his argument on the assumption that there would be a difference in energy states when homologous parts of chromosomes (that carry genes for the same traits) come together versus the case for non-similar lengths of chromosomes.

The principle is the same physically as that accounting for the immiscibility of oil and water. Water molecules attract water molecules, and they also attract oil molecules even more than oil molecules attract each other, but the greater attraction between water molecules for each other forces the oil out. Granted this mechanism, the like-to-like approximation of chromosomes becomes the position of lowest energy, but since it is only *one* of innumerable arrangements, it would be so improbable as not to occur if there were not a further mechanism. The chromosomes as a whole are in movement in the cell fluid, and if two chromosomes happen to touch at some point where they have no homologous parts, we must assume that the energy of interaction is not sufficient for them to remain long in this position; if, however, the parts are homologous, the moment they touch all the other parts up and down from the point of contact will also be homologous, the process of approximation will spread, and it will be no longer possible for the thermal motion to separate them. This may be called the zipper hypothesis of chromosome pairing.[3]

Sage was theorizing about the physical and structural aspects of genetic material, questions soon to become the province of molecular biology; there was also an older tradition continuing within genetics – the study of gene expression – that started with the pioneering observations of Mendel in the nineteenth century. The John Innes Horticultural Institute, where J.B.S. Haldane worked for some years and which was now directed by Darlington, continued the Mendelian approach by concentrating, for example, on the genetically determined chemical reactions that produce plant pigments. British genetics research was modest in scale, and did not compare with what was going on in the Soviet Union under the direction of Nikolai Vavilov. Vavilov had spent two years at the Innes Institute as a researcher just before the First World War, and in 1921, at the age of thirty-six, was picked by Lenin to be the president of the Lenin Academy of Agricultural Sciences. Over the next decade, he built up more than four hundred research institutes and experimental stations across the vast Soviet Union, employing thousands of research workers.[4] Sage knew him quite well, meeting him first at the 1931

Congress on the History of Science in London and then on subsequent visits
to the USSR.

In 1933, Vavilov persuaded Hermann J. Muller, the leading American
geneticist, to come and work with him.[5] It was not a difficult decision for
Muller, who had already jumped from the frying pan of racist Texas, where he
was under FBI surveillance for subversive political activity, into the Nazi-
stoked fire of Berlin. Muller lost no time in establishing his credentials as a
good Marxist, by comparing the favourable opportunities for research in the
USSR with those in the USA, and by delivering a paean on 'Lenin's doctrines
in relation to genetics'. He showed how his approach to genetics was consistent with dialectical materialism, and pledged himself not just to advance the
understanding of genetics through his research, but to apply its fruits to the
improvement of human society.

Vavilov himself had spent his career trying to improve the state of Soviet
agriculture through careful studies of plant genetics, but had been completely
upstaged in Stalin's eyes by Trofim Lysenko, a cunning and ambitious peasant's son from the Ukraine.[6] Lysenko, who had no formal scientific education,
first came to attention in the mid-1920s, when he made extravagant claims for
a technique known as *vernalization*, which involved chilling seeds of wheat
before planting them in the spring. Lysenko promised that yields would be
increased by forty per cent – welcome news in a land where harsh winters and
the collectivization of agriculture had resulted in widespread famine.

Lysenko fabricated results from limited field trials of vernalization; these
were initially accepted at face value by Vavilov and other reputable scientists,
and satisfied a political leadership unconcerned with the truth. Lysenko
exemplified how a peasant could become a hero in the socialist system: he
was put in charge of his own institute in Odessa, made a member of the
Ukrainian Academy of Sciences and, in 1935, awarded the Order of Lenin by
Stalin. By this time, genuine scientists in the USSR were beginning to recognize Lysenko as a charlatan and to point out the damage done by the
uncritical and widespread acceptance of vernalization. Far from being over-
awed by these criticisms, Lysenko went on the offensive, publicly denouncing
Vavilov for distorting the truth and orchestrating attacks on genetics as a
bourgeois indulgence. Sensing that vernalization was no longer worth promoting, Lysenko replaced it with an even more outlandish notion, namely
that he could transform the nature of plants at will, turning winter wheat into
spring wheat for example. An incredulous Vavilov challenged this claim at a
conference by asking, 'You can refashion heredity?' Lysenko calmly affirmed
that he could, before unleashing a tirade against the whole concept of
genetics. As a final irony, he castigated Muller (who had been the first to
demonstrate that genes could be mutated or altered by X-rays), as being guilty

of the 'geneticists' fundamental mistake... they accept the immutability of genes over a long line of generations'. Lysenko and his school, by contrast, could with their plant raising methods 'change the nature of plants in a controlled manner in each generation'.[7]

Lysenko presented some sensational results from his Odessa institute at a meeting of the Lenin Academy of Agricultural Sciences in Moscow in December 1936. Following his unspecified treatment, characteristics acquired by plants could be inherited by the next generation so that winter wheat could be transformed into spring wheat and *vice versa*. Muller, who was a vocal participant at the meeting, forced Lysenko to admit that 'when he claimed the effect of treatment was inherited, he was basing his statement on the fact that only one seed out of a field full survived and that this transmitted the supposedly induced traits'.[8] It was obvious to Muller that the solitary surviving seed could be a contaminant or a mutation, and that Lysenko's one hundred percent success was 'because the number one out of one is 100%'. The schism in Soviet genetics was now public enough to be noticed in the West, and Darlington wrote a news piece for *Nature* in January 1937, reporting

... there was a general attack on the present position of research in genetics. The grounds of the attack were ostensibly twofold. First, geneticists like Muller and Vavilov were said to have ignored the Marxian principle of the unity of theory and practice in failing to keep their work in touch with the needs of farmers. Secondly, the primary assumptions of genetics were said to be invalid. Presumably, in the absence of other evidence, the second contention was deduced from the first. The attack was reinforced by pointing to work like that of Michurin and Lysenko which, unhampered by academic prejudice, has yielded results of immense practical value by methods of trial and error.[9]

The issue concerned Lancelot Hogben, a biologist and old friend of Sage's, whose doubts about Soviet communism, combined with his tetchy nature, were putting him at odds with less sceptical scientists on the left. He wrote to Sage in February 1937, revealing his disenchantment:

You orthodox Marxists are much more pleased if a man thinks the wrong thing with the right religious formulae than whether he is concerned with arriving at correct conclusions. If he has the mischance to do so by employing the lucidities of his native tongue, the only thanks he gets is to be called a Fascist.[10]

Admitting to complete bafflement in the face of Marxist thinking, Hogben characterized dialectical materialism, as 'first stating a plain lie and then stating another plain lie and then applying an elaborate process of casuistry to square one plain lie with the other'. As an example he cited,

... the recent incident over the Genetics Congress in Russia. This has destroyed 50% of the sympathy which some of us would like to build up among the scientific workers for the constructive achievements of the USSR. I believe it is a plain duty to expose this nonsense...

Whatever concerns some British scientists might have registered, inside the USSR the die was cast. Lysenko's outrageous tactics worked to the extent that he found himself elevated to membership of the Supreme Soviet, a position from which he literally looked down on Stalin at Kremlin meetings. To oppose Lysenkoism now called into question the ideology of his detractors, who were painted as fascist sympathizers opposed to the Stalin Constitution. Even before Lysenko's elevation to the highest level of the Soviet system, the terrors had begun for geneticists. Two of Muller's closest colleagues, both of whom had spent time in his Texas laboratory on Rockefeller grants a few years before, suddenly disappeared in 1936. Israel Agol was denounced as 'another Trotskyite bandit' and Solomon Levit, the head of the Medico-Genetics Institute in Moscow, was falsely accused of holding fascist views on eugenics: both men perished in prison.[11] Muller was told not to ask about them by Russian friends. He managed to leave the Soviet Union in September 1937, and with help from Julian Huxley, secured a post at the Institute of Animal Genetics in Edinburgh.

After his accession to the top, Lysenko was complicit in the growing persecution of biologists, who were a small but important group in Stalin's paranoid eyes. The pervasiveness of the threat was such that Muller did not dare to criticize Lysenko even after arriving in Edinburgh, for fear that his words would travel back to the Soviet Union and endanger his former colleagues. He did take note of the attitudes of British biologists and confided to an American friend in December 1937 that 'Hogben and Gordon...are revising their outlook in view of recent happenings in the USSR, and are much upset, but Haldane is 100%'.[12] Indeed Haldane's loyalty to the Soviet system was so complete that he suppressed a mathematical paper on genetics that one of Muller's former students, Vladimir Efroimson, had managed to smuggle out of a Siberian labour camp.[13]

In his 1937 *Nature* article calling attention to the doctrinal threat to the scientists at the Lenin Academy of Agricultural Sciences, Darlington had written that if Lysenko's claims were true 'the tedious methods of plant breeding now practised by orthodox geneticists in Prof. Vavilov's institutions would of course be superfluous'.[14] Lysenko plainly agreed with him because when he finally managed to secure the presidency of the Academy in 1938, his first move was to announce in an article in *Pravda* that the research staff should be cut at least by half to improve productivity, and he put the academicians on notice that 'they were now to follow Party policy rather than to exercise scientific leadership'.[15] The trap was set for Vavilov.

A coordinated campaign against his leadership of the Genetics Institute was launched by Stalin himself in May 1938, repudiating 'the high priests of science [who had] retired into their shells' and demanding an effort 'to smash old traditions, norms and viewpoints'.[16] A *Pravda* editorial called on the Academy of Sciences to oversee the restructuring of recalcitrant institutes; the presidium of the academy made an immediate start and singled out the Genetics Institute for failing to combat hostile class viewpoints on the biology front, and for refusing to acknowledge T.D. Lysenko's works. Lysenko was invited to supervise research at the institute and installed a number of his acolytes. Vavilov was subjected to public humiliation at every opportunity by Lysenko, and his political deviations were minutely recorded by Beria's NKVD [forerunners of the KGB]. With a growing sense of doom, Vavilov courageously remained true to his principles. He told a meeting of scientific workers in Leningrad in the spring of 1939:

We shall go to the pyre, we shall burn, but we shall not retreat from our convictions. I tell you, in all frankness, that I believed and still believe and insist on what I think is right, and not only believe – because taking things on faith in science is nonsense – but also say what I know on the basis of wide experience. This is a fact, and to retreat from it simply because some occupying high posts desire it, is impossible.[17]

He continued to point out the fallacies of Lysenko's theories, and in the summer of 1940 signed a public statement on how Lysenko's dismissal of plant hybridization was invalidated by the success of American breeders in improving their corn harvest by just such methods. This protest may have been the final trigger to Vavilov's arrest on 6th August. Vavilov was tortured by his NKVD interrogator in the Lubyanka prison and eventually signed a false confession. Normally this would be swiftly followed by a summary trial and execution, but for reasons unknown, the process in Vavilov's case was delayed. With pencil and paper, he used the time to write a book on the history of the development of agriculture, until his trial took place nearly a year after his arrest. He was charged with treason, espionage for Britain, and counterrevolution, all of which he denied at the five-minute tribunal hearing. He was sentenced to death by firing squad, but after appeals, this was reduced to twenty years in prison. All this took place against a background of chaos as the German army approached Moscow. Vavilov was transferred to Saratov jail on the banks of the Volga River, where he died of inanition in January 1943.

Whether he ever knew it or not, Vavilov was elected a foreign member of the Royal Society in 1942. Some of the British scientists who were allowed to travel to Moscow in June 1945 for the celebrations at the Academy of Science, asked after him. By November of that year, the fact of his death, but not the circumstances, was known in London; repeated inquiries from the Royal

Society to the Soviet Academy asking about the date and place of his death brought no response. In 1948, Sir Henry Dale, the President of the Royal Society, felt compelled to resign from the Soviet Academy in protest (as did Hermann Muller). Both men decried the sham and obscure doctrine of Lysenkoism that was driving out the sciences of evolution and genetics in the USSR. As Dale wrote:

This is not the result of an honest and open conflict of scientific opinions; Lysenko's own claims and statements make it clear that his dogma has been established and enforced by the Central Committee of the Communist Party, as conforming to the political philosophy of Marx and Lenin ... Since Galileo was driven by threats to his historic denial, there have been many attempts to suppress or to mutilate scientific truth in the interests of some extraneous creed, but none has had a lasting success; Hitler's was the most recent failure. Believing, Mr President, that you and your colleagues must be acting under a like coercion, I can only offer you my respectful sympathy. For my own part, being free to choose, I believe that I should do disservice even to my scientific colleagues in the U.S.S.R., if I were to retain an association in which I might appear to condone the actions by which your Academy, under whatever compulsion, is now responsible for such a terrible injury to the freedom and integrity of Science.[18]

The President of the Soviet Academy, who received Dale's letter, was a physicist, who must have wept when he read these principled words: his name was Sergei Vavilov – he was Nikolai's younger brother.

The climax of Lysenko's campaign to control biological science in the USSR came at a stage-managed conference of the Lenin Academy of Agricultural Sciences in August 1948. Lysenko had survived a period of uncertainty immediately after the war, but retained the patronage of Stalin, who allowed him to pack the Academy with his scientific supporters; Stalin now reaffirmed his public support of Lysenkoism. At the August conference, Lysenko gave a speech, pre-approved by Stalin, in which he denounced several senior biologists and called for proletarian science. His proposals were soon endorsed by the Supreme Soviet – about three thousand biologists were dismissed from their academic posts (some were arrested), and various institutions were closed down. The upheavals were openly reported in *Pravda* and naturally caused comment amongst scientists in the West.

The issue came up in a BBC radio debate between Bernal and Michael Polanyi on 'The organization of science and scientists'.[19] Bernal made his customary case for the central planning of collective research, while Polanyi stressed the need for individualism. He dismissed Bernal's ideas as a wild-goose chase that started a decade before with his book, *The Social Function of Science*, in which Sage espoused Marxist values and suggested that scientific discoveries in Russia were made in response to human need. In Polanyi's opinion, the most important consequence of the planning movement was the fate of Russian scientists, 'who still have to submit to regimentation by planning, [and] remain constantly in danger of falling victim to the machinations of political careerists – men who gain influence on science by pretending to be the fulfillers of Marxism and who may at any moment direct against their fellow scientists the deadly shafts of Marxian suspicion and Marxian invective. The fate of Vavilov and of his many collaborators who succumbed to the planning of science as exercised by Lysenko, can never be absent from the thoughts of any Russian scientist.'[20] Sage did not respond to this point.

The BBC then decided to examine the Lysenko affair, specifically, in a radio broadcast in November 1948. Darlington was one of three scientists who attacked Lysenkoism and its baleful consequences, but the fourth discussant, J.B.S. Haldane, mounted a rearguard defence. He argued against a rush to judgement, likening his adversaries to the jury in *Alice in Wonderland*, giving their verdict before they had heard the evidence. This was somewhat disingenuous since one of the three scientists had interviewed Lysenko, and translated summaries of the August meeting of the Lenin Academy of Agriculture were available. Haldane gave an indication of what level of information he would require when he stated on the subject of Vavilov's death that there were discrepancies in the various accounts circulating, and that he would be satisfied only by an official announcement from the Soviet government.[21]

Haldane was caught in a dilemma between his allegiance to the Soviet Union and his knowledge of scientific facts. His defence of orthodox Mendelian genetics in the broadcast was, however, so *sotto voce* that it was lost in his charitable portrayal of Lysenkoism. *The Daily Worker*, whose editorial board he chaired, had no hesitation in reporting that Haldane had given his complete support to Lysenko. Haldane was furious, but had only himself to blame. A meeting of the Engels Society (a debating club for communist British intellectuals) was called, at which the majority of scientists present were hostile to Lysenkoism. It was left to Bernal, at the end of the meeting, to soothe high tempers and to avoid a vote that might embarrass the Party.[22] The next meeting was a two-day affair with Emile Burns, the communist writer, in the chair and Bernal sitting beside him.[23] Again there was no reconciliation between obedience to the Party and science.

The debate was also carried in print, most prominently in the columns of the *New Statesman*. Waddington wrote articles stating that while he was not convinced about Lysenko's experiments and claims that 'seem so unlikely in view of all our present knowledge that they cannot possibly be accepted until repeated, in other laboratories, and under much more carefully controlled conditions', nevertheless the 'Russians have an arguable (though I do not say convincing) case that the kind of actions they have taken are justifiable'.[24] For this evasive effort, he earned a stinging rebuke from Darlington, who described him as a friend of the Soviet regime seeking 'to release a fog over the Lysenko controversy'.[25] After carefully reviewing what was known about Vavilov's death, Darlington pointed out that the Soviet government 'had put to death eight other leading geneticists'.

Why [he asked] does not the Soviet Government explain officially that all these men are alive and well? Or that they have died natural deaths? Or that they were all spies and traitors – a frequent circumstance? Communists, and friends of the regime outside Russia, would be greatly relieved. The load of shame would be lifted off their shoulders. I suggest that the Soviet Government has not done so, because of the effect such a statement would have *inside* Russia. It would seem a sign of weakness. The disappearance or killing of some individuals always has a general, as well as a particular, value for a government of this kind. It is to terrorise those who remain.[26]

The atmosphere surrounding Lysenkoism was so charged, with the majority of British biologists vehemently against, that Bernal's apparent support for it would no longer go unchallenged. Julian Huxley, who had been an enthusiastic visitor to the Soviet Union in the 1930s, was now deeply troubled about the plight of science and scientists there. He wrote to Bernal in April 1949 in connection with an article he was preparing for *Nature* on the 'Soviet genetics business'.[27] Huxley, the Director General of UNESCO, was concerned that despite the resignations of Dale and Muller from the Academy of Sciences, Bernal was still said to approve of Lysenkoism. Sage responded, with the voice of calm reasonableness, that: 'My opinion on reading the accounts of the controversy is that in general all the facts of orthodox genetics are admitted, but the laws are considered far too simple an interpretation of the facts ... However my judgement in this matter is, of course, very limited.'[28]

Huxley's article appeared in *Nature* in June, and it was a passionate critique of what he saw as a great scientific nation turning its back on the universal and supra-national character of science. To Huxley, the veracity of Lysenko's theories, the fact that Mendelian genetics had been perverted by the Nazis, the need for scientific research to be centrally planned along with the rest of the Soviet economy, even the 'liquidation' of some geneticists by the state were all 'either irrelevant or merely subsidiary to the major issue, which is the official condemnation of scientific results on other than scientific grounds, and therefore the repudiation by the USSR of the concept of the scientific method and scientific activity held by the great majority of the men of science elsewhere'.[29]

Bernal now felt compelled to counter-attack opinions such as Huxley's, which he believed to be alarmist, claiming as they did that Lysenkoism was 'a blow to the liberty of science, as a turning back to confused and antiquated ideas, and as certain to result in the destruction of Soviet science and in the rapid decay of its agriculture'.[30] He viewed the controversy as 'a major intellectual weapon in the cold war'. Sage saw Lysenko's theories and achievements as rooted in practical agriculture and not the product of orthodox academic study: the ideas were 'in essence characteristically socialist as well as characteristically Russian'.[31] He believed that Lysenko's success had been hard-won – 'the result of twenty years of experimentation, discussion and controversies' – and achieved despite the scepticism of more orthodox academics, who had now been won over by his arguments. Lysenko and his ever-increasing band of supporters were the industrious scientists who were going to transform Soviet society and their achievements justified the development of science within the USSR along a separate course.

These men are the scientists of the new socialist world, and we must expect them to appear startling and even repellant to many scientists brought up in the gentlemanly tradition of scholastic research. They are active and purposeful. They are politically educated. The old explicit neutrality of science is not for them. They recognise it as concealing implicitly approval of and assistance to the exploitation of capitalist economy... In the struggle between two world outlooks one cannot occupy an intermediary position.[32]

Huxley dismissed Bernal's essay as 'a specious, if brilliant, piece of apologetics, not an impartial discussion'.[33] He thought Sage had 'unfairly evaded the major issues' such as the legitimacy of the Soviet government in 'officially condemning a whole branch of science as false, anti-scientific, anti-patriotic, etc.', not to mention the dubious scientific validity of Lysenko's work: 'If Professor Bernal were a geneticist instead of a physicist, he would realise that Lysenko's theories are, scientifically speaking, largely nonsense – meaning that they do not make scientific sense.'[34] Huxley was now able to find more common ground with Haldane, who had clarified his own position in the same summer issue of *Modern Quarterly* that carried Bernal's essay. Haldane deplored the 'ill-informed criticism of genetics by supporters of Lysenko' in Britain, and reminded his readers that he was a modern geneticist who believed that 'the hereditary process depends on material objects, called genes, in the nucleus of a cell, and on other objects outside the nucleus'.[35] He stated that genes were neither immortal nor immutable, but if 'they were at the mercy of every environmental change, heredity would be impossible. If they always reproduced their like, evolution, and even the production of domesticated animal and plant varieties would be impossible. Ninety-nine geneticists out of a hundred would agree to this statement.' But Haldane was scornful of those Marxists who 'went so far as to deny that there was a material basis of inheritance... [because] a Marxist can no more deny a material basis for heredity than for sensation or thought'.[36]

Up to this point, Bernal had been careful to couch his argument in moderate language, and his public persona, for example at meetings of the Engels Society, had been placatory. His position, although a minority one within the British scientific community and exasperating to some, had been carefully crafted, but this was all changed by a diatribe he unleashed in August 1949 at a peace conference in Moscow. The meeting was held in the ornate Hall of Columns with huge, garish portraits of Lenin and Stalin serving as the backdrop to the speakers' platform. Sage was there as a representative of the World Federation of Scientific Workers, and while his remarks were not specifically concerned with Lysenko, they left his audience in no doubt about the wickedness of science practised outside the Soviet bloc.

For now in capitalist countries the direction of science is in the hands of those whose only aim is to destroy and torture people so that their own profits may be secured for some years longer. They show this by their choice of weapons, not those of combat against equally armed opponents but weapons of mass destruction, for destroying houses and fields, for poisoning and maiming women and children... The fact is that science in the hands of a decayed capitalism can never be employed usefully, it can only lead to increased exploitation, unemployment, crises and war. It is not astonishing that this should produce in capitalist countries a reactionary attitude to science and inside science itself. Under capitalism war is poisoning science. At the same time there is a move to reject science altogether and to replace it with a mysticism that can easily again turn to the perversions of the Nazis. Already from America has come the call to reduce the population of the world, which can lead logically only to an even more scientific variety of Hitler's gas chambers... Only under capitalism is it true that science can bring no happiness but only destruction. The scientist has no freedom – he is a slave to the masters who have lost their senses.[37]

He praised the Soviet people for serving as the inspiration for 'hundreds of millions of oppressed people of the world' and credited their heroism for saving science and securing its future for mankind; he concluded by greeting 'their great leader and protector of peace and science, Comrade Stalin'. According to the official report, this piece of demagogism brought forth 'stormy and prolonged applause'. No one in the Hall of Columns was to know that within forty-eight hours the first Soviet plutonium bomb would be detonated on the steppes of Kazakhstan; Beria the head of the NKVD was present at the test, and if it had failed, the scientists involved expected to be shot.[38]

Bernal had been preceded on the platform by Sergei Vavilov, President of the Academy of Sciences, who reflected on the horrors of the two world wars and saw the symptoms of another imperialist war beginning against the USSR, under the guise of the Marshall Plan and the new NATO. Turning to the history of science, Vavilov in effect renounced his dead brother by praising Michurin (a horticulturist who had been championed by the Lysenkoists), for charting 'new paths for remaking nature'. He held up the USSR as an example to the rest of the world, for 'under the leadership of Comrade Stalin, brilliant scientist and great statesman, Marxist-Leninist science is a powerful instrument in building Communist society'.[39] Science, he continued, was the 'foundation for a wholesome materialist philosophy; it has strong living contact with our collective farms and the factories of our socialist industry.' Vavilov's peroration, 'Glory to our teacher and leader, the great Stalin', in contrast to Bernal's, seemed to fall flat with the audience, who perhaps detected a note of insincerity.

Sage's speech was immediately picked up by the British newspapers: *The Times* ran a short story headed 'Prof. Bernal praises Mr Stalin' on 29th August. Two days later, the British Association for the Advancement of Science (BAAS) began its annual meeting and released a press statement about Bernal's status as a committee member.

In view of Press reports of statements purporting to have been made by Professor Bernal in Moscow, which could not be reconciled with the scientific aims and objects of the association, it was decided to ask him what was actually said and, in the meantime, to defer the question of his appointment.[40]

Bernal was still in Moscow, spending two days after the peace conference with architects talking about building projects and then the first week of September visiting various scientific institutes. One of these was the experimental farm and greenhouses, where he talked to Lysenko for some hours. He was accompanied by J.G. Crowther, who found the chain-smoking Lysenko 'highly strung', although he appeared to relax when Sage confided in him that he too was the son of a farmer.[41] Sage's notes recording his first impressions of Lysenko stand as a testament to his monumental misjudgment. Viewing him as a 'scientist of the Darwin Rutherford type' who 'cannot accept what is presented [to him] in a mathematical form', Sage thought of Lysenko as 'a poet with vivid imagination [who] forms his own ideas in a qualitative world'.[42] Lysenko was 'antipathetic to formal argument' and had no time for orthodox Mendelian genetics: he left Sage in no doubt that 'if the Mendelists oppose him, he will remove them from office'[43] but it seems Sage preferred not to think of the consequences of such ruthlessness.

When he flew into Northolt Airport on 9th September, Sage found the press waiting for him. He told them that he stood by what he had said in Moscow, but was not prepared to stand by what had been reported until he had seen it. He added: 'The energies of the leading scientists in the capitalist countries are principally devoted to military development. Because 60 per

cent of money devoted to science is in preparation for war, science can hardly
be in any doubt about it.'[44] Speaking a few days later at the conference of
'Soviet Partisans for Peace' in London, Sage was reproachful of BAAS, saying
'I think it is highly irregular that a person who is absent should be judged and
in a limited way condemned, before he is heard.'[45]

Sage received mail accusing him of treason and even an offer from a
gentleman in Gloucestershire of a stipend of £250 per annum, if he would
go and live in Russia. The *News Chronicle* published a robust attack on Sage's
shameless support of Stalin's regime. Sage in turn accused the newspaper of
Goebbels style anti-Soviet propaganda for suggesting that 'millions of the
people live in abject misery and poverty' where on his visit he 'only saw the
happy, well-fed crowds that fill the streets of Moscow at all hours, the good
clothes, the full shops. The contrast with 15 years ago is simply staggering.... The Soviet Union is about as different as anything could be from an
ordered totalitarian state where masses of people are doing precisely what
they are told by an arbitrary higher authority.'[46] The newspaper's columnist,
A.J. Cummings, was not deterred and wrote a second article, 'Prof. Bernal,
These are Facts',[47] saying 'It is now clearer than ever that Professor J.D. Bernal
lives in cloud-cuckoo land.' In a perceptive piece about the Gulag system,
Cummings cited documented evidence of Russian labour camps containing
millions of slaves that have become 'an organic element, a normal component
of the social structure'. He accepted that these were never mentioned in the
Soviet press, but every citizen had friends or relatives who had been a part of
it. Sage was completely unmoved by Cummings' argument and complained to
the editor that the 'facts' quoted by Cummings on labour camps were
'allegations from professed anti-Soviet sources which are unverifiable and
not even self-consistent'.[48] Just like Haldane, Bernal would give credence only
to an official Soviet announcement.

The debate about Soviet science assumed new importance after 23rd
September, when it was announced from Washington that 'within recent
weeks an atomic explosion occurred in the USSR.'[49] American and British
government scientists had detected an increase in radioactive fission products
in the atmosphere, and were able to trace back their time of release to within
an hour. The next public criticism of Sage came from an unexpected quarter.
The Nobel Laureate, Sir Edward Appleton, now Principal of Edinburgh
University, lambasted him in an after-dinner speech, which was fully reported
in *The Times*. His audience was an international one, and he sought to assure
them that there was no country which gave warmer support to scientific
research than Great Britain, and that the fact that most money was given by
way of grants and not by contracts ensured great freedom for university
researchers. He continued:

It is for this reason that the great majority of scientists completely repudiate Professor J.D. Bernal's statement…to the effect that the direction of scientific effort in this country is in the hands of those who hate peace and whose only aim is to destroy and torture people…The facts are that Professor Bernal is receiving a great deal of financial support for his own researches from public funds by way of the Department of Scientific and Industrial Research and the University Grants Committee, such funds being derived from taxes imposed on a predominantly private enterprise society; and if the direction of his scientific work is not in his hands the fault is clearly his.

It would appear that, as in a few other similar cases, there are two Professor Bernals: one is the brilliant natural philosopher of world-wide renown, the other a fervid convert to an extreme political theory. Such a perverse interpretation of the situation as regards research in Britain would never have been made by the former.[50]

Bernal's response in a letter to the editor was good-natured but unrepentant.

Sir, – I can have no quarrel with Sir Edward Appleton reviving for my benefit the fantasy of Jekyll and Hyde, but I can protest that whatever my political views are they have not led me to talk palpable nonsense. When I spoke of the direction of science in capitalist countries – it occurred to no one that I might not be referring to Socialist Britain – the last people I had in mind were the scientists themselves or even the scientific administrators like Sir Edward Appleton. As the reference to profits in the same sentence shows, I could have only meant those politicians and business men, now for the most part in the United States, who control the general direction of science by deciding whether the money will be spent for peace or war. They have decided that 60 per cent or more of the total national expenditure on research and development should be spent on war science. The latest available figures are £300m. out of £500m. in the United States and £67 out of £110m. in Great Britain…Further, as the financial interests of these men are closely linked with war industries, as the Press and political figures allied to them openly treat of war as a method of containing or destroying Communism, I do not feel that I went too far in describing them as enemies of peace. Even now, in our desperate financial situation, we are not only maintaining but actually increasing the number of scientists in war service, and thus holding back indefinitely the possibility of technical improvements in our industry which alone would enable us to survive as a trading nation. I would not criticize the civil section of British scientific effort or suggest that in detail it is not perfectly free. On the other hand, I consider it grossly inadequate in scale and in effective coordination…Complacency rather than criticism is the real danger in British science today.[51]

While it was true that the USA was the main target of Bernal's Moscow attack, he portrayed Britain as its obedient servant, and gave no sign to the Russians that they should regard Britain as a socialist state rather than as a decaying capitalist country. The BAAS had been keeping a vacancy on its council following its summer meeting. Sage sent them a letter in which he recognized that there had been room for misunderstanding in the press reports and gave an assurance that 'it had never been his intention either to state or imply that the scientists responsible for the detailed direction of research in this or any other country were haters of peace'.[52] The council deliberated over the full text of the Moscow speech and the letter before deciding not to re-elect him as one of their number:

The council recognizes the necessity of distinguishing between political statements of its members with which it has no concern and statements on the direction and use of science in this country, and the objection it took last August was solely to certain statements of the latter kind. These appear in Professor Bernal's version of his speech, no part of which he withdraws, and in the view of the council its objections are not removed by his letter.[53]

Sage regretted their decision, which he thought was a political one that would do grave damage to the reputation and future work of the association. A group of his friends circulated a statement deploring the council's decision, which was signed by 244 British scientists. Bernal's response to the association stated:

The essential contention of my speech was that the political and financial direction of science in America and Britain was one towards war... Now the direction of science is a political and not a scientific question, and I cannot but feel that your council has been led in this matter to take up a position which is not in line with the interests and purposes of the association. They [the council] are by implication lending their support to a policy which I believe to be disastrous to science and humanity. This policy is one of using a scientific effort, far greater than is made available for improving the conditions of life of the people of this country, to produce new 'scientific' weapons clearly directed against the peoples of the Soviet Union. These people, a few years back, were our allies and but for their sacrifices, which were far heavier than ours, all decent scientists here would now be in concentration camps or dead.[54]

He suggested that the government's bias towards the military applications of science had already lowered the standard of living for the British people and 'checked the development of scientific teaching and research. It is hindering the applications of science to constructive uses in industry, agriculture, and health at a time when the very existence of the country as an independent power demands their increased use for these purposes.'[55] What Sage failed to see was that the direst consequences of political doctrine on the function of scientists, pure and applied, were taking place in the USSR. Not only had the triumph of Lysenko undermined research in genetics and other biological sciences and led to agricultural catastrophe, but the Lysenkoists were now threatening a similar purge of the natural sciences to root out Western influence or cosmopolitanism, as it was labelled. Andrei Sakharov, who was working at the top-secret Soviet Installation on the development of a thermonuclear weapon, remembered concerted pressure, beginning in late 1949, to stop scientists 'kowtowing to the West'.[56] Under this official campaign, Russians were given credit for discovering or inventing everything, an absurdity encapsulated in a saying of the time, 'Russia, homeland of the elephant.' In 1950, a commission visited the atomic installation to check on the Party loyalty of the senior scientists. Among the questions Sakharov was asked was what he thought about the chromosome theory of heredity. His reply, 'that the theory seemed scientifically correct', caused some suspicious glances among the members of the commission, but Sakharov's importance and reputation allowed this deviancy to be overlooked.[57]

Sergei Vavilov's position as president of the Soviet Academy as well as running FIAN, the physics institute, put him under constant suspicion from the authorities. He died in January 1951, aged sixty; Bernal wrote his obituary for *Nature*. He summarized Vavilov's major research contributions in physical optics, and also recognized his interests in the history and philosophy of science. Noting Vavilov's position as 'a deputy both to the Russian and Union Supreme Soviets', Sage suggested that 'his advice was taken in all problems involving science'.[58] Describing him as a man of quiet dignity whose death was probably due to overwork, Sage evidently decided that any mention of Nikolai Vavilov would not be seemly.

His next obituary essay was far more controversial and, even at the time, objectionable. It came on the death of Stalin in 1953 and was entitled 'Stalin as a scientist'.[59] In retrospect, it is such a grotesque eulogy that friends subsequently writing about Sage have either ignored it,[60] excused it on the basis of the mood of the moment,[61] or suggested, on the basis of no evidence, that it was written by a 'hack' in 'his entourage'.[62] The flavour of the writing can be gathered from the following phrases, which seem to me to reflect Sage's long-standing infatuation with Stalin and his insatiable appetite for communist propaganda.

The greatest figure of contemporary history ... at the same time a great scientist ... his wonderful combination of a deeply scientific approach to all problems with his capacity for feeling and expressing himself in simple and direct human terms ... that great double transformation, the industrialization of the Five Year plans, and the formation of the collective farms is Stalin's most enduring monument ... shallow thinkers, philosophic defenders of 'Western civilization', have accused Stalin of being motivated by love of power, but to those who have followed his thoughts and words, the accusation is only a revelation of utter ignorance ... Stalin's concern for men and women also found expression in his concern for the advancement of

oppressed people and nationalities...his thought and his example is [*sic*] now
embodied in the lives and thoughts of hundreds of millions of men, women, and
children...it has become an indissoluble part of the great human condition.[63]

Stalin died at the beginning of March; had he lived another month or so, he
might have heard about the discovery of the double-helix structure of DNA –
a development that explained the molecular basis of heredity in a way that
was incompatible with Lysenko's theories. Such was the suppression of genetics in the USSR, the idea of the double helix was not given wide currency
amongst scientific groups there until 1956. Bernal immediately saw the
implications of the discovery and a year later had no hesitation in calling it
'the greatest single discovery in biology'.[64]

The discovery of the definitive structure of DNA was made in Bragg's MRC
laboratory in Cambridge by Francis Crick, who had found his way there after
failing to get past Anita Rimel at Birkbeck, and the American biologist James
Watson, who had been recruited to the lab by John Kendrew. It is now a
matter of historical record that in building their model, Watson and Crick
gleaned vital clues from the X-ray diffraction work being done at King's
College, London by Rosalind Franklin. She and the other crystallographers
at King's had benefited from reading Sven Furberg's PhD thesis, describing
how in the DNA molecule, the plane of the bases was almost perpendicular to
that of the sugars. This had led Furberg towards a helical shape for the
molecule with the bases stacked like Astbury's pile of pennies at its core.
Indeed when he returned to Norway in 1952, Furberg constructed one model
of DNA as a single helix that was tantalizingly close to the eventual Watson–
Crick construct.[65]

The historiography of DNA began fifteen years later with the publication of
Watson's account of the discovery in his book, *The Double Helix*. There was an
earlier manuscript, *Base Pairs*, that Harvard University Press considered too
defamatory to be published. Kendrew sent a copy of that to Sage, who enjoyed
it hugely. He wrote to Kendrew:

I have now read the book entitled Base Pairs by Watson. It is an astonishing
production, I could not put it down. Considered as a novel of the history of science
it is unequalled.... It raises many vital problems, not only about the structure of DNA
but about the mechanism of scientific discovery which he shows up in a very bad
light...In England it would be libelous in many places...I never met Watson before
the discovery but if I had I could have told him quite a lot – what impressed me most
is that he did not know, and apparently never tried to find out, what had been done
already in the subject. He is particularly unfair in the contribution of Rosalind
Franklin and does not mention her projection of the helical DNA structure showing
the exterior position of the phosphate groups. I need not mention the complete
absence of a reference to the work of Furberg which contains all the answers to the

structure except the vital one – the double character of the chain and the H-bond base pair linkage.* Effectively, all the essentials of the structure were present in Astbury's original studies, including the negative birefringence and the 3.4 Å piling of the base groups. I should add in my own defence that my weakness was in what he calls the English habit of respect for other peoples' work. There was a tacit understanding. I dealt with biological crystalline substances and Astbury dealt with messy substances . . . I was certainly wrong in this. Astbury was quite clearly incapable of working out the structure. The genetic importance of DNA was apparent to me long before from the work of Caspersson, which Watson hardly mentions. Watson and Crick did a magnificent job, but in the process were forced to make enormous mistakes which they had the skill to correct in time. The whole thing is a disgraceful exposure of the stupidity of great scientific discoveries. My verdict would be the lines of Hilaire Belloc:

> And is it true? It is not true!
> And if it was it wouldn't do.[66]

Bernal was sure that the publication of *Base Pairs* would cause 'a lot of heart burnings in scientific circles and particularly in England, but it makes very good reading and I think would make an even better film because it is so alive and dramatic'. When *The Double Helix* did appear in print two years later, Sage wrote a review that opened with a quote from Lucretius, *De rerum natura*. It is a passage that had he reflected on it two decades before, might have alerted him to the fallacies of Lysenko: 'no species is ever changed, but each remains so much of itself that every kind of bird displays its own specific markings. This is a further proof that their bodies are composed of changeless matter. For if the atoms could yield in any way to change, there would be no certainty as to what could arise and what could not . . . nor could successive generations so regularly repeat the nature, behaviour, habits and movement of their parents.' Sage explained that although Lucretius was writing about the changelessness of atoms, he could, as easily, be arguing for 'the existence of unalterable genes'.[67]

Bernal's name is mentioned only in passing in *The Double Helix*, which he thought was in keeping with his peripheral contribution. Watson referred to the 'legendary' scope of Bernal's brain, and told how watching Crick react to the wartime paper of Bernal and Fankuchen on TMV made him realize that he had to understand the helical theory of X-ray diffraction. Crick, who came to know Bernal better, said that he was the first genius he met with consideration for the feelings of others.

In the later 1950s, Crick and others proceeded to elucidate the genetic code with its triplet base signals determining the sequence of amino acids in a particular polypeptide chain or protein. His reasoning was very like that which Sage had employed in 1931, when he concluded that three-dimensional

---

* Furberg had, in fact, suggested in a 1952 paper that he expected hydrogen bonds to occur in nucleic acids.

replication of protein molecules was just too complicated to be a natural solution. Crick, unlike Sage, never considered a possible two-dimensional solution, but by then he knew 'a lot more about proteins than they knew in 1931'.[68] In 1957, Crick coined what he called the Central Dogma of genetics: not only do nucleic acids determine the specificities of proteins, but 'once "information" has passed into a protein it *cannot get out again*. In more detail, the transfer of information from nucleic acid to nucleic acid, or from nucleic acid to protein may be possible, but transfer from protein to protein, or from protein to nucleic acid is impossible.'[69] A gene became defined as a sequence of DNA that coded for a protein according to the Central Dogma: DNA→RNA→protein: this was almost a universally accepted and dominant concept for thirty years. Most of the experimental data were derived from the study of simple one-cell organisms like the bacterium, *E. coli*, where the Central Dogma still represents the essential story.

For higher organisms, including humans, the story has become far more complicated in recent times.[70] It has been apparent for some years that only about 2 per cent of human chromosomal DNA codes for protein – the other 98 per cent was dismissed as 'junk'. But the 'junk' DNA is proving to have an important regulatory role in gene expression. Some of it encodes for short RNA molecules that do not directly specify proteins themselves, but act as signals to alter the profile of protein production by switching coding genes on and off. This major new area of research is referred to as 'epigenetics' – a term first used by Bernal's bald, pipe-smoking friend, Hal Waddington, in 1942.[71] As Bernal wrote to Huxley in 1949, 'in general all the facts of orthodox genetics are admitted, but the laws are considered far too simple an interpretation of the facts'.

Dorothy Hodgkin, musing on Sage's gullibility about Lysenkoism, said it reflected the fact that he 'held theories lightly'.[72] Her opinion is supported by an essay he wrote early in his career on 'The irrelevance of scientific theory'.[73] In this piece, Sage pointed out dual aspects of a scientific theory that tend to be different for scientists and laymen. Inside science, a theory serves 'to organise existing knowledge and point the way to the acquisition of new knowledge ... Scientific theories are usually taken as true by scientists for emotional reasons in order that they may feel a comfortable exhilaration at their work, but for the working scientist a particular theory is merely a popular champion to be abandoned and ridiculed the moment a new and more effective theory beats it in the field ... [but outside science] scientific theories tend to turn into lay dogmas believed to be true on authority without the possibility of examination, and it is for this reason that it is the more necessary to examine into their origin.' Although, as H.J. Muller wrote to a friend, J.D. Bernal had 'one of the best, if not the best scientific mind in the world',[74] in the case of Lysenkoism, he fell into the role of a trusting layman rather than following the scientific method as he habitually would.

When it came to political theory, for Sage there was only Marxism. He quoted Stalin's interpretation with approval.

Marxism is the science of the laws governing the development of nature and society, the science of the oppressed and exploited masses, the science of the victory of Socialism in all countries, the science of building a Communist society. Marxism as a science cannot stand still, it develops and improves. In its development Marxism cannot but enrich itself with new knowledge – consequently its various formulae and conclusions cannot but change with the passage of time, cannot but be replaced by new formulae and conclusions, which correspond to the new historical tasks. Marxism does not recognise immutable conclusions and formulae, obligatory for all epochs and periods. Marxism is the enemy of all dogmatism.[75]

In Sage's mind, there seemed to be no doubt that human society and behaviour could be cast into a scientific framework provided by Marx so that confident predictions were possible about the way events would turn out. He wrote a short book, *Marx and Science*, in which he reflected on how well 'the actual builders of socialism, Lenin and Stalin, have carried out' the programme laid down by Marx, 'while all their "socialist" detractors, who have done nothing themselves to emancipate their own countries from capitalism, clamour that the Soviet rulers have abandoned true Marxism'.[76] The pseudo-science of Marxism did indeed provide Sage with a sense of comfortable exhilaration that allowed him to overlook its contradictions and horrors. It was a dogma that could not be refuted because it was all-encompassing, convoluted and vague. As we have seen at the time of Stalin's death, Sage poured scorn on the base notion that the dictator was driven by a lust for power. As Alexander Pope said, 'The most positive men are the most credulous.'

16

Peace at Any Price?

The hunger for peace is most ravenous in the aftermath of war. The British public, many of whom could remember the First World War – the war to end all war – emerged from the Second World War weary from privations but thankful to have survived. Their suffering did not compare with that of the Poles or the Soviets or indeed the citizens of the two countries subjected to the most ferocious bombing campaigns – Germany and Japan. Modern warfare was no longer confined to the armed forces, and as one of the Chiefs of Staff remarked to Bernal, by the end of WW2, weapons determined strategy: strategy no longer dictated weapons.[1] The new spectre of the atom bomb, as Bernal said at the time, 'implicitly changed the whole existence of man in this universe'.[2] While conceding that 'the immediate effects, however horrible, have been decisive in ending the war' Bernal suggested that 'the possibilities of further destructive use are in every man's mind'.[3] Bernal had more reason than most to worry about such a catastrophe from his involvement in the revision of the Tizard report, with its analysis of a nuclear exchange between the UK and the USSR.

Prime Minister Attlee was as alert as any statesman to the danger of nuclear proliferation: in the autumn of 1945, he suggested in a thoughtful letter to President Truman that they should meet to discuss the pressing need for international regulation.[4] A summit was held in November between the US and its two wartime allies most involved with the Manhattan Project: Britain and Canada. The three leaders called for 'effective enforceable safeguards' against the use of atomic energy for destructive purposes and recommended that a commission should be set up by the United Nations. In the meantime, Truman moved to wrest control of the US nuclear programme from the military and place it with an Atomic Energy Commission that would be answerable to Congress. During this process, the American relationship with the British and Canadians became estranged to suit two opposing factions: the US military (personified by General Groves) who did not want to share their apparent monopoly with any third party, and liberal politicians who thought that any preference shown now might prejudice subsequent international negotiations with the USSR in particular. Sir James Chadwick, the chief British scientist on the Manhattan Project, sensed as early as December 1945 in Washington 'the cohesive forces which held men of diverse opinions together during the war are rapidly dissolving: any thought of common effort or even of common purpose with us or with other peoples is becoming both weaker in strength and rarer to meet.'[5]

Broadcasting on the BBC in March 1946, Sage made a plea for men of faith in the future to take up the new challenge that confronted the world.

We are afraid of another war which can only occur if we deliberately sabotage the effective international collaboration of which the United Nations Organisation is the first embodiment. The real danger does not come from the Soviet Union or the atom bomb, or from the inherent wickedness of man, or from our intrinsic inability to co-operate in building a new world based on common effort for the common good. It comes from those who do not want this kind of world: those who talk of wars and rumours of wars: those who have discovered the special values of 'western civilization', the defence of which we can now take up from the defeated Germans. These are the enemies of promise: these are the real heirs to the Nazis. Unless we can stop them splitting the world into two camps in men's minds, the fatal division will grow and war will be inevitable.[6]

A UN conference on international atomic energy policy was scheduled for June. The Americans assembled an impressive team of politicians, administrators and scientists (with J. Robert Oppenheimer making the most influential contribution). The British approach was low-key: they were to be represented by Chadwick and two senior diplomats, Sir Alexander Cadogan and Lord Inverchapel (previously Ambassador in Moscow now the Ambassador to the US). Bernal was in New York just before the UN conference started and wrote an impression of 'The American Scene'[7] as an unnamed correspondent for the *New Statesman*. He was uncomplimentary about President Truman, who attempted 'at intervals to re-create the old enthusiasm for the policies of Roosevelt, but it is clear that he neither understands them nor really believes in them'. Nor was it just the president who was drifting – there was a 'lack of any real government', the country had lost its purpose and the economy was suffering through the lack of effective central planning. Sage also detected the appearance of a native form of fascism, 'it shows itself in violent "Red" baiting and fomenting racial antagonisms – anti-Semitic and anti-Negro. The Rankin Committee...is pursuing un-American activities with Star Chamber methods...Everywhere the Catholic Church and the national minorities that it controls are working up feeling scarcely distinguishable from incitement to war against the Soviet Union.' But what really struck him was a recent Gallup Poll showing a large growth in the fear of war.

From the fourteen per cent who a year ago thought there would be another war in the next twenty-five years, the proportion is now seventy-five per cent . . . and of course there is no doubt whom the next war will be against. The presence of the atomic bomb has had the paradoxical effect, in the one country that possesses it, of increasing the feeling of insecurity. The majority of the Americans do not think of themselves as using the atomic bomb but of what will happen if it is used against them: hence the hysteria about secrecy and spy scares.

Bernal took encouragement from the recent formation of the Federation of American Scientists (FAS), organized by those who had worked on the Manhattan Project and were now dedicated to using their special knowledge of the effects of nuclear weapons to inform the world of the unprecedented danger it faced. The FAS announced themselves to be 'overwhelmingly in favor'[8] of their government's plan for the international control of atomic energy when it was first announced in April, although like Chadwick, they were uneasy about the choice of the elderly financier, Bernard Baruch, to present the plan to the UN. The central tenet of the original US plan was to place all dangerous activities that could result in the manufacture of atomic weapons under the control of an international agency. The agency would control the world supplies of uranium, construct and operate all plutonium separation plants and nuclear reactors, and have powers to license and inspect nuclear operations in individual countries. In his presentation to the UN, Baruch modified the original American plan to include a provision for unspecified punishment of transgressor nations that could not be avoided by the use of a Security Council veto. The Soviet delegation, led by Andrei Gromyko, countered with their own proposals for an international ban on the production, stockpiling and use of atomic weapons. Any existing bombs were to be destroyed within three months of the end of the convention.

As the talks were getting underway, there was a sense of idealistic optimism in many quarters that the establishment of an international Atomic Development Authority would assist countries to reap the energy benefit of atomic power, while keeping the world safe from the proliferation of atomic weapons. The *New Statesman* saw the Baruch plan as another step towards a World Government; while there were two rival forms of government – liberal democracy and communism – each of which seemed to demand the eclipse of the other, the 'A[tomic] d[evelopment] a[gency] is the crux on which turns the issue of whether these two worlds can come together into One World.'[9] After six months of fruitless debate, the UN conference, for which there were so many hopes at the outset, ended in stalemate. For this, many blamed Baruch's intransigence, but each side distrusted the other to the extent failure seems to have been inevitable.[10] As the convention was sitting, the Soviets were pushing ahead as fast as they could on the secret development of their own weapon. Their plan called for the US to destroy its stock of weapons and made no provision for international inspections – the Americans and the rest of the world were expected to put their trust in Uncle Joe. The Baruch plan, on the other hand, would have subjected the Soviets to international inspection and control before the US had to cede its own nuclear monopoly (which Stalin could not imagine them giving up).

While the idea of world government continued to gain support among the American public (a Gallup poll in August 1946 showed a majority in favour of a proposition to turn the UN into a world government 'with power to control the armed forces of all nations, including the United States'[11]), the atmosphere in the White House was cooling. The commander-in-chief was not going to allow a communist tyrant to gobble up countries that had so recently been freed from a Nazi tyranny, at the cost of so many American lives. Earlier in the year, Truman sent a blunt message to the Kremlin after the Soviet Union had failed to withdraw troops from Iran, despite the Iranians protest to the UN. This was one of a litany of complaints in his diary for September 1946: 'Reds, phonies and... parlor pinks can see no wrong in Russia's four and one half million armed forces, in Russia's loot of Poland, Austria, Hungary, Rumania, Manchuria... But when we help our friends in China who fought on our side it is terrible... When Russia occupies Persia for oil that is heavenly.'[12] His mood was not improved by reading the Clifford–Elsey intelligence report on Soviet foreign policy. The one-hundred-page document identified 'a direct threat to American security' resulting from the Soviet Union's apparent preparations for 'war with the leading capitalistic nations of the world'.[13] The report was so forceful and provocative that Truman confiscated all twenty extant copies, telling Clifford that 'if it leaked it would blow the roof off the White House, it would blow the roof off the Kremlin'.[14] Resolved to take a tough line with the Soviets, Truman was more convinced than ever of the importance of atomic weapons to balance the growing deficit in US conventional forces in Europe. Appeals from the FAS to keep atomic energy negotiations going at the UN, and 'to pursue every avenue toward one world'[15] fell on deaf ears in Washington. The Truman administration would be more influenced by Edward Teller than by Albert Einstein.

Within weeks of the war ending, Attlee had formed a British 'Atom Bomb Committee' (disguised as 'Gen 75') on the largely unspoken assumption that in order to remain in the first rank of nations, an atomic weapon would need to be produced with its casing stamped 'Made in Britain'. As the USA withdrew cooperation and disregarded promises given in wartime about the free exchange of ideas on atomic matters, the question of an independent British bomb became more acute. The decision to proceed was taken on 8th January 1947 by a committee of just six men, meeting in the greatest secrecy.

The most influential opinion was that of Ernest Bevin, the turbulent Foreign Secretary, who had been a consistent supporter of a British weapon when other economic ministers had expressed doubt. His motivation was not to counter any potential threat from the Soviets, but a desire to be treated as equals by the USA. He told the other politicians at the meeting: 'We could not afford to acquiesce in an American monopoly of this new development.'[16] Patrick Blackett, a member of the Advisory Committee on Atomic Energy, sensing the course that his political masters were taking, circulated another document opposing the development of a British atomic weapon. He had presented a detailed, closely argued, memorandum a year earlier suggesting that Britain should publicly renounce such an effort, at least for a period of some years, in the interests of her own security and European stability, and to avoid the costly diversion of scientists and technicians from a civil nuclear programme. His 1945 memorandum was dismissed by Attlee as the work of a layman in political and military problems and was rejected out-of-hand by the Chiefs of Staff. His second attempt to steer Britain towards a non-nuclear defence policy in February 1947 did lead to two meetings with the Prime Minister, but no change of heart.[17]

In the winter of 1947, a prolonged period of freezing weather threatened to shut down the British economy. Bread rationing, which had not been necessary in either world war, had been imposed a few months earlier, and public misery was now compounded by transport strikes and fuel shortages. Unemployment quickly rose to fifteen per cent. On 10th March there was a major parliamentary debate on the crisis: the government proposed economic planning units for each of its departments and called for controls on wages, profits and dividends. The country needed to recognize that austerity 'had to be accepted as a long-term condition of the peace'.[18] Three days later, *The Times* published a letter from Bernal pointing out that the government 'tacitly assumed that the industry and agriculture of our country must be carried out along existing lines'.[19] He continued:

There is no mention of the possibility of using technical development and scientific research to raise our productivity without the use of additional materials and manpower. Yet this is a perfectly feasible method, as was amply demonstrated in the war, and a determined effort to use our scientific resources to the full might, in the next critical two or three years, provide just that margin which would make the difference between disaster and prosperity... During the course of the war, however, it was found that the value of the scientists was as great, if not greater, in examining and advising on many and varied problems of warfare and supply, and particularly the evolution of the methods of operational research. These methods could be applied immediately to our present industrial problems: to increasing, for example, coal production; to diminishing waste in the use of coal and power; to improving the effectiveness of the transport system, of building and generally increasing the admittedly low technical efficiency of our productive industry. The methods are known, the men who can use them and largely created them are still available. All that is required is the impulse to set them in action.

In May, Bernal succeeded Blackett as the president of the Association of Scientific Workers (AScW). He continued to make frequent speeches calling on the government to make greater use of science and technology in the service of British industry and agriculture. The government, however, was under the kind of unremitting strain that does not foster innovation. In July, when the international conversion of currencies was restarted, a disastrous run on sterling started. After it had continued for a month, Chancellor of the Exchequer Dalton wrote to Prime Minister Attlee:

We are running out of foreign exchange, and if this goes on much longer, *we shall not be able to go on buying anything*... We must reduce the armed forces... There is nothing more inflationary than having all these non-productive people absorbing supplies of all kinds.[20]

On the day that Attlee received this alarming letter, *The Times* published another letter from the president of the AScW, bemoaning the large share of the national scientific research budget (65 per cent) devoted to military purposes. Bernal took his figures from the government's published statistics, and argued that the present allocation of resources to the services must be reduced in the light of 'the absolute shortage of scientific and technical manpower' in the UK. To cut spending on fundamental scientific research or teaching would be 'suicidal' given that 'the fundamental reason for the crisis, the relatively low efficiency of British industry, is a long-term one' and nothing must compromise 'the supply of workers or ideas for 10 or 15 years ahead... In our present serious situation the urgency for an intense and well-directed scientific and technical effort is undeniable.'[21] In making his case, Sage had used a figure of £76.5 million for total government spending on scientific research. What was never disclosed by the Attlee administration was the expenditure of an additional £100 million over the next four years on the atomic weapon project.[22]

One country where government policy was strongly influenced by a nuclear physicist of the first rank was France. An avowed communist, like many of his countrymen, Joliot-Curie was appointed head of the new Atomic Energy Commission (CEA), and was instrumental in formulating the French declaration at the 1946 UN conference that France had no intention of making nuclear weapons. He soon became an outspoken critic of US atomic policy and in late 1946 condemned their bomb tests in the Pacific as 'a miserable idea'.[23] We have seen how he and Bernal were the prime movers behind the foundation of the World Federation of Scientific Workers (WFSW) with its stated aim 'to work for the fullest utilization of science in promoting peace and the welfare of mankind'.[24] The two men supported this proposition with great enthusiasm, but both recognized that they could not just rely on their scientific reputations to influence events; the campaign for peace would require mass political action on an international scale.

The first significant event came about partly as a result of Joliot-Curie's connections through marriage. He was approached by some Polish intellectuals to set up a bilateral peace conference. The meeting was to be held in Poland and soon attracted such interest that it became the World Congress of Intellectuals for Peace. Bernal found an invitation waiting for him at Birkbeck on his return from the first international congress of the International Union of Crystallography at Harvard in August 1948. He had been selected as a delegate to an international geology conference in London at the end of the month, but instead flew out to Poland. The peace congress was to be held in Wroclaw – previously Breslau, a Silesian city that the Soviets had largely flattened just three years earlier, in a siege lasting eighty days.[25] Ivor Montagu, Sage's comrade from Cambridge communist days, recalled the scene with an optimism sustained by the fact that he had to stay there only for three days:

At no conference before or since have I seen so exalted and so assorted a galaxy of celebrities, in so appropriate a setting. The city was a heap of ruins. Rising above the rubble, approached precariously by planks over mud, was the germ of an art gallery; blazing posters vied with brilliant ceramics. At a café table in the open, Picasso sketched Polish citizens and the Pole Feliks Topolski sketched Picasso. Within the hall, poets, sculptors, musicians, architects, scientists and theologians, historians and political journalists, priests and film directors, parliamentarians and former prime ministers jostled to speak.[26]

Had Montagu cared to know, the desperate citizens of Wroclaw, who had emerged from their cellars to face the looting and rapes of the Soviet army, were now experiencing the coercion, mass arrests and political executions needed to bring about monolithic Stalinist rule. The Polish organizers found that they were searched 'no less than seven times, and the headquarters of the Congress was packed with secret servicemen'.[27] Joliot-Curie was unable to attend, but his wife, Irène, chaired the first day of the meeting, when she had to listen to lengthy reports from each nation represented. She could not understand the Russian contribution by a writer named Alexander Fadeyev because there was no translation available. After repudiating American imperialism, he seemed to be carried away on a wave of professional envy, denouncing not only American writers like T.S. Eliot and Eugene O'Neill, but Jean Paul Sartre and André Malraux – the darlings of Parisian intelligentsia.

'If hyenas could type and jackals could use a fountain pen they would write such things', he said.

About one quarter of the British party of forty were scientists, with Bernal and Haldane being described as 'the big guns'.[28] Haldane remained silent, while Bernal 'harped on a favourite theme: the obstacles a new arms race would present to humanity's chance to benefit from scientific cooperation'.[29] The Oxford historian, A.J.P. Taylor likened the seemingly endless speeches to 'an exhausting process of mass hypnosis . . . reaching a climax in a unanimous resolution against American Fascism'.[30] It was Taylor, who endeared himself to the Poles and infuriated Soviet and British communists alike with his own scintillating, extempore, speech that culminated with this memorable passage:

All peoples ask for freedom from oppression – freedom from arbitrary arrest, freedom from a secret police, freedom to speak their opinion of their own government as well as of others. If we defend this, we defend also the peace of the world and we offer the people of the world what they want. But even if I spoke only for myself, I would still say without intellectual freedom, without love, without tolerance, the intellectual cannot serve humanity.[31]

Taylor and Julian Huxley, who thought that half the speeches made were more likely to promote war than peace, were among the eleven who voted against the long, final resolution that included reference to 'a handful of self-interested men in America and Europe who have inherited fascist ideas of solving all problems by force of arms'. Sage was one of four hundred and twenty-six voting in favour. After returning to London, Bernal wrote praising the Congress and its final manifesto, warning that the US was preparing 'a war for complete world domination', in which 'nothing of the panoply of Fascism is lacking'.[32] Taylor and seven other members of the British group at the Congress published a letter in the *New Statesman*, explaining why they were unable to accept the conclusions reached at Wroclaw.

Two ways of life are in conflict throughout the world and it should be the task of intellectuals to resolve the conflict by peaceful means. We feel the implication of the resolution that one side alone is to blame to be a waste of a great opportunity. We believe that, though we were in a minority at the Congress, we represent the majority of men and women throughout the world.[33]

Taylor actually believed that the Soviets were sincere in their expectation of immediate attack by the US and were entitled to defend their convictions. In return, he thought it was essential for Western intellectuals to stand up for their values, and 'try to restore a culture which is neither Soviet nor American but the heritage of all humanity'.[34] At the time of the Congress, less than two hundred miles to the north-west of Wroclaw, the Berlin airlift had been in operation for about two months, giving a real edge to the opinions expressed.

Bernal thought that the real importance of the Congress could be gauged from the distortion and suppression it received in the British press. He defended Fadeyev's forcible and harsh speech as the authentic voice of the Soviet Union, reminding the Congress that Hitler had been defeated only by the heroic efforts of the Red Army and Soviet people. Now the world was having to face the danger of another war because of 'the avowed imperialists of the United States of America, who could not tolerate the liberation that had already occurred in Eastern and to some degree in Western Europe, and who wished to make a world again safe for capitalism, even if it meant rebuilding the whole edifice of fascism which the war had overthrown'.[35] The value of Fadeyev's speech was to prevent the Congress wasting time 'with generalities about the desirability of peace' and to emphasize that 'the fight for peace could only be carried out effectively by those who accepted along general lines the analysis that he had given'. Speakers like A.J.P. Taylor, who were, in Bernal's opinion, oblivious to the harsher realities of the present world, 'confused the beliefs and desires of the people of the United States and Britain with the plans and actions of the most powerful groups that controlled their governments. The Marshall Plan appeared to Taylor as a great gesture of generosity from the American people. This is certainly what the American people have been taught to believe and for the most part honestly do believe. Nevertheless, the intention of the Marshall Plan is revealing itself more and more as an economic annexe of the Truman policy of countering Communism and imposing reactionary governments by bribes and threats.'[36]

Bernal's one-sided views caused some long-standing allies to lose patience. Nevill Mott, a professor of physics in Bristol who was an implacable opponent of atomic weapon research and an active member of AScW, insisted on taking the chair when Sage came to speak in November. He did not think anyone ought to get away with the 'impudent assumption of peace as a communist specialty'.[37] Writing about the occasion to his mother, he said:

My remarks from the chair were listened to in stony silence but provoked Bernal into a passionate defence of Soviet policy which is just what I wanted. Loud applause for B. But all the same – with some of my young physicists there, it *must* be made clear that Bernal's conclusions (organise a will to peace among the peoples of the west) only follows from his premises (the sole danger to peace comes from the U.S.).

Mott felt about the AScW the way that many scientists did about the new WFSW – that it was a communist-dominated organization, and he decided to resign his membership. Bernal does not seem to have been a card-carrying member of the CPGB at this stage, but continued to wear his party loyalty on his sleeve. He wrote frequently for *Modern Quarterly*, the journal so despised by Orwell, and started to take an interest in a new editorial assistant there, Margot Heinemann. She was in her mid-thirties, petite, with a strong handsome face and curly hair. She knew more about Sage than he realized at first, because she had been an undergraduate at Newnham College during the early 1930s. She once had him pointed out to her in the street by a friend, 'There's Bernal, he's the cleverest man of his generation.' Her reply, 'What that man with the green face?' caught his appearance when 'he had been pushing life too hard'.[38] Margot converted to communism after seeing the hunger marchers pass through Cambridge in 1934 and because she felt convinced by the popular front case against the rise of fascism. At Cambridge, she read English and fell in love with John Cornford, the romantic revolutionary and history scholar of Trinity College. Cornford went to fight with the International Brigade and was killed in Spain in 1937, but not before he had written some remarkable poetry and letters to Margot. In her grief, she immersed herself in political activity and worked in the labour research department of the TUC for the next twelve years. She became closely involved in the setting up of the National Union of Mineworkers and even wrote a book called *Britain's Coal* towards the end of the war.

Sage invited her to Torrington Square for a drink, before going out to dinner and, if all went according to plan, to bed. When he came down to meet her at the front door, he found her standing in a pool of blood – she had stepped on a broken milk bottle and cut her heel. So their first date started with him fetching the first aid kit from the lab and cleaning her wound. Within a few months, he had moved into her flat just off Haverstock Hill, almost within sight of Margaret Gardiner's house. Margot was the daughter of German Jewish immigrants and liked to say that she came 'from a long line of married people'.[39] Like Cornford, she preferred to be a monopoly capitalist in love if not in politics, but decided that she would rather have part shares in Bernal than the whole of a lesser man. Her parents were understandably worried about her choice, but Harry Pollitt, the general secretary of CPGB, who had taken a protective stance towards Margot since Cornford's death, promised her father that if Sage did not treat her right, 'He would knock his bloody block off.'[40]

In February 1949, Bernal was one of a host of leading British intellectuals invited to a world peace conference at the Waldorf-Astoria hotel in New York. He accepted but was concerned that Blackett, whose presence he felt was necessary to give the British delegation weight, had refused. Bernal wrote to Harlow Shapley, the Harvard astronomer who was organizing the conference, regretting that he had been unable to persuade Blackett to change his mind; he explained that Blackett 'has an antipathy to large meetings, publicity,

journalists, etc.'[41] Sage was planning to take Anita Rimel with him and the
Fankuchens were going to sponsor their visas. Anita was especially looking
forward to the trip; she had struck up a long-distance friendship with Dina
Fankuchen and the two formed a Society of 'Women who had never been to
bed with Sage', with Dina as president and Anita as treasurer. It may have been
around this time that Anita sent her a telegram saying 'You are now president
AND treasurer of the society.'

Bernal was invited to give lectures in Boston, Chicago, Philadelphia and
Washington,[42] which would be helpful in paying for the trip, but the FBI had
been taking an interest in his anti-American speeches. Senator Joseph
McCarthy's relentless anti-communist campaign had not yet taken off, but
there were already widespread concerns about communists holding university
posts.[43] At the last minute, Sage was summoned to the American Embassy in
London and asked his political views. 'I said they were perfectly well known'[44]
he told reporters later, 'The whole proceedings took half a minute' and his
visa was revoked. This represented a major turnaround from eighteen months
earlier, when he had gone to the Embassy to receive the Medal of Freedom
with bronze palm for his 'very meritorious service in scientific research and
development' during the war. There were protests to Dean Acheson, the
Secretary of State and speeches were made in the House of Commons about
the incident. Shapley, who had decided to make Sage the guest of honour at
the conference dinner, pointed out that the American government were
excluding the man 'who helped to plan the D-Day invasion of Normandy'.[45]

Bernal was allowed to travel to Paris in April 1949 for the World Congress
of the Partisans of Peace. It was a hybrid communist peace event with Joliot-
Curie as president, and Bernal, a prime organizer and vice-president. Stalin's
ministry of global propaganda, the Cominform, lent its support and predicted that 'the Peace Congress will become an historic landmark'.[46] The
French government, made nervous by the communists' ascension to power
in China, refused entry visas for over three hundred delegates, mostly Chinese, who were then accommodated at a parallel meeting in Prague. There
were still over two thousand people packed into the Salle Pleyel on 20th April,
when Joliot-Curie took the stage to thunderous applause and launched into
his peace offensive. He told the audience:

We are not here to ask for peace, but to impose it. This congress is the reply of the
peoples to the signers of the Atlantic pact [NATO]. To the new war they are preparing,
we will reply with a revolt of the peoples.[47]

In the opinion of *The Economist*, Joliot-Curie set the defiant, belligerent
tone for the conference.[48] Their editorial likened the atmosphere to the
Nuremberg rallies held under the symbol of Picasso's dove rather than Hitler's

swastika. In communist eyes, 'the purpose of congress delegates is not to think but to listen, not to discuss but to agree; they assemble not to confront ideas but to demonstrate solidarity. So the Partisans of Peace were summoned not to seek ways of understanding between governments and conciliation between peoples but to organize resistance and hostility to the Atlantic Pact.' Paul Robeson, the great American bass, apart from singing 'Ole Man River' gave an incendiary speech, which cost him his passport; he accused the US government of pursuing policy 'similar to that of Hitler and Goebbels'.[49]

During the meeting, it was announced that Nanking had fallen to the communist forces of Mao Zedong, news that was received by the audience with 'delirious enthusiasm'. When a British delegate, Harvey Moore KC, pointed out that to advocate peace meant opposing war including the most horrible form, civil war, he was received in silence. The audience hissed him when he suggested that delegates to a peace congress should oppose the civil war in China. They froze when he continued that 'in countries where there was no liberty and no free access to independent courts the state of things was favourable to war and not to peace'.[50] On balance, the French writer, Jean Genet, thought the Paris Peace Congress was 'the most concentrated inflammatory anti-American propaganda effort in this part of Europe since the beginning of the cold war'.[51] The Soviet reaction to the Partisans of Peace was one of immense satisfaction: Ilya Ehrenburg writing in *Pravda* saw the Paris meeting as a turning point when the imperialist 'howling' about the atomic bomb had 'been drowned by human voices'.[52]

Soon after the Paris congress, Bernal returned to France for a holiday with his son Martin. They toured around taking bus rides and, when there were no buses, accepting lifts on the backs of lorries. They visited the Joliot-Curies at their home at Sceaux, south of Paris, where Sage and Frédéric spent some evenings swapping wartime stories in the local bar. What especially impressed the twelve-year-old Martin about Joliot-Curie was not that he was a Nobel Laureate and a Resistance hero, but his claim to be able to eat for nothing in any patisserie because his grandfather had been the pastry chef to Napoleon III.

In August, Sage flew to Moscow where he gave his infamous rant in the Hall of Columns. The geopolitical landscape was undergoing rapid seismic shifts, many due to events in the nuclear world, that would reshape not only the Cold War but also, for example, Anglo-American relations and American domestic politics. The detection of the first Soviet nuclear explosion in September caused dismay in Washington and ended any possibility of restraint in the nuclear arms race. In October, Truman learned of the concept of the hydrogen bomb from his National Security Council and he immediately instructed his Atomic Energy Commission 'to go to it and fast'.[53] The public announcement that the US would develop 'the so-called hydrogen or super-bomb' followed at the end of January 1950. Truman's mundane language made it sound like a new highway construction project rather than a device with the potential for ending the human race. There were immediate protests from the world community of scientists, many of whom had realized that such a bomb was a possibility and were informed enough to admit that its effects were essentially incalculable. At that time, the weapon was still a mass of unsolved equations, but its dark threat was overpowering. Sage wrote to Linus Pauling, 'we are all very glad to see the stand you have made against the criminal lunacy of the hydrogen bomb'.[54]

The American monopoly on the H-bomb was destined to be much shorter than their four-year term for fission weapons. On 22nd September 1949, the day before Truman broke the news of the first atomic test in the USSR, the FBI opened a file on the naturalized British scientist, Klaus Fuchs; they had deciphered a 1944 KGB message that indicated information on gaseous diffusion from Los Alamos had been transmitted through the British Mission in New York.[55] So impressive was Fuchs' work on the Manhattan Project that he was asked to stay on at Los Alamos after the war ended. Such was his strength as a theoretician that Edward Teller invited him to a secret conference in April 1946 to discuss the feasibility of a thermonuclear weapon that became known as the Super. At the end of May, Fuchs and von Neumann filed a joint patent for an implosion process to ignite the Super.[56] After his arrest in London in February 1950, Fuchs 'laughingly' claimed that the idea was his and not von Neumann's; from that point, the FBI suspected the Soviets might already be at work on a hydrogen bomb.

The decision to proceed with the hydrogen bomb and concerns about the Soviet programme placed further barriers to true cooperation in nuclear weapon development between the Americans and the British. Washington was not amused when Attlee suggested his War Minister, Sage's old friend John Strachey, who had been a CPGB member as recently as 1944, should head an inquiry into the Fuchs affair.[57] Aside from worries about security, the threat posed by Soviet nuclear weapons now impelled the US to stockpile as many bombs as possible. The UK was seen as vulnerable to Soviet attack so that it made sense to accumulate raw material on the North American continent; it would be more efficient to concentrate production facilities there as well.[58]

The USSR, with justification, saw itself as the potential target of this rapidly growing American nuclear arsenal. Until the Soviets achieved an adequate parity of atomic weapons, there was a necessity for them to discourage any American attack by any means possible. The burgeoning peace movement in Western Europe was seen as their top priority, and the Cominform declared soon after the Paris Congress that 'The struggle ... for the organization and consolidation of the forces of peace against the forces of war should now become the pivot of the entire activity of the Communist parties and democratic organization.'[59] The Cominform wanted the Partisans of Peace to be reinforced by recruits from the proletariat, trades unions, youth and women's organizations as well as scientists, writers and political figures. The Soviets wanted active peace efforts, grounded in Marxist philosophy. An international peace campaign led by communists might reduce the risk of a US attack, and also mollify the war-weary masses in the newly subjugated states of Eastern Europe.

In October 1949, Bernal addressed a meeting of the British–Soviet Society in London. He referred to 'the state of war hysteria and panic which had been spread in the countries of the West'[60] during the two weeks since the announcement of the Soviet bomb test. This reaction was particularly acute in the US, a country he characterized as 'under the domination of a very small but very effective set of people'. He estimated the American expenditure on nuclear weapons to be $13 billion, with large private corporations having a double interest in the programme – one economic, the other political. By contrast, the USSR was applying the major part of its scientific effort to 'the enormous task of building up the country', (implying the military portion of its research budget was tiny). The 'sharp increase in international tension and in demands for further armaments' that followed the news of the Soviet bomb made 'the strongest case for the policy, steadily advocated by the Soviet Union, of abolishing all weapons of mass destruction and of general disarmament'.

The Partisans of Peace next convened under Joliot-Curie's leadership on 15th March 1950 in Stockholm. The major achievement of this meeting was the launching of the Stockholm Peace Appeal, a document drawn up by the Soviet writer Ilya Ehrenburg that was palatable to 'all men of goodwill throughout the world' (who were expected to sign it) without displeasing Stalin. The short text called for 'the absolute banning of the atomic bomb', 'strict international control to ensure implementation of this ban', and the recognition that first use of the weapon would be 'a crime against humanity' for which the government responsible would face punishment befitting a war criminal.[61] Joliot-Curie was the first to sign the Appeal. On his return to France, he gave an impassioned speech at the Communist Party Congress, promoting the Stockholm Appeal as a means to avoid the 'war of aggression which is being prepared against the Soviet Union' and pledging that 'Communist scientists [like him] would never give a scrap of their science to make war against the Soviet Union'.[62] By the end of the month, the French government now committed to developing its own bomb, dismissed him from his post as High Commissioner for atomic energy.

In January 1950, Stalin sent a telegram to his ambassador in Pyongyang informing Kim Il Sung, the communist leader of North Korea, that he would 'assist' in the reunification of Korea by military means. In May, Mao Zedong added his encouragement, saying that unification by peaceful means was not possible and that Kim Il Sung should not be afraid of the Americans who 'will not enter a third world war for such a small territory'.[63] On Sunday 25th June, the North Korean army crossed the 38th parallel and quickly captured Seoul. President Truman immediately pledged US forces to defend the South, as did the UK and France in turn. Undaunted, the Partisans of Peace continued to make arrangements for their next gathering, scheduled for Sheffield in November.

The British Peace Committee (chairman, Ivor Montagu) was in charge of making arrangements. They depended on volunteers to find accommodation for the large numbers expected to attend. Ully Harris, Martin Bernal's old nanny, was recruited through the Holborn branch of CPGB and spent four weeks working hard in Sheffield. While the official delegates would stay in hotels, their support staff would need to be billeted in homes. Adverts were placed in local newspapers; food rationing was still in force, and Ully had to ask prospective hosts 'whether they would give them some supper – some cocoa and a bit of bread and cheese'.[64]

The communist partisanship of the Partisans of Peace had been the source of unease amongst some intellectuals since the Wroclaw conference. Patrick Blackett had written to Joliot-Curie before the Paris Congress pointing out that the danger of the 'Western Powers waging a preventative war, relying on the supposed decisive character of atomic bombs'[65] had lessened since the height of the Berlin crisis the previous year. He urged the peace movement to adopt Fabian tactics and play for time to encourage military realism to take hold rather than expend energy on distant problems. Einstein, who had sent a message to Wroclaw that was subsequently doctored by the organizers, now informed Joliot-Curie that he would not be attending the Sheffield conference. 'I must confess frankly', he said, 'that I cannot believe in the present situation manifestations of such kind will help to bring genuine peace nearer.'[66] There was also some fierce criticism in the *Sheffield Telegraph*.

The Sheffield Congress is the last place for peace lovers to find themselves. It is not concerned with peace at all. We got a clue to its real purpose by studying the records of the small group of communists and fellow travellers who direct it. These include people who urge the Greek guerillas to fight their elected government; who urge the Malayan bandits to attack our troops and murder our civilians; who justify the aggression of North Korea against South Korea. They are surely the most bloodthirsty peace lovers in history. The campaigns which they support have only one thing in common. Common to them all is the fact, that, if successful, they would increase the power of the Soviet Union relative to the power of the free world.[67]

The author of this hard-hitting article had, until a few months earlier, been a junior minister at the Foreign Office (he lost his seat in the 1950 general election). His name was Christopher Mayhew and he was a particular favourite of Attlee's. It was Mayhew who first persuaded Bevin (after the Foreign Secretary had been publicly humiliated by Molotov at the UN in 1947) to set up an agency within the Foreign Office to counter the Cominform by producing anti-communist propaganda. The resultant Information Research Department (IRD) was initially intended to spread material about communist misdeeds abroad, but was soon drawn into a more defensive, domestic role as well; it attempted to block CPGB members from infiltrating trade unions, youth organizations and the BBC. The Information Research Department made use of the writing talents of Malcolm Muggeridge and George Orwell, and subsidized the publication of *Animal Farm* internationally.[68] In 1949, the cachectic Orwell passed a blacklist of three dozen or so 'crypto-communists and fellow travellers' to the IRD. One entry read: Bernal, Professor J.D. (Irish extraction): Scientist (physicist), Birkbeck College, London University. Scientific staff of Combined Operations during the war. 'Science and Society.' Qy. open C.P.? Very gifted. Said to have been educated for R.C. priesthood. I am pretty sure he is an open member.[69] It was probably the IRD who persuaded the Home Office to refuse visas for the permanent officers, like Joliot-Curie, and many other delegates two days before the Sheffield Congress was due to start.

Bernal heard the news of the bans from Ivor Montagu on Saturday morning, 11th November. They spent the rest of the day trying to sort out the tremendous confusion and held a lively press conference. This had two advantages: to instruct those delegates who were in Britain to proceed to Sheffield as originally planned, and to give the Congress maximum publicity. Bernal was back in his office early on the Sunday morning and spent the day sending telegrams and exploring alternatives. He asked Stan Lenton to organize drinks for a party in his Torrington Square flat that evening. Late in the afternoon he broke away from the office to meet an important foreign delegate, who was arriving in London – Pablo Picasso. Picasso was already in England because the Arts Council was sponsoring an exhibition of his paintings in London and they had obtained his visa. Bernal had dinner with Picasso and a few French delegates who had made it into the country. Picasso felt rather chagrined that he been allowed into England, when Joliot-Curie had not. On returning to Torrington Square, they found a handful of Soviets waiting for them, including Vsevolod Pudovkin the film director; others drifted in and the party started. Bernal's main anxiety soon became whether the drink would hold out![70]

Sage slipped away from the party with Picasso and Pudovkin to give them a tour of the crystallography laboratory downstairs. 'Both were interested in quite different ways. Pudovkin as a scientist, and Picasso by the form and colours of the crystals. He was struck by the resemblance of his pictures to some of our Fourier diagrams and wondered if he put them [his pictures] through the machine backwards, they would come out as crystals.'[71] They returned upstairs to find that the flat was packed and Lenton's bar in the kitchen was under considerable strain. Sage asked Picasso whether he would scribble something for him on the wall. They were in the living room, which was divided from the kitchen by a thin partition wall; the only light came from a small, naked, bulb suspended from the low ceiling. Picasso stood on a chair so that he could draw on the wall space above the bookshelves. He took a multicolour grease pencil from his pocket and 'began with a swish of line that immediately became a real face, but had a devil's horns, closed, blind eyes and a shut little mouth'.[72]

The artist climbed down from the chair and stepped back into the throng to look at his work. He 'shook his head, pounced on the wall and turned the horns into a laurel wreath, opened the devil's eyes and widened his mouth until he looked like an anxious god'.

On reflection he said sympathetically, 'Il a l'air solitaire' and started to draw him a friend. This time there were no changes, no hesitation – a long undistorted face, free of tricks such as double profiles.

He stepped down again, and somebody shouted out, 'What's it got to do with peace?', so he added a pair of angel's wings.

A few days later, some decorators arrived from the university and had to be firmly persuaded by Lenton not to paint over the only Picasso mural in England. Sage wrote in confessional tones to the Director of the National

Gallery, 'I have acquired, almost accidentally, on my wall a large drawing by Picasso which I would very much like you to see'.[73]

Early in the morning after the great party, Bernal, Picasso and Montagu took the train to Sheffield. It was a beautiful, bright, day in London and Picasso talked about his father painting doves. The idyllic mood was rather spoiled by arriving in Sheffield, which looked 'grim' in the pelting rain. There was no reception committee, and small groups made their own way to the vast, empty conference hall. Some members of the press turned up to take photographs. Bernal was approached by a city official, who showed him a warrant giving permission for Special Branch policemen to be present at the private meeting. Sage informed him 'we were under no obligation to be there ourselves'.[74] Thanks to the press coverage, several hundred people came to the hall, with Bernal now taking Joliot-Curie's role as chairman. When he asked, 'Who would like to fly to Warsaw for this world peace conference?' (this is what he and Montagu had arranged with Soviet contacts), 'a forest of hands shot up'. There were then 'very good speeches' which went on until 10.30 pm, and Bernal felt heartened by the spirit of the meeting. At the end he auctioned a dove that Picasso had drawn. It was knocked down for twenty guineas – 'the maximum appreciation of the industrial north'.[75]

Arriving back in London the following afternoon, Sage took Picasso on a tour of London in his small car. It was Picasso's first visit since 1919. That evening there was a reception organized by the Arts Council at Topolski's studio, where Sage found artists, critics, filmmakers – 'the greatest congregation of British intellectuals ever' – though Picasso did not arrive until most guests were leaving.

Bernal was up at 5.30 am the next day to fly with a small group to Warsaw. Their flight to Prague via Frankfurt was delayed so that they did not get to Germany until early afternoon. After refuelling, the plane was taxiing to take off when the tail wheel slipped off the runway into deep mud. They walked back to the terminal, feeling 'slight anxiety because we were in American territory'.[76] Any concern was dispelled by a very agreeable lunch, when Sage struck up a conversation with a cockney bricklayer, who had been elected as a delegate to the conference by his trade union. Sage ranged over the history of bricks, construction methods through antiquity, and the great efficiency of Soviet building methods. When they were walking back to the plane, the bricklayer sidled up to Francis Aprahamian, a communist Cambridge student of the 1930s and now Bernal's personal research assistant at Birkbeck, to ask, "Who did yer say he was?' 'Professor Bernal.' "as he bin a Brickie?"[77]

They flew into Prague at dusk, where they were greeted by a large contingent of singing boys and girls. The final leg of the journey to Warsaw was an extremely bumpy flight in an unheated Polish plane. On arrival, Sage was whisked away in a limousine to the city centre. At midnight, he found himself being ushered through grand anterooms with fine paintings, finally coming to a dining room 'where Joliot was a third of the way through an extremely good dinner. It was the Belvedere Palace, the President's residence.'[78] Sage sat down to what would be the only proper meal he would eat in Warsaw, and they plunged into discussions about the conference. They were soon joined by Chinese and Soviet representatives and finished at 4 am local time. After a short sleep, Sage was driven by chauffeur through the devastated city and was naturally interested to see what reconstruction was taking place. The hall for the Congress was a factory shed that had been rapidly converted in the previous few days by 1,500 workers. It was impossible to see from one end to the other; side rooms were partitioned by cloth and Sage was worried about the fire hazard. There was a 'massive Chinese delegation', others from Europe he had never met, as well as old friends. Sage discovered a buffet behind the platform with tea, cold meat and fish, open all hours; he lived exclusively off this for the remainder of his stay.

The two thousand Partisans of Peace renamed themselves the World Peace Council (WPC) and elected Joliot-Curie their first president by acclamation. Bernal was to be one of the vice presidents. Fadeyev treated the crowd to his trademark vitriol, accusing the Americans of turning Korea 'into a desert of ruins and ashes, flooding the country with the blood of children, and performing all sorts of fascist bestialities, similar to those that led to the Nuremberg Trial'.[79] The fact that the simultaneous translation service was not working properly did little to dampen enthusiasm. That evening, Bernal and Joliot-Curie were guests in the President's box at the theatre, where they watched a visiting troupe of amateur Russian dancers performing to the music of two accordians. They used the long periods of inactivity on the stage to discuss the strategy for the WPC and the restoration of intellectual life.

The next morning, Sage got up very early to prepare his speech. The second day of the conference opened with a procession of Polish mothers who had lost sons in the war, farm workers, youth organizations, and finally industrial workers. Most of the British delegates arrived in Warsaw that afternoon, and immediately complained about the makeshift arrangements, which rather annoyed Sage. In the evening, he made the mistake of going to the theatre again – a tedious 1870 Polish light opera, which he abandoned after the second act at 2 am.

Word reached Warsaw University that Sage was at the conference and he was invited to address the students. He agreed to do this on Sunday morning, before the conference started, explaining that he needed to keep to a tight schedule. He was taken to a covered courtyard, where there was an audience he estimated to be six to eight thousand. They were 'in every possible aperture, hanging on the pillars and crawling over the rafters of the roof so it appeared to me that they might drop on us at any moment'.[80] He then endured an official welcome 'in fluent Polish' that lasted for an hour and when he rose to speak, he lost further time because of the students' enthusiastic applause. He spoke to them on the theme of rebuilding.

He arrived at the conference an hour-and-a-half late to find that it had still not started, so he decided to go on a tour of Warsaw to see the reconstruction for himself. In the face of tremendous destruction, he could see that there was very little steel or heavy equipment available – far less than in the UK or the USSR. Most of the work was done using wood and small machines; there were some concrete blocks for larger buildings. Despite the obstacles, he judged the results 'magnificent' and was particularly impressed with cooperative housing estates that incorporated shops and laundries. Although there was central heating (a rarity in British buildings) he was told that it was turned on only for a few hours a day because of fuel shortages.

He returned to the conference hall to find that the new draft of his speech, left with a typist in the morning, had not been touched. The level of chaos reminded him of the Duchess's croquet party in *Alice*: there were no interpreters and the few typewriters available had Polish keyboards. Things were no better the next morning when he returned to deliver the speech; even his handwritten version could not be found. Just as he was being introduced and starting to walk to the podium, Francis Aprahamian saw it on the translator's desk – she had denied having it. He grabbed it and gave it to Sage who was then heard in dead silence – most of the delegates could not understand English and the British delegation, still sulking, showed no interest: 'There was a slightly staggered kind of clapping at the end but I felt really that all the effort had been completely wasted.'[81]

On Monday afternoon, he talked to some Polish intellectuals about Copernicus, about whom most of them knew nothing. He then returned to the Congress to supervise the drafting of the final resolution, which took until 3 am. A ten-point statement was issued with the first priority being a termination of the Korean War and the withdrawal of foreign armies from Korean soil. The strategic goal of 'the unconditional banning of all means of atomic, bacteriological and chemical weapons, poisonous gases, radio-active and all other means of mass extermination'[82] ranked no higher than point seven. In his writings, Bernal was plainer: 'The effective prohibition of the atom bomb is the first and absolutely necessary condition for any serious move to peace.'[83] In spite of 'the enormous extent of propaganda for the "cold war", especially in the United States', Bernal believed that 'negotiation on the basis of mutual respect, leading to a peaceful co-existence of the economic systems of capitalism and socialism, could proceed free from the threat of sudden destruction by the atom bombs'. The deadlock between world leaders could be broken by the massive demonstration of the popular will embodied in the simple language of the Stockholm Appeal. The people had come to see that 'the preparations for atomic warfare had ceased to be merely criminal; they were becoming suicidal'. If the issue could be restricted to a ban on atomic weapons, there was an opportunity to unite 'those who take one side or the other in the Korean struggle, those who support and those who deplore the war in Malaya, those who think of the U.S. as a probable aggressor and those who fear aggression from the Soviet Union, those who believe in free enterprise, the welfare state or socialism'.

By the time of the next large WPC meeting in Berlin in the summer of 1952, Bernal was disappointed that popular demand had not been more successful in forcing the issue of nuclear disarmament at the UN. This failure, in his opinion, was largely due to the US policy of accelerated rearmament, in pursuit of 'a new Holy War against communism to liberate Europe, restore Chiang Kai Chek and open the door to American enterprise'.[84] Still Bernal reaffirmed in his speech a belief in 'a policy of comprehensive, fair, practicable and rapid disarmament which involved quantitatively the substantial reduction by one third to one half of all armed forces, armaments and armament industry; qualitatively, the entire prohibition of weapons of mass destruction, including all forms of atomic and bacteriological warfare.' To achieve these ambitious ends, a system of inspection and control that would supply ample security to participating countries needed to be in place within a year. There were signs that Bernal was moving closer to the type of pragmatic approach espoused by Blackett; he told the audience that he had 'made the mistake of being too academic about disarmament in the past. It should be presented as a practical solution to particular problems such as the Korean War.'

In 1952, there was another, more personal, international appeal that captured the support of many left-wing activists: the campaign to free Julius and Ethel Rosenberg, who had been found guilty of espionage in the US in April 1951. The judge, when handing down their death sentences, held them responsible for 'the Communist aggression in Korea' because their treachery had put 'into the hands of the Russians the A-bomb, years before our best scientists predicted Russia would perfect the bomb'.[85] Portrayed as 'the first victims of American fascism', the pair maintained their innocence and hoped that public outcry might save them. Julius wrote to Ethel in March 1952: 'We must soberly realize that our only hope rests with the people.'[86] They wrote letters from Sing Sing to their supporters, claiming to speak for peace; these messages were amplified in Europe by the Cominform, determined to maximize anti-American sentiment.

Julius Rosenberg was identified as the central figure of a wartime Soviet spy ring, codename *Enormoz*, by cryptographers working on *Venona* material. These intercepted signals were too valuable and secret to use at the Rosenbergs' trial. Instead Julius' role in transmitting atomic secrets to the Soviets was mainly established by the evidence of Ethel's brother, David Greenglass and his wife Ruth. Ethel was convicted solely on their testimony. From August 1944, David Greenglass had worked as a machinist at Los Alamos, fabricating the high-explosive lenses that were so crucial in the implosion design of the plutonium bomb. He described this process and other details of the bomb design to his brother-in-law at the end of the war.

Sage evidently wrote to the Friends of the Rosenbergs Committee in early October 1952, and received an excited response, saying that his was the first letter they had received 'from a scientist abroad' and gave them 'a real lift'.[87] This was followed two days later by a letter from the Rosenbergs' attorney asking him to review the case against them, particularly the evidence of David Greenglass. Bernal's view was that the information that Greenglass might have passed to Julius Rosenberg was of 'a very low order' and did not constitute 'the secret of the atom bomb'.[88] He suggested that the principle of convergent implosion or hollow charge had been known for 60 years, and it would be the first method to be explored 'by any intelligent designer if faced by the problem of rapidly compressing a volume of material'.[89] Sage subsequently spoke at a public rally in London to save the Rosenbergs – a contribution again noted by the FBI. Another speaker was Dennis Pritt, a communist, King's Counsel, MP for Hammersmith and leading member of the British Peace Committee. He subsequently helped Bernal to file an affidavit with the American court. In the affidavit, Bernal gave his academic credentials and pointed out his expertise in high explosives as a result of his war work. In an attempt to minimize the impact caused by Greenglass's evidence, Bernal stated that: 'The principle of the converging shock wave is not a new one. It has been utilized in practice as far back as 1792. It was rediscovered by Admiral Munroe of the US Navy in 1888, it is known as the Munroe effect and was widely publicized at that time and later...' There were, he said, British patents dating from 1911, and the shaped charge was the principal mechanism of the tank-destroying bazooka.

Whether Bernal's evidence was ever considered in the Rosenbergs' appeal is not clear, but it did not help them. The Supreme Court refused to order a retrial, which prompted Bernal to write a long letter to Einstein, railing against the injustice of their case and asking him to use whatever influence he had on their behalf. The Rosenbergs had become emblems of the Cold War. Their deaths in the electric chair pleased Stalin's regime because they were innocent victims of American fascism in the eyes of millions, and, by the same token, the executions served to demonstrate the resolve of the new Eisenhower administration against communism.

What might have puzzled Stalin was that the Rosenbergs were executed without confessing their guilt: such loose ends would never be permitted under his rule. From 1948 onwards, he had become increasingly concerned that Jews in the Soviet Union represented an internal threat to his iron grip on the state. He embarked on a secret pogrom and in August 1952, after interminable torture and a closed trial, the members of the Jewish Antifascist Committee were shot. They were guilty of bourgeois nationalism and of being used as the tools of American intelligence to undermine the Soviet system. Their families, exiled in Siberia and Kazakhstan, were only informed of the executions three years later. At the meeting of the Presidium of the Central Committee in December 1952, Stalin proclaimed that 'every Jew is a potential spy for the United States'.[90] The fate of the Jewish Antifascist Committee was intended to be but a grisly prelude to the systematic persecution and deportation of Soviet Jewry. A glimpse of this was seen in the West when, in January 1953, news of the Doctors Plot was announced from Moscow. This implicated many leading physicians, mostly Jewish, in a conspiracy to kill Soviet leaders on the instructions of American, British and Zionist intelligence agencies. Stalin had orchestrated the campaign, and was frustrated with the time it took his security forces to extract the necessary confessions. Accusing the KGB of working 'like waiters in white gloves' he ordered the chief investigator to 'beat them, beat them, beat them with death blows'.[91] When Stalin died in March, the surviving doctors were released and *Pravda* even reported the fact. At the time, Churchill wrote to Eisenhower that 'nothing impressed me so much as the doctor story' which he thought must have 'cut very deeply into communist discipline and structure'.[92]

The doctor story and the narrowly averted pogrom caused little comment in the West, and not all the comment was sympathetic – physicians in France, for example, saw fit to denounce their Soviet colleagues.[93] The Rosenberg case, by contrast, had become an international cause célèbre. The indignation about the Rosenbergs' conviction and subsequent execution stemmed from a feeling that their trial was unfair and that they had been denied their individual rights. But such individual rights had no meaning in the USSR (nor for that matter in Mao Zedong's China), where they were subsumed by the state. It was precisely this lack of individual rights that made the massive Stockholm Appeal doubly meaningless. By the time of the Warsaw Congress, according to Montagu,[94] the total number of signatures gathered had reached 473,154,259. Of these, nearly three quarters were either from China or the USSR – states where there was no such thing as free opinion and where, in any event, the rulers were indifferent to the desires of the people. The number of

British signatures was 1,343,340, which was less than ten per cent of those collected in France. Bernal was disappointed that the British had been 'the slowest to answer the call of Stockholm'.[95] He was right that 'this is little indication of the spirit of our people' who desired peace and the avoidance of nuclear war as fervently as any other nation. What Sage could not see was that the British public were rightly suspicious of the motives behind the Stockholm Appeal and were exercising innate caution.

As part of the celebrations for Stalin's seventieth birthday in December 1949, it was decided to establish a committee to award an annual Stalin Peace Prize. The winners would receive a gold medal and 100,000 roubles. Bernal was a committee member, and in 1951 the first prize was given to Joliot-Curie. In 1952, Sage nominated his old colleague from the Royal Institution, Kathleen Lonsdale, who was a Quaker and a pacifist – she did not win. On 21st December 1953, Bernal was one of ten winners. His photograph was on the front page of *Pravda* and he was accurately described as 'a progressive scientist who wants the achievements of science to serve human progress and peace'.[96]

17

The Physical Basis of Life

Even in the darkest days of World War Two, the BBC adhered to Lord Reith's maxim of informing, educating and entertaining the public. In March 1942, as part of a series 'Science lifts the veil', Sir William Bragg interviewed Sage about 'The problem of the origin of life'. It had been Bragg who arranged for Bernal to give a series of lectures on 'The molecular architecture of biological systems' at the Royal Institution in 1938, and the broadcast was to some extent a summary of those talks. Bernal again referred to the gap between the molecular world studied by biochemists and the larger objects that could be seen under the microscope – the gap in which most structures important for life exist. In addition to the ultracentrifuge and X-ray diffraction, there was by 1942 a new tool for exploring the gap: the electron microscope. Bernal explained how the Tobacco Mosaic Virus (TMV) that he studied by X-ray diffraction had now been visualized directly by electron microscopy (he tactfully omitted to mention that this work took place in Berlin).

Bragg asked Bernal whether viruses are alive or not. Chuckling, Bernal replied he would rather not say 'because my colleague Dr Pirie, who has done so much of this work on viruses and has written a cutting essay on the meaninglessness of the term "life" would never let me hear the end of it'.[1] What the acerbic Pirie wrote was:

We have now examined destructively the various qualities which might be used to define the word 'life' and we have found that they are individually inadequate for even an approximate definition...combinations of two or three qualities, though they might be drawn up to exclude all obviously non-living systems, will also exclude some which are, if not typically living, at least generally included in that category.

Until a valid definition has been framed it seems prudent to avoid the use of the word 'life' in any discussion about border-line systems and to refrain from saying that certain observations on a system have proved that it is or is not 'alive'.[2]

Instead of offering Bragg a definition, Bernal preferred to quote Engels, one of his favourite philosophers of science, as saying that 'Life is the mode of action of proteins' – which had become the credo for his own research programme.

Beginning in 1929, Astbury in Leeds had made pioneering X-ray studies of wool in its natural and stretched states, which he christened the α-and β-forms. He surmised that in its unstretched α-form, the wool protein fibre was folded, and that this property was shared by other keratins such as hair, feather, and even the porcupine quill. From fuzzy X-ray photographs of fibrous proteins, Astbury observed that the diffraction pattern repeated itself every 5.15 Å along the longitudinal axis of α-keratin fibres. He emphasized this fact in a letter to Sage as early as February 1931: 'The important fact is that the main periodicity of alpha-hair is about 5.15 Å.'[3] 5.15 Å was the distance that would dominate thinking about protein structure for the next two decades.

For the first year or so, Astbury worried about how proteins that were chemically diverse could adopt an identical physical form, as revealed by X-ray diffraction patterns. This was why he urged Bernal, 'night and day, to get me the dimensions of the *molecules* of glycine, alanine, leucine, glutamic acid and arginine'.[4] He wanted to know the exact sizes of the constituent amino acid residues so that he could understand how they would fit together in an α-chain. But by the time he published some pictures of the structure of feathers in 1932, Astbury was more relaxed. He wrote to Sage:

I am no more worried about the problem of why proteins can have such varying chemical analysis, and yet be the same thing and give the same X-ray photos. It seems to me that this is the first definite proof that proteins are really and truly gigantic molecules built to patterns of heroic proportions. I can see now quite clearly the structural basis of life – I couldn't see it from silk or wool, the pattern was (apparently) too small – out of all the possible permutations of the protein chain, it seems to me, now that we have demonstrated the ease with which even the patterned permutations are built, then all the other permutations are not only equally possible, but also more probable. Anything and everything can happen – in fact, almost everything <u>has</u> happened.[5]

In his 1947 Guthrie lecture delivered to the Physical Society in London, Bernal reflected on how his work, Astbury's, and that of Hopkins' Dunn Laboratory had reinforced Engels' dictum about proteins being the essence of life. He claimed that scientific advances had made this hypothesis more precise, but his exposition of the subject was almost as speculative as Astbury's breathless letter had been.

So many of the chemical reactions occurring in living systems have been shown to be catalytic processes occurring isothermally on the surface of specific proteins, referred to as enzymes, that it seems fairly safe to assume that all are of this nature and that the proteins are the necessary basis for carrying out the processes that we call life. Now although since the great work of Fischer we know that the proteins consist of various combinations of some twenty amino acids, we still do not know the precise structure of any of them. But we do know that they have a precise structure, and we have a reasonable hope of determining it in the not so very distant future. It is perhaps significant that though the number of different proteins may be counted in tens of millions, this represents an insignificant proportion of the possible combination of twenty amino acids. The most likely explanation is that certain sub-units containing the same amino acids in the same order must occur over and over again.[6]

The eagle-eyed Pirie still managed to object to the vital role that Sage seemed to grant proteins as a force in the evolution of life. Pirie wrote 'I think proteins are only a necessary part of present-day life because they work better, as matches work better than flint and steel. There is no reason to think of them as original.'[7] Bernal hastened to agree that there must have been 'proto-proteins with a smaller number and simpler arrangement of amino acids . . . that did inefficiently some, but just enough, of the things proteins do today'. Regardless of Pirie's point, Bernal maintained that the present day 'very sophisticated and highly differentiated' protein molecules governed the processes of life. When the lecture was subsequently published, Pirie dismissed it as 'unsatisfactory', in a review titled 'Vital blarney'. He did say, in Sage's defence, that some had compared it to Schrödinger's short book *What is Life?* but it was not as bad as that! Tongue-in-cheek, he advised Sage to stick to his lasts of crystallography, politics, building, bomb-damage, ethics, history etc., for which he needed as many arms as Briareus.* Pirie thought Sage wrote with such authority and conviction on those subjects that 'we must put down to pure Irish whimsy his decision to write a book on life'.[8]

While Astbury and Bernal trusted that the structure of proteins would emerge over time from X-ray diffraction studies of these large, complicated molecules, Linus Pauling at Caltech took the opposite tack that it was first necessary to establish as much detail as possible about the molecular structure of the constituent amino acids and in particular to understand how they linked together. Coming to X-ray crystallography from a chemistry background, Pauling had also embraced quantum theory, and by the late 1930s was the world's leading authority on chemical bonds. In 1937 he recruited a research fellow from the Rockefeller Institute, Robert Corey, to come to work with him in California; they decided to launch a systematic attack on the molecular structure of amino acids and small peptide molecules by X-ray diffraction. When Pauling reviewed the published literature on the subject, the only worthwhile paper he could find was Bernal's from 1931. In that short publication, Sage had promised 'a detailed account of the crystallographic investigation with a discussion of its chemical implications will be published at a later date'[9] – which it was by Corey in 1938!

---

* Briareus, or Aegaeon, in Greek mythology, was one of the three hundred-armed, fifty-headed Hecatoncheires (sons of Poseidon and Gaea).

One of the substances that Bernal studied in 1931, at Astbury's behest, was the ring-shaped diketopiperazine molecule. He had concluded, correctly, that diketopiperazine is 'built from centro-symmetrical, almost flat, hexagonal molecules linked together in ribbons by their residual electrical forces'.[10] Corey confirmed Bernal's finding that the molecule was indeed flat, and then extended the earlier work by accurately determining the lengths and angles of the inter-atomic bonds. He went on to establish that the C–N peptide bond in all the structures he analysed was planar – the atoms adjacent to peptides bonds had to lie in the same plane, a crucial constraint on any protein structure.[11]

Pauling's intention had been to use his 'knowledge of structural chemistry to predict the dimensions and other properties of a polypeptide chain and then to examine possible conformations of the chain, to find one that would agree with the X-ray diffraction data'.[12] Despite many hours of strenuous thought, the solution eluded Pauling until he was laid low by sinusitis, while a visiting professor to Oxford in March 1948. Bored with reading detective stories, he asked his wife for a pencil, a piece of paper and a ruler. He set out to sketch a polypeptide chain that would be spiral in shape, yet would show no rotation on either side of a peptide bond. The whole structure would be stabilized by hydrogen bonds on the outside of the spiral. Pauling rolled his paper up and found that these conditions would all be met by a spiral containing about 3.7 amino acid residues per twist, in a pattern that repeated every 5.4 Å. The idea of a non-integral pattern was novel, but not impossible: the larger objection lay in the miniscule discrepancy between 5.4 Å, and Astbury's well-established 5.1 Å.

Work on protein structure in the British schools of X-ray crystallography was a dispiriting business in the late 1940s. At Oxford, the wartime work on penicillin had diverted Dorothy Hodgkin away from insulin; her next pick was the vitamin B12 molecule – medically important and much smaller than insulin. At Birkbeck, Bernal had brought Carlisle a tube containing several hundred crystals of ribonuclease from a Rockefeller chemist, Moses Kunitz, who had been the first to crystallize the enzyme. The enzyme was recovered from the pancreas of cows and appeared to be chemically stable and rather small (molecular weight 13,000), making it a promising candidate for X-ray analysis. As it turned out, Carlisle and his group would take twenty years to obtain the definitive structure of ribonuclease.[13] Even at Cambridge, the redoubtable Perutz was reluctantly facing 'the stark truth that the years of tedious labour, the many nights of interrupted sleep and the appalling strain of measuring the intensities of thousands of little black spots by eye had brought me no nearer to the solution of the structure of haemoglobin, and that I wasted some of the best years of my life trying to solve a seemingly insoluble problem'.[14]

In 1949, Perutz did find evidence of an Astbury-type 5.1 Å repeat in crystals of horse haemoglobin which led him to conclude 'rashly that the structure of haemoglobin consisted of a set of close-packed, α-keratin-like polypeptide chains'.[15] His colleague, John Kendrew, who had just started studying the smaller myoglobin molecule from horse muscle, soon made the same interpretation of that protein. Perutz and Kendrew were the only two permanent members of the MRC Unit at the Cavendish Laboratory, where Sir Lawrence Bragg was still the chief. One day Bragg arrived in their lab 'armed with a broomstick into which he had hammered a helical pattern of nails repeating at intervals of 5.1 cm along its axis, representing what he suspected was the repeat of amino acid residues along the fibre axis of α-keratin'.[16] Kendrew and Perutz attempted to build models, with either two, three or four amino acid residues per turn of the helix, but none was a good fit. Even without knowing Corey's finding that the peptide bond was always planar, the angles of the bonds in their models seemed to be under strain. Bragg remained optimistic that they were on the verge of a breakthrough and he wrote to Sage about it:

Perutz, Kendrew and I have been rather excited lately because we feel we are getting somewhere with the nature of the actual protein chain. . . . If we accept Perutz's results about the spacings along the chains and the distances between them, it implies that we have got to fit 3 amino acid residues per 5 Å of length, and the possibilities boil down to very few. . . Incidentally, Perutz has tried to make models of the Astbury chain, and they do not seem to work too well.[17]

When the Cambridge group eventually published the inconclusive results of their modelling work, Pauling read the paper and immediately saw its flaws. Bragg's group had not been restrictive enough in applying modern chemical concepts, and he now felt the time had come to publish his own model even though he had no experimental data of his own to support it. He alerted Bernal to the new model in a letter dated 13th June 1951:

Have you seen the series of 8 papers that Professor Corey and I have got out on the structure of proteins? They are in the April and May issues of the Proceedings of the National Academy of Sciences. I think that there is very little doubt about the correctness of these structures. So far we have not found any configurations of polypeptide chains in proteins other than those described in these papers.[18]

Sage was not entirely convinced.

I have read your papers with Corey with the greatest interest and I certainly think that you have made the point that it is not necessary that the residues should follow each other along the chain with any regular crystallographic repeats. On the other hand, I am rather doubtful on the basis of Carlisle's work here, that any structure with as many as 3, let alone 3.7, residues per turn can be fitted into the data for some crystalline proteins such as ribonuclease and chymotrypsin. The number we get by estimation of the number of chains and the periodicities along the chain, in this case about 5.4 Å, indicates a figure much more like 2.[19]

To Max Perutz, who had been so frustrated by trying to build models for Bragg that would comply with Astbury's concept of α-keratin, Pauling's announcement of his α-helix with a fractional number of amino acids per complete turn was revelatory. He was 'thunderstruck by Pauling and Corey's paper. In contrast to Kendrew's and my helices, theirs was free of strain ... the structure looked dead right.'[20] But there were no experimental data to support it. Perutz thought about the Pauling model in terms of a spiral staircase with each amino acid residue as a separate step. Each step would be 1.5 Å high and 'according to diffraction theory, this regular repeat should give rise to a strong X-ray reflection of 1.5 Å spacing from planes perpendicular to the fibre axis.'[21] Why had no one, Astbury in particular, ever seen these reflections? The answer came in a flash – Astbury always orientated his protein fibres with their long axis perpendicular to the X-ray beam (in fact, an oblique angle was required) and his flat plate camera had too narrow an aperture to capture the image.

In mad excitement, I cycled back to the lab and looked for a horse hair that I had kept tucked away in a drawer. I stuck it on a goniometer head at an angle of 31° to the incident X-ray beam; instead of Astbury's flat plate camera I put a cylinderical film around it that would catch all reflections with Bragg angles of up to 85°.[22]

After exposing the horse hair in the X-ray beam for about two hours, Perutz developed the film, with 'his heart in his mouth', and there were the lines he predicted. A week after Bernal had written his letter expressing reservations to Pauling, *Nature* published a letter from Perutz offering the first experimental substantiation of the α-helix.[23] In this letter, Perutz included some preliminary results showing that even the globular haemoglobin molecule contained stretches of α-helix.

Perutz continued to worry about the discrepancy between Astbury's 5.1 Å and Pauling's 5.4 Å. The answer was supplied by his PhD student, Francis Crick, in 1952 when he came to the lab 'with two rubber tubes around which he had pinned corks with a helical repeat of 3.6 corks per turn and a pitch of 5.4 cm. He showed me that the two tubes could be wound around each other to make a double helix such that the corks neatly interlocked. This shortened the pitch of the individual chains, when projected onto the fibre axis, from 5.4 to 5.1 cm, as required by the X-ray pattern of α-keratin.'[24] In 1952, Crick referred to this arrangement as a 'coiled coil'[25] – the double helix would be next year's model.

In the summer of 1951, there was a meeting of the leading British protein researchers at the Cavendish. Crick was going to make his first presentation in such exalted company and was understandably nervous. His supervisor, Perutz, spoke before him and described the latest findings on haemoglobin. When Bernal rose to comment on Perutz's talk, Crick was astonished by his mild manner:

I regarded Bernal as a genius. For some reason I had acquired the idea that all geniuses behaved badly. I was therefore surprised to hear him praise Perutz in the most genial way for his courage in undertaking such a difficult and, at that time, unprecedented task and for his thoroughness and persistence in carrying it through. Only then did Bernal venture to express, in the nicest possible way, some reservations.[26]

When Crick did speak, his contribution was daring. His theme 'broadly speaking, was that they [the X-ray crystallographers] were all wasting their time and that...almost all the methods they were pursuing had no chance of success'.[27] The barrier to progress that Crick analysed more rigorously than some of his teachers was the old problem of the phases of the diffracted X-rays. This is a complicated mathematical concept, but a crude analogy would be with setting the correct focus of a light microscope. The spots in an X-ray diffraction pattern gives some measure of intensity, but without knowledge of the peaks and troughs of the reflected X-ray waves, Crick realized that no worthwhile three-dimensional representation of protein molecules would ever be possible. A solution to the phase problem had been successfully applied in the 1930s to solve the relatively simple structure of an organic dye by introducing a heavy atom, nickel, into its crystal. The principle of what became known as *isomorphous replacement* is that by adding a heavy atom (which gives a strong diffraction) to an identical position in all unit cells of a crystal, a measurable change will be produced in the diffraction pattern. Comparison of this new heavy atom pattern with that of the native crystal allows the phase of each spot to be determined mathematically: the added heavy atom will make each spot in the pattern stronger or weaker depending on phase.

Bernal had raised the possibility of applying the isomorphous replacement method to protein structure in his 1939 talk at the Royal Institution:

Unfortunately, however, direct analysis of these X-ray photographs [of protein crystals] is rendered impossible by the fact that we can never know the phases of the reflections corresponding to the different spots. The ambiguity introduced in this way can only be removed by some physical artifice, such as the introduction of a heavy atom or the observation of intensity changes on dehydration, which have not hitherto been carried out in practice.[28]

Crick, despite his junior status, was more forceful at the 1951 Cavendish meeting. He had confided in Kendrew what he was going to say, and Kendrew suggested that he title his talk 'What mad pursuit', which he did.

Bragg was furious. Here was this newcomer telling experienced X-ray crystallographers, including Bragg himself, who had founded the subject and been in the forefront of it for almost forty years, that what they were doing was most unlikely to lead to any useful result. The fact that I clearly understood the theory of the subject and indeed was apt to be unduly loquacious about it did not help.[29]

At the time, Crick felt that Bernal was not paying attention, but in later years he found that Bernal was the only one to remember that he had given his colleagues 'a very necessary jolt' in the right direction. A few months later, the leading British protein investigators decided to invite Pauling to London to defend the α-helix model to all at a Royal Society meeting. The date was set for 1st May 1952, but the guest of honour was prevented from attending by the US State Department, who refused to grant him a passport because they believed him to be a communist. In his introductory talk as chairman of the meeting, Astbury clung tenaciously to the primacy of his 5.1 Å repeat distance and was concerned that the 'Pauling–Corey spiral' failed to conform to this experimental fact. A pair of papers from Caltech followed, but Pauling's assistant, Eddie Hughes, who delivered the second one in Pauling's stead was flustered by lack of preparation and the grandeur of the venue; for the rest of the afternoon, he had to endure British scientists 'telling us what was wrong'[30] with Pauling's model. Bernal, in his talk,[31] expressed some scepticism about Pauling's claim 'that purely chemical considerations do, in the case of proteins, limit almost to one model the possible configuration of the protein chain. It can only be said at this stage that however well this model can account for the data for fibrous proteins – natural and synthetic – it has not yet been fitted satisfactorily to any globular protein.' Whatever their reservations about Pauling's model of protein structure, the British scientists were unanimous in their resentment that he had been barred from coming to England, and Bernal sent a letter of protest to the State Department signed by thirty other scientists.

In time, Sage came to view Pauling's irrational (non-integer) α-helix as a revolutionary event in the field of molecular biology, and thought that the only thing wrong with the hypothesis was the unstated implication that 'the α-helix was an important structural feature of *all* globular proteins. If it had been stated as *some* globular proteins, it would have been correct as well as illuminating.'[32] Again Sage gave credit to Crick for pointing out the notion he shared with most other crystallographers in the early 1950s – that globular proteins consisted of rods of polypeptides arranged parallel to each other – was demonstrably false. Sage gave his own perspective on these historical developments in a letter to Kendrew towards the end of his life.

The term 'Molecular Biology' was introduced by W.T. Astbury, the founder of protein analysis, for his own X-ray studies of wool structure. His genius, going far ahead of his observations, enabled him to divine – and to divine correctly – the basic structure of a linear polymer, thus leading on to the structures of all proteins, globular and chain alike, and those of the helices of nucleic acids. This is the keystone of the Crick–Watson discovery. Astbury was prevented from reaching this degree of comprehension by his obstinate adherence to two rather than three-dimensional models. The Astbury fold is now forgotten in favour of the Pauling alpha-helix.

This invasion of three-dimensional thinking into molecular structure was to do to biology what Pasteur had done in founding stereochemistry. Both are examples of the ultimate simplification of the complication of biological structures in terms of metrical distances and angles, of nature copying art, the molecular hypothesis.[33]

Crick was lured away from the exacting tedium of protein crystallography by Kendrew's post-doctoral student, Jim Watson, to build models of DNA. It was left to Perutz to exploit the isomorphous replacement method. When Bernal had first suggested the idea of introducing a heavy atom into proteins for the purpose of X-ray analysis, he had not bothered to calculate whether it would have a measurable effect in such large molecules. There was also the practical difficulty of trying to grow crystals with the added heavy atom. Sage had suggested to Dorothy Hodgkin in 1935 that she substitute cadmium for zinc in her insulin crystals[34] – but she was unable to obtain any crystals at all. Even if she had, she would have been disappointed because cadmium was not heavy enough to make a measurable difference. Perutz made a crucial observation:

A chance experiment made me realize that in the diffraction pattern of haemoglobin, the scattering contributions of most of the atoms were extinguished by interference. So that for any one reflection fewer than one per cent of the electrons contributed. Substitution with heavy atoms to solve the phase problem was nothing new, but we all thought one would never be able to measure the contribution of the heavy atom among the thousands of light atoms in the protein. But I measured the fraction of the incident beam that is scattered by a haemoglobin crystal, and this measurement led me to realize that most of the scattering contributions of light atoms were extinguished by interference; but if I had a heavy atom, all its electrons would be concentrated at a point and they would all scatter in phase, and so they would make a measurable contribution.[35]

Then Perutz had a stroke of luck. In the spring of 1953 he received reprints of a paper from a researcher at Harvard, Austin Riggs, who was studying sickle cell anaemia. Riggs had introduced mercury atoms into haemoglobin and found that it made virtually no difference to its oxygen carrying capacity: Perutz immediately 'realized that attachment of the mercury atom must leave the structure intact'. He now had his heavy atom and a way of incorporating it into haemoglobin. The experimental work was completed in about a month. Perutz demonstrated 'that attaching two mercury atoms to a molecule of haemoglobin would produce subtle differences in the intensities of the diffracted rays, and from these differences [he] was able to derive the positions of the mercury atoms and then the phases of one set of reflections in haemoglobin. This really was the discovery which opened the whole field of protein structure.'[36] Unlike Watson and Crick with the double helix, Perutz did not feel the breath of scientific rivals on his neck and carefully wrote a set of full-length papers for the *Proceedings of the Royal Society*. He felt 'there was not the remotest possibility of anybody else doing the same thing: there were so few crystallographers around and the astonishing thing was that when the papers appeared, nobody else had a go.'[37]

Perutz had succeeded in obtaining the first accurate picture of the haemoglobin molecule, but it was only a two-dimensional image: the result 'was a triumph but unfortunately it was totally uninterpretable'.[38] Such a complex molecule gives a tangle of overlapping elements when projected onto a plane. It would take Perutz several more years of innovative effort before the first three-dimensional model of haemoglobin emerged. Kendrew, using analogous techniques for the simpler myoglobin molecule, achieved the distinction of the first detailed protein structure in 1958. They were jointly honoured with the Nobel Prize for chemistry in 1962. They shared the platform with Crick, Watson and Maurice Wilkins who were in Stockholm to collect their medicine or physiology prizes.

Sage was delighted by their accolades and does not seem to have been troubled by the slightest prick of envy. Perutz wrote to him:

Dear Sage,

I was touched by your good wishes, and not only because it was you who started me off, but because of the many occasions when your visits filled me with fresh enthusiasms and determination to carry on. I wish that you who opened up the field could also have had the thrill of solving the first structure, and I always regard with great admiration your gracious and genuine pleasure in seeing John and me doing the job, and now getting this tremendous reward for it.[39]

The remainder of the letter was taken up with a novel observation made by his PhD student, Hilary Muirhead, of a subtle change in the configuration of human haemoglobin when it combined with oxygen – news which Perutz found as exciting as the Nobel Prize itself.

Kendrew wrote an equally affectionate letter to Sage.

...I'm always grateful that it was you, during the war, who more than anyone awoke biological interests in a chemist tired of chemistry: and as to the bomb in the jungle, I've been dining out ever since on the story... Anyway, after being a renegade chemist all these years I now seem to be a respectable one once more and as to you, it seems to me that you've fathered five Nobel Prizes this year alone. Yours ever, John Kendrew[40]

Crick, only fifteen years younger than Sage, revealed his awe of Bernal's stature by telling him that 'Watson and I have always thought of you as our scientific "grandfather", fortunately perennially young.'[41]

The revolutionary discoveries that emerged from the MRC Unit for Molecular Biology were the fruits of creative individuals and small groups toiling in cramped and shabby conditions. When a young South African physicist wishing to study biomolecules by X-ray crystallography came to Cambridge in 1949 on an 1851 Exhibition Scholarship, Bragg told him that there was no room in the Unit. To this day, Aaron Klug does not know whether the Unit was really full, or whether Bragg was just disappointed by the previous research student from South Africa. Instead Klug 'finished up doing a PhD in a very dull subject – phase transitions in steel – a problem left over from the war'.[42] While the subject was not what Klug would have chosen, it proved to be invaluable experience for his future. He developed mathematical techniques and physical models for the kinetics of phase changes in solids. This work led his supervisor to recommend Klug to F.J.W. Roughton, the Professor of Colloid Science, who was interested in the diffusion of oxygen into red blood cells and its reaction with haemoglobin. Klug saw this simultaneous diffusion–chemical reaction in terms of a phase change in haemoglobin, and he developed the mathematical equations to describe its kinetics. After about a year working with Roughton, Klug successfully applied for a Nuffield research fellowship, which brought him to Birkbeck College and Bernal at the end of 1953.

Klug and his Nuffield research assistant joined Carlisle's team working on the enzyme, ribonuclease. This was proving to be an endlessly challenging task, made more difficult by the fact that Carlisle was labouring under two misapprehensions. One, due largely to Bernal, was that the phase problem might be avoided by placing more reliance on the strong X-ray reflections (which Bernal called *constellations*) that resulted from the most salient and regular features of a protein molecule. Bernal had aired this approach at the 1952 Royal Society meeting, suggesting that it could provide a shortcut to seeing the essential features of a protein structure. In the middle of a mathematical paper, he threw in a couplet from Donne's elegy on an ugly woman to illustrate his point:[43]

> *Though all her parts be not in their usual place*
> *She hath yet an Anagram of a good face*

Carlisle's second error was to assume that ribonuclease was predominantly an α-helix. Klug, fresh from Cambridge, had no doubt that isomorphous replacement was the only remedy to the phase problem and that no mathematical gimmick would solve the complex structures of proteins, with their thousands of atoms. On the question of α-helical features, Klug devised a mathematical search programme to analyse Carlisle's photographs of ribonuclease and concluded that the molecule did not contain any significant amounts of α-helix. Klug's quiet, unassuming manner cloaks a formidable intellect, which in his youth was accompanied by a precocious self-confidence. Carlisle refused to believe that this young upstart knew what he was talking about and so they parted company.

Klug was 'banished upstairs to the attic at 21 Torrington Square',[44] while Carlisle kept his research assistant. He found himself in the next room to Rosalind Franklin, who had moved to Birkbeck from King's College in March 1953. Her first task had been to write up her crucially important crystallographic work on DNA, but Bernal's intention was that she should switch to virus research, starting with Tobacco Mosaic Virus (TMV).[45] She had been deeply unhappy at King's and even though she was pleased to escape to Birkbeck, she still felt isolated. In a letter written in December 1953, she reflected on her move:

For myself, Birkbeck is an improvement on King's, as it couldn't fail to be. But the disadvantages of Bernal's group are obvious – a lot of narrow-mindedness, and obstruction directed especially at those who are not Party members. It's been very slow starting up... I'm starting X-ray work on the viruses (the old TMV to begin with).[46]

The appearance of Klug, who was pleasant and scientifically alert, transformed Rosalind's Birkbeck career – she now had someone she liked and trusted, working alongside her. Like Margot Heinemann, Rosalind was the product of a famous British girl's school and Newnham College. Both women were Jewish and similar in physique, but where Margot was self-confident and radical, Rosalind was shy and withdrawn. She was also immune to Bernal's predatory charm and disapproved of his promiscuous behaviour. Although Sage was now living with Margot and their baby daughter, Jane, he still used his flat at Torrington Square for quick liaisons. Sometimes his wife, Eileen, came to see Sage and there might be audible crying and swearing. When Rosalind moved to a new office on the second floor of No. 22 she could not fail to see various women come down the stairs from the flat and indicated her disgust to Klug.[47] But she and Sage soon developed a mutual respect for each other as scientists.

Rosalind Franklin impressed Klug as a brilliant experimenter. This did not just mean that she was deft with her fingers, but that she first planned methodically how she was going to proceed and then carried out her work with patience and dedication. In his Nobel lecture many years later, Klug stated: 'It was Rosalind Franklin who set me the example of tackling large and difficult problems.'[48] Both Franklin and Klug were new to virus work and the natural starting point for them was the earlier series of papers written by Sage and Fan. There was the earliest Cambridge paper, co-authored by Bawden and Pirie, that had first identified the nucleic acid component (RNA) of TMV and the 'quasi-regular' assembly of protein sub-units that constituted the virus particles. In their second paper, Bernal and Fankuchen described more fully a technique for orientating the virus particles and mounting them for X-ray exposures (which were as long as 400 hours).[49] These practical details would form the basis of Franklin's experiments, although she now had better X-ray tubes and cameras than Bernal and Fan used, and was able to obtain finer photographs with shorter exposure times.

The key difficulty remained the interpretation of the numerous spots obtained on the photographs. In 1937, Bernal struggled to fit the patterns he and Fan saw into a traditional crystal model. He wrote that 'normally, crystallinity presupposes an indefinite repetition of identical units in three-dimensional space. These [TMV] proteins appear not to possess this degree of regularity.'[50] In late 1952, an important breakthrough was made by Jim Watson in Cambridge. He was trying his hand at X-ray crystallography for the first time, after he and Crick had built a model of DNA that was so bad, Bragg ordered them to do something else. Again starting from the pre-war experiments of Bernal and Fankuchen and having 'pilfered'[51] their 1941 paper from the library, Watson took X-ray photographs of TMV and proposed that it was a helical structure.[52] He was able to reach this conclusion only because Crick and others had derived the mathematical theory of helical diffraction that predicted that a helical molecule would give rise to an X-shaped diffraction pattern. When Watson took his results to Birkbeck, Sage looked at the photographs and said, 'It [TMV] looks like a pineapple.'[53]

Klug applied himself to the helical nature of TMV and to the key question of the shape of the protein sub-units and how they were arranged together. Bernal showed a great interest in this: Watson's pictures were quite similar to those that he and Fan had obtained. In his photographs, Bernal had concentrated on a series of smeared lines, in which every third line appeared especially strong. He had wondered whether this resulted from a rotational pattern that repeated every 120 degrees. Now he would come up to Klug every few days and say: 'Tell me again, why isn't it a simple screw axis?'[54] Klug would explain the X-ray diffraction theory of helices to him in a physical way. 'He would grasp it physically, Bernal could do mathematics if he wanted to, he was just too busy. He took an interest and would come running up the stairs, every now and again, and say: "What's new?" I would never answer him, but under my breath say that "We're still struggling with what's old".'[55]

Looking back, Klug thinks that Bernal 'had all the right ideas about biomolecular research', but that as a chief he did not pay enough attention to details. This was probably inevitable given the multiplicity of his talents and his ubiquity. Anita Rimel would get very angry if anyone took Sage his mail; she once attacked Alan Mackay for doing this, saying, 'Don't you know he is not allowed to have his own letters, he only makes a mess of it and loses them.'[56] Lenton assumed the role of departmental accountant in addition to being the head technician. He collected about fifty invoices per month, for which Sage just signed the cheques without question. Lenton understood the Customs procedures for importing equipment. In July 1950, Bernal visited Berlin as an invited guest at the 250th anniversary celebrations of the German Academy of Science. He visited Katie Dornberger-Schiff in East Berlin and she agreed to send one of her goniometers to Birkbeck. Lenton normally took charge of importing equipment and was asked to step in by Anita, when the goniometer was impounded by Customs. He went to the airport office and found that Sage had filled out the Customs form: instead of writing 'No commercial value' he had entered the word 'Priceless'.

Sage was once asked whether he ran his lab on communist lines. He said he had advanced socially only as far as the state of feudalism so that people had to plough the Lord's land for half the time and for the other half, they could plough their own.[57] The dilapidated buildings in Torrington Square, crammed with workers from different departments, caused their own problems. Rosalind Franklin frequently wrote notes to Bernal[58] complaining about the pharmacy department pouring large quantities of ether down the sink, oblivious to the fire risk, and on another occasion flooding her laboratory on the first floor. Safety was not a priority – in one lab there were beakers used for brucine (a poisonous alkaloid like strychnine). There was a handwritten notice next to them: DO NOT USE FOR COFFEE.[59]

During the early 1950s, Sage carried out virtually no original work himself, but would occasionally show glimpses of his mastery of crystallography. One day he asked Klug for a microscope and mounted an inky blue crystal of azulene; Klug was amazed by the amount of information Sage extracted in this simple way. The crystals are diamond-shaped with one acute corner truncated: Sage thought that many crystallographers had misinterpreted the axis of symmetry, and he wrote a brief note to *Nature* pointing out their error.[60] Mackay, who was by now an assistant lecturer in the department and studying iron oxides, had a similar experience of Sage's astounding ability with a light microscope. 'He could look at the interference pattern from a crystal in polarized light, and it might look pinkish in one place and he would say "I can see the molecules lined up in a particular direction" – he inferred directly from the asymmetry of the optical scattering that's how molecules must be aligned.'[61]

Although his personal finances remained haphazard, Sage was adept at attracting grant money to his department. Franklin's original Turner and Newall Fellowship ended at the end of 1954, and Sage managed to secure funding from the Agricultural Research Council to pay her salary, purchase equipment and to provide salaries for two research workers. The first to arrive was John Finch, a shy young physicist from King's College, London, who wanted to make the transition to research with potential application to medicine. He was joined in July 1955 by Kenneth Holmes, freshly graduated from Cambridge, who wrote to Bernal for a research job because he did not think he would get a good enough degree to be taken on at the Cavendish. Rosalind took them both on as doctoral students, but as she had no official University of London status, Bernal was their nominal supervisor.

The money from the ARC could not change the rabbit warren layout of Torrington Square. Franklin wrote a note of despair to Sage reminding him that 'my desk and lab are on the fourth floor, my X-ray tube in the basement, and I am responsible for the work of four people distributed over the basement, first and second floors on two different staircases'.[62] To her, one obvious improvement would be to move Jim Jeffery and his cement group, but when she put this to him with her typical brusqueness, Jeffery instantly declined her offer. She could not understand why he was so unreasonable, and it was left to Klug to explain to her gently that Jeffery 'was here before you came along' and was not going to give up his territory.[63] Her group continued to expand steadily and grabbed small workspaces where they could. Close international ties were forged with two other centres working on TMV: Tübingen in Germany and Berkeley in California. Both labs provided Franklin with TMV material that she used to establish further fundamental details about the virus, but a problem arose with her British supplier, Bill Pirie.

Pirie, whom Klug came to regard as a professional sceptic, took exception to a paper by Franklin in which she, correctly, pointed out that infective TMV particles were all the same length and consisted of identical protein sub-units. Pirie could not accept such simple regularity and wrote a scalding letter to her.[64] He also refused to send any more TMV to Birkbeck. Franklin and Klug did not ask Bernal to intercede on their behalf with his querulous friend, but decided to grow their own TMV through the University's Botanical Unit. In the meantime, they were working with a TMV preparation from Berkeley in which mercury atoms were incorporated into the viral protein to make it more amenable to X-ray analysis. The Berkeley group using electron microscopy had shown that TMV could re-assemble itself, *in vitro*, from its component protein and RNA into biologically active virus particles (an experiment hailed in the press as creating life in a test tube).

Franklin acquired some new X-ray tubes from France, which enabled her to focus the beam down to very small dimensions while maintaining high spatial resolution. The Beaudouin tubes, which were difficult to use, were again housed in the basement, where condensation dripping from the pipes often caused Franklin to operate under an umbrella.[65] Despite working in these slum conditions, Franklin's Birkbeck group provided the most detailed picture yet of the ultrastructure of the rod-shaped virus: it was a hollow, knobbly, protein helix with a thread of RNA deeply embedded within it, probably following the line of the helix throughout the length of the virus particle.[66] These findings were presented at a landmark meeting in March 1956, one of a series sponsored by the Ciba Foundation, in London. It was a select international gathering of the world's leading virus researchers. Bernal did not attend, but Birkbeck was well represented by Franklin and Klug. At the meeting, Crick and Watson teamed up again to explore, with their trademark brilliance, the assumption that the amino acid sequence in the protein of progeny viruses is determined by the genetic specificity of the infecting virus, and not to any significant extent by the genetic machinery of the infected host cell. They asserted that there was no direct means of copying the protein subunits from one generation of virus to the next: the amino acid sequence was controlled by the molecular structure of the RNA of the infecting virus, expressed through a relatively simple code (they estimated that three consecutive bases in the RNA molecule would specify one amino acid in the viral protein coat).

Two weeks before the Ciba meeting, Crick and Watson had just published a paper in *Nature* attempting to answer the question 'Why are all viruses either rods or spheres?'[67] Starting with TMV, the most studied virus, they were struck by the regularity and symmetry of the protein sub-units bound together in a helix: 'This feature is the clue to the general principle which we can apply whenever, on the molecular level, a structure of a definite size and shape has to be built up from smaller units; namely, that the packing arrangements are likely to be repeated again and again – and hence the sub-units are likely to be related by symmetry elements'.[68] Were there corresponding sub-units that locked together in a regular way to form the protein shell of spherical viruses? Two early papers from Bernal suggested that there might be repeated symmetries for both tomato bushy stunt virus (TBSV) and turnip yellow mosaic virus (TYMV). Now there was evidence from Donald Caspar, an American friend of Watson's working in the MRC laboratory at the Cavendish, that TBSV showed icosahedral symmetry (a high degree of symmetry that approximates to a sphere), and that each spherical shell probably comprised sixty (or a multiple of sixty) sub-units. Crick and Watson pointed out that this was one of three symmetrical arrangements that would automatically form a spherical shell. The question now became 'how are the sub-units arranged?' Crick and Watson's analogy was to find identical shapes that could be fitted together to cover the surface of a tennis ball.

Although Caspar carried out his X-ray crystallography in Cambridge, the stimulus and the materials for it resulted from a visit to Birkbeck. He talked to Klug about spherical viruses and the two of them raided the laboratory refrigerator. There they found vials of TBSV and TYMV left over from Bernal's own experiments, many years before. They agreed that Caspar should take the tomato virus while Klug and his research student, John Finch, would work with the turnip virus. The turnip yellow virus that Klug chose had a larger unit cell than did tomato bushy stunt virus and proved harder to solve. Eventually, both spherical plant viruses were shown to have icosahedral symmetry – with 180 sub-units symmetrically packed into a regular polyhedron.

Franklin's group at Birkbeck was at the leading edge of biomolecular research as Bernal reminded their sponsor, the Agricultural Research Council. Writing to the ARC chairman, Lord Rothschild, Sage emphasized that the group's 'results which are beginning to show the precise relation of nucleic acid to the protein component are... at the very centre of interest of bio- logical structure analysis and are already beginning to tie up with the struc- ture of such components such as microsomes and chromosomes'.[69] As a result of Sage's intervention, the ARC (who had been niggardly in their support of Franklin) agreed to renew their grant for one more year. In an effort to secure future funding, Franklin took the novel step of applying to the US Public Health Service for support. Within months, she was rewarded with an annual grant of £10,000 – a sum so large that the London University Senate assumed it was to be spread over three years. If they had understood that the money was for one year, Klug was told that they would have refused the grant because it created unacceptable inequality between the different research groups at Birkbeck.[70] Until now all the structural research in England had been carried out on plant viruses: in her application to the US Public Health Service, Franklin indicated that she wished to venture into field of animal viruses. She had spent time at various US laboratories in the summer of 1956, and two of her colleagues in Berkeley offered her samples of the newly crystallized polio virus to study. She approached Bernal about this new work and he wrote to the Master of Birkbeck, Lockwood, for his permission in July 1957, pointing out that 'In view of the extremely small amounts of infective material with which she will be dealing, and the very careful precautions she will be taking, there could be no objection to the research being carried out.'[71]

Bernal was wrong in this assurance. Rosalind Franklin asked Stan Lenton to procure '20 lbs. of cotton wool, 20 gallons of formaldehyde and six empty biscuit tins'.[72] When he asked her what this was all for, he was told 'Live polio virus'. Although polio vaccination was available in England by this time, memories of summer polio epidemics were fresh, and the news that live polio virus was going to be brought into the dilapidated Birkbeck laboratories caused a great deal of alarm among the staff, especially those with children. There was also the presence of Werner Ehrenberg, the physicist who was crippled as a result of childhood polio, as a visible reminder of the danger. Bernal called a departmental meeting that lasted for four hours; although he thought the actual risk was negligible he arranged for the virus to be stored at the nearby London School of Hygiene and Tropical Medicine.

By this time, Franklin was seriously ill with ovarian cancer and had undergone surgery. She did start work with the polio crystals, but was frustrated because when she mounted them in capillary tubes for X-ray study, the crystals would rapidly disappear. The crystals were in a very dilute salt solution and Franklin came to the conclusion that the crystals were interacting with metal ions that leached from the glass of the capillary tube.[73] She wrote to glass specialists in Sheffield requesting neutral glass, free of any metal, but before this could be supplied she became too ill to work. She died in April 1958 at the age of thirty-seven, and Sage wrote a heartfelt obituary in *The Times*, calling 'her early and tragic death ... a great loss to science'. Drawing on his characteristic ability to make scientific subjects understandable to the layman, Bernal gave a masterly summary of her career. In a later obituary in *Nature*, he referred to the 'extreme clarity and perfection' of her work. At a time when there was little public awareness of DNA and no controversy about the discovery of its structure, Bernal thought it worthwhile to attempt to 'disentangle' her contribution to the work. He credited her with 'the technique of preparing and taking X-ray photographs of the two hydrated forms of deoxyribonucleic acid and by applying the methods of Patterson function analysis to show that the structure was best accounted for by a double spiral of nucleotides, in which the phosphorus atoms lay on the outside'.[74] Paying tribute to her qualities as a scientist and a human being, Sage wrote:

Her photographs are among the most beautiful X-ray photographs of any substance ever taken. Their excellence was the fruit of extreme care in preparation and mounting of the specimen as well as in the taking of the photographs. She did nearly all this work with her own hands. At the same time, she proved to be an admirable director of a research team and inspired those who worked with her to reach the same high standard. Her devotion to research showed itself at its finest in the last months of her life. Although stricken with an illness which she knew would be fatal, she continued to work right up to the end.[75]

Franklin's legacy to Birkbeck was the talented research group of Klug, Finch and Holmes who, thanks to her, were now financially secure for the next few

years. With the generous US funding, they were able to buy better X-ray sets
and a powerful centrifuge for spinning down virus particles into concentrated
solutions (Franklin's technique had been to hang the virus solutions from the
ceilings in bags and rely on evaporation and gravity to do their slow work).[76]
In California, scientists had succeeded in preparing better quality crystals of
polio virus and offered some to Klug. The offer came from Carlton Schwerdt
and when Klug accepted, Schwerdt said he and his wife were coming to
London and would bring the crystals with them. Patsy Schwerdt was an
attractive woman, 'one of these marvellous, bubbly, American extraverts
who could disarm anybody'.[77] On their arrival at Heathrow airport, Schwerdt
gave his wife the Dewar flask to carry. When she was asked by a Customs
Officer what she had in the flask, she said 'Some polio virus.' The Officer
responded in panic, 'You can't bring that in here.' Smiling demurely, she
reassured him that the contents were safe because they were only crystals, and
he waved her through!

Again the crystals were kept at the School of Hygiene and Tropical Medicine. Klug thought of an alternative to the glass capillary problem that
plagued Franklin, when she first attempted to work with polio crystals. He
noticed that researchers in Jeffery's group at Birkbeck enclosed cement pow-
ders in capillaries made of quartz to withstand high temperatures. He decided
to try quartz for the polio crystals and found that the crystals remained intact.
There was still resistance at Birkbeck to working on polio and the most
powerful rotating anode X-ray tube was at the Royal Institution, where Sir
Lawrence Bragg was now president. Klug decided that the best X-ray photographs would be obtained at the RI, but this meant carrying the virus crystals
across central London. Working with Finch, he mounted the crystals into
quartz capillaries, which were then placed on a platform and covered with a
dome. Quartz is tougher than glass, and thin glass tubes containing formalin
were also placed on the platform so that if the sealed container were dropped,
the glass would shatter and the formalin would kill any free virus. Klug
demonstrated this apparatus to the Chief Medical Officer who approved it.
Klug decided that the safest way to travel the short distance from Bloomsbury
to Piccadilly was on the Underground.

The Californian workers had observed that polio crystals started to deteriorate after an hour at room temperature, so Klug and Finch made sure that
theirs were always kept cold. They kept a jet of freezing dry air playing on the
crystal during the X-ray exposures of 20 hours or more so that the crystal
temperature never rose above 5°C. By this technique and with the use of the
rotating anode X-ray tube, they were rewarded with photographs of exquisite
detail, showing a greater degree of crystal perfection than had been previously
observed with any other virus. Klug took the photographs to show Sage whose

immediate reaction surprised him: 'These photographs are worth ten thousand pounds', he said. Klug then realized that Bernal needed to raise money constantly to keep the Biomolecular Laboratory running, and the photographs would be valuable tokens for that purpose. Finch and Klug published their findings in June 1959, announcing that the polio virus is constructed with icosahedral symmetry, (just like turnip yellow mosaic virus). In their 1956 paper, Crick and Watson had set out the advantage for the protein coat of a virus to be constructed from a large number of small protein molecules (the simpler the protein sub-unit, the less genetic coding information required to produce it). Finch and Klug now took this evolutionary argument a step further, suggesting that perhaps all spherical viruses would prove to have icosahedral symmetry. This was because an icosahedral arrangement 'allows the use of the greatest possible number, namely, 60, of identical structural units in building the framework' of the virus. Assuming the purpose of the protein coat is just to protect the genetic material within the virus, there is another way in which the icosahedral shape delivers the greatest bang for the virus's buck. Finch and Klug pointed out: 'If it is required to "enclose" a space around a point by a symmetrical arrangement of small identical units, it can be shown that the ratio of the number of sub-units to the volume enclosed is smallest if icosahedral symmetry is employed.'[78]

The icosahedron is one of five regular polyhedra,* described by Plato and sometimes known as the Platonic bodies. Despite their great antiquity, their shapes have never lost their fascination; in the twentieth century, their most prominent exponent was perhaps Buckminster Fuller – the self-taught, American designer, inventor and architect of the geodesic dome. In the late 1950s, Klug read a biography of Buckminster Fuller and wrote to him about the similarities between the icosahedral structure of viruses and geodesic domes. The next time he was in London, Buckminster Fuller visited Birkbeck and had a long conversation with Klug. Inspired by the American's thoughts, Klug applied the architectural principles to viral structure – a fusion of art and science that must have delighted Sage. In what has become a classic paper in molecular biology, Caspar and Klug wrote:

The solution we have found was, in fact, inspired by the geometrical principles applied by Buckminster Fuller in the construction of geodesic domes. The resemblance of the designs of geodesic domes to icosahedral viruses had attracted our attention at the time of the poliomyelitis work. Fuller has pioneered in the development of a physically orientated geometry based on the principles of efficient design. Considering the structure of the virus shells in terms of these principles, we have found that with plausible assumptions on the degree of quasi-equivalence required, there is only one

---

* A polyhedron is any solid shape bounded by plane or flat surfaces

general way in which iso-dimensional shells may be constructed from a large number of identical protein sub-units, and this necessarily leads to icosahedral symmetry. Moreover, virus sub-units organized on this scheme would have the property of self-assembly into a shell of definite size.

The basic assumption is that the shell is held together by the same type of bonds throughout, but that these bonds may be deformed in slightly different ways in the different, non-symmetry related environments. Molecular structures are not built to conform to exact mathematical concepts, but, rather, to satisfy the condition that the system be in a minimum energy configuration.[79]

The Torrington Square houses were meant to provide temporary accommodation for about five years, but the crystallography group would be trapped there for nearly twenty. More than a decade after any bombs had fallen on London, the war's greatest expert on structural damage was in receipt of the following message from the Clerk of Birkbeck College: 'I feel sure that you will be relieved to learn that there are no immediate prospects of the spontaneous collapse of the northern external wall of 22 Torrington Sq.'[80] Bernal first wrote to John Lockwood, Master of Birkbeck, in 1951 suggesting that X-ray crystallography be spun off from physics as a separate department. Five years later, he was still pressing the point, with no success; he also wanted to set up a separate department of computing under Booth. He pointed out to Lockwood that 'the very existence of crystallography teaching and research [in the University of London] is dependent on me personally'.[81] Sage was not seeking to magnify his own importance, but warning the Master that crystallography and computing were vital support services for other branches of science and if they were not formally organized, there could be a resulting financial burden on Birkbeck.

Faster progress was made in Cambridge, the country's other major molecular biology centre, where the laboratories were as scattered and poorly housed as at Birkbeck. The Medical Research Council was persuaded by the remarkable accomplishments of Watson and Crick, Perutz and Kendrew to build a new facility, away from the mediaeval colleges in the heart of the city. The elements of X-ray crystallography, electron microscopy, biochemistry and virology were to be housed in new purpose-built laboratories, under one roof. The MRC Laboratory of Molecular Biology opened in 1962 under Perutz's chairmanship. The MRC offered Klug and his Birkbeck virology group space in the new Cambridge facility. The American grant that Franklin had secured for them in 1957 ran out in 1961. The move was supported by Bernal, although as the pioneer in the field of virus structure, he must have been sad to see them go. Klug, who went on to win the Nobel Prize for Chemistry in 1982 and to become President of the Royal Society, still regards Bernal as the godfather of the MRC Laboratory of Molecular Biology and the man who virtually invented the subject.

18

History and the Origins of Life

Bernal's friends were among the most important science writers of their time. Restricting the group to those who worked in England, and leaving aside C.P. Snow and J.G. Crowther who lived by their pens, they were remarkable for the range, quality and volume of their collective output. Haldane inherited H.G. Wells' mantle as the best popular writer about science, but even he could not match the sales of Lancelot Hogben whose *Mathematics for the Million: A Popular Self-Educator* is estimated to have sold over half a million copies during its four editions.[1] The doyen of the set was Joseph Needham, who abandoned his own career as an embryologist during the Second World War and devoted the remainder of his life to a landmark study of China, concentrating on the history of scientific development and the influence played by Chinese religion, politics and customs. Over a period of forty years, Needham published successive volumes of *Science and Civilization in China*, the early numbers of which were eagerly read, and often reviewed, by Sage. Needham came to believe that the predominance of Chinese science and technology for fifteen hundred years and its subsequent eclipse by European science from the seventeenth century onwards could be understood only in terms of differences between the social and economic systems of China and the West – an historical approach stimulated by his conversations with Bernal in Cambridge before the war.[2]

The first volume of Needham's monumental work appeared in 1954, coinciding with Bernal's own *Science in History*. Bernal's was also an encyclopaedic book, in which he examined the interplay of science and society from prehistoric man to the present; it had its origins in a series of lectures on 'Science in social history' that he had given in 1948 at Ruskin College, Oxford. He started by considering the character of science and its emergence from evolving techniques such as hunting, agriculture, and pottery – 'the mystery of the craftsmen' – and from theory such as 'the lore of the priest'.[3] The first five hundred pages were taken up with the development of science from the Stone Age through the early centres of commercial and cultural activity such as Babylon, India and Egypt, to ancient Greece, and then back to the Middle East, where during the barbarian age of Europe, new discoveries were made in 'a brilliant synthesis under the banner of Islam'. The new knowledge and techniques spread to mediaeval Europe, giving rise to what he saw as four major periods of advance: the Renaissance in Italy, the intellectual ferment leading to the Enlightenment (starting with Galileo and ending in Newton), the Industrial Revolution in Britain and the Revolution in Paris, and finally the accelerating pace of twentieth-century discoveries. At each stage of the story, Sage reminded his reader of the way in which social and economic change shaped science, and how science in turn altered human history.

The task of writing the book enthralled and, at times, threatened to overwhelm Sage. Much of it was dictated from his prodigious memory, and it was left to Francis Aprahamian to check and supply extra facts. The whole manuscript was rewritten half a dozen times, with Anita Rimel typing each new version and providing the index. Even for Sage, it was an ambitious undertaking that he justified in part as 'a first attempt to sketch out the field, if only to stimulate, through its omissions and errors, others more leisured and better qualified to produce a more authoritative picture'.[4] He did think though that his experience as a busy scientist, who had participated in some critically important work, gave him an advantage over a professional historian. Klug remembers how consumed Sage was by the preparation of the book – a project that he regarded as equal in importance to any of the experimental research going on at Birkbeck at the time.[5]

The first part of the book, in addition to being an historical account of science, was meant to buttress the Marxist view of the world that would then be used in a prescriptive way in the second part. Much of this was material, familiar from his previous writings, on the impending divorce of science from worn-out capitalism and the hope of a happier second marriage to socialism. The planning of science would go hand in hand with the central control of society, to the mutual benefit of both. In 1954, he still stoutly supported the baseless ideas of Lysenko (who would enjoy the enthusiastic patronage of Khrushchev in the USSR for another decade) against the genetic theories of Mendel. As details of the genetic code became irrefutable facts in the late 1950s, Bernal became more interested in the molecular approach to genetics and evolution, and Lysenko's name disappeared from later editions of the book.

During the four years between the first and second editions, Khrushchev's denunciation of Stalin at the twentieth congress of the Soviet communist party meant that party followers world-wide had to revise their outlooks. This adjustment was taken seriously by British communists, who also had to come to terms with events in Hungary. As part of the cosmetic repairs, Beria (the despicable chief of the NKVD who was executed within months of Stalin's death) soon had his name expunged from official Soviet history, being replaced by an entry on the Bering Sea. Bernal was visited at Birkbeck by

N.V. Belov, an old friend, who was Professor of Crystallography at Gorki University. Bernal brought Belov to his office to meet some of his younger colleagues. Belov's eye was caught by the Soviet encyclopaedia that Sage had on his shelves. Reaching for the volume containing BE, Belov remarked, 'There have been some changes.' Turning the pages, he smiled and said 'Ah, Bernal, he is still all right!'[6]

By 1965, when the third edition of *Science in History* appeared, Sage had to rewrite the chapters on 'Science in our time' to reflect the revolution in molecular biology, the rapid developments in electronics and computing, and the advent of the Space Age. An optimistic tone prevailed, based on the past successes of science which he hoped would now be brought to the peoples emerging from colonial rule. Yet he was concerned that the benefits of science were unevenly spread, and that there was still widespread hunger in the world because underdeveloped countries depended on subsistence agriculture, without access to modern techniques or chemical fertilizers. In his new preface, Sage wrote:

Actually the differences between the standards of living of the peoples in the developed and the under-developed world is not yet diminishing: it is increasing in a way that seems bound to lead to a crisis, and there is always the danger that a crisis of this sort might itself set off a first world nuclear war. This crisis can and must be avoided, but it can be avoided only by the efforts of the peoples themselves of all countries. For that they must get the necessary education and find the capital to build themselves a scientific and industrial complex which can provide for their needs.[7]

Just three years later, when the final, illustrated, edition came out, his mood was much more pessimistic. Far from beginning to narrow, he saw the gap between rich and poor nations widening even more.

While science is playing a larger and larger part in the advanced industrial countries, it is stagnant or even receding in those parts of the world which contain the bulk of its population. The effect of this is to bring about for the first time the possibility that humanity will extinguish itself by war or famine. Science, as it is now being used, contributes to making such a horrifying prospect not only possible but almost certain, and up till now there has been little evidence of factors that will cause this process to reverse. This vast prospect of Nemesis, however imminent, has caused little alarm and produced virtually no efforts to deal with it. It would seem that there is a universal tacit conspiracy to avoid thinking about it by those responsible for creating the situation in the advanced countries, and the victims' complaints are met with indifference and repression.[8]

These words were written at the height of the Vietnam War, and Bernal placed most of the blame for science losing its way in the world on the USA. With their calm discussions of 'megadeaths' and 'overkill', the 'men of Big

Science are being reduced to the worst kind of savage imaginable. Moreover, behind them lies a population whose values have been mentally corrupted by the policy and ideology of anti-communism.[9] There was a second Industrial Revolution at hand that was based largely on electronics and automation, and a few American corporations were threatening to gain control of the global economy by their mastery of these developments. He could not see how this American infiltration could be arrested, especially by the 'old capitalist powers, such as England, France and Germany... on account of their small size and outdated methods'.[10]

It is now evident that the real source of wealth lies no longer in raw materials, the labour force or machines, but in having a scientific, educated, technological manpower base. Education has become the real wealth of the new age.[11]

How much more difficult it would be for countries of the Third World to establish their own autonomous industries. The post-colonial countries were in a race against the onset of famine; while they might receive some genuine aid from the socialist countries, Bernal thought that ideally they 'should rely on their own resources of materials and men. In other words, they will have to pull themselves up by their own boot-straps'.[12]

The sweep of *Science in History* was tremendous, and Sage realized that he had to compromise on the depth of his scholarship if the book was to be coherent. It grew from a single tome of 867 pages in 1954 to four volumes of 1,328 pages in the fourth edition, published in 1968. There remained one prehistoric question that was so intriguing he explored it separately – the origin of life. His first serious consideration of the topic came in the 1947 Guthrie lecture, referred to in the last chapter. In 1946, he had visited Princeton and talked to Einstein about the underlying unity, in terms of its biochemical processes, of life on Earth. As a result of their discussion, Sage came to the view that 'life involved another element, logically different from those occurring in physics at that time, by no means a mystical one, but an element of *history*. The phenomena of biology must be... contingent on events. In consequence, the unity of life is part of the history of life and, consequently, is involved in its origin'.[13]

The origin of life was a subject that had been opened up in the nineteenth century by Darwin, Pasteur and Thomas Huxley, but which remained essentially speculative and not the province of any particular branch of science. In other words, it was perfect for Sage. Claiming to be fully aware of his own inadequacy, he listed the attributes necessary to make any headway on the problem: the researcher would need 'to be at the same time a competent mathematician, physicist, and experienced organic chemist, he should have a very extensive knowledge of geology, geophysics and geochemistry and, besides all this, be absolutely at home in all biological disciplines'.[14] Other than Sage, J.B.S. Haldane was probably the scientist who came closest to satisfying these qualities, and it was he who had made a notable contribution to the subject in 1929. In a short article, he considered how a chemical environment might have arisen that would be conducive to the origin of life, and his essential thesis was encapsulated in three sentences: 'When ultra-violet light acts on a mixture of water, carbon dioxide and ammonia,' he wrote, 'a vast variety of organic substances are made, including sugars, and apparently some of the materials from which proteins are built up . . . Before the origin of life they must have accumulated until the primitive oceans reached the consistency of hot, dilute, soup . . . The first living or half-living things were probably large molecules synthesized under the influence of the Sun's radiation, and only capable of reproduction in the particularly favourable medium in which they originated'.[15]

Although Haldane did not know it at the time, some similar ideas had been published in the USSR in 1924 by a botanist and biochemist named Alexander Oparin. Oparin proposed the evolution of complex carbon and nitrogen compounds in the Earth's primitive ocean, and further suggested that it was possible that those organic compounds then aggregated together into larger molecules, eventually forming gels.[16] In his original pamphlet, Oparin had assumed that oxygen was present in the Earth's primitive atmosphere, whereas Haldane thought there was 'little or no oxygen' (but plenty of carbon dioxide and ammonia) so that 'the chemically active ultra-violet rays from the Sun were not, as they are now, mainly stopped by ozone (a modified form of oxygen) in the upper atmosphere, and oxygen itself lower down'.[17] Oparin later agreed that the primordial atmosphere lacked elemental oxygen. Such a reducing atmosphere would stabilize organic (carbon-rich) compounds and also meant that the first organisms would depend on fermentation for their energy metabolism.

In his Guthrie lecture, Bernal underpinned his ideas with two kinds of scientific data – 'the geochemistry and physico-chemistry of the cooling planet, and the organic chemical composition common to all existing living organisms.' He viewed the process of life developing as 'a play divided into a prologue and three acts'.

The prologue introduces the scene on the surface of the primitive earth, and the first group of actors of an entirely inorganic kind which must start the play. The first act deals with the accumulation of chemical substances and the appearance of a stable process of conversion between them, which we call life; the second with the almost equally important stabilization of that process and its freeing from energy dependence on anything but sunlight. It is a stage of photosynthesis and of the reappearance of molecular oxygen and respiration. The third act is that of the development of specific organisms, cells, animals and plants, from these beginnings. All we have hitherto studied in biology is really summed up in the last few lines of this act, and from this and the stage set we have to infer the rest of the play.[18]

Bernal had one major reservation about the Oparin–Haldane hypothesis that the evolution of organic molecules into proto-proteins and other building blocks of living organisms took place in the primordial soup of the ocean. He was worried about the problem of extreme dilution – how would the simple molecules, perhaps containing one carbon atom, ever come together with a dozen or more similar molecules in such a vast setting to form a complex aggregate? While there might be some concentration in pools and lagoons, he had a novel theory:

It has occurred to me, however, that a much more favourable condition for concentration, and one which must certainly have taken place on a very large scale, is that of adsorption in fine clay deposits, marine and freshwater.[19]

The role of clay appeared plausible to Sage on the general grounds that 'there is probably today more living matter, that is protein, in the soil and in the estuarine and sea-bed clays than above the surface or in the waters'. There were also new specific experimental findings to bolster his theory. Electron microscopy had revealed that fine-grained clay comprised thin sheets of aluminium silicate that gave 'an enormous effective adsorptive surface'. What was more, there was chemical evidence that a wide variety of organic compounds were preferentially adsorbed on such surfaces in an orderly way so that relatively high concentrations could be achieved. The regular arrangement of molecules as they attached to the clay surface would encourage chemical interactions: the 'simpler molecular compounds could be made to undergo complex polymerization, polymerization to such an extent that the macromolecules produced might be able to exist in a colloid form even without the clay, and become . . . enzymes in their turn'.[20]

Clay was not the only material on which Bernal thought adsorption of carbon-based molecules might have occurred. In his mind, quartz was another potential scaffolding for macromolecules, and it had an additional attraction over clay: it was a mineral with handedness – its crystals have either a right-handed or a left-handed twist. Reminding his audience that Pasteur had shown that living organisms characteristically do not contain mirror-image molecules, whereas 'normal chemical processes produce right-handed and left-handed molecules with equal facility', Bernal suggested that the twist of the quartz crystal would restrict macromolecular assembly to molecules of the same handedness. The asymmetry of life was a fundamental point in Haldane's theory too, for he wrote:

It is probable that all organisms now alive are descended from one ancestor, for the following reason. Most of our structural molecules are asymmetrical, as shown by the fact that they rotate the plane of polarized light, and often from asymmetrical crystals. But of the two possible types of any such molecule, related to one another like a right and left boot, only one is found throughout living nature . . . There is nothing, so far as we can see, in the nature of things to prevent the existence of looking-glass organisms built from molecules which are, so to say, the mirror-images of those in our own bodies . . . If life had originated independently on several occasions, such organisms would probably exist. As they do not, this event probably occurred only once, or, more probably, the descendents of the first living organism rapidly evolved far enough to overwhelm any later competitors when these arrived on the scene.[21]

When *The Physical Basis of Life* was published, Bernal included an appendix given over to critical comments made by Pirie, in a letter after the original Guthrie lecture appeared. Pirie was put out that these private remarks should appear in public – not because he did not stand by his arguments, but because he was concerned they were carelessly expressed. When he saw the book, Pirie wrote to Sage complaining that he had written his observations in a hurry and may have been 'tight' at the time. He went on: 'Continually I complain, in political fields, that you write thoughtlessly with errors of phrasing',[22] and now Sage was making him inadvertently guilty of the same lapses of style. Pirie[23] had a deep love for the English language and often contributed to the *Oxford English Dictionary.** Pirie closed his letter with a threat: 'If you publish this letter I will sue you'! Unabashed, Sage sent the following reply:

Dear Bill,

It never occurred to me that you were tight, or, even if you were, you could ever have forgotten yourself so far as not to express yourself in perfect English! . . . I should have asked you and I am very sorry now that I did not because you might have produced longer and even more controversial comments.

As we have seen, Pirie took some revenge in his review, 'Vital blarney'. He used the review to amplify one of his major reservations about Bernal's thesis.

The framer of a hypothesis, or speculation, about the origin of life labours under the difficulty, not only that he does not know what raw material he has to work with, but also that he does not know what types of substance he must arrange to have synthesized. Professor Bernal assumes that, in the beginning, proteins were essential. He assumes this partly because they are components of some living organisms now, and partly on the authority of Engels. I have already argued against the dogma that proteins are essential, but the dogma dies hard and the case may be argued further.

---

* His *OED* credits include the printed use of 'bugger' in its colloquial sense from a letter he wrote to *The Listener* about a conversation between himself, Haldane and Carl Sagan.

The statement that all living organisms contain protein is unproven; fewer than 0.1 per cent of the present-day species have been examined for protein, not many more have even been shown to contain nitrogen. It may well be that all present-day species do contain proteins; this will demonstrate that protein-based mechanisms have proved more efficient than others and in the course of 2,000 million years of evolution have ousted them. Present-day conditions tell us nothing about the qualities necessary or desirable at the beginning.[24]

The debate, laced with personal barbs, was too good to be allowed to rest, and the editors of *New Biology* asked Sage for a rejoinder to 'Vital blarney'. Bernal restricted the banter, which by now had a distinct edge, to his opening paragraph:

One of these days I will see a review by N.W. Pirie of a scientific work of which he thoroughly approves. It will no doubt be a study by an expert in the field which explores, very precisely and with every reasonable precaution, a circumscribed subject and expresses the result in an orderly way with due allowance for any possible foreseen or unforeseen error. It will certainly never be anything I write. To be criticized by Pirie therefore does not surprise me and is no mark of distinction. However, in his delight in castigating the impudence of anyone – not even a biochemist – who pretends to knowledge about the origin of something that does not exist, he has allowed himself to express opinions of his own of an extravagance of scepticism that far exceeds anything he charges against me, and it is these rather than his criticisms of my efforts that require to be answered. The burden of Pirie's review was that firstly I had said nothing new, or even nearly new, for what I had said had been better said fifty to a hundred years ago, further, insofar as I had said anything else it was unproven or wrong, and lastly, that not being a professional biochemist I had no right to say anything at all on the subject.[25]

It seemed to Bernal that Pirie's objection to speculative inquiry into the origin of life on the basis 'You cannot be right because you do not know enough' was an attempt to obstruct the progress of science. In Bernal's mind, the question had moved from the one that confronted the Victorians like Huxley – *whether* life originated from a previous inorganic state – to the question of *how* it did so. He did not deride the Victorians ideas – indeed he quoted a newly discovered passage written by Charles Darwin in 1871 that seemed to anticipate the Oparin–Haldane hypothesis with its discussion of a 'proteine compound' emerging from 'some warm little pond, with all sorts of ammonia and phosphoric salts, light, heat, electricity etc., present'. In *The Physical Basis of Life*, Sage was merely trying to chart *a* process by which organic material could have arisen from inorganic compounds that was in keeping with the modern laws of biochemistry, geochemistry and physics. He made no claim that this was *the only way* life could have started, but thought it was 'churlish and self-defeating to disparage what we know and to refuse to try to put facts in a reasonable order because we do not know all of them to start with'.[26]

16. Sage in 'the very doubtful disguise of a naval officer' for his aborted second visit to the Normandy beaches. Seated to his right is Capt. T. A. Hussey RN

17. Sage in Ceylon 1944 next to Lord Mountbatten (wearing his naval cap)

18. The Birkbeck crystallography research group in the Faraday Lab at the Royal Institution in 1946. From left to right standing: Sam Levene, Jim Jeffery, John Hirsch, Geoffrey Pitt, Helene Scouloudi; seated: Anita Rimel, Werner Ehrenberg, Desmond Bernal, Helen Megaw, Harry Carlisle

19. Sage meets Comrade Lysenko in 1949 but seems unable to look him in the eye. J.G. Crowther, the science journalist, is wearing the Panama hat

20. Margot Heinemann

21. 21–22 Torrington Square just before the houses were demolished in 1966. Bernal's flat was at the very top of No. 22 on the left. The fire that blackened the wall of No. 21 started in the chemistry department

22. Sage with Nobel laureates Irène and Frédéric Joliot-Curie and Sir C.V. Raman in India, 1950

23. Leading virus crystallographers at a conference in Madrid, 1956.
Left to right: Anne Cullis, Francis Crick, Don Caspar, Aaron Klug, Rosalind Franklin, Odile Crick and John Kendrew

24. Sage and Linus Pauling (centre) in Moscow in 1957 for Oparin's conference on the origins of life

25. Jane Bernal holds her parents' hands as they march in support of the London bus strike, June 1958

26. Bernal listens intently as Khrushchev addresses the World Congress on General Disarmament and Peace for over 2 hours in Moscow, July 1962. Mme Blum is on Bernal's left and Paul Robeson two seats to her left

27. Sage constructs his first ball-and-spoke model of liquid structure, confident that he will be interrupted every few minutes so that the model would be disordered

At about the time Bernal was writing these words, a graduate chemistry student at the University of Chicago, Stanley L. Miller, set out to replicate the primordial environment in a simple laboratory experiment.[27] He was inspired to carry out the experiment by his supervisor, Harold Urey, a Nobel Laureate in chemistry, who had lately become interested in the origin of life and had reached the conclusion that the prebiotic atmosphere would have been a reducing one, conducive to the synthesis of organic molecules. Miller set up a closed apparatus of tubes and flasks, in which he boiled water (the ocean) and circulated the resultant water vapour with reducing gases (ammonia, hydrogen and methane thought to have existed in the primitive atmosphere) past an electrical discharge or spark (to represent lightning). After the first twenty-four hours of circulation, the water became 'noticeably pink' and 'by the end of the week the solution was deep red'. When this primordial tomato soup was analysed, it was found to contain at least two amino acids, glycine and alanine, in surprisingly large (milligram) quantities. As Haldane would have predicted, the amino acids in Miller's flask were equally distributed into the left- and right-handed forms; the exclusive presence of the L form in living organisms remained to be explained.

Miller elegantly demonstrated that the organic building blocks of life could have arisen as a result of electrical excitation of the primitive atmosphere (he thought that ultraviolet light from the Sun would be an equally effective source of energy but could not test that idea in his glass apparatus). His two-page report in *Science* cited just three references – by Oparin, Urey and Bernal. Miller's experiment transformed the whole subject of the origin of life from armchair speculation into a new branch of experimental science, in a flash.

While Miller had shown that the Oparin–Haldane hypothesis was plausible, he could not prove that these chemical reactions were actually taking place in the prebiotic phase of life. Bernal thought it was 'now indisputable' that organic molecules could have arisen in this way and 'their presence in organisms is strong presumptive evidence for the pre-existence of the reducing atmosphere from which Miller synthesized them'.[28] Sage also interpreted the appearance of red-coloured substances, capable of absorbing light, in Miller's experiment as opening the way to photosynthesis. He remained concerned about the problem of concentration of the primitive molecules necessary for their chemical interaction – the issue that had led him to propose clay as a means of absorbing organic molecules and holding them in close quarters. It now appeared to him that if polymers consisting of a thousand atoms or so could be achieved, they would bind layers of water molecules 'provoking the formation of macroscopic colloidal aggregates ... The water held in this way has properties intermediate between those of ice and of ionic solution. It possesses mechanical rigidity, but ions and even small molecules such as sugars can diffuse through it except for the portion within one or two water molecule diameters of the particle... Protein molecules are particularly suited for the formation of such water-holding colloids and it seems to me that the evidence is still strong that they or some smaller polypeptides were the first substances in the evolution of life fitted for this role'.[29]

Pirie, as one might expect, was far less impressed than Sage with the significance of Miller's report. He believed that the set of chemical reactions observed in that experiment were of relevance only if the currently accepted model of the physical creation of the Earth and its subsequent development held sway. He had little confidence in that model because, in his words, 'Every few years a new theory of the origin of the earth appears and with it new probabilities about the primitive atmosphere... some suggest an oxidizing and some a reducing atmosphere. Until substantial unanimity has been reached and maintained on this point, we can only speculate about the types of molecule that would have been present in the surface layers, because the factors that lead to different conclusions about the atmosphere lead also to different conclusions about the surface... The attitude of mind that leads people to erect a new dogma on the "Stop Press" news from astronomy and physics is similar to that of the child who, seeing copyists at work in an art gallery, said 'What do they do with the old pictures when the new ones are finished?'[30]

Pirie's essay also contained a few more gibes against Sage, who was given the right of reply. While not attempting to conceal his differences with Pirie, he seemed to be tiring of their argument.

Pirie is certainly entitled to have another crack at me and I can only object at misrepresentation. I am not quite so ignorant as he makes me out to be, only more wrong-headed. Ancient authorities impress him more than they do me...Nor do I think science is really like painting. The new pictures in science may or may not be so well painted as the old, but they have something in them that the old simply did not have. Our art should consist in fitting the new facts in, not rejecting them out of hand. With his positive propositions I am, however, in almost complete agreement, particularly with his ideas on the evolution of molecules. I would not try to limit biopoesis [Pirie's term for the making of life] to our particular brand, but I think we are more likely to find out this kind first as we know something of the beginning from geochemistry and the end from biochemistry.[31]

The point Bernal was making in the last sentence was that emerging evidence from astronomers and geochemists as to the mode of formation of the planet from condensation of cosmic dust, together with the chemical composition and likely temperature of its surface, should act as a guide to the chemical reactions that could have taken place initially. At the other end, biochemical processes of present-day life and the cellular organelles such as nuclei, mitochondria and membranes where they take place, should have precursors in primitive life forms. Indeed 'we should look for close relations between chemical processes likely to take place on the surface of a newly formed planet and those occurring in organisms, particularly the most common processes which are also likely to be the oldest'.[32]

Pirie thought Sage's line of reasoning was sophistry. He believed that the uniformity of present-day organisms in their chemical composition and metabolism was often exaggerated, and what were the dominant biochemical pathways now might have completely replaced the earliest, primitive, mechanisms. He summarized his position thus:

Every biopoesis on Earth starts with the same Geochemistry; my contention is that they may have used different aspects of it. [Pirie thought one of his greatest contributions was to add an *s* to *origin*.] The final result is present-day Biochemistry; but my contention is that we may be emphasizing the wrong aspects of it. Alongside the now well-understood protein and carbohydrate mechanisms there are many that we look on as bizarre and unusual. It may well be that these resemble the primitive mechanisms; the commonly made assumption that those mechanisms which are quantitatively most important now, are the primitive ones, is wholly arbitrary. The facts of Geochemistry and Biochemistry do not define any particular route between the beginning and the present position.

Fortunately for Sage, he was not restricted to an exclusive debate with Pirie on the origin of life. Other scientists were now attracted to the subject, encouraged no doubt by Miller's successful experiment. Bernal received word from Oparin that he was planning an international conference in Moscow in the summer of 1957. Sage gave some thought to what he might speak about, and decided that he should give two papers. The first would be a general paper on 'Ideas on the principles of the study of the origin of life'. In this lecture, he would emphasize the critical importance of physical coherence as expressed in gels and coacervates (featureless blobs of jelly proposed by Oparin as precursors of living cells); the origin and place of polymer formation; the mutual biochemical reactions of nucleic acids, purines, sugars and fats; and finally the role of the different kinds of molecules in producing the structures observable in viruses and cells. He would attempt to relate the above with aspects of geochemical and geophysical evolution.[33] The second lecture would concentrate more on geometric structure of macromolecules related to the origin of life. Sage also made some suggestions about scientists Oparin should invite: John Randall from King's College, Rosalind Franklin, Dorothy Hodgkin, Crick and Watson amongst them.

Sage had a chance to rehearse his lectures at Oparin's institute during a visit to the USSR in September 1956. It was an unsettling time for Stalinists – the waves from Khrushchev's sudden indictment of the cult of personality and of the Stalin-era state crimes were rocking the previously unshakable Soviet edifice. Sage was joined on this trip by Alan Mackay, who remembers that their official translator, a lecturer in English at Moscow University, had a distinctly cockney accent. Although Bernal was still treated as an honoured guest, he commented to Mackay that his lavish suite of rooms at the Hotel Moskva was poor compared to the accommodation on his previous visits, when his sitting room had not only contained a grand piano, but a stuffed bear proffering a box of matches.[34]

The first international symposium on 'The origin of life on the earth' attracted more than forty scientists from sixteen countries to Moscow in August 1957. Bernal addressed them in the first session and proposed a schema for the stages by which life might have begun. He did not believe that his framework was 'the correct one or that it may not require drastic modification, but I do urge that it is better in such a Congress to have before it some pattern than none'.[35] He reiterated his belief in the principle proposed by Sir Charles Lyell, the Victorian geologist and friend of Darwin, who 'tells us to search in the present world for processes which may have occurred in the past'. In the context of the origin of life, Bernal thought that this meant more than just searching for the origin of the materials of the organic world in the inorganic, but that there should also be continuity of the basic chemical processes like oxidation–reduction and hydrolysis–condensation reactions. As to the materials, he was struck that the commonest, stable, elements of the earth's crust such as silicon and aluminium play almost no role in biochemistry, whereas the soluble simple ions such as potassium and magnesium and the labile atoms of sulphur, phosphorus and iron are key.

While accepting Pirie's point that there may have been other radically different forms of life, now long extinct, Bernal thought that this just meant scientists were restricted to studying the origin of the one form of life that now existed on Earth. In his opinion, this could be traced only by working backwards: attempting to work forwards from any initial inorganic origins would be futile because there were too many possible lines to be followed.

There may well be potential biochemical cycles that would have solved the problems of the formation of life and reproduction of organisms as well as, and even better than, those actually evolved. But biochemical evolution differs from that of organisms in that variant forms, if not actually incorporated in the common biochemical pattern, became absolutely extinct. There is only one *dominant* chemical pattern of life.[36]

With Pirie in the audience, Sage now even proposed a working definition of life: *the embodiment within a certain volume of self-maintaining chemical processes.* The problem confronting them was how such a system could establish itself, starting from available inorganic materials and subsequently reproduce and evolve. He sub-divided this large question into four inter-related but distinct problems:

1. The problem of the external source of free energy to keep the system going;
2. The problem of the facilitation of the energy interchanges within the system, where an isothermal condition implies some catalysis; [biochemical processes take place without the input of heat that would be necessary in the absence of enzymes]
3. The problems of the means of holding the system together and in the more complicated cases, such as bacterial and nucleated cells, of how all parts of the organism can maintain their individuality while being in constant chemical relation with each other;
4. The problems of reproduction with its almost, but never quite exact, duplication of organisms as shown in evolving species, pose the further problem of the normal transference, with occasional modification, of specific guiding patterns.

Sage gave the audience reasons to be optimistic: the exact composition of the Earth's original atmosphere did not have to be known before considering the emergence of organic molecules; the efficiency of primitive proto-enzymes was probably extremely low; and the first natural polymers would not need to have a high degree of regularity to permit the formation of colloidal proto-cells.

Pirie, in his presentation,[37] came close to agreement on some points with Sage – for example, he did not think discussions on biopoesis should wait for more accurate data on the original composition of the Earth's surface. He was also ready to concede that it seemed likely that all present life-forms were protein-based, although he still thought this irrelevant to any discussion about the origins of life. He introduced a novel idea, illustrated by two cones joined apex to apex (like a narrow-wasted egg-timer), that in the beginning there was chemical diversity and structural simplicity. As inefficient chemical processes disappeared, there was a point of maximal simplicity (the narrow waist) where life originated and thereafter the biochemistry became simplified as protein-based organisms ascended, resulting in morphological complexity and chemical uniformity.

So struck was Pirie with his own picture of biopoesis that it took pride of place in a summary of the Moscow symposium that he wrote for *Nature*. Nor could he resist a clever dig at Sage: 'Argument about evolution presents many intellectual pitfalls for the imprudent. J.D. Bernal fell into some of them with consequent inversion. This was the position in which, according to Engels, Marx found Hegel. Marx put Hegel on his feet and put posterity in his debt by making the Dialectic useful. I would like to perform a like service for my friend.'[38] His friend reacted as follows:

N.W. Pirie's characteristic and entertaining account of the symposium in Moscow on the origin of life mainly consists of an exposition of his views on the subject and a metaphysical criticism of a minor part of my own contribution to the discussion.[39]

Where Pirie had made his familiar complaint that the Victorian intellectuals like Huxley and Tyndall 'had a clearer grip on the nature of the problem', Sage was encouraged that 'so many distinguished and active scientists in fields ranging from astrophysics to genetics...had come together to discuss a subject of such wide scope and importance'. In his single-page report, Sage was able to give *Nature*'s readership a much fuller and more detailed account of the meeting than Pirie managed in more than double the number of words. Sage ended by saying 'I hope these remarks may do something to enlarge Pirie's view of the symposium, but they still are far from doing justice to the wealth of information presented and the interesting discussions that ensued.'[40]

Pirie's familiar name was 'Bill', bestowed by his parents after 'Kaiser Bill' in recognition of their son's youthful belligerence and nonconformist ways. He never outgrew these traits and took pride in his 'distrust of authority and majority opinion'.[41] At times, this scepticism meant he rejected new facts such as Franklin's structure of TMV or the genetic code, and his prickliness caused unease among the younger molecular biologists. Sage was an established figure, who was not threatened by Pirie's sniping, and did not take offence at the personal insults – although he would have preferred a more cerebral debate. He regretted that the controversy with Pirie was not very productive because it was 'largely due to a difference in temperament'.[42] Pirie wrote over forty articles on the origins of life over a sixty-year period, and ultimately came to regard them as 'extremely repetitive'.[43]

At Bedford School, Bernal's housemaster gave him the title of 'Astronomer Royal', and as a schoolboy he wrote his first scientific paper on the theory of comets.[44] The paper was lost and never published, but gave Bernal a general feeling for reciprocal space that helped him to develop so rapidly as an X-ray crystallographer. His astronomical interests were reawakened in connection with the origins of life in the early 1960s, when some American scientists announced that they had identified biogenic hydrocarbons, similar to animal products like butter, in the carbonaceous material of a meteorite that had fallen to earth nearly a century before in France. The Orgueil meteorite had been carefully examined at the time by Pasteur himself, who attempted to culture any indigenous microorganisms from its interior and found none. Naturally the conclusion of the American scientists (Nagy, Meinschein and

Hennessy) 'that biogenic processes occur and that living forms exist in regions of the universe beyond the earth' caused an enormous amount of public excitement. Although the trio were reliable scientists, Bernal, writing in *Nature*, could see a disadvantage to the amount of publicity they received.

There is a danger that this [publicity] will, in serious scientific circles, cause the observations of the three authors to be overlooked, which would be a great mistake, for whatever the interpretation put on them they are of cardinal importance to science... The major question that arises, therefore, is as to the interpretation of the results. Though the mass spectroscopic evidence indicates a composition of meteoritic hydrocarbons within the range of those given by material of organic origin on the Earth, from this it only follows that the meteorite material *may* be of organismal origin and not that it *must* be so... If the material is derived from life, this must have occurred on the planetary parent body from which by general consensus we believe meteorites to have been derived by fragmentation.[45]

Soon after the original announcement about long hydrocarbon molecules in the Orgueil meteorite came another, even more astonishing, discovery. Bart Nagy, a chemist, had brought a microbiologist, George Claus, into the research and they found evidence of microscopic particles in the Orgueil meteorite and a second meteorite, the Ivuna, which resembled fossilized algae.[46] These organized elements showed some staining with biological agents and appeared to Claus to have some morphological structures like the double membrane of a cell wall. A group from Chicago tried to replicate the findings of the New York team and did find similar round particles which 'appeared to possess a clear double wall, as described by Claus and Nagy, but since the thickness of this wall could be changed by slight adjustment of the focus, the "wall" may be an optical illusion'.[47] They carried out a detailed chemical analysis of the particles and found that their composition was 'strikingly different from that of any known fossil or living organism'. The discovery of fossils in meteorites had been announced once before in the late nineteenth century, and the Chicago group were unimpressed by the morphological evidence which depended on 'a great deal of subjective judgement'. To them a purely inorganic mode of origin for the organized elements seemed perfectly possible.

Sage was asked by *Nature* to comment on this unfolding story. He had had the opportunity, when Claus visited Britain, to examine some of the Orgueil material and was convinced by what he saw: 'Anyone who had seen it under a microscope with varied depths of focus would be inclined to accept its organic character, yet so far no similar object has been found among protozoa, algae or even pollen grains.'[48] Nor did Sage believe that the particles represented contamination from terrestrial sources, a significant counter-claim being made by many, because identical contamination was 'highly improbable' in meteorites that had fallen as far apart as France and Tanzania. It seemed possible that the carbonaceous material was either the product of extrater-restrial life processes or, if it had an inorganic origin, a possible source for the origin of life. It could no longer be assumed that life 'must have originated on Earth, though it does not follow that it may not have'.[49] Claus thought that although the 'organisms' from the meteorites were not similar to any terres-trial single-cell organisms, they did appear to have similar biochemistry because they reacted with Feulgen stain (as do nucleic acids); there was also evidence that different meteorites contained 'substances extremely similar to amino acids and purines'.[50] This raised the possibility that life forms, wher-ever they originated, followed similar biochemical pathways. In his view, the work of Claus and Nagy, while shattering many of his own assumptions, opened 'the way to the solution of problems hitherto unthought of'.

When Klug vacated his attic office at 21 Torrington Square to move to Cambridge, he was replaced not by a molecular biologist, but by a young geochemistry researcher named John Kerridge. The transition reflected Ber-nal's enthusiasm about the origin of life, which was a new subject for experimentation, whereas protein and virus research, while still absorbing, had passed beyond the pioneering stage. Kerridge was due to start work in January 1961, but found himself invited to the departmental Christmas party two weeks earlier. He arrived, a little shy as an outsider, and found the party going full blast. Sage quickly caught sight of him and waved him over. He said to Kerridge, 'Meet a friend of mine, Linus Pauling' and left the PhD student talking to the Nobel Laureate. Kerridge was hired to analyse carbonaceous meteorites in order to elucidate the mineralogy of their parent asteroids, and thereby provide clues about the conditions in which extra-terrestrial life might have emerged. As he started his researches, he was given the usual warning by others that he might hear more than one set of footsteps ascend-ing to Bernal's flat above his office during the evenings, at which point he should discreetly leave lest his innocence be ruined.

In 1963, Sage was invited to a select conference on the origins of life held in Wakulla Springs, under the auspices of Florida State University and NASA. He was unable to attend because of illness, but his paper was read *in absentia*.[51] He reminded the audience that the problem confronting them was no longer confined to the origins of life on Earth, but needed to include 'the origin of prelife states of complex carbon and nitrogen compounds' that could have taken place inside the solar system or even beyond it. Although recent claims about carbon-based substances on meteorites being produced biologically were highly controversial, Bernal believed the study of meteorites was important if only because the geological history of the Earth was so turbulent, with its continental drifts and mountain building, that the meteorites offered a unique opportunity to analyse primitive carbon compounds. But, he said, carbonaceous meteorites might not contain carbon molecules as such, rather an amorphous mass of carbon, nitrogen, hydrogen and oxygen like char. Bernal reported that Kerridge, at Birkbeck, had shown that the primary form of carbon in meteorites tended to be associated with low-temperature hydrated silicates (some similar to asbestos); the rounded particles or chondrules within carbonaceous meteorites contained water but with a higher deuterium content (heavy water) than found on Earth.

Whatever the mysteries about the initial synthesis of complex organic compounds, Sage thought that the next stage in biopoesis was 'the most obscure and the most speculative'.[52]

Starting from an equilibrium mixture of carbon–nitrogen compounds, such as can be produced by the action of ionizing radiation acting on small molecules, how did it actually proceed to develop the features we now call those of life? Stage 2, as I see it, whatever the origin in space or the atmosphere of the equilibrium mixture, was played out here on Earth and in particular as part of the Earth's hydrosphere, whether in free water or in mud banks.

The most interesting question, in his opinion, was: 'How did the basic elements of molecular reproduction themselves originate?' The ability of complex biochemical molecules to reproduce is essential to life. Present-day life depended on the reproduction of nucleic acids and the production of proteins – functions that take place within specific structural sites or organelles within the cell. The revolution in biology wrought by Watson and Crick had resulted in increased understanding of these mechanisms which, through their very perfection, made it 'more difficult to see how they could have come into existence spontaneously together with their function'. Reproduction did not mean the occasional division of a complete organism into two or the emergence of a new bud.

It is evident that reproduction applies not so much to the whole organism as to every moment of its metabolism. The reproduction of nucleic acids and the production of protein molecules is essential to all vital processes as we meet them now. We can also say that they are essential to the actual structures of life, to organisms, and to the making of subcellular structures now revealed by the electron microscope and followed in detail by the studies of cytochemistry that also depend on this nucleic acid–protein cycle.[53]

One possible answer to the problem of how cell membranes and organelles arose, in Bernal's opinion, was as a consequence of crystallization of identical small molecules. This would imply that the production of identical or nearly identical protein molecules preceded the appearance of internal cell architecture. He cited his own and Rosalind Franklin's work on the structural subunits of TMV as an example of how such construction might take place. There was an important distinction between the possible modes of biopoesis (which depend on logic and chemistry) and the actual genesis of life (which must take account of the fossil record and the present biochemistry of life). Perhaps as an aside to Pirie, who was at the conference in Florida, Sage observed that:

Many people have argued and some still do, that the whole of life is a highly improbable process. In fact, it would not be difficult to prove that life could not exist; it would be far easier than to demonstrate that it must exist. But, as we have life and, indeed, are life, we have to accept it and, therefore, explain it.[54]

The philosophy of employing probability at all was critically examined by Peter Mora, a biochemist from the National Institutes of Health, in a paper titled 'The folly of probability'. In his contribution, Mora also questioned the adequacy of the scientific method, especially the reductionism of physics, to comprehend something as inherently complex as life. Bernal read this paper, which he found to be salutary, but he could not bring himself to agree with Mora's negative conclusions. Bernal, in his written comments, agreed with Mora that the present laws of physics 'are insufficient to describe the origin of life'. To Mora, Sage continued,

this opens the way to teleology, even, by implication, to creation by an intelligent agent. Now both of these hypotheses were eminently reasonable before the fifteenth or possibly even before the nineteenth century. Nowadays they carry a higher degree of improbability than any of the hypotheses questioned by Dr Mora. If he thinks that he has shown conclusively that life cannot have originated by chance, only two alternatives remain. The first is that it did not arise at all, and that all we are studying is an illusion. This is the old argument of Parmenides, whose logic led him to believe that the Universe is *One* and that any apparent multiplicity is illusory. The other alternative is that life *is* a reality but that we are not yet clever enough to unravel the nature of its origin which seems to me admittedly *a priori* more probable.[55]

Bernal's essential point was that the debate on the origin of life had moved on from the metaphysical stage to one where the phenomenon of life was being analysed in terms of its underlying biochemistry. Pirie, who chaired that session of the conference, congratulated Mora for setting people thinking, but was 'surprised at the improbably large number of occasions on which my reaction was almost the precise opposite to yours'!

Bernal published *The Origin of Life* in 1967 as a book for 'the normal, intelligent reader' giving a summary of current ideas as well as incorporating the historic essays of Oparin and Haldane as appendices.[56] Since the study of the origin of life raised more questions than it answered, he revived a very old kind of practice – the inclusion of unanswered queries. He had done the same thing for his paper to the Florida conference in 1963, where he had listed 32 questions for the audience to think about. In the book, Sage attempted to answer his own questions. He stuck to the view that the elementary organic substances, whether formed on Earth or arriving by meteorite, became converted into the more complex molecules of life in the surface water of the Earth, probably adsorbed onto clay or some other mineral. In answer to the key question 'How did the basic elements of molecular reproduction themselves originate?' Sage offered the following answer.

The bases and amino acids were formed presumably abiotically and then selected. Some of the base and sugar phosphates have acted as protocoenzymes and were subsequently polymerized into nucleic acids. An intermediate stage in which short lengths of nucleic acids were attached to particular amino acids probably intervened, leading to the formation of transfer RNA, and hence to the whole process of replication.[57]

At the Moscow conference, a decade earlier, Bernal had first suggested the primacy of RNA over DNA in biopoesis.[58] His reason for believing so was that DNA-containing structures always seem to be contained within a membranous envelope such as the cell nucleus, whereas RNA is found in the general milieu of the cell and may be a more versatile molecule. The notion of RNA as the key molecule for replication and also as an agent to catalyse the synthesis of proteins was an idea whose time had come in the late 1960s. It was written about by Carl Woese in his 1967 book, *The Genetic Code*, and suggested independently by Crick in Cambridge and Leslie Orgel at the Salk Institute for Biological Studies in San Diego. Subsequently, there has been the discovery of ribozymes, enzymes made of RNA, and the RNA world remains a popular view of how DNA–RNA–protein life got started.[59] Bernal's name should perhaps be added to the list of the originators of this theory.

Sage regarded the idea first put forward in his 1947 Guthrie lecture that the polymerization of small organic molecules floating in the primitive soup into more complex biochemical substances was facilitated by adsorption onto fine clay particles as his most original contribution. In the late 1970s, it was shown that amino acids coated onto clay surfaces can link up into short chains that resemble modern biological proteins.[60] And just as he had suggested in the same lecture that quartz might impart handedness to any macromolecules assembled on its asymmetrical facets, experiments at the Carnegie Institution in 2000 showed that calcite (limestone) attracts left-handed and right-handed amino acid molecules differentially to its mirror-image crystal faces.[61] Dorothy Hodgkin told a story about two of Sage's friends marvelling at his versatility. One asked, 'How is he, what is he doing now?' 'I don't know' the second replied, 'The world is his oyster.' 'Rather' said the first 'is the universe his oyster – the world is his pearl.'[62] More than half a century after he proposed the clay hypothesis, a paper was published that extended his idea to outer space – after analysing several meteorites (including the Orgueil), the authors (who even referred to Bernal's *The Physical Basis of Life*) concluded that 'the meteoritic organic matter is strongly associated with clay minerals. This association suggests that clay minerals may have had an important trapping and possibly catalytic role in chemical evolution in the early solar system prior to the origin of life on the early Earth.'[63]

19

Marxist Envoy

Soon after the war, Sage wrote that 'the day of the wandering scholar is over'.[1] He then spent much of the next twenty years attempting to revive the tradition. In addition to the triennial International Union of Crystallography meetings, invitations to speak at foreign universities, and his globe-trotting for the World Peace Council and the World Federation of Scientific Workers, he took several lengthy trips to nations that interested him. These visits were usually at the invitation of the national science academy of the country in question, and the ostensible reason for the visit would be a one-man review of their leading centres of science and technology. For emerging countries with limited resources, Sage represented expertise in physics, chemistry, crystallography, materials science and metallurgy, the building industry and agriculture. He was indefatigable and cheap. As a scientist, he regarded himself as a world citizen and was determined to do all he could to bring the benefits of pure and applied science to developing lands. If the places were not established communist states like China and the USSR, they were often ex-colonial nations that appeared ripe for conversion to some form of socialism, when, of course, the planning of science would become a central edict. For Sage, the visits offered an unrivalled opportunity to make friends and learn more about the culture of foreign parts – there would be excursions to historic sites and museums, where more than one head curator was gently corrected about their exhibits.

His first post-war visit to the USSR was in the summer of 1949, beginning with the Soviet Peace Congress in the Hall of Columns. After the Congress was over, he spent several days touring construction sites in Moscow, talking to architects and civil engineers. Tens of thousands of Muscovites were living in barracks, and Nikita Khrushchev, the Moscow party chief, was in charge of an emergency programme to build apartment blocks that succeeded, in no small measure, because of the bold decision to use prefabricated reinforced concrete.[2] Bernal was impressed with the speed at which the buildings were erected and wrote several articles praising the construction techniques on his return to London. He spent the first week of September visiting scientific institutions in Moscow and giving lectures; for the second week he repeated this effort in Leningrad. He wrote to Sergei Vavilov, President of the Soviet Academy of Sciences, saying he had noticed 'an enormous improvement in material means for science since his last visit in 1934'. He hoped for better communication with Soviet scientists and looked forward to exchange visits. He had canvassed support for the WFSW at the various institutes he visited. He closed his letter with 'best wishes for a glorious future for Soviet science in the common service of mankind'.[3] It was on this trip that he met Lysenko and took such a rosy view of his qualities.

After a term spent teaching and supervising research at Birkbeck, Sage was invited by the Indian Academy of Science to speak at its annual meeting in Bombay at the end of December.[4] He was met at Bombay airport by Professor Sir C.V. Raman, founder and president of the Indian Academy, and director of the new Raman Institute of Research in Bangalore. After dropping his small suitcase at the Taj Hotel, Sage was taken straight to the new Institute of Nuclear Research, housed in what used to be the Royal Yacht Club, where he learned about their research on cosmic rays. Raman drove him up to the Malabar Hill, where he stood in the hanging gardens and watched the sun set over the city. Raman told Sage about his early life, growing up in an academic family in southern India; Sage was amused that he had decided to shorten his name to Raman from Venkataraman so that any scientific contribution he made might be more easily remembered. This certainly paid off when he discovered the Raman effect of scattered light in 1928.

Dinner that evening was at the home of some wealthy Parsees, who had invited other leading figures from the meeting as well as local dignitaries. Among the guests were the Joliot-Curies, and Sage spent time comparing notes on the USSR with Frédéric, who had been there three months earlier. Sage also talked to the editor of a progressive Bombay newspaper, from whom he formed the impression that the Congress government had little control over business activity in the city, but were using the police to suppress communism.

The chief minister of Maharashtra state opened the Academy meeting with a speech in which he referred several times to Bernal's book *The Social Function of Science*. This led to its author being subjected to 'a mass attack of autograph hunters' and multiple invitations to speak at Indian colleges. After the morning session, Bernal found himself at the Governor General's house for lunch along with Sir Robert Robinson, the Oxford chemistry professor and President of the Royal Society, who was also an invited speaker at the Academy meeting. Protocol would not permit Sage to leave before the Governor General and so he had no chance to prepare his lecture. Indeed he only just managed to arrive back at the meeting in time to deliver his talk on 'X-ray analysis and organic chemistry' at 5pm. Following Bernal's lecture, there were some good presentations by Indian scientists on textiles (but Bernal was disappointed that these contained no X-ray work).

Bernal talked to many of the Indian scientists at the meeting, and this was probably the occasion when he met G.N. Ramachandran, who had just completed a PhD under Peter Wooster's supervision at Cambridge. Ramachandran, the recently appointed Professor of Physics at Madras University, always credited Bernal with steering him towards the structure of collagen as a worthwhile research topic. In Madras, the Central Leather Research Institute was virtually next door to Ramachandran's laboratory, and in 1954 he was the first to describe collagen's triple helix formation.[5]

On the drive from the Governor General's house to the site of the meeting, Sage was depressed by the condition of Indian housing that he passed – 'miserable lean-tos and shacks made mostly out of old rags and bits of wood, worse than anything I have seen in West Africa'.[6] The peasants, he learned, paid rent to black market landlords. He cornered the chief minister that evening at a reception in 'the most exquisite grounds of an extremely wealthy Parsee businessman' to suggest how their situation might be alleviated by modern building techniques, but found that the premier 'took a most defeatist attitude'.

Sage left the Taj Hotel on the morning of 2nd January, after 'a certain amount of difficulties about tipping the numerous beggars, dhobi men, porters, page boys etc. that surrounded our departure'.[7] He drove south-east to Poona to attend another science congress, which Pandit Nehru, the leader of the newly independent India, was expected to attend. Sage knew Nehru well from pre-war Bloomsbury parties. That evening after the dinner, Nehru drew him aside and 'we started a conversation on the proper utilization of science in India'. After ten minutes, they were interrupted by Nehru's aide-de-camp 'who moved me onto the Governor's wife'. She was 'rather a terrifying character not at all fitting into the scheme of vice-regal propriety'[8] and he did not succeed in escaping from her for the rest of the evening. Sage returned to his residence, and Nehru dropped in just before midnight with the artist Felix Topolski, who was staying with him in order to make sketches of India and Indian characters. Both men were tired and they held a rather 'desultory and unsatisfactory conversation'.

Bernal soon formed the impression that young Indian scientists were very keen and also tended to exaggerate the importance of foreign visitors. Word spread that he was writing a report for government, and one morning he was woken by a phone call from M.R. Patel, a dissident scientist, who dismissed governmental plans for organizing science as 'moonshine'. In Patel's opinion, Nehru displayed an over-optimistic attitude to large-scale projects, and corruption and nepotism were rife within his administration. At the Poona conference, Bernal lectured on structure of proteins, and attended the annual meeting of the Indian Association of Scientific Workers with Joliot in the evening. Following that meeting, he went to dinner with a colleague from the war, General Daya Ram

Thapar, the head of the Indian Army medical service. They discussed the tensions between India and China, and Sage admired the General's even temper as he was berated by his wife and daughter* for his opinions.

The next three days were given over to sightseeing, with Sage taking a particular delight in the caves of Maharashtra, which involved some hot and steep hiking. The caves, cut into rock, are Buddhist monasteries that contain elaborate sculpture. He was taken to the Bhandarkar Oriental Research Institute where a few elderly learned scholars were preparing an edition of the Mahabharata, the epic Hindu text. The scholars had already been toiling for thirty years and expected to be finished in another sixty. Sage felt a pang of sympathy for them and noted that their labours received only 'niggardly government support'.

He flew from Poona to Aurangabad in order to visit the cave temples of Ajanta and Ellora. At the hotel after dinner, Sage played ping-pong, but 'soon saw that we were getting in the way of a bevy of extremely charming young ladies. As we gave way to them, one of them came up to me and asked in French if she had the honour of addressing M. Joliot-Curie. I said I couldn't quite be that, but we started a conversation and then when Joliot did turn up, I said, I would be charmed to introduce you but I don't know your name and she said "My name is Miss Mistry." It was in fact nothing mysterious ... it is a very common Parsee name. The family consists entirely of ten Miss Mistrys ...'[9]

The following morning, they drove across the Deccan plateau, through villages of brick and mud and banyan trees to Ajanta, an old town with a great wall and magnificent gate. They walked along a gorge to get to the line of caves, which are cut into the hillside, and were greeted by the curator himself – 'an earnest young man ... whose tendency toward popular exposition rather spoilt the archaeological interest of the trip.'[10] After driving the two hundred or so miles back to Bombay, Bernal flew to Calcutta with the Joliot-Curies.

Calcutta struck him as little changed from his previous visit four years earlier, 'as vast a city as ever with the open garbage piles in the road being nibbled at by the ever-present sacred cows, which wandered in and out of houses'.[11] The city was living up to its reputation as the incubator of revolution in India, and Bernal sensed an atmosphere of danger due to bomb-throwing outrages and frequent armed police raids. He visited Presidency College, where he was impressed by the quality of biochemical research on vitamins and hormones. He gave a lecture on building techniques at an engineering college before flying to Benares, a city where the buildings seemed to lean drunkenly and be about to slip into the Ganges. He watched people bathing in the river, unconcerned by the corpses being dipped in the water before cremation on the Ghat.

---

* Romila Thapar, the General's daughter, became one of India's most distinguished historians.

From Benares he flew to Delhi, where he had dinner with an economics professor, who told him about the difficulties of financing foreign debt and the problems of industrialization. The economy was in a critical state, and short-term speculators hindered government planning. Sage lectured on the history and teaching of science, and visited physics and agricultural institutes. He had another unsatisfactory interview with Nehru:

This was not a very happy affair because, first of all, he was himself obviously very depressed in his obsession for the Congress and secondly because I had nothing very encouraging to tell him about science or its applications. I asked him very pointedly what his real policy was and he answered me in the most evasive way, implying that he was not really a free agent and that he should be congratulated not so much on what he had done but what he had prevented from happening.[12]

Bernal found time for a short visit to Ceylon, where once again he fell for the lush, green beauty of the landscape. He lectured to large audiences on the origins of life, building methods, and peace. Then he returned to Calcutta once more for a huge peace meeting, where he received an embarrassing number of garlands. His speech was interrupted by insects and 'unrestrained loudspeakers from neighbouring houses'. He was able to watch the sunrise before flying home.

Bernal made another major trip to the Eatern Bloc in the early spring of 1951. He flew in bad weather from Prague to Lwow in occupied Poland. There he was met by a woman from VOKS (the society for the promotion of cultural activity with foreign countries) and ate an austere Soviet dinner of strong sausage, biscuit and tea for 'the excessive price of 12 roubles'.[13] Things looked up after he arrived in Moscow and booked into the vast Hotel Metropol. The next day he visited a crystallography department that reminded him strongly of Birkbeck because the scientists were attempting to work amidst a crew of plasterers and painters – pieces of furniture and apparatus were pushed into odd corners of the laboratory. He visited the Ministry of Forest Plantation, where he was completely taken in by projects that were based on Lysenko's specious theories. There was a visit to a superb historical museum where his eye was taken by daggers from Central Asia, dating from the third century, which had bronze blades and cast iron handles.

For his first three evenings in Moscow, Sage went to the cinema (where the film was the usual dull Soviet fare about the grain harvest), the Bolshoi and a puppet theatre. He was enraptured by the puppet show, in which a university professor fell in love with a much younger champion swimmer. To impress her, the professor pretended to be a diver and performed a daring four-and-one-half somersault dive, which resulted in him being carted off to hospital. The swimmer came to visit him, and when he confessed to being a university professor, he got the girl!

There was a Soviet peace meeting going on, and he met up with the journalist Ilya Ehrenburg and Pablo Neruda, the Chilean poet. They took the night train to Leningrad together and stayed in luxury at the Astoria Hotel. Apart from spending hours at the peace meeting, Bernal visited construction sites and scientific departments, squeezed in an evening at the ballet and a tour of the Hermitage, before returning to Moscow to attend a meeting of the Stalin Peace Prize jury. Sage wondered how many other men shared the peculiar distinction of taking part in committee meetings at the Kremlin, the White House and 10 Downing Street. He was taken to see the tower blocks of Moscow University being built with great speed by the Red Army. There were meetings with the Minister for Power Stations on electricity generation and supply problems, and on irrigation schemes.

In the autumn of 1953, Sage led a delegation of British scientists, invited to the USSR by the Soviet Academy of Sciences.[14] The party included Dorothy Hodgkin, Olga Kennard and the Oxford mathematician Henry Whitehead. Sage flew into Moscow some hours later than the main party, and as soon as he arrived they were all swept into a grand banquet with the Soviet academicians. The numerous courses were interspersed by increasingly loquacious toasts and speeches.[15] Sage then repaired to the grandest suite of rooms at the Metropol Hotel, at the end of a corridor two hundred yards long, where the pipes had to travel such a distance that there was never any hot water. Among the scientists Sage visited was Madame Olga Lepeshinskaya, then over eighty years old, who disputed the cellular theory of life and was a fervent supporter of Lysenko. He did not seem to register any objection to her preposterous theories, perhaps because they were embraced by the state. Sage made the now customary journey from Moscow to Leningrad on the night express. Olga Kennard remembers him coming straight from the Kremlin and sitting up all night drinking vodka as he talked about Stalin (who had died about six months earlier). When the train drew into the station, he said to her, 'Olga, let's creep out the back way and I will show you Leningrad.' They walked everywhere and Sage showed her everything – the Hermitage, the architecture – while giving a tremendous exposition on the art and history of the city. In the end, he said 'Olga, I think we had better go back because those poor people have been waiting for me.' They returned to the station to find a welcoming party still standing there, clutching small bunches of flowers wrapped in newspaper.[16] Later during the trip, Sage flew to Tiflis in Georgia to make a pilgrimage to Stalin's birthplace.[17]

Bernal was a frequent visitor to Hungary in the early 1950s, and was there as the official guest of the Hungarian Academy of Sciences in April 1954. He gave three public lectures and visited most of the scientific and technical institutes in Budapest. The head of the physics department, Professor Lajos

Jánossy, had worked at Birkbeck before the war and then transferred to Manchester with Blackett to continue research on cosmic rays. In Budapest he had a laboratory with meticulous temperature and air current controls, designed originally for cosmic ray work that he was now using to study quantum effects in electromagnetic fields. He was researching into the coherence of light and showed Bernal an elegant experiment demonstrating that there is 'absolutely no correspondence between reflected and refracted waves in the light striking a glass mirror'.[18] Sage was taken with the enthusiasm of the university lecturers he met, but sensed that science in Hungary was being held back by the continued after-effects of the war, language difficulties, and the large teaching load. The Hungarians' contact with Soviet science could not yet replace, he thought, contact with 'the science in the older capitalist countries'.

The centre that impressed him most in Budapest was the Biomedical Institute, where he was fascinated by research on the structure and ageing of *elastin*, the rubbery protein that allows the lungs and blood vessels to stretch and relax. Elastin, a generally indigestible protein, is readily broken down by the enzyme, *elastase*, and the researchers in Budapest showed that this process was accelerated for aged elastin. The implication to Sage was that 'the young or newly formed elastin is the most highly polymerized and that some kind of depolymerisation process, presumably some kind of chain breaking, oxidation, cross-linking or other break is occurring very very slowly with time. I saw an analogy with this and the process which diminishes the elasticity of the lens of the eye, also progressive and apparently quite normal. The problem is really an extremely interesting one, because it does suggest that there is, over and above any pathological ageing, a perfectly natural ageing of tissue itself.'[19]

Sage had been in Hungary three years earlier and was struck by the improvements in the standard of living since his last visit; there was a common *joie de vivre*, people were well dressed and there were many excellent, popular restaurants. After the death of Stalin, the hard-line communist, Matyas Rakosi, was replaced as prime minister by the more liberal figure of Imre Nagy. Nagy had loosened state control of the news media and encouraged public debate about economic and political reform. Bernal was there for the Liberation Day celebrations on 4th April and enjoyed the folk dancing and the firework display over the Danube. Reflecting on the scientific effort in the country, he thought it was showing signs of promise, despite some inevitable unevenness and lack of organization. There were some canvassing a change-over to a more Soviet-style approach, but on balance Sage thought 'they will have to find their own way to suit the conditions. I do not feel that an exact copy of the Soviet system is called for here. The major difficulty as I see it in Hungary, or indeed any country of that size, is the attempt to build on a set of natural resources which are inevitably limited and ill-balanced: in contrast, for instance with a very large country like the Soviet Union, where any imbalance locally is easily made up for by materials from somewhere else.'[20]

In September 1954, Sage was in Moscow again to collect his Stalin prize at the Kremlin. In his acceptance speech, he referred to the success of the peace movement in laying the foundation of a permanent settlement and holding off war. He reminded his audience that, in an atomic age, men could no longer live in hostility to each other. 'Friendship and cooperation became the conditions of survival', he said.[21] Once the stocks of fissile materials were released from military sources, he was optimistic that a rapid increase in available energy from atomic sources would be possible:

That would mean first of all water where it was wanted through irrigation and pumping, unlimited steel and other materials, the end of hard toil and repetitive tasks, the cure of disease and the pushing back of life itself... We cannot allow it to be taken from us by a small group of narrow, embittered and frightened men who would rather hold this power back, would rather use it for destruction in order to preserve their petty interests, their own boasted way of life, which the new life would so completely surpass.[22]

There were some frustrations attached to being a hero of the Soviet Union. He complained to his friend Ilya Ehrenburg:

I have been given a room in a far too luxurious hotel... A programme has been worked out for the few days that I can spend in Moscow: a ride in the Metro, Gorky Street and on Sunday to see the architecture of the agricultural exhibition. This is my eighth visit to Moscow. I know a dozen clever, interesting people in this city, but instead of giving me the opportunity to talk to them, when there are so many engrossing things happening in the world, I am being treated like a sacred cow.[23]

But there were compensations. Sage's request for a personal interview with Khrushchev was immediately granted, and the meeting took place in the Kremlin on 25 September. Khrushchev, who had been promoted a year earlier to first secretary of the Central Committee of the Communist Party had ruthlessly consolidated his grip on power. By the summer of 1954, it was becoming clear, at least within the USSR, that he was the new boss. With his old ally, Georgy Malenkov, Khrushchev had engineered the arrest of Beria in June 1953 and his execution six months later. He then set about eclipsing Malenkov, who had been Stalin's heir apparent. Stalin put Malenkov in charge of agriculture after the war; in 1952 as Stalin's mouthpiece, he announced that the grain crisis was over – a falsehood that Khrushchev would cunningly exploit. The 1952 harvest was, in fact, smaller than it had been before World War I.[24]

In August 1953, with Stalin dead, Malenkov made some rather more enlightened suggestions to improve the woeful state of agriculture: the state should increase prices paid for produce, taxes should be lowered, and peasants' smallholdings should be liberalized.[25] Malenkov, whose two sons were both scientists, went even further, recommending a review of pure and applied science in the USSR. Later he would renounce Lysenko as a charlatan. Khrushchev, who was unwilling to cede control of agriculture to Malenkov, gave a major speech of his own at the Central Committee plenary meeting in September 1953, proposing even more ambitious changes. Without needing to refer directly to Malenkov, Khrushchev took every opportunity to remind audiences of the 1952 statement that the grain problem had been solved, whereas the official government statistics now pointed to a crisis in Soviet farming. During the spring of 1954, Khrushchev displaced Malenkov from the seat of honour at Kremlin meetings of the Presidium, and asserted his own authority.

At his 1954 Kremlin meeting, Bernal's first question was about the grain crisis, and the comments it had sparked in the West about the failure of collectivization. Khrushchev answered, 'Enemies of the Soviet Union are trying to use our criticisms of shortcomings in the sphere of agriculture for their own ends, to put their own meaning into the criticism. Indeed, we sharply criticize our shortcomings in agriculture. However, this is not a kind of self-flagellation prompted by morbid repentance.'[26] He emphasized that the Central Committee did it to educate the workers, to train them and to eliminate problems more rapidly. He saw no contradiction between Stalin's statement at the 18th Party Congress and Malenkov's at 19th Party Congress claiming that the grain problem had been solved and the current push for agricultural reform. Both leaders were right, he told Sage, 'when they said we have enough grain to assure bread for the population'. The task was to satisfy demand for best quality goods to the broad masses (which in capitalist countries, he pointed out, would lead to profiteering). 'The Socialist way is to develop production and continue the policy of reducing prices', he reminded his attentive visitor.

Bernal's second question was about a new Soviet policy to build rural power plants. In his opinion, it seemed that these relatively small plants were 'essentially uneconomic, as they involve higher capital costs than the giant plants you are building'. Khrushchev conceded that the power they produced was much more expensive, but it was still advantageous to collective farms to build small electric stations, because industry took the output from the big ones. By generating their own power, the farmers could use it for their own needs, and run equipment to increase the mechanization of agriculture. Khrushchev thought that as a national grid for distribution was developed, even the farms would obtain their power from large stations. In his answer to Bernal's next question about the allocation of resources in agriculture,

Khrushchev took the opportunity to emphasize his view of the Soviet Union as a whole rather than balancing the needs of one region with another.

While the content of Bernal's interview was quite limited, it was noteworthy as one of the only direct contacts between the new Soviet leader and a Westerner. The international situation was extremely tense – the Soviets exploded their H-bomb in 1953 and seemed to the West to possess an overwhelming superiority of conventional forces in Europe. So when a summary of Bernal's interview was published in *The Times* and the *New York Times* three months later, it provided an almost unique opportunity for Kremlin watchers to glimpse Khrushchev in a spontaneous exchange of ideas. Some of them found the delay in releasing the transcript to be significant, reflecting friction within the Kremlin: Bernal thought it was just because he (and Khrushchev) had been away in China.

The reason for the visit to China was to celebrate the fifth anniversary of the People's Republic. It was Khrushchev's first trip abroad as Soviet leader, and he held talks with Mao Zedong and Zhou Enlai. Sage had been invited by the Chinese Academy of Sciences and was to carry out an extensive survey of science and technology in the country, as well as to take part in the festivities. His journey from Moscow to Peking was more makeshift than that of Khrushchev and his entourage. Flying off the day after his Kremlin interview, the first leg of the journey was about 750 miles south-east to Sverdlovsk. There he had an amusing talk with an interpreter, who was a fan of Mark Twain; Sage explained many words and phrases to him, not found in the Russian dictionary.[27] The other passengers on the plane were a Bulgarian delegation, who had visited Moscow and were now also going to Peking. They took off again at sunset, and were able to see the large factories around the city, before flying through the Siberian night to Novosibirsk, where they landed at dawn. This sprawling city, where the Trans-Siberian railway crosses the River Ob, was an important transportation centre. A sumptuous banquet was laid on for the important visitors, but they just had time to swallow some soup before taking off again. They flew east, a few hundred miles north of the border with Mongolia. Their destination was Irkutsk, a city in eastern Siberia, which they approached in the pink dawn light, flying over range upon range of the Altay mountains.

Sage enjoyed breakfast with a young woman interpreter before resuming what he described as the 'most beautiful and exciting air trip ever'.[28] There were mountains, lakes, forests, grassy hills and dry valleys as they flew south into Mongolia. They landed at Ulan Bator and were received by a deputation in a ceremonial yurt that was identical to those Sage had read about, except for the addition of a wooden door, and an iron stove instead of an open fire. Ornamental rugs hung on the walls and silks lined the roof – their patterns were those that had existed for many thousands of years. There was plenty of local fiery spirit to drink, but little food on offer. As a consequence, Sage found it difficult to stay awake over the Gobi Desert, which appeared from the air to consist mostly of red and yellow patches of rock and clay.

The further east they flew, the more signs of habitation they saw. First there were small villages with square, flat-roofed houses and small enclosures (always on the windward side, Sage noted). Then came forts and walled cities, some grasslands and soon a modern town with a church. The Great Wall appeared 'stretching up and down and round, and winding like a Chinese dragon over the fantastic hills as far as the horizon to the east and the west'.[29] Then came the Great Plain of China, covered with trees, and at last Peking 'with its walls, its great palace in the middle, the lakes that go through it from north to south, the pagodas, the whole plain around dotted with other buildings, old and new, palaces, factories and universities'. They landed at an airfield five miles from the city, near the ancient Summer Palace.

The Bulgarian delegation was let off the plane first, and Sage had to remain in his seat while formalities were completed on the tarmac. He listened to a band playing what he took to be the Bulgarian and Chinese anthems, watched the inspection of a guard of honour through his window and then sat while lengthy speeches were exchanged. Eventually he was allowed to leave the plane, and enjoyed his own 'very discreet reception' by a small group from the Academy of Sciences. He was driven into the city, very excited to have arrived and be so close to the teeming peasants: 'endless rows of donkey carts – very reminiscent of Ireland – people with baskets slung over their backs on poles, with an enormous impression of people and people and people, all busy, all dressed very much alike – blue or black – men and women hardly different. . . . then the first impressions of the city itself – the wall with its many-storied towers'.[30] The sun was setting and suddenly he was overcome with fatigue – the last few miles of the journey felt interminable. Entering the city at last, he was struck by 'streets very wide but so full of people and so covered with shops of all kinds, with bustle, with more bicycles than Cambridge'.[31]

The car dropped him at the Peking Hotel, 'a vast rather colonial edifice with nothing Chinese about it', and from his room he could see crowds gathering with flags to celebrate the new constitution that had been declared that day. He went straight into a banquet, 'which seemed to last a long time and probably did'. He loved authentic Chinese food 'crisp, delicious and so varied'. Toast after toast was drunk with warm wine and after dinner, he went out into streets, full of people dancing and singing in the 'most confused, delightful and spontaneous way imaginable'. He got to bed at midnight.

He woke late the next morning and received a visit from Felix Aprahamian and Ivor Montagu, who had travelled from London. They spent the day sightseeing together, and naturally their first destination was the Forbidden City, or Emperors' Palace, which they entered through the Tiananmen Gate. Awestruck they strolled across the five marble bridges in the first courtyard and came to successive courtyards of 'ever increasing dignity'. Sage was moved by the extraordinary effect of repetition and symmetry in the architecture. The pavilions and halls were all constructed from wood, which surprised him; their decorations with red lacquer, dragons, phoenixes, and the sweeping, gold-tiled roofs contrasted brilliantly with the grey roofs of the dismal buildings in Peking. Thinking no doubt of Jane, his baby daughter in London, Sage was delighted by a group of small children in the first courtyard, 'sitting on the ground with their bare behinds'. He noted with satisfaction, 'The Chinese have a most practical system of maintaining a slit in the trousers, while we stuff them with nappies'.[32]

Sage decided that his favourite art was from the Sung period 'when art depicted the lives of ordinary people, and in such a wealth of figure and gesture that made it all become enormously alive'. Later, he found how little life had changed in the succeeding seven or eight centuries in terms of everyday implements. In a museum in the Forbidden City, he made his first acquaintance with that great piece of Chinese machinery – the crossbow lock – 'the ancestor of all military lock mechanisms and of such mundane articles as the common typewriter.' His only regret was that his friend, Joseph Needham, was not with him to illuminate the experience.

The next day he visited the Temple of Heaven, where he found the architecture to be of the same order as St Peter's or the Taj Mahal. He reflected on the naïve preoccupation of the Chinese with astrology: 'so peculiar that people so wrapped, as they were, in careful calendrical observations should ever have bothered to go beyond the elements of astronomy, and it was only when these astrological aspects had been forgotten that the real advances in astronomy were to come.' That evening there was a reception given by Zhou Enlai. The entertainment was provided by Bulgarian and Indonesian dancers, who looked like fairies, dressed in silk. Among the guests were mayors of Chinese cities, and the Dalai Lama. The gregarious Zhou Enlai showed 'terrific *joie de vivre*, shaking hands and drinking toasts'. Mao himself came and said a few words to the assembled company. Bernal's spirits were dampened by news from England of the Labour Party Conference, where a controversial vote on the rearmament of West Germany had just passed by a very narrow majority. He wrote up his interview with Khrushchev after the banquet, so that Aprahamian could take it back to London.

The next morning, Sage set off for the Summer Palace with Ivor Montagu and his wife. There they were confronted by a 'mounting set of horrors of bad taste' – restorations undertaken by officials not by artists and archaeologists.

In the afternoon, he went to the parliament house to hear about the new constitution and listened to four hours of speeches in various languages by foreign envoys, including Khrushchev. Sage was excited by the auspices for Liberation Day: the Korean War was over, the IndoChina war in Vietnam appeared settled after the Geneva Conference in June, and prospects for economic production and peace around the world were, he thought, better than ever.

On Liberation Day, 1st October, Sage got up before dawn. He breakfasted in his room on fried eggs, which the Chinese insisted on giving him as a foreigner – 'always three, always cold.' He put on his suit and pinned the Stalin medal on his lapel, before making his way through jam-packed streets to the stand reserved for foreign delegates. Two little schoolgirls led the procession, followed by ranks of troops and then 100–200 people passed every second for four hours. There were trades unionists, miners carrying picks, textile workers, railwaymen, steel workers, peasants, and then different religious groups. The mood was one of humour, gaiety, and ease. There were balloons, banners, streamers and whistles adding to performances by dancers, athletes, and a final troop of tough, well-drilled school sports teams. 'Chairman Mao and others smiling and extending a greeting, which was clearly taken up by each group as they passed the grandstand. It was the most intimate linking of the people with their leader because one thing seems to be clearer than anything else in China – the simple affection that Mao creates.'

In his overexcited state, Sage decided that Peking was one of the cleanest and liveliest cities in the world. He thought that the Chinese economy, in which nothing was wasted, was extraordinary. He saw 'in one little back street they are occupied with stone rollers in rolling out galvanized iron quite flat and then in another part of the workshop rolling it up again to make drainpipes out of it'.[33] These peasants were the forerunners of Mao's Great Leap Forward, in which the modernization of China was to be forced by the spread of industrialization throughout the country. As an economic strategy, it was indeed extraordinary, and caused millions of useful tools and household utensils to be melted down to produce millions of tons of poor quality steel, useless for any industrial purpose, at the cost of enormous labour and energy consumption.

As part of the nationalist celebrations, there were exhibitions from various other countries and Sage went to see the Soviet one. Although there were electron microscopes, spectroscopes and computers on display, demonstrating the scientific excellence of the USSR, he was disappointed that the cultural element was represented by rooms full of old pictures and Russian books. The following week was taken up with more sightseeing around the city, preliminary visits to various scientific institutes and some adventurous tours.

He took an overnight train to inspect the Kuangting water reservoir, where workers had constructed a dam by hand, moving two billion cubic metres of earth and facing it with stone. The work was scheduled to be completed within three years, and Sage observed 'nothing bigger than small concrete mixers, and with stone cutting, shifting and earth shifting done by gangs. There was plain evidence of very finely-built workers villages including not only canteens but a theatre ... When it is completed it will be a good if somewhat minor source of power for the Peking area, but will also serve for a great deal of irrigation ...'[34]

A few days later, Sage was in the hills to the west of the city and insisted on hiking up them, dressed in his suit, in sweltering weather. From the crest of the main ridge, he was rewarded by magnificent views in all directions: to the north, ridge after ridge as far as the Great Wall; higher mountains to the west; to the south, the river on which the dam was being built, as well as iron works and the Marco Polo bridge; to the east, the Ming tombs and the city itself, shrouded in haze. He descended through a wooded valley, rather steep and rocky, with a stream gushing from under rock. He came across a little temple, the Temple of Quiet Happiness. As he was walking through a village, he heard a child cry for the first time since he had been in China – it was a little girl who had fallen and cut her face. This small incident made him reflect on the most remarkable change in New China – 'an internal human and moral change in the people.'

Sage became friendly with a man called Rewi Ali, whom he found 'amusing and enlightening'. The pair took breakfast together and Rewi would tell him about Chinese history as well as modern China. One morning, he discussed agriculture and land reform in China. From the first year of communist rule, the redistribution of land to peasants and the punishment of exploitative landlords were given a high priority as a way to bring revolutionary fervour to the rural areas and to guarantee loyalty to the Party. Rewi told Sage that the policy of liquidating landowners was exaggerated because out of several thousand in his area, only three had been executed.

Bernal began a series of lectures at the Institute of Applied Physics, given to huge audiences. He found the first lecture on teaching and research in crystallography 'rather heavy going' because everything he said had to be translated and written on the blackboard in Chinese characters. The second lecture, a day later on crystallographic apparatus and technique, was more practical and he thought more successful. That night there was a full moon and Sage went back to the Forbidden City with Mr Wu from the Academy of Sciences. They persuaded the night watchman to let them inside and enjoyed walking round in magical conditions. 'Incongruously, Mr Wu still wanted to talk about crystallography and this occupied us all the way back to the hotel.'[35]

The next evening Bernal gave a four-hour talk on dislocations in metals, attracting the biggest audience yet and provoking the liveliest discussion.

He spent 15th October touring the huge Peking University and was invited to give more lectures to the physics and chemistry departments. The Arts faculty also asked him to contribute to a meeting that they were planning to mark the tercentenary of the death of the English writer, Henry Fielding. The following day Bernal gave a five-hour talk on the social function of science at the Peking Library. After his week of lectures, Sage was taken to the site south-west of the city where the bones and teeth of Peking Man, *homo erectus*, had been excavated. These remains were found in caves at the edge of the plain and Bernal was impressed with the number of bear and hyena bones in the same caves, suggesting that life had been brutal and short. The pace of his activities increased again over the next week as he visited various national laboratories, the Ministry of Heavy Industry, and gave lectures on subjects ranging from 'The origin of life' to 'Recent advances in understanding of the role of hydrogen in inorganic and organic substances'.

Nehru brought an Indian delegation to Peking for the Liberation Day celebrations. The end of his visit was marked by an official banquet and he insisted on taking Sage as his guest. Sage found himself sitting with Dutch and Pakistani diplomats, and was intrigued that the Dutch Ambassador was van Zeeman, the nephew of the discoverer of the Zeeman effect.* An even more pleasant surprise was the Ambassador's attractive young wife, with whom he had a lively conversation about opera and cooking in Peking. At the end of the evening, Nehru took his guest back to the French Embassy, where he was staying, and the two sat up for hours discussing science in China. Nehru asked Sage to stop in New Delhi on his journey home. The day after the banquet, Bernal went to the Fielding celebration at the university and gave his talk on 'Fielding and the Industrial Revolution'.

His hosts loaded more and more onto Sage's broad shoulders, and he was so engrossed by everything he saw that it never occurred to him to protest. He had now been in Peking for a month and was still able to produce a new lecture every day. One of the modern customs that amused him was the sight of mass physical exercise. He thought that 'exercises in China are very much what prayers are to the Mohammedans – something which goes on regularly three times a day'. Before leaving Peking, Bernal made a radio broadcast. He told the listeners that he never expected to see such a scientific effort built in such a short time. The history of science in China was much older than in Europe, but 'the new science of China can be said to date almost entirely from

---

* Described by Peter Zeeman in 1896, atomic line spectra are altered in a strong magnetic field.

the liberation in 1949'. It was an enormous effort, 'compared with anything
elsewhere and even to a certain extent compared with what is going on in the
Soviet Union and the other popular democracies today, the scale of effort in
China is really stupendous'.[36] He thought that the Chinese authorities were
essentially copying the Soviet model of institutes attached to specific industries and attempting to have everything in place in just five years.

On 12th November he embarked on the two-day train journey south to
Nanking. He had two companions from the Academy of Sciences – Mr Wu
and Mr Chien. Loudspeakers in their compartment blared Chinese opera
incessantly as they sped over the Yellow River and across the flooded Yangtze
plain. The chef on board would come and discuss menus with the two
Chinese; Bernal found that they could not possibly eat all the delicious
chicken and pork that he prepared for them. When the train needed to
cross the wide Yangtze River itself, there was no bridge and it was loaded
onto a ferry. Arriving in Nanking in the afternoon, Bernal managed to visit
four scientific institutes before retiring to bed with a fever, looking very green
indeed. The next morning a doctor was called and visited with 'a very demure
nurse called Miss Chien', who took his pulse and temperature and gave him
some 'rather peculiar medicine'. He dozed for the rest of the morning, but the
temptation of seeing the Suchow Opera got him out of bed. He watched four
plays, with the common theme that women have the best of life, which so
delighted him that he felt perfectly cured. Over the next few days he paid
official visits to the observatory, the institutes of soil research, palaeontology,
geophysics, geography, botany and history as well as reviewing university
laboratories of physics, chemistry, geology and biology. He sailed down the
Yangtze, taking note of the great number of junks on the river, to see a
fertilizer factory. There he saw that, just as at a steel works he had visited in
the north, the production process was quite automated, but the finished
product was all manhandled.

On 17th November, Bernal's party took their leave of Nanking and caught
the train to Shanghai. The next few days were taken up with the customary
site visits and long evening lectures. He made a one-day visit to the beautiful
city of Hangzhou, where he held meetings with scientists and was taken to see
Buddhist and Taoist temples, and the local museum, where the greatest
treasure on view was the magic fish bowl. This is a bronze bowl, which
when filled with water and has its handles suitably rubbed, produces four
jets of water rising about two feet from the surface. It was clear to Sage that 'it
is a question of ultrasonic vibrations. The attendant did it magnificently. My
scientific knowledge only produced a few drops of water.'[37] Sage by now was
addicted to Chinese opera and would try to attend a production in each new
city: among his favourites were 'Chang Yu boils the sea' and the 'Lohan coin'.

He spent his last few days in the People's Republic in Canton, the gateway to China. As usual, the time was packed with university and museum visits. As he was about to board the train for Kowloon, Wu and Chien asked him for an honest appraisal of their hospitality. Sage was touched by their earnestness but did manage one criticism. He told them they should be careful not to ask other foreign scientists to work continuously from 6 am until midnight, because people were not used to it. In reply, Chien and Wu said that he had worked them too hard!

The train to Kowloon ran alongside what he thought must be one of the most beautiful coasts in the world and gave the impression of passing a series of holiday resorts. After two months in mainland China, the affluence and brashness of Hong Kong came as a shock to his senses. He was met at the station by a number of reporters eager to hear about the state of science in China. Bernal sat down and gave them a lengthy account, which was generously carried in the newspapers, in a way it would not have been in England. One of his first impressions of Hong Kong was of the enormous prevalence of every kind of religious institute. He presumed 'this is partly a kind of reflux of the missionary movement from the rest of China, but I cannot imagine anywhere, even in Spain, that has a higher density of religious establishments'.[38]

From Hong Kong, Sage flew to India, where at the invitation of Sir Shanti Swarup Bhatnagar FRS, the Minister for Science, he carried out another detailed review of the country's scientific institutes in a hectic three-week tour. He also took the opportunity to address the plenary session of the All-India Congress for Peace, where he appealed for cooperation with those political leaders who were demanding an absolute ban on atom and H-bombs. In an interview with the *Indian Express* newspaper in Madras, Sage was asked to compare scientific progress in India with that in China. He replied that 'science progress in India, though good, was not fast enough as compared to China'. When the reporter wondered whether this was due to the different political systems, Sage stated that both countries had mixed economies, but in China the government was in control of things. He wondered who in India was in such control.[39] He flew back to London on New Year's Day 1955, having been away for over three months, with more information about technological developments in the USSR, China and India stored in his head than any Western government agency could match.

Khrushchev's devastating speech exposing some of the crushing inhumanity of Stalin's regime (in which he served throughout) was made in a closed session of the communist party congress in February 1956. In March, Bernal attended a small meeting of the European Cultural Association in Venice, where he seems to have been baited at every turn by Stephen Spender, the writer who had become an active anti-communist.[40] According to Spender, one of the interpreters asked how it was that Bernal 'who is so logical in every way, so objective, and who also has a sense of humour, can be so completely illogical and unobjective whenever the discussion comes round to Communism?'[41] Spender asked Sage what he thought about Stalin. He replied, 'We seem to have made some very serious mistakes.' When Spender suggested that such mistakes were inevitable under communism, Bernal stated that he still preferred communism to the alternative system. When asked why, he referred to the 'utter unnecessary misery and waste and lack of opportunity that exists in the world as it is at present . . . One person who is greedy and dishonest who gets into a strong position can undo the good done by hundreds.'

Copies of Khrushchev's speech began to circulate through the Warsaw Pact countries during the spring, and the CIA had a copy in early April.[42] The world at large was apprised of its content by the *New York Times* in June, and naturally the report triggered considerable doubts amongst communists and Stalin's loyal supporters in the West. Within the Soviet bloc, Khrushchev's words were misinterpreted by some to signal imminent political reform. In Hungary, where there had already been some relief from the Stalinist grip, the speech encouraged bolder action towards a more liberal society. Anti-Soviet demonstrations started by students at the end of October 1956 quickly attracted mass support, and the reformer Nagy promised the far-reaching democratization of Hungarian public life. He formed a coalition government and asked the UN to guarantee Hungary's neutrality and to shield it from the USSR. Nagy called for the Soviet troops to be withdrawn and stated that Hungary would withdraw from the Warsaw Pact. The challenge to the authority of the USSR was unmistakable and after some initial hesitation, Khrushchev took decisive action. He ordered the Red Army to crush the uprising, which they did within the first few days of November, killing several thousand Hungarian citizens in the process.

The brutality of the Red Army came as a shock to some Soviet sympathizers in Britain, who had been spared any press coverage of its liberation of Berlin a decade earlier. One of Bernal's friends described him as looking 'haggard and wretched' at the time.[43] Dorothy Hodgkin said he was in tears and went to the Soviet Embassy to lodge his protest, for which he was rebuked by his friend Harry Pollitt, General Secretary of the CPGB.[44] Aaron Klug went to a meeting arranged by the Fabian Society at University College to discuss the Soviet invasion of Hungary. Bernal was one of the speakers and it was the first time Klug heard him make a political speech – just as at Cambridge before the war, Bernal never talked politics in the laboratory. Klug was amazed by Sage's opening statement, 'Ever since June, we have known that things have been going on in Soviet Russia.'[45] Klug was incredulous. He thought back to his boyhood in South Africa, when he had read all about the Soviet show trials in the newspapers and said to himself, 'Ever since June – I have known it since 1938, when I was 11 years old!'

Bernal was in Budapest six months after the Revolution and spent his first night there with an old friend, the Marxist philosopher, George Lukács. Lukács, who spent many years exiled in the USSR before and during the Second World War, had been appointed Minister of Culture in Nagy's very short-lived administration. Nagy would be executed for attempting to overthrow the 'democratic state order', but Lukács' luck held and he was merely deported to Bulgaria for a few months. Sage was apprehensive about what condition Lukács might be in, as a result of his recent experiences, and was relieved to find him 'as cheerful, alert and intelligent as ever. His only comment on his exile was "We enjoyed the conditions of pure communism. We had no money but were given everything we asked for." He showed no sign of suffering, bitterness or disillusion, rather, a philosophical cheerfulness and a determination to master the situation by understanding it.'[46] Bernal accompanied Lukács and his wife to a neighbourhood restaurant. When they walked in 'many heads turned and there was much whispering and smiling but no overt demonstration. If Lukács is back, things must be easier was what I gathered from the general atmosphere.'[47]

Bernal wrote several articles about his visit, in which he attempted to reassure the worried fellow travellers and socialists of England. In a disgraceful piece in the *New Statesman*, he sought to justify the Soviet invasion on the grounds that it quelled a nascent anti-Semitism in Hungary.[48] His article in *Tribune*, on reconstructing Hungary's economy and science, offered the following analysis of what had gone wrong in a country that just three years earlier displayed such spirit and affluence.

The economic roots of the troubles of last year lay in the policy of attempting far too much...hence the pressure on the workers with a harshly operated piece work system; hence the pressure on the peasants for deliveries which left them with little of their own produce; hence, at one remove, the police tyranny needed to enforce these unpopular measures. What is now being planned is a more realistic industrial system which concentrates on the lines in which Hungarian industry has had long experience, such as diesel engines or electrical machinery, or where they have special natural resources such as aluminium ore.[49]

Suggesting that the media coverage of the uprising had exaggerated its effects, Sage explained that there had been little physical damage, and what there was had already been repaired. There was more good news: 'deliveries of grain from the Soviet Union and improved relationships with peasants...more food available than for many years past.' The curfew was over, there were no troops on the streets and few armed police. Belief in the correctness of Marxism should not be shaken by recent events because as Lukács explained to Bernal:

> ...the major weakness in the further development of Marxism had been its subordination, during much of the Stalin era, to the service of immediate political and economic requirements with the consequent neglect of an adequate Marxist analysis of the great and positive social achievements of the Soviet peoples. Lukács reasserted his faith in the basic superiority of the socialist system, which even despite the great mistakes that had been made, had already achieved so much.[50]

There was brief reference in the *Tribune* article to Hungary's scientists, and he covered their status more fully in a short note in *Nature*.[51] Pointing out that there had been minimal disruption to university life, Sage recounted the flourishing research work being undertaken by Jánossy and others.

> More significant, however, than the continuation of work in progress is the effort that is now being made to re-organize the whole scientific activity of the country to eliminate the errors and distortions of the past and to bring it into relation with a more realistic planning of industry and agriculture. In this replanning, scientists are playing a much more important part than formerly, for it is realized that the undertaking of the over-ambitious and misdirected industrial enterprises of the former regime could have been avoided if responsible scientific and technical advice had been taken in the first place.

In his view, Hungary was now set fair to emulate the successes of Switzerland and Denmark as a small country with a buoyant, specialized economy, underpinned by a strong research effort in pure and applied science. Nearly half a century later, the younger generation of Hungarian scientists are frustrated by 'the grip that the old guard, and its Soviet-era thinking, still has on the Hungarian scientific establishment'.[52]

Mao Zedong initially advised Khrushchev against invading Hungary to suppress the revolution, believing that the working class of Hungary would achieve this by themselves.[53] Mao came to view Khrushchev as a leader of limited ability, lacking in 'revolutionary morality', and never forgave him for his criticism of Stalin.[54] Khrushchev's words struck too close to home – Mao's style of ruling could be characterized by the same 'cult of personality' charge: he and Stalin displayed the same paranoia in their need for absolute adulation. At the time of the Hungarian uprising, Mao indicated that free speech for intellectuals in China would be encouraged, saying 'Let a hundred flowers bloom' and 'a hundred schools of thought contend'. When this unleashed a torrent of criticism about the Party and the irrelevance of Marxism to Chinese life, he smartly reversed course in the summer of 1957 with an 'Anti-Rightist campaign' to purge dissident intellectuals, 'the poisonous weeds' who lurked amongst the flowers.[55]

Not lacking in 'revolutionary morality' himself, Mao set China on a radical course to catastrophe. Known as the Great Leap Forward, it was a policy based on Mao's faith in the limitless capacity of the peasantry to produce steel and food, if they were efficiently organized. In 1958, existing land cooperatives were merged into communes of 50,000 people for whom the state would provide childcare, cooking and medical services. All private ownership of land was abolished and even farm animals were collectivized. Agricultural techniques were based on Lysenko's theories, coupled with some of Mao's own nostrums such as planting seeds close together – 'with company they grow easily.'[56] Instead of the giant harvest, blithely predicted by Mao, there was famine. The harsh reality was concealed in official reports from the communes, which were euphoric in tone, and grain exports were doubled. By the following summer, stories of widespread starvation were commonplace, but the only government official who dared bring them to Mao's attention, the Minister of Defence, Peng Dehuai, was accused of 'factional activity' and dismissed from his post. Where Party officials had predicted a doubling or trebling of yields in 1959, the harvest was 30 million tonnes less than the previous year's, partly due to severe floods in July. Government statistics, nevertheless, showed a considerable increase.[57] It is estimated that approximately 30 million people starved to death between 1958 and 1962 as a result of the Great Leap.

The 1959 harvest coincided with the tenth anniversary celebrations of the founding of the People's Republic, and once again Sage found himself rubbing shoulders with communist leaders in Peking. His first impression was how much modernization had occurred since his last visit, with wide roads now leading into the city from a modern airport. Khrushchev was nominally the guest of honour, but was treated with utter contempt by the hosts because of his recent criticism of the Great Leap and his refusal to supply China with a prototype atomic bomb.[58] As Sage was watching the firework display from the Gate of Heavenly Peace, he was approached by a tall Russian, who asked 'Anglichani?' Sage nodded and the Russian said 'Bernal'. 'I had to admit it, and he said "Nikita Sergeyevich wants to speak to you."'[59] Bernal followed to where Khrushchev was just taking leave of Mao. Bernal had a friendly exchange with the Russian leader, and the two agreed to have a serious talk on the morrow. He also saw Zhou Enlai, who promised him an interview later. Finally he spoke to Mao, who enquired after his book *Science in History*, which had just been translated into Chinese.

Bernal's son, Martin, now in his early twenties and an outstanding Orientalist, was a postgraduate student in Peking, and that evening they were reunited. Martin took his father to a party, where Sage soon abandoned a more adult gathering to join the younger generation and learned to rock and roll. He went to bed at 2.30 am and rose at 6 am to meet Ho Chi Minh, who was on a diplomatic mission to raise support for the communist struggle in Vietnam. Later that morning, he had his promised meeting with Khrushchev. As we shall see, Bernal found that the two politicians held divergent views on the situation in SE Asia, and Khrushchev was forthcoming about the cold war. After a late lunch, Sage visited an agricultural show, where the techniques of modern farming and the large communes were being celebrated – with no mention of the disastrous harvest.

The schedule for the following week was a familiar one for Sage, visiting schools, scientific institutes, tractor works and a massive construction project where thousands were toiling to dam the Yellow River. The cultural highlight was a visit to the ancient capital of Xian with its huge Buddhist pagodas, dating from the Tang dynasty. Sage and Martin flew back to Peking in rough weather. At one stopover, they were given a banquet of chicken, duck, mutton, beef and fish. Sage arrived in Peking feeling ill and depressed. His spirits were further dampened by an undiplomatic message from Zhou Enlai, saying that 'he did not see any value in seeing me'.[60]

Before leaving China, Bernal was taken to the showpiece Yellow Ridge Commune, about 15 miles from Peking. Started in 1958, it was smaller than many Great Leap communes. In total there were 26,000 people living there, engaged in agriculture as well as operating 26 small factories. Bernal thought the commune did not have enough new buildings, and the factories were on a primitive scale, but with introduction of electric power, he could imagine productivity improving and a high standard of living for the peasants. Martin, by this time, was becoming disillusioned with Mao and the Great Leap Forward because he had heard many stories about the famine in rural areas. He thought that the optimistic official statistics were fraudulent. He raised these doubts with his father, and Sage agreed that the government figures were neither valid nor accurate.[61] Back in London, Martin's mother, Margaret Gardiner, asked Bernal what he would do if Martin were to be arrested in China. He replied that he would go straight to Mao Zedong and demand his release.[62]

Just as the late 1950s was a period of upheaval for the Soviet Empire, it saw the rapid unravelling of the British Empire. The independence of India had been the first step in 1947, and a decade later decolonization spread to Africa. Ghana, previously the Gold Coast, was one of the first nations to gain independence and was eager to establish institutions with an African face. Dorothy Hodgkin's husband, Thomas, was a leading spokesman for the cause of African nationalism and formed friendships with many future leaders, including Kwame Nkrumah, the first President of Ghana. Hodgkin was experienced in the field of adult education and it was natural that Nkrumah should turn to him for advice on reforming Ghana's university system. Hodgkin wrote to Sage in the summer of 1960, asking him to serve on a small advisory committee to redesign the tertiary education system so that it would relate 'as closely as possible to the needs of modern Ghana and modern Africa [and] take the place of the existing (strongly Cambridge influenced) model, which dates from the colonial period'.[63] Sage naturally accepted the invitation, and a visit to Ghana was arranged for the Christmas vacation.

Bernal's fellow commissioners were from the USA, the USSR and Sierra Leone; he found them to be agreeable company and Mr Botzio, a Ghanaian government minister appointed to be commission chairman, was 'genial and conscientious'. Following a formal dinner on their first evening together in Accra, Sage sat on a terrace under the stars, drinking brandy and coffee, talking and reflecting on the notion of 'translating the spirit of Cambridge into the barbarities of the Gold Coast'.[64] This was one of the few moments of relaxation in what would be three weeks of intensive work. Botzio made it clear from the outset that the two main government aims were to increase the numbers of students and to appoint more Africans to university staff positions.

Before visiting any universities, the commissioners went to two schools. The first, a middle school, reminded Sage of a village school in China: 'bare walls and everything reduced to extreme simplicity.'[65] He was impressed by the domestic science teaching – no nonsense about modern methods but an old cooking pot on three lumps of clay. They also went to Achimota College, which had very good staff and excellent buildings. It was a private school, whose alumni filled all the top technical and administrative positions in the country. Just as in Hong Kong, the influence of Christian missionaries was strongly in evidence, with hymn singing everywhere.

Thomas Hodgkin joined them for their first visit to Legon University, just outside Accra. Bernal visited the science departments, which were well staffed and equipped, but produced very few students. He was especially interested in the Geology Department, where two devoted English scientists had spent much time revealing the strange Precambrian rock strata underlying central Ghana. They were going to be supplanted by a team of thirty Soviet geologists, and Bernal was optimistic that soon 'we really will get to know something about the country'.[66] He wondered how the Ghanaians were going to convert from tribalism to socialism. At the medical school, he heard about high childhood mortality due to protein malnutrition; he had already seen a university farm, where, despite heroic efforts, the animal stock did poorly. Thinking back to his own boyhood at Brookwatson, he immediately grasped the impossibility of raising cattle where there was a severe water shortage and no way of making dry fodder such as hay.

New Year's Eve found Sage improvising new dances in a packed ballroom at Kumasi, the capital of the Asanti region. He was impressed by the Kumasi College of Technology, where students could qualify with external degrees in engineering from the University of London, and there were also schools of pharmacy, architecture and building. On 3rd January, the commissioners flew further north and visited a tribal village. Sage noticed the cleanliness of the round huts. They were taken to see a sacred pool, where some boys were teasing a crocodile with a live chicken on a string. The crocodile eventually caught the chicken and swallowed it in one gulp. The American commissioner expressed her horror at this outcome, until Sage reminded her that she had eaten chicken for supper the night before, and from the chicken's point of view, there was not much difference. It was a poor area, where boys were used to herd cattle and drive them south to the cities for sale. There was not much enthusiasm, Sage noted, for educating girls.

The commissioners visited the small, but relatively wealthy city of Ho, in the Volta region. In Ho, Bernal was encouraged to find some co-educational schools. The commissioners visited a juice bottling plant run by a woman, who told them 'if you have been to the co-ed school, you can stare in the eyes of the boy and kick him out!'[67] Back in Accra, they met Nkrumah for the first time, and he displayed a lively interest in the educational programme. The commissioners spent one day revising a draft report, which Sage had finished writing at 3.30am, and the final version was delivered to Nkrumah on 11th January.

The report's central recommendation was to create two independent universities, one in Legon and the second in Kumasi, with a training college in Cape Coast. It also called for the Africanization of the staff as rapidly as was compatible with maintaining the quality of teaching and research. Nkrumah's administration adopted it immediately and caused some ill feeling by sacking some lecturers without compensation, and abruptly discontinuing certain courses. Their radical approach found favour with the *Ghanaian Times*, which applauded the end of the reactionary, bourgeois university system. The newspaper told its readers that 'Africa is in revolutionary ferment. Our institutions of higher learning cannot stand still.'[68] Confident in the future, the editorial writer eagerly anticipated the teaching of economics and history from an African perspective, and the advent of socialist economic planning. Nkrumah persuaded Thomas Hodgkin to become the first Director of the Institute of African Studies at the University of Ghana in Legon, (although Hodgkin and the commission had called for the elimination of European staff). He also appointed an Irishman, Connor Cruise O'Brien, as the Vice-Chancellor, but soon came to regret this when O'Brien resisted Nkrumah's crude attempts at increased state control of the University.[69]

In May 1963, Bernal was asked to advise on a new professor of physics for the University of Ghana. There were five candidates, and Bernal said that his top choice was Alan Nunn May, 'a most distinguished physicist'.[70] May had become a communist while a Cambridge undergraduate in the thirties; during the war, he worked as a member of the British nuclear research team in Canada. After the war, he was the first atomic spy to be unmasked and served six years hard labour for supplying secrets to the Soviets. In his recommendation, Bernal referred to this interruption to May's career as resulting from an act of conscience against the misuse of science, and suggested that without it, May would have risen to the top in modern physics. With Bernal's support, May was appointed and served the University well as professor and Dean until he retired in 1976.

Sage undertook his last great adventure at the age of sixty, when he travelled to South America in January 1962. He was invited to speak at a summer school at the University of Concepción on the rugged Pacific coast of Chile. It was, he soon found, a country where geology played a prominent role – there had been a devastating earthquake two years earlier, mining was the major industry, and the Andes range and numerous volcanoes were testament to the earth's prehistoric upheavals. It was a landscape that excited him from the moment he saw the rising sun over the peaks of the Andes. After a breakfast discussion at his Santiago hotel about 'the present state of the life-in-meteorites problem', Sage was driven up into the mountains, where 'the scenery became more and more grand' as they ascended to 10,000 feet, and he caught sight of the snow-covered peak of a volcano at 21,000 feet.[71] On his second day in Chile, he flew from Santiago south-west to Concepción and the bright weather afforded him 'a magnificent view of the Andes as a set of more or less isolated peaks'. On arrival, he 'plunged right into the business of the summer school, a large hall which was in the Institute of Jurisprudence, of course without any such things as blackboards or screens [but] with a very considerable audience'.[72]

The summer school finished after Bernal had been there for about a week. A philosophy professor from Santiago gave a closing lecture which 'lasted an hour and a half and gave the most gloomy impression of civilization and its doom... I, luckily was chosen to express the views of the invited guests which I did more optimistically and forcibly in a quarter of an hour.'[73] He was in a rush because friends had promised to take him on a hike in the volcanic region about seventy miles from Concepción. Travelling by bus and lorry along increasingly primitive and dusty roads, they passed through rich farmlands where they saw horsemen mounted on silver saddles; they also came across extremely poor peasants, who were using ox-carts with solid wooden wheels made exactly like those shown in paintings from Sumerian times.

Rising at 5.30 am the next morning, Sage was fascinated by the variety of hot springs close to the hotel – 'some of mud, some of water, some with steam blowing through cold water, many of gas, largely sulphurous depositing sulphur salt, boracic acid and other chemicals along the holes, and always changing their position so that the whole ground was speckled in different colours, deep reds, blacks, purples, yellows, greens, by various effects of manganese, iron and, curiously enough, specific algae which only grew in the very hot water.' The really serious climb of the day started after breakfast, emerging above the tree-line into hot sun, over ridges and down into valleys of spectacular beauty, with hot and cold streams running through them every few yards. Bernal had never seen such lush grassland that was not used by cattle, and everywhere there were flowers. The ground rose so steeply that every hundred yards or so they came across new kinds of flowers, gentians and an enormous number of bright species they could not identify. Working their way up towards the peak of the volcano, which although covered in parts with snow and ice was still steaming, they managed to get above the snow-line before turning back. Down at the hotel there was just time to take a cool bathe in a pool, from where they could see all the surrounding mountains, before the long trudge to the nearest town, Chilan. There, Bernal boarded a bus to Concepción and then Santiago. On eventually reaching his hotel in Santiago, he felt he had spent 'a fairly complete twenty-hour day'.

He was up early the next morning to give a series of lectures at the Institute of Physics. After a delicious lunch in the shade of ilex trees, drinking Chilean wine and talking about the problems of Latin America and the native Indians, he returned to the university to give two more lectures, one on molecular biology and one on the origin of life. These ran over time so he was late for a talk to the Chilean Peace Committee.

This meeting lasted rather longer than I expected, in fact until well after 11 o'clock, after which I was driven across town to a hill... the last bit of the Andes which is still left in Santiago. There I went to the house of my old friend Pablo Neruda, the national poet of Chile who is still revered even when he is considered politically subversive. Pablo Neruda has built himself a fantastic house on this hill with all the rooms naturally on different levels, separated by stone staircases [and] through the garden with a little stream flowing through it making ponds with goldfish... I thought I had arrived, of course, long after they had had their dinner, but, after talking for about three-quarters of an hour, he said 'I think it is about time we went down to dinner now.' So we went down these staircases into another room where we were served a real Chilean dinner with lots of roast meat and other things, more wine and more conversation. I started making excuses that it was a bit late but I was not released until about one-thirty in the morning.

The next afternoon Bernal flew over the Andes to the neighbouring country of Argentina and stayed in Buenos Aires for the last few days of January. Buenos Aires he found to be a more chaotic and bustling city than Santiago, reflecting to some extent the Italian influence there versus the German heritage of Chile. Although he regarded Argentina as a police state, he was pleasantly surprised that he was able to go to the House of Deputies and have informal discussions with a number of politicians about the problems of Latin America, particularly the foreign policy of the new Kennedy administration that had just been unveiled at a conference at Punta del Este in Uruguay. He noted that political life in Buenos Aires was rather exciting because the military had just issued an ultimatum to the president to disavow Castro's Cuba or be removed from office. Bernal was lionized by the illegal Argentine peace organization, who gave a four-hour dinner in his honour, attended by academics, trade unionists, students and representatives of women's movements. The following night, he addressed a clandestine peace meeting, where he first had to listen to 'four rather long and very flattering speeches from various kinds of delegates describing my capacities and virtues'. Feeling 'extremely embarrassed', he kept his own remarks short and then received 'such prolonged applause that [he] had to stop it by saying that it would not be allowed in the Soviet Union because it would indicate a "cult of personality"'.[74]

The final stop on his South American tour was Rio de Janeiro, 'an incredibly beautiful place'. While he had not seen a single African face in Chile or Argentina, in Rio 'as a result of slavery which was only abolished in 1890, about half the population is black and, as it seems to be the case, despite the idea that there is no racial inequality, they seem to be doing all the rough jobs'. The whole trip had taken only two weeks, but during that time Bernal made some very astute observations about the conditions of the countries he visited. All three nations depended on American capital to such an extent that he thought they were all colonies of the new imperialism. Chile was the most extreme in both its geography and its economy.

Chile is a country with enormous material resources – minerals, water-power, agriculture, forests and fisheries – all largely unused, a development held back by local feudalism. Forty families own between them nearly all the good land, and foreign countries, largely the United States, own and export all the minerals. Ninety per cent of the resources of the country are foreign owned. On the peasant holdings, conditions are unbelievably primitive for the New World. There are few modern roads; transport is by ox-cart, some even have solid wheels which were out of date in the fourth millennium B.C. I saw peasants reaping with sickles and threshing the corn under ox hooves on a threshing floor.

There is little industry apart from mining. The coal mining towns along the coast are in a state of great depression and unemployment...the general depression is showing itself in the standard of living. Infantile mortality, which had fallen to 96 per thousand in 1953, now stands at 125.

These may seem fairly chronic conditions for a Latin American country and the conditions in Chile are better than in most; there is a higher degree of literacy, 80 per cent, a more democratic tradition and neither the army nor the church are as powerful as in other South American republics. What is new is the realisation, most vocal among the educated but spreading throughout the whole people, that all this is unnecessary and could quickly be changed.

American policy towards Latin America in the 1950s was driven by the doctrine of anti-communism, and in Chile, at least, had effectively supported the existing oligarchy. Castro's revolution in 1958 heightened US concerns that the socially unstable countries on the South American continent might turn to communism. Kennedy decided on a more activist approach, the 'Alliance for Progress', under which the US administration would support social reform in Latin America, but in return would expect those countries to shun Cuba. This was the deal that had been pushed through at the Punte del Este conference, but Kennedy's good faith was immediately beached at the Bay of Pigs. Castro, forced into the arms of the Soviets, declared himself a 'Marxist-Leninist'.[75]

The military presence was especially obvious to Bernal in Argentina, where an army of 150,000 was needed to preserve the ruling class. He was sceptical about Kennedy's overtures to the South American countries and his ability to bring down Castro.

The uneasy equilibrium that now exists here [Argentina] and elsewhere in Latin America, is between these vested interests and the popular forces demanding land reform and an end to foreign exploitation either by direct ownership or by the rigging of prices.

For all this Cuba is the touchstone. Those who have reason to fear the example of what Fidel Castro has done there, will support the United States policy of exclusion and embargo with the hope that this will bring about his collapse. But they do so without enthusiasm or much hope, for every step that they make along this path weakens their support from their own people, while military intervention against Cuba would bring about the most violent reactions.

The much boosted 'Allianza per il progresso' has not proved a very effective lever. The 'progress' part has been quietly dropped; there is no evidence of any land reform or diminution of foreign interests, while the promised money benefits have been slow in arriving and carry too visible strings, as Punta del Este showed. Crushing Castro will not solve the endemic problems, political or economic, of Latin America and Castro is as far as ever from being crushed.[76]

It seems that Sage just did not have the time to visit Cuba. He received an invitation to go there in 1960 – Che Guevara, as President of the Cuban National Bank, wrote to ask him to come on a fact-finding tour and to give his 'frank opinion' on the problems to be faced. He said that Castro's government could arrange to use his 'valuable services'.[77] Bernal replied that he was 'most encouraged by the resurgence of popular liberties in Cuba and by the way in which the Cuban people, together with their leader, are determined to redress the economic misery of their country'.[78] He said that he would be privileged to help, but ultimately nothing came of the exchange of letters.

Bernal's brief but penetrating observations of life in Latin America at the beginning of 1962 would inform his view of the Cuban missile crisis, just as his deeper contacts in China and the USSR gave him a unique perspective on the developing rift between Khrushchev and Mao Zedong.

20

Peacebroking

Just as the dropping of the atomic bombs on Japan acted as the immediate stimulus for the disarmament movement after the war, the US thermonuclear weapon test at Bikini atoll on 1st March 1954 re-ignited global fear. The device, fuelled by lithium and an isotope of hydrogen, was at least one thousand times more powerful than the fission bomb dropped on Hiroshima. Its yield was also three times bigger than the Americans expected, because the scientists who developed it at Los Alamos had overlooked an important nuclear fusion reaction.[1] The underwater explosion vaporized much of the atoll and caked the crew of the Japanese fishing boat, *Lucky Dragon*, with radioactive fallout though they were 80 miles away, outside the exclusion zone. The test had been preceded by the announcement of a new strategic policy of 'massive retaliation' by the US Secretary of State, John Foster Dulles, in January.

Bertrand Russell, the elder statesman of mathematics and philosophy in England, felt compelled to sound the alarm that mankind was in danger of exterminating life on the planet through the development of the H-bomb. He gave a talk on 'Man's Peril' at Christmas 1954 on BBC radio, which attracted a good deal of public comment. Among the hundreds of letters received by Russell was one from Joliot-Curie in his capacity as president of the World Federation of Scientific Workers (WFSW). In his opinion, Joliot-Curie said, 'The danger that faces humanity appears so terribly real that I believe it essential for scientists whom people respect for their eminence to come together to prepare an objective statement on the matter.'[2] Taking up this suggestion, Russell wrote to Einstein asking if he could recruit scientists in America to join the campaign to bring home to people and governments the looming disaster of war in the thermonuclear age. Two days before his sudden death in April 1955, Einstein replied to Russell endorsing his proposed message; this was announced to the world as the Russell–Einstein Manifesto in London later that summer.

Sage proposed Russell, an ardent anti-communist, for the 1955 Stalin Peace Prize, but warned his fellow committee members that he would probably refuse it.[3] Bernal continued to be convinced that the major nuclear danger came from the US – with some reason. The US National Security Council had pledged secretly in October 1953 to 'consider nuclear weapons to be as available for use as other munitions' in the case of war with the USSR or China.[4] Bernal seemed to sense this covert American policy, when addressing a public meeting in Holborn Town Hall in March 1955:

The truth is that there exists a very definite intention in some quarters to use these weapons. The pretence of using them only for retaliation has been dropped, and military commanders are boasting of their incorporation in normal military establishments. Therefore, there are people who will always find reasons for saying that control is not possible. It follows that the answer to the problem of the abolition of atomic weapons lies not in devising more ingenious methods of control, but in beginning to establish control. This will not be done as long as there is the intention to use the nuclear weapons, but when that intention is dropped, control will be easy. The people know this. They know that the 'grand deterrent' wanted by Churchill and Eisenhower is not what they want themselves, and for this reason they are resisting certain official policies. A remarkable feature of the situation is the extreme reluctance of the governments of both Britain and the US to state that they will not use the bomb first. Apparently they are too scrupulous to make a statement they may not keep.[5]

At the beginning of March, there had been a defence debate in parliament, centering on Britain's decision to produce her own H-bomb. Prime Minister Churchill defended the policy as necessary to reinforce the Western world's deterrence against the communist bloc; he held out the hope that 'safety will be the sturdy child of terror, and survival the twin brother of annihilation'.[6] The main political rift was not between Churchill's government and the Labour opposition, but within the ranks of the Labour party, where Aneurin Bevan accused Attlee of 'a monstrous evasion of a cataclysmic issue'.[7] Small anti-bomb organizations began to spring up, some endorsed by church leaders and trade unions – women's groups in north London (where Sage was living with Margot Heinemann) were particularly active. At this pivotal time, Bernal felt that it was his duty as a scientist to 'study the facts about the effects of nuclear weapons and to use every means at [his] disposal to communicate them'.[8]

There was a World Assembly for Peace in Helsinki in June 1955, which Labour MPs were forbidden to attend. Bernal, of course, was there and regretted that the ban had resulted in the British contingent being almost entirely communist. He spoke about the overwhelming threat posed by the H-bomb with its unprecedented destructive power that

... is so horrible and so extensive that it has almost served to prevent any intelligent reaction to it. With disasters of this magnitude the human mind is fascinated and paralysed. People cannot bear to believe it and rather tend to await it passively like the predicted end of the world. But this cannot be our attitude for if man brings universal destruction about by his own efforts he will stand self-condemned in that last judgment. We in the peace movement must not allow ourselves to be terrified or hypnotized but rather we must think clearly and act deliberately. Exaggeration and apathy have equally to be avoided. . . . we must however clearly distinguish between those who prepare for atomic war which they see as inevitable and the far greater number who have been persuaded that the production of atomic bombs in some way guarantees peace. We must find ways to make it clear to them that the mere existence of such weapons is a permanent threat to peace and inevitably increases international tension . . . The central case is that these weapons are inhuman in themselves and that their use cannot be tolerated whatever the excuse . . . Atomic bombs are evil things, whatever government makes them – American, Soviet or British.[9]

Bernal's main sphere of activity remained the Soviet-funded World Peace Council (WPC), on which he had served as vice-president since its inception in 1949. By the mid-1950s non-aligned peace organizations were beginning to emerge that infuriated the WPC by pointing out the USSR, and not just the USA, posed a nuclear threat to the world. The prominent Methodist leader, Rev. Donald Soper, denounced the WPC and its national spin-off, the British Peace Committee, as organs of Russian propaganda in a letter to *Tribune*. He cautioned peace lovers in England against 'allowing themselves to become the well-meaning but inevitable pawns of the Russian Party line, with its insist-ence that war is the original sin of the Western powers and that peace is the immaculate conception of the Soviet bloc'.[10] As if to illustrate Soper's point, the WPC found no contradiction in condemning the Anglo-French invasion of Suez, while excusing the Soviet repression of the Hungarian uprising on the grounds that 'serious divergences and . . . opposing theses have not permitted the formulation of a common opinion'.[11] The need for a better image did strike some within the USSR. One of Bernal's fellow committee members for the Stalin Peace Prize, Dimitry Skobeltzyn, suggested changing the name to the Lenin Peace Prize. Sage wrote to Academician Skolbeltzyn saying that he was 'not very enthusiastic about the project as it seems to me somewhat too obvious a change from the name which has now become a liability'.[12]

Many British communists did leave the Party over Hungary and threw their lot in with the Labour Party instead. They supported the Bevanite wing in its unsuccessful attempt to make unilateral nuclear disarmament official Labour policy, and then joined other activists to form the Campaign for Nuclear Disarmament (CND), with Bertrand Russell as its president. At Easter 1958, CND was one of the groups who took part in the first Aldermaston march, to the site of the Atomic Weapons Research Establishment.[13] The marchers, who included Sage, Margot Heinemann and Jane, had an extra spring in their steps because the Soviets had just announced a unilateral suspension of nuclear tests, for an unspecified period. One of their prime motives for doing so was to mobilize public opinion and increase 'pressure on the USA and England' to follow suit.[14]

Joliot-Curie had been in poor health for some years: he once complained that 'many were the days when I felt like death, but just had to go on. I noticed this particularly in travel abroad. Everyone was kind, but it was only my conscience that kept me going.'[15] He was depressed when he wrote to Bernal in January 1954, reflecting on the recent loss of his sister: 'I am now the last of a family of six children, and it is painful no longer to have witnesses with whom I can exchange memories of my parents and my childhood.'[16] His wife, Irène, died in the spring of 1956 (like her mother, a victim of radiation-induced leukaemia). Two years later, Joliot-Curie summoned up his energies to make a final visit to Moscow, where he had a long meeting with Khrushchev in the Kremlin. Joliot-Curie found him an exciting character – more sympathetic than other world leaders. He thought Khrushchev wanted to inject some liberalism into Soviet affairs but realized that there had to be strict limits, if the ultimate control of the Party was to be preserved. Khrushchev told Joliot-Curie that the WPC should act on principle, even if this meant going against the USSR at times; he also warned of the rapid development of nuclear affairs in China.[17]

Word reached Bernal that his great friend died in Paris on 14th August 1958. After a State funeral, Joliot-Curie's body was laid to rest next to Irène's in a small cemetery at Sceaux. The streets outside were packed with thousands of people, standing in the rain. The main eulogy was delivered by Bernal, in French, on behalf of the WPC. He told the crowds that Joliot qualified as a great man of the twentieth century on two counts. He was firstly 'a scientist [who] contributed to fundamental discoveries, which have shown how to liberate the giant forces of the atom'; secondly 'by his public actions he waged a fight so that these forces do not doom mankind to destruction, but assure it benefit by liberating it of age-old ills'.[18] It was Joliot-Curie, Bernal said, who more than anyone else reminded scientists of the saying of Rabelais: 'Science without conscience is nothing but the ruin of the soul.'

Sage spoke from the heart and in doing so moved not only the French crowd but also his colleagues from the WPC, who immediately demanded that he should take on the presidency. In Joliot-Curie's house that afternoon, he said that he could not be president in rank, but, 'if he must, he would be in function'.[19] It was not in Sage's nature to refuse the challenge, but he must have realized that he was adding the load of a diplomat to those of a senior academic and still creative scientist – not forgetting he was also the father of a five-year-old daughter. Three days into Bernal's presidency, Eisenhower announced that from 31st October the US would suspend nuclear tests for one year. The Soviet moratorium of March had succeeded to the extent that the United States appeared 'in the eyes of the world as a "warmonger"', Eisenhower told the French foreign minister at the time.[20]

Bernal gave his first presidential address to the WPC, on home turf in Moscow, six months after Joliot-Curie's funeral. Under the inspirational leadership of Joliot, he said, the WPC had mobilized public opinion among hundreds of millions to make them understand the dangers of war. In the past decade, the WPC had not only stopped the outbreak of a new world war, but helped to bring to an end serious wars in Korea and Vietnam.[21] He was to change his optimistic view on Vietnam during his trip to China that autumn, when he met Ho Chi Minh. Ho Chi Minh contrasted the intolerable conditions in South Vietnam under the US-backed government with those in the North, where the peasants were reaping the benefits of reorganization along Leninist lines. He told Sage that the government of South Vietnam was 'utilizing the refined methods of tyranny, combining the worst of the Nazi's methods of direct brutality with the legal and inquisitorial methods of American McCarthyism. At the same time the economic conditions in South Vietnam were desperate owing to the effects of American imports and suppression of native industries, and the general diminution of agricultural productions so that the country which had been one of the major rice-exporting countries of the world was now being forced to import rice.'[22]

Ho Chi Minh told Bernal that he was very concerned that Laos, whose royal army was supported by the US, would enter the war against the Vietcong. If they did, he thought China might well be drawn in as well. He urged Bernal to inform world public opinion about what was really happening in South Vietnam, Laos and Cambodia.

Sage had spent the night before meeting Ho Chi Minh dancing to rock and roll music in Peking, and had no time to rest before setting off to see Khrushchev later that morning. The Soviet leader had just completed a barnstorming tour of the USA, which was just one reason why Mao Zedong was angry with him. The two communist leaders did not manage a civil word between them, and Khrushchev decided to leave on the third day of his official visit.[23] It seems probable that his meeting with Bernal was the most relaxed and substantive discussion of his trip. In the circumstances, it was not surprising that Khrushchev advised Bernal that the WPC would have to deal with China direct and not look to the Soviets as intermediaries. Not knowing how dispirited Khrushchev was as a result of the spiteful atmosphere, Sage found him very vague and formed the impression that he would have to do everything for himself. Mao's interpreter said of the visit that 'Mao saw himself as the bullfighter and Khrushchev as the bull',[24] but the Soviet leader, who had such a mercurial temper, was measured and thoughtful in his conversation with Bernal. He pointed out that the Chinese were 'very new at the game' and fairly trustworthy, but must not be expected to adopt diplomatic methods at this stage of their development.[25] He said to Sage 'we were very like that ourselves when we were 10 years old'.

On the subject of the crises in SE Asia, Bernal found that Khrushchev attached far less significance to Laos than Ho Chi Minh did. The Soviet leader did not think that widespread war arising from Vietnam was likely, but that priority should always be given to disarmament, and if one could get relaxation in the West it was bound to spread sooner or later to the East. Sage was perhaps surprised when Khrushchev 'stated that these problems had *not* been discussed between him and President Eisenhower'[26] during his recent US visit. As far as the peace movement was concerned, Khrushchev thought the WPC should support an immediate major campaign on disarmament and also insist on the great powers coming together at a summit – a meeting that he had been calling for since the previous year. Bernal formed the impression that Khrushchev 'was obviously anxious not to compromise relaxation in the West by any openly anti-imperialist or anti-American policy'.[27] Khrushchev's trip to the US had convinced him that the time was right for a summit, but he did not expect immediate success. He told Bernal he was prepared to wait for years for the achievement of a complete disarmament programme and for settlement of outstanding questions such as Germany. Again he did not think that Germany, where he wanted America to recognize East Germany and not to install nuclear weapons in West Germany, would lead to a crisis in the near future.

As a result of his talks with Khrushchev, Sage began 1960 in an optimistic frame of mind. At a WPC meeting in January, he commented that the popular momentum towards nuclear disarmament and a test ban treaty was going to be difficult for the advocates of the Cold War to resist. Those advocates had not yet surrendered and were fighting a tough delaying action, notably in Geneva where an agreement to end nuclear testing had 'been stalled on a pettifogging technical point of difference'.[28] Sage advertised for a peace secretary in *The Daily Worker* and interviewed a middle-aged woman of child-like intensity, named Vivien Pixner. She was a good organizer and a talented linguist, fluent in French and German. When she accepted the job, she mentioned that there was no phone at her home. Sage said you must have a phone, 'Get in touch with the Post Office and explain that you will be working for Professor Bernal. The phone will be installed very quickly because MI5 will want to listen to our conversations.'[29] She did as she was instructed, and the phone arrived with none of the usual delays.

Nowhere was the battle over a test ban treaty more evenly balanced than in Washington. There were powerful political arguments on both sides – the doves pointed to public fear over radioactive fallout and the arms race, and 1960 was an election year. The hawks were worried that the British would sign an unenforceable agreement with the Soviets, and that the Soviets would simply cheat in the absence of effective monitoring. At the Pentagon, there was concern about the supposed 'missile gap' (with the US lagging the Soviets). The stunning success of the Sputnik programme in 1957 reinforced anxieties about Soviet technical capabilities. Attempting a compromise within his own administration, Eisenhower announced that the USA would not be bound by its moratorium on testing after 1959, but would not resume tests without warning and would continue to negotiate in Geneva for a treaty.[30] Bernal wrote to Eisenhower, regretting his statement that the USA was free to resume weapons' testing. He told the President that the WPC believed the difficulties cited over verification were political rather than technical.[31]

The nuclear silence that had lasted over a year was broken not by the USSR or the USA, but by France making its conspicuous entry into the nuclear club in early February 1960. Oblivious to protests in Paris and throughout Africa, the French detonated a fission device in the Sahara desert. Sage reacted as though he had been betrayed by an old friend:

The world has heard with indignation of the explosion of the first French atomic bomb, despite appeals voiced in the UN and by many governments and peoples to refrain from such a step. The peoples of Africa will not readily forgive this action carried out on their soil in defiance of their express wishes.

This action occurring as it does in the midst of a truce on tests by the major atomic powers and when negotiations were reaching a decisive stage can only do harm . . . The real glory of France would have been to adhere to the declaration of the French Government before the UN in 1946 that it would use atomic energy only for peaceful purposes. This was the spirit of the great scientist Frédéric Joliot-Curie who had done so much to help France to master the new powers of science. It is a sad and retrograde step.[32]

At the end of 1959, Khrushchev decided that the USSR had enough rockets of sufficient range that it could 'virtually shatter the world' and this emboldened him to make a radical cut in conventional troop strength.[33] In the first few months of 1960, he was looking forward to a summit of the great powers to be held in Paris in May. He was confident that there would be an agreement over Germany and on banning nuclear tests. But his hopes and any prospect of detente with the Eisenhower administration crashed with the American U-2 spy plane shot down near Sverdlovsk on May Day. Eisenhower had reluctantly authorized the provocative, high-altitude photoreconnaissance missions over the Russian heartland to monitor progress in building and deploying inter-continental ballistic missiles (ICBMs). Khrushchev, whose explosive anger often got the better of his statesman's brain, went to Paris intent on humiliating Eisenhower, and the summit never started. The prospect of an international nuclear treaty vanished, and Khrushchev's attempt to rekindle it at a press conference in Austria on 8th July seemed lame. He wished to 'raise the peoples, raise the masses for struggle against those who slow down solution of the disarmament question'.[34] Sage did his best to heed the WPC paymaster's call, and the next day proposed a worldwide campaign, like the great Stockholm petition of 1950 to convene a world disarmament conference, but this time there were no signatures collected.

At the beginning of 1961, Eisenhower's Republican administration was succeeded by the Democrat one led by J.F. Kennedy. Eisenhower's valedictory speech warned of the dangers of the 'military-industrial complex', while Kennedy in his inaugural address made a plea to 'begin anew the quest for peace, before the dark powers of destruction unleashed by science engulf all humanity in planned or accidental self-destruction'. He held out a small olive branch to Khrushchev, when he stated 'both sides [are] overburdened by the cost of modern weapons, both rightly alarmed by the steady spread of the deadly atom, yet both racing to alter that uncertain balance of terror that stays the hand of mankind's final war'. In private, Eisenhower had become 'entirely preoccupied by the horror of nuclear war',[35] but this did not stop him from telling Kennedy that he thought a resumption of underground tests was necessary. Kennedy at his first press conference announced that he had set up a group to work towards a new test ban treaty and his administration lost no time in questioning the prevailing doctrine of 'massive retaliation'. Despite this he remained wary of anti-nuclear activists, especially those funded by communists, and it is doubtful whether he took any notice of the letter he received from Sage urging him to pursue disarmament and a reduction of world tension. Bernal wrote: 'The world cannot live indefinitely under a balance of terror. The powers of destruction are already only too ample. To attempt to guard against their use by increasing them is a proved way to disaster.'[36]

The Western nuclear powers that entrusted their national security to nuclear weapons remained suspicious of anti-nuclear campaigners and of outspoken scientists like Blackett, Bernal and Pauling. Non-aligned nations were not threatened by them and some statesmen, for instance Nehru, became significant critics of the arms race themselves. In March 1961, Bernal made a short visit to New Delhi to attend a meeting organized by the WPC. He warned a huge crowd on the Ramlila Grounds that nuclear war in the past few months had acquired a new kind of military logic. Although there were enough bombs to kill the world population 10 times over, some in the US wanted more.

The idea is what is called the first strike must be sufficient to destroy all methods of nuclear retaliation . . . an excessively dangerous doctrine in itself because it puts an absolute premium on the country that is first to strike. All that is required is a moral excuse, and this moral excuse is furnished by the theory of what is called 'the pre-emptive attack', that is: if a country, let's say the USA, claims to have found out from its intelligence agencies, from its U-2's, or spies or in one way or another, that for instance the Soviet Union intends to attack within a matter of days, [it] attacks first in order to prevent the Soviet attack.[37]

Sage stated that he had read this theory in many books 'for his own misery', and feared that it carried a lot of weight with the new US government. At a separate meeting with the Indian Peace Council, he expressed misgivings about the new Kennedy administration. In his view, the crucial test of Kennedy would be his actions over disarmament, and 'so far, words in favour of disarmament have been balanced by further increases and acceleration of actual and potential armaments such as Polaris and Minutemen'. President Kennedy had just increased the defence budget to include an extra two dozen Polaris submarines and double the number of Minutemen ICBMs. Bernal's feeling was that 'the new sophisticated and pseudoscientific military thinking which is now dominant in the Kennedy administration may contain dangers greater even than the old brutal threats of massive retaliation of the days of Dulles'.[38] Kennedy was, in fact, repelled by the first-strike strategy and urged Robert McNamara, his Defense Secretary, to 'repeat to the point of boredom' in his speeches that the US would use nuclear weapons only in response to a direct attack or an attack on their allies, and had no intention of waging preventive war.[39] Kennedy was, however, fearful that Khrushchev wanted to push the US into a nuclear conflict; he was not reassured after meeting the Soviet leader for the first time in Vienna, in June, and told a reporter from *Time*, 'I never met a man like this. [I] talked about how a nuclear exchange would kill seventy million people in ten minutes and he just looked at me as if to say "So what?" My impression was that he just didn't give a damn if it came to that.'[40]

Khrushchev was determinedly belligerent throughout his meeting with President Kennedy in Vienna and showed none of the thoughtful reflection that was evident when he met Bernal in China. Within weeks of the Vienna meeting, the Soviets stopped any serious negotiation at the Geneva test ban talks, and Khrushchev proposed cutting the American, British and French access to West Berlin. Khrushchev's aims were to stop the torrent of refugees, who were leaving the communist bloc via Berlin, and to prevent the eventual reunification of Germany. Kennedy was determined to avoid the extremes of a meek withdrawal from Berlin or escalation of the crisis into a nuclear ex-change. He sought to beef up US Army numbers without delay. On 13th August 1961, East German security guards began building the barbed-wire barrier between East and West Berlin that would become solidified as the

Berlin Wall. In response to demands for action, Kennedy dispatched Vice-President Johnson to West Berlin and reinforced the US garrison there. The president of the WPC released a press statement referring to the 'closing of the inter-zonal boundary' in Berlin. He regretted the vigorous efforts 'made by certain statesman and public figures, particularly in West Berlin, to whip up hostile feelings and to create an atmosphere in which war can become conceivable, despite the horrors that would attend it in this age of H-bomb missiles.'[41] Bernal was reassured by the Soviets saying that they had 'no intention of encroaching on the freedom of the people of West Berlin or of putting obstacles in the way of access to West Berlin'. There was, therefore, no *casus belli*, and the American and Soviet positions seemed 'eminently negotiable'. In fact, both Kennedy and Khrushchev found some relief in the construction of the Wall.

Khrushchev, who at the time regarded Kennedy as a weakling, chose this moment to resume nuclear weapons' testing. This action brought oblique criticism from Bernal and the WPC: 'Lovers of peace throughout the world will deeply regret that the Soviet Government has however reluctantly found it necessary to resume the testing of nuclear weapons . . . The decision arises as a consequence of the continual attempts on one side to deal with political and negotiable proposals by threats of force.'[42] Bernal laid the blame for the escalation in the nuclear stakes squarely on the NATO powers, whose preparations with respect to Polaris, multiplication of atomic bases on foreign soil and strengthening of Federal German forces all pointed to an acute danger of war. Bernal also wrote to Kennedy, Khrushchev, British Prime Minister Macmillan and General de Gaulle privately appealing to them to stop the testing. Khrushchev replied that the Soviet Union had made multiple efforts at the UN and elsewhere to abandon testing, to which the West responded with more threats. His letter continued:

To renounce in such a situation the carrying out of measures to strengthen the defence of our country, the perfecting of the nuclear weapon and consequently its testing would mean weakening the defensive capacity of the Soviet Union and the countries of the socialist commonwealth, and I would say, weakening the position of all peoples in the world who are striving to avert war.[43]

Khrushchev said he was prepared to respond to the WPC call to renounce weapons testing when others did. The other leaders did not respond to Bernal's letter. Privately, Kennedy was appalled by the prospect of resumed testing, but felt that the Russians were completely untrustworthy, since they had been actively preparing for their latest series of atmospheric tests while negotiating in bad faith in Geneva. Macmillan, who was convinced that Khrushchev wanted to avoid nuclear war, tried unsuccessfully to persuade

Kennedy to keep the Geneva talks going. Kennedy's ambivalence was plain in his indecisive instructions to the Atomic Energy Commission, but ultimately the need to signal US determination to stand up to Moscow led him to authorize a resumption in testing in the spring of 1962. At a press conference in Washington, Kennedy stated that the failure to reach an agreement on the cessation of nuclear testing that might have been an important step in easing the tension and preventing nuclear proliferation was the greatest disappointment of his first year as President.[44]

Although Bernal was committed to the WPC, he was well aware of the increasing popularity of international peace groups that were not aligned with any particular political system (although they all tended to have socialist or world government sympathies). Bernal's close identification with communist-funded organizations like the WPC and the WFSW effectively precluded him from Pugwash, the most important international scientists' group against nuclear weapons. At times differences between the communist and non-aligned groups could be sharp. When Bertrand Russell was invited to a WPC meeting in 1959, he responded scathingly: 'Could you let me see any pronouncement of the World Council protesting against militaristic imperialism in East Germany, Hungary and Tibet? The greatest contribution that could be made towards ending the Cold War would be the abandonment of militaristic imperialism by Russia and China.'[45] Whatever Bernal's personal loyalties, his inclination was always towards inclusiveness: he tended to like people even if he did not agree with them. There was also the geopolitical reality that an overtly communist peace movement was bound to fail in North America and Western Europe.

In September 1961, a 'Peace Pugwash' was held in London. This was an event painstakingly arranged by Bernal, Canon Collins (the clerical head of Britain's CND), and Homer Jack, an American Unitarian minister who was the executive director of SANE (National Committee for a Sane Nuclear Policy) in New York. Although the Peace Pugwash was generally considered a success, one leading American pacifist remarked to Collins that while 'people like Professor Bernal may be looking for a "united" world peace movement' he thought such an attempt would be 'disastrous'.[46]

In an attempt to build on the spirit of the London meeting, Bernal decided that WPC should organize a World Congress on General Disarmament and Peace in Moscow in July 1962. He wrote in an appeal leaflet in January.

People everywhere are protesting more and more vigorously against the threat of nuclear annihilation. Yet that threat remains and grows. New ways must be found to unite mankind in action to banish nuclear weapons from the world. 1962 can be the year when the governments, urged forward by their peoples, reach agreement on the first genuine measures of disarmament.

Disarmament – general, complete and controlled, including the destruction of nuclear weapons – is the most urgent need of our time. It is an essential step to a world without war.

Sage chaired a preparatory meeting in Sweden in May; the WPC were expecting 2,000 delegates from 90 countries to come to the Congress. There was a list of international sponsors that included politicians (Anwar Sadat, Jomo Kenyatta and Che Guevara, the Cuban Minister of Industry), scientists (among whom Linus Pauling was the most prominent), writers (Sartre and Neruda) and artists (Picasso and Shostakovich). Albert Schweitzer agreed to be a sponsor, but wrote from Africa to say he could not come to Moscow to participate because 'it is impossible for me to leave my hospital in July, which I regret, but my heart will be with you... Public opinion all over the world must know that this movement exists and that it goes on fighting for peace in order to create a public opinion which will make it possible to realize peace.'[47] Delegates' travel expenses were to be met by a charitable fund set up by the WPC, while the Soviet Peace Committee would provide additional money to cover living costs.

The Americans started atmospheric tests again in April, and the French continued their series of underground explosions in the Sahara. Bernal accused these two governments (but not the Soviets) of 'riding roughshod over world public opinion' and thereby forging 'a new spiral in the nuclear arms race'.[48] The UN Disarmament Committee was still in session in Geneva, but not making any perceptible progress. Bernal wrote to all the governments involved, inviting them to either send representatives or written reports to Moscow setting out their views. One of the few to respond was the French government, which ironically had decided to take no further part in the Geneva talks. As an explanation of their position, the French sent Bernal a copy of de Gaulle's recent press conference, in which he said that France wanted to ban the means of delivery of atomic weapons (rockets, bombers and submarines) but saw no prospect of that happening. Until such time there was such reciprocal disarmament, France would continue to test atomic weapons. De Gaulle also seemed piqued that the UN had invited so many governments to Geneva (eighteen), and said that were the conference to be confined to the four nuclear powers, 'France would participate in it whole-heartedly.'[49]

One of the governments that de Gaulle would have excluded was India's, and Pandit Nehru found himself torn between agreeing with his old friend Bernal that 'disarmament is not only essential but is feasible', and not wanting to make any gesture that might compromise the Geneva talks. He thought it was clear that disarmament 'is a matter intimately connected with the fears and apprehensions of countries and cannot be dealt with purely on the logical level. There is far too much of threats from one country or the other and boastfulness of its strength. It is this attitude that has to be changed.' Yet Nehru dare not send a representative to the Moscow congress, because that might have political implications that could impede any actual progress in Geneva. He told Sage, 'Any pressures exercised from other directions might well result in stiffening of attitudes.'[50]

The World Congress on General Disarmament and Peace convened in Moscow on Monday 9th July. Bernal had courted leaders of non-aligned peace groups with the promise that their messages would be heard in the conference hall and published in the Soviet press. As a result, independent groups from Austria, Canada, Denmark, France, Great Britain, India, Italy, Norway, Sweden and West Germany joined the communist bulk of the WPC delegates. Only one US group decided to attend, but individual leaders of the American peace movement, like the Paulings and Homer Jack, came as Bernal's personal guests. In all there were over 2,200 people from 120 countries. Bernal gave the opening address in French, and Khrushchev spoke for two-and-a-half hours at a special session on the first afternoon. Homer Jack was bitterly disappointed by what he heard.

It was a belligerent, cold war, *tour de force*. Only the Soviet Union wanted peace. The West was warlike. Khrushchev was wildly applauded by most delegates. He had an opportunity to give a constructive speech to an international gathering, but he chose instead to give the kind of address he would normally give to the Supreme Soviet.[51]

In his own remarks to the plenary session, Jack contrasted the peace movement in the United States which 'speaks to its government' with the peace organizations of the Soviet bloc that 'espouse the policies of their governments, whether these governments happen to be developing greater bombs or calling for disarmament'.[52] The generally sullen audience cheered when he declared that West Germany should not be allowed to rearm or to have nuclear weapons, but hissed when he challenged the WPC to match their criticism of the US with a condemnation of forthcoming Soviet tests.

Canon Collins said that he had agreed to lend his name to the conference because he believed that the WPC intended to give full scope for reasonable dialogue, and thought that Khrushchev's claim that the USSR had a monopoly of peaceful intentions was not helpful. In his view, 'the USSR made a grave error, whatever reasons may have been advanced by her military advisers, in resuming her testing of nuclear weapons last autumn'.[53] Another CND leader, the left-wing Labour MP, Sydney Silverman, also dared to criticize Khrushchev. He said 'It is really of no assistance for the two great nations, whose quarrel may tear the earth to pieces, merely to shout contemptuous slogans one against the other... [Khrushchev's] speech gives little hope [because he suggests] that the Soviet Union has always been right and never made a mistake.'[54] Bertrand Russell suggested that every disarmament negotiator from the West, including President Kennedy, should state that 'I am firmly convinced that a nuclear war would be worse than the worldwide victory of communism'[55] and every negotiator from the East, including Nikita Khrushchev, should say the same about the worldwide victory of capitalism. Such dissident opinions had never been heard at a WPC conference before, and Jack thought that much of the credit belonged to Bernal for being 'scrupulous in allowing freedom of speech inside the meeting'.[56]

Freedom of speech outside the meeting was an entirely different matter. *Pravda* gave a one-sided account, concentrating on material that was in line with Soviet policy and omitting any criticism of Khrushchev, the USSR or even the WPC. Representatives of the Committee of 100, a group of luminaries set up by Russell in Britain to implement a programme of civil disobedience, decided to hold an anti-nuclear demonstration in Red Square. They handed out a few leaflets couched in unilateralist terms to astonished Muscovites, before being led away by police. The demonstration was planned for Friday 13th July, and two banners were painted, one in English one in Russian reading: 'We condemn Anglo-American tests. We demand no further Soviet tests. Let all people act against the tests.' The march was due to start in the lobby of the Moskva Hotel, and two hundred marchers were going to pass the US, French and British embassies before returning to Red Square.

The head of the Soviet Peace Committee, Yuri Zhukov, urged the Committee of 100 to call it off, saying it would put the embassies at risk, that pamphlets affronted the Soviet authorities and would play into the hands of hard-liners. It was agreed to stay within Red Square and not to hand out more pamphlets. In the event twenty-five brave souls marched, and there were twenty-five foreign press in front of Lenin's tomb who took photographs. Within one minute of the banners being unfurled, they were confiscated by three Soviet citizens (who were probably from the secret police).[57] The following week, *Pravda* carried a vigorous denunciation of the small protest by Zhukov, accusing a 'handful' of foreigners of going out of their way to be arrested or beaten up so that 'they could write in the papers that peace champions were maltreated in the Soviet Union'.[58]

Russell was convinced by the events in Moscow that for the time being 'any fruitful cooperation between the peace movements of East and West is unlikely'.[59] By contrast, Sage in his closing address to the Congress took a much more sanguine view: 'This Congress has been unique for the free expression that has been given everywhere to all views, both by word of mouth and in writing. I hope we shall stick to that principle and develop it further.' He thought the major political lesson was that the wind of disarmament and the wind of national independence have got to blow together.[60]

In his opening address, Bernal had referred several times to Cuba, and the threat to its independence evinced by the abortive CIA-backed invasion at the Bay of Pigs the previous year. While the Congress was going on in Moscow, the first ship left the USSR carrying the vanguard of what was planned to be 50,000 troops to Cuba. Their task on arrival would be to construct concrete launching pads for dozens of ballistic missiles with nuclear warheads that were to follow in October. The perilous scheme had been hatched by Khrushchev that spring, in part as a response to Kennedy's placing of Jupiter missiles with nuclear warheads in Turkey, in part to deter any future American attempt to unseat Castro, and to force the USA, by throwing 'a hedgehog down Uncle Sam's pants', to come to terms over Berlin. He also wanted to demonstrate to the world that the USSR, not China, was still the communist top dog.[61] On the morning of 16th October, Kennedy was shown photographs taken by a U-2 reconnaissance plane over Cuba two days before that revealed conclusive evidence of the missile launch pads, as well as crated Soviet bombers capable of delivering nuclear bombs. The world seemed poised on the brink of nuclear war. The American public did not learn of the crisis until Kennedy made a sombre television address to the nation on 22nd October, in which he condemned the Soviets for lying about their installation of offensive weapons in Cuba, demanded that they should be removed and announced that the US Navy would quarantine Cuba to prevent any more weapons from arriving.[62]

The WPC responded immediately with a message to the UN Security Council, claiming that 'the orders given to the US Navy to stop and search all shipping to Cuba are completely illegal'.[63] Bernal pointed out that the USSR and other socialist countries had been ringed for years with nuclear bases without producing the 'hysterical military reaction which the US government is now exhibiting'. He urged the Security Council not to back US but to condemn it. The message closed by predicting a US invasion of Cuba.

With the Soviets racing ahead with missile-site construction and the assembly of their bombers, while still denying they had any missiles in Cuba, the UN Secretary, U Thant, suggested a two- to three-week delay in both the quarantine of Cuba and the Soviet arms shipments.[64] Kennedy had no intention of being 'impaled on a long, negotiating hook'[65] and did not flinch. Khrushchev, believing a US invasion of Cuba to be imminent, began to pull back from the abyss. He eventually agreed to remove all Soviet weapons, following Kennedy's secret offer to take the Jupiter missiles out of Turkey within months.

Two nights after Khrushchev announced his decision to retreat from Cuba to save the world from nuclear catastrophe, Bernal spoke about the crisis at a WPC committee meeting.

Everybody has been so frightened of nuclear war that ten times as many people as before are aware of its danger and the resources of the peace movements in the world demanding disarmament will be increased . . . The foiling of this attack on Cuba alone shows the importance of defending national independence. It was the national independence of Cuba at stake, successfully defended not only by the people of Cuba themselves, but by the diplomatic and military help they received from the Soviet Union. This example will encourage other countries who wish to assert independence to do so successfully.[66]

Sage was apparently unable to see or to admit that it was Khrushchev's recklessness that had provoked the Cuban crisis. Philip Morrison, an American physicist who worked on the Manhattan Project and subsequently became a leading critic of nuclear weapons, complained about an article that the WPC president had written on the confrontation over Cuba. Saying the piece was incomplete and dishonest and 'too tendentious to be sober politics', Morrison asked 'Are you sure that WPC is not more left than the Kremlin?'[67] Morrison said he expected a rapprochement soon between the US and the USSR, and 'would hope the WPC could play a role, not necessarily more neutral, but at least more objective'.

One of the outcomes of the big World Congress on General Disarmament and Peace in Moscow was that the non-aligned groups from various countries discussed the prospect of forming their own world federation. A meeting was convened to explore this development at Oxford University in early January 1963. Forty non-aligned peace groups from eighteen countries sent delegates, who pledged to oppose 'the testing, manufacture, and possession of nuclear arms by all nations'.[68] Canon Collins, without consulting the conference organizers, invited Bernal to bring ten WPC observers to the meeting.[69] When news of this arrangement reached various national groups, they were furious. Some of the US delegates had been granted visas on the express grounds that they were attending a non-communist conference, and they objected strongly before the meeting started. This raised the left's reflex cry of 'McCarthyism', but when a vote on the issue was taken the Australians, Belgians, French, Italians, New Zealanders, West Germans and Yugoslavs all said they wanted nothing to do with an organization that participated in the Cold War, and the WPC observers were excluded. Sage's friend, Ilya Ehrenburg, who was waiting with other would-be observers at the Russell Hotel in London, threatened the hapless Collins that 'the attitude shown to the WPC representatives would make it impossible for the Soviet Peace Committee to

cooperate further with the organizations represented at Oxford'.[70] Attempting
to mollify the WPC, another invitation was issued for them to come to
Oxford after the main meeting was over, which Bernal in an open letter called
'a deliberate rejection'. Fleet Street enjoyed the spat and the *Daily Telegraph*
ran the headline 'Canon Collins Stops Russian Gatecrashers', oblivious to the
point that the poor Canon had invited them.

The peace groups at Oxford coalesced into the International Confederation
for Disarmament and Peace (ICDP), and their first task was to come to the
Russell Hotel to bury the hatchet with the WPC. Homer Jack read out a letter of
apology to Ehrenburg, who refused to accept it because he said it should have
been addressed to Bernal.[71] Although Bernal issued a press statement that the
meeting between the two groups had been cordial and friendly, the atmosphere
was rancorous; Bernal said he did not trust Jack and did not want any further
discussions with the new group. Over the next few months, the WPC's constituents lost no opportunity to attack the ICDP, and Bernal warned Khrushchev in August that such non-aligned groups 'are really anti-Soviet'.[72]

The WPC soon found itself under attack on a second front. The Chinese
had been unimpressed by what they saw as Khrushchev's 'adventurism'
followed by his 'capitulationism' over Cuba.[73] One small way for the Chinese
to show their contempt for the USSR was to attack the WPC. In May 1963,
Bernal received a telegram from the China Peace Committee criticizing the
evasive way that the WPC was run and threatening to discontinue financial
support because the WPC was not doing enough to counter American
imperialism. Through its actions, it had 'become increasingly detrimental to
[the] defence of world peace'.[74] Sage must have felt that his truest friend for
world peace was Pope John XXIII, whom he congratulated warmly for his
encyclical 'Pacem in Terris'. After reading it, Bernal sent the following message
to the Vatican.

Peace workers the world over welcome with great joy your historic encyclical Pacem in
Terris. It gives them immense encouragement and renewed heart to pursue the great
humanitarian goals you enumerate...immediate ending of nuclear tests, banning of
nuclear weapons, halting of the arms race, progress towards complete and controlled
world disarmament, and an end to racial discrimination and the denial of human
equality.[75]

The machinations of the various peace groups became irrelevant after the
Cuban missile crisis because both Kennedy and Khrushchev recognized the
advantages of reaching an agreement to end nuclear testing. This message was
carried to Moscow in December 1962 by Norman Cousins, the editor of the
Saturday Review who had been one of the founders of SANE with Homer
Jack. Khrushchev freely admitted to Cousins that the Cuban crisis had scared

him – 'Of course I was scared. It would have been insane not to be scared.'[76] Yet despite hopes on both sides that a test ban treaty could forestall global proliferation of nuclear weapons (especially in China), serious negotiations did not start until the early summer, when they were given life by Kennedy's speeches at home and on his European tour. The Partial Test Ban Treaty was signed by the Americans, British and Russians in the Kremlin on 25th July 1963. The French refused to take part. Khrushchev had seen no reason to include China, on the verge of possessing nuclear weapons, and his refusal to allow international inspections meant that underground testing was still permissible. While much of the world breathed a sigh of relief, the Chinese denounced it as a 'dirty treaty'. Liao Cheng-chih, the vice-chairman of the China Peace Committee, called it 'a big conspiracy in which the imperialists and their hangers-on join hands against the socialist countries, against China and against the forces of peace of the whole world'.[77] Bernal sent a message of congratulations to the three world leaders that he thought reflected the over-whelming feelings of the WPC membership.

Limited test ban agreement is welcomed by millions of peace supporters as halting poisoning of the environment and as a vital step towards the abolition of all nuclear weapons and towards general disarmament.[78]

He was outraged when the Americans immediately started underground testing again, in what he viewed as a direct blow against the spirit if not the letter of the Treaty. He stated simply that 'The resumption of underground nuclear testing by the US government within a few hours of the conclusion of the Moscow partial test ban agreement is an affront to humanity.'[79] The American action was bound to inflame the Chinese further, and Bernal was already concerned that their open hostility towards the Treaty might cause the WPC to break up. He wrote to Khrushchev asking him for his advice on how to handle the Chinese, saying that above all he wanted to follow Joliot-Curie's principle of promoting peace all over the world.[80] Khrushchev answered that while the WPC should not align itself with the policy of any government or party, Bernal must 'know what a dangerous position the Chinese leaders are taking in problems of war and peace. Their statements against peaceful co-existence of states with different social systems, against the banning of thermonuclear tests, against disarmament, against other important problems concerning the relaxation of international tension undermine in effect the foundation of the world peace movement, the unity of its ranks. The world public opinion will not understand it, if the WPC in such a situation failed to express its attitude to the stand taken by Peking, which is inconsistent with the basic principles of the movement. It seems to me that one should not resort to their style and form of polemics, but what is necessary is to explain profoundly and seriously to all the forces of peace, the Chinese public opinion included, the great harm that this position is inflicting to peace.'[81]

In general, Khrushchev was optimistic after the signing of the 'Moscow Treaty'. He told Bernal he would be sending two comrades, 'K. and V.' to London to discuss its implications with him. Khrushchev was aware that Sage had been ill: he was very complimentary about the achievements of the WPC under Bernal's presidency, and sent his 'wholehearted wishes for the speediest and complete recovery'.

In fact Sage was not well enough to attend the next WPC presidential committee meeting later in September, but did send a message to his colleagues. He referred to the Partial Test Ban Treaty as something that 'in itself may not be very much, but as a sign for the future it can be made a turning point from which we may never have to regress ... We cannot be, logically, for or against a treaty on the grounds that it may or may not be followed up. It is our business to see that it is followed up.'[82] In an attempt to placate those who saw the Treaty as fixing the lead that the US already held in the arms race, a lead that they might extend through underground testing, Bernal said that he had 'gone very carefully into its technical and military implications, and can find no basis for the view that it will give the US a one-sided military advantage'. Referring to China, he warned that 'No disarmament policy can be fully effective unless negotiated with and unless participated in by the government of the People's Republic of China.' He encouraged the WPC to bring maximum pressure to bear on the UN and its member states so that China could take its rightful place in the UN and in the disarmament talks. In his opinion, 'the participation of this great nation, comprising a quarter of the human race, is indispensable for the solution of world problems'.

At a subsequent WPC conference in November, Liao Cheng-chih angrily attacked the WPC for telling 'the oppressed nations and peoples to disarm ... [as] a fraud with no other aim than to make the world peace movement abandon its task of fighting against imperialism'.[83] Liao was barracked by the Soviets during his speech, which earned them a rebuke from Bernal, but there was no way to straddle the widening split in communist ideologies. The following summer at the World Conference against Atomic and Hydrogen bombs, the Chinese poured scorn on the idea that 'nuclear weapons rather than imperialism headed by the United States'[84] was going to cause a nuclear war. In October 1964, China exploded its first atomic bomb and was roundly condemned by the WPC, with its built-in Soviet majority, for adding 'to the radioactive contamination of the atmosphere'[85] and to the risk of nuclear proliferation.

Sage thought, above all, 'the partial test ban agreement gives great encouragement to the peace forces, and to people generally, for it shows them that their consistent action over many years can achieve results. Thus, it heartens them for further struggle.'[86] While the first part of this statement was almost certainly true – the popular peace movements did have a significant influence on the behaviour of their governments – the second part was not. The period of the late fifties and early sixties was the high-water mark for the world peace movement. One reason surely was the Partial Test Ban Treaty reduced the environmental and public health risks and therefore the general level of fear. Only the truly committed kept up the campaign against nuclear weapons.

During the early 1960s, Bernal made frequent references to the escalating war in Indochina. He first wrote to President Johnson in 1964 to express his 'bewildered disappointment' at the decision to increase greatly the number of US troops in Vietnam, while recognizing that the new President had inherited this problem from his 'predecessor'. He urged him instead to start negotiations based on the 1954 Geneva agreement in order to alleviate the great suffering of the Vietnamese people and the mounting losses.[87] A year later, Bernal was no longer bewildered, but angry:

All who cherish peace and humanity must condemn the brutal abominations of President Johnson's war in Vietnam. Gas and napalm are used against combatants and non-combatants alike in South Vietnam . . . Savage air attacks, mounting in weight and range, are carried out on the flimsiest of pretexts, against the Democratic Republic of [North] Vietnam, a country with which America is nominally at peace . . . The world looks on in horror at the US Government's violation of all canons of international law.[88]

At the eighth WPC conference, in Helsinki in July 1965, on 'Independence and general disarmament', the Vietnam War was Sage's primary concern. In his opening address to the 1,500 delegates, he characterized the conflict as 'a particularly brutal war of aggression . . . being waged by American forces against the people of both South and North Vietnam, one which threatens to escalate into a nuclear world war'.[89] He went on to lambaste US foreign policy.

The US government, and those who support it, would do well to remember that no solution will be acceptable to world opinion which does not secure, as well as peace, the full independence of the people of Vietnam; and that the people of South Vietnam are in no way represented by the series of military puppets, paid for and armed by the US, but by the National Liberation Front which has united, in spite of the most terrible sufferings, the heroic people of South Vietnam and is in fact already the effective government of four-fifths of the country . . . As the conflict develops, its ultimate purpose is becoming clearer. Taken in conjunction with official statements and other actions of the US government, particularly its interference in Latin America . . . we have to face the application of a conscious doctrine which is bound to lead to war and tyranny. This, now exercised by President Johnson, follows that of

Presidents Truman and Kennedy – and it is that the US has the right to intervene, at any time, in any part of the world which the President thinks is being endangered by communism; that communism represents any type of government displeasing to the head of the US and . . . by definition, communism is always produced by subversion from China or Russia, or both. In other words, the US is asserting the right, backed by force and money, to establish in every part of the world only governments of which it approves. It is an assertion by the US government of absolute world domination, of the domination of US capital, which characterizes the so-called 'free world'.[90]

To him, a scientist, it was 'a particular tragedy that in 20 years since the end of the last world war, when immense progress has been made in the means of production and the powers given by science are greater than they have ever been, the peoples of the world should still be living for the most part in a state of poverty and anxiety'.[91] For this state of affairs he blamed 'the pre-occupa-tion of the old industrialized powers with war preparations, and the un-checked operation of economic exploitation, which by controlling raw material prices, hinders the development of the newly liberated countries, and reduces to an absurdity the "aid" which has been grudgingly given to them'.

During his speech, Bernal said he would be stepping down as president of the WPC, when the congress was over. At the final session, an emotional Pablo Neruda recited a poem he had written to mark the occasion. In the last stanza, Neruda called out 'Bernal! Bernal! And doves will fly'[92] but, in his own closing speech, Bernal was anything but dovish. Whereas he had always argued for negotiations rather than continued fighting as a way to settle international disputes, he could not bring himself to support Johnson's call for uncondi-tional discussions over Vietnam. Dismissing the President's suggestion as 'meaningless and hypocritical', Bernal stated that he was content to wait for 'actual military developments in Vietnam and . . . world public opinion, to which this Congress has made a notable contribution' to force the US evacuation from South Vietnam before any negotiations.[93] During his open-ing speech just five days earlier, he had been applauded for saying, 'The first principle of the World Council of Peace is to stop wars in being.' Once again, as in the Hall of Mirrors in 1949, he could not resist milking the cheers from a communist audience with blazing anti-American rhetoric.

After he stepped down from the presidency, Bernal prepared a sober assessment of the future role of the WPC. He deplored the loyalist tendency to believe that 'all is for the best in the best of all possible peace movements (ours), and that anyone who dares to lay a finger on its structures and methods is a liquidationist and a pessimist'.[94] Instead he pointed to the need to break down the 'monolithic principle of obtaining unanimous de-cisions, policies and universal actions'. Its demise would be a hopeful sign because it would reflect the passing of the harsh rigidities of the worst Cold War period and 'a return to the healthy diversity of ideas and policies which is normal in a world made up of so many different countries, civilizations and cultures...It is essential to realise that this is an inevitable, irreversible development and that no useful purpose will be served by trying to turn back the tide at a command, in the manner of the early Danish King of England, Canute.' The WPC would have to learn to live with the increasingly diverse peace movements emerging outside of the communist bloc.

Critics of the WPC, both at the time and subsequently, have dismissed it as an arm of the Soviet regime, a sham organization. There is no doubt that it served an important foreign policy role for the USSR, especially in the early years when the US held an overwhelming advantage in nuclear weaponry. But for all its ridiculous posturing, fraudulent petitions and bombastic meetings, through the leadership of Joliot-Curie and Bernal, the WPC may have had an important restraining influence on Khrushchev in particular. In his farewell speech at Helsinki, Sage reflected that 'following the example of my predecessor Frédéric Joliot-Curie and many of the other great scientific workers for peace such as Bertrand Russell and Linus Pauling, we have not altogether failed...to get across to the people of the world the knowledge which alone can ensure that the dangers of war will be averted'.[95] However difficult it may be to make any elected statesman accept unwelcome or disconcerting information (as for example Patrick Blackett found with Prime Minister Attlee), it is incontrovertibly harder to persuade a totalitarian leader to the same truths. Only the bravest and most charismatic citizens within the system, for example Andrei Sakharov and Peter Kapitza in the USSR, would dare to broach the subject, and most outside experts would be dismissed as enemies. Joliot-Curie and Bernal genuinely believed in communism and were accepted, on a personal level, by Khrushchev as friends of the Soviet Union. If its first two presidents were even partly responsible for Khrushchev's realization that 'it's one thing to threaten with nuclear weapons, it's another to use them',[96] the WPC did not exist completely in vain. According to Khrushchev, neither Castro nor Mao Zedong seemed to comprehend the insanity of nuclear war.

President Kennedy's summer reading for 1962 included Barbara Tuchman's bestseller *The Guns of August*, which brilliantly reconstructed the start of World War One.[97] Kennedy could not put out of his mind a conversation between two German leaders on the outbreak of that war. 'How did it all happen?' asked one. The other replied, 'Ah, if only one knew.' Kennedy told his White House staff that he was determined to prevent two survivors of a nuclear war having the same conversation. During the half-century between 1914 and the Cuban Missile Crisis, the speed of communication between international statesmen had increased dramatically, but the content still depended on the bluff and quirks of human psychology. If Kennedy and Khrushchev had not managed to stop pulling on the ends of the rope in which the knot of war was tied, as Khrushchev said, 'reciprocal extermination' would begin.[98] Whereas the world survived the horrors of the First World War, which is still spawning new histories, nuclear war would not allow any literary legacy. As Bernal wrote in his 1958 book, *World Without War,*

Those killed outright will be the luckiest; far more will die in lingering agony from burns and radiation sickness. There will be little hope of help and it will be of little help when it comes. Overall there will be the general horror of the bursting, searing bombs, crushed and burnt bodies, greater than anything imagined in the hells of the Middle Ages, and the longer horror of recovering for a few of the immediate survivors...Nuclear war would not mean a simple, clean end to civilization, such as indeed as could happen from an explosion of the sun, but rather a painful creeping back into some form of life of the maimed and crazed remnants of humanity in the least-affected areas such as Tristan da Cunha or Tierra del Fuego, which will also be the least likely to retain the creative possibilities of civilization. It means a setback of hundreds or perhaps thousands of years. Yet I do not believe it means a complete destruction of civilization, because this has been sufficiently diffused, and enough will be kept of the principles of science, even in remote places, to start again without having to retrace all the steps from the Stone Age.[99]

21

Order and Disorder

Both at home and abroad, Sage had close contacts with a wide range of scientists, reflecting the diversity of his own interests and the interdisciplinary nature of X-ray crystallography. He was an inspirational figure to colleagues everywhere – Linderström Lang, who was the protein chemist in charge of the outstanding Carlsberg Laboratory in Copenhagen, told Perutz, 'When Bernal comes to see me, I feel that my research is really worthwhile.'[1] Given how much time and effort Bernal spent as an unpaid consultant in science and technology to countries like China, India, and Russia in the 1950s, it would have been understandable if he had no enthusiasm left for the same role at home. He had, after all, written *The Social Function of Science* to stimulate others to think about the way science contributed to the British economy and way of life; he had done his best to revitalize research in England after the war, both at Birkbeck and by his frequent visits and talks at other universities. At the start of 1956, when he was still unable to persuade the university authorities that a separate department of crystallography needed to be established at Birkbeck, he decided it was time to review the whole issue of how scientific research was funded and organized in Britain. He sent out a memorandum to two hundred of the country's leading scientists, politicians and university administrators. In his preamble, he made it clear that he was concentrating on the future of pure scientific research rather than on the subsequent economic and social application of scientific discoveries.

The vitality of the economy of Britain depends ultimately on that of fundamental scientific research. No amount of attention to applied research and technology can take the place of fundamental research. That is not only in the long run in the provision of radically new ideas, but also in the short run in providing the answers to key questions as they arise.[2]

While he did not think there had been any falling off in the quality of scientific research in Britain, he was concerned that the piecemeal system of funding within the university system meant that in future Britain was likely to fall behind both the USA and the USSR. He listed four major practical obstacles to current research:

1. lack of technical assistance;
2. inadequate research staffing;
3. lack of up-to-date equipment;
4. shortage of modern laboratories.

The bulk of university research funding came from the University Grants Committee (UGC) and Bernal thought that this funding should be increased to allow individual universities to develop more ambitious research programmes. He also suggested that a parallel National Research Committee should be established, where a panel of leading scientists would direct extra money to promising research projects. There should, in addition, be more direct sponsorship from industry and individual government departments to the universities.

About seventy individuals replied to Bernal, and their attitudes diverged widely. One university administrator thought that scientists were very poor at exploiting the existing facilities at their disposal due to a mixture of 'uninterest and incompetence'. He had obviously never set foot in the Torrington Square laboratories. There were many who were broadly in sympathy with Bernal's proposals. This was not surprising – since the publication of *The Social Function of Science* in 1939, the notion that science should be centrally planned to meet the needs of society had attracted supporters under the banner of 'Bernalism'. There were still some who adhered to the opposing viewpoint, articulated most clearly by Michael Polanyi, that a scientist should be allowed to investigate whatever subject interested him or her, untrammelled by any outside control. Sage recounted the reply he received from one of 'our most productive scientists':

I have never been able to plan a research, and set out the plan, and justify it, or apparently justify it, as is required by a scientific committee, such as a Research Council. If ever I had a plan, it was somewhere deep down in the sub-conscious, and I could not have told even myself, let alone anybody else, what I hoped might come out, still less what did in fact come out.[3]

This unnamed professor told Sage that he simply approached his university for money and made do with what they gave him, valuing most of all the complete freedom to follow where his instincts led him. Another professor who wrote a friendly reply was Sir Solly Zuckerman, who by now was combining a career at Birmingham University with the chairmanship of various government committees concerned with science and technology. He suggested that he and Sage should meet to discuss the issues raised: Zuckerman's prime concern was that the universities were going to find it increasingly difficult to compete with industry for talented research workers.

Bernal's memorandum was well received by several influential Labour MPs, who saw it as a foundation on which to build a modern science policy. Harold Wilson discussed its content with the nuclear physicists in his Liverpool constituency and 'they very much confirmed my prima facie view on reading your report that it is on the lines we should press for'.[4] Wilson had also passed the document onto Jim Callaghan, who had responsibility for science in the shadow cabinet. Callaghan incorporated several of Bernal's ideas in a House of Commons speech in June.[5] The new leader of the Labour Party was Hugh Gaitskell, a frequent participant at the Tots and Quots dinners before and during the war, who was well acquainted with scientists like Bernal, Blackett and Zuckerman. These Labour MPs saw science policy as a mechanism for modernizing Britain, when they came to power, and as a way to gain power, by outshining the Conservative government studded with classicists and knights from the shires.

The development of Labour Party science policy was led by the unlikely figure of Marcus Brumwell, a flamboyant comrade in the finest champagne-and-caviar mould. He owned Stuarts Advertising Agency in Mayfair, where he would sometimes oblige Sage by finding jobs for young women in need.[6] In May 1956, Sage sent Brumwell memoranda on fundamental and applied science policy.[7] Apart from the well-worn complaints about inadequate financing of fundamental research, especially when compared with the lavish amounts spent on military research, Bernal identified the nation's old-fashioned education system as the root cause of the shortage of qualified researchers and technicians. He recommended three broad policy improvements for a future Labour government to make:

1. mobilize existing resources by reducing restrictions and shifting funding from the military;
2. plan greater use of science in industry and agriculture, and stimulate research in medicine and the social sciences;
3. remould the education system.[8]

Brumwell organized a series of dinners at the Reform Club and Brown's Hotel, where scientists in sympathy with the Labour Party would have a chance to brief interested politicians and to thrash out policy ideas. Blackett and Zuckerman were two key members of the group; Sage would sometimes attend, but more often wrote the policy menu for the evening. Over a period of two years, the opinions expressed at these dinners were refined into a draft Labour Party policy document. Bernal sent six pages of comments on the draft to Brumwell, saying he found it to be 'remarkably lacking in a quantitative approach. We want far more facts and figures.'[9] He objected to the myth promoted by the Labour Party research department that 'most of our distinguished scientists made their way from humble beginnings' which was 'hardly true, though some did'. A more substantive criticism was the document's omission of 'the chemical industry, which underpins modern agriculture as well as plastics and pharmaceuticals'. Bernal noted that the nationalized coal industry invested £64 million on research during a period when the private chemical industry invested 700 million: he thought nationalized industries ought to be setting an example. The document was rewritten by C.P. Snow and was ready for the summer of 1959, when Gaitskell and Wilson both came to a dinner at Brown's and announced that they were very satisfied with it.

Unfortunately for the Labour Party, the British electorate chose to believe Prime Minster Macmillan that autumn, when he told them that 'You have never had it so good.' Brumwell wrote to Bernal thanking him for all his hard work, which had impressed Gaitskell and Wilson and opened their eyes to the possibilities of modern science.[10] Brumwell did his best to keep the lines of communication open over the next few years, but Wilson was the only politician to attend the dinners, and often his interest seemed rather superficial. In November 1962, Brumwell sent a letter to Gaitskell on behalf of the group, voicing their frustration that although lip service was being paid to science, it still had a very low priority in practice. To remedy this, Brumwell wanted Gaitskell to appoint a shadow minister exclusively for science and to ensure at least two other MPs attended their meetings. It would fall to Wilson to make these changes as the new Labour leader after Gaitskell's untimely death at the start of 1963.

Wilson immediately promoted Richard Crossman from the backbenches to become shadow Minister for Higher Education and Science. Wilson had particular respect for Blackett, and he would become the primary figure, with Crossman, in revitalizing Labour's approach to science and technology. The spirit was caught by Wilson in his landmark 'white-hot technology revolution' speech to the Party conference in Scarborough in 1963. Bernal wrote to Crossman saying that he 'thoroughly and enthusiastically' agreed with most of what Wilson said, but was worried about certain plans, 'such as putting large research institutes under separate ministries, where research will have a low priority because they are overwhelmed with quotidian problems'.[11]

Sage was too red for the white-hot technology revolution. While Zuckerman, who had been Chief Scientist at the Ministry of Defence since 1960, would in addition become scientific adviser to the Cabinet Office in the new Labour government, and Blackett was offered the new Ministry of Technology to run, Sage was not even admitted to a Labour Party conference on science in London. He was invited originally by Crossman himself, who then withdrew the invitation, saying he had exceeded his powers by inviting him without the proper authorization. Sage took the snub in good heart.

Dear Crossman,

Naturally, I was somewhat upset at receiving your second letter, but I cannot say I was as surprised by it than I was at receiving the original invitation . . . Some method, surely, could be devised whereby those who do not agree with certain aspects of the Labour Party policy such as Polaris submarines or mixed manned forces could be consulted on relatively non-controversial subjects such as science.[12]

Crossman did include Bernal as one of five FRSs on a government working party, headed by Robert Maxwell MP, on government, science and industry. Within months, Bernal's health would deteriorate to the extent that he was no longer able to fulfill any official duties. There was therefore no prospect of him being appointed to Crossman's Council on Science Policy. This body did include several of his friends, in particular Blackett, John Kendrew and Lord Rothschild. When their report appeared in 1966, it seemed to sound the death knell of Bernalism. Sage wrote to Blackett objecting to the statement in the report that there was a 'misconception that the advance of scientific knowledge itself can be directed from the centre'. Sage thought this statement 'very largely destroys the object of the report' because no alternative was offered. He still believed it was 'possible to identify certain growth points such as electronics, computers and biochemistry, materials science that ought to be given special support'. The report, mindful of Britain's sluggish economy, also stated that the 15% rate of increase in scientific growth was unsustainable and should be cut – an opinion Sage derided as 'entirely deplorable as well as unnecessary'.[13]

It is easy to forget that amongst his extra-curricular activities, Bernal also held a university chair in physics and was therefore responsible for a great deal of administration and some teaching. He was able to achieve this by delegating freely, for example to Stan Lenton, but above all by letting Anita Rimel run his life. From 1951, the physics department at Birkbeck was housed in a new building in Malet Street, next to the Senate House. On the entry door to Sage's ground floor office was a sign 'ANITA RIMEL SECRETARY' under which the title 'PROFESSOR J.D. BERNAL' appeared in much smaller letters. She was the sentinel at his gate, and in order to meet him you had to persuade her that you would not waste her professor's precious time. He also had an emergency escape route through a backdoor that connected to the Physics Staff Room, where four of his lecturers had their desks. They became quite used to the professor beating a hasty retreat, after receiving a warning signal from Anita.[14] With his own staff, Sage was generous with his time and encouragement; this extended to the student body (who came to lectures in the evenings because nearly all of them held fulltime jobs). Under Bernal, the physics department was the first to allow student representation on committees.

The atmosphere amongst the staff was generally excellent, but there was inevitably friction on occasion, most notably involving Rosalind Franklin in the completely inadequate accommodation of 21–22 Torrington Square. The most celebrated complaint came not from a staff member but from an overseas student, James Julian Ben Sammy. He had been the outstanding student at a missionary school in Trinidad and was sponsored to come to Birkbeck as a fee-paying student. He spent three years (instead of the usual two) obtaining an ordinary BSc in physics and then stayed on for another three to obtain a Special BSc. Sammy thought he deserved a first-class degree and when he did not receive one, he sued Birkbeck for breach of contract, fraud and professional negligence. The case came to trial in the High Court with Sammy appearing as the plaintiff in person. It quickly became the best farce in London and was extensively reported in *The Times* Law Report.[15] The judge allowed him a great deal of latitude in the way he questioned witnesses from Birkbeck, but snapped when Sammy asked the Registrar if he knew the game of cricket. Sage was naturally called as a witness and was conspicuously kind to Sammy. Far from obtaining a first, it emerged that Sammy obtained a bare pass mark after Bernal had persuaded the other members of the examination board that he deserved special consideration because he was so far from home and worked hard.

During the 1950s, Bernal managed to publish four books (counting the two editions of *Science in History* as one book). The output from his department included 155 research papers, several of which were fundamental contributions to crystallography (on molecular biology as well as on silicates and cement). Fifteen research students gained PhD's and 47 received MSc's, mostly in X-ray crystallography. Apart from running his own department, Bernal was the chairman of the University of London board of studies in physics. Far from resting on his laurels, Bernal had been thinking and writing about the origin of life; in 1957 he decided to take up research into the structure of liquids again.

At first blush, the phrase 'structure of liquids' might seem an oxymoron, since it is their fluidity and ability to take on the shape of any container that commonly defines liquids. They have no inherent, durable structure, but at any instant the atoms in a liquid will occupy certain positions in space. Those positions, however, are continuously changing and do not form any symmetrical pattern. Bernal made his first attempt at a molecular theory of liquid structure[16] in the 1930s, a few years after he and Fowler had proposed their revolutionary model of the structure of water. In his theoretical treatment, Bernal confined himself to consider the case of a liquid consisting of single, identical atoms, rather than say water, where the shape of the constituent molecules and their association by hydrogen bonds make the analysis even more complicated. It was axiomatic to Bernal that one of the main characteristics of the liquid state, its fluidity, resulted from 'the irregularity of distribution of its component atoms or molecules and the capacity of those distributions to change under the influence of heat or the mechanical stress'. He pointed out that 'a liquid differs fundamentally from a solid in that its configuration is not even approximately constant, but is a function of the temperature and pressure'.[17] Any attempt at quantifying the irregular structure of even the simplest monatomic liquid foundered for the lack of any adequate statistical technique of three-dimensional geometry. Sage was 'baffled by the difficulty of describing irregularity'.[18]

During the intervening two decades, the problem had largely been the province of mathematical physicists, who either approached the liquid state as an extension of dense gases or as an imperfect solid, resulting in theories that Sage found 'fundamentally unsatisfying as a crystallographer, however much they might appeal to a physical chemist or a mathematician'.[19] He had begun to think in much more everyday terms, for example saying that atoms in a liquid 'have more elbow room [than in a solid] and they are not so particular about their partners'.[20] What he wanted was a more graphic picture of liquid structure, as it might exist for an instant.

One approach, which was now certainly fashionable after the success of Watson and Crick, was to build models. Although Bernal had not relied heavily on model building in his previous research (unlike Lawrence Bragg, for example, going back to the 1920s), he kept a variety of models in the lab, which he regarded as a basic necessity to help thinking about problems in three dimensions.[21] There had been other major breakthroughs in structural biology that seemed relevant to liquids. The α-helical structure of proteins, with its non-integral number of amino acids per turn, described by Pauling and Corey, had freed crystallographers from the mental tyranny of regular shapes. Watson and Crick's subsequent work on the structure of spherical viruses, with their icosahedral symmetry, had taught crystallographers that although two-, three-, four- or six-fold symmetry were necessary to produce ordered, repeating structures, five-fold symmetry existed in nature even though it could not be propagated as a lattice structure. At Birkbeck, there were very talented researchers (Aaron Klug on the organic side and Alan Mackay on the inorganic) who were thinking deeply about three-dimensional geometry, and discussing their ideas with Bernal (and with Buckminster Fuller).

While all these ideas were buzzing in Bernal's head, the actual stimulus to return to liquid structure research came during a lecture on ultra-hard alloys by Charles Frank, a professor from Bristol University. As Frank was explaining how tungsten and other metal atoms were arranged in quasi-regular shapes, including some with five-fold symmetry, Sage's brain made the knight's move from hard metals to liquids. Frank was a solid-state physicist, who made important observations about dislocations and other microscopic imperfections in crystals, whereas Bernal was intent on chasing down the fundamental irregularity in the structure of liquids. To help in this research, he used the services of John Mason, a Birkbeck laboratory demonstrator newly arrived from New Zealand.

One of Bernal's first decisions was to build the type of ball-and-spoke model that was very familiar to all chemists in the context of solid crystals. Whereas X-ray scattering studies of solid crystals give information on specific atomic positions in a lattice, similar measurements of liquids give information on the distances between pairs of atoms. The statistic that describes the distribution of these pair distances is known as the *radial distribution function*. Spokes for the model were cut to different lengths that represented interatomic distances found in liquids, in accordance with the radial distribution function – each length of spoke was made a different colour. The model had to be free of any long-range order or pattern. Sage described his first attempt, 'I tried to do this in the first place as casually as possible, working in my own office, being interrupted every five minutes or so and not remembering what I had done before the interruption.'[22] By constructing the model, Bernal had converted one-dimensional data on the radial distribution of distances between atoms in a liquid into three dimensions. Although there was, by design, no regularity in the model, on inspection he could find a variety of irregular shapes such as semi-octahedra and tetrahedra. Looking at the model, he drew a distinction between arranging atoms (or building blocks) in a neat *pile*, as was the case in crystal lattices, versus a disorganized *heap*, as in a liquid. For a given volume, you have fewer atoms in a heap than you do in a pile.

Bernal then asked himself the question of how the irregular polyhedra in his model fitted together. He imagined sitting on one atom and identifying all its immediate neighbours. By bisecting each spoke connecting the home atom with its neighbours, another irregular polyhedron will be formed. Mason came up with a way of creating such unusual shapes. He took a number of balls of plasticine and dusted them with chalk to stop them from sticking together. He then put the balls inside a football bladder and sucked the air out using a vacuum pump. This had the effect of pushing the soft spheres together, until they completely occupied all the remaining space. On cutting the balloon open, the plasticine spheres had squashed into 'very beautiful and shapely polyhedra'.[23] Sage was delighted to find that he was replicating an experiment carried out in 1727 by the Reverend Stephen Hales, who compressed peas in an iron pot. Hales wrote in his *Vegetable Staticks* that the peas 'formed into pretty regular Dodecahedrons'.[24] The plasticine was a little too soft and could be easily distorted on handling, and Mason improved the experiment by using beeswax instead and putting the spheres inside meteorological balloons that he found in Australia.[25]

Bernal and Mason counted the number of faces on each squashed sphere, as well as the number of sides or edges per face. The average number of faces was 13.5, and the commonest number of sides to a face was five – yet no two shapes were the same. The number of faces corresponded to the number of neighbouring atoms; in his ball-and-spoke model the average number of neighbouring atoms was 13.6. Sage was delighted when the great geometer, Donald Coxeter from Toronto University, took an interest after visiting Birkbeck. He analysed mathematically the packing of quasi-equal polyhedra in space and calculated the average number of faces to be 13.56.

Sage unveiled his new models and ideas at a Friday evening discourse at the Royal Institution in October 1958. He started with what he called 'some rather childish experiments to explain earlier and naïve views of liquid structure', emphasizing the quality of fluidity, which earlier workers had taken as their point of departure. He told the enraptured audience that he thought this was 'a delusive path' and he intended to start from 'the static and molecular structural properties of liquids'.[26] His ball-and-spoke model was on view, and Mason repeated the experiment with a balloon of beeswax balls. Pointing out that no two polyhedra were identical, Bernal emphasized the predominance of five-sided faces on them.

Now you can see how very shocking such an arrangement would be to a crystallographer because it is impossible to fit these five-sided figures together in any regular way... in other words such an arrangement of points is radically different from a crystal – I could not get a regular from an irregular structure except by a very marked transition of the same nature as that between one crystalline structure and another... This explains why melting is a marked phase transition occurring at a definite temperature and with a relatively large latent heat. My analysis would show that it is impossible to pass in a continuous way from a crystalline solid to its corresponding liquid.

Only towards the end of the talk did Sage come to the actual question of fluidity. He then showed how spontaneous movement or diffusion of atoms through the liquid could result from the changes in the irregular polyhedra of neighbouring atoms. In his view, '*it is not the fluidity of a liquid that gives rise to its irregularity. It is its irregularity that gives rise to its fluidity.*'[27] He concluded the talk with a mock apology to 'the modern theoretical physicists for introducing such a simple way of looking at things, but I believe on the whole that it is better to start with a model that has some resemblance to reality'.

He did concede that to be useful, his model would need to be translated into mathematical terms. What was needed, he thought, was a new branch of mathematics called *Statistical Geometry*. But 'up till now it has been very difficult to attract pure mathematicians to this and when I have tried to do so,' he continued, 'some of them say the problem is too difficult and others say it is too trivial'.[28] He was encouraged by the start Professor Coxeter had made and hoped others would follow suit. In fact, he persuaded his eldest son, Mike, to write programs for the London University computer that generated a dense spatial model of a random distribution of points.

In 1958, Sage was elected a foreign member of the Soviet Academy of Sciences (along with his great friend Linus Pauling), nearly completing his sweep of scientific academies behind the Iron Curtain. He had already collected memberships of those in Hungary, Poland, Romania, and Bulgaria; Czechoslovakia and the German (East) Academy would soon follow. In 1959, he received the prestigious Grotius gold medal in international law (which historically is a strong form guide to the Nobel Peace Prize). By contrast, the honours accorded him in his own country were meagre, given his influence and fame. In 1962, the Royal Society did appoint him as Bakerian lecturer (a great distinction to add to his Royal Medal of 1946).

The annual Bakerian lecture, which dates back to 1775, is the Society's premier lecture in the physical sciences. Bernal again chose for his topic 'The structure of liquids'. He wrote to the Clerk of Birkbeck in February asking for access to the derelict 20 Torrington Square so that Mason could build him a large model in preparation for the lecture at the Royal Society.[29] He explained that the model was expected to take up 2–3 cubic yards of space. When no permission was forthcoming, he gave another laboratory technician, Ian Cherry, approval to use rooms in No. 20 and told him just to drill a hole through from No. 21 to bring in an electricity cable.[30] Cherry designed a special jig for the model construction, and when it was finished two or three years later, it was so big (about 4 cu. yd.) that it was entombed in a back room of No. 20 until the houses were finally demolished in 1966. For his Bakerian lecture, Bernal had to be content to show an earlier model built by Lenton and Mason. He extended his description of the modelling and mathematical work that had been going on at Birkbeck, and concluded that he and his colleagues had now substantiated the original concept of a liquid 'being essentially a *heap* of molecules, that is, being *homogeneous* and *continuous* without containing hypothetical regular inner structures'.[31]

For the second time in his career, Sage had changed the way scientists thought about liquids. There is little doubt that the subject appealed to his sense of history. He had begun his earlier discourse at the Royal Institution with the following words.

Of all the states of matter the liquid is the least understood and yet it is the one out of which, according to the Ancients at least, all other forms of matter were made. To go no further back than Thales,* the belief that the universe was created out of water is the beginning of modern science and philosophy.[32]

His research returned him to the study of geometry, one of his first loves, and required him to draw on concepts that he first learned as an undergraduate at the feet of Mr Grace in Peterhouse. The realization that there was no long-range order in liquid structure was a mathematical inconvenience, but this was not a reason to reject his model. Indeed, Dorothy Wrinch's cyclol hypothesis of protein structure, based almost entirely on mathematical neatness, failed because it could not account for the physical complexities of protein structure. The extension of X-ray crystallography first to biological substances and now to liquids called into question the whole definition of what 'crystalline' meant. In Bernal's opinion, biomolecular studies had 'broken formal crystallography, shattered it completely'.[33]

We clung to the rules of crystallography, constancy of angles and so forth, the limitation of symmetry notations to two-, three-, four- and six-fold, which gave us the 230 space groups, as long as we could. Bragg hung on to them, and I'm not sure whether Perutz didn't too, up to a point, and it needed Pauling to break them with his irrational α-helix. And so there are no rules, or the old rules are enormously changed. What we have called crystallography is a particular, small branch of crystallography, three-dimensional lattice crystallography. We are seeing now a generalized crystallography, although it hasn't been written up as such. But I think we have many elements of many chapters of generalized crystallography in the works of Cochran, Klug, Caspar and so forth. Any kind of a repeat organization is a crystal in this general sense. Protein chains are examples of it, so is DNA, and RNA. They have their own inner logic, the same kind of logic but a different chapter of the logic that applies to the three-dimensional regular lattice crystals.

He went on to consider the structural hierarchy of biological forms, starting with the particle ('which one might say has no dimension'), and then the fibre (one-dimension), the membrane (two-dimensions) and finally a three-dimensional structure (which is not a regular crystal). He considered the issue of identity, which the biologists had first studied in the context of genetics, and proposed that biological structures were 'combinations of arrangements of quasi-identical particles'. The key here was his favourite distinction between heaps and piles.

You can make a heap out of anything, no matter what it is, but you cannot make a pile of things that are not more or less the same – you see every day piles of oranges, piles of apples. Another word that comes in all languages . . . is the article 'an': an apple, an

---

* Thales of Miletus (*c.*560 BC) made predictions of eclipses (which Bernal thought were on the basis of earlier observations of the Babylonians) and believed that all matter derived from water, dividing itself into air above and earth beneath.

orange. It is not always true, but by and large everything for which you could use that article is a quasi-identical object: it can be made into a pile. I can even apply this to an amino acid, or a nucleotide. These quasi-identities have most surprising results. They enable you to build structures, and they also enable the structures to build themselves. That cannot be done unless there is quasi-identity. I cannot go into the details of how much 'quasi' is allowed; it is something I do not know. Two per cent is allowed, 10 per cent is just off, but somewhere in between those you can build piles.[34]

Although liquids were heaps of atoms, they displayed repeated signs of five-fold symmetry in isolated regions. Mackay listened to Bernal's strictures about five-fold symmetry being a violation of classical crystallography rather than being incompatible with the laws of nature. Just as there was good evidence that irregular five-fold structures were common to the structure of viruses and liquids, Mackay postulated that they might occur in inorganic solids. His prediction was born out in the early 1980s with the discovery of quasi-crystals in aluminium–iron alloy.[35] Forty years after Sage sensed the arrival of generalized crystallography, a professor of chemistry wrote about the concept of 'crystal' in *Nature*, saying that the key issue 'is not how one defines crystal but how one should define order'.[36] He built his case on the divergences from classical X-ray crystallography made necessary by the discoveries of quasi-crystals, biological and liquid structures. All these phenomena can be traced back to Sage's Birkbeck department. As Sage's friend Nikolai Belov wrote, 'His last enthusiasm was for the laws of lawlessness'.[37]

Although Bernal received the *Proceedings of the Soviet Academy of Sciences* as a foreign member, he did not read (or speak) Russian, and was probably unaware of a series of ten papers from the Institute of Surface Chemistry that appeared there between 1962 and 1966. The lead author on these publications was Boris Deryagin, a surface chemist who was well respected in the West. The subject of the reports was an anomalous form of water that his group claimed to have produced in quartz capillary tubes. They thought that in this form of water, the H_2O molecules were connected together in some novel way that accounted for physical properties such as boiling and freezing points, very different from those of ordinary water. Deryagin was invited to a meeting of the Faraday Society, held in Nottingham in September 1966, giving him the opportunity to present anomalous water to an international audience of chemists.

In his talk, Deryagin made some revolutionary claims that occasioned surprisingly little comment at Nottingham, where the audience may have had difficulty understanding him, or was perhaps reluctant to criticize one of the few Soviet scientists to attend a meeting in the West, or was merely dozing. While it was known that the solid wall of a container forces liquid molecules coating the surface to line up in layers, Deryagin proposed much more than a surface effect, and one that the molecules remember even in the vapour phase.

What was more, the denser anomalous water was the stable form of water – 'The usual state of water and certain other liquids is thermodynamically metastable', he said.[38] The implications of this remark are staggering. Deryagin seemed to be suggesting that, over a long period of time, all the water on the planet would revert from its common but metastable state of H_2O into the lowest energy state of anomalous water (which he claimed was 15 times more viscous than ordinary water and had a boiling point approaching 200°C). If Deryagin were correct, it was a reasonable assumption that anomalous water would occur naturally, perhaps in conjunction with silicates such as quartz.

Over the next two years, a few British laboratories set out to see if they could replicate the Russian experiments. One of these was the crystallography department at Birkbeck, where Bernal selected his PhD student, John Finney, to undertake the exacting task. Finney was a Cambridge physics graduate, who had learnt the principles of classical X-ray crystallography from Helen Megaw. He was to be Bernal's last PhD student, in a distinguished line going back to Helen Megaw, and the first male one whose hair-length matched the professor's. When he came for interview, he was shown the liquid ball-and-spoke model in 20 Torrington Square and asked to find the order in it. After studying the ping-pong balls and coloured spokes for some minutes, he turned to Bernal and said softly 'I can't see any order in it.'[39] Sage congratulated him and said he was hired. Finney's main work would be to produce a satisfactory 3-D model of a real liquid, but divining for anomalous water would become a major diversion.

Deryagin was invited back to Britain in 1968 and visited Birkbeck on 2nd May, when he took part in a discussion that was tape-recorded. Bernal asked the Russian how he thought anomalous water formed, and Deryagin admitted:

This is the most unclear point of the work. We have only two points clear, that this water may appear on the condensation of vapour but not as the result of direct contact of liquid water from quartz. Liquid water does not transform in some of our kind of water even after prolonged contact even at raised temperature; but in the form of vapour it can be modified.[40]

After some practical questions from Finney, Sage asked, 'Have you any idea what the structure is of this new kind [of water]?' Deryagin replied, 'No, we do not know. But it may be a ring [of H_2O molecules] or a square or it may be tetrahedral.' Deryagin was convinced that the phenomenon was real and depended on changes at the molecular level. When Sage somewhat rashly stated, 'In my opinion, this is the most important physico-chemical discovery of this century.' Deryagin jumped in. 'I am very glad to hear you say this. I would like to ask you something. Would it be possible for you to write something later about your opinion on the significance of this work, as you are the principal specialist on the physics and chemistry of water? It would be very important for me to get such an estimate.'[41] One of Deryagin's reasons for wanting Bernal's support was that he was having difficulty in persuading any Western scientific journal to publish his results, and praise from Sage would no doubt enhance his reputation at home as well.

After more speculation from Deryagin on the possible biological effects of anomalous water and its possible presence in high atmospheric clouds, he was brought back to earth by a sceptical Finney.

Finney: Are you talking in terms of water which is partially modified and water which is fully modified, and so presumably most of the time you are dealing with a mixture of water.

Deryagin: Yes. We always prepare a mixture of water, partially modified, but after we continue the evaporation it would become strongly modified water. We can also do the inverse. We can take strongly modified water and mix, not very quickly; sometimes it lasts one week, because the coefficient of the diffusion of the molecules of this modified water in ordinary water. It is about five or ten times lower than the coefficient of self-diffusion in ordinary water. So the diffusion is a slow process.

Finney: Can you actually say you can prepare water which is 100 per cent modified or do you not know this? Can you say: This water is 100 per cent modified. Have you any way of telling, any way of measuring the degree of modification?

Deryagin: Well, the degree of modification is not so precisely measured . . . [42]

The Soviet Embassy in London put out a press release about Deryagin's visit to Birkbeck and included some mention of anomalous water. Paul Barnes, who was just completing a PhD at Cambridge on the properties of ice surfaces, read the newspaper story. He had heard Deryagin lecture at the Cavendish Laboratory and decided to apply for a job at Birkbeck so that he could join Bernal's team working on anomalous water. The Americans, ever watchful of Soviet science, became interested too, and Finney was given a 'rather splendid lunch at the US Embassy'[43] by a liaison scientist for the US Office of Naval Research (ONR). In February 1969, the ONR held a symposium in Washington to discuss anomalies in the properties of liquid water. The promise of government research dollars was enough to overcome previous scepticism, and several American laboratories started work on the subject. A report appeared in *Nature* from a group of chemists at the Unilever Research Laboratories at Port Sunlight, who thought that they might have evidence for a trace of anomalous water in ordinary water treated according to Deryagin's method. Finney and the Birkbeck group were having no success at all; in an article 'Polymerized water – is it or isn't it' in May 1969, Finney wrote 'By not fitting in with existing ideas, anomalous water could trigger off an important advance . . . If only we could make a thimbleful, the problem would very quickly be resolved.'[44]

The same month that Finney's article appeared, there seemed to be a definite breakthrough as a result of collaboration between the British Ministry of Technology and an American spectroscopist, Ellis R. Lippincott, who served as a senior consultant to many US government departments. They found that the spectroscopic fingerprint of anomalous water was quite different from that of ordinary water and stated that anomalous water '*must* consist of polymer units' that they thought would be four water molecules linked in a square pattern.[45] Over the next few months, the popular press in Europe and the USA would be full of stories about this weird 'polywater' (as it was now termed). The polywater fever was stoked by a letter to *Nature* from a scientist at Wilkes College, Pennsylvania, who, having been convinced of the existence of polywater, regarded it as potentially 'the most dangerous material on earth'.[46] This 'unduly alarmist and misleading letter' earned him an immediate rebuke from the Birkbeck group, who were 'currently trying to sort out the chaos surrounding the phenomenon'.[47]

Contrary to the data which Dr Donahoe quotes as fact, remarkably little is still known about the precise properties of the substance, and it is still not certain that it even exists... There is still no adequate explanation of the phenomenon, and no coherent picture of its properties. One of the greatest difficulties in even accepting the existence of a more stable phase is its apparent absence in nature. Indeed, this is the most persuasive evidence of its inability to grow at ordinary water's expense, for it has stood the test of billions of years. The classic conditions for its formation – a quartz surface and greater than 95 per cent humidity – are very widespread in nature, yet no anomalous water has been detected. If it can grow at the expense of ordinary water, we should already be a completely dead planet... By all means draw attention of scientists to the dangers of their work, but make sure it is a real danger before alarming everybody else.

The debate over polywater continued with considerable publicity for the next year or so. At Birkbeck, it remained elusive unless the strict conditions of the experiment were relaxed. In Finney's words, they became convinced polywater was 'a load of junk' and in 1971 published an article 'Polywater and polypollutants'[48] in which they attributed the phenomenon to gross impurities, introduced as a result of ignorance or carelessness. The accompanying *Nature* editorial, 'Polywater drains away' provided the epitaph, although Deryagin continued to believe in his discovery and wrote to Bernal suggesting his team was incompetent and should be fired. While Sage had shown initial enthusiasm for anomalous water, and his words about it being 'the most important physico-chemical discovery of this century' have been quoted against him,[49] he never repeated the remark in public and took the responsible course of seeing whether Deryagin's work could be replicated. His own major contribution to the structure of liquids resulted from throwing off orthodoxy, and such startling new observations about anomalous water, from a credible source, were bound to intrigue him. His attitude was infinitely less reprehensible than it had been over Lysenko's sham genetics.

By the time the controversy over polywater was settled, Sage was no longer an active participant. His last public appearance on the stage of science, which he had graced over five decades, came at a Ciba symposium on 'Principles of biomolecular organization' in London in June 1965. He was invited to open the meeting, which brought together not only the cream of molecular biologists from Cambridge (Crick, Finch, Holmes, Huxley, Kendrew, Klug, and Wilkins) but a contingent from Harvard, led by Watson and Caspar. In his opening remarks, Sage dwelt on the development of generalized crystallography and raised the flag of Bernalism for the last time – recommending that thought should be given to the future arrangement of molecular biology, which was 'in some need of the application of a science of science'.[50]

Over the next three days, he listened to fifteen lengthy papers on the structural organization of cells and their components. Each talk was followed by rapier-like exchanges between the young giants of the field, who would often ask Sage for his opinion or refer to his work. At the end of the meeting, Crick asked him to give his impressions, and lawlessness was much in evidence in Sage's unscripted remarks.[51]

A meeting like this gives me great encouragement because it is an example of absolutely random processes which seem to yield results. I may have come here with some ideas of organizing this work in order to improve its yield, but these ideas have been amply dissipated in the course of the discussion. We have had here a highly sophisticated participation from what have been called by D.J. de Solla Price the 'high-level scientific commuters' or the 'scientific jet set'. I have spent a long time trying to get these things organized only to conclude, first of all that no one wants to organize them, and, secondly that there is no proof that if one did organize them they would be any better.

He could not quite abandon his need to plan, and questioned whether molecular biology was being studied in enough centres (with enough resources), whether it was attracting enough young scientists and if it was reporting results in an accessible fashion.

One element involved in this is free energy, which in this case can be equated with money. Presumably we all know how to spend the money when we have it, and the point is to extract it. One of the great problems in the whole of science is to what degree is science to be considered as a criminal activity? There is big criminal activity and small criminal activity, and through the whole history of science – it does not matter on what scale – the scientist is forced to do something. He has two problems: how to do it, and how to raise the money for it, which consists – and this is why I call it criminal – in finding some way of dressing the thing up so as to extract money from the people who have it, by persuading them that it is going to do something quite different from what it is really going to do...

I have come to this conference from another conference which was concerned entirely with the moon. It was very interesting because, of course, no one knew what it [the moon] was like; they all disagreed but they all agreed that within three years they would know what it was like and, therefore, this was their last chance of blowing off their ideas on the subject. Quite seriously, the moon is a very good money-raiser. I think the ratio in the US is 7:3 for money spent going to the moon and money spent on all the rest of science put together.

Seriously though, the problem is, is there a money problem? Is there a communication problem? There is an enormous increase in publication each year, and although you may be able to produce 50 per cent more papers per annum, it is doubtful whether you could read them. It is also doubtful whether there is any use reading them. The whole object of a meeting like this is to avoid having to read papers; it is really a sorting process. If you read one in a hundred or one in a thousand of the papers you will find out the state of the field – you will get a good random sample . . . It was pointed out, for example, that the one-to-one combination of Watson and Crick did not need anyone else at that stage . . . there are certain strategies, and the thing about strategies in science is that you engage in them first, and you find out about their existence afterwards . . . A cook does not know how he produces his results, but you know whether he has produced them . . .

The advance of science is really a nucleation phenomenon. Someone gets an idea that something would be worth doing, and he does it; if he fails nothing more is heard about it, but if he succeeds, then hundreds of people do it, and that may be the way science advances. I am interested in these methods, but from a specialist point of view, to find out how science works.

Sage returned to some of these ideas in a conversation with Aaron Klug. He told Klug that he had begun to realize that there were two ways of organizing science: one was planning it strategically and getting all the right elements in, the other was the Rockefeller Principle. Klug asked him what the Rockefeller Principle was, and he replied 'Oh, the Rockefeller just gives money to people who look good and have interesting ideas, irrespective of the nature of the project as long as it's something that appears to be important and generally in the right field.'[52] After the war, Sage had planned the Birkbeck department and succeeded in establishing the prototype for future molecular biology departments by including computing, X-ray crystallography, protein chemistry and other elements. He was less concerned about the staff appointments. It was Klug's impression the success of the Cambridge MRC Laboratory of Molecular Biology, so evident at the Ciba conference, persuaded Sage that a better method might be to recruit the brightest young people and let them follow their own interests. It was, after all, the way Sage moved science forward.

22

Years of Struggle

Bernal and Margot Heinemann were well matched: both shared a passion for literature and politics. The 1950s was probably Bernal's most stable decade domestically, although he was far from settled into a conventional style of life. Soon after Jane was born, they moved to a house in Highgate (a move probably financed from the Stalin Peace Prize). The house was not lavish and the family's material needs were met by Sage's professorial salary of over £2,000 per annum. In the 1950s, it was quite shocking for an unmarried couple to be living together and raising a child, let alone when the man was still married to another woman. There were also the added complexities that attached to being a communist household – although such a distinction mattered less in London than it did in communist states.

Like all Bernal's 'wives', or principal women, Margot had to be forgiving and independent – and she was. She jokingly referred to herself as 'a genius's moll'.[1] Such were the demands on Bernal's time, there were often periods when he played his role as father *in absentia*. Take 1957, the year before Bernal succeeded Joliot-Curie to the presidency of the WPC and dramatically increased his commitment to the peace movement. There were no long trips, but the extent of his foreign travel during the year was extraordinary, even for a scientist of international renown. In April he was in Hungary; during the summer vacation, he attended the Congress of the International Union of Crystallography (IUCr) in Montreal in July and the international conference on the origin of life, organized by Oparin in Moscow in August. He was back in Moscow in November 1957 as the guest of honour at a two-day meeting held by the Academy of Sciences to discuss his book *Science in History*.[2] In between those two visits, he had attended the Comenius international meeting in Prague and a WPC committee meeting in Stockholm. He was not just an observer at any of these events, delivering scientific papers at the summer meetings in Montreal and Moscow and long addresses at the others. His travel arrangements were made by Anita Rimel. Klug remembers going into the office one day, when she was on the phone to Helsinki airport (a stop en route to Moscow) saying, 'The professor will be arriving at Helsinki and please make sure there is some hot soup waiting for him.'[3]

The day after flying back from Moscow in November, Bernal chaired a day-long meeting at the Royal Society on the physics of water and ice.[4] His opening remarks were cogent and expectant, and he displayed an undiminished ability to integrate fresh information in his discussion of a paper read by Dr B.J. Mason, from Blackett's department at Imperial College. Mason reported how ice crystals grown carefully from supersaturated water vapour at controlled temperatures took on different shapes – plates, needles, hollow prismatic columns – but could not explain the mechanism. The chairman came to his assistance:

If Dr Mason does not venture an explanation of the phenomena of the different morphological forms of ice formed at different temperatures, I will take the risk of putting forward one which, to be honest, I only thought about this morning. If it is right, and I think there should be fairly simple means of testing it, it would apply in general to all crystallizations from the vapour which occur in conditions not far removed from equilibrium ... [5]

Sage went on to expound a thermodynamic approach to the phenomenon (which occurs naturally in snowflake formation), and explained that his hypothesis was based on a paper he had heard on the formation of quartz crystals, at the Montreal IUCr congress that summer. In his closing remarks to a meeting that he clearly enjoyed, he admitted that he was both humble and anxious to push on with research in the face of continued ignorance about the essential properties of the commonest of all liquids, water.

When Sage was at home, he took delight in the company of Jane and her friends. He would return from trips with wonderful presents and a fund of entertaining stories. He was good at assessing children's interests. When Martin was young, Sage read the whole of H.G. Wells' *Outline of History* to him. With Jane, he encouraged her curiosity about natural history, and they would discuss the names and types of plants, animals and birds. Invertebrates were included, and if Jane said 'Yuk' when faced with a creepy-crawly, he would tell her, 'It's just a question of scale: everything is beautiful if you just get the right scale.'[6] At her birthday parties, he would provide the entertainment with science tricks, which were wildly popular with her friends. He would bring home a flask of liquid nitrogen from the lab and freeze a rose, before shattering it with a hammer. He would set fire to steel wool in pure oxygen and tell the audience about Priestley's dramatic life. For many years, Jane was confident that her father knew everything until she uncovered one or two gaps, such as music. When she was about ten years old, Jane sang in a school production of Noye's Fludde. Sage came and wept throughout, 'making noises like a sea-lion',[7] to the distraction of the audience. If they went to a museum, a small crowd would often gather round to hear Sage's commentary, assuming him to be the curator.

Summer holidays were usually spent in West Cornwall, on the same beaches he had gone to with Mike and Egan in the thirties, and Martin early in the war. The journey from London would involve multiple diversions to see friends, such as Dorothy Hodgkin in Oxford, as well as prehistorical sites – the Rollright stones, Avebury and Stonehenge. His archaeological pastime in Cornwall was to investigate small subterranean passages, known as fogous, that date from the Iron Age. Many fogous would be too small for him to enter, and Jane, inspired by stories of children discovering cave paintings and other art treasures, acted as his willing accomplice.

Any decent holiday spot had to have rocks emerging from the ground. One year, Sage was in Budleigh Salterton, where he was told there was uranium in the rocks.[8] While he was taking samples with a hammer and cold chisel, some local boys came along and asked him what he was doing. Instead of shooing them off, he squatted on his haunches, and drawing diagrams with the chisel in the sand, proceeded to give a condensed lecture on radioactivity without using long words or being patronizing. On another holiday in the West Highlands of Scotland, Sage took everyone to a bleak, windswept, road construction site, where an *unconformity* in the rock strata had just been revealed.[9] He scrambled up the cliff to take a closer look, watched by a line of small, cold, children who had been grounded by their mothers.

The Christmas rituals caused Sage some difficulties. On Christmas Eve, he would often go with Margot and Jane to have dinner at Margaret Gardiner's house in Hampstead. Margaret, by this time, was completely relaxed about her relationship with Sage. She once introduced herself to someone as 'Mrs Bernal', to be told that she did not look like the Mrs Bernal the person knew. 'Oh', she said, 'There are hundreds of us.' Sage's legal wife, Eileen, was living in rural Suffolk with a female companion, named Foffie; on Christmas afternoon, Sage would drive up to see her, Mike and Egan.

He still retained the flat at Birkbeck, which could be used to arrange a social life in parallel. One Christmastime, Eileen's presence there saved the lab from serious damage. As Bernal wrote in a letter of complaint: 'On Boxing Day afternoon, Mrs Bernal, who was fortunately in the building at 21 Torrington Square, noticed water coming down from the second floor occupied by the Chemistry Department Lab.'[10] She phoned Stan Lenton, who came in from home and spent five hours locating the leak from a perished rubber waste pipe. In Bernal's opinion the condition of the Torrington Square houses 'is approaching one of criminal negligence'. There was danger to a large number of people, and the potential for major scandal since, he thought, the insurers might reject any claim in the event of fire or personal injury. He urged the removal of the chemistry department, and suggested the Master should call an emergency meeting of all heads of department. It was a very cold winter and there were many more leaks from frozen pipes; Lenton became understandably resentful about the amount of time he spent mopping up, and complained to Bernal that 'the primary cause of flooding is the neglectful and irresponsible methods of the chemistry department and their chaotic water and waste pipes'.[11] There was another serious flood in May that ruined papers, an X-ray set and cameras.

When the crystallography group first moved into the Torrington Square houses in 1948, they were meant to provide temporary accommodation for five years or so, until a purpose-built lab materialized. Bernal spent many hours reviewing plans and making suggestions for a new crystallography department, but by the early 1960s the timetable for the lab was perpetually five years late. Yet the mere spectre of a new building meant that the College was extremely reluctant to spend any money repairing Torrington Square. Ever since the appointment of John Lockwood as Master in 1951, Bernal had been petitioning to have crystallography made a separate department from physics. Lockwood was a classicist, who had become an experienced university administrator and also served as the Vice-Chancellor of London University during the late 1950s. He was about the same age as Bernal, and the two men shared an interest in the organization of tertiary education in postcolonial Africa. But they did not get on and found themselves on opposite sides in a debate about the future of Birkbeck College. Lockwood favoured ending the tradition of part-time students and thought the College should move to a new site away from central London.[12] For once, Sage found himself in the role of the traditionalist. According to College folklore, Lockwood was right-wing, anti-science, and blind to the world-class crystallography department that Bernal had built up.

Even in the late 1950s, many of the crystallography staff were still idealistic about communism and, like Sage, quite open about their political views. He would visit the CPGB headquarters in King Street after returning from trips behind the Iron Curtain, and would also give a lunchtime talk about his experiences to the Birkbeck staff. John Mason, the lab steward, listened to accounts of how good things were in the Soviet Union with distaste.[13] Mason had become friendly with Dr Douglas Dakin, the Registrar of Birkbeck, as a result of commuting together on the Underground. He knew that Dakin was anti-communist as a result of his wartime experience with the army intelligence corps in Yugoslavia. In 1961, Britain was rocked by the Portland spy case, when several Russian spies were convicted of stealing secrets from the naval underwater weapons research establishment. This triggered a memory in Mason's brain from Bernal's last lunchtime talk on the USSR, when he alluded to some anti-submarine research that he had seen. Wondering whether this could be connected to the Portland material, Mason mentioned it to Dakin. Dakin still had contacts with the intelligence services and arranged a meeting for Mason. It took place in the Lyons teahouse in the Strand, where Mason talked to an anonymous man he presumed to be from MI5. At the end of the rather inconsequential story, the agent just said, 'So you had a hunch about the submarine work.'[14]

A few days later, Anita Rimel came into Mason's room and said, 'The Professor wants to see you.' Mason thought this was odd because their rooms were close together and normally Sage would just walk over to speak to him. As soon as he entered the office, he could tell that there was something wrong because Bernal would not look at him, but stared down at his desk. An argument ensued and Mason lost his temper. Bernal said quietly, 'You can go now', and never referred to the incident again. Mason was convinced that Bernal had learned of his interview, and that the information must have come from within MI5.

There is no way of knowing whether Dakin communicated any concerns about Bernal to the Master – if he did, it would have hardened Lockwood's dislike for Sage. Regardless of the antipathy between Sage and the Master, the very success of the physics department created a severe case of academic jealousy amongst the smaller departments (most notably the chemistry department), and this, as much as Lockwood's influence, thwarted Bernal's plans.

By 1962, Sage had persuaded the Academic Board to approve the separation of crystallography from physics, but during the summer vacation, the Governors resolved to ask the Academic Board to reconsider this decision. Sage learned of the change, when he returned from the tumultuous World Congress on Disarmament and Peace in Moscow and must have been stunned by the news. He discovered that Professor W.G. Overend of the chemistry department (and Dean of the Science Faculty) had persuaded the Governors to set up an inquiry into the future of X-ray crystallography in teaching and research. Sage wrote to J. Monteath Robertson, Professor of Chemistry in Glasgow and a distinguished crystallographer himself, to explain that Overend was predicting the demise of X-ray crystallography as a separate discipline.

The view expressed here is that whereas it did have some interest twenty years ago, it has now become so much a routine matter that it should be left to appropriate people in the departments of physics, chemistry or geology. Naturally, while I welcome the spread of crystallographers into these departments – I feel no chemistry department is complete without someone who can do a crystal analysis – I do not think this is enough, and more specifically I feel that there should be at least two or three centres in the country which are centres of crystallographic research, where new methods may be developed and new fields opened up.[15]

Bernal asked for a letter of support, which was quickly forthcoming. Robertson began by saying, 'I must confess to feeling rather shocked that this matter should be raised at all, or questioned at all, in view of the ever growing importance of the subject.'[16] The fact that Robertson had been made President of the Chemical Society was some recognition of the crucial importance of crystallography, he thought. He agreed wholeheartedly with Sage, and believed Birkbeck to be one of the most important centres in the UK. Armed with this letter and others like it, Bernal went on the counteroffensive and pointed out that the separation into two departments had been adopted as official policy for the 1962–67 quinquennium, but not put into practice due to shortage of funds. He thought that it was up to those who now objected to the policy to show cause as to why it should be altered.

A meeting of the Academic Committee was arranged at Birkbeck for 1st November. The opposition was led by Overend and the professor of zoology, W.S. Bullough. During the meeting, Lenton smuggled a note into Sage because he heard on the radio that Perutz and Kendrew had been awarded the Nobel Prize for Chemistry in recognition of their X-ray analysis of haemoglobin and myoglobin. Despite this piece of intelligence, the outcome was not a clear-cut victory for Bernal. The committee did recommend the establishment of a chair in crystallography within the department of physics, but in order that the situation might be clarified, crystallography should remain with physics until 1967. Bernal and his staff were extremely disappointed by this compromise, which would further delay the establishment of a separate department. The staff registered their grievances with Sage, fearing that the previous 'lack of active protest against our slum conditions has been taken by the authorities as acquiescence'. Their overriding complaint was 'the filth and squalor of the buildings 21–22 Torrington Square'. There had been no redecorating since 1955, and they had to cope with dirt, dust, floods, storage of flammable liquids under wooden stairs, and a blocked toilet on the third floor. Given there was no prospect of a new lab before 1966, they suggested that temporary buildings should be erected. In a show of loyalty to Sage they said: 'Privately, we are resolved to increase the quality and quantity of our research to exhibit our conditions as an even bigger disgrace to the University than they are at present.'[17]

Sage's difficulties at Birkbeck prompted him to write a paper on the future of X-ray crystallography that he intended to present at the IUCr congress in Rome the following year.

I have felt for some time that the position of what we have called X-ray crystallography, but might be more correctly called structural diffractometry, or structure determination by diffraction, requires consideration by the Group ... Until now, as we all know, progress has depended largely on the accidents of university appointments and on the ability and drive of individuals ... the subject had the inestimable advantage of starting in this country with the combined abilities of the Braggs, which gave it a long lease of life, first at the Royal Institution, and Manchester and Cambridge. [They attracted] young men of exceptional enterprise and scientific ability, who were subsequently appointed to chairs of physics and chemistry.[18]

He warned that the first generation of students of the original masters was now reaching retiring age. There needed to be more concerted effort to establish the subject as a regular part of teaching, not necessarily in all universities, but at least in a sufficient number of them. There was no established chair in crystallography in Britain and there were only two institutions (Cambridge and Birkbeck) that provided regular courses lasting more than a year. But, he wrote, 'the continuity of both these schools is at the moment threatened'.[19]

From the time he was a boy at Brookwatson, Sage opted out of the quotidian chores of life. He rarely set foot inside a shop – Margot or Anita bought his clothes for him. At Birkbeck or at conferences, he would usually wear a suit with a waistcoat, but preferred an old tweed jacket and baggy flannel trousers. He hated to have his hair cut. Stan Lenton often picked him up from Highgate in the mornings and drove him to Birkbeck. By the early 1960s, Sage's prewar Austin was showing its age, and Lenton finally persuaded him that he should buy a new car. Sage gave him a bundle of banknotes and told him to choose one. When Lenton asked him what make of car he wanted, Sage replied, 'I know nothing about cars. I am sure you will know what suits.'[20] Francis Aprahamian functioned as his amanuensis for non-technical writing, and Anita Rimel dominated the content of his working day. Jane remembers, as a small child, listening to her father taking a phone call at home from Anita: 'Yes, Anita.' 'No, Anita.' 'I am sorry, Anita.' 'I will try not to do that again, Anita' he said apologetically. She turned to her mother and asked, 'Is Anita Daddy's teacher?'[21] For Anita, he was *the* Professor and nothing was good enough for him. The scene at Torrington Square in the early 1960s was caught by a writer, who came to interview Sage about his role in planning Overlord.

We sat on two old wooden Windsor chairs, warming our knees before a small, asthmatic gas-fire, which, before the war, cost a few shillings. The floor was covered with old brown linoleum: the surroundings – in a late Georgian private house, requisitioned by the University authorities – far from luxurious. Dr Bernal's secretary, leading me through the house, along uncarpeted corridors, past open doors, past finger-printed walls of dingy distemper – the air sour with the rank smell of the Student – muttered irritably: 'Only a little while more. It's a crying shame they have to ask him to see people – *and* work – in such surroundings. In a civilized country, they'd see to it that he'd be properly housed.[22]

Anita never married, and looking after Sage was her life. She could not help but resent any new figure, especially a female, who might come between her and the professor. Vivien Pixner felt this antagonism as soon as she became his peace secretary in 1960. Sage asked that foreign trips should be arranged to combine WPC work with a scientific meeting, when possible; according to Anita's diary, it was usually impossible. The first time it was tried, Sage was flying to Rome with Vivien for a WPC committee meeting, and arranged to speak to the Italian Academy of Science on the structure of liquids. He arrived at the airport, cradling a cardboard box with a large ball-and-spoke model packed inside. At the check-in, he realized that he had left his suitcase at home. Vivien's first job in Rome was to go out and buy him a change of clothes and toiletries.[23]

Sage's life was always full to overflowing. His mental drive was rooted in a strong constitution, but he constantly pushed himself to the point of exhaustion. As he got into his sixties, he seemed surprised that sometimes his body could no longer keep up. When he was spending twenty-hour days in Chile in 1962, he noticed that walking high in the Andes was a real physical effort. His main exercise in England, apart from summer walks along cliff tops in Cornwall, was the annual Aldermaston march. At Easter 1963, he had to rest after going about five miles and sat for three hours watching the thousands of marchers go by. He decided to seek medical attention and went to the National Hospital for Nervous Diseases in Queen Square. He was admitted as a private patient at the end of May under Dr Kremer. After blood tests and X-rays, Kremer diagnosed cervical spondylosis, a degenerative disorder of the neck that can compromise blood flow to the brain and cause limb weakness. He recommended a soft collar, which Sage wore for about a week, finding it extremely uncomfortable; as a method of spinal fixation, it struck him as 'ad hoc and crude'.[24] He wrote the neurologist a note asking whether the collar needed to be worn continuously and saying that he was unimpressed by the single paper he had been able to find in the *British Medical Journal* supporting the therapy. He wanted to know:

1. Is there any proved medical benefit to be got by fixing the vertebrae of the cervical spine?
2. If beneficial, what is the optimum position?
3. Having settled the desirable position and the amount of freedom to be allowed, the design should be left to competent mechanical designers, whether or not they have any orthopaedic experience.[25]

He had been invited as a guest speaker to a Gordon Research Conference on cell structure and metabolism in June. The Gordon Conferences are designed to be stimulating and informal affairs, where innovative thinking is encouraged by publishing no proceedings and by guaranteeing that ideas expressed will remain off the record. The conferences are traditionally held at New England prep schools, and the thought of spending a few days in rural New Hampshire seemed very attractive at the end of what had been a frustrating academic year in London. Sage was invited to speak on the 'Properties of water and its role in biological systems'. The opportunity was too good to miss and he thoroughly enjoyed the conference. In his lecture, he likened the structure of the cell to a Dutch seventeenth-century city, where there were many gates in the wall, but at any time few would be open.[26] The analogy appealed to Herman Barendsen, a post-doctoral physical chemist from Groningen, who struck up a friendship with Sage. On the last afternoon of the conference, the pair took a canoe onto the Connecticut River in nearby Vermont and spent four hours paddling in quite strong currents.

Greatly invigorated, Sage made his way to New York, which was experiencing an intense heat-wave. He boarded the plane to fly back to London and found himself 'wedged between the fattest people' on board.[27] The plane was held on the tarmac for two hours, during which time there was no ventilation, and Sage found it very difficult to breathe. After they took off, he ate 'the very inferior meal provided' and could not sleep. When he went to the toilet at the rear of the plane, he stumbled in the doorway but thought it was due to tail vibration. He found he had to hang onto the seatbacks to return to his place. Breakfast was served, and he could not grip the coffee cup. On arrival at Heathrow, he had to struggle with his luggage through customs and then queued to get a bus to Victoria station.

Stan Lenton had driven to the airport to meet him, but there was no arrival information about the New York flight; after waiting for four hours, he returned to Birkbeck. There was a phone message to pick Sage up from Victoria, and when Lenton saw him, there was clearly something wrong: 'The prof wasn't with it, didn't react and just slumped into the back seat.'[28] Lenton drove him to Birkbeck where Sage immediately went to a meeting of the Academic Board. Eric Hobsbawm, who was there, remembered that he 'looked like death' and noticed that his speech seemed slurred.[29] The future of crystallography was again on the agenda, but Bernal felt too tired to continue. His last words before leaving the meeting were 'I object.' He walked slowly to his office, where he signed letters and started to read the mail that had accumulated. He dragged himself upstairs to his flat and fell into a deep sleep.

When he awoke an hour later, he felt very strange and knew that he had suffered a stroke because he could not move his right side, nor walk or speak properly. He crawled into the next room and his symptoms improved considerably. Eileen called to see him and arranged for him to be admitted to the National Hospital in Queen Square straightaway. While waiting for the ambulance to collect him, Sage attempted to monitor his condition by repeatedly signing his name and walking around the room to see if he could avoid bumping into the furniture. Once in hospital, he felt comparatively cheerful, and reflected on his past life and what he might expect for the rest of it. He hoped to be able to tidy up his work on liquid structure. His condition steadily improved over the next few days. He wrote his scientific will, leaving problems for others to solve.

Dr Kremer decided that he should have a cerebral angiogram, an investigation that required a general anaesthetic. Sage pointed out to the anaesthetist that his last experience of one had been in Ireland in 1905, when he had his tonsils removed. 'He assured me that anaesthetics had improved out of all recognition in the interval. That may be so as far as unconsciousness is concerned because it worked perfectly... [afterwards] I felt iller and more sick than I have ever been even in the worst sea storms.'[30] The angiogram showed no abnormality and Sage was discharged. He went to stay with his friend, the actor Miles Malleson, who lived in a large house in nearby Rugby Street so that the hospital physiotherapists could attend him. Miles had divorced Eileen's friend, Joan, years before, and was remarried to a much younger woman. Sage, much to Miles' amusement, took a shine to her. The tryst was interrupted by toothache and a fever. Arrangements were made for Sage to go into the private Italian Hospital, next door to the National. He was 'assured that it was a civic hospital but when I got there it was full of nuns. The room was very clean and neat and rather forbidding. As I sat there while Anita put my things away, I thought what a complete waste of time and life it was to be there.' Sage walked out, 'moving with surprising rapidity', until he was well out of sight and sound of the hospital.[31]

At the end of July, Eileen took him to Stoneland Park in West Sussex to recuperate. They stayed in a bungalow with a beautiful rose garden, which Sage enjoyed. It was while he was there that the partial test ban treaty was signed in Moscow. Unfortunately, the toothache returned to plague him, until he persuaded a dentist to extract the tooth even though X-rays showed no abscess. He spent the remainder of the summer vacation in St. Ives with Margot and Jane. He was vexed by the Chinese attitude to the WPC, and exchanged letters with Khrushchev. Ivor Montagu came to visit him to be briefed for an upcoming WPC committee meeting in Helsinki. Montagu described Sage's attitude to rest.

Before lunch he had one walking up the hilly point, puffing to keep pace, desperately trying not to miss what he said about signs of possible life in hundreds-of-millions-of-years-old Canadian meteorites. At last Desmond was prevailed upon to return home to sleep after lunch. Using the opportunity I got into bathing shorts and sneaked across the sand for a swim. Suddenly I heard a shout and there was Desmond similarly clad, insecurely testing his footing at the water's edge.[32]

Bernal was soon knocked over by a wave and found it difficult to get back up, but nothing could lessen his lifelong habit of pushing himself. The International Union of Crystallography held its triennial meeting in Rome in September; they elected Bernal to be president of the organization, in his absence.

He would need all his tenacity of spirit to survive the next term at Birkbeck. When the original decision to split the physics department during 1962 had been made, Ehrenberg had been given a personal chair in order for him to become the new head of the smaller physics department. As a corollary to this, the University appointed Sage to a new chair in crystallography, starting on 1st October 1963, even though the College had decided no split would now take place before 1967. In a remarkably cynical gesture, Overend now wrote to Sage to inform him that physics could not have two representatives on the heads of department meetings, and he would be inviting Ehrenberg alone.[33] Sage immediately complained to the Master that this snub was 'actuated by a narrow and exclusive spirit'. As the senior professor of 25 years standing, he thought it would be 'vexatious and injurious' to the College to exclude him from these most important discussions on the future and suggests he might appear in a personal capacity: 'Such a compromise might meet the immediate situation and prevent these administrative and constitutional points from causing more bitterness in the College that they have already done.'[34]

Overend's miserable tactic backfired, and Bernal's cause was taken up by many who had previously been agnostic on the future of crystallography. The Academic Board met on 3rd December and voted 22–5 to support Bernal's suggestion that the Governors again consider the setting up of an independent department of crystallography. Bernal pointed out at the meeting that his illness left him unable to cope with running the physics department, but he could still manage the smaller crystallography department. In Hobsbawm's opinion, 'now the cause of Bernal was the cause of all adversaries of Lockwood'. He sensed that Bernal's colleagues were moved by his physical plight and revolted by 'the idea that his wishes should be refused in such circumstances'.[35] In February 1964, the Professoriate Committee voted narrowly to create a separate department of crystallography before the next academic year, and in July the University Senate amended the terms of Bernal's chair so that he would become Head of the Department of Crystallography. In Hobsbawm's words:

Crystallography at Birkbeck thus survived Bernal. The whole miserable episode is an example of the tangled and trivial civil wars with which anyone with experience of colleges and universities will be familiar... It is difficult for anyone who was involved in these disputes at the time, or who surveys the record impartially, to look back on them with anything but a sense of shame. They forced a scientist of extraordinary gifts to pursue his and his colleagues' work under constant threat of strangulation, in constant uncertainty about its very survival.[36]

More good news followed later in 1964, when Dorothy Hodgkin won a Nobel Prize. Sage had first proposed her for the Chemistry Prize in 1956, only to be told that he was supposed to be recommending a scientist for the Physics Prize. So in 1957 he proposed her for the Physics Prize, and again in 1959 (when he also suggested Charles Frank from Bristol).[37] When news of her overdue success reached London, Sage wrote a celebratory piece for the *New Scientist*. A few years earlier, Paul Ewald had written to Bernal after reading Dorothy's paper elucidating the complex structure of vitamin B_{12}. Ewald said, 'if you had not done anything in science but to train this woman your name should never be forgotten'.[38] While singing her praises, Sage uncharacteristically exaggerated how much of the work she had carried out in his lab at Cambridge. Describing her as 'one of these masters [*sic*] whose method of work was as exciting and beautiful to follow as the results that flowed from it', Sage went on to say that 'wherever she went she won acclaim, far beyond the understanding of her work, by her rare sweetness and generosity. If ever a Nobel Prize has been fully and fairly won, it is this one.'[39]

Dorothy, for her part, always maintained that Sage should have shared the prize with her. In her opinion, it was impossible to overstate his influence and inspiration. The crystallographers in Cambridge gave Dorothy a lunch, and Bernal was able to attend. Although he was incapable of jealousy, Olga Kennard noticed how depressed he was, surrounded by the likes of Crick, Kendrew and Perutz. He admitted to her that he would have enjoyed some official recognition for himself, and realized that he had given away so many fruitful ideas to others.[40]

Sage decided to step down as president of the WPC at the Helsinki congress in July 1965. He stayed with some friends in a small house on the outskirts of the city and was taken in to the meetings every day. The long hours of speeches and argument exhausted him. While he was there, word reached him that John Lockwood, who had done so much to hinder his plans at Birkbeck, had died unexpectedly. Although he had been introduced to Mrs Lockwood only once or twice, Bernal insisted on missing a session of the congress to write her a letter of condolence. As he explained to Ann Synge, who was with him, 'she would expect a letter from me and would be upset if I didn't write, and one shouldn't wantonly upset people when they are bereaved'.[41]

The precipitating factors for Bernal's stroke in the summer of 1963 are easy to identify. He had taken four hours of unaccustomed exercise and was probably still dehydrated when boarding the plane. Sitting in the heat, breathing foul air and then being immobile in a low-oxygen environment for a total of ten hours, with no liquid intake, were conditions sure to make his circulation sluggish. The *coup de grace* may have been attending the contentious committee meeting, when his blood pressure shot up. He made a good recovery, suggesting that the event was thrombotic – a blockage that subsequently cleared (he was treated with intravenous heparin at the National Hospital). Unfortunately, his blood pressure remained dangerously high – a year later it was 160/112 – despite being under the care of one of the country's leading specialists, Max Rosenheim at University College Hospital. While in Cornwall in 1965, one of the blood vessels in the right side of his brain could no longer withstand the surges of pressure, and burst. The result was immediate and complete paralysis of his left arm and leg (in addition to the residual weakness on the other side from the first stroke). Even more devastating for the man whom Perutz described as the most brilliant conversationalist he ever met, was the realization that he could no longer speak clearly.

He was transferred from sunny Cornwall to the dreary surroundings of St. Ann's Hospital, Tottenham. Eileen wrote love letters to him every day and made plans to move from Suffolk to London so that she could help to look after him. There were letters from old friends and colleagues such as Barbara Hepworth, Aaron Klug and Solly Zuckerman. There was also a letter from 14 Rugby Street:

Darling heart... Des my love take care. We'll talk and love – soon, soon. I love you more than I can understand. Your Polly. PS Miles (who is in Moscow) sent all wishes to you.[42]

Poor Polly felt jilted by Sage earlier in the summer, when she wrote to ask:

What sort of idiot do you take me for? Forgive any note of bitterness... ring me and blow kisses. Most women buy a new hat under these circumstances but – privately – I never wear a hat. Thank God you need a licence to buy a gun. Love [xxx]

After languishing in St Ann's for a month, Sage scrawled his frustrations on an envelope.

My room is in danger of being cluttered up with old papers. My voice is getting worse not better. I find it most depressing. I cannot get my ideas across...[43]

Eileen set up home at 44 Albert Street in Camden, where his sister, Gigi, lived in a flat upstairs. Eileen and Margot had no reasons to like each other, but for Bernal's sake they came to a civilized arrangement for his care. Margot worked as a teacher at Camden School for Girls, and it was agreed that Sage should live with Eileen during the week and come to Highgate for the weekends and school holidays. Anita Rimel would often help out, and was one of the few who could understand his distorted speech. Gigi kept to herself upstairs.

When Sage resigned from the WPC in July 1965, he was still the president of the International Union of Crystallography and was hoping to attend their next congress in Moscow the following summer. He had been closely involved with the planning, and indeed had received some criticism from the conference programme committee for always acceding to the wishes of the USSR National Committee without consultation.[44] Following his second stroke, his old friend Kathleen Lonsdale took over the presidency from him, and it was clear that he would not be able to travel to Moscow. He wrote to Katie Dornberger in Berlin regretting that he would be unable to attend and enclosed an abstract for a paper on 'The Range of Generalized Crystallography' that he hoped someone would read at the congress. He told Katie that the paper was intended 'to explain the structures of proteins, nucleic acids and a variety of cell contents such as flagella, muscle fibres and virus surfaces whether cylindrical or polyhedral'.[45] The main emphasis was the consideration of linear, sheet-like and 3-D structures in living forms. He had been thinking about cell organelles that 'exist in 3-D aggregates which lack a true lattice, but which nevertheless can be made to fill space approximately. The one- and two-dimensional structures of the generalized type are much simpler and much more akin to restricted crystallography. The helical cylinder which when unrolled has the appearance of an infinite, regular, 2-D lattice, is one such form. It would seem to occur even in the inorganic field with the tubes of asbestos . . . where a non-integral helix is imposed by sterical considerations. Similar but different principles are applied to the quasi, irregular filling of polyhedra, which Klug particularly has studied in the so-called spherical viruses. Here the irregularity is shown by the fact whereas most of the molecules have identical coordination, usually 6-fold planar coordinates, some of them, for instance in the adeno virus, have 5-fold coordinates in the form of flat pyramids.' One of the consequences 'is the concept of self-assembly of identical but polyvalent particles. It is possible to conceive particles which are not spherical but are covered by a number of attachment points. When held together such spheres can adhere appearing to satisfy rules . . . These are what I call the arrangement of self-assembly which depend only on the properties of the particle. There may be more than one such arrangement for given identical particles and of course an infinite number of arrangements when the parts are different . . . It is for us a fortunate accident that atoms and ions themselves mostly lack these different assembly valencies and so only show the simplest kind of structures, readily forming indefinite 3-D lattices.'

Despite the recent catastrophic insult to his legendary brain, Sage was still thinking with great subtlety. He sent a short message to the IUCr congress, in which he referred to the sweep of Nobel Prizes by the 'co-founders of molecular biology' in 1962 and Hodgkin's 1964 prize. He expressed the opinion that 'the foundation of molecular biology is an event in the whole history of science comparable with that of Darwin's theory of evolution or Dalton's atomic theory'. Bernal was in everyone's thoughts in Moscow. Belov, who was elected as the next IUCr president, sent a message saying that Sage's 'very absence served to emphasize your part as not only our temporal leader, but predominantly spiritual, world's crystallographer Number 1 ... the most universal crystallographer'.[46] Belov added that he became a crystal chemist only after hearing Bernal lecture in Leningrad in 1935.

Sage paid homage of his own to Lawrence Bragg when the Royal Society awarded Bragg the Copley Medal in November 1966. Bragg had always remained a faithful supporter of Bernal's, although uncomprehending of his politics. Bernal wrote to him, saying:

This is only to congratulate the Society for giving you at last the Copley, which you have deserved many times over. It cannot really at this stage mean much to you, as you and the whole scientific world know what you have done. Crystal structures may seem now an old story, and it is, but you, its only begetter, are still with us. Three new subjects, mineralogy, metallurgy, and now molecular biology, all first sprang from your head, firmly based on applied optics. You can afford to look back on it all with justified feelings of pride and achievement.[47]

Sage reached the official retirement age of 65 years in May 1966. It was the end of an era in crystallography at Birkbeck – not only because he would no longer be in charge, but new laboratories were finally ready and the Torrington Square houses were to be demolished. Lenton saw the wreckers arrive and immediately feared for the Picasso mural. He ran into Sage's office, and Sage told him to stop them. When Lenton asked how, he was told 'Shoot the bloke if you like.'[48] Lenton successfully intervened and suggested that before cutting the lathe and plaster wall, it should be backed by plaster of Paris to prevent it crumbling. The College readily agreed that the drawing was Bernal's property. In a display of punctiliousness that reflected years of devoted committee work, Sage wrote to the College secretary to point out, 'I appreciate that the College has given me permission to dispose of the drawing as I wish, but I am not sure how to proceed with regard to obtaining the permission of the University Authorities regarding the removal of the wall itself.'[49] The mural was donated to the new Institute of Contemporary Art and returned to Birkbeck many years later.

Bernal remained interested in world affairs and was disturbed by what he saw. There were reactionary generals imposing counter-revolution in South America, Algeria and Indonesia, all backed by the CIA: 'If my head and my voice were clearer, I would write a great article on this subject; that is why I am praying that I may be able to say what is in my head before I die.'[50] He wrote multiple drafts of an essay 'Enormity or logic and hypocrisy in the ultimate solution'[51] that would be published in part in an obscure French journal. The opening paragraph sets a dark tone, but was informed by more than his own sense of impending death.

This is the most pessimistic essay. It should be impossible, all my friends say, to write anything about world politics without indicating a hopeful solution and showing what we must do to achieve it. But I cannot do this and I do not see it is logically necessary. Death and birth may be indeed inescapable for the world of man as well as for every individual in it. There may be no limit to human folly and callousness. But we ought to know what we are in for: and not in a distant, unimaginable future, but within forty years from now. Many now alive may see the beginning of the end of humanity, a self-destructive consequence of evolution, biological and social.

The looming force that preoccupied him was the population explosion and the coincident food shortage. His concerns were reinforced by reading the proceedings of a conference held at the California Institute of Technology in March 1967 on 'The next ninety years'. The first signs of the crisis would be seen in the Third World, but even there it would not be uniform – there would be degrees of want.

One of the symptoms is the spread of shanty-towns, as in the Bustees of Calcutta or the Favelas of Rio de Janeiro, where thousands of people go because it is even harder to live in the countryside and where, without roads, water, fuel or drainage, they manage somehow to find a life for themselves and their many children. There also is the greatest discrepancy between ostentatious wealth and abject poverty. It is also in those areas that there is the greatest degree of internal instability, wars, revolutions, and military coups sedulously fostered by the American CIA, [who] cannot deal with the conversion of the dying centres of the US cities themselves into urban ghettos.[52]

In his opinion, the economic priorities of the wealthy prevented any effective action from being taken.

Little can be done because the one source of wealth, the land, is in the hands of big landlords who invest their profits abroad, and industry and trade is in the hands of foreign companies who exploit people to great profit for their shareholders. The overall picture is the unfavourable terms of trade for the Third World countries who have to sell their raw materials cheap and buy their machinery dear, ensuring that the rich get richer and the poor get poorer.

Standing out against this grim picture are the Socialist States, either established ones like Russia or China, or newly-liberated ones like Algeria, Cuba and Syria.[53]

Bernal was again chary about foreign aid as the answer. First, military aid was steadily increasing compared with civilian aid, but more importantly 'it is very difficult to imagine how such aid would benefit the people of the underdeveloped nations'. While he did not foresee the socialist kleptocrats, who would divert so much aid money from Africa and the Middle East over the next three decades, he identified the essential problem: how do aid programmes make provisions 'for lowering the burdens these people have to suffer from native landlords and wealthy men who invest their capital and profits in Europe, or for providing dollars to invest in industry or the improvement of agriculture'.[54] Exacerbating all these problems, in his opinion, was the US's intention to rule the world so that 'nothing must be done to interfere with the position or property of the foreign trusts, nor must the status of friendly wealthy people, local landlords or military personalities in the client countries be interfered with in any way'.

While he mentioned the provision of fertilizer and agricultural machinery for the Third World, Bernal seemed convinced that the bulk of the necessary food supply would have to come from North America. The fact that the rich did not need the poor for their own survival presented 'the most frightful assault on the Puritan conscience . . . If some African tribe is the first victim of world starvation, and if it is widely publicized, as it is very likely to be, there will be such a broad-based protest as may even make the defender of the cruel burning up of villages with napalm and the destruction of crops in Vietnam, [L.B.J.] ultimately change his mind. But he will have to deal, in the sequel, with a series of agonizing decisions where it will be evident that anti-Communism is not enough, and that not everybody in the world can be a good American.'[55]

Sage saw no easy or palatable solution. He did not believe that mankind was ready to starve quietly, but the present measures to deal with the population explosion were pathetically futile and useless. He often quoted Swift's 1729 'Modest Proposal to the Peoples of Ireland' – a satirical solution by which the starving peasants would sell their numerous children to the rich to be eaten, thereby increasing the supply of meat and enriching themselves in the process. What was required now, in Bernal's view, was 'an economic and social revolution affecting the whole world and particularly the poorer three-quarters of it in Asia, Africa and Latin America'.

It implies abolition of large estates owned by landlords, and of foreign organizations which are sending their profits out of the country. With them must go the reactionary governments which protect both these. This justifies, insofar as it succeeds, the worldwide revolutions preached by Che Guevara and Mao Tse Tung. The Third World must awake and free itself by its own efforts.[56]

He repeated many of these points when disagreeing with 'an optimistic forecast' about the Year 2000 by Max Steinbeck of the East German Research Council. Regardless of any birth control measures, Sage agreed that the world population would be five billion by 2000 but 'the chances of providing all these people with food and roofs over their heads are most improbable'.[57] The only examples that gave him heart were the improvements made in Cuba and North Korea over the previous decade.

In December 1967, apparently in an effort to clarify his own thoughts, Sage wrote a comparison of Chairman Mao and the Soviets, who had been locked in mutual hostility for some years. In his opinion, Mao was aiming for nothing less than the complete moral, economic and political transformation of humanity.[58] The Maoists were dedicated to completing the Cultural Revolution, and this required the active loyalty of every citizen. The nationwide inquisition in China was designed to search out and denounce people who still clung to old cultural customs and ideas. Given the opportunity for varying interpretations of Mao's dicta and the continual round of denouncements, Bernal thought it was amazing that there was any order at all and not complete anarchy. He suspected there was a secret cadre organizing operations. The economic effects of the revolution were hard to gauge because no statistics had been published for years, and Sage thought on balance that 'the changes for good or bad have not been very great'.[59]

When it came to the Soviets, the purpose of their contemporary policies was 'even more difficult to grasp than the Chinese'. Kosygin had replaced Khrushchev in 1964, but there did not seem to have been any fundamental change in direction, and while there were probably reasons to depose his friend, Sage did not understand what they were. Khrushchev's guiding principle had been to seek peaceful co-existence with states of different economic and political systems, and he had been dedicated to spreading disarmament. While the Soviets had been prepared to support countries in South America and the Middle East that openly defied the US, they had, at the same time, sought a general détente with the US, especially in the area of nuclear non-proliferation.

It has been a regular policy of the Soviet Union to avoid as far as possible, and with no regard to 'face', any direct confrontation which might lead to the outbreak of nuclear war. This policy denounced as it has been in Peking, has guided the Soviet actions in the latest events, especially after war in the Middle East. The war against Israel went very badly for the Arab cause, but was not considered by the Soviet Union worth starting a nuclear war about. Although the Chinese government violently criticized it, it is evident, at the same time, that they themselves have not taken action in the face of much more evident threats by US forces on their own boundaries in S. China. Despite the speeches about America being only a paper tiger, they have themselves submitted in this case to what they have called nuclear blackmail.[60]

He wrote a separate note for the WPC about the 1967 Arab–Israel war, which he saw as a foretaste of 'a vaster conflict between Western capitalist states and the whole of the underdeveloped world'.[61]

The full tragedy of the Balfour Declaration in 1918 [*sic*] in setting up the State of Israel, aroused at the time and ever since the bitterest resentment of the impoverished Arabs, and the very successes of the Israeli State only serve to embitter them still further. They found that the setting up in their countries of an imitation, subsidized Europe was a constant reminder of their own economic inferiority, and, added to the historic hatreds between Jew and Arab was enough to provoke the most bitter reprisals.

This in itself will be enough to set up a new form of the old division of the whole world between the haves and the have-nots, the affluent and the starving peoples. The war between them may very well be long-drawn out with many reversals of fortune. On the one side there is massive power and money, on the other there are many millions of people, but they are not yet awakened to the reality of the situation.[62]

In the aftermath of a brilliant victory by Israel, Sage thought that the 'imperial world' would be convinced of the value of the bridgehead it had set up in the Middle East, but warned that it might become a 'wasting asset'. He predicted that the natural sympathy for the Israelis in the West following the Nazi atrocities might not last for long, and that if the Israeli government did not succeed in the very difficult task of obtaining from the Arab countries full recognition and guarantees against future aggression, the very existence of Israel would remain threatened.

In 1967, Sage could still read scientific papers and was active to some degree in the crystallography department at Birkbeck. Colleagues at Cambridge, especially Olga Kennard, would write or come to see him and tell him about progress (in her case on the burgeoning Crystallographic Data Centre). Max Perutz drove to Highgate one weekend, and brought his latest electron density maps of horse haemoglobin for Sage to see. The maps were at 2.8 Å resolution and showed the positions of the individual amino acid residues in the haemoglobin molecule. Sage was delighted that the pictures were so clear.[63] Despite the kindness of old friends, Sage began to feel cut off from his world. He wrote to Rosenheim asking about his prognosis. He asked whether there had been any progress in stroke therapy and questioned whether it was worthwhile continuing with physiotherapy since there had been no improvement in his walking for two years. At one point he had managed to move around with two walking sticks, but was now essentially confined to a wheelchair. He worried about the strain on Eileen, who took him to his appointments, and also 'the demoralizing effect on physiotherapists, who are most devoted and take endless trouble, but have seen no improvement for so many months.'[64] He wondered when he might expect a fatal stroke to carry him off. Rosenheim was sympathetic, but unable to supply any answers.

Bernal's health continued to decline, and he required considerable assistance with everyday activities. Margaret Gardiner came to see him occasionally and sent the following description to Zuckerman.

You do know, don't you, what a wretched case [*sic*] he's in. His speech is virtually unintelligible to all except those who are with him constantly and he can only walk horribly slowly, by being hoisted up on to a kind of baby pusher affair – and then he has to be helped down again. As it appears that his mind isn't at all affected, the frustration and humiliation is immense, poor devil. People tend – inevitably I suppose – to treat him like a child or an idiot, or just avoid him because seeing him is too painful and difficult.[65]

Margaret reflected that Sage's wayward habits were now coming to his rescue: 'various "wives" – no one of whom could have supported the full burden of caring for him – now share it (with a certain acerbity) between them!'[66] The acerbity was not confined to the 'wives'. Margot rented a flat in Swanage for their 1968 summer holiday, and Anita stayed with friends nearby so that she could help out with Sage's care. But neither the accommodation nor the social arrangements worked smoothly. The flat was poorly equipped for a man who was immobile and needed help to go to the toilet. And there was conflict between Anita and Margot occasioned by the communist crisis of the summer – the invasion of Czechoslovakia. It was reminiscent of Hungary twelve years before, but the number of British communists who supported this latest example of repression of 'socialism with a human face' was markedly diminished. Those who favoured the Soviet invasion were known as 'tanks'. Margot was resolutely 'anti-tank', whereas Anita was fiercely 'tank'.[67]

Anita's devotion to the Soviet cause was absolute and concealed a terrible secret. In the 1930s, her sister, Pearl, married a Dutchman, George Fles, and the couple emigrated to Stalin's Russia.[68] Anita liked George (although she disapproved of the state of marriage) and would write to him. She enclosed with her letters articles about the Soviet system that she wanted his opinion about. When he was arrested for counter-revolutionary crimes in 1937, these articles (including some about Trotsky) formed the central case against him and sealed his fate. Pearl fled with her young son to the US, and many years later learned that George died in 1939 in the gulag.

Although Sage had resigned from the presidency of the WPC three years earlier, no recognizable successor had emerged and he was still regarded as the moving spirit of the organization. Following requests from the WPC, Anita, abetted by Ivor Montagu, made frequent attempts to get him to sign press statements and letters endorsing the Soviet invasion. He refused.[69] When he returned to London, Sage slowly set out his thoughts using an electric typewriter his American cousin, Persis, had given him and which was now his main instrument of expression. Referring to 'the stupid and illegal movement of Soviet military units into Czechoslovakia on the night of August 21st',[70] Bernal suggested it implied that any deviation from strict CPSU orthodoxy would be regarded as 'a reactionary plot' to be suppressed by whatever means necessary. While questioning whether 'the steps taken in Czechoslovakia were really necessary in the light of the whole international situation', he still believed that the USSR had been provoked 'by reactionary forces acting both externally and internally on the orders of the American government'. *Pravda* sought to explain the Soviet action under the doctrine of 'peaceful counter-revolution'. Bernal did not think the crisis in Czechoslovakia would serve as a *casus belli* in the West because the US government clearly accepted that the country lay in the Soviet sphere of interest. Acceptance of the new status quo would 'save the peace but at the expense of the new-found freedoms of the Czech people'. The whole affair might be an indicator of growing openness in Soviet society.

It is particularly hard that the Czechs should have to bear the burden of the occupation and to accept the virtual validity of the doctrine of 'peaceful counter-revolution' which they have done so little to further themselves; but the Soviet rulers whose suspicions, nourished by the cold war, really originated it, are intensifying their reactionary policies. Now, at last, however, there is some evidence that the Russian people – and not just the rulers – are reacting to the events in Czechoslovakia. It must be difficult for them, despite the propaganda barrier, to understand why Russian soldiers and those of their allies should be sent suddenly and without explanation to occupy the territory of what they have been told had been a model socialist state. The barrier that has served to shelter the ordinary people from outside events is beginning to break down.[71]

Sage was probably unfamiliar with the Russian word *glasnost*.

Paul Barnes started his studies on polywater at Birkbeck in October 1968, but did not meet Bernal for some weeks. He noticed that staff at the college spoke about the old professor with 'a mixture of love, awe and apprehension'.[72] Harry Carlisle, still working on ribonuclease, had taken over as head of the crystallography department on Bernal's retirement two years earlier. But everyone, especially Carlisle, still worked in Bernal's shadow. Barnes was invited to join a small group who were going to Albert Street to report on progress to Sage. He noticed in the car on the way that Carlisle was anxiously poring over papers and results – he presumed that he was one of those highly active scientists who could not bear to waste even 15 minutes of his precious research time. On arrival, they were ushered into a waiting room by Anita, and Carlisle was the first to be admitted to the inner sanctum. After some minutes, Barnes was astonished to hear a strangulated cry of 'More results'. It was then his turn to go in with Finney and Cherry to discuss the polywater project, where of course there were no positive results. Bernal's frustration was immediately evident. He turned to Barnes, the new boy, and asked through Anita, what he was going to do about this sorry state of affairs. Barnes, his brain working feverishly, suggested that he would try to seed the elusive polywater between narrowly spaced plates rather than in capillary tubes as Deryagin had done. This random proposal found favour with Sage, who then proceeded to hold up Barnes as an example to the others on how the problem should be tackled.

Within months Sage suffered another stroke and had a heart attack (which was the only time Jane thought he was afraid). He was now completely dependent on the care of others and essentially speechless. He spent measureless days watching television and was incapable of any outward expression. In 1968 he endowed an annual lecture to be given at Birkbeck in his name, asking that the lectures should reflect some 'aspect of the purpose of the College and the lecturers should be in sympathy with those purposes'. The inaugural lecture was given by Dorothy Hodgkin in October 1969, with Patrick Blackett in the chair, but Sage was too ill to attend.

Visitors to Albert Street became fewer. Jane would come to see her father every afternoon on her way home from school. Although she could not be sure that he understood what she was saying, she would describe her day to him in loving detail. Just occasionally she would be rewarded with a reaction, as when she was talking about her A-level biology course and evolution, and Bernal suddenly uttered 'Axolotl'. In 1970, Olga Kennard dedicated the first two volumes of *Molecular Structures and Dimensions*, produced at the Cambridge Crystallographic Centre, to Bernal. She carried the books to Camden for Sage to see. Eileen said to him 'If you realize what Olga has brought, just raise your hand.' Sage tried to kiss Olga's hand. On his seventieth birthday, tributes poured in from around the world. Linus Pauling sent the following message:

For 50 years he has, over and over again, astounded the scientific world by his extraordinarily original and fertile concepts, which show a depth of understanding and brilliance of thought possessed, in my opinion, by no other living man. He is one of the greatest men in the world. I am glad to have him as my friend.[73]

Desmond Bernal stopped breathing on 15th September 1971. By his own lights, cut off from all communication with the world, he had been as good as dead for the previous two years. When he was contemplating the transformation of the human frame in *The World, the Flesh & the Devil*, Sage mused that consciousness might escape the close-knit organism, 'ultimately perhaps resolving itself entirely into light'.[74] His was one of the brightest stars.

Postscript

In *The Social Function of Science*, Bernal wrote about science and culture. He observed that the separation whereby 'a highly developed science stands almost isolated from a traditional literary culture, is altogether anomalous and cannot last'.[1] For mixing to occur, science would have to shed the 'dryness and austerity' that 'had led to its widespread rejection by those of literary culture'. Certainly the scientific method, a critical way of thinking that depended ultimately on experimental verification of facts, could be included in general education, but there was a common lacuna in the understanding of human creativity, whether in the arts or science.

The really positive part of science, the making of discoveries, lies outside the scientific method proper, which is concerned with preparing the ground for them and with establishing their reliability. Discoveries are usually unthinkingly attributed to the operations of human genius, which it would be impious to attempt to explain. We have no science of science.[2]

Sage expected that science, over time, would lead to a more complete understanding of the world and form a universal backdrop to human activity, gradually incorporating history, the literary and visual arts. Two decades after he wrote this, his vision was so far from being realized that his rotund friend C.P. Snow, the novelist and civil servant, was able to make great play out of 'The two cultures'.[3] In his Rede Lecture at Cambridge University, Snow cast physical scientists at one pole and writers at its opposite, where there was total incomprehension of science. This incomprehension gave a pervasive unscientific flavour to the traditional culture, which in turn, Snow thought, was threatening to become anti-scientific. In *The Social Function of Science*, Bernal had identified 'romantic reactionaries' as one group who reject science, as a result of an understandable dislike of the despoiled nature of contemporary civilization and 'an idealization of the mediaeval world which is usually seen from the castle rather than from the hut'.[4] Snow proposed that scientists have 'the future in their bones' and the traditional culture (still in the ascendancy in the West) responded by wishing that the future did not exist. To illustrate his point, Snow compared Orwell's *1984* (which, in a strange interpretation, he stated as demonstrating the 'strongest possible wish that the future should not exist'), to Bernal's *World Without War*. In 1959, Snow believed that a scientific revolution, characterized by the introduction of electronics, atomic energy and automation, was already underway: his analysis was broadly anecdotal and, within the context of a lecture, necessarily less detailed than Bernal's treatment of the societal transition in *The Social Function of Science*. Like Bernal, Snow thought 'the Russians have judged the situation sensibly' in their approach to education and training.

'The two cultures' became an instant classic on both sides of the Atlantic, and established Snow as an authority on Western civilization. Snow did nothing to dispel the notion that he was the only man capable of spanning the great divide between the intellectual camps. This proved too much for F.R. Leavis, the acidulous Cambridge English don. While he stood at the lectern to give the 1962 Richmond Lecture in Cambridge, Leavis seemed to be on the bridge of a battleship, directing all its firepower onto the luxury yacht, *Two Cultures*, with its skipper Charles Snow at the helm. In Leavis's estimation, Snow was 'intellectually as undistinguished as it is possible to be' and his Rede lecture exhibited 'an utter lack of intellectual distinction and an embarrassing vulgarity of style'.[5] Assuring his audience that as a novelist, Snow 'doesn't exist; he doesn't begin to exist. He can't be said to know what a novel is', Leavis picked on one theme from the Rede Lecture.

Such a phrase as 'they have the future in their bones' (and Snow repeats it) cannot be explained as a meaningful proposition, and in that sense has no meaning. It emerges spontaneously from the cultural world to which Snow belongs and it registers uncritically (hence the self-evident force it has for him) its assumptions and attitudes and ignorances ... And Snow rides on an advancing swell of cliché: this exhilarating motion is what he takes for inspired and authoritative thought.[6]

Having predicted that Snow would leave no trace as a novelist, Leavis admitted to 'the gravest suspicion regarding the scientific one of Snow's two cultures'. His remarks were printed in detail in *The Spectator* and led to an avalanche of letters, mostly (but not all) in support of Snow. Prominent amongst these was one from Sage, who defended Snow as a scientist ('a brilliant physical chemist') who had voluntarily abandoned a research career because he 'was more interested in scientists, as people, and in their effect on the world they lived in [*sic*]'.[7] Perhaps it was fortunate that Margot Heinemann wrote separately to defend Snow as a novelist. Sage was quite effective at demolishing Leavis's method of logic: 'there are no premises or arguments and the conclusions are simple assertions on the authority of Dr Leavis himself, speaking as an unchallengeable representative of the Great Tradition of English culture.'

After the startling success of 'The two cultures', C.P. Snow was invited to deliver the Godkin Lectures at Harvard University in December 1960. He chose for his title 'Science and government',[8] which no doubt Leavis would have dismissed as typically portentous. In fact, the lectures comprised mostly a lively narrative about the friendship, and the subsequent intense dislike, between Henry Tizard and Lord Cherwell. The two leading antagonists of the area bombing policy had both died a short time before, and this was the first public airing of the great wartime controversy. Snow could not help reminding the audience at frequent intervals that he was both a novelist and a senior civil servant. He gave the dispute a moral dimension, asking whether those responsible for the bombing offensive had 'resigned their humanity'. In England, it provoked passionate argument, especially after a series of articles in *The Times* by R.V. Jones, an Oxford-trained physicist, called 'Scientists at war – Lindemann vs. Tizard'. In the spring of 1961, Sage was away in India and the Soviet Union and so missed the start of the debate. He wrote to Snow, on his return, asking if this was 'a private fight or can anyone join in?'[9]

Snow had based his account on personal knowledge of Tizard and Cherwell, and on Tizard's papers. In his long letter to Snow, Bernal set out his own involvement with the setting up of the Butt Report and the general atmosphere at Bomber Command in 1941. He also told Snow about the Hull and Birmingham survey that he had conducted with Zuckerman. Where Snow merely stated in his lecture that Cherwell's scientific judgment about bombing policy had been wrong, Bernal was less bloodless and saw Cherwell's advocacy of area bombing as dishonest and deliberately misleading. But overall Bernal approved of Snow's account, as did Blackett, who wrote that Snow had correctly emphasized Cherwell's fanatical character that had led to his complete belief in the efficacy of bombing to 'the almost total exclusion of wider considerations'.[10]

Sage was contemplating his own letter to *The Times*, and sent a draft to Solly Zuckerman, hoping that he might co-sign it. Zuckerman, at the time, was Chief Scientific Adviser to the Ministry of Defence, where undoubtedly he would encounter, on a regular basis, senior RAF officers who had risked their own lives and lost many friends during the bombing of Germany. Zuckerman made the following observation to Bernal: 'I'm amazed at the partial truths that are emerging about the 1942 change in bombing policy. My files are complete – and I have a fear that both Charles Snow and Patrick Blackett are jumping much further than the facts at their disposal justify. Have you any of the 1942 papers still?'[11] A few weeks later, Zuckerman wrote again to say that he had unearthed a crucial note from Tizard to Sir Archibald Sinclair, the Air Minister, dated 20th April 1942, in which Tizard concedes 'I should like to make it clear that I don't disagree fundamentally with the bombing policy, but I do think that it is only likely to be decisive if carried out on the scale envisaged by the Air Staff.'[12] Snow had not seen, and later chose to disregard, this document. Blackett certainly had deep moral misgivings about the targeting of civilians in modern war, and Bernal thought the longer area bombing was continued the less justifiable it became. But in 1942, the dispute had been waged on operational and not moral arguments. To some extent dissuaded by Zuckerman, Bernal decided not to add his voice to the chorus attacking Cherwell.

In January 1972, Lords Blackett, Snow and Zuckerman each spoke at a memorial service for Bernal organized by Birkbeck College. Snow spoke grandly and with warmth of Bernal the man and the scientist. At one point, he ventured to say that his Irishness was not important, provoking an outburst from Gigi, who shouted out, 'Our boys are being killed in Derry.'[13]

Zuckerman's contribution was the most surprising. After reviewing his joint work with Sage during the early years of the war, he came to the following passage.

There are many apocryphal stories about Bernal's war activities, but most miss the real point. He made no contribution to the conduct of actual military operations. He neither designed a new type of radar, a bomb nor a depth charge. He did not contribute to the emergence of nuclear weapons. The artificial harbour, Mulberry, was not his idea. He planned no assaults, nor did he go on any. His great contribution was to exercise in Combined Operations Headquarters the same kind of general catalytic influence, which he was already doing in the Ministry of Home Security. He imparted a point of view, a way of seeing things – the same quality which characterized his whole life as a scientist.[14]

Contrast these begrudging words with those Bernal wrote about Zuckerman in a book review, a few years earlier. As a result of security vetting, Bernal found it 'a most impersonal book' in which there was 'no reference to the enormous contribution which he [Zuckerman] himself made to the theory and practice of the war effort'.[15] He was, Bernal wrote, 'the first of the new military scientists, a field which was virtually created in the last war'.

It can in fact be said that the final victory on the Western Front was very largely due to his collaboration with the air force under Lord Tedder... Sir Solly's career is marked by extraordinary persistence and steady advancement. It calls to mind that of his predecessor, Lord Cherwell, who exemplified the kind of influence which Snow characterizes as 'Court science', and who entirely depended on personal loyalty to his patron, Sir Winston Churchill. Sir Solly is a contrast to Cherwell in most ways, although he, too, depends very much on his ability to get on with people. This has been exercised not on one patron but many – the Service Chiefs to start with, but the scientific world as well... If he had a fault, it was being too easily influenced by the military opinion of the time. He was King Log to Cherwell's King Stork.*

All branches of the Bernal family were shocked by Zuckerman's unleavened remarks. After all, Bernal's wartime stories, especially about the build-up to

---

* A reference to Aesop's fable 'The frogs desiring a king'. Jove sent them first a large log, which they found they could dance on with impunity. The frogs asked for a real king who would rule over them. Jove sent a stork, who gobbled them up. 'Better no rule than cruel rule.'

D-Day, were often recounted at social gatherings; indeed, they had featured in the recent obituaries. Nor were they the only ones disappointed by the tenor of Zuckerman's address. He sent a copy of his speech to Mountbatten, who thanked him for his 'brilliantly written piece', but said 'I don't think you have made it clear how very highly I thought of him.'[16] Snow, whom Zuckerman had little time for, was outraged and wrote to Margot Heinemann saying, 'Typical Solly, small-minded.'[17] Margaret Gardiner was angry with Zuckerman and sent him a copy of Bernal's unpublished D-Day diaries. Eileen took up the matter with Mountbatten, who wrote to Zuckerman again to express his concerns. Zuckerman replied, referring to Eileen as 'the authentic Mrs Bernal', saying that he happened to know that the obituary in *The Times*, which implied that Bernal went to the Normandy beaches before D-Day, was 'totally wrong'.[18] He agreed that it did appear that Bernal was taken over and landed on the Normandy coast on D-Day+3. 'I was sent by the Mrs Bernal who wrote to me after the Memorial Meeting a copy of a personal account he had written, apparently shortly after this trip, which struck me as pretty fanciful in places.' He doubted whether Bernal could have wandered about the beaches without being arrested or blown up.

Margaret Gardiner was one of Solly's oldest and closest friends: indeed the two had been lovers in the early 1930s. But in his letter to Mountbatten, she was dismissed as 'the Mrs Bernal'. This was not the first time, nor would it be the last, that Margaret reproached Solly for his attitude towards Sage. In 1968, the Queen appointed Zuckerman to the Order of Merit.* Bernal wrote him a note of congratulation,[19] in his painfully slow scrawl.

I may join, but with a slight difference, the notes of your various Establishment friends on your OM. I am sure that scientifically and technically it was fully deserved, I saw you demonstrating it in France and the Med, but I at least must deplore the uselessness of so much good science being devoted to the war science even when used against the Nazis...At any rate, as you can see, I am without the means or time to do the job myself so reluctantly must give it up. I must pass it back to you. Anyhow it was good fun while it lasted. So in memories of past work together. D.

It was oddly expressed, but plainly affectionate in tone. Zuckerman wrote to Margaret about what a strange letter it was, which prompted her graphic description of how Sage had been ravaged by the two strokes. Several years later Zuckerman was preparing to write the first volume of his memoirs, and had obviously talked to Margaret about them. She wrote him a note saying,

---

* The OM is the most exclusive honour, restricted to 24 members at any given time. Association with Bernal was no bar: Dorothy Hodgkin, Blackett, Mountbatten, Zuckerman, Perutz and Klug all received OMs.

'I have been saddened, loving you both, by your bitterness about Des, though I can to some extent understand it as well as understanding his total unawareness of having caused it. I hope it won't be too strongly perpetuated in your memoirs.'[20] Zuckerman replied immediately to assure her that most references to Bernal would be written with admiration.

In the autumn of 1977, Zuckerman discussed Bernal's role in Operation Overlord with Tom Hussey, the naval captain who had been the CXD (Coordinator of Experiments and Development) at Combined Operations HQ, to whom he and Bernal first reported. Hussey made some enquiries and confirmed to Zuckerman that 'Bernal crossed to Normandy, disguised as a badly dressed junior naval officer on or about D-Day+4. He wanted to see the damage done by air bombardment and, in particular, rockets. Also, of course, slopes of beaches and their bearing capacities.'[21] Hussey wrote again in December to cast further doubt on Bernal's role.

As regards Bernal, I agree with all you say. My directorate had NO knowledge of the plans for the landings in Normandy apart from the knowledge that they would take place somewhere around Arromanches – no date or time or fireplan was known to us.

Our job was to answer any problems put by the planners as how to overcome beach obstacles, mines, flat beaches and so on. In these problems Bernal was hard working and useful.[22]

About a year later, Maurice Goldsmith, who was writing a biography of Bernal, contacted Zuckerman and inadvertently fuelled the obsession with Bernal's wartime roles. Goldsmith had met Bernal in the early 1950s when he was working at UNESCO in Paris. Subsequently he had written a number of books on science and technology, and a biography of Joliot-Curie. He coedited with Alan Mackay *The Science of Science*, a collection of essays to mark the 25th anniversary of the publication of *The Social Function of Science*. Goldsmith had told Bernal towards the end of his life that he was going to write his biography. Sage made it clear to Eileen, Margot and others that he did not want Goldsmith as his biographer. When Goldsmith started his research, he was able to interview many of Bernal's friends, colleagues and lovers, but then in his words 'the order came to pull down the curtain on me'.[23] He was refused permission to look at Bernal's papers, C.P. Snow was engaged to persuade him not to discuss Sage's love life and a letter was sent round to likely contacts asking them not to cooperate with Goldsmith.

Goldsmith sent Zuckerman a draft of his chapter on Bernal's wartime exploits, and Zuckerman sent him critical, detailed, comments in return. The core of these concerned Operation Overlord.

COHQ was concerned with many of the technical matters relating to an invasion – some major ones like Mulberry – but I am practically certain that no Combined Ops.

Officer and certainly no COHQ civilian had anything whatever to do with the operational planning in which the Navy, Army and Air Force had to get together.

Bernal was never on the ULTRA list. Nor was he on the list called BIGOT which had to do with the actual planning. Not only was Bernal not on the two lists, neither was the senior officer on whose staff he served. Apart from Mountbatten himself, very few people in COHQ were cleared for ULTRA. In the five months of planning for the invasion, beginning on 1 January 1944, in which I was involved with Tedder and Leigh Mallory, I hardly ever met Bernal, to whom I had been warned not to talk.

The account which you give . . . is, I can recognize, taken partly from a memorandum Bernal wrote and gave to Margaret Gardiner sometime after the landings, partly on the paper he gave in Caen in the 1950s, and partly on what he told Bernard Fergusson.

Some time ago I had occasion to check the first document and I am afraid it turned out to be very fanciful . . . You say that he did not go in with the first assault troops but he went in later that afternoon. He didn't. What is more, Bernal would not have known before D-Day that the assault was going to take place when it did. Bernal was not taken over to France until D+4; he would have been shot by our own troops had he done what he said he did in the document, namely to wander off on his own two miles inland, not knowing about mine fields etc. I have checked all these points with the man who is described as the 'Commodore' who took Bernal to France.

. . . I have always been puzzled by the Walter Mitty in Bernal, coming out as it did in that piece he wrote for Margaret Gardiner and some of the things he did later. That his memory played him false was clear when, in the early 1960s, he wanted me to join him in an attack on Cherwell.[24]

When Goldsmith attempted to keep a dialogue with Lord Zuckerman, he received a withering response implying that Zuckerman was merely trying to prevent him making a fool of himself by writing about matters he did not understand.

What is wrong with what you are proposing is that you could not know that Bernal was not cleared for ULTRA: nor do I believe you would know how to set about the research to discover whether he was; nor do I believe you would have known about BIGOT. Unless you are prepared to do your own research, I fear that you cannot use my information in the way you suggest in your note 2. So far as note 1 is concerned it is not a 'suggestion' that Bernal was not taken over to France until D-Day+4. It happens to be a fact. What is more, I did not, in my contribution to the Memorial meeting in 1972, make any reference to Bernal's visit to the Normandy beaches; that is your own embellishment.[25]

Zuckerman knew that Goldsmith had been in touch with Mountbatten, and he wrote to him ('My dear Dickie') to warn him that he was 'somewhat circumspect as I had had one or two exchanges with him [Goldsmith] in the past, and as I also happen to know that his enterprise was not welcomed by at least one of Bernal's "widows"'.[26]

I am sure you have never seen the fanciful document, which Bernal wrote and gave to one or two of his girl-friends shortly after D-day. It is clearly the document from which Goldsmith got the view that Bernal had taken charge of a boat that was foundering, etc. etc. I saw this imaginative piece of writing because it was sent to me in protest about a sentence which I included in my contribution to a Memorial Meeting about Bernal, and in which I said Bernal's main contribution was his immense intellectual power and the fact that he was a ferment in so far as he kept asking questions and making people think. I added that Bernal neither planned any operations nor went on any. It was this remark which resulted in my being sent the document which he had written after D-Day, and in which he claimed to have gone over with somebody who he described as 'the Commodore'.

As the Commodore was obviously Tom Hussey, and as I know that Bernal was regarded as a security risk, and that he was neither on any of the operational planning staffs (whose papers were code-named BIGOT-TOP SECRET), and as I was practically certain that Bernal had never been cleared for 'ULTRA', I got in touch with Tom in order to check my memory.[27]

Zuckerman enclosed copies of Hussey's letters and pointed out that 'Bernal could never have known when D-Day was going to be since the decision was, as you know, taken at the last moment by Eisenhower, but with all ships loaded and waiting.' Zuckerman also wrote to Hussey to put him on guard about Goldsmith, 'an author for whom I haven't got much time'.[28]

In the face of this concerted campaign and with very limited access to any primary documents, it is not surprising that Goldsmith was persuaded that Bernal's own accounts of D-Day were unreliable. In his book he wrote: 'Was there something of the Walter Mitty in him? I am satisfied that he did not go over on D-Day.'[29]

When a Fellow of the Royal Society dies, one of his colleagues writes an authoritative biographical memoir, detailing his life and scientific achievements. In Sage's case, this task fell to Dorothy Hodgkin, and it was one she laboured over for nearly a decade. Zuckerman wrote to her just before she finished it, explaining that he and Sage 'parted rather abruptly' after the war.[30] He warned her that he had carefully checked Bernal's D-Day diaries and his version of events 'is perhaps fifty percent fact and fifty percent fiction'. She was in a quandary because she had written the original obituary for *The Times*, in which she credited Sage not only with a leading role in planning D-Day, but even suggested that he had taken part in the secret reconnoitres of the beaches before the invasion. She was well aware of the resentment caused by Zuckerman at the memorial service, and was now faced with a restatement of his view – given after 'a most careful check'. She turned to Mountbatten for help and he provided his own memories of Bernal's war work. But Mountbatten had also been subjected to Zuckerman's forceful opinions and had seen all the correspondence with Hussey. He wrote a detailed account of Bernal's activities up to the Quadrant Conference in 1943, but could not rely on his memory after that, because, of course, he went to South East Asia then. He concluded instead by saying that he thought Bernal's natural generosity had led to his great contribution to the war effort not being properly appreciated, 'but those of us who really knew what he did have an unbounded admiration for his contribution to our winning the war'.[31]

So was Zuckerman correct that Bernal's account of D-Day was largely fantasy? The contemporaneous documents would suggest not. First there are the cryptic notes in a filofax that show from August 1943 onwards Bernal was aware of Overlord and frequently prepared briefings, beach tests and charts in connection with it. There were frequent references to TIS (Theatre Intelligence Section) where he worked on maps and examined aerial photographs, and there were meetings with senior military figures such as Admiral Ramsay at the Chiefs of Staff Supreme Allied Command. Although Zuckerman and Bernal did not see much of each other in the first part of 1944, Bernal's diary shows that both men met with the Chief of Combined Operations on 11th April. Further, despite Hussey's remark that Bernal had no knowledge of any fire plan, the diary entry for 16th April records a discussion with Zuckerman 'on bombing policy for Overlord, analysis of fire plan and damage to beaches and on preparations for operational research'.[32] He met again with Zuckerman on 25th April 'on mines, intelligence and bombardments'. Logan Scott-Bowden, who so courageously carried out the beach surveys and samplings, told me 'Bernal was crucial to the planning of D-Day. He was in charge of it in a way.'[33] His assessment is amply supported by the documentary evidence.

This still leaves the question as to whether Bernal landed on the beaches on D-Day+2, as he claimed in his account. Hugh Bunting, a young crop scientist who knew Bernal from the Association of Scientific Workers, remembered catching a train at Basingstoke to go to London, just before D-Day. By mistake, he got into the first-class buffet or club car where he saw 'the extraordinary sight of Bernal in naval uniform with lots of brass and a cap too small for him'.[34] Bunting reasoned that Bernal 'had been dressed for a possible situation in which it was necessary (Geneva Convention) that he should appear, if captured, as an officer, not as a civilian. And on a train coming from the south-west, at a time when it was well known that preparations for a second front were underway, the possible conclusions were obvious. But not a word was said – we were too far from each other even for a verbal greeting. And I skeedaddled out of the coach as fast as I could.'

There was one other incidental witness – Peter Danckwerts who shared an office at COHQ with Sage during 1944. Many years later, Danckwerts recalled that Bernal's desire to be on the beaches by D-Day+1 almost caused a breach of security. He also said that even after having his hair shorn and kitted-out with boots and battledress, Sage did not cut 'a particularly military figure'.[35]

Bernal's diary for 1944 provides the strongest evidence to support his version of events. There is one entry for D-Day: 'Fragmentation panel (mechanical engineers)'. Presumably this was a committee appointment that day. For nearly every day up to 6th June, the diary is crammed with notes. For the period 7–15th June the diary is essentially blank, after which the events of everyday are recorded again. Sage realized that he could have been taken prisoner, in which case he would not want to have a diary in his pocket, showing that he was privy to the military plans. On Sunday 18th June, Bernal's diary indicates that he embarked for Normandy a second time with Capt Menzies and Mr Monk. There is a photograph of him in uniform on what appears to be a motor launch. At the British Mulberry harbour, he transferred to a cruiser, *HMS Mauritius*, where for the next three days he rode out the great midsummer storm that completely destroyed the American Mulberry harbour. He was unable to land and the *Mauritius* sailed for England on 21st June, arriving at 18.00hr when the sea was still so rough that it was 'impossible to get a boat alongside'.[36] Sage eventually got ashore and returned to London. The next day he records a meeting with 'Capt. Hussey, the Commodore and CCO on further investigations in relation to possible future landings'.[37]

In Bernal's account of his trip to Normandy immediately after D-Day (which is so detailed and vivid that to invent it would have required a talent for fiction that was never expressed anywhere else in Bernal's writings), he referred to the Commodore who accompanied him. Zuckerman assumed that the Commodore was Hussey (he wrote to Mountbatten, 'the Commodore was obviously Tom Hussey'[38]) and when Hussey denied sailing with Bernal on D-Day, in Zuckerman's mind, Bernal's account was disproved. But the diary entry for 22nd June plainly indicates that Capt. Hussey and the unnamed Commodore were two different people.

In November 1944, COHQ issued a series of reports on the technical aspects of the landing. They were cogently written and included fresh details that would have been quickly obliterated by the fighting and breakout from the beachhead. Bernal's diary for September 1944 shows that one of his top priorities before leaving for Burma was preparing Overlord reports.

Zuckerman convinced himself that Bernal invented his D-Day role because he wanted to believe it. Having done so, he took deliberate steps to make sure that Bernal's first biographers dared not contradict his opinion. Nor was Bernal the only major scientist from that era to earn a posthumous smear from Zuckerman. Writing of Blackett, another scientist he admired, Zuckerman implied that he, like Bernal, was a well-recognized security risk by 1944. But Bernal's diary is littered with references to Blackett leading up to

D-Day, with the last one coming on 25th May, 'discussions with Blackett on the assault'.

Both Bernal and Blackett were members of the Tizard committee during 1944–5 that reported to the Chiefs of Staff on weapons development and the future of warfare, strongly suggesting that they had not been labelled as security risks. When Julian Lewis was working on his Oxford DPhil history thesis 'British Military Planning for Post-War Strategic Defence, 1942–47' he approached Zuckerman about Bernal's involvement in the highly sensitive revision of the Tizard report that examined the consequences of a nuclear exchange between Britain and the USSR. Zuckerman wrote to him saying Bernal could not possibly have taken any active part 'because by 1945 he was certainly regarded as a security risk'.[39] Lewis stood his ground and replied that 'it is clear that Bernal was fully involved in the revision of the Tizard report – as COHQ representative and a member of the original ad hoc committee...I am fairly sure that the security aspect was simply over-looked.'[40]

Zuckerman was a vain man, whose talent and ambition propelled him to achieve all the honours that England has traditionally bestowed on her best scientists. Having arrived from South Africa as a penniless medical student, half a century later he was in the House of Lords, retained his own office in the Cabinet Office and was a confidant of the Royal Family. Yet it was not enough for Solly to succeed – he needed his friends to fail. In the 1966 book review, before rightly crediting Zuckerman with huge influence on the air strategy that made the invasion of Europe successful, Bernal reminded readers that 'Solly Zuckerman was a distinguished scientist in his own right before he became involved in the last war.'[41]

His work on the sexual life of the primates was cited by his commanding officer at Combined Operations, Lord Mountbatten, to the late King George VI as having annoyed the Archbishop of Canterbury – a joke His Majesty failed to appreciate. He has also done valuable work on the sexual cycle of woman, one of the subjects which is now in the forefront of the controversy on the pill. His work in these fields brought him the Chair of Anatomy at Birmingham University, where he reorganized the whole course of medical education.[42]

By contrast, Zuckerman devoted not one word to Sage's scientific achievements at the 1972 memorial service. He knew that, as a scientist, he was not in the same class as Bernal (or Blackett) and it bothered him. But Bernal was a scientists' scientist. From the rarefied ranks of Nobel Laureates who knew him, I have compiled the following list of those who expressed admiration or even awe of Bernal's creativity and vision as a scientist: Lawrence Bragg, Albert Szent-Györgyi, Hermann Muller, Patrick Blackett, Linus Pauling, Francis

Crick, John Kendrew, Max Perutz, James Watson, Maurice Wilkins, Dorothy Hodgkin and Aaron Klug. There may well be others one should add to this dozen, such as his close friends Frédéric Joliot-Curie and Cecil Powell, but I have just not come across any encomiums from them. Pauling, whose unique achievement of winning both Chemistry and Peace Prizes might well have been emulated by Sage, said it best in the obituary he wrote.

I met Bernal first in the spring of 1930, in his laboratory in Cambridge. He impressed me then as the most brilliant scientist that I had ever met, and I have retained this impression, which was substantiated by the many later discussions that I had with him. He was astonishingly quick in grasping a new idea, and was often able to contribute an illuminating insight, based on the breadth of his knowledge and his extraordinary ability to see interconnections between apparently rather distant fields of science...Bernal must be considered one of the greatest intellectuals of the 20th century.[43]

It was another Noble laureate, Sir Edward Appleton, who put his finger on the central paradox of Bernal's life. He saw 'two Professor Bernals: one is the brilliant natural philosopher of worldwide renown, the other a fervid convert to an extreme political theory.'[44] Although Sage was amused by this description and was quick to jest about his Jekyll and Hyde image, Appleton was making a serious charge. It was repeated even more pointedly by A.J. Cummings, the *News Chronicle* journalist, who dared to tell Sage in 1949 that the Soviet system, to which he was so devoted, contained millions of slaves in the gulags as 'an organic element, a normal component of the social structure'. When he could not refute Cummings' facts, Sage wrote to his editor dismissing them as 'allegations from professed anti-Soviet sources which are unverifiable and not even self-consistent'.

Appleton's description of him was accurate, and the possible reasons underlying Bernal's unshakeable beliefs mystified those of his friends who did not share them. To Max Perutz it seemed to be a question of faith. It is clear from Bernal's undergraduate diaries that his overnight conversion to socialism coincided with his withdrawal from the Catholic Church. Arthur Koestler described the spiritual ecstasy of his own overnight conversion to communism in Germany during the 1930s.

To say that one had 'seen the light' is a poor description of the mental rapture which only the convert knows ... The new light seems to pour from all directions across the skull; the whole universe falls into a pattern like the stray pieces of a jigsaw puzzle assembled by magic at one stroke. There is now an answer to every question, doubts and conflicts are a matter of the tortured past ... Nothing henceforth can disturb the convert's inner peace and serenity – except the occasional fear of losing faith again, losing thereby what alone makes life worth living, and falling back into the outer darkness.[45]

Perutz concluded that Bernal 'must have been one of those characters who needed an absolute belief'.[46] Just as tragic world events test the faith of Catholics, Sage was distressed by Hungary in 1956, but in Perutz's view he could not 'face the wrench of not being communist'. However, his misgivings were shown only to a few close friends, like Dorothy Hodgkin, who were presumably experiencing similar emotions of their own. Perhaps the most egregious example was when Martin Bernal questioned his father about the veracity of Chinese official statistics in 1959, and Sage agreed that they were invalid and inaccurate. It is now known, but largely overlooked, that the famine Martin sensed in its earliest stages resulted in the deaths of 60–70 million people. It is ironic that thousands of those intellectuals who attended Bernal's wonderful lectures in China would starve to death, after being dismissed from their posts and sent to labour in the fields.

Aaron Klug takes a different view of Bernal's political convictions. He described walking one day with Bernal from Birkbeck to University College. They passed a church, and 'Bernal gave a description of the church, the history of the Church of England and the Reformation; he gave a little ex-tempore account of the Anglican revolution. I could see the way he spoke about it, he spoke with the long eye of history.'[47]

In the long eye of history, if you think of all the brutalities, the murders, Henry VIII breaking away from Rome, all those kind of things, we don't think kindly of those things, yet we think it has all been for the good. It is really a view that history is progressive and that you have to put up with the blemishes. I didn't know him well enough to know whether in the middle of the night, he began to have doubts.[48]

Klug does not believe that Bernal could have thought all those who perished in Stalin's show trials of the 1930s were spies or counter-revolution-aries rather than victims of an ideological struggle. But he might have believed that the collectivization of agriculture was a reform, rather like the setting up of mediaeval land enclosures or the advent of industrialization – to be associated with short-term pain before ultimately improving the lot of the peasants. The bloodshed would be accepted by history as another necessary price of progress, in Bernal's mind.

In 1954, his friend from undergraduate days, Kingsley Martin wrote a sketch of Bernal for the *New Statesman* that contained elements of both the Perutz and Klug views.

Bernal was not the man to do without a religion. His romantic temperament demanded an ideal to give sanction and purpose to the duty of investigating and changing the very imperfect world around him ... post [First World] war Cambridge was in every way destructive of Catholicism. It did nothing to satisfy the need for social change ... and the universal aspiration to put an end to war. Most able young men became Socialists of some kind. Bernal was not of a temper to be satisfied with the moderation of British Labour. Only Communism satisfied his needs, since he thought it alone had the proper attitude towards Science. Bernal was an unorthodox, because anti-liberal, recruit to the line of idealists from Condorcet to H.G. Wells, whose faith was Progress through Science ... He appears uninfluenced by such questions as whether millions of people really live in and die miserably in Siberian labour camps. If such things happen in the Soviet Union they are part of the necessary historical process. If he is bothered by the preposterous and cruel nonsense of the purges, whereby the children of the Revolution periodically devour each other, he maintains an obedient silence ... He cannot allow himself to admit faults in Moscow: that would set at war within himself the romantic and scientific sides of his nature which are integrated in his Communism.[49]

Martin was surely right that science and communism were two sides of the same Bernal coin. Both carried the promise of a better world, but one face was counterfeit. Sage was a visionary who did not confine himself to one sphere of human activity. His predictions about the course of science (stating, for example in the 1920s, that X-ray crystallography would reveal the structure of proteins and the secrets of life) were no more audacious than his confidence that communism would reorder society, banishing the inequalities that he found so unjust. But his theoretical speculations about molecular structure were far more insightful than his prognostications about the transformation of society. Like many Western intellectuals between the wars, Sage was blinded by the imperfections of his own country to the horrors of Stalinism. When science and communism came into direct conflict in the Lysenko affair, Sage betrayed his scientific principles. In his activities with the World Peace Council, he was an instrument of Soviet foreign policy, whether he realized it or not. He continued to believe in the world revolution, almost until the end of his life, despite the mounting evidence of communism's moral and economic bankruptcy in country after country. He would never have accepted historian Richard Pipes' verdict that 'Communism was not a good idea that went wrong; it was a bad idea.'[50]

Max Perutz was amused that Bernal was such an outspoken advocate of the central planning of science because Bernal 'was a man who never planned anything. He was totally disorganized.'[51] His personal life was certainly colourful and chaotic, and like his science career, unlikely to suffer imitation. Sage did form deep attachments to some women, but would always be on the lookout for sexual adventure (even after his first stroke). The first time she ever heard Bernal's name, Margaret Gardiner was on a train in France talking to an Englishman, who asked her if she believed in 'sexual varietism'. When she confessed ignorance about the term, he said 'There is a wonderful chap that I know in Cambridge who believes in sexual varietism.' The chap was Desmond Bernal. Margaret would later discover something of Bernal's devotion to sexual varietism, but saw that he would never abandon anyone if he could help it – she said he was faithful in his fashion. Margaret thought he 'felt a sort of moral compulsion ... to give everybody their turn, you know, and to expect the others to accept it'.[52]

Sage's life was so crowded that he sometimes could not avoid letting his friends down. Zuckerman experienced this in North Africa in 1943 and seems to have been strangely scarred by it. In the second volume of his memoirs, published in 1988, Zuckerman related in some detail how he turned on Bernal at a dinner party at home in the early 1950s. Understandably irritated by Bernal's repeated predictions of the fall of liberal democracy and its replacement by a Marxist society, Zuckerman said he 'didn't give a damn about Bernal's politics' and that he had no intention of conforming to the rationally designed framework that Bernal was proposing. Zuckerman described Sage becoming more and more silent, 'his big head sinking into his chest'.[53] Zuckerman regarded the one-sided row as the end of their friendship; Sage thought no more of it, and always referred to Solly Zuckerman as his friend.[54] He never attempted to convert colleagues or friends to the communist cause – he had no need to because he believed the Marxist revolution was inevitable. That is not to say that some were not drawn to communism after being dazzled by Sage.

Whatever his faults, Bernal always tried to see the best in people, and until becoming depressed towards the end of his life, remained optimistic about the human race. He would always strive to be courteous towards others, whether they were delegates to a WPC conference giving a three-hour speech at one am in a language he did not understand, or scientists who did not agree with his ideas, or his political opponents. His essential humanity was always displayed in the company of children. He would never talk down to them – nor to bricklayers, taxi drivers and farmers – preferring instead to use the brilliance of his exposition to allow them to glimpse the world through his eyes.

Desmond Bernal led a fascinating and complex life, which seemed linked to history from the time he came of age in a deeply divided Ireland. He avoided the Great War and survived the Spanish influenza. As a young scientist he was fortunate to cross paths with some of the greatest figures of the day; his imagination and brilliance shaped the development of crystallography and led to molecular biology. His ideas changed the course of science, and he inspired a generation of younger researchers, who went on to glittering success. Sage was a renaissance figure – widely read, steeped in history and literature, and a notable authority on architecture and the visual arts. He was a pioneer in thinking systematically about the integration of science with society, and even though many of his predictions in that sphere have not come to pass, he clearly foresaw the emergence of Big Science. His objective studies of the effects of bombing on cities stood the test of time, and the D-Day invasion might well have taken a different course without his diverse contributions. He instantly understood, like many of his war-hardened colleagues, the devastating threat of nuclear weapons, and he devoted himself to calling for their abolition. In doing this, he was unbalanced in his assessment of the one-sided nature of the threat from America, but Bernal's opinions on the use of nuclear weapons and his contacts with Khrushchev may have helped the Soviet leader to step back from the abyss during the Cuban missile crisis. Bernal was the first to utter the phrase 'weapons of mass destruction' that looms so large today. In all these activities, he was the quintessential twentieth-century Sage of science.

Notes

Bernal's voluminous papers (JDB papers), meticulously organized and catalogued by the late Brenda Swann, are held in the Manuscript Department of Cambridge University Library. I am grateful to the Syndics of the Library for permission to quote from them.

NOTES TO CHAPTER 1

1. Bernal, J.D. *Microcosm*. Undated document. JDB Papers, B.4.1.
2. *San Jose Daily Mercury* (26/3/1900).
3. Hodgkin, D.M.C. (1981). Microcosm: the world as seen by John Desmond Bernal. *Proceedings of the Royal Irish Academy*, **81B**, 11–24.
4. Hruby, D.D. (1965). *Mines to Medicine*. San José, California.
5. Hodgkin, D.M.C. (1980). John Desmond Bernal, 1901–1971. *Biographical Memoirs of Fellows of the Royal Society*, **26**, 17–84.
6. Kee, R. (1982). *Ireland*. Little Brown and Co., Boston.
7. See note 5.
8. See note 3.
9. See note 6, p. 124.
10. See note 1.
11. Bernal, E (25/4/37). Letter to J.D. Bernal. JDB Papers, O.2.1
12. See note 1.
13. Ibid.
14. Ibid.
15. Miller, J.J. Undated family notes. JDB Papers, O.1.3.
16. See note 1.
17. Bernal, J.D. (1954). *Four stories for Boris Polevoi*. JDB Papers, B.4.68.
18. Ibid.
19. Bernal, J.D. (1909). Diary. JDB Papers, O.23.1.
20. See note 1.
21. See note 5.
22. Bernal, J.D. (11/11/11). Letter to Aunt Mod. JDB Papers, O.2.2.
23. See note 1.
24. Ibid.
25. Bernal, J.D. (5/10/14). Letter to E. Bernal. JDB Papers, O.2.2.
26. Bernal, J.D. (1915). Diary. JDB Papers, O.23.1.
27. Bernal, J.D. (1916). Diary. JDB Papers, O.23.1.
28. See note 6, p. 137.

29. Foster, R.F. (1988). *Modern Ireland 1600–1972*. Allen Lane, London.
30. Ferguson, N. (1998). *The Pity of War*. Allen Lane, London.
31. See note 29, p. 474.
32. See note 6, p. 153.
33. See note 27.
34. Pais, A. (1991). *Niels Bohr's Times*. Clarendon Press, Oxford.
35. Bernal, J.D. (1917). Character book. JDB Papers, O.23.1.
36. Bernal, J.D. (1917). Diary. JDB Papers, O.23.1.
37. See note 34, p. 132.
38. See note 36.
39. Ibid.
40. Ibid.
41. Ibid.
42. Ibid.
43. Gilbert, M. (1994). *The First World War*. Henry Holt, New York.
44. Ibid, p. 391.
45. Bernal, J.D. (1918). Diary. JDB Papers, O.23.1.
46. Ibid.
47. See note 6, p. 178.
48. See note 45.
49. See note 6, p. 177.
50. Ref. 45.
51. Ibid.
52. Ibid.
53. Ibid.
54. Ibid
55. Ibid.
56. Ibid.
57. Bernal, G. (1971). Interview with E. Bernal. JDB Papers, P.6.1.
58. See note 1.
59. See note 45.
60. Ibid.
61. Balibar, F. (1993). *The Science of Crystals*. McGraw-Hill, New York.
62. Story Maskelyne, N., Miers, H.A., Fletcher, L. et al. (1901). The structure of crystals. *Report of the British Association for the Advancement of Science*, 297–337. John Murray, London.
63. Ref. 45.
64. Synge, A. (1999). Early years and influences. In B. Swann and F. Aprahamian (eds.) *J.D. Bernal*, pp. 1–16. Verso, London.
65. Bernal, J.D. (1919). Diary. JDB Papers, O.23.1.
66. Ibid.
67. Ibid.
68. See note 6, p. 124.
69. See note 65.

NOTES TO CHAPTER 2

1. Thomson, J.J. (1937). *Recollections and Reflections*. Macmillan, New York.
2. Bernal, J.D. (1919). Diary. JDB Papers, O.23.1.
3. Ibid.
4. Ibid.
5. Bernal, J.D. *Microcosm* (undated manuscript). JDB Papers, B.4.1.
6. Ibid.
7. Gilbert, M. (1991). *Churchill: A Life*. Henry Holt, New York.
8. Dowie, J.A. (1975). 1919–20 is in need of attention. *Economic History Review*, pp. 429–50.
9. Moynahan, B. (1997). *The British Century*. Weidenfeld and Nicolson, London.
10. Ferguson, N. (1998). *The Pity of War*, p. 400. Allen Lane, London.
11. Martin, K. (1966). *Father Figures*. Hutchinson, London.
12. Lovell, A.C.B. (1975). P.M.S. Blackett. *Biographical Memoirs of Fellows of the Royal Society*, 21, 1–115.
13. See note 2.
14. Ibid.
15. See note 5.
16. See note 2.
17. Ibid.
18. Snow, C.P. (1964). J.D. Bernal, a personal portrait. In M. Goldsmith and A. Mackay (eds.) *The Science of Science*, pp. 19–29. Souvenir Press, London.
19. Bernal, J.D. (1920). Diary. JDB Papers, O.23.1.
20. Dobb, M. (1978). Random biographical notes. *Cambridge Journal of Economics*, 2, 115–20.
21. Hobsbawm, E. (1967). Maurice Dobb. In C.H. Feinstein (ed.) *Socialism, Capitalism and Economic Growth*, pp. 1–12. Cambridge University Press.
22. Kee, R. (1982). *Ireland*, p. 180. Little Brown and Co., Boston.
23. See note 2.
24. Ibid.
25. See note 19.
26. Ibid.
27. See note 22, p. 182.
28. Foster, R.F. (1988). *Modern Ireland 1600–1972*, p. 498. Allen Lane, London.
29. See note 19.
30. Todd, J.A. (1958). John Hilton Grace. *Biographical Memoirs of Fellows of the Royal Society*, 4, 93–7.
31. Motz, L. and Weaver, J.H. (1993) *The Story of Mathematics*. Plenum Press, New York.
32. See note 19.
33. Ibid.
34. See note 31.

35. See note 19.
36. Ibid.
37. Bernal, J.D. (23/2/20). Letter to E. Bernal. JDB Papers, O.2.1.
38. See note 19.
39. Slobodin, R. (1997). *W.H.R. Rivers*. Sutton, Stroud.
40. See note 5.
41. Sargant Florence, P. (1968). The Cambridge Heretics (1909–1932). In A.J. Ayer (ed.) *The Humanist Outlook*, pp. 225–39. Pemberton, London.
42. Ibid, p. 228.
43. See note 11, p. 102.
44. See note 2.
45. See note 19.
46. Bernal, J.D. (1921). Diary. JDB Papers, O.23.1.
47. See note 19.
48. Ibid.
49. Ibid.
50. Ibid.
51. See note 22, p. 185.
52. See note 19.
53. Ibid.
54. Ibid.
55. Ibid.
56. Ibid.
57. Ibid.
58. Ibid.
59. Hankins, T.L. (1980). *Sir William Rowan Hamilton*. Johns Hopkins University Press, Baltimore.
60. Hargittai, I. and Hargittai, M. (1994). *Symmetry: A Unifying Concept*. Shelter Publications, Bolinas, California.
61. Ewald, P.P. (1962). *Fifty Years of X-ray Diffraction*. International Union of Crystallography, Utrecht.
62. Ibid, p. 343.
63. See note 46.
64. Ibid.
65. Ibid.
66. Ibid.
67. Ibid.
68. Bragg, W.L. (1920). The arrangement of atoms in crystals. *Philosophical Magazine*, **40**, 169–89.
69. See note 46.
70. Ibid.
71. Hodgkin, D.M.C. (1980). Microcosm: the world as seen by John Desmond Bernal. *Proceedings of the Royal Irish Academy*, **81**, 11–24.
72. Ibid.

73. See note 11, p. 111.
74. See note 46.
75. Montagu, I. (1970). *The Youngest Son.* Lawrence and Wishart, London.
76. Hutt, A. (1972). Interview with E. Bernal, JDB Papers, P.6.1.
77. See note 46.
78. Ibid.
79. Ibid.
80. Ibid.
81. See note 19.
82. See note 46.
83. Ibid.
84. http://geometry.ma.ic.ac.uk/bernal/sprague.html.
85. See note 46.
86. Ibid.
87. Ibid.
88. Bernal, J.D. (1922). Diary. JDB Papers, O.23.1.
89. Synge, A. (1999). Early years and influences. In B. Swann and F. Aprahamian (eds.) *J.D. Bernal,* pp. 1–16. Verso, London.
90. See note 88.
91. Bernal, J.D. (1922). Undated letter to E. Bernal. JDB Papers, O.2.1.
92. Wootton, B. (1980). Saving the world. *London Review of Books, 19 June–2 July.*
93. Author's interview with Brenda Swann, 8/3/00.
94. Lucas, N.B.C. (1972). Reminiscences of Bernal. Emmanuel College Archives.
95. Hodgkin, D.M.C. (1980). John Desmond Bernal, 1901–1971. *Biographical Memoirs of Fellows of the Royal Society,* 26, 17–84.
96. See note 46.
97. Bernal, J.D. (1923). Diary. JDB Papers, O.23.1.
98. See note 46.
99. See note 10, p. 142.
100. Ibid.
101. Bernal, E. (1923). Letter to J.D. Bernal, 24 January. JDB Papers, O.2.1.
102. Bernal, J.D. (1923). The analytical theory of point systems (unpublished paper). JDB Papers, A.4.1
103. Ibid.
104. See note 95.

NOTES TO CHAPTER 3

1. Brown, A.P. (1997). *The Neutron and the Bomb.* Oxford University Press, Oxford.
2. Hodgkin, D.M.C. (1980). John Desmond Bernal, 1901–1971. *Biographical Memoirs of Fellows of the Royal Society,* 26, 17–84.
3. Andrade, E.N. da C. (1943). William Henry Bragg (1862–1942). *Obituary Notices of Fellows of the Royal Society,* 4, 277–92.

4. Bragg, W.H. and Kleeman, R. (1905). On the α particles of radium, and their loss of range in passing through various atoms and molecules. *Philosophical Magazine*, 10, 318–40.

5. Bragg, W.H. (1907). Letter to E. Rutherford. Rutherford's papers, Cambridge University Library.

6. Ewald, P.P. (ed.) (1962). *Fifty Years of X-ray Diffraction*. International Union of Crystallography, Utrecht.

7. Ibid, pp. 59–60.

8. Bragg, W.L. (1992). *The Development of X-ray Analysis*. Dover, New York.

9. Bragg, W.H. (1921). The structure of organic crystals. *Proceedings of the Physical Society, London*, 34, 33–50.

10. Ibid.

11. Bernal, J.D. (1962). My time at the Royal Institution, 1923–27. In P.P. Ewald (ed.) *Fifty Years of X-ray Diffraction*. International Union of Crystallography, Utrecht.

12. Bernal, J.D. (1963). William Thomas Astbury (1898–1961). *Biographical Memoirs of Fellows of the Royal Society*, 9, 1–35.

13. Hodgkin, D.M.C. (1975). Kathleen Lonsdale (1903–1971). *Biographical Memoirs of Fellows of the Royal Society*, 21, 447.

14. See note 11.

15. Ibid.

16. Caroe, G.M. (1978). *William Henry Bragg, 1862–1942*. Cambridge University Press, Cambridge.

17. Bernal, J.D. (1924). The structure of graphite. *Proceedings of the Royal Society, London, A*, 106, 749–73.

18. See note 11.

19. Ibid.

20. See note 17.

21. Ibid.

22. Bernal, J.D. (1920). Diary. JDB Papers, O.23.1.

23. See note 11.

24. Bernal, J.D. (1926). On the interpretation of X-ray, single crystal, rotation photographs. *Proceedings of the Royal Society, London, A*, 113, 117–60.

25. Patterson, A.L. (1962). Experiences in crystallography – 1924 to date. In P.P. Ewald (ed.) *Fifty Years of X-ray Diffraction*. International Union of Crystallography, Utrecht.

26. Author's interview with M. Perutz, 5/3/00.

27. See note 11.

28. See note 12.

29. Ibid.

30. Lonsdale, K. (1962). Crystallography at the Royal Institution. In P.P. Ewald (ed.) *Fifty Years of X-ray Diffraction*. International Union of Crystallography, Utrecht.

31. Steward, F. (1999). Political formation. In B. Swann and F. Aprahamian (eds.) *J.D. Bernal*. Verso, London.

32. Bernal, J.D. (1925). Diary. JDB Papers, O.23.1.

33. Ibid.

34. Ibid.

35. Bernal, J.D. (1926). Diary. JDB Papers, O.23.1.

36. Carswell, I. (1972). Letter to E. Bernal. JDB Papers, P.6.1.

37. Ibid.

38. Bernal, E. (8/2/26). Letter to J.D. Bernal. JDB Papers, O.2.1.

39. Bernal, E. (4/5/26). Letter to J.D. Bernal. JDB Papers, O.2.1.

40. Ibid.

41. Gilbert, M. (1991). *Churchill: A Life*, pp. 474–9. Henry Holt, New York.

42. See note 35.

43. Moynahan, B. (1997). *The British Century*, p. 158. Weidenfeld and Nicolson, London.

44. See note 35.

45. Ibid.

46. Lampe, D. (1959). *Pyke, The Unknown Genius*. Evans Brothers, London.

47. See note 35.

48. See note 31.

49. See note 35.

50. See note 43.

51. See note 31.

52. See note 35.

53. Bernal, J.D. (1927). Diary. JDB Papers, O.23.1.

54. Bernal, J.D. *Microcosm*. Undated document. JDB Papers, B.4.1.

55. Bernal, J.D. (1928). The complex structures of the copper–tin intermetallic compounds. *Nature*, 122, 54.

56. See note 2.

57. Pye, W.G. & Co. (23/3/28). Letter to J.D. Bernal. JDB Papers, J.188.

58. See note 2.

59. See note 38.

60. Bernal, G. (29/8/26). Letter to J.D. Bernal. JDB Papers, O.2.1.

61. Bernal, E. (30/5/27). Letter to J.D. Bernal. JDB Papers, O.2.1.

62. Bernal, E. (1/6/27). Letter to J.D. Bernal. JDB Papers, O.2.1.

63. Bernal, J.D. (18/8/27). Letter to E. Bernal. JDB Papers, O2.1.

64. See note 12.

65. Bragg, W.H. (21/7/27). Letter. JDB Papers, J.13.

66. Snow, C.P. (1964). J.D. Bernal, a personal portrait. In M. Goldsmith and A. Mackay (eds.) *The Science of Science*, pp. 19–29. Souvenir Press, London.

67. Bernal, E. (8/10/27). Letter to J.D. Bernal. JDB Papers, O.2.1.

68. Bernal, Gofty (2001). Telephone interview with author.

69. Bernal, E. (17/10/27). Letter to J.D. Bernal. JDB Papers, O.2.1.

NOTES TO CHAPTER 4

1. Bernal, J.D. *Microcosm*. Undated document. JDB Papers, B.4.1.
   All subsequent quotations in this chapter are from this unpublished source, unless otherwise indicated.
2. Bernal, J.D. (1929). *The World, the Flesh & the Devil*. Routledge & Kegan Paul, London; reprinted by Indiana University Press 1969.
3. Clarke, A.C. (2000). *Greetings, Carbon-Based Bipeds*. St. Martin's Griffin, New York.
4. Bernal, J.D. (1929). *The World, the Flesh & the Devil*. Kegan Paul and Co., London.
5. Ibid, p. 5.
6. See note 1.
7. See note 4, p. 11.
8. Ibid, p. 12.
9. Ibid, p. 15.
10. Ibid, p. 16.
11. Bernal, J.D. *Travelling to the moon*. Undated document. JDB Papers, B.4.11.
12. Ibid.
13. See note 4, p. 30.
14. Ibid.
15. Ibid.
16. Clark, R.W. (1968). *JBS: The Life and Work of JBS Haldane*. Coward-McCann, New York.
17. Haldane, JBS (1923). *Daedalus, or Science and the Future*. Kegan Paul Trench Trubner, London.
18. See note 4, p. 30.
19. Ibid, p. 31.
20. Ibid, p. 43.
21. Ibid, p. 47.
22. Ibid, p. 49.
23. Ibid, p. 51.
24. Ibid.
25. Ibid, p. 57.
26. See note 1.
27. Ibid.
28. See note 4, p. 58.
29. Ibid, p. 74.
30. Ibid, p. 75.
31. Ibid, p. 77.
32. Ibid, p. 78.
33. Ibid, p. 79.
34. Ibid, p. 77.
35. Wilson, D. (1983). *Rutherford: Simple Genius*. Hodder and Stoughton, London.

36. Conquest, R. (2000). *Reflections on a Ravaged Century.* W.W. Norton, New York.
37. Bernal, J.D. (1930). Unholy alliance. Reprinted in *The Freedom of Necessity* (1949), pp. 102–7. Routledge & Kegan Paul, London.
38. Ibid.
39. Ibid.
40. Bernal, J.D. (1949). *The Freedom of Necessity*, p. vii. Routledge & Kegan Paul, London.

NOTES TO CHAPTER 5

1. Wilson, D. (1983). *Rutherford: Simple Genius*, p. 591. Hodder and Stoughton, London.
2. Oliphant, M.L. (1972). *Rutherford – Recollections of the Cambridge Days*, p. 38. Elsevier, Amsterdam.
3. Hutchinson, A. (20/9/27). Letter to J.D. Bernal. JDB Papers, J.95.
4. Hutchinson, A. (21/9/27). Letter to J.D. Bernal. JDB Papers, J.95.
5. Lanham, A. (1972). Interview with E. Bernal. JDB Papers, P.6.2.
6. Pais, A. (1991). *Niels Bohr's Times.* Oxford University Press.
7. Bernal, J.D. (1927). Diary. JDB Papers, O.23.1.
8. Ibid.
9. Ibid.
10. Ibid.
11. Bernal, J.D. (1928). *On the present state of crystal structure studies.* Unpublished document. JDB Papers, A.4.5.
12. Ibid.
13. Kapp, H. (1972). Letter to E. Bernal. JDB Papers, P.6.1.
14. Olby, R. (1994). *The Path to the Double Helix: The Discovery of DNA.* Dover Publications, New York.
15. Polanyi, M. (1962). My time with X-rays and crystals. In P.P. Ewald (ed.) *Fifty Years of X-ray Diffraction*, pp. 629–36. International Union of Crystallography, Utrecht.
16. Mark, H.F. (1993). *From Small Organic Molecules to Large.* American Chemical Society, Washington.
17. See note 14, p. 34.
18. Tanford, C. and Reynolds, J. (2001). *Nature's Robots: A History of Proteins.* Oxford University Press, Oxford.
19. Svedberg, T. (1927). The ultracentrifuge. In *Nobel Lectures – Chemistry, 1922–1941.* Elsevier, Amsterdam.
20. See note 18, pp. 164–75.
21. Astbury, W.T. (12/9/28). Letter to J.D. Bernal. JDB Papers, J.2.
22. See note 14, p. 43.
23. Bernal, J.D. (2/2/29). Letter to W.T. Astbury. JDB Papers, J.2.
24. Astbury, W.T. (22/2/29). Letter to J.D. Bernal, JDB Papers, J.2.
25. Bernal, J.D. (28/2/29). Letter to W.T. Astbury. JDB Papers, J.2.

26. Bernal, J.D. (1929). The problem of the metallic state. *Transactions of the Faraday Society*, **25**, 367–79.

27. Pauling, L. (1981). Early work on chemical bonding in relation to solid state physics. *Proceedings of the Royal Society, London, A*, **378**, 207–18.

28. Bernal, J.D. (1968). Development of science and technology in the 21st century (unpublished lecture). JDB Papers, B.4.106.

29. Kapitza, P. (1928). The study of the specific resistance of bismuth crystals and its change in strong magnetic fields and some allied problems. *Proceedings of the Royal Society, A*, **119**, 358–86.

30. MacKay, A.L. (1979). The pre-history of zone-refining. *Trends in Biochemical Science*, **4**, N33.

31. Bernal, J.D. (1929). Unpublished note on the Royal Institution Conference of X-ray crystallographers. JDB Papers, L.1.

32. Astbury, W.T. (16/9/29). Letter to J.D. Bernal. JDB Papers, J.2.

33. Ewald, P.P. (1962). The consolidation of the new crystallography. In P.P. Ewald (ed.) *Fifty Years of X-ray Diffraction*, pp. 696–706. International Union of Crystallography, Utrecht.

34. Bernal, J.D. (1963). William Thomas Astbury (1898–1961). *Biographical Memoirs of Fellows of the Royal Society*, **9**, 1–35.

35. Astbury, W.T. (25/2/30). Letter to J.D. Bernal. JDB Papers, J.2.

36. See note 14, p. 51.

37. Astbury, W.T. (26/3/30). Letter to J.D. Bernal. JDB Papers, J.2.

38. See note 34.

39. Astbury, W.T. and Street, A. (1931). X-ray studies of the structure of hair, wool, and related fibres. *Philosophical Transactions of the Royal Society*, **230A**, 75–101.

40. Ibid.

41. See note 37.

42. Astbury, W.T. (7/10/30). Letter to J.D. Bernal. JDB Papers, J.2.

43. Bernal, J.D. (22/1/31). Letter to W.T. Astbury. JDB Papers, J.2.

44. Astbury, W.T. (23/1/31). Letter to J.D. Bernal. JDB Papers, J.2.

45. Ibid

46. Bernal, J.D. (23/2/31). Letter to W.T. Astbury. JDB Papers, J.2.

47. Bernal, J.D. (1931). The crystal structure of the natural amino acids and related compounds. *Z. Kristallogr. Kristallgeom.*, **78**, 363–9.

48. Snow, C.P. (1964). J.D. Bernal, a personal portrait. In M. Goldsmith and A. Mackay (eds.) *The Science of Science*, pp. 19–29. Souvenir Press, London.

49. See note 14, p. 250.

50. Ibid.

51. Bernal, J.D. (1930). The place of X-ray crystallography in the development of modern science. *Radiology*, **15**, 1–12.

52. Bragg, W.L. (5/3/31). Letter to E.R. Rutherford. Rutherford papers, B416. CUL.

53. Zuckerman, S. (1978). *From Apes to Warlords*. Hamish Hamilton, London.

54. See note 51.

55. Zuckerman, S. (10/6/31). Letter to J.D. Bernal. JDB Papers, J.267.

56. Bernal, J.D. (29/6/31). Letter to W.T. Astbury. JDB Papers, J.2.

57. Astbury, W.T. (2/7/31). Letter to J.D. Bernal. JDB Papers, J.2.

58. Bernal, J.D. (1932). Crystal structures of vitamin D and related compounds. *Nature*, **129**, 277–8.

59. Rosenheim, O. (4/5/32). Letter to J.D. Bernal. JDB Papers, J.199.

60. Hodgkin, D.M.C. (1980). John Desmond Bernal, 1901–1971. *Biographical Memoirs of Fellows of the Royal Society*, **26**, 17–84.

61. Wersky, G. (1978). *The Visible College*. Holt, Rinehart and Winston, New York.

62. Bernal, J.D. (1931). Notes for the International Congress on the History of Science. JDB Papers, A.4.7.

63. Ibid.

64. Ibid.

65. Ibid.

66. Ibid.

67. Abir-Am, P.G. (1987). The biotheoretical gathering, trans-disciplinary authority and the incipient legitimation of molecular biology in the 1930's. *History of Science*, **25**, 1–70.

68. Needham, J. (1971). Desmond Bernal: a personal recollection. *Cambridge Review*.

69. Bernal, J.D. (1954). *The structure of water* (unpublished). JDB Papers, B.4.68.

70. Fowler, R.H. and Bernal, J.D. (1933). Note on the pseudo-crystalline structure of water. *Transactions of the Faraday Society*, **29**, 1049–56.

71. Bernal, J.D. and Crowfoot, D. (1933). Crystalline phases of some substances studied as liquid crystals. *Transactions of the Faraday Society*, **29**, 1032–49.

72. See note 60.

73. Wooster, N. (1972). Letter to E. Bernal. JDB Papers, P.6.1.

74. Megaw, H. (1972). Letter to E. Bernal. JDB Papers, P.6.2.

75. Bernal, J.D. and Megaw, H. (1935). The function of hydrogen in intermolecular forces. *Proceedings of the Royal Society, London, A*, **151**, 384–420.

76. Astbury, W.T. (13/7/32). Letter to J.D. Bernal. JDB Papers, J.2.

77. See note 60.

78. Astbury, W.T. (13/1/33). Letter to J.D. Bernal. JDB Papers, J.2.

79. Astbury, W.T. (1/5/34). Letter to J.D. Bernal. JDB Papers, J.2.

80. Bernal, J.D. and Crowfoot, D. (1934). X-ray photographs of crystalline pepsin. *Nature*, **133**, 794–5.

81. Astbury, W.T. (16/5/34). Letter to J.D. Bernal. JDB Papers, J.2.

82. Ibid.

NOTES TO CHAPTER 6

1. Wood, N. (1959). *Communism and British Intellectuals*. Columbia University Press, New York.

2. Moynahan, B. (1997). *The British Century*. Weidenfeld and Nicolson, London.

3. MacDonald, R. (1992). We are not on trial. In B. MacArthur (ed.) *The Penguin Book of Twentieth-Century Speeches*, pp. 107–9. Viking, London.

4. Zuckerman, S. (1978). *From Apes to Warlords*. Hamish Hamilton, London.

5. Ibid, p. 394.

6. See note 1, pp. 84–6.

7. Haden Guest, C. (1939). *David Guest*. Lawrence and Wishart, London.

8. Cohen, S. (1971). *Bukharin and the Bolshevik Revolution*. Oxford University Press, Oxford.

9. Holmes, C. (1972). Bukharin in England. *Soviet Studies*, pp. 86–90.

10. Quoted in note 9, pp. 124–5.

11. Hessen, B. (1971). The social and economic roots of Newton's Principia. In N. Bukharin et al. (eds.) *Science at the Cross Roads*. Frank Cass, London.

12. Bernal, J.D. (1931). Science and society. Reprinted in *The Freedom of Necessity* (1949). Routledge & Kegan Paul, London.

13. Thomas, H. (1973). *John Strachey*. Eyre Methuen, London.

14. See note 11.

15. See note 9.

16. See note 12.

17. Bernal, J.D. (1931). *What is an intellectual* (unpublished). JDB Papers, B.4.13.

18. Ibid.

19. Ibid.

20. Swann, B. and Aprahamian, F. (1999). *J.D. Bernal: A Life in Science and Politics*. Verso, London.

21. Penrose, B. and Freeman, S. (1986). *Conspiracy of Silence: The Secret Life of Anthony Blunt*. Grafton Books, London.

22. See note 7, p. 94.

23. See note 12.

24. Huxley, J. (1932). *A Scientist Among the Soviets*. Chatto & Windus, London.

25. Ibid, p. 21.

26. Ibid, p. 59.

27. Ibid, p. 51.

28. Bullard, J. and Bullard, M. (2000). *Inside Stalin's Russia: The Diaries of Reader Bullard, 1930–4*. Day Books, Oxfordshire.

29. Crowther, J.G. (1970). *Fifty Years with Science*. Barrie & Jenkins, London.

30. Muggeridge, M. (1974). *Chronicle of Wasted Time: The Greenstick*. William Morrow, New York.

31. Sheehan, H. (1985). *Marxism and the Philosophy of Science*. Humanities Press, New Jersey.

32. Bernal, J.D. (1954). *The structure of water* (unpublished). JDB Papers, B.4.68.

33. Ibid.

34. Wersky, G. (1978). *The Visible College*. Holt, Rinehart and Winston, New York.

35. See note 29, p. 86.

36. Quoted in note 34, p. 148.

37. Ibid.

38. Carswell, I. (1972). Letter to E. Bernal. JDB Papers, P.6.1.
39. Hendry, J. (1984). *Cambridge Physics in the Thirties*. Adam Hilger, Bristol.
40. See note 13, p. 112.
41. Auden, W.H. (1933). *Poems (No. XXII)*. Faber and Faber, London.
42. See note 21, p. 87.
43. Bernal, J.D. (1933). The scientist and the world today. Reprinted in *The Freedom of Necessity* (1949). Routledge & Kegan Paul, London.
44. Ibid.
45. Boyle, A. (1979). *The Fourth Man*, p. 74. Dial Press, New York.
46. See note 21, p. 89.
47. See note 9.
48. Levy, H., Fox, R. et al. (1934) *Aspects of Dialectical Materialism*. Watts & Co., London.
49. See note 34, p. 167.
50. See note 48, p. 1.
51. Ibid, p. 89.
52. Ibid, p. 107.
53. Howarth, T.E.B. (1978). *Cambridge Between Two Wars*. Collins, London.
54. See note 48, pp. 91–2.
55. See note 53.
56. Snow, C.P. (2000). *The Search*. House of Stratus, London.
57. Ibid, p. 183.
58. Ibid, pp. 195–6.
59. Gardiner, M. (2000). Interview with the author.
60. Gardiner, M. (1988). *A Scatter of Memories*. Free Association Books, London.
61. Ibid, p. 241.
62. Ibid, p. 247.
63. Ibid, p. 248.
64. Carswell, J. (1983). *The Exile: A Life of Ivy Litvinov*. Faber and Faber, London.
65. See note 60, p. 250.
66. Ibid, p. 256.
67. Ibid, p. 258.

NOTES TO CHAPTER 7

1. Churchill, W.S. (1948). *The Second World War – The Gathering Storm*. Cassell, London.
2. Werskey, G. (1978). *The Visible College*. Holt, Rinehart and Winston, New York.
3. Bernal, J.D. (1933). The scientist and the world today. Reprinted in *The Freedom of Necessity* (1949). Routledge & Kegan Paul, London.
4. Werskey, G. (1969). Nature and politics between the wars. *Nature*, 224, 462–72.
5. Editorial (1933). Science in parliament. *Nature*, 132, 981–3.
6. See note 2, p. 235.
7. See note 3.

8. Ibid.

9. See note 2, pp. 339–42.

10. Burhop, E.H.S. (1964). Scientists and public affairs. In M. Goldsmith and A. Mackay (eds.) *The Science of Science*. Souvenir Press, London.

11. Minutes of the Academic Freedom Committee (1935). JDB Papers, L.7.

12. Hill, A.V. (1933). International status and obligations of science. *Nature*, 132, 952–4.

13. Goldsmith, M. (1980). *Sage: A Life of J.D. Bernal*. Hutchinson, London.

14. See note 2, p. 226.

15. Eastern Daily Press (19/8/35). JDB Papers, L.8.

16. See note 3.

17. Steward, F. (1999). Political formation. In B. Swann and F. Aprahamian (eds.) *J.D. Bernal: A Life in Science and Politics*. Verso, London.

18. Bernal, J.D. (1947). Paul Langevin (1872–1946). *Nature*, 159, 798–9.

19. See note 12, p. 126.

20. Tilly, C. (1986). *The Contentious French*. Harvard University Press, Cambridge, MA.

21. Bradshaw, D. (1997). British writers and anti-fascism, part I. *Woolf Studies Annual*, 3, Page University Press, NY.

22. Ibid.

23. Minutes of FIL meeting, 9/2/36. Collection Add 9369, Cambridge University Library.

24. See note 21.

25. Ibid.

26. Moynahan, B. (1994). *The Russian Century*. Random House, New York.

27. Wigner, E.P. and Hodgkin, R.A. (1977). Michael Polanyi (1891–1976). *Biographical Memoirs of Fellows of the Royal Society*, 23, 413–37.

28. Polanyi, M. (1935). Soviet economics – fact and theory. Reprinted in *The Contempt of Freedom* (1940). Watts, London.

29. Polanyi, M. (1936). Truth and propaganda. Reprinted in *The Contempt of Freedom* (1940). Watts, London.

30. Ibid.

31. Polanyi, M. (25/3/35). Letter to J.D. Bernal. JDB Papers, J.182.

32. Bernal, J.D. (11/4/35). Letter to M. Polanyi. JDB Papers, J.182.

33. Blythe, R. (1983). *The Age of Illusion*. Oxford University Press, Oxford.

34. Conquest, R. (2000). *Reflections on a Ravaged Century*. Norton, New York.

35. Bradshaw, D. (1998). British writers and anti-fascism, part II. *Woolf Studies Annual*, 4, Page University Press, NY.

36. See note 2, p. 225.

37. Calder, R. (1999). Bernal at war. In B. Swann and F. Aprahamian (eds.) *J.D. Bernal: A Life in Science and Politics*. Verso, London.

38. Huxley, A. (8/8/36). Letter to J.D. Bernal. JDB Papers, J.96.

39. See note 2, p. 229.

40. Wilkins, M.H.F. (1988). Fortunate failures I don't regret. *The Scientist*, 2[3], 14.

41. See note 37.

42. Stewart, G. (1999). *Burying Caesar.* Weidenfeld & Nicolson, London.
43. Foulkes, C.H. (1937). Air raid precautions. *Nature,* **139,** 606–8.
44. Bernal, J.D., Fremlin, J., Glasstone Shirley, et al. (1937). Air raid precautions. *Nature,* **139,** 760–1.
45. See note 2, p. 230.
46. Bernal, J.D. (1937). Supplement on A.R.P. *New Statesman and Nation.*
47. Crowther, J.G. (1970). *Fifty Years with Science.* Barrie & Jenkins, London.
48. *New Statesman,* 27/8/38.
49. Rolph, C.H. (1973). *Kingsley.* Gollancz, London.
50. Article on J.B.S. Haldane, *The Listener,* 2/11/67.
51. Whittaker, C. (1999). Building tomorrow, in B. Swann and F. Aprahamian (eds.) *J.D. Bernal: A Life in Science and Politics.* Verso, London.
52. See note 2, pp. 232–3.
53. Bernal, J.D. (19/2/69). Letter to D. Woodman. JDB Papers, J.254.
54. Bernal, J.D. (1938). Science and national service. *Nature,* **142,** 685–7.
55. See note 37, p. 165.
56. Zuckerman, S. (1978). *From Apes to Warlords.* Hamish Hamilton, London.
57. Civil Defence Research Committee (1939). *Nature,* **143,** 847.
58. Eady, W. (6/4/39). Minute on Civil Defence Research Committee. HO 45/21876, PRO.
59. Minutes of Civil Research Committee. (12/5/39). HO 45/21876, PRO.
60. Conquest, R. (1990). *The Great Terror: A Reassessment.* Oxford University Press, Oxford.
61. Gardiner, M. (2000) Interview with the author.

NOTES TO CHAPTER 8

1. Ferry, G. (1998). *Dorothy Hodgkin: A Life.* Granta Books, London.
2. Bernal, J.D. (undated). *A framework for his own autobiography.* JDB Papers, O.1.1.
3. Ibid.
4. See note 1, p. 111.
5. Ibid, p. 113.
6. Dale, H. (19/3/35). Letter to D. Crowfoot. D. Hodgkin Archive, B.105, Bodleian Library, Oxford.
7. See note 1, p. 86.
8. Bernal, J.D. (11/9/35). Letter to A. Windaus. JDB Papers, J.252.
9. Crowfoot, D. (26/6/36). Letter to J.D. Bernal. JDB Papers, J.89.
10. See note 1, p. 104.
11. Ibid., pp. 119–20.
12. Bernal, J.D. (1936). Report on 'X-ray crystallography and the chemistry of sterols'. JDB Papers, J.89.
13. See note 2.
14. See note 1, p. 123.
15. Ibid, p. 127.

16. Bragg, W.L. (14/10/35). Letter to J.D. Bernal. JDB Papers, J.14.

17. Pirie, N.W. (1973). Frederick Charles Bawden (1908–72). *Biographical Memoirs of Fellows of the Royal Society,* **19,** 19–59.

18. Bawden, F.C., Pirie, N.W., Bernal, J.D. and Fankuchen, I. (1936). Liquid crystalline substances from virus-infected plants. *Nature,* **138,** 1051–2.

19. Bernal, J.D. (1964). Professor Isadore Fankuchen (obituary). *Nature,* **203,** 916–17.

20. See note 17.

21. See note 18.

22. Ibid.

23. Bernal, J.D. (24/7/37). Letter to W.T. Astbury. JDB Papers, J.2.

24. Bernal, J.D., Fankuchen, I. and Riley, D. (1938). Structure of the crystals of tomato bushy stunt virus preparations. *Nature,* **142,** 1075.

25. Pirie, N. (1938). Undated letter to J.D. Bernal. JDB Papers, J.181.

26. Bernal, J.D. and Fankuchen, I. (1941). X-ray and crystallographic studies of plant virus preparations, parts I, II, & III. *Journal of General Physiology,* **25,** 111–65.

27. Ibid.

28. Author's interview with Max Perutz, Cambridge, March 2000.

29. Ibid.

30. Olby, R. (1994). *The Path to the Double Helix: The Discovery of DNA.* Dover Publications, New York.

31. Perutz, M.F. (4/12/37). Letter to J.D. Bernal. JDB Papers, J.178.

32. Perutz, M.F. (1997). *Science is Not a Quiet Life: Unravelling the Atomic Mechanism of Haemoglobin.* World Scientific, Singapore.

33. Bernal, J.D., Fankuchen, I. and Perutz, M. (1938). An X-ray study of chymotrypsin and haemoglobin. *Nature,* **141,** 523–4.

34. See note 32, p. 36.

35. Megaw, H. (undated). *A note on crystallography at Cambridge since 1929.* JDB Papers, B.4.11.

36. Crowther, J.G. (1970). *Fifty Years with Science.* Barrie & Jenkins, London.

37. See note 30, pp. 252–3.

38. Megaw, H (1972). Letter to E. Bernal. JDB Papers, P.6.2.

39. Abir-Am, P.G. (1987). The biotheoretical gathering, trans-disciplinary authority and the incipient legitimation of molecular biology in the 1930s. *History of Science,* **25,** 1–70.

40. See note 30, p. 234.

41. Snow, C.P. (2000). *The Search.* House of Stratus, London.

42. See note 39.

43. Ibid.

44. See note 30, p. 116.

45. Wrinch, D. (1936). The pattern of proteins. *Nature,* **137,** 411–12.

46. See note 30, p. 57.

47. Bernal, J.D. (13/4/37). Letter to W.H. Bragg. JDB Papers, J.13.

48. Bernal, J.D. (13/11/38). Letter to D. Wrinch. JDB Papers, J.258.

49. Wrinch, D. (1939). A discussion on the protein molecule. *Proceedings of the Royal Society, London, A,* **170**, 40–79.

50. Pirie, N. (1938). Undated letter to J.D. Bernal. JDB Papers, J.181.

51. Hager, T. (1995). *Force of Nature: The Life of Linus Pauling.* Simon & Schuster, New York.

52. Bernal, J.D. (14/12/38). Letter to W.L. Bragg. JDB Papers, J.14.

53. Bernal, J.D. (14/12/38). Letter to I. Langmuir. JDB Papers, J.119.

54. Bragg, W.L. (12/12/38). Letter to J.D. Bernal. JDB Papers, J.14.

55. Bernal, J.D. (19/12/38). Letter to W.L. Bragg. JDB Papers, J.14.

56. Bernal, J.D. (1939). Vector maps and the cyclol hypothesis. *Nature,* **143**, 74–5.

57. Bernal, J.D. (1939). Structure of proteins. *Nature,* **143**, 663–7.

58. Ibid.

59. Tanford, C. and Reynolds, J. (2001). *Nature's Robots: A History of Proteins.* Oxford University Press, Oxford.

60. Bragg, W.L. (10/11/36). Letter to J.D. Bernal. JDB Papers, J.14.

61. See note 41, pp. 185–6.

62. Bernal, E. (25/4/37). Letter to J.D. Bernal. JDB Papers, O.2.1

63. Bradshaw, D. (1998). British writers and anti-fascism, part II. *Woolf Studies Annual,* 4, Page University Press, NY.

64. Gardiner, M. (2000). Interview with the author.

65. Bernal, J.D. (1937). Catalogue of sculpture by Barbara Hepworth, Lefevre Gallery. JDB Papers, B.3.30.

66. Hepworth, B. (1937). Undated letter to J.D. Bernal. JDB Papers, J.84.

67. Hepworth, B. (1971). Undated letter to E. Bernal. JDB Papers, P.6.2.

68. Bernal, J.D. (1937). Art and the scientist. Reprinted in *The Freedom of Necessity* (1949). Routledge & Kegan Paul, London.

69. Bernal, J.D. (1937). Architecture and science. Reprinted in *The Freedom of Necessity* (1949). Routledge & Kegan Paul, London.

70. See note 64.

71. Malleson, J. (undated). Letter to J.D. Bernal. JDB Papers, J.159.

72. Bernal, J.D. (1938). *Notes on molecular architecture of biological systems.* JDB Papers, A.4.22.

73. Hobsbawm, E. (1999). Bernal at Birkbeck. In B. Swann and F. Aprahamian (eds.) *J.D. Bernal,* pp. 1–16. Verso, London.

74. Bernal, J.D. (1937). Undated curriculum vitae. JDB Papers, C.2.

75. Bernal, J.D. (28/4/38). Letter to M.F. Perutz. JDB Papers, J.178.

76. Bragg, W.L. (31/10/38). Letter to J.D. Bernal. JDB Papers, J.14.

77. Bernal, J.D. (3/11/38). Letter to W.L. Bragg. JDB Papers, J.14.

78. Frisch, O.R. (1979). *What Little I Remember.* Cambridge University Press, Cambridge.

79. Hodgkin, D.M.C. (1980). John Desmond Bernal, 1901–1971. *Biographical Memoirs of Fellows of the Royal Society,* **26**, 17–84.

80. Bernal, J.D. (1939). *The Social Function of Science.* Routledge & Kegan Paul, London.

81. Author's interview with B. Swann, March 2000.
82. See note 51, p. 247.
83. Polanyi, M. (1939). Rights and duties of science. Reprinted in *The Contempt of Freedom* (1940). Watts, London.
84. Ibid.
85. Ibid.
86. Galison, P. and Hevly, B. (1992). *Big Science: The Growth of Large-scale Research*. Stanford University Press, California.
87. Le Fanu, J. (1999). *The Rise and Fall of Modern Medicine*. Little Brown and Co., London.

NOTES TO CHAPTER 9

1. Notes on visit to USA (1939). JDB Papers, L.13.
2. Bernal, J.D. (27/7/39). Letter to I. Fankuchen, Fankuchen Collection, AIP Archives.
3. Bernal, J.D. (1939). Science teaching in general education. Reprinted in *The Freedom of Necessity* (1949). Routledge & Kegan Paul, London.
4. Ibid.
5. Bernal, J.D. (undated). *A framework for his own autobiography.* JDB Papers, O.1.1.
6. Author's interview with B. Swann, March 2000.
7. Bernal, J.D. (12/9/39). Letter to E. Cohn, Fankuchen Collection, AIP Archives.
8. See note 6.
9. Research in civil defence. (1939). *Nature*, **143**, 869–70.
10. Haldane, J.B.S. (1938). *A.R.P.* Gollancz, London.
11. Minutes of Sub-Committee A, Civil Defence Research (1939). HO 195/17. PRO.
12. Bernal, J.D. (25/11/39). Letter to P. Ewald. JDB Papers, J.41.
13. Zuckerman, S. (1978). *From Apes to Warlords*. Hamish Hamilton, London.
14. Carlisle, C.H. (1981). Dorothy and cholesteryl iodide. In G. Dodson, J.P. Glusker and D. Sayre (eds.) *Structural Studies on Molecules of Biological Interest*, pp. 30–4. Clarendon Press, Oxford.
15. Bernal, J.D. (1940). Letter to Rockefeller Trustees. D. Hodgkin papers, C.67.
16. Bernal, J.D. (1940). Undated letter to I. Fankuchen, Fankuchen Collection, AIP.
17. Ferry, G. (1998). *Dorothy Hodgkin: A Life*. Granta Books, London.
18. Churchill, W.S. (1939). Appendix L, the black-out. In *The Second World War – The Gathering Storm*. Cassell, London.
19. See note 5.
20. Hopkinson, T. (1982). *Of This Our Time*. Hutchinson, London.
21. Notes on the Tots and Quots. Zuckerman archive, SZ/TQ/1–2.
22. Ibid.
23. Crowther, J.G. (1970). *Fifty Years with Science*. Barrie and Jenkins, London.
24. Ibid, pp. 214–18.
25. Bernal, J.D. (4/4/40). Memorandum to R. Stradling. JDB Papers, D.3.
26. Ibid.

27. Blyth, R.C. (1940). Diary of visit to France. JDB Papers, D.3.

28. See note 13, pp. 116–17.

29. See note 27.

30. Minutes of Explosives Research Committee (10/5/40). WO 195/161. PRO.

31. Huxley, J.S. (1940). Science in war. *Nature*, 146, 112–13.

32. See note 6.

33. Wheeler-Bennett, J.W. (1962). *John Anderson*. Macmillan, London.

34. Ibid, p. 240.

35. Perutz, M.F. (1998). Enemy alien. In *I wish I'd Made You Angry Earlier*. Oxford University Press.

36. Internment of alien scientific workers (25/5/40). *Nature*, 145, 796.

37. Bernal, J.D. (25/7/40). Letter to L. Pauling. Ava Helen and Linus Pauling Papers, Oregon State University.

38. See note 11.

39. Hartley, A.B. (1959). *Unexploded Bomb*. W.W. Norton, New York.

40. Ibid, p. 19.

41. Bernal, J.D. (1962). The place of speculation in modern technology and science. In I.J. Good (ed.) *The Scientist Speculates*, Heinemann, London.

42. Lowe, J.C.W. (30/5/40). Letter to H.J. Gough. UXB Committee, Ministry of Supply. WO/195/184.

43. See note 39, p. 23.

44. See note 39, pp. 45–6.

45. See note 39, pp. 24–5.

46. See note 11.

47. Danckwerts, P.V. (1983). In the land of the giants. *New Scientist*, 904.

48. Fitzgibbon, C. (1971). *London's Burning*. Macdonald & Co., London.

49. See note 13, p. 131.

50. Bernal, J.D. (1954). Wartime stories. JDB Papers, B.4.68/3.

51. Ibid.

52. Ibid.

53. Ibid.

54. Snow, C.P. (1964). J.D. Bernal, a personal portrait. In M. Goldsmith and A. Mackay (eds.) *The Science of Science*, pp. 19–29. Souvenir Press, London.

55. See note 13, p. 131.

56. See note 23, p. 222.

57. See note 13, p. 399.

58. See note 21.

59. Bernal, J.D. (1940). The physics of air raids. *Proceedings of the Royal Institution of Great Britain*, 31, 262–79.

60. Ibid.

61. Miscellaneous cutting (4/12/40). JDB Papers, D.5.

62. See note 5.

63. See note 20, p. 183.

64. Rees, G. (1972). *A Chapter of Accidents*. Chatto and Windus, London.

65. Muggeridge, M. (1973). *Chronicles of Wasted Time: The Infernal Grove*. Collins, London.
66. Ibid, p. 107.
67. West, N. (1999). *Venona*. Harper Collins, London.
68. See note 64.

NOTES TO CHAPTER 10

1. Hastings, M. (1979). *Bomber Command*. The Dial Press, New York.
2. Baldwin, S. (1932). The bomber will always get through. In B. MacArthur (ed.) *The Penguin Book of Twentieth-Century Speeches* (1986). Viking, London.
3. Gilbert, M. (1991). *Churchill: A Life*. Henry Holt, New York.
4. Wilson, T. (1995). *Churchill and the Prof*. Cassell, London.
5. Thomson, G.P. (1958). Frederick Alexander Lindemann, Viscount Cherwell. *Biographical Memoirs of Fellows of the Royal Society*, 4, 45–71.
6. Ibid.
7. Medawar, J. and Pyke, D. (2001). *Hitler's Gift*. Arcade Publishing, New York.
8. Churchill, W.S. (1948). *The Second World War – The Gathering Storm*. Cassell, London.
9. See note 3, p. 512.
10. Clark, R.W. (1965). *Tizard*. The MIT Press, Cambridge, MA.
11. See note 3, p. 536.
12. See note 10.
13. See note 10, p. 125.
14. See note 3, p. 631.
15. See note 4, p. 8.
16. Fitz Gibbon, C. (1971). *The Blitz*. Allan Wingate, London.
17. Bernal, J.D. and Garwood, F. (1940). An investigation of probable air raid damage. Ministry of Home Security, R.C. 107. Zuckerman Archive.
18. Ibid.
19. Ibid.
20. Neillands, R. (2001). *The Bomber War*. Overlook Press, New York.
21. Churchill, W.S. (1949). *The Second World War, II – Their Finest Hour*. Cassell, London.
22. Ibid, pp. 332–3.
23. Author's interview with R. Brittan and U. Harris, June 2000.
24. Zuckerman, S. (1978). *From Apes to Warlords*. Hamish Hamilton, London.
25. Watkins, K. Undated note. JDB Papers, O.1.2.
26. Watkins, K. (1971). Letter to E. Bernal. JDB Papers, P.6.2.
27. Churchill, W.S. (1950). *The Second World War, III – The Grand Alliance*. Cassell, London.
28. Ibid, p. 340.
29. Bernal, J.D. (1941). Present-day science and technology in the USSR. *Nature*, 148, 360–1.

30. See note 20, p. 53.
31. Bernal, J.D. (11/4/61). Letter to C.P. Snow. JDB Papers, J.217.
32. Ibid.
33. Ibid.
34. Ibid.
35. Ibid.
36. See note 27, pp. 451–2.
37. See note 24, p. 398.
38. Ibid.
39. Ibid, p. 140.
40. Zuckerman, S. (1975). Scientific advice during and since World War II. *Proceedings of the Royal Society, London, A*, **342**, 465–80.
41. See note 24, p. 141.
42. See note 31.
43. Ministry of Home Security Report 2770 (1942). *Quantitative study of the total effect of air-raids.* Zuckerman archives, SZ/OEMU/57/1.
44. Ibid.
45. Ibid.
46. Bernal, J.D. (1942). Diary. JDB Papers, D.1.
47. See note 3, p. 716.
48. See note 10, pp. 309–10.
49. Ibid.
50. Ibid.
51. Crook, P. (2003). The case against area bombing. In P. Hore (ed.) *Patrick Blackett: Sailor, Scientist, Socialist.* Frank Cass, London.
52. Blackett, P.M.S. (1962). *Studies of War.* Hill and Wang, New York.
53. Butt, D.M. (1942). Letter to S. Zuckerman. Zuckerman archives, SZ/OEMU/2/1/9.
54. See note 4, p. 74.
55. See note 43.
56. See note 10, pp. 311–12.
57. Ibid.
58. Webster, C. and Frankland, N. (1961). *The Strategic Air Offensive Against Germany.* Vol I. HMSO, London.
59. See note 10, pp. 311–12.
60. See note 10, pp. 231–2.
61. See note 10, p. 244.
62. Colville, J. (1986). *The Fringes of Power.* W.W. Norton, New York.
63. See note 10, p. 293.
64. See note 3, pp. 718–20.
65. Ibid.
66. Ibid.
67. Air Ministry Commentary. (1942). *The total effects of air raids.* Zuckerman archive, SZ/OEMU/18/2.
68. See note 58, p. 336.

69. Ibid, p. 366.
70. Ibid, p. 371.
71. Bernal, J.D. (1948). Note to P. Blackett. JDB Papers, J.9.
72. See note 31.
73. Ibid.

NOTES TO CHAPTER 11

1. The Brains Trust Number 50 (7/12/41). JDB Papers, B.5.5.
2. Bernal, J.D. (1942). The freedom of necessity. Reprinted in *The Freedom of Necessity* (1949). Routledge & Kegan Paul, London.
3. Ibid, pp. 4–5.
4. Ibid, p. 6.
5. Ibid, pp. 67–8.
6. Bernal, J.D. (1942). Conference on science and the war effort. *Nature*, **149**, 71.
7. See note 5.
8. Hodgkin, D.M.C. (1980). John Desmond Bernal, 1901–1971. *Biographical Memoirs of Fellows of the Royal Society*, **26**, 17–84.
9. Lampe, D. (1959). *Pyke, The Unknown Genius*. Evans Brothers, London.
10. Ibid, p. 88.
11. Mountbatten, L. 'Memories of Desmond Bernal' in note 8.
12. www.standto.com/qorbruneval.html.
13. Zuckerman, S. (1978). *From Apes to Warlords*. Hamish Hamilton, London.
14. Harris, J. (ed.) (2001). *Goronwy Rees: Sketches in Autobiography*. University of Wales Press, Cardiff.
15. See note 11.
16. Villa, B.L. (1989). *Unauthorized Action: Mountbatten and the Dieppe Raid*. Oxford University Press, Oxford.
17. See note 13, p. 153.
18. Bernal, J.D. (undated). *A framework for his own autobiography*. JDB Papers, O.1.1.
19. See note 14, p. 95.
20. See note 9, p. 111.
21. See note 9, p. 120.
22. Ibid.
23. Hamilton, N. (1981). *Monty: The Making of a General*. Hamish Hamilton, London.
24. Ibid, p. 555.
25. See note 16, p. 46.
26. See note 13, p. 157.
27. Naval Intelligence Records, Dieppe Raid. ADM 199/2465, PRO.
28. Watkins, K. (1971). Letter to E. Bernal. JDB Papers, P.6.2.
29. See note 27.
30. Ibid.
31. Campbell, J.P. (1993). *Dieppe Revisited*. Frank Cass, London.

32. Notes on the Tots and Quots. Zuckerman archive, SZ/TQ/1–2.
33. See note 9, p. 123.
34. Mark, H.F. (1993). *From Small Organic Molecules to Large*. American Chemical Society, Washington.
35. Ibid, p. 100.
36. See note 9, p. 128.
37. Bernal, J.D. (1942). Diary. JDB Papers, D.1.
38. See note 16.
39. Author's interview with Martin Bernal, 2001.
40. See note 13, p. 153.
41. Perutz, M.F. (1998). Enemy alien. In *I Wish I'd Made You Angry Earlier*. Oxford University Press.
42. Ibid, p. 83.
43. Churchill, W.S. (7/12/42). Minute to General Ismay for COS Committee. ADM 1/15236, PRO.
44. Bernal, J.D. (1942). Memorandum on research and development, HABBAKUK. ADM 1/15236, PRO.
45. Bernal, J.D. (1942). Habbakuk: general conclusions. ADM 1/15236, PRO.
46. Bernal, J.D. (1943). Habbakuk: note on practicability of scheme – 8 Jan 43. ADM 1/15236, PRO.
47. Middle East Operations Research. WO 32/10150. PRO.
48. Clark, R.W. (1965). *Tizard*. The MIT Press, Cambridge, MA.
49. Notes of the ninth informal meeting of independent scientific advisers. 15/12/42. SZ/BSu/1/1/8. Zuckerman Archive.
50. Ibid.
51. Outgoing cypher message (21/12/42) Vice-CAS to AOC-in-C. SZ/BSu/1/1/10. Zuckerman Archive.
52. Under-Secretary War Office to Director of Medical Services (31/12/42). SZ/BSu/1/1/20.
53. See note 13, p. 161.
54. Ibid.
55. See note 18.
56. See note 13, p. 162.
57. Peyton, J. (2001). *Solly Zuckerman: A Scientist Out of the Ordinary*. John Murray, London.
58. Ibid, p. 48.
59. Vice-Chief Air Staff to HQ RAF, Middle East (23/12/42). SZ/BSu/1/1/11. Zuckerman Archive.
60. See note 13, p. 162.
61. See note 41, p. 84.
62. Zuckerman, S. (1943). North Africa Journal. SZ/BSu/1/7. Zuckerman Archive.
63. See note 18.
64. See note 13, p. 166.
65. Zuckerman, S. (27/12/71). Letter to J. Kendrew. Kendrew Papers, O.2.

66. See note 13, p. 164.

67. Author's telephone interview with N. Waddleton (2005).

68. Author's interview with Max Perutz, Cambridge (2000).

69. Bernal, J.D. (1943) Undated letter to S. Zuckerman. SZ/BSu/1/1/33, Zuckerman Archive.

70. See note 18.

71. Ibid.

72. Ibid.

73. Bernal, J.D. (1943). Diary. JDB Papers, D.1.

74. See note 41, p. 89.

75. Bernal, J.D. (1943). *Brief summary of progress of research work in Canada*. ADM 1/15236. PRO.

76. Mountbatten, L. (1943). Cable to Bernal and Pyke. ADM 1/15236, PRO.

77. See note 41, p. 85.

78. Perutz, M. (6/4/43). Letter to G. Pyke. ADM/15236, PRO.

79. Bernal, J.D. and Pyke, G. (1943). Undated message to CCO. ADM 1/15236. PRO.

80. See note 18.

81. *Evening Standard*, 24/5/43.

NOTES TO CHAPTER 12

1. Davie, M. (ed.) (1976). *The Diaries of Evelyn Waugh*. Little, Brown and Co., Boston.

2. Minutes of Habbakuk Committee (27/5/43). ADM 1/15236, PRO.

3. Harrison, M. (1965). *Mulberry: The Return in Triumph*. W.H. Allen, London.

4. Churchill, W.S. (1952). *The Second World War, V: Closing the Ring*. Cassell, London.

5. See note 3, p. 82.

6. Churchill, W.S. (1951). *The Second World War, IV: The Hinge of Fate*. Cassell, London.

7. See note 3, p. 136.

8. Steer-Webster, V.C. (31/12/63). Letter to J.D. Bernal. JDB Papers, J.224.

9. Fergusson, B. (1961). *The Watery Maze*. Collins, London.

10. Perutz, M.F. (1998). Enemy alien. In *I Wish I'd Made You Angry Earlier*. Oxford University Press.

11. Minutes of Habbakuk Committee (15/7/43). ADM 1/15236, PRO.

12. See note 10, p. 91.

13. See note 9, p. 285.

14. Bernal, J.D. (1943). Diary. JDB Papers, D.1.

15. Minutes of COS meeting (7/8/43). CAB 121/154, PRO.

16. See note 9, p. 286.

17. Mountbatten, L. (1999). Memories of Desmond Bernal. In B. Swann and F. Aprahamian (eds.) *J.D. Bernal*. Verso, London.

18. Aprahamian, F. (1971). Interview with E. Bernal. JDB Papers, P.6.2.

19. See note 14.
20. Ziegler, P. (1985). *Mountbatten.* Alfred A. Knopf, New York.
21. Minutes of COS meeting (9/8/43). CAB 121/154, PRO.
22. Ibid.
23. Gilbert, M. (1991). *Churchill: A Life.* Henry Holt, New York.
24. Bernal, J.D. (undated). *A framework for his own autobiography.* JDB Papers, O.1.1.
25. Bernal, J.D. (1943). Filofax notes. JDB Papers, D.1.
26. Minutes of COS meeting (19/8/43). CAB 121/154, PRO.
27. See note 4, p. 81.
28. Lampe, D. (1959). *Pyke, The Unknown Genius.* Evans Brothers, London.
29. COS minute to Vice-COS (23/8/43). ADM 1/15236, PRO.
30. See note 28, pp. 147–8.
31. See note 24.
32. London to Washington cable (1943). ADM 1/15236, PRO.
33. Bernal, J.D. (6/9/43). Letter to Lord Mountbatten. MB1/C24/1, Broadlands Archives, University of Southampton.
34. See note 17, p. 193.
35. See note 10, p. 95.
36. See note 17, pp. 193–4.
37. Air Ministry Signal (15/12/43). ADM 1/15217, PRO.
38. Bernal, J.D. (9/10/43). Letter to Lord Mountbatten. MB1/C24/3, Broadlands Archives, University of Southampton.
39. See note 28, p. 175.
40. See note 9, p. 295.
41. Calder, R. (1999). Bernal at war. In B. Swann and F. Aprahamian (eds.) *J.D. Bernal.* Verso, London.
42. Kenn, M.J. (1991). Ralph Alger Bagnold, 1896–1990. *Biographical Memoirs of Fellows of the Royal Society,* 37, 57–68.
43. See note 41, p. 179.
44. See note 3, p. 108.
45. Bernal, J.D. (1955). Scientific Preparations for the Normandy landings. Lecture to the French Association for the Advancement of Science, Caen. JDB Papers, A.3.130.
46. See note 25.
47. See note 3, p. 108.
48. See note 3, p. 107.
49. Ibid.
50. See note 45.
51. Ramsay, B.H. (2/11/43). Memo to CCO and COSSAC on naval reconnaissance of the enemy coast. ADM 1/13066, PRO.
52. Author's interview with L. Scott-Bowden (2004).
53. Ibid.
54. Ibid.
55. Miller, R. (1993). *Nothing Less than Victory.* Michael Joseph, London.

56. Ibid.
57. Bernal, J.D. (7/1/44). Letter to Lord Mountbatten. MB1/C24/6, Broadlands Archives, University of Southampton.
58. Bernal, J.D. (1944). Desk Diary. JDB Papers, D.1.
59. See note 9, p. 303.
60. COHQ Overlord Bulletin Y/35 (1944). *Underwater obstacles.* HS8/286. PRO.
61. See note 58.
62. See note 45.
63. Map of North Coast of France. JDB Papers, D.8.
64. See note 45.
65. See note 3, p. 109.
66. See note 3, p. 110.
67. See note 58.
68. See note 4, pp. 518–19.
69. Ibid.
70. Gardiner, M (2000). Interview with the author.
71. See note 60.
72. See note 3, p. 260.
73. See note 58.
74. See note 60.
75. See note 58.
76. See note 60.
77. Ibid.
78. See note 45.
79. See note 59.
80. See note 58.
81. Danckwerts, P.V. (1983). In the land of the giants. *New Scientist*, 904.
82. Bernal, J.D. (1944). The Normandy landings. JDB Papers, B.4.68/3.
83. Ibid.
84. Ibid.
85. Ibid.
86. Ibid.
87. Ibid.
88. Ibid.
89. Ibid.
90. COHQ Overlord Bulletin Y/34 (1944). *Underwater obstacles.* HS8/286. PRO.
91. See note 82.
92. Ibid.
93. Ibid.
94. Ibid.
95. Ibid.
96. Ibid.
97. Ibid.
98. Ibid.
99. See note 60.

100. COHQ Overlord Bulletin Y/36 (1944). HS8/286. PRO.
101. COHQ Overlord Bulletin Y/39 (1944). *Navigational aspects of the assault.* HS8/286. PRO.

NOTES TO CHAPTER 13

1. Ziegler, P. (1985). *Mountbatten.* Alfred A. Knopf, New York.
2. Bernal, J.D. (6/9/43). Letter to Mountbatten. MB1/C24/1, Broadlands Archives.
3. Ibid.
4. Bernal, J.D. (9/10/43). Letter to Mountbatten. MB1/C24/3, Broadlands Archives.
5. See note 1, p. 251.
6. Lampe, D. (1959). *Pyke, The Unknown Genius.* Evans Brothers, London.
7. Ibid, p. 163.
8. Bernal, J.D. (7/1/44). Letter to Mountbatten. MB1/C24/3, Broadlands Archives.
9. Bernal, J.D. (7/1/44). Operational Research Organisation – South East Asia. MB1/C24/7, Broadlands Archives.
10. Bernal, J.D. (1944). Desk Diary. JDB Papers, D.1.
11. Kendrew, J.C. (12/2/44). Letter to J.D. Bernal. Kendrew papers, B.7.
12. Burma Campaign. WO 203/531. PRO.
13. Ibid.
14. See note 11.
15. See note 10.
16. See note 6, p. 167.
17. See note 10.
18. See note 1, p. 279.
19. Bernal, J.D. (undated). *A framework for his own autobiography.* JDB Papers, O.1.1.
20. Bernal, J.D. (1944). Pocket diary. JDB Papers, D.1.
21. Churchill, W.S. (1954). *The Second World War, VI: Triumph and Tragedy.* Cassell, London.
22. See note 19.
23. Ibid.
24. Calder, R. (1999). Bernal at war. In B. Swann and F. Aprahamian (eds.) *J.D. Bernal.* Verso, London.
25. Kendrew papers, B.17.
26. Kendrew, J.C. (1972). Tribute to Bernal at Birkbeck memorial meeting. Kendrew Papers, L.149.
27. Ibid.
28. See note 24, p. 189.
29. See note 20.
30. See note 19.
31. Allen, L. (1984). *Burma, The Longest War.* St. Martin's Press, New York.
32. See note 19.
33. Bernal, J.D. (11/12/44). Letter to Lord Mountbatten. Mountbatten Archives, MB1/C24/9.

34. Ibid.

35. Ibid.

36. See note 10.

37. Lewis, J. (2003). *Changing Direction*. Frank Cass, London.

38. Ibid, pp. 180–1.

39. Zuckerman, S. (1978). *From Apes to Warlords*. Hamish Hamilton, London.

40. Ibid, pp. 216–58.

41. See note 10.

42. See note 39, p. 321.

43. Brown, A. P. (1997). *The Neutron and the Bomb*. Oxford University Press, Oxford.

44. Churchill, W.S. (19/4/45). Minute to General Ismay. PREM3/139/11A, PRO.

45. See note 37, p. 187.

46. See note 37, p. 183.

47. See note 37, p. 184.

48. *The Times*, 15/6/45.

49. Lord Woolton (18/6/45). Letter to J.D. Bernal. JDB Papers, H.27.2.

50. Anderson, J. (14/7/45). Letter to J.D. Bernal. JDB Papers, H.27.2.

51. See note 37, p. 189.

52. Bernal, J.D. (1945). New frontiers of the mind. Reprinted in *The Freedom of Necessity* (1949). Routledge & Kegan Paul, London.

53. Ibid.

54. Science in the post-war world (For and against, 7). BBC Overseas, Eastern, 3/9/45. JDB Papers, B.5.14.

55. Oliphant, M.L. (1/10/45). Letter to Sir James Chadwick. CHADI 25/1, Chadwick Papers.

56. Ibid.

57. See note 37, p. 194.

58. See note 37, pp. 222–41.

59. Ibid.

60. Revision of the Tizard Report, January 1946, reproduced as Appendix 4 in note 37.

61. Bernal, J.D. (1946). Atomic energy and international security. Reprinted in *The Freedom of Necessity* (1949). Routledge & Kegan Paul, London.

62. The Warner Memorandum (2/4/46) FO 371/56832, reproduced as Appendix 6 in note 37.

63. See note 58.

64. Ibid.

65. See note 37, p. 223.

66. See note 37, p. 224.

67. Bernal, J.D. (1945). Belief and action. Reprinted in *The Freedom of Necessity* (1949). Routledge & Kegan Paul, London.

68. Unsigned editorial. (1946). *Polemic*, **3**. Reprinted in S. Orwell and I Angus (eds.) *The Collected Essays, Journalism and Letters of George Orwell* (1968). Secker and Warburg, London.

NOTES TO CHAPTER 14

1. Gordon Jackson, H. (8/2/42). Letter to J.D. Bernal. JDB Papers, C.1.1.
2. Gordon Jackson, H. (10/3/42). Letter to J.D. Bernal. JDB Papers, C.1.1.
3. Bernal, J.D. (13/3/42). Letter to H. Gordon Jackson. JDB Papers, C.1.1.
4. Bernal, J.D. (30/10/42). Letter to H. Gordon Jackson. JDB Papers, C.1.1.
5. Bernal, J.D. (1945). Draft scheme for a biomolecular centre (unpublished). JDB Papers, C.1.2.
6. Tizard, H. (7/3/45). Letter to J.D. Bernal. JDB Papers, C.1.2.
7. Bernal, J.D. (1945). The future of X-ray analysis. *Nature*, **155**, 713–15.
8. Ibid.
9. Ferry, G. (1998). *Dorothy Hodgkin: A Life*. Granta Books, London.
10. Bernal, J.D. (4/7/45). Letter to H. Tizard. JDB Papers, C.1.2.
11. Booth, A.D. (1997). An autobiographical sketch. *Annals of the History of Computing*, **19**(4), 57–63.
12. Bernal, J.D. (27/11/45). Letter to I. Fankuchen. Fankuchen Collection, AIP.
13. See note 11.
14. Booth, A.D. (2003). Unpublished information to the author.
15. Hutchins, J. (1997). From first conception to first demonstration: the nascent years of machine translation, 1947–1954. *Machine Translation*, **12**(3), 195–252.
16. Astbury, W.T. (23/1/31). Letter to J.D. Bernal. JDB Papers, J.2.
17. *To Professor J.D. Bernal from his staff*. (1951). Unpublished document. JDB Papers, C.1.2.
18. Olby, R. (1994). *The Path to the Double Helix: The Discovery of DNA*. Dover Publications, New York.
19. Ibid, p. 337.
20. Furberg, S. (1950). The crystal structure of cytidine. *Acta Crystallographica*, **3**, 325–33.
21. Author's telephone interview with S. Lenton, 6/12/03.
22. Ibid.
23. Gardiner, M (2000). Interview with the author.
24. Beckett, F. (2004). *Stalin's British Victims*. Sutton, London.
25. Crick, F. (1988). *What Mad Pursuit*. Basic Books.
26. Bernal, J.D. (1941). Research organisation in the building industry. JDB Papers, B.4.114.
27. Ibid.
28. Bernal, J.D. (1944). Building Research Station – notes and correspondence. DSIR 4/1632. PRO.
29. Bernal, J.D. (1946). Shrinkage and cracking of cementive materials. *Nature*, **158**, 11–14.
30. Ibid.
31. Bernal, J.D. (1946). Swelling and shrinking. *Transactions of the Faraday Society*, **42B**, 1–5.
32. Ibid.

33. Ibid.
34. See note 17.
35. Mackay, A.F. (2001). Interview with the author.
36. Bernal, J.D. (1946). Science in building. BBC Home Service. JDB Papers, B.5.27.
37. Bernal, J.D. (1945). The housewife. BBC Home Service. JDB Papers, B.5.16.
38. Bernal, J.D. (1945). The organization of building. *The Builder*, CLXIX, 400–2.
39. Ibid.
40. See note 36.
41. Hennessy, P. (1993). *Never Again*. Jonathon Cape, London.
42. Ibid, p. 170.
43. Bernal. J.D. (1962). Modern science in architecture. *Architectural Association Journal*, 78, 156–60.
44. Whittaker, C. (1999). Building tomorrow. In B. Swann and F. Aprahamian (eds.) *J.D. Bernal*. Verso, London.
45. Huxley, J. (1945). Science and the United Nations. *Nature*, 156, 553–6.
46. Bernal, J.D. (1945). A permanent international scientific commission. *Nature*, 156, 557–8.
47. Ibid.
48. Crowther, J.G. (1970). *Fifty Years with Science*. Barrie and Jenkins, London.
49. McLachlan, D. (1983). The 1946 conference in London. In D. McLachlan and J.P. Glusker (eds.) *Crystallography in North America*. American Crystallographic Association.
50. Bernal, J.D. (1953) Molecular asymmetry. In *Science and Industry in the Nineteenth Century*. Routledge & Kegan Paul, London.
51. Ibid, p. 218.
52. Bernal, J.D. (1939). *The Social Function of Science*. Routledge & Kegan Paul, London.
53. Bernal, J.D. (1945). Information service as an essential in the progress of science. Reprinted in *The Freedom of Necessity* (1949). Routledge & Kegan Paul, London.
54. Ibid.
55. Ibid.
56. Kendrew, J.C. (1948). Undated notes on scientific literature survey. JDB Papers, H.27.1.
57. Author's interview with Martin Bernal, Ithaca, 2001.
58. Lampe, D. (1959). *Pyke, The Unknown Genius*. Evans Brothers, London.
59. East, H. (1998). Professor Bernal's 'insidious and cavalier proposals': the Royal Society scientific information conference 1948. *Journal of Documentation*, 54(3), 293–302.
60. Ibid.
61. Pirie, N.W. (10/5/48). Letter to J.D. Bernal. JDB Papers, H.27.1.
62. Bernal, J.D. (23/6/48). Letter to *The Times*.
63. Ibid.
64. *The Times* (29/6/48).
65. See note 59.
66. Ibid.
67. Ibid.

68. See note 59.
69. Garfield, E. (1982). J.D. Bernal – the Sage of Cambridge. *Current Contents*, **19**, 5–14.
70. Ibid.
71. Ibid.
72. Bragg, W.L. (1948). Recent advances in the study of the crystalline state. *British Association for the Advancement of Science*, **5**, 165.
73. Author's interview with Dr Olga Kennard, Cambridge, 2004.
74. See note 17.
75. Bernal, J.D. (8/2/51). Letter to J. Lockwood. JDB Papers, C.1.2.
76. Kendrew, J.C. (1972). Tribute to Bernal at Birkbeck memorial meeting. Kendrew Papers, L.149.

NOTES TO CHAPTER 15

1. Waddington, C.H. (1969). Some European contributions to the prehistory of molecular biology. *Nature*, **221**, 318–21.
2. Bernal, J.D. (1940). The cell and protoplasm. *American Association for the Advancement of Science*, **14**, 199–205, Washington.
3. Ibid.
4. Harland, S.C. and Darlington, C.D. (1945). Obituary of Prof. N.I. Vavilov. *Nature*, **156**, 621–2.
5. Carlson, E.A. (1981). *Genes, Radiation and Society: The Life and Work of H.J. Muller.* Cornell University Press, Ithaca.
6. Soyfer, V.N. (1994). *Lysenko and the Tragedy of Soviet Science.* Rutgers University Press, New Jersey.
7. Ibid, pp. 87–9.
8. See note 5, p. 231.
9. Darlington, C.D. (1937). Genetic theory and practice in the USSR. *Nature*, **139**, 185.
10. Hogben, L. (25/2/37). Letter to J.D. Bernal. JDB Papers, J.88.
11. Conquest, R. (1990). *The Great Terror.* Oxford University Press, Oxford.
12. See note 5, p. 250.
13. See note 5, p. 243.
14. See note 9.
15. See note 6, p. 120.
16. See note 6, p. 122.
17. See note 6, p. 136.
18. Dale, H.H. (22/11/48). Resignation from the Academy of Sciences of the USSR, reproduced in Zirkle, C. (1949). *Death of a Science in Russia.* University of Pennsylvania Press, Philadelphia.
19. Script of 'The organization of science and scientists'. BBC Third Programme (16/9/48).
20. Ibid.
21. Langdon-Davies, J. (1949). *Russia Puts the Clock Back.* Victor Gollancz, London.

22. Almond, G.A. (1954). *The Appeals of Communism.* Princeton University Press, Princeton, NJ.

23. Ibid, p. 316.

24. Waddington, C.H. (1948). Lysenko and the scientists. *New Statesman,* **36,** 566.

25. Darlington, C.D. (1949). The Lysenko controversy. *New Statesman,* **37,** 81–2.

26. Ibid.

27. Huxley, J. (13/4/49). Letter to J.D. Bernal. JDB Papers, J.97.

28. Bernal, J.D. (12/5/49). Letter to J. Huxley. JDB Papers, J.97.

29. Huxley, J. (1949). Soviet genetics: the real issue. *Nature,* **163,** 935–42.

30. Bernal, J.D. (1949). The biological controversy in the Soviet Union and its implications. *Modern Quarterly,* 4(3), 203–17.

31. Ibid, p. 204.

32. Ibid, p. 211.

33. Huxley, J. (1949). *Heredity East and West (Postscript 1).* Henry Schuman, New York.

34. Ibid.

35. Haldane, J.B.S. (1949). In defence of genetics. *Modern Quarterly,* 4(3), 194–202.

36. Ibid.

37. Bernal, J.D. (1949). Speech to the Soviet Peace Conference. JDB Papers, E.2.5.

38. Holloway, D. (1994). *Stalin and the Bomb.* Yale University Press, New Haven.

39. Vavilov, S. (1949). Speech to the Soviet Peace Conference. JDB Papers, E.2.5.

40. *The Times* (1/9/49).

41. Crowther, J.G. (1970). *Fifty Years with Science.* Barrie & Jenkins, London.

42. Bernal, J.D. (1949). Unpublished notes on visit to USSR. JDB Papers, L.31.

43. Ibid.

44. *The Times* (10/9/49).

45. *The Times* (12/9/49).

46. Bernal, J.D. (14/9/49). Letter to the *News Chronicle.* JDB Papers, H.2.2.

47. Cummings, A.J. (16/9/49). Prof. Bernal, these are facts. *News Chronicle.*

48. Bernal, J.D. (17/9/49). Letter to the *News Chronicle.* JDB Papers, H.2.2.

49. Rhodes, R. (1995). *Dark Sun.* Simon & Schuster, New York.

50. *The Times* (4/10/49).

51. *The Times* (8/10/49).

52. *The Times* (5/11/49).

53. Ibid.

54. *The Times* (8/11/49).

55. Ibid.

56. Sakharov, A. (1990). *Memoirs.* A.A. Knopf, New York.

57. Ibid, p. 135.

58. Bernal, J.D. (1951). Academician S.I. Vavilov. *Nature,* **168,** 679.

59. Bernal, J.D. (1953). Stalin as a scientist. *Modern Quarterly,* **8,** 133–42.

60. Hodgkin, D.M.C. (1980). John Desmond Bernal, 1901–1971. *Biographical Memoirs of Fellows of the Royal Society,* **26,** 17–84.

61. Rose, H. and Rose, S. (1999). Red scientist. In B. Swann and F. Aprahamian (eds.) *J.D. Bernal: A Life in Science and Politics.* Verso, London.

62. Goldsmith, M. (1980). *Sage: A Life of J.D. Bernal*. Hutchinson, London.
63. See note 59.
64. Bernal, J.D. (1954). *Science in History*. C.A. Watts and Co., London.
65. Olby, R. (1994). *The Path to the Double Helix: The Discovery of DNA*. Dover Publications, New York.
66. Bernal, J.D. (20/12/66). Letter to J.C. Kendrew. JDB Papers, A.3.222.
67. Bernal, J.D. (1968). The material theory of life. *Labour Monthly*, **50**(7), 323–6.
68. Crick, F.H.C. (2001). Letter to the author.
69. See note 65, p. 432.
70. Mattick, J. (2004). The hidden genetic program of complex organisms. *Scientific American*, **291**(4), 60–7.
71. Wu, C.-T., and Morris, J.R. (2001). Genes, genetics and epigenetics: a correspondence. *Science*, **293**, 1103–5.
72. Ferry, G. (1998). *Dorothy Hodgkin: A Life*. Granta Books, London.
73. Bernal, J.D. (1929). The irrelevance of scientific theory. Reprinted in *The Freedom of Necessity* (1949). Routledge & Kegan Paul, London.
74. See note 5, p. 262.
75. See note 59.
76. Bernal, J.D. (1952). *Marx and Science*. Lawrence and Wishart, London.

NOTES TO CHAPTER 16

1. Bernal, J.D. (1958). *World Without War*. Routledge & Kegan Paul, London.
2. Bernal, J.D. (1945). New frontiers of the mind. Reprinted in *The Freedom of Necessity* (1949). Routledge & Kegan Paul, London.
3. Ibid.
4. Brown, A.P. (1997). *The Neutron and the Bomb*. Oxford University Press, Oxford, pp. 299–320.
5. Ibid.
6. Bernal, J.D. (1946). The challenge of our time. Reprinted in *The Freedom of Necessity* (1949). Routledge & Kegan Paul, London.
7. Bernal, J.D. (1946). The American scene. *New Statesman*, **XXXI**, 390–1.
8. Wittner, L.S. (1993). *The Struggle Against the Bomb: Vol. I, One World or None*. Stanford University Press, Stanford.
9. Towards world government. *New Statesman* (15/6/46).
10. Holloway, D. (1994). *Stalin and the Bomb*. Yale University Press, New Haven.
11. See note 8, p. 79.
12. Rhodes, R. (1995). *Dark Sun*. Simon & Schuster, New York.
13. Ibid, pp. 280–1.
14. Ibid.
15. See note 8, p. 64.
16. Gowing, M. (1974). *Independence and Deterrence*. Macmillan, London.
17. Ibid, pp. 183–4.
18. Harris, K. (1982). *Attlee*. Weidenfeld & Nicolson, London.
19. Bernal, J.D. (13/3/47). Letter to *The Times*.

20. See note 18, p. 346.
21. Bernal, J.D. (23/8/47). Letter to *The Times.*
22. See note 16, p. 406.
23. See note 8, p. 112.
24. Goldsmith, M. (1976) *Frédéric Joliot-Curie.* Lawrence and Wishart, London.
25. Davies, N. and Moorhouse, R. (2002). *Microcosm: Portrait of a Central European City.* Jonathon Cape, London.
26. Montagu, I. (1999). The peacemonger. In B. Swann and F. Aprahamian (eds.) *J.D. Bernal.* Verso, London.
27. See note 25, p. 448.
28. Taylor, A.J.P. (2/9/48). Intellectuals at Wroclaw. *Manchester Guardian.*
29. See note 26.
30. See note 28.
31. See note 25, pp. 449–50.
32. Bernal, J.D. (18/9/48). Letter to the *New Statesman,* **XXXVI,** 238–9.
33. Ref. 25, p. 450.
34. Ref. 28.
35. Bernal, J.D. (1948). Wroclaw and after. *Modern Quarterly,* 4(1), 5–26.
36. Ibid.
37. Mott, N. (1986). *A Life in Science.* Taylor & Francis, London.
38. Author's interview with Jane Bernal (2003).
39. Ibid.
40. Ibid.
41. Bernal, J.D. (25/2/49). Letter to H. Shapley. JDB Papers, L.30.
42. Bernal, J.D. (9/3/49). Letter to I. Fankuchen. Fankuchen Collection, AIP.
43. Bird, K. (1998). *The Color of Truth.* Simon & Schuster, New York.
44. *New York Times,* 23/3/49.
45. *New York Times,* 24/3/49.
46. See note 8, p. 177.
47. See note 8, p. 178.
48. Fifth column in Paris. (30/4/49). *The Economist.*
49. See note 8, p. 178.
50. See note 48.
51. See note 8, pp. 179–80.
52. Ibid.
53. See note 12, p. 381.
54. Bernal, J.D. (15/2/50). Letter to L. Pauling. JDB papers, J.175.
55. See note 12, p. 375
56. See note 12, pp. 252–3.
57. Aldrich, R.J. (2001). *The Hidden Hand.* John Murray, London.
58. See note 16, pp. 282–5.
59. See note 8, pp. 180–1.
60. Atomic warfare. *The Times* (8/10/49).
61. See note 26.
62. See note 24, pp. 162–3.

63. Weathersby, K. (1996). New Russian documents on the Korean War. *Cold War International History Project*, 6–7.
64. Author's interview with Renée Brittan and Ully Harris. (2000).
65. See note 24, pp. 186–7.
66. See note 8, p. 208.
67. Mayhew, C. (1998). *A War of Words*. I.B. Tauris, London.
68. See note 57, pp. 443–63.
69. Hitchens, C. (20/8/99). Qy. open C.P.? Very gifted. *Times Literary Supplement*.
70. Bernal, J.D. (1950). Warsaw, second World Congress on Peace. JDB Papers, E.1.5.
71. Ibid.
72. Interview with Bernal by Lena Jeger. *Guardian* (19/7/60).
73. Bernal J.D. (9/5/51). Letter to E. Rawlins. JDB Papers, J.204.
74. See note 70.
75. Ibid.
76. Ibid.
77. Aprahamian, F. (1972). Letter to E. Bernal. JDB Papers, P.6.2.
78. See note 70.
79. See note 8, p. 184
80. See note 70.
81. Ibid.
82. See note 8, pp. 184–5.
83. Bernal, J.D. (1950). Peace or war? *Modern Quarterly*, 5(4), 291–4.
84. Bernal, J.D. (1952). Speech to WPC meeting in Berlin, 1–5/7/52. JDB Papers, E.2.6.2.
85. See note 12, pp. 479–80.
86. See note 12, pp. 519–23.
87. Freistadt, H. (10/10/52). Letter to J.D. Bernal. JDB Papers, I.30.
88. Bernal, J.D. (22/10/52). Letter to H. Freistadt. JDB Papers, I.30.
89. Ibid.
90. Brent, J. and Naumov, V.P. (2003). *Stalin's Last Crime*. Harper Collins, New York.
91. Ibid, pp. 216–17.
92. Ibid, p. 1.
93. Conquest, R. (2000). *Reflections on a Ravaged Century*. W.W. Norton, New York.
94. See note 26.
95. See note 83.
96. Stalin peace prize. JDB Papers, J.23 and O.7.1.

NOTES TO CHAPTER 17

1. Bernal, J.D. (1942). The problem of the origin of life. *BBC radio broadcast*.
2. Pirie, N.W. (1937). The meaningless of the terms 'life' and 'living'. In J. Needham and D.R. Green (eds.) *Perspectives in Biochemistry*. Cambridge University Press, Cambridge.
3. Astbury, W.T. (23/1/31). Letter to J.D. Bernal, JDB Papers, J.2.
4. Ibid.

5. Astbury, W.T. (3/10/32). Letter to J.D. Bernal, JDB Papers, J.2.

6. Bernal, J.D. (1951). *The Physical Basis of Life.* Routledge and Kegan Paul, London.

7. Ibid, p. 71.

8. Pirie, N.W. (1952). Vital blarney. *New Biol.,* 12, 106–12.

9. Bernal, J.D. (1931). The crystal structure of the natural amino acids and related compounds. *Z. Kristallogr. Kristallgeom.,* 78, 363–9.

10. Ibid.

11. Olby, R. (1994). *The Path to the Double Helix: The Discovery of DNA.* Dover Publications, New York.

12. Pauling, L. (1996). The discovery of the alpha helix. *Chem. Intell.,* 2(1), 32–8.

13. Carlisle, C.H. (1978). Serving my time in crystallography at Birkbeck. Valedictory Lecture, Birkbeck College.

14. Perutz, M.F. (1997). *Science is Not a Quiet Life: Unravelling the Atomic Mechanism of Haemoglobin.* World Scientific, Singapore.

15. Ibid, p. 40.

16. Ibid, p. 45.

17. Bragg, W.L. (7/2/49). Letter to J.D. Bernal. JDB Papers, J.14.

18. Pauling, L. (13/6/51). Letter to J.D. Bernal. Ava Helen and Linus Pauling Papers, Oregon State University.

19. Bernal, J.D. (22/6/51). Letter to L. Pauling. Ava Helen and Linus Pauling Papers, Oregon State University.

20. Perutz, M.F. (1998). *I Wish I'd Made You Angry Earlier.* Oxford University Press, Oxford.

21. Ibid, pp. 174–5.

22. Ibid.

23. Perutz, M.F. (1951). New X-ray evidence on the configuration of polypeptide chains. *Nature,* 167, 1053.

24. See note 20.

25. Crick, F.H.C. (1952). Is α-keratin a coiled-coil? *Nature,* 170, 882.

26. Crick, F.H.C. (1988). *What Mad Pursuit.* Basic Books, New York.

27. Ibid, pp. 48–50.

28. Bernal, J.D. (1939). The structure of proteins. *Nature,* 143, 663–7.

29. See note 26, pp. 48–50.

30. Hager, T. (1995). *Force of Nature: The Life of Linus Pauling.* Simon and Schuster, New York.

31. Bernal, J.D. (1953). The use of Fourier transforms in protein crystal analysis. *Proceedings of the Royal Society, London, B,* 141, 71–84.

32. Bernal, J.D. (1968). The pattern of Linus Pauling's work in relation to molecular biology. In A. Rich and N. Davidson (eds.) *Structural Chemistry and Molecular Biology.* W.H. Freeman, San Francisco.

33. Bernal, J.D. (1969). Letter to J.C. Kendrew. JDB Papers, J.41.

34. Hodgkin, D.M.C. (1980). John Desmond Bernal, 1901–1971. *Biographical Memoirs of Fellows of the Royal Society,* 26, 17–84.

35. Author's interview with M.F. Perutz, Cambridge, March 2000.

36. Ibid.

37. Author's interview with M.F. Perutz, Cambridge, March 2000.
38. Ibid.
39. Perutz, M.F. (19/11/62). Letter to J.D. Bernal. JDB Papers, J.178.
40. Kendrew, J.C. (1962). Undated letter to J.D. Bernal. JDB Papers, J.109.
41. Crick, F.H.C. (1/11/62). Letter to J.D. Bernal. JDB Papers, J.24.
42. Author's interview with A. Klug, Cambridge. (2003).
43. See note 31.
44. See note 42.
45. Maddox, B. (2002). *Rosalind Franklin: The Dark Lady of DNA.* Harper Collins, London.
46. Ibid, p. 231.
47. See note 42.
48. Klug, A. (1982). From macromolecules to biological assemblies. *Nobel lecture.*
49. Bernal, J.D. and Fankuchen, I. (1937). Structure types of protein crystals from virus infected plants. *Nature,* 139, 923.
50. Ibid.
51. Watson, J.D. (1968). *The Double Helix.* Penguin, London.
52. Watson, J.D. (1954). The structure of tobacco mosaic virus. *Bioc. et Biophys. Acta,* 13, 10–19.
53. Author's telephone interview with J.D. Watson. (2004).
54. See note 42.
55. Ibid.
56. Author's interview with A.F. Mackay, London. (2001).
57. Ibid.
58. Franklin, R. (1955). Letters to J.D. Bernal. JDB Papers, C.1.2.
59. See note 56.
60. Bernal, J.D. (1956). Symmetry of azulene crystals. *Nature,* 178, 40.
61. See note 56.
62. Franklin, R.E. (20/11/55). Letter to J.D. Bernal. JDB Papers, C.1.2.
63. See note 42.
64. See note 45, pp. 251–2.
65. Klug, A. (1968). Professor Bernal and virus research at Birkbeck College (unpublished). JDB Papers, C.9.
66. Franklin, R.E., Klug, A. and Holmes, K.C. (1957). X-ray diffraction studies of the structure and morphology of tobacco mosaic virus. In G.E.W. Wolstenholme and E.C.P. Millar (eds.) *CIBA Foundation Symposium on the Nature of Viruses.* Little, Brown & Co., Boston.
67. Crick, F.H.C. and Watson, J.D. (1956). Structure of small viruses. *Nature,* 177, 473–5.
68. Ibid.
69. See note 45, p. 291.
70. See note 42.
71. See note 45, p. 298.
72. Lenton, S. (1971). Letter to E. Bernal. JDB Papers, P.6.1.
73. See note 42.

74. Bernal J.D. (1958). Dr Rosalind E. Franklin (obituary). *Nature*, **182**, 154

75. Ibid.

76. See note 65.

77. See note 42.

78. Finch, J.T. and Klug, A. (1959). Structure of poliomyelitis virus. *Nature*, **183**, 1709–14.

79. Caspar, D.L.D. and Klug, A. (1962). Physical principles in the construction of regular viruses. *Cold Spring Harbor Symp. Quant. Biol.*, **27**, 1–24.

80. Caraffi, A. (2/7/56). Letter to J.D. Bernal. JDB Papers, C.1.2.

81. Bernal, J.D. (3/1/56). Letter to J. Lockwood. JDB Papers, C.1.2.

NOTES TO CHAPTER 18

1. Keynes, M. (1999). Lancelot Hogben, FRS (1895–1975). *Notes Rec. R. Soc. Lond.* **53**, 361–9.

2. Needham, J. (1964). Science and society in East and West. In M. Goldsmith and A. Mackay (eds.) *The Science of Science.* Souvenir Press, London.

3. Bernal, J.D. (1954). *Science in History.* Watts and Co., London.

4. Ibid., p. 2.

5. Author's interview with A. Klug, Cambridge. (2003).

6. Ibid.

7. Bernal, J.D. (1965). *Science in History* (3rd edn), Watts and Co., London.

8. Bernal, J.D. (1968). *Science in History* (4th edn), Penguin Books, Harmondsworth.

9. Ibid, pp. 16–17.

10. Ibid.

11. Ibid.

12. See note 7, p. 18.

13. Bernal, J.D. (1967) *The Origin of Life.* Weidenfeld and Nicolson, London.

14. Bernal, J.D. (1951). *The Physical Basis of Life.* Routledge and Kegan Paul, London.

15. Haldane, J.B.S. (1929). The origin of life, reproduced in note 13.

16. Oparin, A.I. (1924). The origin of life, reproduced in note 13.

17. See note 15.

18. See note 14, p. 28.

19. See note 14, p. 34.

20. See note 14, pp. 34–8.

21. See note 15.

22. Pirie, N.W. (24/5/51). Letter to J.D. Bernal. JDB Papers, J.181.

23. Pierpoint, W.S. (1999). Norman Wingate Pirie (1907–1997). *Biographical Memoirs of Fellows of the Royal Society*, **45**, 399–415.

24. Pirie, N.W. (1952). Vital blarney. *New Biol.*, **12**, 106–12.

25. Bernal, J.D. (1952). Keep off the grass. *New Biol.*, **13**, 120–6.

26. Ibid.

27. Miller, S.L. (1953). A production of amino acids under possible primitive earth conditions. *Science*, **117**, 528–9.

28. Bernal, J.D. (1954). The origin of life. *New Biol.*, **16**, 28–40.

29. Ibid.

30. Pirie, N.W. (1954). On making and recognizing life. *New Biol.*, **16**, 41–53.

31. See note 28.

32. Ibid.

33. Bernal, J.D. (17/7/56). Letter to A.I. Oparin. JDB Papers, L.58.

34. Mackay, A.L. (2004). Letter to author.

35. Bernal, J.D. (1959). The problem of stages in biopoesis. In A.I. Oparin, A.G. Paynshii, A.E. Braunshtein and T.E. Pavlovskaya (eds.) *The Origin of Life on the Earth*, pp. 38–53. Macmillan & Co., New York.

36. Ibid.

37. Pirie, N.W. (1959). Chemical diversity and the origins of life. In A.I. Oparin, A.G. Paynshii, A.E. Braunshtein and T.E. Pavlovskaya (eds.) *The Origin of Life on the Earth*, pp. 76–83. Macmillan & Co., New York.

38. Pirie, N.W. (1957). The origins of life. *Nature*, **180**, 886–8.

39. Bernal, J.D. (1957). The origins of life. *Nature*, **180**, 1220.

40. Ibid.

41. See note 23.

42. See note 13.

43. See note 23.

44. Bernal, J.D. Undated autobiographical notes. JDB Papers O.1.1.

45. Bernal, J.D. (1961). Significance of carbonaceous meteorites in theories on the origin of life. *Nature*, **190**, 129–31.

46. Claus, G. and Nagy, B. (1961). A microbiological examination of some carbonaceous chondrites. *Nature*, **192**, 594.

47. Fitch, F., Schwarcz, H.P, Anders, E. (1962). 'Organized elements' in carbonaceous chondrites. *Nature*, **193**, 1123–5.

48. Bernal, J.D. (1962). Comments. *Nature*, **193**, 1127–9.

49. Ibid.

50. Ibid.

51. Bernal, J.D. (1965). Molecular matrices for living systems. In S.W. Fox (ed.) *The Origins of Prebiological Systems*, pp. 65–88. Academic Press, New York.

52. Ibid.

53. Ibid.

54. Ibid.

55. Bernal, J.D. (1965). Comments on 'The folly of probability'. In S.W. Fox (ed.) *The Origins of Prebiological Systems*, pp. 52–6. Academic Press, New York.

56. See note 13.

57. See note 13, Appendix 4.

58. See note 35.

59. Orgel, L.E. (1994). The origin of life on the Earth. *Scientific American*, **271**, 53–61.

60. Hazen, R.M. (2001). Life's rocky start. *Scientific American*, **284**, 77–85.

61. Ibid.

62. Hodgkin, D.M.C. (1980). John Desmond Bernal, 1901–1971. *Biographical Memoirs of Fellows of the Royal Society*, **26**, 17–84.

63. Pearson, V.K., Sephton, M.A., Kearsley, A.T. et al. (2002). Clay mineral-organic matter relationships in the early solar system. *Meteorites & Planetary Science*, 37, 1829–33.

NOTES TO CHAPTER 19

1. Bernal, J.D. (1946). International scientific organization. Reprinted in *The Freedom of Necessity* (1949). Routledge & Kegan Paul, London.
2. Taubman, W. (2003). *Khrushchev – The Man and His Era*. W.W. Norton, New York.
3. Bernal, J.D. (1949). Letter to S. Vavilov. JDB Papers, L.31.
4. Bernal, J.D. (1949–50). Unpublished notes on visit to India. JDB Papers, L.33.
5. Balaram, P. and Ramaseshan, S. (2001). A 'Nobel Class' Scientist – G.N. Ramachandran. *Current Science*, 80(8), 909–11.
6. See note 4.
7. Ibid.
8. Ibid.
9. Ibid.
10. Ibid
11. Ibid.
12. Ibid.
13. Bernal, J.D. (1951). March–April visit to the USSR. JDB Papers, L.38.
14. Bernal, J.D. (1953). USSR delegation, 17/9–2/10/53. JDB Papers, L.44.
15. Ferry, G. (1998). *Dorothy Hodgkin: A Life*. Granta Books, London.
16. Author's interview with Dr Olga Kennard, Cambridge, 2004.
17. See note 14.
18. Bernal, J.D. (1954). Notes on visit to Hungary. JDB Papers, L.40.
19. Ibid.
20. Ibid.
21. *The Daily Worker* (24/9/54).
22. Ibid.
23. Quoted in Wersky, G. (1978). *The Visible College*. Holt, Rinehart and Winston, New York, p. 318.
24. See note 2, p. 242.
25. See note 2, pp. 260–1.
26. Transcript of interview with N.S. Khrushchev (25/9/54). JDB Papers, L.46.
27. Bernal, J.D. (1954) Unpublished account of visit to China. JDB Papers, L.48.
28. Ibid.
29. Ibid.
30. Ibid.
31. Ibid.
32. Ibid.
33. Ibid.
34. Ibid.

35. Bernal, J.D. (1954) Unpublished account of visit to China. JDB Papers, L.48.
36. Ibid.
37. Ibid.
38. Bernal, J.D. (1954). Visit to Hong Kong. JDB Papers, L.50.
39. *Indian Express* (3/1/55). JDB Papers, L.51.
40. Spender, S. (1978). *The Thirties and After.* Random House, New York.
41. Ibid, p. 143.
42. See note 2, p. 284.
43. Carswell, J. (1971). Letter to E. Bernal. JDB Papers, P.6.1.
44. See note 15, pp. 385–6.
45. Author's interview with A. Klug, Cambridge. (2003).
46. Bernal, J.D. (1957). Notes on visit to Hungary. JDB Papers, L.40.
47. Ibid.
48. Bernal, J.D. (1957). Hungary revisited. *New Statesman,* LIII, 641 & 738.
49. Bernal, J.D. (1957). I talk with George Lukacs. *Tribune,* 7, 20 May.
50. Ibid.
51. Bernal, J.D. (1957). Science in Hungary. *Nature,* 179, 939.
52. Schienmeier, Q. (2004). Dreaming on the Danube. *Nature,* 427, 94–5.
53. See note 2, p. 297.
54. See note 2, p. 339.
55. Spence, J. and Chin, A. (1996). *The Chinese Century.* Harper Collins, London.
56. Glover, J. (2000). *Humanity: A Moral History of the Twentieth Century.* Yale University Press, New Haven.
57. Ibid, p. 287.
58. See note 2, pp. 392–3.
59. Bernal, J.D. (1959) Unpublished account of visit to China. JDB Papers, L.61.
60. Ibid.
61. Author's interview with M. Bernal, Ithaca. (2001).
62. Author's interivew with M. Gardiner, London. (2000).
63. Hodgkin, T.L. (8/6/60). Letter to J.D. Bernal. JDB Papers, G1.1.
64. Bernal, J.D. (1960–1). Unpublished notes on visit to Ghana. JDB Papers, L.67.
65. Ibid.
66. Ibid.
67. Ibid.
68. *Ghanaian Times* (6/6/61). JBD Papers, L.61.
69. See note 15, p. 348.
70. Correspondence with Ghana University. JDB Papers, J.61.
71. Bernal, J.D. (1962). Unpublished notes on visit to South America. JDB Papers, L.69.
72. Ibid.
73. Ibid.
74. Ibid.
75. Roberts, J.M. (1999). *The Twentieth Century.* Viking, New York.
76. See note 71.

77. Che Guevara, E. (12/4/60). Letter to J.D. Bernal. JDB Papers, J.69.
78. Bernal, J.D. (28/4/60). Letter to E. Che Guevara. JDB Papers, J.69.

NOTES TO CHAPTER 20

1. Rhodes, R. (1995). *Dark Sun.* Simon & Schuster, New York.
2. Clark, R.W. (1978). *The Life of Bertrand Russell.* Penguin Books, Harmondsworth.
3. Notes on the Stalin Peace Prize Committee. JDB Papers, J.23.
4. Wittner, L.S. (1997). *The Struggle Against the Bomb: Vol. 2, Resisting the Bomb.* Stanford University Press, Stanford.
5. Bernal, J.D. (26/3/55). Speech on long term effects of nuclear weapons. JDB Papers, B.3.216.
6. Arnold, L. (2001). *Britain and the H-Bomb.* Palgrave, Basingstoke.
7. Harris, K. (1982). *Attlee.* Weidenfeld & Nicolson, London.
8. See note 5.
9. Bernal, J.D. (1955). Notes on Helsinki World Assembly for Peace (22–29 June). JDB Papers, E.2.9.
10. Soper, D. (4/2/55). Letter to *Tribune.*
11. See note 4, p. 88.
12. Bernal, J.D. (30/8/56). Letter to D. Skobeltzyn. JDB Papers, J.23.
13. Mercer, P. (1986). *'Peace' of the Dead.* Policy Research Publications, London.
14. See note 4, p. 172.
15. Goldsmith, M. (1976). *Frédéric Joliot-Curie.* Lawrence and Wishart, London.
16. Ibid, p. 224.
17. Ibid.
18. *The Daily Worker,* 21/8/58.
19. Montagu, I. (1999). The peacemonger. In B. Swann and F. Aprahamian (eds.) *J.D. Bernal.* Verso, London.
20. See note 4, p. 182.
21. Bernal, J.D. (1959). Notes on WPC meeting in Moscow, 21–25 Feb. JDB Papers, E.2.12.
22. Bernal, J.D. (1959). Notes on visits to China and Soviet Union. JDB Papers, L.62.
23. Taubman, W. (2003). *Khrushchev – The Man and His Era.* W.W. Norton, New York.
24. Ibid, p. 394.
25. See note 22.
26. Ibid.
27. Ibid.
28. Bernal, J.D. (1960). Notes on WPC meeting. JDB Papers, E.2.13.
29. Author's telephone interview with V. Pixner. (2004).
30. See note 4, p. 408.
31. Bernal, J.D. (14/1/60). Letter to D. Eisenhower. JDB Papers, E.1.59.
32. Bernal, J.D. (17/2/60). WPC press statement. JDB Papers, E.12.1.
33. See note 22, p. 498.

34. See note 4, p. 342.

35. See note 4, p. 402.

36. Bernal, J.D. (25/1/61). Letter to J.F. Kennedy. JDB Papers, E.1.59.

37. Bernal, J.D. (1961). Speech at New Delhi. JDB Papers, E.1.30.

38. Bernal, J.D. (1961). Notes on meeting with Indian Peace Council, 24–28 Feb. JDB Papers, E.2.14.

39. Dallek, R. (2003). *An Unfinished Life*. Little Brown and Co., Boston.

40. Ibid, p. 347.

41. Bernal, J.D. (21/8/61). WPC press statement on Berlin crisis. JDB Papers, E.12.1.

42. Bernal, J.D. (31/8/61). WPC press statement on resumption of Soviet nuclear tests. JDB Papers, E.12.1.

43. Khrushchev, N.S. (25/11/61). Letter to J.D. Bernal. JDB Papers, E.1.54.3.

44. See note 39, pp. 462–3.

45. See note 4, pp. 314–15.

46. Ibid.

47. Schweitzer, A (29/4/62). Letter to J.D. Bernal. JDB Papers, E.2.15.1.

48. Bernal, J.D. (11/5/62). WPC press statement. JDB Papers, E.12.1.

49. de Gaulle, C. (15/5/62). Press conference on UN Disarmament Committee. JDB Papers, E.2.15.2.

50. Nehru, P. (1/6/62). Letter to J.D. Bernal. JDB Papers, E.2.15.2.

51. Jack, H.A. (1962). The Moscow conference for general disarmament and peace. JDB Papers, E.2.15.4.

52. See note 4, pp. 316–17.

53. Collins, J.L. (1962). Speech to world congress on general disarmament and peace. JDB Papers, E.2.15.3.

54. Silverman, S. (1962). Speech to world congress on general disarmament and peace. JDB Papers, E.2.15.3.

55. Russell, B. (1962). Speech to world congress on general disarmament and peace. JDB Papers, E.2.15.3.

56. See note 51.

57. Ibid.

58. See note 4, p. 318.

59. Ibid.

60. Bernal, J.D. (14/7/62). Speech to world congress on general disarmament and peace. JDB Papers, E.2.15.3.

61. See note 23, pp. 529–77.

62. See note 39, pp. 558–9.

63. Bernal, J.D. (23/10/62). WPC message to UN Security Council. JDB Papers, E.12.1.

64. See note 39, pp. 558–9.

65. Ibid, p. 566.

66. Bernal, J.D. (28/10/62). Speech to WPC presidential committee. JDB Papers, E.2.15.3.

67. Morrison, P. (30/12/62). Letter to J.D. Bernal. JDB Papers, E.1.59.

68. See note 4, pp. 302–5.

69. Collins, J.L. (14/12/62). Letter to J.D. Bernal. JDB Papers, E.11.6.2.
70. Ehrenburg, I. (5/1/63). Letter to J.L. Collins. JDB Papers, E.11.6.2.
71. Notes of WPC observers group (1963). JDB Papers, E.11.6.2.
72. Bernal, J.D. (21/8/63) Letter to N.S. Khrushchev. JDB Papers, E.1.54.3.
73. See note 23, p. 578.
74. See note 4, pp. 310–11.
75. Bernal, J.D. (12/4/63). Telegram to Pope John XXIII. JDB papers, E.1.51.
76. See note 23, p. 583.
77. See note 4, pp. 310–11.
78. Bernal, J.D. (5/8/63). Telegram to Kennedy, Khrushchev and Macmillan. JDB Papers, E.2.17.
79. Bernal, J.D. (4/9/63). WPC press statement. JDB Papers, E.12.1.
80. See note 72.
81. Khrushchev, N.S. (6/9/63). Letter to J.D. Bernal, JDB Papers, E.1.54.3.
82. Bernal, J.D. (18/9/63). Message to WPC presidential committee. JDB Papers, E.2.17.
83. See note 4, pp. 310–11.
84. Ibid.
85. Ibid.
86. See note 82.
87. Bernal, J.D. (24/4/64). Letter to L.B. Johnson. JDB Papers, E.1.59.
88. Bernal, J.D. (23/3/65). End American inhumanity in Vietnam. *WPC press statement.* JDB Papers, E.12.1
89. Bernal, J.D. (10/7/65). Opening speech at eighth World Congress for Peace, Helsinki. JDB Papers, E.2.20.3.
90. Ibid.
91. Ibid.
92. Neruda, P. (1965). Untitled poem to Bernal. JDB Papers, E.2.20.4.
93. Bernal, J.D. (15/7/65). Closing speech at eighth World Congress for Peace, Helsinki. JDB Papers, E.2.20.3.
94. Bernal, J.D. (1965). Memo on the structure, organization and working methods of the WPC. JDB Papers, E.3.45.
95. See note 93.
96. See note 23, pp. 529–77.
97. See note 39, p. 505.
98. See note 23, pp. 529–77.
99. Bernal, J.D. (1958). *World Without War.* Routledge & Kegan Paul, London.

NOTES TO CHAPTER 21

1. Author's interview with Max Perutz, Cambridge, March 2000.
2. Bernal, J.D. (1956). Future of fundamental research in Britain, JDB Papers, F.1.1.
3. Ibid.
4. Wilson, J.H. (24/4/56). Letter to J.D. Bernal. JDB Papers, F.1.4.
5. Callaghan, J. (23/6/56). Letter to J.D. Bernal. JDB Papers, F.2.

6. Author's interview with Renée Brittan, June 2000.

7. Bernal, J.D. (1956). Memos on Labour science policy. JDB Papers, F.2.

8. Ibid.

9. Bernal, J.D. (1958). Comments to J.R.M. Brumwell on Labour policy for science. JDB Papers, F.2.

10. Brumwell, J.R.M. (19/2/60). Letter to J.D. Bernal. JDB Papers, F.8.

11. Bernal, J.D. (22/11/63). Letter to R.H.S. Crossman. JDB Papers, F.9.

12. Bernal, J.D. (3/3/64). Letter to R.H.S. Crossman. JDB Papers, F.9.

13. Bernal, J.D. (1966). Notes sent to P.M.S. Blackett on the report of the Council on Scientific Policy. JDB Papers, F.12.

14. Author's interview with Peter Trent, June 2001.

15. *The Times,* Law Reports, 27–30/10/59.

16. Bernal, J.D. (1937). An attempt at a molecular theory of the liquid state. *Transactions of the Faraday Society,* **33**(1), 27–40.

17. Ibid.

18. Bernal, J.D. (1959). The structure of liquids. *Proceedings of the Royal Institution of Great Britain,* **37**, 355–93.

19. Bernal, J.D. (1964). The structure of liquids (Bakerian Lecture 1962). *Proceedings of the Royal Society, London, A,* **280**, 299–322.

20. Bernal, J.D. (1960). The structure of liquids. *Scientific American,* **203**(2), 125–33.

21. Mackay, A. (2005). Note to the author.

22. See note 18.

23. See note 19.

24. Ibid.

25. Author's telephone interview with John Mason. February 2004.

26. See note 18.

27. Ibid.

28. Ibid.

29. Bernal, J.D. (23/2/62). Letter to A. Caraffi. JDB Papers, C.1.3.

30. Cherry, I. (1972). Interview with E. Bernal. JDB Papers, P.6.1.

31. See note 19.

32. See note 18.

33. Bernal, J.D. (1966). Opening remarks. In G.E.W. Wolstenholme and M. O'Connor (eds.) *Principles of Biomolecular Organization.* Little Brown and Co., Boston.

34. Ibid.

35. Hargittai, I. and M. (2000). *In Our Own Image.* Plenum, New York.

36. Desiraju, G.R. (2003). In search of clarity. *Nature,* **423**, 485.

37. Quoted in note 35, p. 148.

38. Franks, F. (1981). *Polywater.* MIT Press, Cambridge.

39. Author's interview with John Finney, February 2004.

40. See note 38, pp. 47–51.

41. Ibid.

42. Ibid.

43. See note 38, p. 57.

44. See note 38, pp. 65–83.

45. Ibid.
46. Donahoe, F.J. (1969). Anomalous water. *Nature*, **224**, 198.
47. Bernal, J.D., Barnes, P., Cherry, I.A. and Finney, J.L. (1969). Anomalous water. *Nature*, **224**, 393–4.
48. Barnes, P., Cherry, I., Finney, J.L., and Peterson, S. (1971). Polywater and poly-pollutants. *Nature*, **230**, 31–3.
49. Cohen, I.B. (1985). *Revolution in Science*. Harvard University Press.
50. See note 33.
51. Bernal, J.D. (1966). General discussion. In G.E.W. Wolstenholme and M. O'Connor (eds.) *Principles of Biomolecular Organization*. Little Brown and Co., Boston.
52. Author's interview with A. Klug, Cambridge. (2003).

NOTES TO CHAPTER 22

1. Author's interview with Jane Bernal, London. (2003).
2. Goldsmith, M. (1980). *Sage*. Hutchinson, London.
3. Author's interview with A. Klug, Cambridge. (2003).
4. Bernal, J.D. (1958). Contributions to a discussion on the physics of water and ice. *Proceedings of the Royal Society, London, A*, **247**, 421–538.
5. Ibid.
6. See note 1.
7. Ibid.
8. Sprague, L. (1971). Letter to E. Bernal. JDB Papers, P.6.1.
9. See note 1.
10. Bernal, J.D. (11/1/63). Letter to A. Caraffi. JDB Papers, C.1.3.
11. Lenton, S. (1963). Note to J.D. Bernal, JDB Papers, C.1.3.
12. Hobsbawm, E. (1999). Bernal at Birkbeck. In B. Swann and F. Aprahamian (eds.) *J.D. Bernal*. Verso, London.
13. Author's telephone interview with J. Mason. (2004).
14. Ibid.
15. Bernal, J.D. (4/10/62). Letter to J.M. Robertson. JDB Papers, C.1.3.
16. Robertson, J.M. (17/10/62) Letter to J.D. Bernal. JDB Papers, C.1.3.
17. Protest letter from Bullen, Carlisle, Jeffery, Lenton, Mackay. (16/1/63). JDB Papers, C.1.3.
18. Bernal J.D. (1962). Note on Structural Diffractometry. JDB Papers, H.19.1.
19. Ibid.
20. Author's telephone interview with S. Lenton. (2003).
21. See note 1.
22. Harrison, M. (1965). *Mulberry: The Return in Triumph*. W.H. Allen, London.
23. Author's telephone interview with V. Pixner. (2004).
24. Bernal, J.D. (1963). Account of illness. JDB Papers, O.10.1.
25. Ibid.
26. Bernal, J.D. (1963). Notes on Gordon Conference. JDB Papers, L.70.
27. See note 24.
28. See note 11.

29. See note 12.
30. See note 24.
31. Ibid.
32. Montagu, I. (1999). The peacemonger. In B. Swann and F. Aprahamian (eds.) *J.D. Bernal*. Verso, London.
33. Overend, W.G. (29/11/63). Letter to J.D. Bernal. JDB Papers, C.1.3.
34. Bernal, J.D. (29/11/63). Letter to J.W. Lockwood. JDB Papers, C.1.3.
35. See note 12.
36. Ibid.
37. Correspondence with Nobel nominating committee. JDB Papers, H.21.
38. Ewald, P. (11/4/58) Letter to J.D. Bernal. JDB Papers, H.19.1.
39. Bernal, J.D. (1964). Dorothy Hodgkin and the structure of natural compounds. *New Scientist*, **416**, 351.
40. Author's interview with Olga Kennard. (2004).
41. Synge, A. (1971). Letter to E. Bernal, JDB Papers, P.6.1.
42. See note 24.
43. See note 24.
44. MacGillavry, C. (4/9/64). Letter to J.D. Bernal. JDB Papers, H.19.1.
45. Bernal, J.D. (7/3/66). Letter to K. Boll-Dornberger. JDB Papers, H.19.1.
46. Belov, N. (15/8/66). Letter to J.D. Bernal, JDB Papers, H.19.1.
47. Phillips, D. (1979). William Lawrence Bragg. *Biographical Memoirs of Fellows of the Royal Society*, **25**, 75–143.
48. See note 18.
49. Bernal, J.D. (20/5/66). Letter to A.J. Caraffi. JDB Papers, O.6.
50. Bernal, J.D. (1966). Unpublished thoughts. JDB Papers, B.4.97.
51. Bernal, J.D. (1967). Enormity or logic and hypocrisy in the ultimate solution. JDB Papers, B.4.101.
52. Ibid.
53. Ibid.
54. Ibid.
55. Ibid.
56. Ibid.
57. Bernal, J.D. (1968). The year 2000. JDB Papers, E.14.15.
58. Bernal, J.D. (1967). Mao and the Russians (unpublished notes). JDB Papers, B.4.103.
59. Ibid.
60. Ibid.
61. Bernal, J.D. (1967). What the Middle East confrontation means to the world. E.14.14.
62. Ibid.
63. Author's interview with M. Perutz. (2001).
64. Bernal, J.D. (17/11/67). Letter to M. Rosenheim. JDB Papers, O.10.4.
65. Gardiner, M. (11/5/68). Letter to S. Zuckerman. Zuckerman archive, SZ/CSA/100/2.

66. Ibid.
67. See note 1.
68. Beckett, F. (2004). *Stalin's British Victims*. Sutton, London.
69. See note 1.
70. Bernal, J.D. (1968). The doctrine of 'peaceful counter-revolution' and its consequences. JDB Papers, B.4.108.
71. Ibid.
72. Barnes, P. (2005). Letter to the author.
73. Pauling, L. (1971). 70th birthday tribute to Bernal. JDB Papers, J.175.
74. Bernal, J.D. (1929). *The World, the Flesh & the Devil*. Routledge & Kegan Paul, London; reprinted by Indiana University Press 1969.

POSTSCRIPT

1. Bernal, J.D. (1939). *The Social Function of Science*. Routledge and Kegan Paul, London.
2. Ibid, p. 411.
3. Snow, C.P. (1959). *The Two Cultures and the Scientific Revolution*. Cambridge University Press, Cambridge.
4. See note 1, p. 155.
5. Leavis, F.R. (1962). *Two Cultures? The Significance of C.P. Snow*. Chatto & Windus, London.
6. Ibid, p. 18.
7. Bernal, J.D. (23/3/62). The two cultures. The *Spectator*.
8. Snow, C.P. (1961). *Science and Government*. Harvard University Press, Cambridge.
9. Bernal, J.D. (11/4/61). Letter to C.P. Snow. JDB Papers, J.217.
10. Blackett, P.M.S. (1961). C.P. Snow's account of the role of two scientists in government. *Scientific American*, **204**, 192.
11. Zuckerman, S. (17/4/61). Letter to J.D. Bernal. JDB Papers, J.267.
12. Zuckerman, S. (1/5/61). Letter to J.D. Bernal. JDB Papers, J.267.
13. Author's interview with Martin Bernal. (2001).
14. Zuckerman, S. (1972). Tribute to J.D. Bernal. Zuckerman archive, SZ/CSA/100/2/10.
15. Bernal, J.D. (1966). Military scientist. *New Statesman*, LXII, 173–4.
16. Mountbatten, L. (29/1/72). Letter to S. Zuckerman. Zuckerman archive, SZ/CSA/100/2.
17. Author's interview with Jane Bernal, London. (2003).
18. Zuckerman, S. (22/4/72). Letter to L. Mountbatten. Zuckerman archive, SZ/CSA/100/2.
19. Bernal, J.D. (26/4/68). Letter to S. Zuckerman. Zuckerman archive, SZ/CSA/100/2/7.
20. Gardiner, M. (5/5/77). Letter to S. Zuckerman. Zuckerman archive, SZ/CSA/100/2.
21. Hussey, T.A. (3/10/77). Letter to S. Zuckerman. Zuckerman archive, SZ/CSA/100/2.
22. Hussey, T.A. (22/12/77). Letter to S. Zuckerman. Zuckerman archive, SZ/CSA/100/2/43.
23. Goldsmith, M. (1980). *Sage*. Hutchinson, London.

24. Zuckerman, S. (20/2/79). Letter to M. Goldsmith. Zuckerman archive, SZ/CSA/100/2.

25. Zuckerman, S. (3/3/79). Letter to M. Goldsmith. Zuckerman archive, SZ/CSA/100/2/41.

26. Zuckerman, S. (7/3/79). Letter to L. Mountbatten. Zuckerman archive, SZ/CSA/100/2/42.

27. Ibid.

28. Zuckerman, S. (2/4/80). Letter to M. Goldsmith. Zuckerman archive, SZ/CSA/100/2/43.

29. See note 23, p. 111.

30. Zuckerman, S. (22/3/80). Letter to D. Hodgkin. Zuckerman archive, SZ/CSA/100/2/45.

31. Hodgkin, D.M.C. (1980). John Desmond Bernal, 1901–1971. *Biographical Memoirs of Fellows of the Royal Society*, **26**, 17–84.

32. Bernal, J.D. (1944). Diary. JDB Papers, D.1.

33. Author's telephone interview with L. Scott-Bowden. (2004).

34. Bunting, A.H. (2001). Letter to the author.

35. Danckwerts, P.V. (1983). In the land of the giants. *New Scientist*, 904.

36. See note 32.

37. Ibid.

38. See note 26.

39. Zuckerman, S. (14//2/81). Letter to J.M. Lewis. Zuckerman archive, SZ/CSA/100/2/51.

40. Lewis, J.M. (17/2/81). Letter to S. Zuckerman. Zuckerman archive, SZ/CSA/100/2/51.

41. See note 15.

42. Ibid.

43. Pauling, L. (1972). Bernal's contributions to structural chemistry. *Scientific World*, **2**, 13–14.

44. *The Times* (4/10/49).

45. Koestler, A. (1949). In R.H.S. Crossman (ed.) *The God that Failed*. Harper, New York.

46. Author's interview with Max Perutz. (2000).

47. Author's interview with Aaron Klug. (2003).

48. Ibid.

49. Martin, K. (1954). Old chrysanthemum. *New Statesman*, **XLVII**, 286–7.

50. Pipes, R. (2001). *Communism*. Modern Library, New York.

51. See note 46.

52. Author's interview with Margaret Gardiner. (2000).

53. Zuckerman, S. (1988). *Monkeys, Men and Missiles*. Collins, London.

54. See note 17.

Index